ORGANiSATiON DEVELOPMENT & CHANGE

ORGANiSATiON DEVELOPMENT & CHANGE

ASiA PACiFiC EDITiON

DIANNE M. WADDELL__THOMAS G. CUMMINGS__CHRISTOPHER G. WORLEY__

THOMSON
™

Australia . New Zealand . Canada . Mexico . Singapore . Spain . United Kingdom . United States

Level 7, 80 Dorcas Street
South Melbourne Victoria 3205

Email highereducation@thomsonlearning.com.au
Website http://www.thomsonlearning.com.au

Previously published by South-Western Thomson Learning as *Organization Development and Change* by Thomas G.
Cummings and Christopher G. Worley, in 2001.
Authorised adaptation of the seventh edition by South-Western Thomson Learning.

Adaptation first published in 2000
Second edition published in 2004
This edition published in 2007
10 9 8 7 6 5 4 3 2 1
12 11 10 09 08 07

National Library of Australia
Cataloguing-in-Publication data
Waddell, Dianne, 1949–.
Organisation development and change.
3rd ed.
Bibliography.
Includes index.

ISBN 978 0 17 013280 0.

1. Organizational change. I. Cummings, Thomas G. II.
Worley, Christopher G. III. Title.
302.35

Publishing manager: Michael Tully
Senior Publishing editor: Dorothy Chiu
Project editor: Chris Wyness, Nathan Katz
Developmental editor: Penelope Goodes
Production controller: Deepa Travers, Zoe Whatmore, Adele Psarras
Text designer: Olga Lavecchia
Cover designer: Olga Lavecchia
Editor: Pete Cruttenden
Photo researcher: Karen Forsythe, CopperLeife
Indexer: Russell Brooks
Cover image by Getty Images
Typeset in 9.5/11 pt Sabon by KnowledgeWorks Global Ltd.
Printed in China by CTPS

This title is published under the imprint of Thomson.
Nelson Australia Pty Limited ACN 058 280 149 (incorporated in Victoria)
trading as Thomson Learning Australia.

The URLs contained in this publication were checked for currency during the production process.
Note, however, that the publisher cannot vouch for the ongoing currency of URLs.

Contents

List of applications

Preface

Change management is a complex and multifaceted process, often with confusion as to 'organisation development' and 'organisation transformation'. It would be an oversimplification if the role and responsibilities of change managers could be divided into neat, simple and succinct modules that could be successfully replicated in every context. In reality this is not the case. Change management is also becoming more crucial in gaining the competitive advantage that is the goal of most organisations.

Organisation development is an integrated and sometimes intricate balance of dealing with people within an organisational context. Even where there is chaos there must be planning. Interventions, including interpersonal, sociotechnical, human resource and structural, often cannot be easily delineated from each other. It is more an interdependency of functions that, once started, is ongoing and evolving. These interventions may often be unpredictable but must be co-ordinated and place considerable demand on managers where they have to be 'all things to all people at all times' in a chaotic, unpredictable and volatile environment.

Writing a book about change management is a challenge, as is the task of management itself. There has been very constructive feedback from previous editions and all have highlighted the need to emphasise that the world of managing people and processes continues to change dramatically. There is no doubt that managers are faced with conflicting challenges of understanding and motivating an increasingly diverse workforce, being open and accountable to a wide range of stakeholders, planning for the future in an increasingly changing environment, considering the ethical implications of decision making, and much more.

For students studying change management, the prospect of managing others in a changing environment may be daunting. While it is interesting and somewhat 'straightforward' to become a change agent, the added pressure of supervising or managing change interventions can be stressful. *Organisation Development & Change* is written with students in mind – preparing students for the challenges that lie ahead. With many current case studies, exercises and support material, the challenges of managing change are presented in a real-life manner. There is no 'one method fits all' panacea for managing change, so this book discusses the 'smorgasbord' of approaches from which to choose with the intention of designing successful and harmonious change processes.

The contributors to this book merge their vast experience in teaching management at university with their first-hand management experience and consulting to a wide variety of organisations. Students are the beneficiaries of this experience, as *Organisation Development & Change* draws these groups together, with the emphasis on heightening the learning experience for students. Students entering a management position, or contemplating change management as a specialisation, will be exposed to a variety of issues in this text. Lessons learnt will provide a strong grounding for our future managers.

The success of such a project as this relies on the contribution of many who have been supportive of this third edition. To acknowledge everyone would be a difficult task, nevertheless there are those who spring immediately to mind. Peer reviews have played a very significant role in helping refine the content and pedagogy of this book and without their valuable contribution we would not be able to produce such an outcome. Their comments were instrumental in enabling me to change perspectives and gave me the courage to confront the challenges.
I would like to thank sincerely the following colleagues:
Jerry Anway, Christian Heritage College
Allan Cadwaller, UCOL

Paul Corcoran, University of the Sunshine Coast
Ray Gordon, University of Southern Queensland
Cherie England, James Cook University
Judith McMorland, University of Auckland
Franceen Reihana, Unitech
Colleen Rigby, Waikato University
Amanda Roan, University of Queensland

My special appreciation and recognition extends to John Molineux, James Latham, Margaret Heffernan and Anne Smyth who worked on the special issues section of the book. I realise that writing such chapters is very time-consuming and often brings little reward. Nevertheless, I admire their professionalism and commitment as this gave the book an extra dimension and a thematic approach to the issues.

For their contribution to the key instructional support items such as the Testbank, the PowerPoint slides and the Instructor's Manual, I wish to thank Dr Ramanie Samaratunge (Monash University), Deb Stewart (Victoria University) and Dr Linda Glassop (Deakin University), respectively.

These tasks are often burdensome but they were very generous in sharing their expertise in education and learning.

It would be remiss not to acknowledge my appreciation of the team at Thomson Learning for their patience, understanding and, at many times, their persistence. Dorothy Chiu and Penelope Goodes have provided unending support during the tough times, especially when trying to reach deadlines. Both have worked consistently hard on making sure all aspects of the book come together physically, and they were able to keep me on schedule when most would have despaired. Peter Cruttenden, the manuscript editor, was able to make sense out of what I wrote and translate it into something more coherent and well structured. Again his professionalism was a further motivator to 'get things done'.

As writing a textbook bites considerably into personal and family time, I would also like to thank those special people in my life: Denis, Paul, Megan, Suzy and especially my new grandson Kit. In particular I would like to thank my two special research assistants, my sister Joan Ryan and my daughter Corie Waddell.

Of course this would not be possible without the support and understanding of my work colleagues and students at Deakin University who were often the 'victims' of my tantrums and a sounding board for ideas.

Di Waddell
Melbourne
December 2006

RESOURCES GUIDE

FOR THE STUDENT

As you read this text you will find a wealth of features in every chapter to enhance your study of organisation development and change and help you understand its applications.

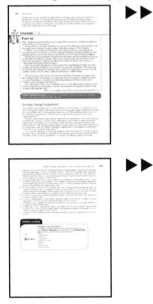

▶▶ In every chapter, *Application boxes* featuring local companies, situations and organisational practices help you to relate the theory to a real-world business environment. Each *Application box* is accompanied by a *Critical Thinking Question* to encourage you to think critically and debate the issues.

▶▶ Included with this text is a passcode that gives you a FREE four-month subscription to InfoTrac College Edition. At the end of each chapter you will find a list of search terms called *Online reading* that you can use to help guide you through InfoTrac. This online library will provide you with access to full-text articles from hundreds of scholarly and popular periodicals. Don't restrict yourself to the search terms provided throughout the book, think of your own search terms and expand your understanding of organisation development and change.

At the end of each chapter you'll find several learning tools to help you to not only review the chapter and key concepts but to help you extend your learning.

End-of-chapter summaries provide a review of each chapter's important concepts and help you to check your comprehension.

Review questions enable you to test your comprehension of the key concepts in each chapter.

Discussion and essay questions encourage you to question, analyse and apply the concepts you have learnt, either independently or in a group situation.

FOR THE INSTRUCTOR

Thomson Learning is pleased to provide you with an extensive selection of electronic and online supplements to help you lecture in organisation development and change.

ExamView® Testbank CD ROM

ExamView helps you create, customise and deliver tests in minutes for both print and online. The Quick Test Wizard and Online Test Wizard guide you step by step through the test-creation process. The program also allows you to see the test you are creating on the screen exactly as it will print or display online. With ExamView's complete word-processing capabilities, you can add an unlimited number of new questions to the bank, edit existing questions and build tests of up to 250 questions using up to 12 question types. You can now export the files into Blackboard or WebCT.

Instructor's Manual and PowerPoint Presentation on CD-ROM

The Instructor's Manual provides you with a wealth of content to help set up and administer an organisation development and change subject. It includes learning objectives, solutions to problems in the text and suggested further reading. Also included on the CD-ROM are PowerPoint presentations to accompany *Organisation Development and Change*. Use these slides in your lectures to reinforce key principles.

Artwork CD-ROM

The Artwork CD-Rom includes digital files of graphs, tables and diagrams from the text that can be used in a variety of media. Use them in WebCT or Blackboard, PowerPoint presentations or copy them onto overheads.

For updates and news relating to *Organisation Development and Change*, 3e please go to the companion website at:

▶▶ **www.thomsonlearning.com.au/waddell3e**

Case matrix

CASE TITLE	CASE AUTHORS	MANUFACTURING	SERVICE
Northern Stock Feed Supplies	Cheryl England, James Cook University	●	
Qantas Airlines	Quamrul Alam, Monash University		●
Clothing Company Pty Ltd: Maintaining An Organisation's Culture During A Period Of Rapid Growth	Lindy Henderson, University of Newcastle, Glenda Strachan, Griffith University and John Burgess, University of Newcastle		
Teaching and Technology: University of the Sunshine Coast	Selina Tomasich, University of the Sunshine Coast and Paul Corcoran, University of the Sunshine Coast		
Canterbury Precision Engineers Ltd: Implementing Quality Management Improvements in a Smaller Firm	Tom Batley, University of Otago	●	
The Office of Redeployment and Retraining, WA	Eric Walton, University of Western Australia, and Ken Williams		
Facilitating Change: A Nursing Documentation Review	Katrina Perroud, Caulfield General Medical Centre, Anita Romsdal, Canan Tzelil, Erika Watercutter and Mustafa Manager		●
Australian Customs Service: Implementation of a Container X-ray System	Belinda Incani, Australian Customs Service, Mandy Mustapic and Sibel Toremis		
Rural Ambulance Services	Harvey Griggs, Central Queensland University, and David Lyster, Rural Ambulance Victoria		
Large-scale Change and Australian Universities: Views from the Academic Heartland	Richard Winter, Australian National University		●
Changing HR Practices in China: CableCo	Cherrie Jiuhua Zhu	●	
Pilkington: An Organisation in Transition	Brendan Barrett, Chantelle Cook and Melissa Williams	●	
Managing Strategic Change at Energize	Michael Duncan and V. Nilakant		●
Employee Relations at Centrelink	Sarah Turberville and Rowena Barrett		
World Vision Australia: A Not-For-Profit Organisation	Rowan Lewis and Di Waddell		
Water Industry Reform - Stopping the Leaking Tap?	Amanda Pyman, Ivan Mathieson, Alec Craig and Kathleen Doherty		●
The Acquisition of Heatane by Elgas	Renae Richards and Natalie Smith	●	
Self-Managed Work Teams as a Management Tool	Peter Benazic, Judy Pool and Cathy Williams		
Call Centre Relocation: Advantage Credit Union	Paul Bolton, Philip Carr, Kylie Davenport, Kent Hansen and Theo Tolkis		●
Melbourne City Parking and Traffic	Olivia Tsen and Chulanga Jayawardanai (with contributions by Paul Wilson)		
Changes in Telstra's Field Workforce	Warrick Coad, Susan Foley, Libby Hanson, Sue McConnell and David Vickers		●
Guardian Pharmacies Australia Limited	Anthony Paula, Alex Bradilovich, Bernadette Ivkovic and David Lyster		
Stanley Australia	Christopher Andrews, Lee O'Mahoney and John Bourke	●	
Qenos: The Kemcor–Orica Joint Venture	Steven Coulton, Anne Duncan, Jague Lee and Sari Sitalaksmi	●	
Disability Service: Inevitable Structural Change	David Brett, Wendy Cox, Suzanne Diprose, Cynthia Loquet and Robert Moore		

Left margin labels: For 2e; WEBSITE CASES AVAILABLE AT WWW.THOMSONLEARNING.COM.AU/WADDELL3e For 1e

* Please note that all cases are integrated case studies that can be used in any order. This is a guide only, to identify topics and therefore chapter content that is predominant to each case study.

GOVERNMENT/ NOT FOR PROFIT	RETAIL	CONSUMER GOODS	INDUSTRIAL GOODS	MULTINATIONAL CORPORATION	SMALL-MEDIUM SIZED COMPANY	RELATES TO CHAPTERS*
		●	●		●	3, 9, 10, 11, 15
						9, 10, 11, 12
	●					7, 9, 10
●						2, 8, 10
			●		●	2, 3, 4, 5, 6, 7, 8, 9
●						3, 4, 7, 8, 9, 10
						4, 5, 6, 7, 8
●						2, 4, 5, 6, 8, 10, 11
●						3, 4, 6, 7, 8, 9, 10
						4, 5, 8, 9, 11
			●	●		8, 9, 11
			●	●		4, 5, 6, 7, 8, 9, 10, 11
						2, 3, 4, 6, 7, 8, 10, 11
●						4, 7, 8, 9, 10
●						2, 5, 6, 8, 9, 11
						4, 7, 8, 10, 11
			●			2, 4, 6, 7, 8, 11
●						2, 3, 4, 5, 6, 7, 8, 10
						4, 5, 6, 7, 8, 9, 10
●						2, 4, 5, 6, 7, 8, 11
						2, 5, 7, 8, 9
	●					3, 4, 6, 7, 8, 9
		●	●			4, 8
			●	●		6, 8, 9, 11
●						2, 6, 8, 10, 11

Acknowledgements

The following extracts and diagrams have been printed with permission:
Howard E. Aldrich, *Organizations and Environments*, Prentice-Hall, 1979. Reprinted edition forthcoming in 2008, Stanford University Press, "Business Classics" series, new forward written by the author, p. 300; S. Appelbaum and B. Shapiro, 'The ABCs of EAPS', *Personnel*, 66(1989): 39–46. Reprinted with permission, *Workforce* 1989. Copyright Crain Communications Inc. www.workforce.com, p. 283; Carolyn Barker, 'Innovative advantage', *Management Today*, Sept. 2004, p. 8; Bureau of Meteorology, http://www.bom.gov. au/weather/qld, p. 450; Reprinted from *Business Horizons*, Vol. 16. Copyright 1973, with permission from Elsevier, p. 274; Copyright © 1959 and by the Regents of the University of California. Reprinted from *California Management Review*, Vol. XII, No. 2, Fig. 1. By permission of the Regents, pp. 219, 380, and Copyright © 1983 by the Regents of the University of California. Reprinted from the California Management Review, 28:3 by permission of the Regents, p. 219; From ACADEMY OF MANAGEMENT EXECUTIVE: THE THINKING MANAGER'S SOURCE by K. CAMERON, S. FREEMAN AND A. MISHRA. Copyright 1991 by ACADEMY OF MANAGEMENT (NY). Reproduced with permission of ACADEMY OF MANAGEMENT (NY) in the format Textbook via Copyright Clearance Center, p. 223; Adam Carey, 'Listen to the voice of the hive', *The Age*, 3/10/2006, pp. 136–7; *Systems Thinking, Systems Practice*, John Wiley & Sons, Peter B. Checkland, Chichester 1981. Copyright John Wiley & Sons Ltd. Reproduced with permission, p. 385; Cameron Cooper, 'Leadership: Part Two: Brad Sugars: Action international business coaching', *Management Today*, Mar. 2006, p. 30; From *Organization Development and Change* (ISE), 8e, by Cummings/Worley, 2005. Reprinted with permission of South-Wester, a division of Thomson Learning: www.thomsonrights.com, pp. 156–7; Reprinted from D. Denison and G. Spreitzer, 'Organizational culture and organizational development: A competing values approach', in *Research in Organizational Change and Development*, 5e, eds R. Woodman and W. Posmore, p. 4, Copyright 1991, with permission from Elsevier, p. 327; Catherine Fox, 'Flaky Biz', *Boss Magazine, Australian Financial Review*, 13/4/06, p. 14; Leon Gettler and Barry Fitzgerald, 'Ethics of the axe', *The Age*, 11/6/05, pp. 222–3; J. Gibson, J. Ivancevich and J. Donnelly Jr, *Organizations: Behaviors, Structure, Processes*, 8e, Plano, TX, Business Publications, 1994. Reproduced by permission of the McGraw-Hill Companies, p. 286; Amanda Gome, 'Different ambition', *Business Review Weekly*, Feb. 2–8, 2006, pp. 277–8, and 'Man amid controversy', *Business Review Weekly*, 9–15 Feb. 2006, pp. 77–8; *Managing Organisational Change*, F. Graetz & M. Rimmer, John Wiley & Sons Australia, Ltd; © 2006. Reprinted with permission of John Wiley & Sons Australia, p. 432; Michelle Grattan & Tim Colebatch, 'Let women fight: Call goes out Senator joins recruitment debate', *The Age*, 2/10/2006, p. 148; 'Training: a release of positive energy', *Insurance Age*, 1/1/06, pp. 94–5; David James & Emily Ross, 'Leadership: The change agents', *Business Review Weekly*, Mar.–Apr. 2005, pp. 52–3; David James, 'Ideas and issues: keep clear', *Business Review Weekly*, 11/5/06, p. 84, 'Leading indicators', *Business Review Weekly*, 25/8/05, pp. 319–20, and 'Mobile battleground', *Business Review Weekly*, 11–17 May 2006, pp. 349–50; Vicki Jayne, 'People Issues: How to run the talent show', *Management*, 19, 1/8/06. © 2006 3Media, pp. 5–6; John Kavanagh, 'Swipe-card squeeze', *Business Review Weekly*, 8–14 Jun. 2006, pp. 302–3; M. Lacey, 'Internal Consulting: Perspectives on the Process of Planned Change', *Journal of Organizational Change Management*, 8(1995):76. © 1995. Republished with permission, Emerald Group Publishing Limited, www.emeraldinsight.com, p. 54; From 'Productivity and the quality of work life', Edward E. Lawler, III, and Gerald E. Ledford, Jr., *National Productivity Review*, Winter 1981–82, pp. 23–36. Reproduced by permission of John Wiley & Sons, p. 233–4; Reproduced by permission of E. Lawler, S. Mohrman and T. Cummings, Center for Effective Organizations, University of Southern California, p. 111; Reproduced by permission of the publisher from Edward Lawler III, 'Increasing worker involvement to enhance organizational effectiveness: Design features for a participation system'; in P. Goodman and associates, *Change in Organizations*, San Francisco, Jossey-Bass, 1982, p. 238; R. Likert, *New Patterns of Management*, New York, McGraw-Hill, 1961. Reproduced by permission of the McGraw-Hill Companies, p. 12; Simon Lloyd, 'Software replaces crystal ball', *Business Review Weekly*, 20/4/2006, pp. 115–16; Julie Macken, 'Shut up and listen', *Boss Magazine, Australian Financial Review*, 2002, pp. 112–13; From EVALUATION REVIEW by MACY & MERVIS. Copyright 1982 by SAGE PUBLICATIONS INC JOURNALS. Reproduced with permission of SAGE PUBLICATIONS INC JOURNALS in the format Textbook via Copyright Clearance Center, pp. 160–1, 162; 'Australia Post heads the charge', *Management*

Today, Jan–Feb 2005, p. 324, and 'New Leader Tips', *Management Today*, May 2004, p. 191; Tom McKaskill, 'Change Management', *Business Review Weekly*, 20–26 Apr. 2006, pp. 12–13; 'Management: Stress: coping strategies for employers', *Metalworking Production*, 22/5/06, www.metalworkingproduction.co.uk, pp. 289–90; Lisa Murray and Scott Rochfort, 'Norris ready to rise to the challenge', *Sydney Morning Herald*, 21/6/05, pp. 231–2; Harry Onsman, 'Busted: the more things change', *Boss Magazine, Australian Financial Review*, 2002, pp. 107–8; Derek Parker, 'Leading through change', *Management Today*, April 2006, pp. 337–8; Jeffrey Pfeffer & Robert I. Sutton, *Hard Facts: Dangers half-truths & total nonsense*, Harvard Business School Press, 2006. Reproduced by permission of Harvard Business School press, p. 38; Real Estate Institute of Australia, www.reia.com.au, p. 67; Emily Ross, 'Catching the Sol train', *Business Review Weekly*, 8–14 Dec. 2005, pp. 332–3, 'Ideas & Issues: The meetings divide', *Business Review Weekly*, 27/4/06, p. 195, 'Leadership: Change Merchant', *Business Review Weekly*, 6/10/05, pp. 52–3, and 'Retail resurrection', *Business Review Weekly*, 8/6/06, p. 309; N. Russell-Jones, *The Managing Change Pocketbook*, Management Pocketbooks, London, 1999, p. 430; R. Sarah, T. Haslett, J. Molineux, J. Olsen, J. Stephens, S. Tepe and B. Walker, 'Business action research in practice: A strategic conversation about conducting action research in business organizations', *Systemic Practice and Action Research*, 15:6, 2002. Reproduced with permission from Springer Science & Business Media, p. 398; Jane Searle, 'Small Talk', *Business Review Weekly*, Oct. 27–Nov. 2 2005, pp. 126–7; Reprinted from *Organizational Dynamics*, 10, Summer 1981, H. Schwartz and S. Davis, 'Matching corporate culture and business strategy', p. 38, Copyright 1981, with permission from Elsevier, p. 326; from *The Fifth Discipline* by Peter Senge, published by Century. Reprinted by permission of The Random House Group Ltd., p. 383; Stephen J. Smith, 'How to make a decision about mergers and acquisitions', *Journal of Business Forecasting*, July 2005, Vol. 24, Iss. 2, p. 11, p. 354; Reproduced with permission from W. Snyder and T. Cummings, 'Organisation learning disorders: Conceptual model and intervention guidelines', Copyright © The Tavistock Institute, London, UK, 1998, by permission of Sage Publications Ltd., p. 336; Article extracts by courtesy of SPH/*The Business Times*, pp. 58–9; The State of Queensland, Department of Primary Industries and Fisheries, 1995–2005., pp. 448, 449; Amita Tandukar, 'Culture clash: a fictional case study', *Business Review Weekly*, 25/5/06, pp. 357–8, 'Innovation: Insurers play catch-up', *Business Review Weekly*, 13/4/06, pp. 227–8, 'Knowhow: Political animals', *Business Review Weekly*, 25/5/06, pp. 198–9, and 'Lift Performance', *Business Review Weekly*, 17/11/05, pp. 263–4; Tim Treadgold, 'Theory meets reality', *Business Review Weekly*, 24–30 Nov. 2005, pp. 166–7; Adapted from MP de Val & CM Fuentes, 2003, 'Resistance to change: A literature review and empirical study', *Management Decision*, 41(2), pp. 148–55. Republished with permission, Emerald Group Publishing Limited, www.emeraldinsight.com, p. 436; 'Aker Kvaerner-Clough wins $111m Boddington gold contract', *WA Business News*, 24/4/06 © Business News Pty Ltd, pp. 360–1; D. Waddell, *E-Business in Australia: Concepts and Cases*, Sydney, Pearson Education Australia, 2002. Reproduced by permission of Pearson Education Australia, p. 2; Jacqui Walker, 'Think Ahead', *Business Review Weekly*, Feb.–Mar. 2006, pp. 35–6; Nicholas Way, 'The human factor', *Business Review Weekly*, 4/5/06, pp. 269–70; L. White and M. Rhodeback, 'Ethical dilemmas in organization development: A cross-cultural analysis', Figure 1, *Journal of Business Ethics*, 11(1992): 663–70. With kind permission from Kluwer Academic Publishers, p. 60; David Williamson, 'Challenge of the sea now translates into "ripple effect" coaching skills', *The Western Mail*, 27/5/06, p. 46; Graham Willgoss, 'People: People Management: Case Study—The challenge of expansion', *Third Sector*, 22/3/06. This article first appeared in Third Sector, the leading UK weekly magazine for and about charities and the voluntary sector www.thirdsector.co.uk, pp. 304–5; Angie Wong, 'A past master at logistics', *South China Morning Post*, 4/2/06, pp. 241–2.

Every attempt has been made to trace and acknowledge copyright holders. Where the attempt has been unsuccessful, the publisher welcomes information that would redress the situation.

About the authors

Dianne Waddell, Doctor of Philosophy (Monash), Master of Education Administration (Melbourne), Bachelor of Education (Melbourne) and Bachelor of Arts (La Trobe), is Associate Professor and Director of Management and Human Resources Programs at Deakin University. She is responsible for the development, implementation and evaluation of postgraduate courses, and teaches in the areas of quality management, change management and strategic management. These subjects are offered both on-campus off-campus. Dianne has published and presented papers on 'Resistance to change', 'Leadership', 'E-business', 'Quality management' and 'Forecasting for managers' and has taught in both public and private education systems for many years, as well as presenting specifically designed industry-based courses.

Margaret Heffernan, OAM, Bachelor of Education (Melbourne), Bachelor of Business (Dist. RMIT) Master of Arts (Monash), is a lecturer in the RMIT University Business Portfolio (School of Management), Australia. Her work has enabled her to contribute to global education and the integration of Western and Confucian Management education in Melbourne, Singapore and Hong Kong. This increased awareness of cultural diversity has enabled her to develop more meaningful resources and experiences for tertiary students, especially in the areas of change management, organisation communication and human resource management. Margaret is a contributing author to a HRM text and has written a book for the gynaecological cancer sector.

James Latham, Bachelor of Arts (Hons), Master of Arts in Organisation Psychology (Lancaster), PhD (Curtin), is a lecturer in Organisation Studies and Leadership at Swinburne University of Technology. He began his career as a tradesman in the utilities industry and has extensive industrial experience of organisation change in the utilities, chemical and technical education sectors of industry. He has a particular interest in non-management human factors of organisation development with particular emphasis on discourse and relationships. James's research is in the field of relationships and discourse with an emphasis on social construction methods.

John Molineux, Bachelor of Business in Personnel Management, a Graduate Diploma in Management, a Master of Management in Organisational Systems, and a Doctorate of Philosophy in Management, is an experienced human resources manager. For over 30 years, he has worked in a range of human resources, personnel and change management roles in several Australian government departments and agencies. His doctoral thesis used an action research methodology to implement a systemic approach to cultural change in a large Australian government agency. John is currently a Chartered Member of the Australian Human Resources Institute and a member of the Australia and New Zealand Academy of Management.

Anne Smyth is a Senior Lecturer in the School of Management RMIT University. She works as an educator, consultant and researcher in the fields of management and leadership development, organisational change and transition, and human resource management. She approaches her work in these areas through the use of reflective practice, action learning and action research, and is particularly interested in helping managers and organisations review and strengthen their practice. She has considerable experience in managing and teaching in international education programs in the Asian region.

iNTRODUCTiON

 Change as evolutionary and revolutionary processes

1

CHANGE AS EVOLUTiONARY AND REVOLUTiONARY PROCESSES

Organisations today are confronted almost daily with the need for change. It remains one of the few constants in an increasingly unpredictable and complex environment and one of the more significant and demanding issues facing managers today. As the environment changes, organisations must adapt if they are to be successful. Under these pressures, companies are downsizing, re-engineering, flattening structures, going global and initiating more sophisticated technologies. A major challenge facing organisations today is to develop a management style and culture that will enable them to cope with the challenges and opportunities they face. Irrespective of whether the change has to do with introducing new technology, a reorganisation or new product development, it is important for leaders to have a sound understanding of change issues and theories to help guide their actions.[1]

Kimberley (cited in endnote 1) noted that despite spanning a period of more than half a century, the change literature is complex and fragmented, characterised by the diversity of approaches and opinion. She observes that there is no one universal change model and no one best way of successfully implementing change. As a consequence she designed a mind map that charted a course through organisational change theory. This very useful approach is presented in Figure 1.1.

It becomes apparent from the figure that, for the purposes of sustainability, organisations need to be able to implement both incremental and transformational change. 'This requires organisational and management skills to compete in a mature market (where cost, efficiency and incremental innovation are key) and to develop new products and services (where radical innovation, speed and flexibility are critical).'[2] Thus, managers today are required to master both incremental and revolutionary change.

But in all probability managers have their own intuitive approaches to bringing about change – the change models they carry inside their heads. A personal theory of change would therefore include any assumptions, biases and paradigms that influence their beliefs about what should change and how change should occur. However, in order to successfully implement change, managers should at least be cognisant of various perspectives on change and the thinking that underpins them.

There is a metaphor for change: a pendulum that swings from incremental and planned change (organisation development) to dramatic and unplanned change (organisation transformation). Although organisation transformation (OT) receives headlines in the media it is often organisation development (OD) that is the desired state for organisations. Where OT is a reactive, and sometimes dramatic, response to external pressures, OD is the preferred option for organisations that are introspective and wish to continually improve their products and services in an incremental manner.

This is a book predominantly about OD, the desired state: a process that applies behavioural science knowledge and practices to help organisations achieve greater effectiveness, including increased financial performance and improved quality of work life. It must also be noted that OD differs from other planned change efforts, such as technological innovation, training and development or new product development, in that the focus is on building the organisation's

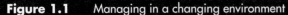

Figure 1.1   Managing in a changing environment

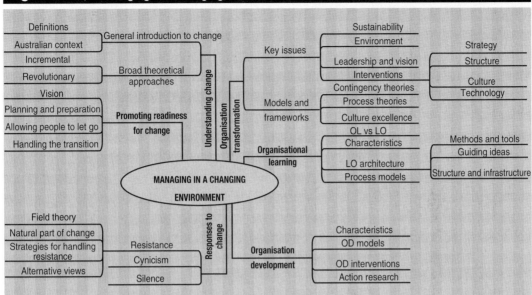

Source: D. Waddell, *E-Business in Australia: Concepts and Cases,* Sydney, Pearson Education Australia, 2002.
Reproduced by permission of Pearson Education Australia.

ability to assess its current functioning and to achieve its goals – OD is process-oriented not outcome-oriented. Moreover, OD is oriented to improving the total system – the organisation and its parts in the context of the larger environment that impacts on them.

This book reviews the broad background of OD and examines assumptions, strategies and models, intervention techniques and other aspects. Whereas OT is considered in more detail in Part 5, transformation strategies are more 'ad hoc' and company-specific such that a text with this focus on evolution of change could not encompass the revolutionary concepts with any depth.

This chapter provides an introduction to OD, describing the concept of OD itself, and explains why OD has expanded rapidly in the past 50 years, both in terms of people's needs to work with and through others in organisations and in terms of organisations' needs to adapt to a complex and changing world. It briefly reviews the history of OD and describes its evolution into its current state. This introduction is followed by an overview of the rest of the book.

WHAT IS ORGANISATION DEVELOPMENT?

OD is both a professional field of social action and an area of scientific inquiry. The practice of OD covers a wide spectrum of activities, with seemingly endless variations upon them. Team building with top corporate management, structural change in a local council and job enrichment in a manufacturing firm are all examples of OD. Similarly, the study of OD addresses a broad range of topics, including the effects of change, the methods of organisational change and the factors that influence OD success.

A number of definitions of OD exist and are presented in Table 1.1. Each definition has a slightly different emphasis. For example, Burke's description focuses attention on culture as the target of change; French's definition is concerned with OD's long-term interest in, and use of, consultants; Beckhard's and Beer's definitions address the process of OD; while Dunphy and Stace refer to the 'soft' approaches. The following definition incorporates most of these views and is used in this book:

> Organisation development is a systemwide application of behavioural science knowledge to the planned development and reinforcement of organisational strategies, structures and processes for improving an organisation's effectiveness.

Table 1.1	Definitions of organisation development

- Organisation development is a planned process of change in an organisation's culture through the utilisation of behavioural science technology, research and theory (Warner Burke).[3]
- Organisation development refers to a long-range effort to improve an organisation's problem-solving capabilities and its ability to cope with changes in its external environment with the help of external or internal behavioural-scientist consultants, or change agents, as they are sometimes called (Wendell French).[4]
- Organisation development is an effort (1) planned, (2) organisation-wide, and (3) managed from the top to (4) increase organisation effectiveness and health through (5) planned interventions in the organisation's 'processes', using behavioural science knowledge (Richard Beckhard).[5]
- Organisation development is a system-wide process of data collection, diagnosis, action planning, intervention and evaluation aimed at: (1) enhancing congruence between organisational structure, process, strategy, people and culture; (2) developing new and creative organisational solutions; and (3) developing the organisation's self-renewing capacity. It occurs through the collaboration of organisational members working with a change agent using behavioural science theory, research and technology (Michael Beer).[6]
- Organisation development is a 'soft' approach that describes a process of change undertaken in small incremental steps managed participatively (Dexter Dunphy and Doug Stace).[7]

This definition emphasises several features that differentiate OD from other singular approaches to organisational change and improvement, such as technological innovation, training and development, and organisation evolution.

First, OD applies to an entire system, such as an organisation, a single plant of a multiplant firm, or a department or work group. This contrasts with approaches that focus on one or few aspects of a system, such as a training and development model or a 'one off' technological innovation. In these approaches, attention is narrowed to individuals within a system or to the improvement of particular products or processes.

Second, OD is based on behavioural science knowledge and practice, including microconcepts such as leadership, group dynamics and work design, and macro-approaches such as strategy, organisation design and international relations. These subjects distinguish OD from such applications as technological innovation, which emphasise the technical and rational aspects of organisations. These approaches tend to neglect the personal and social characteristics of a system. In addition, the behavioural science approach to change acknowledges the individual's influence over an organisation's destiny. More deterministic perspectives, such as organisation evolution, discount the influence of organisation members on effectiveness.

Third, whereas OD is concerned with planned change, it is not, in the formal sense, typically associated with business planning or technological innovation nor, in the deterministic sense, often associated with organisation evolution. Instead, OD is more an adaptive process for planning and implementing change than a blueprint for how things should be done. It involves planning to diagnose and solve organisational problems, but such plans are flexible and often revised as new information is gathered about the progress of the change program. If, for example, the performance of international managers was seen to be a concern, a reorganisation process might begin with plans to assess the current relationships between the international divisions and the corporate headquarters, and to redesign them if necessary. These plans would be modified should the assessment discover that most of the international managers' weak performance could be attributed to poor cross-cultural training prior to their international assignment.

Fourth, OD involves both the creation and the subsequent reinforcement of change. It moves beyond the initial efforts to implement a change program to a longer-term concern for stabilising and institutionalising new activities within the organisation. For example, the implementation of self-managed work teams might focus on ways by which supervisors could give workers more control over work methods. After the workers had been given more control, attention would shift to ensuring that supervisors continued to provide that freedom, including the possible rewarding of supervisors for managing in a participative style. This attention to reinforcement is similar to training and development approaches that address maintenance of new skills or behaviours, but differs from other change perspectives that do not address how a change can be institutionalised.

Fifth, OD encompasses strategy, structure and process changes, although different OD programs may focus more on one kind of change than another. A change program aimed at modifying organisation strategy, for example, might focus on how the organisation relates to a wider environment and on how those relationships can be improved. It might include changes in both the grouping of people to perform tasks (structure) and the methods of communicating and solving problems (process) used to support the changes in strategy. Similarly, an OD program directed at helping a top-management team become more effective might focus on interactions and problem-solving processes within the group. This focus might result in the improved ability of top management to solve company problems in strategy and structure. Other approaches to change, such as training and development, typically have a narrower focus on the skills and knowledge of organisation members.

Finally, OD is oriented to improving organisational effectiveness. This involves two major assumptions. First, an effective organisation is able to solve its own problems and focus its attention and resources on achieving key goals. OD helps organisation members gain the skills and knowledge necessary to conduct these activities by involving them in the process. Second, an effective organisation has both high performance – including quality products and services, high productivity and continuous improvement – and a high quality of work life. The organisation's performance is responsive to the needs of external groups, such as stockholders, customers, suppliers and government agencies, that provide the organisation with resources and legitimacy. Moreover, it is able to attract and motivate effective employees who then perform at high levels.

This definition helps to distinguish OD from other applied fields, such as management consulting, operations management or new product development. It also furnishes a clear conception of organisation change, a related focus of this book. Organisation change is a broad phenomenon that involves a diversity of applications and approaches, including economic, political, technical and social perspectives. Change in organisations can be in response to external forces, such as market shifts, competitive pressures and radical new product technologies, or it can be internally motivated, such as by managers trying to improve existing methods and practices. Regardless of its origins, change does affect people and their relationships in organisations and so can have significant social consequences. For example, change may have a negative connotation or be poorly implemented. The behavioural sciences have developed useful concepts and methods for helping organisations deal with these problems. They help managers and administrators to manage the change process. Many of these concepts and techniques are described in this book, particularly in relation to managing change.

Organisation development can be applied to managing organisational change. However, it is primarily concerned with change that is oriented to transferring the knowledge and skills needed to build the capability to achieve goals, solve problems and manage change. It is intended to move the organisation in a particular direction, towards improved problem solving, responsiveness, quality of work life and effectiveness. Organisation change, in contrast, is more broadly focused and can apply to any kind of change, including technical, managerial and social innovations. These changes may or may not be directed at making the organisation more developed in the sense implied by OD. Application 1.1 compares employment to running a variety show where you cannot keep the audience glued to their seats because there is a risk that the enterprise would fail.

APPLICATION 1.1

PEOPLE ISSUES: HOW TO RUN THE TALENT SHOW

Engagement is something Harold Hillman is pretty good at. The American-born director of organisation development and talent management for Fonterra certainly kept those attending a recent NZIM breakfast presentation on full alert as he explained how to 'hold onto and develop your best talent'.

Even Hillman's job title is a sign of the times – traditional HR just doesn't cut it in a world that's having to try much harder to attract and retain the talent needed to sustain competitive advantage.

▷▷

His recipe for getting it right involves reprogramming the entire cultural DNA of an organisation – something he's excited to be part of in a 'visionary' company like Fonterra.

'Organisations,' he notes, 'are a reflection of the people who work in them.'

That's why creating a learning organisation is a vital aspect of the talent retention mix.

'If you're going to have an organisation where leaders thrive, you have to be explicit about building a learning organisation,' says Hillman. 'Good leaders are good learners, so building capability is imperative.'

A fan of organisational development authors Chris Argyris and Peter Senge, Hillman points out that hiring smart people is only the starting point; unless they're working in an environment where questioning is encouraged, they can be pretty good at making dumb decisions.

It's all about encouraging quality conversation and minimising the impact of what he refers to as the 'left-hand column' effect. That's what's in your head and influencing the discussion – but is not what is overtly discussed (that's in the right-hand column). So for every two people, there are really three conversations, which can add up to a lot of unexpressed decision influencers when it comes to team decision making. More worryingly, the left-hand component rises exponentially around the boardroom table, says Hillman: 'Where they're making multi-million dollar decisions, people tend to have bigger left-hand columns and their decisions get dumber.'

One of the problems is that the more senior people get, the more they impose unrealistic expectations around what they're supposed to know – and may even worry about being exposed as frauds.

'You need to position leaders as effective questioners,' says Hillman. That leads to more open and productive conversation – and the quality of conversation is important to the quality of decisions emerging from it.

At most board tables, the ratio of advocacy to enquiry is about 9:1 – and that needs to change, says Hillman.

A learning organisation also encourages a greater sense of engagement, and employees (particularly in the Gen Y category) need to feel they're in a role and a company where they can contribute – where their efforts make a difference. That's not a hard thing to achieve, says Hillman.

His three drivers for generating engagement are: line of sight (can employees see how their individual effort contributes to organisational goals?); personal growth (how are they getting smarter in that role and in that business?); and perspective (they're entitled to have an opinion about the work they do). Employers whose attitude to shopfloor or junior workers is 'we don't pay you to think' is a mentality that needs to be shaken off, says Hillman, as it leads to employee disengagement – and there's already too much of that about.

Surveys show that around 70% of the workforce doesn't look forward to coming to work; that, he says, is a concerning figure.

Hillman also spoke about the relationship between leadership and change, and the need to understand the dynamics of change, as represented by the 'sigmoid curve' (a tool popularised by management guru Charles Handy). Simply put, it is being able to recognise when a natural growth cycle is close to peaking – and before it starts declining.

'The trick is getting people to do something different just at the moment when everything seems to be working really well,' says Hillman.

That's when reinvention is needed to jump on the next growth cycle, and these cycles keep getting shorter: 'Every 18 months, you need to look at something to sustain momentum – this is where engagement is vital.'

Source: Vicki Jayne, 'People Issues: How to run the talent show', *Management*, 19, 1/8/06. © 2006 3Media.

Critical Thinking Question: 'The trick is getting people to do something different just at the moment when everything seems to be working really well.' What other considerations should there be besides the need for sharing knowledge before implementing change?

Why study organisation development?

In the previous editions of this book we argued that organisations must adapt to increasingly complex and uncertain technological, economic, political and cultural changes. We have also argued that OD can help an organisation create effective responses to these changes and, in many cases, proactively influence the strategic direction of the firm. The rapidly changing conditions of the past few years confirm these arguments and accent their relevance. According to several observers, organisations are in the midst of unprecedented uncertainty and chaos, and nothing short of a management revolution will save them.[8] Three major trends are shaping change in organisations: globalisation, information technology and managerial innovation.[9]

First, globalisation is changing the markets and environments in which organisations operate as well as the way they function. New governments, new leadership, new markets and new countries are emerging and creating a new global economy. The development of the European Union has developed and strengthened an internal market; the demise of the Soviet Union has allowed the development of countries such as Kazakhstan, now a major provider of commercial minerals; and the growth of nationalism and religious fervour in Asia and the Middle East has had far-reaching, international effects resulting in economic and political turmoil.

Second, information technology such as e-business is changing how work is performed and how knowledge is used. The way an organisation collects, stores, manipulates, uses and transmits information can lower costs or increase the value and quality of products. Electronic data interchange, for example, directly connects two organisations, allowing instantaneous exchange of sales data, pricing, inventory levels and other information. This can be used to adjust manufacturing scheduling, service delivery, new product development activities and sales campaigns. In addition, the ability to move information easily and inexpensively throughout and between organisations has fuelled the downsizing, delayering and restructuring of firms. High-speed modems and laptop computers have allowed for a new form of work known as telecommuting: organisation members can work from their homes or cars without ever going to the office. Finally, information technology is changing how knowledge is used. Information that is widely shared reduces the concentration of power at the top of the organisation. Decision making, once the exclusive province of senior managers who had key information, is shared by organisation members who now have the same information. The concept of work needs redefinition and the relationship between business and customer is less delineated – business to business (B2B) versus business to consumer (B2C) and now business to employee (B2E).

Third, managerial innovation has both responded to the globalisation and information technology trends and accelerated their impact on organisations. New organisational forms, such as networks, clusters, strategic alliances and virtual corporations, provide organisations with new ways of thinking about how to manufacture goods and deliver services. The strategic alliance, for example, has emerged as one of the indispensable tools in strategy implementation. No single organisation – not even BHP Billiton, Lend Lease or Western Mining Corporation – can control the environmental and market uncertainty it faces. Many CEOs of Australian companies share this viewpoint. For example, Richard Pratt of Amcor is prominent when the debate concerning the environment is regularly to the forefront. Qantas has extended its Australian operations into the global market by allying with Oneworld. In addition, new methods of change, such as downsizing (right sizing, creating job opportunities, etc) and re-engineering, have radically reduced the size of organisations and increased their flexibility, while new large group interventions, such as the search conference and open space, have increased the speed with which organisational change can take place.

Managers, OD practitioners and researchers argue that these forces are not only powerful in their own right but also interrelated. Their interaction makes for a highly uncertain and chaotic environment for all kinds of organisations, including manufacturing and service firms and those in the public and private sectors. There is no question that these forces are profoundly impacting on organisations.

Fortunately, a growing number of organisations are undertaking the kinds of organisational changes needed to survive and prosper in today's environment. They are making themselves more streamlined and nimble, and more responsive to external demands. They are involving employees in key decisions and paying for performance rather than time. They are taking the initiative in innovating and managing change, rather than simply responding to what has already happened.

Organisation development is playing an increasingly important role in helping organisations change themselves. It is helping organisations to assess themselves and their environments and to revitalise and rebuild their strategies, structures and processes. OD is helping organisation members go beyond surface changes to transform the underlying assumptions and values that govern their behaviours. The different concepts and methods discussed in this book are increasingly finding their way into government agencies, manufacturing firms, multinational corporations, service industries, educational institutions and not-for-profit organisations. Perhaps at no other time has OD been more responsive and practically relevant to organisations' needs if they are to operate effectively in a highly complex and changing world.

Organisation development is obviously important to those who plan a professional career in the field, either as an internal consultant employed by an organisation or as an external consultant practising in many organisations. A career in OD can be highly rewarding, providing challenging and interesting assignments that involve working with managers and employees to improve their organisations and their work lives. In today's environment, the demand for OD professionals is rising rapidly. For example, consulting has been the biggest area of growth for Australia's 'Big Five' accounting practices, and it now represents 25–30% of their total worldwide billings. The owners of fast-growing companies are making more use of consultants, and 58% increased the use of their services. This would indicate that career opportunities in OD should continue to expand in Australia.

Organisation development is also important to those who have no aspirations to become professional practitioners. All managers and administrators are responsible for supervising and developing subordinates and for improving their departments' performance. Similarly, all staff specialists, such as accountants, financial analysts, engineers, personnel specialists or market researchers, are responsible for offering advice and counsel to managers, and for introducing new methods and practices. Finally, OD is important to general managers and other senior executives as it can help the whole organisation be more flexible, adaptable and effective.

Organisation development can help managers and staff personnel perform their tasks more effectively. It can provide the skills and knowledge necessary for establishing effective interpersonal and helping relationships. It can show personnel how to work effectively with others in diagnosing complex problems and devising appropriate solutions. It can help others become committed to the solutions, thereby increasing the chances of their successful implementation. In short, OD is highly relevant to anyone who has to work with and through others in organisations.

Application 1.2 demonstrates how organisations, through all levels, need to recognise that organisational innovation is a key driver for change if they are to succeed.

APPLiCATiON 1.2

INNOVATIVE ADVANTAGE

According to the CEO of AIM Qld & NT, Carolyn Barker, at the very core of organisational innovation is the concept of renewal. She says that clever organisations are able to turn the renewal process into a core competency, one that underpins organisational strategy through aligned vision, mission and values, and this lays at the heart of a healthy organisational culture.

'Right here and in the future, cutting costs and remaining efficient will be mandatory for corporate health but those strategies alone will not ensure continued survival. Today, organisations of all sizes rely on customer service as their chief differentiator, but that, too, will be commoditised and no longer a competitive advantage.'

Sustainable competitive advantage and long-term profits will only be built through innovation that is strategic and continuous. There are four essential supporting mechanisms for innovation: idea generation, operational management, entrepreneurship and leadership.

We must remember that leadership of the innovation process is not confined to the top tiers of the organisation. It is important that leaders at all levels be involved in and aligned with the process. This is recognising those who have cultural influence within the organisation and engaging their participation as innovation champions.

It is important to ask oneself necessary questions such as:
- What is your current level of innovation, and that of your competitors?
- Does current innovation relate to client needs?

- How much innovation is needed for survival?
- Do your organisational systems help or hinder the innovation process?
- Do you need to restructure?

Managers must examine their own role in the innovation process – their personal ability and willingness to step outside of the square.

Source: Carolyn Barker, 'Innovative advantage', *Management Today*, Sept. 2004.

Critical Thinking Question: 'Right here and in the future, cutting costs and remaining efficient will be mandatory for corporate health but those strategies alone will not ensure continued survival.' Is this statement true? Why or why not?

A SHORT HISTORY OF ORGANISATION DEVELOPMENT

A brief history of OD will help to clarify the evolution of the term as well as some of the problems and confusions that have surrounded its development. As currently practised, OD emerged from five major backgrounds or stems, as shown in Figure 1.2. The first was the growth of the National Training Laboratories (NTL) and the development of training groups, otherwise known as sensitivity training or T-groups. The second stem of OD was the classic work on action research conducted by social scientists who were interested in applying research to the management of change. An important feature of action research was a technique known as survey feedback. Kurt Lewin, a prolific theorist, researcher and practitioner in group dynamics and social change, was instrumental in the development of T-groups, survey feedback and action research. His work led to the initial development of OD and still serves as a major source of its concepts and methods. The third stem reflects the work of Rensis Likert and represents the application of participative management to organisation structure and design. The fourth background is the approach that focuses on productivity and the quality of work life. The fifth stem of OD, and the most recent influence on current practice, involves strategic change and organisational transformation.

Figure 1.2   The five stems of OD practice

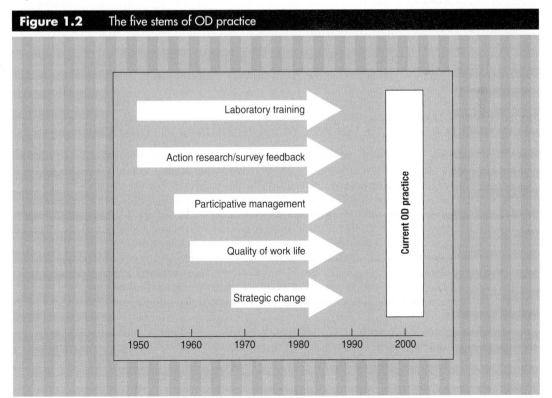

Laboratory training background

This stem of OD pioneered laboratory training or the T-group: a small, unstructured group in which participants learn from their own interactions and evolving dynamics about such issues as interpersonal relations, personal growth, leadership and group dynamics. Essentially, laboratory training began in the summer of 1946, when Kurt Lewin and his staff at the Research Center for Group Dynamics at the Massachusetts Institute of Technology (MIT) were asked by the Connecticut Interracial Commission and the Committee on Community Interrelations of the American Jewish Congress for help in research on training community leaders. A workshop was developed, and the community leaders were brought together to learn about leadership and discuss problems. At the end of each day, the researchers discussed privately what behaviours and group dynamics they had observed. The community leaders asked permission to sit in on these feedback sessions, to which the researchers finally gave their assent. Thus, the first T-group was formed, in which people reacted to data about their own behaviour. The researchers drew two conclusions about this first T-group experiment: (1) feedback about group interaction was a rich learning experience, and (2) the process of 'group building' had potential for learning that could be transferred to 'back-home' situations.[10]

A new phenomenon arose in 1950 when an attempt was made to have T-groups in the morning and cognitive-skill groups (A-groups) in the afternoon. However, the staff found that the high level of carry-over from the morning sessions turned the afternoon A-groups into T-groups, despite the resistance of the afternoon staff members, who were committed to cognitive-skill development. This was the beginning of a decade of learning experimentation and frustration, especially in the attempt to transfer skills learned in the T-group setting to the 'back-home' situation.

Three trends emerged in the 1950s: (1) the emergence of regional laboratories, (2) the expansion of summer program sessions to year-round sessions, and (3) the expansion of the T-group into business and industry, with NTL members becoming increasingly involved with industry programs. Notable among these industry efforts was the pioneering work of Douglas McGregor at Union Carbide, of Herbert Shepard and Robert Blake at Esso Standard Oil (now Exxon), and of McGregor and Richard Beckhard at General Mills. Applications of T-group methods at these three companies introduced the term 'organisation development' and led corporate personnel and industrial relations specialists to expand their roles to offer internal consulting services to managers.[11]

Applying T-group techniques to organisations gradually became known as 'team building': a process for helping work groups become more effective in accomplishing tasks and satisfying member needs.

Action research and survey feedback background

Kurt Lewin was also involved in the second movement that led to OD's emergence as a practical field of social science. This second background refers to the processes of action research and survey feedback. The action research contribution began in the 1940s with studies conducted by social scientists John Collier, Kurt Lewin and William Whyte, who discovered that research needed to be closely linked to action if organisation members were to use it to manage change. A collaborative effort was initiated between organisation members and social scientists to collect research data about an organisation's functioning, analyse it for causes of problems, and devise and implement solutions. After implementation, further data were collected to assess the results, and the cycle of data collection and action often continued. The results of action research were twofold: members of organisations were able to use research on themselves to guide action and change, and social scientists were able to study that process to derive new knowledge that could be used elsewhere.

A key component of most action research studies was the systematic collection of survey data, which were subsequently fed back to the client organisation. Following Lewin's death in 1947, his Research Center for Group Dynamics at MIT moved to Michigan and joined with the Survey Research Center as part of the Institute for Social Research. The institute was headed by Rensis Likert, a pioneer in the development of scientific approaches to attitude surveys. Likert's doctoral dissertation at Columbia University, 'A technique for the measurement of attitudes', was the classic study in which he developed the widely used, five-point 'Likert Scale'.[12]

In an early study of the institute, Likert and Floyd Mann administered a company-wide survey of management and employee attitudes at Detroit Edison.[13] Over a two-year period beginning in 1948, three sets of data were developed: (1) the viewpoints of 8000 non-supervisory employees about their supervisors, promotion opportunities and work satisfaction with fellow employees; (2) similar reactions from first- and second-line supervisors; and (3) information from higher levels of management.

The feedback process that evolved was an 'interlocking chain of conferences'. The major findings of the survey were first reported to the top management and then transmitted throughout the organisation. The feedback sessions were conducted in task groups, with supervisors and their immediate subordinates discussing the data together. Although there was little substantial research evidence, the researchers intuitively felt that this was a powerful process for change.

In 1950, eight accounting departments asked for a repeat of the survey, and this generated a new cycle of feedback meetings. Feedback approaches were used in four departments, but the method varied, with two of the remaining departments receiving feedback only at the departmental level. Because of changes in key personnel, nothing was done in two departments.

A third follow-up study indicated that more significant and positive changes (such as job satisfaction) had occurred in the departments that were receiving feedback than in the two departments that did not participate. From these findings, Likert and Mann derived several conclusions about the effects of survey feedback on organisation change, and this led to extensive applications of survey-feedback methods in a variety of settings. The common pattern of data collection, data feedback, action planning, implementation and follow-up data collection in both action research and survey feedback can be seen in these examples.

Participative management background

The intellectual and practical advances from the laboratory training and action research/survey-feedback stems were closely followed by the belief that a human-relations approach represented a one-best-way to manage organisations. This belief was exemplified in research that associated Likert's participative management (System 4) style with organisational effectiveness.[14] This framework characterised organisation as having one of four types of management systems:[15]

- *Exploitative authoritative* systems (System 1) exhibit an autocratic, top-down approach to leadership. Employee motivation is based on punishment and occasional rewards. Communication is primarily downward, and there is little lateral interaction or teamwork. Decision making and control reside primarily at the top of the organisation. System 1 results in mediocre performance.
- *Benevolent authoritative* systems (System 2) are similar to System 1, except that management is more paternalistic. Employees are allowed a little more interaction, communication and decision making but within limited boundaries defined by management.
- *Consultative* systems (System 3) increase employee interaction, communication, and decision making. Although employees are consulted about problems and decisions, management still makes the final decisions. Productivity is good, and employees are moderately satisfied with the organisation.
- *Participative* group systems (System 4) are almost the opposite of System 1. Designed around group methods of decision making and supervision, this system fosters high degrees of member involvement and participation. Work groups are highly involved in setting goals, making decisions, improving methods and appraising results. Communication occurs both laterally and vertically, and decisions are linked throughout the organisation by overlapping group membership. Shown in Figure 1.3, this linking-pin structure ensures continuity in communication and decision making across groups by means of people who are members of more than one group – the groups they supervise and the higher level groups of which they are members. System 4 achieves high levels of productivity, quality and member satisfaction.

Figure 1.3   The linking pin

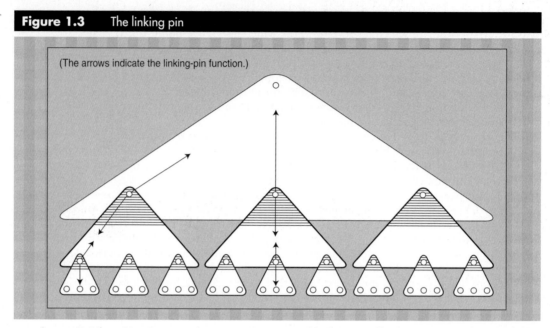

(The arrows indicate the linking-pin function.)

Source: R. Likert, *New Patterns of Management*, New York, McGraw-Hill, 1961. Reproduced by permission of the McGraw-Hill Companies.

Likert applied System 4 management to organisations, using a survey-feedback process. The intervention generally started with organisation members completing the profile of organisational characteristics.[16] The survey asked members for their opinions about both the present and ideal conditions of six organisational features: leadership, motivation, communication, decisions, goals and control. In the second stage, the data were fed back to different work groups within the organisation. Group members examined the discrepancy between their present situation and their ideal, generally using System 4 as the ideal benchmark, and generated action plans to move the organisation towards System 4 conditions.

In Application 1.3, Tom McKaskill warns that business owners will one day face the prospect of selling up, and they will have to tell their staff.

APPLiCATiON 1.3

CHANGE MANAGEMENT

In an environment in which a substantial number of owner-managers are nearing retirement and intend to sell their businesses, the problem of how and when to inform their employees about an impending sale of the business can be stressful. Many owners are concerned about the effect on morale, and if they handle the situation poorly, they will lose the very people who contribute to the value of the business.

It is not unreasonable for an employee to be fearful of the changes that take place when a business is sold. People fear change, and few employees will have positive feelings about the sale of the business. Naturally, the owners of the business do not want to lose employees before they sell. They appreciate the uncertainties surrounding an impending sale can be disruptive and choose not to announce the sale. On the other hand, they would feel disloyal to their employees by not informing them that a sale of the business is probable.

Jonathan Levie, of the Hunter Centre for Entrepreneurship at the University of Strathclyde, Glasgow, recently conducted a series of interviews with serial entrepreneurs who have sold several businesses. His findings show that entrepreneurs are polarised on this issue. Some believe firmly that the sale negotiations should be conducted in secret, and that the less notice employees have about the impending sale the better. Others strongly recommend taking employees into their confidence well before the event so that they can prepare themselves for the anticipated changes.

Employees told at the last minute that a business is being sold can often feel resentful or betrayed. They feel that they have given their best efforts to an owner who did not trust them enough to share the most important change that will happen to the business, and therefore to them. This could result in the employees resigning or intentionally undermining the company in the eyes of potential buyers, believing their efforts are no longer valued.

Employees who are qualified and have good employment prospects are less concerned about change. If they are made redundant, they know they can readily find another job. On balance, I would recommend actively involving employees in the process.

Source: Tom McKaskill, 'Change Management', *Business Review Weekly*, 20–26 April 2006.

Critical Thinking Questions: When should employees become involved in the change process? How involved should they be?

Productivity and quality-of-work-life background

Projects to improve productivity and the quality of work life (QWL) were originally developed in Europe during the 1950s. Based on the research of Eric Trist and his colleagues at the Tavistock Institute of Human Relations in London, this approach examined the technical and human sides of organisations and how they interrelated.[17] It led to the development of the sociotechnical systems methods of work design that underlie many of the employee involvement and empowerment efforts occurring in Australia today.

Early practitioners in the United Kingdom, Ireland, Norway and Sweden developed work designs that were aimed at better integrating technology and people. These QWL programs generally involved joint participation by unions and management in the design of work, and resulted in work designs that gave employees high levels of discretion, task variety and feedback about results. Perhaps the most distinguishing characteristic of these QWL programs was the development of self-managing work groups as a new form of work design. These groups were composed of multiskilled workers who were given the necessary autonomy and information to design and manage their own task performances.

In Australia today, top management keeps employees motivated by a combination of good financial rewards, an interesting environment and challenging projects. The staff are also given feedback about their own work and kept informed about the company's situation.

Gradually, QWL programs expanded beyond individual jobs to include group forms of work and other features of the workplace that can affect employee productivity and satisfaction, such as reward systems, work flows, management styles and the physical work environment. This expanded focus resulted in larger-scale and longer-term projects than the early job-enrichment programs and shifted attention beyond the individual worker to work groups and the larger work context. Equally importantly, it added the critical dimension of organisational efficiency to what had been up to that time a predominant concern for the human dimension. The economic and human-resource problems that faced Australia during the 1980s have further reinforced this focus upon organisational efficiency.

At one point, the productivity and QWL approach became so popular that it was called an ideological movement. International conferences were aimed at identifying a coalition of groups from among unions and management that supported QWL ideals of employee involvement, participative management and industrial democracy. Some Australian companies adopted the Japanese method of management and employee participation, which involved the spread of quality circles. Ford was one such company. Popularised in Japan, quality circles are groups of employees trained in problem-solving methods who meet regularly to resolve work environment, productivity and quality-control concerns and to develop more efficient ways of working.

Finally, the productivity and QWL approach has gained new momentum by joining forces with the total quality movement advocated by W. Edward Deming[18] and Joseph Juran.[19] In this approach, the organisation is viewed as a set of processes that can be linked to the quality of products and services, modelled through statistical techniques and continuously improved.[20] Quality efforts at Toyota, Sheraton and Ericsson, along with federal government support through the establishment of the Business Excellence Awards, have popularised this strategy of organisation development. Application 1.4 identifies non-traditional forms of management to improve the likelihood of successful change.

APPLiCATiON 1.4

Flaky biz

Weird, indulgent, oppressive? What are we to make of the rush towards non-traditional methods for getting the most out of our workers?

Ducking off for your lunchtime meditation? Or perhaps it's the office yoga class? And there is still time to get tickets for Deepak Chopra's (spiritual writer) latest seminar on 'SynchroDestiny'.

It's hard to pinpoint quite when the business world started to embrace some decidedly non-corporate practices and activities as part of its employee development repertoire. Whether it's New Age-style seminars to get in touch with your spiritual side or become more emotionally intelligent.

Most fall into a few broad streams: the personal transformation quest, the team-building program, and the health and well-being initiatives. They all have a long lineage, with connections to some of the major psychological, self-help and philosophical movements, plus the major theories on organisational development of the last century.

When she worked at the professional services firm PWC, Sandy Blackburn-Wright, now head of culture and learning at Westpac, was surprised at the popularity of meditation: 'We were using McKinsey for culture-change work and there was a strand on the high-performance mind. It was all meditation really. It was the partners' (Westpac) favourite part of culture change.'

…

Fads come and go in this arena, and at the moment Buddhism for business and yoga at work, plus bonding through cooking classes, are having their time in the spotlight. A range of Australian companies, from banks to consultants, are offering their employees the chance to zone out at lunchtime, or get a massage at the keyboard.

This is big business. The promise of redemption and success through personal 'awakening' holds enormous appeal for growing numbers of people, with some of the most popular techniques being co-opted by the corporate world.

Source: Catherine Fox, 'Flaky Biz', *Boss Magazine*, *Australian Financial Review*, 13/4/06.

Critical Thinking Question: Comment on how successful will these strategies be in the future. Can you anticipate any difficulties? Why/why not?

Strategic change background

The strategic change background is a recent influence on OD's evolution. As organisations and their technological, political and social environments became more complex and more uncertain, the scale and intricacies of organisational change increased. This trend has produced the need for a strategic perspective from OD and has encouraged planned change processes at the organisation level.[21]

Strategic change involves improving the alignment in an organisation's environment, strategy and organisation design.[22] Strategic change interventions include efforts to improve both the organisation's relationship to its environment and the fit between its technical, political and cultural systems.[23] The need for strategic change is usually triggered by some major disruption to the organisation, such as the lifting of regulatory requirements, a technological breakthrough or a new CEO from outside the organisation.[24]

One of the first applications of strategic change was Richard Beckhard's use of open systems planning.[25] He proposed that an organisation's environment and its strategy could be described and analysed. Based on the organisation's core mission, the differences between what the environment demanded and how the organisation responded could be reduced and performance improved. Since then, change agents have proposed a variety of large-scale or strategic change models.[26] Each of these models recognises that strategic change involves multiple levels of the organisation and a change in its culture, that it is often driven from the top by powerful executives and that it has important impacts on performance.

The strategic change background has significantly influenced OD practice. For example, the implementation of strategic change requires OD practitioners to be familiar with competitive strategy, finance and marketing, as well as team building, action research and survey feedback. Together, these skills have improved OD's relevance to organisations and their managers.

EVOLUTION IN ORGANISATION DEVELOPMENT

Current practice in organisation development is strongly influenced by these five backgrounds, as well as by the trends that shape change in organisations. The laboratory training, action research and survey feedback, and participative management roots of OD are evident in the strong value focus that underlies its practice. The more recent influences (the quality-of-work-life and strategic change backgrounds) have greatly improved the relevance and rigour of OD practice. They have added financial and economic indicators of effectiveness to OD's traditional measures of work satisfaction and personal growth.

Today, the field is being influenced by the globalisation and information technology trends described earlier. OD is being carried out in many more countries and in many more organisations that operate on a worldwide basis, and this is generating a whole new set of interventions as well as adaptations to traditional OD practice.[27] In addition, OD must adapt its methods to the technologies now being used in organisations. As information technology continues to influence organisational environments, strategies and structures, OD will need to manage change processes in cyberspace as well as face to face. The diversity of this evolving discipline has led to tremendous growth in the number of professional practitioners, in the kinds of organisations involved with OD and in the range of countries within which OD is practised.

The expansion of the OD network is one indication of this growth. OD divisions have been set up by many training and development organisations, and courses are being taught at Australian universities at postgraduate and undergraduate levels; for example, the Australian Graduate School of Management (University of Sydney), which offers the Graduate Certificate in Change Management.[28]

In addition to the growth of professional societies and educational programs in OD, the field continues to develop new theorists, researchers and practitioners who are building on the work of the early pioneers and extending it to contemporary issues and conditions. Included among the first generation of contributors are Chris Argyris, who developed a learning and action–science approach to OD;[29] Warren Bennis, who tied executive leadership to strategic change;[30] Edgar Schein, who continues to develop process approaches to OD, including the key role of organisational culture in change management;[31] Richard Beckhard, who focused attention on the importance of managing transitions;[32] and Robert Tannenbaum, who continues to sensitise OD to the personal dimension of participants' lives.[33]

Among the second generation of contributors are Warner Burke, whose work has done much to make OD a professional field;[34] Larry Greiner, who has brought the ideas of power and evolution into the mainstream of OD;[35] Edward Lawler III, who has extended OD to reward systems and employee involvement;[36] Newton Margulies and Anthony Raia, who together have kept our attention on the values underlying OD and what they mean for contemporary practice;[37] and Peter Vaill and Craig Lundberg, who continue to develop OD as a practical science.[38]

Included in the newest generation of OD contributors are Dave Brown, whose work on action research and developmental organisations has extended OD into community and societal change;[39] Thomas Cummings, whose work on sociotechnical systems, self-designing organisations and transorganisational development has led OD beyond the boundaries of single organisations to groups of organisations and their environments;[40] Max Widen, whose international work in industrial democracy draws attention to the political aspects of OD;[41] William Pasmore and Jerry Porras, who have done much to put OD on a sound research and conceptual base;[42] and Peter Block, who has focused attention on consulting skills, empowerment processes and reclaiming our individuality.[43] Other newcomers who are making important contributions to the field include Ken Murrell and Joanne Preston, who have focused attention on the internationalisation of OD;[44] Sue Mohrman and Gerry Ledford, who have focused on team-based organisations and compensation;[45] and David Cooperrider, who has turned our attention towards the positive aspects of organisations.[46] In Australia there are such centres as the Centre for Corporate Change in the Australian Graduate School of Management at the University of New South Wales and the Centre for Workplace Culture Change at RMIT University, both of which actively contributed to the body of research. These academic contributors are joined by a large number of internal OD practitioners and external consultants who lead organisational change, such as the Australian Institute of Training and Development.[47]

Many different organisations have undertaken a wide variety of OD efforts. Many organisations have been at the forefront of innovating new change techniques and methods, as well as new organisational forms. Larger corporations that have engaged in organisation development include General Electric, General Motors, Ford, Corning Glass Works, Intel, Hewlett-Packard, Polaroid, Procter & Gamble and IBM. Traditionally, much of this work was considered confidential and not publicised. Today, however, organisations have increasingly gone public with their OD efforts, sharing the lessons with others.

Organisation development work is also being done in schools, communities and local, state and federal governments. A system that encourages staff at Casey Institute of Technical and Further Education (TAFE) to learn from one another has won its designer, Stuart Williams, a prestigious individual achievement recognition award from the Australian Human Resources Institute (AHRI). It requires all departments to provide six hours of training to fellow staff members annually.[48] The University of Technology in Sydney (UTS) is awarding testamurs to employees of AMP who sign up for its workplace-based program. Described as a revolutionary step by AMP management, the initiative is designed to assess work performance in terms of academic criteria. The award courses, from the faculties of business or mathematical and computer sciences, are based on performance agreements negotiated between AMP, UTS and the employee.[49]

Organisation development is increasingly international. As well as in South-East Asia, it has been applied in the United States, Canada, Sweden, Norway, Germany, Japan, Israel, South Africa, Mexico, Venezuela, the Philippines, China (including Hong Kong), Russia and the Netherlands. These efforts have involved such organisations as Saab (Sweden), Norsk Hydro (Norway), Imperial Chemical Industries (England), Shell Oil Company (The Netherlands), Orrefors (Sweden) and Alcan Canada Products.

Although it is evident that OD has vastly expanded in recent years, relatively few of the total number of organisations in Australia are actively involved in formal OD programs. However, many organisations are applying OD approaches and techniques without knowing that such a term exists.

OVERVIEW OF THE BOOK

This book presents the process and practice of organisation development in a logical flow, as shown in Figure 1.4. In Part 1, Chapter 1 provides a comprehensive overview of OD that describes the process of planned change, those who perform the transition and the various types of interventions. Part 2 covers an overview of OD, the process of OD and OD interventions. In particular, Chapter 2 discusses the nature of planned change and presents some models that describe the change process. Planned change is viewed as an ongoing cycle of four activities: entering and contracting; diagnosing; planning and implementing; and evaluating and institutionalising. Chapter 3 describes the OD practitioner and provides insight into the knowledge and skills needed to practise OD, and the kinds of career issues that can be expected.

The book continues with the next three chapters describing the process of organisation development. Chapter 4 characterises the first activity in this process – entering an organisational system and contracting with it for organisation development work – and presents the steps associated with the next major activity of the OD process: information gathering. This involves helping the organisation to discover causes of problems and suggesting areas for improvement. Chapter 4 also presents an open systems model to guide diagnosis at three levels

Figure 1.4   Overview of the book

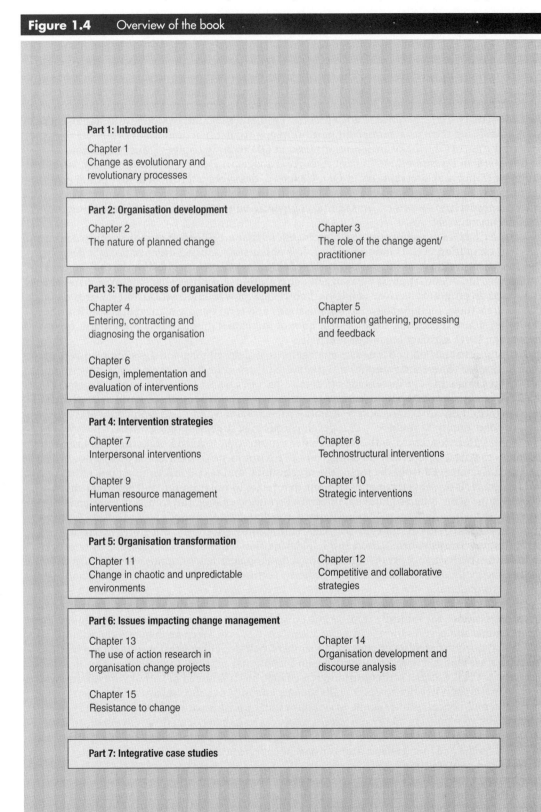

Part 1: Introduction

Chapter 1
Change as evolutionary and
revolutionary processes

Part 2: Organisation development

Chapter 2
The nature of planned change

Chapter 3
The role of the change agent/
practitioner

Part 3: The process of organisation development

Chapter 4
Entering, contracting and
diagnosing the organisation

Chapter 5
Information gathering, processing
and feedback

Chapter 6
Design, implementation and
evaluation of interventions

Part 4: Intervention strategies

Chapter 7
Interpersonal interventions

Chapter 8
Technostructural interventions

Chapter 9
Human resource management
interventions

Chapter 10
Strategic interventions

Part 5: Organisation transformation

Chapter 11
Change in chaotic and unpredictable
environments

Chapter 12
Competitive and collaborative
strategies

Part 6: Issues impacting change management

Chapter 13
The use of action research in
organisation change projects

Chapter 14
Organisation development and
discourse analysis

Chapter 15
Resistance to change

Part 7: Integrative case studies

of analysis: the total organisation, the group or department, and the individual job or position. Chapter 5 reviews methods for collecting, analysing and feeding back diagnostic data. Chapter 6 addresses issues concerned with the third activity: designing, planning, implementing and evaluating change. It finishes with an overview of the intervention design process. Major kinds of interventions are identified, and the specific approaches that make up the next four parts of the book are introduced. It discusses the process of managing change and identifies key factors that contribute to the successful implementation of change programs. The chapter also describes the final activity of the planned change process: evaluating OD interventions and stabilising or institutionalising them as a permanent part of organisational functioning.

Part 4 presents the major interventions used in OD today. Chapters 7 and 9 concern interpersonal interventions and human resource management interventions. These are the oldest and most traditional interventions in OD. Chapter 7 describes interpersonal and group process approaches: T-groups, process consultation and team building. It also presents more system-wide process approaches, such as organisational confrontation meetings, intergroup relations and large-group interventions.

Chapter 8 reviews technostructural interventions that are aimed at organisation structure and at better integrating people and technology. It is about restructuring organisations; it describes the alternative methods of organising work activities as well as processes for downsizing and re-engineering the organisation. It also suggests interventions for improving employee involvement. These change programs increase employee knowledge, power, information and rewards through parallel structures, high-involvement organisations and total quality management. It describes change programs directed at work design, both of individual jobs and of work groups, for greater employee satisfaction and productivity.

Chapter 9 focuses on performance management and developing and assisting members of an organisation. These interventions are traditionally associated with the personal function in the organisation and have increasingly become a part of OD activities. Process management is a cycle of activities that helps groups and individuals set goals, appraise work and reward performance. It discusses three interventions – career planning and development, workforce diversity and employee wellness – that develop and assist organisation members.

Chapter 10 is concerned with strategic interventions that focus on organising the firm's resources to gain a competitive advantage in the environment. These change programs are generally managed from the top of the organisation and take considerable time, effort and resources. It presents three interventions that relate to organisation and environment relationships: open systems planning, integrated strategic change and transorganisational development. Open systems planning is aimed at helping an organisation to assess its environment and develop strategies for relating to it more effectively. Integrated strategic change infuses strategy formulation and implementation with the OD perspective to improve organisation performance. Transorganisational development helps organisations to form partnerships with other organisations in order to perform tasks that are too complex and costly for them to undertake alone.

In Part 5, Chapter 11 looks at change in chaotic and unpredictable environments. It describes three interventions for radically transforming organisations: culture change, self-designing organisations and organisation learning. Culture change is directed at changing the values, beliefs and norms shared by organisation members. Self-designing organisational interventions are concerned with helping organisations gain the internal capacity to fundamentally alter themselves. Finally, organisation learning is a change process aimed at helping organisations develop and use knowledge to continually change and improve themselves.

Chapter 12 concerns an example of organisational transformation that focuses on dramatically reorganising an organisation's resources to gain a competitive advantage in the environment. It presents four interventions having to do with competition, including integrated strategic change and mergers and acquisitions, and strategies of collaboration, including alliances and networks.

Part 6 (Chapters 13, 14 and 15) is concerned with issues impacting on the evolution and revolution of change management. Chapter 13 revisits action research as an approach to planned change, which was first discussed in Chapter 2. The action research model underlies most current methods of planned change and has long been identified with the practice of organisational development. In particular, John Molineux provides an understanding of action research in organisational change, including: its essential components, its cyclical nature, benefits and problems, and the importance of reflection. The author also develops a systemic understanding of action research, and how it can operate in a context of complexity and non-linearity. When students have completed the chapter, they should be able to review and understand certain models used in conjunction with an action research change program, including Soft Systems Methodology, a model of strategic human resource management used for cultural change, and the FMA model of reflection.

Chapter 14 explains the concepts of discourse and discourse analysis. This chapter further reviews how language and discourse regulation impact on change initiatives. James Latham identifies communities of discourse in organisations and explains how the core and peripheral members impact on OD. By the completion of this chapter, students will be challenged to explore ways in which discourse processes can assist and/or hinder OD and change initiatives, as well as how they link to OD techniques and practices.

Chapter 15 revisits the debate on resistance to change. Margaret Heffernan and Anne Smythe emphasise that resistance to change is a complex issue that is caused by many factors and is often driven by the paradigm or framework that each individual or department is operating within. It is important to be mindful that resistance is to be expected when implementing organisational change, that it can be overt or covert and that it has both positive and negative impacts on organisations' outcomes. In fact it is crucial to be more aware that 'resistance' is one of a range of human responses to the change management process, that it can be managed and worked with effectively, and that it requires committed leadership. Students should be aware that the effective management of resistance requires management and leadership skills, and appropriate human resource development strategies and support mechanisms to be put in place.

Part 7 provides a selection of case studies, which are instances of change where organisations have been impacted by a variety of circumstances. They are integrative and aim to assist with understanding the ramifications of change strategies on the organisation.

SUMMARY

This chapter introduced OD as a planned change discipline concerned with applying behavioural science knowledge and practice to help organisations achieve greater effectiveness. Managers and staff specialists must work with and through people to perform their jobs, and OD can help them form effective relationships with others. Organisations are faced with rapidly accelerating change, and OD can help them cope with the consequences of change. The concept of OD has multiple meanings. The definition provided here resolves some of the problems with earlier definitions. The history of OD reveals its five roots: laboratory training; action research and survey feedback; participative management; productivity and quality of work life; and strategic change. The current practice of OD goes far beyond its humanistic origins by incorporating concepts from organisation strategy and structure that complement the early emphasis on social processes. The continued growth in the number and diversity of OD approaches, practitioners and involved organisations attests to the health of the discipline and offers a favourable prospect for the future.

ACTIVITIES

Review questions

1. Define organisation development and organisation transformation. How are they different? Is it possible for these approaches to coexist? Why? Why not?

2. Organisation development attempts to help an organisation cope with various aspects of the organisation's environment. What are these aspects? Give current examples of OD and explain its value to the organisation.

▷▷

③ What is the meaning of 'T-group', and when was the first one formed? Has the concept changed over time?

④ What is the assumption that underlies the use of survey feedback in OD? Why is it important to distinguish this from other forms of survey? What is the value of survey feedback in an action research approach to change?

⑤ What is the most distinguishing characteristic of QWL? Explain the relationship between QWL and TQM.

⑥ What is productivity? What factors have an effect on productivity? Give current examples of these factors.

⑦ With what functional considerations do practitioners need to be familiar if they are to create strategic change? Strategic change has often been confused with organisation transformation – why has that been the case?

Discussion and essay questions

① Discuss the value of planned change and explain why it is necessary. Use examples throughout your response to support your understanding.

② Compare and contrast the five 'stems' of organisation development: laboratory training, action research/survey feedback, participative management, quality of work life and strategic change. Include in your answer the circumstances that are most conducive to the success of these strategies.

③ Outline the key events in the history and evolution of organisation development. What do you see to be the future directions of the field? How would you suggest that practitioners proactively promote or facilitate the evolution of OD?

④ Identify a company/corporation that has undergone or is undergoing organisational development or change. Identify the steps taken and, with the benefit of hindsight, make recommendations to improve the process.

NOTES

1 D. Waddell, *E-business in Australia: Concepts and Cases* (Sydney: Pearson Education Australia, 2002): 23.
2 M. Tushman and C. O'Reilly, 'Ambidextrous organisations: Managing evolutionary and revolutionary change', *California Management Review*, 28 (Summer 1996): 11.
3 W. Burke, *Organization Development: Principles and Practices* (Boston, MA: Little Brown, 1982).
4 W. French, 'Organization development: objectives, assumptions, and strategies', *California Management Review*, 12 (February 1969): 23–34.
5 R. Beckhard, *Organization Development: Strategies and Models* (Reading, MA: Addison-Wesley, 1969).
6 M. Beer, *Organization Change and Development: A Systems View* (Santa Monica, CA: Goodyear Publishing, 1980).
7 D. Dunphy and D. Stace, *Beyond the Boundaries* (Sydney: McGraw-Hill, 1994).
8 J. Naisbitt and P. Aburdene, *Re-inventing the Corporation* (New York: Warner Books, 1985); N. Tichy and M. Devanna, *The Transformational Leader* (New York: John Wiley and Sons, 1986); R. Kilmann and T. Covin, eds, *Corporate Transformation: Revitalizing Organizations for a Competitive World* (San Francisco: Jossey-Bass, 1988); T. Peters, *Thriving on Chaos: Handbook for a Management Revolution* (New York: Alfred A. Knopf, 1987); J. Kotter, *Leading Change* (Cambridge, MA: Harvard Business School Press, 1996).
9 T. Stewart, 'Welcome to the revolution', *Fortune* (13 December 1993): 66–80; C. Farrell, 'The new economic era', *Business Week* (18 November 1994).
10 L. Bradford, 'Biography of an institution', *Journal of Applied Behavioural Science*, 3 (1967): 127; A. Marrow, 'Events leading to the establishment of the National Training Laboratories', *Journal of Applied Behavioural Science*, 3 (1967): 145–50.
11 W. French, 'The emergence and early history of organization development with reference to influences upon and interactions among some of the key actors', in *Contemporary Organization Development: Current Thinking and Applications*, ed. D. Warrick (Glenview, IL: Scott, Foresman, 1985): 12–27.
12 ibid., 19–20.

13 F. Mann, 'Studying and creating change', in *The Planning of Change: Readings in the Applied Behavioural Sciences*, eds W. Bennis, K. Benne and R. Chin (New York: Holt, Rinehart and Winston, 1962): 605–15.

14 R. Likert, *The Human Organization* (New York: McGraw-Hill, 1967); S. Seashore and D. Bowers, 'Durability of organizational change', *American Psychologist*, 25 (1970): 227–33; D. Mosley, 'System Four revisited: some new insights', *Organization Development Journal*, 5 (Spring 1987): 19–24.

15 ibid.

16 ibid.

17 A. Rice, *Productivity and Social Organisation: The Ahmedabad Experiment* (London: Tavistock Publications, 1958); E. Trist and K. Bamforth, 'Some social and psychological consequences of the longwall method of coal-getting', *Human Relations*, 4 (January 1951): 1–38.

18 M. Walton, *The Deming Management Method* (New York: Dodd, Mead and Company, 1986).

19 J. Juran, *Juran on Leadership for Quality: An Executive Handbook* (New York: Free Press, 1989).

20 'The quality imperative', *Business Week*, Special Issue (25 October 1991).

21 M. Jelinek and J. Litterer, 'Why OD must become strategic', in *Research in Organizational Change and Development*, 2, eds W. Pasmore and R. Woodman (Greenwich, CT: JAI Press, 1988): 135–62; P. Buller, 'For successful strategic change: blend OD practices with strategic management', *Organizational Dynamics* (Winter 1988): 42–55; C. Worley, D. Hitchin and W. Ross, *Integrated Strategic Change* (Reading, MA: Addison-Wesley, 1996).

22 Worley, Hitchin and Ross, *Integrated Strategic Change*, ibid.

23 R. Beckhard and R. Harris, *Organizational Transitions: Managing Complex Change*, 2nd edn (Reading, MA: Addison-Wesley, 1987); N. Tichy, *Managing Strategic Change* (New York: John Wiley and Sons, 1983); E. Schein, *Organizational Culture and Leadership* (San Francisco: Jossey-Bass, 1985); C. Lundberg, 'Working with culture', *Journal of Organization Change Management*, 1 (1988): 38–47.

24 D. Miller and P. Freisen, 'Momentum and revolution in organisation adaptation', *Academy of Management Journal*, 23 (1980): 591–614; M. Tushman and E. Romanelli, 'Organizational evolution: a metamorphosis model of convergence and reorientation', in *Research in Organizational Behaviour*, 7, eds L. Cummings and B. Staw (Greenwich, CT: JAI Press, 1985): 171–222.

25 Beckhard and Harris, *Organizational Transitions*, op. cit.

26 T. Covin and R. Kilmann, 'Critical issues in large scale organization change', *Journal of Organization Change Management*, 1 (1988): 59–72; A. Mohrman, S. Mohrman, G. Ledford Jr, T. Cummings and E. Lawler, eds, *Large Scale Organization Change* (San Francisco: Jossey-Bass, 1989); W. Torbert, 'Leading organizational transformation', in *Research in Organization Change and Development*, 3, eds R. Woodman and W. Pasmore (Greenwich, CT: JAI Press, 1989): 83–116; J. Bartunek and M. Louis, 'The interplay of organization development and organization transformation', in *Research in Organizational Change and Development*, 2, eds W. Pasmore and R. Woodman (Greenwich, CT: JAI Press, 1988): 97–134; A. Levy and U. Merry, *Organizational Transformation: Approaches, Strategies, Theories* (New York: Praeger, 1986).

27 A. Jaeger, 'Organization development and national culture: where's the fit?' *Academy of Management Review*, 11 (1986): 178; G. Hofstede, *Culture's Consequences: International Differences in Work-Related Values* (London: Sage, 1980); P. Sorensen Jr, T. Head, N. Mathys, J. Preston and D. Cooperrider, *Global and International Organization Development* (Champaign, IL: Stipes, 1995).

28 http://www2.agsm.edu.au.

29 C. Argyris and D. Schon, *Organizational Learning* (Reading, MA: Addison-Wesley, 1978); C. Argyris, R. Putnam and D. Smith, *Action Science* (San Francisco: Jossey-Bass, 1985).

30 W. Bennis and B. Nanus, *Leaders* (New York: Harper and Row, 1985).

31 E. Schein, *Process Consultation: Its Role in Organization Development* (Reading, MA: Addison-Wesley, 1969); E. Schein, *Process Consultation, 2: Lessons for Managers and Consultants* (Reading, MA: Addison-Wesley, 1987); E. Schein, *Organizational Culture and Leadership*, 2nd edn (San Francisco: Jossey-Bass, 1992).

32 Beckhard and Harris, *Organizational Transitions*, op. cit.

33 R. Tannenbaum and R. Hanna, 'Holding on, letting go, and moving on: understanding a neglected perspective on change', in *Human Systems Development*, eds R. Tannenbaum, N. Margulies and F. Massarik (San Francisco: Jossey-Bass, 1985): 95–121.

34 W. Burke, *Organization Development: Principles and Practices* (Boston: Little, Brown, 1982); W. Burke, *Organization Development: A Normative View* (Reading, MA: Addison-Wesley, 1987); W. Burke, 'Organization development: then, now, and tomorrow', *OD Practitioner*, 27 (1995): 5–13.

35 L. Greiner and V. Schein, *Power and Organizational Development: Mobilizing Power to Implement Change* (Reading, MA: Addison-Wesley, 1988).

36 E. Lawler III, *Pay and Organization Development* (Reading, MA: Addison-Wesley, 1981); E. Lawler III, *High-Involvement Management* (San Francisco: Jossey-Bass, 1986).

37 A. Raia and N. Margulies, 'Organization development: issues, trends, and prospects', in *Human Systems Development*, eds R. Tannenbaum, N. Margulies and F. Massarik (San Francisco: Jossey-Bass, 1985): 246–72; N. Margulies and A. Raia, 'Some reflections on the values of organizational development', *Academy of Management OD Newsletter*, 1 (Winter 1988): 9–11.

38 P. Vaill, 'OD as a scientific revolution', in *Contemporary Organization Development: Current Thinking and Applications* (Glenview, IL: Scott, Foresman, 1985): 28–41; C. Lundberg, 'On organisation development interventions: a general systems–cybernetic perspective', in *Systems Theory for Organisational Development*, ed. T. Cummings (Chichester: John Wiley and Sons, 1980): 247–71.

39 L. Brown and J. Covey, 'Development organizations and organization development: toward an expanded paradigm for organization development', in *Research in Organizational Change and Development*, l, eds R. Woodman and W. Pasmore (Greenwich, CT: JAI Press, 1987): 59–87.

40 T. Cummings and S. Srivastva, *Management of Work: A Socio-Technical Systems Approach* (San Diego: University Associates, 1977); T. Cummings, 'Transorganizational development', in *Research in Organizational Behaviour*, 6, eds B. Staw and L. Cummings (Greenwich, CT: JAI Press, 1984): 367–422; T. Cummings and S. Mohrman, 'Self-designing organizations: towards implementing quality-of-work-life innovations', in *Research in Organizational Change and Development*, 1, eds R. Woodman and W. Pasmore (Greenwich, CT: JAI Press, 1987): 275–310.

41 M. Widen, 'Sociotechnical systems ideas as public policy in Norway: empowering participation through worker managed change', *Journal of Applied Behavioural Science*, 22 (1986): 239–55.

42 W. Pasmore, C. Haldeman and A. Shani, 'Sociotechnical systems: a North American reflection on empirical studies in North America', *Human Relations*, 32 (1982): 1179–204; W. Pasmore and J. Sherwood, *Sociotechnical Systems: A Source Book* (San Diego: University Associates, 1978); J. Porras, *Stream Analysis: A Powerful Way to Diagnose and Manage Organizational Change* (Reading, MA: Addison-Wesley, 1987); J. Porras, P. Robertson and L. Goldman, 'Organization development: theory, practice, and research', in *Handbook of Industrial and Organizational Psychology*, 2nd edn, ed. M. Dunnette (Chicago: Rand McNally, 1990).

43 P. Block, *Flawless Consulting* (Austin, TX: Learning Concepts, 1981); P. Block, *The Empowered Manager: Positive Political Skills at Work* (San Francisco: Jossey-Bass, 1987); P. Block, *Stewardship* (San Francisco: Berrett-Koehler, 1994).

44 K. Murrell, 'Organization development experiences and lessons in the United Nations development program', *Organization Development Journal*, 12 (1994): 1–16; J. Vogt and K. Murrell, *Empowerment in Organisations* (San Diego: Pfeiffer and Company, 1990); J. Preston and L. DuToit, 'Endemic violence in South Africa: an OD solution applied to two educational settings', *International Journal of Public Administration*, 16 (1993): 1767–91; J. Preston, L. DuToit and I. Barber, 'A potential model of transformational change applied to South Africa', in *Research in Organizational Change and Development*, 9 (Greenwich, CT: JAI Press, in press).

45 S. Mohrman, S. Cohen and A. Mohrman, *Designing Team-Based Organizations* (San Francisco: Jossey-Bass, 1995); S. Cohen and G. Ledford Jr, 'The effectiveness of self-managing teams: a quasi-experiment', *Human Relations*, 47 (1994): 13–43; G. Ledford and E. Lawler, 'Research on employee participation: beating a dead horse?', *Academy of Management Review*, 19 (1994): 633–6; G. Ledford, E. Lawler and S. Mohrman, 'The quality circle and its variations', in *Productivity in Organizations: New Perspectives from Industrial and Organizational Psychology*, eds J. Campbell, R. Campbell and associates (San Francisco: Jossey-Bass, 1988); A. Mohrman, G. Ledford Jr, S. Mohrman, E. Lawler III and T. Cummings, *Large Scale Organization Change* (San Francisco: Jossey-Bass, 1989).

46 D. Cooperrider and T. Thachankary, 'Building the global civic culture: making our lives count', in *Global and International Organization Development*, eds P. Sorensen Jr, T. Head, N. Mathys, J. Preston and D. Cooperrider (Champaign, IL: Stipes, 1995): 282–306; D. Cooperrider, 'Positive image, positive action: the affirmative basis for organising', in *Appreciative Management and Leadership*, eds S. Srivastva, D. Cooperrider and associates (San Francisco, CA: Jossey-Bass, 1990); D. Cooperrider and S. Srivastva, 'Appreciative inquiry in organizational life', in *Organizational Change and Development*, 1, eds R. Woodman and W. Pasmore (Greenwich, CT: JAI Press, 1987): 129–70.

47 S. Marinos, 'Getting down to business beyond 2000', *The Age* (24 February 1998): 6.

48 C. Rance, 'Recognition for Casey learning system', *The Age* (20 September 1997): 12.

49 A. Hepworth, 'Yearning for more learning', *The Australian Financial Review* (5 June 1984): 4.

Online reading

INFOTRAC® COLLEGE EDITION
For additional readings and reviews on organisation development, explore
InfoTrac® College Edition, your online library. Go to **www.infotrac-college.com**
and search for any of the InfoTrac key terms listed below:
- Behavioural science
- Planned change
- Action research
- Participative management

INFOTRAC

ORGANiSATiON DEVELOPMENT

2

THE NATURE OF PLANNED CHANGE

The increasing pace of global, economic and technological development makes change an inevitable feature of organisational life. However, change that happens to an organisation can be distinguished from change that is planned by organisation members. In this book, the term 'change' will refer to planned change. Organisation development is directed at bringing about planned change in order to increase an organisation's effectiveness. It is generally initiated and implemented by managers, often with the help of an OD practitioner, from inside or outside the organisation. Organisations can use planned change to solve problems, to learn from experience, to adapt to external environmental changes, to improve performance and to influence future changes.

All approaches to OD rely on some theory about planned change. These theories describe the different stages through which planned change may be effected in organisations and explain the temporal process of applying OD methods to help organisation members manage change. In this chapter, we first describe and compare three major theories of organisation change: Lewin's change model, the action research model and contemporary adaptations to action research. These three approaches, which have received considerable attention in the field, offer different concepts of planned change. Next we present a general model of planned change that integrates the earlier models and incorporates recent conceptual developments in OD. This model has broad applicability to many types of planned change efforts and serves to organise the chapters in this book. We then discuss different types of change and how the process can vary according to the change situation. Finally, several critiques of planned change are presented.

THEORIES OF PLANNED CHANGE

Conceptions of planned change have tended to focus on how change can be implemented in organisations.[1] Called 'theories of changing', these frameworks describe the activities that must take place in order to initiate and carry out successful organisational change. In this section, we describe and compare three different theories of changing: Lewin's change model, the action research model and contemporary approaches to change.

Lewin's change model

One of the early fundamental models of planned change was provided by Kurt Lewin.[2] He conceived of change as a modification of those forces that keep a system's behaviour stable; specifically, the level of behaviour at any moment in time is the result of two sets of forces: those striving to maintain the status quo and those pushing for change. When both sets of forces are about equal, current levels of behaviour are maintained in what Lewin termed a state of 'quasi-stationary equilibrium'. To change that state, one can increase those forces pushing for change, decrease those forces that maintain the current state or apply some combination of both. For example, the level of performance of a work group might be stable because group norms maintaining that level are equivalent to the supervisor's pressures for change to higher levels. This level can be increased either by changing the group norms to support higher levels of performance or by increasing supervisor pressures to produce at higher levels. Lewin suggested that modifying those forces that maintain the status quo produces less tension and resistance than increasing forces for change, and consequently is a more effective strategy for change.

Lewin viewed this change process as consisting of three steps, which are shown in Figure 2.1(A):

1   *Unfreezing.* This step usually involves reducing those forces that maintain the organisation's behaviour at its present level. Unfreezing is sometimes accomplished through a process of 'psychological disconfirmation'. By introducing information that shows discrepancies between the behaviours desired by organisation members and those behaviours currently exhibited, members can be motivated to engage in change activities.[3]

2   *Moving.* This step shifts the behaviour of the organisation, department or individual to a new level. It involves the development of new behaviours, values and attitudes through changes in organisational structures and processes.

3   *Refreezing.* This step stabilises the organisation at a new state of equilibrium. It is frequently accomplished through the use of supporting mechanisms that reinforce the new organisational state, such as organisational culture, norms, policies and structures.

Lewin's model provides a general framework for understanding organisational change. Because the three steps of change are relatively broad, considerable effort has gone into elaborating them. For example, the planning model (developed by Lippitt, Watson and Westley) arranges Lewin's model into seven steps: scouting, entry, diagnosis (unfreezing), planning, action (movement), stabilisation and evaluation, and termination (refreezing).[4] Lewin's model remains closely identified with the field of OD, however, and is used to illustrate how other types of change can be implemented. For example, Lewin's three-step model has been used to explain how information technologies can be implemented more effectively.[5]

Action research model

The action research model focuses on planned change as a cyclical process in which initial research about the organisation provides information to guide subsequent action. Then the results of the action are assessed to provide further information that will guide further action, and so on. This iterative cycle of research and action involves considerable collaboration between organisation members and OD practitioners. It places heavy emphasis on data gathering and diagnosis prior to action planning and implementation, as well as careful evaluation of the results after action has been taken.

Action research is traditionally aimed both at helping specific organisations to implement planned change and at developing more general knowledge that can be applied to other settings.[6] Although action research was originally developed to have this dual focus on change and knowledge, it has been adapted to OD efforts in which the major emphasis is on planned change.[7] Figure 2.1(B) shows the cyclical phases of planned change as defined by the action research model. There are eight main steps:

1   *Problem identification.* This stage usually begins when a key executive in the organisation, or someone with power and influence, senses that the organisation has one or more problems that might be alleviated with the help of an OD practitioner. In one case, the quality manager of an electronics plant had been involved with OD before, but it took her almost a year to persuade the plant manager to bring in a consultant.

2   *Consultation with a behavioural science expert.* During the initial contact, the OD practitioner and the client carefully assist each other. The practitioner has his or her own normative, developmental theory or frame of reference and must be conscious of those assumptions and values.[8] Sharing them with the client from the beginning establishes an open and collaborative atmosphere.

3   *Data gathering and preliminary diagnosis.* This stage is usually completed by the OD practitioner, often in conjunction with organisation members. It involves gathering appropriate information and analysing it to determine the underlying causes of organisational problems. The four basic methods of gathering data are interviews, process observation, questionnaires and organisational performance data (unfortunately, often overlooked). One approach to diagnosis begins with observation, proceeds to a semistructured interview and concludes with a questionnaire to measure precisely the problems identified by the earlier steps.[9] When gathering diagnostic information, it is

Figure 2.1 Comparison of planned change models

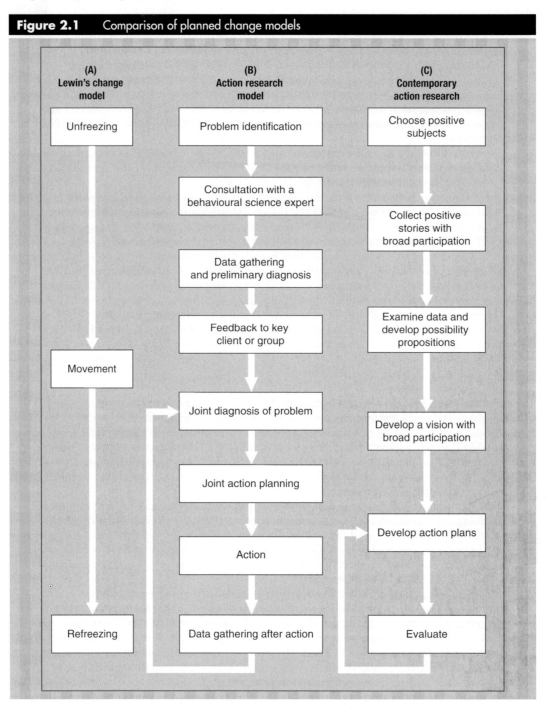

possible that OD practitioners may influence members from whom they are collecting data. In OD, 'every action on the part of the ... consultant constitutes an intervention' that will have some effect on the organisation.[10]

4   *Feedback to key client or group.* Because action research is a collaborative activity, the diagnostic data are fed back to the client, usually in a group or work-team meeting. The feedback step, in which members are given the information gathered by the OD practitioner, helps them to determine the strengths and weaknesses of the organisation or the department under study. The consultant provides the client with all relevant and useful data. Obviously, the practitioner will protect those sources of information

and, at times, will withhold data if the group is not ready for the information or if the information would make the client overly defensive.

5 *Joint diagnosis of problem.* At this point, members discuss the feedback and explore with the OD practitioner whether they want to work on identified problems. A close interrelationship exists among data gathering, feedback and diagnosis as the consultant summarises the basic data from the client members and presents the data to them for validation and further diagnosis. An important point to remember, as Schein suggests, is that the action research process is very different from the doctor–patient model, in which the consultant comes in, makes a diagnosis and prescribes a solution. Schein notes that the failure to establish a common frame of reference in the client–consultant relationship may lead to faulty diagnosis or to a communications gap whereby the client is sometimes 'unwilling to believe the diagnosis or accept the prescription'. He believes 'most companies have drawers full of reports by consultants, each loaded with diagnoses and recommendations which are either not understood or not accepted by the "patient"'.[11]

6 *Joint action planning.* Next, the OD practitioner and the client members jointly agree on further actions to be taken. This is the beginning of the moving process (described in Lewin's change model), as the organisation decides on how best to reach a different quasi-stationary equilibrium. At this stage, the specific action to be taken depends on the culture, technology and environment of the organisation; the diagnosis of the problem; and the time and expense of the intervention.

7 *Action.* This stage involves the actual change from one organisational state to another. It may include installing new methods and procedures, reorganising structures and work designs, and reinforcing new behaviours. These actions typically cannot be implemented immediately, but require a transition period as the organisation moves from the present to a desired future state.[12]

8 *Data gathering after action.* Because action research is a cyclical process, data must also be gathered after the action has been taken in order to measure and determine the effects of the action and to feed the results back to the organisation. This, in turn, may lead to rediagnosis and new action.

Application 2.1 suggests that great organisations are built on the foundation of the sales function. The old McKinsey 7-S framework can be adapted to create a winning organisation.

APPLiCATiON 2.1

THE 7-S FORMULA FOR SALES SUCCESS

Great organisations are built on the foundation of the sales function. The old McKinsey 7-S framework can be adapted to create winning sales organisations.

There are no shortcuts to success. Or so goes the old adage … Strong organisations are built on the foundation of strong sales teams. No matter how wonderful your product or service is, if it does not reach the distribution network or customers it is of no use and cannot benefit the organisation.

… Many years ago, McKinsey, one of the world's best-known management consultants, had suggested a 7-S framework for organisations to succeed. This model was central to the popular book *In Search of Excellence*. Many companies have adopted the model globally and it has helped build great organisations … it is strongly recommended that sales teams master this 7-S framework to stay ahead.

Shared goals. Goals are dreams with deadlines, said Diana Scharf Hunt. Shared goals are central to the foundation of successful sales organisations. To be successful in sales, one must ensure that the goal is clear and shared with every stakeholder.

… I, therefore, took up the task of explaining the 'how' of achieving the goals. Detailed actions plans were worked out for each market and each product category so that collectively we would generate the kind of growth we were targeting. It was the detailing which made the team realise the potential available and made them all go out and achieve the goals … It is my firm belief that without being clear on the 'how' part of achieving goals, one cannot expect the team to deliver. It is the responsibility of the leader to communicate comprehensively both the 'what' and the 'how' to succeed.

▷▷

Best and Smart. Even when goals are decided, we need to ensure they are SMART (Specific, Measurable, Achievable, Rewarding and Time-bound). Further, they should be simple and short to ensure better buy-in among team members.

... 'Strategy without tactics is the slowest route to victory; tactics without strategy is the noise before defeat,' said Sun Tzu. Strategy can best be defined as a choice made from the alternatives available to execute or accomplish the goal ... hence making the right choice after a careful consideration of alternatives available is the essence of strategy.

...

Need for focus. The implications of choice are awesome ... yet we had to choose because we could not afford to do everything ... 'in strategy it is important to see distant things as if they were close and to take a distanced view of close things.' In strategising, evaluating alternatives and choosing responsibly calls for thorough knowledge ... Strategy is the starting point for all actions and hence a sound, balanced strategy is a must. The ability to strategise is a critical skill that a sales team and its leader need to have, or acquire.

...

The right pace. Speed or pace in executing what has been decided upon, without compromising on quality, is what makes the difference between long-term success and failure ... 'If I had eight hours to chop down a tree, I'd spend six hours sharpening my axe', said Abraham Lincoln. Sharpening an axe is similar to sharpening our minds ... to succeed in sales, several important skills are necessary: conceptual, planning, communication, problem-solving, creative, persuasive, decision making, interpersonal, motivating and leadership skills.

Skill-building. We need to develop each of the above skills if we wish to emerge a leader in sales and to make our teams successful ... At Nerolac, we achieved consistent success in the market due to the focus we had on developing our skills ... 'Management works in the system; leadership works on the system', said Stephen R Covey. There is a system to everything in life.

Putting in a system. [To] achieve success in the short term, one can operate even by whims and fancies with some tactical moves. But to achieve success in the long term and sustain it, it is essential to have adequate systems in the set-up. Systems should form a basis of working ... 'Man's mind, once stretched by a new idea, never regains its original dimension', said Oliver Wendall Holmes Jr ... Jack Welch, former CEO of GE, said 'Stretch means that we have to try for huge gains while having no idea on how to get there – but our people figure out ways to get there.'

Service dimension. A sales team needs to service all its clientele well – from dealers and retailers to distributors, franchisees, wholesalers, sales associates and direct customers – in order to establish strong relationships, which in turn help them sustain success. In addition, the sales team also needs to service and support other functions related to sales, namely production, customer service, quality, planning, marketing, distribution/logistics, finance, collection, R&D, etc, to provide seamless service to customers ... While one can claim that we require more attributes to succeed than what has been used in the model here, I believe that the 7-S framework covers all the essential elements, and will be able to help a team perform better than others who do not have such a focused approach.

Source: G. Dhananjayan, *Indian Management* (May 2005): 54.

Critical Thinking Questions: Do you think the 7-S framework covers all the essential elements required for the success of the organisation? If not, what elements are missing? What do you think Sun Tzu meant when he said: 'Strategy without tactics is the slowest route to victory; tactics without strategy is the noise before defeat'?

Contemporary adaptations to action research

The action research model underlies most current approaches to planned change and is often identified with the practice of OD. Action research has recently been extended to new settings and applications, and consequently researchers and practitioners have made the requisite adaptations to its basic framework.[13]

Trends in the application of action research include the movement from smaller sub-units of organisations to total systems and communities.[14] In these larger contexts, action research is more complex and political than in smaller settings. Therefore, the action research cycle is co-ordinated across multiple change processes and includes a diversity of stakeholders who have an interest in the organisation. (We describe these applications more thoroughly in Chapter 10.)

Action research is also increasingly being applied in international settings, particularly in developing nations in the southern hemisphere.[15] Embedded within the action research model, however, are Western assumptions about change. For example, action research traditionally views change more linearly than Eastern cultures, and it treats the change process more collaboratively than Latin American and African countries.[16] To achieve success in these settings, action research needs to be tailored to fit their cultural assumptions.

Finally, action research is increasingly being applied to promote social change and innovation.[17] This is demonstrated most clearly in community-development and global social-change projects.[18] These applications are heavily value-laden and seek to redress imbalances in power and resource allocations across different groups. Action researchers tend to play an activist role in the change process, which is often chaotic and conflictual.

In view of these general trends, action research has undergone two key adaptations. First, contemporary applications have substantially increased the degree of member involvement in the change process. This contrasts with traditional approaches to planned change where consultants carried out most of the change activities, with the agreement and collaboration of management.[19] Although consultant-dominated change still persists in OD, there is a growing tendency to involve organisation members in learning about their organisation and how to change it. Referred to as 'participatory action research',[20] 'action learning',[21] 'action science'[22] or 'self-design',[23] this approach to planned change emphasises the need for organisation members to learn about it first-hand if they are to gain the knowledge and skills to change the organisation. In today's complex and changing environment, some argue that OD must go beyond solving particular problems to helping members gain the necessary competence to continually change and improve the organisation.[24]

In this modification of action research, the role of OD consultants is to work with members to facilitate the learning process. Both parties are 'co-learners' in diagnosing the organisation, designing changes and implementing and assessing them.[25] Neither party dominates the change process. Rather, each participant brings unique information and expertise to the situation, and together they combine their resources to learn how to change the organisation. Consultants, for example, know how to design diagnostic instruments and OD interventions, while organisation members have 'local' knowledge about the organisation and how it functions. Each participant learns from the change process. Organisation members learn how to change their organisation, to refine and improve it. OD consultants learn how to facilitate complex organisational change and learning.

The second adaptation to action research is the promotion of a 'positive' approach to planned change.[26] Referred to as 'appreciative inquiry', this application of planned change suggests that all organisations are to some degree effective and that planned change should focus on the 'best of what is'.[27] This assumption challenges the dominant metaphor that organisations are problems to be solved.[28] Rather, appreciative inquiry helps organisation members understand and describe their organisation when it is working at its best. That knowledge is then applied to creating a vision of what the organisation could be. Because members are heavily involved in creating the vision, they are committed to changing the organisation in that direction. Considerable research on expectation effects supports this positive approach to planned change.[29] It suggests that people tend to act in ways that make their expectations occur; a positive vision of what the organisation can become can energise and direct behaviour to make that expectation come about.

These contemporary adaptations to action research are depicted in Figure 2.1(C). Planned change begins with choosing positive aspects of the organisation to examine, such as a particularly effective work team or a new product that has been developed and brought to market especially fast. If the focus of inquiry is real and vital to organisation members, the change process itself will take on these positive attributes. The second step involves gathering data about the 'best of what is' in the organisation. A broad array of organisation members is involved in developing data-gathering instruments, collecting information and analysing it. In the third stage, members examine the data to find stories, however small, that present a picture of the future that is truly exciting and possible. From these stories, members develop 'possibility propositions' – statements that bridge the organisation's current best practices with ideal possibilities for future organising.[30] This redirects attention from 'what is' to 'what might be'. In step four, all relevant stakeholders are brought together to construct a vision of the future and to devise action plans for moving in that direction. Finally, implementation of those plans proceeds similarly to the action and evaluation phases of action research described previously. Members make changes, assess the results, make necessary adjustments and so on as they attempt to move the organisation towards the vision.

Application 2.2 presents a case study of the entrepreneur Brad Sugars who emphasises the value of 'systematic methodology' as a planned process of change.

APPLiCATiON 2.2

BRAD SUGARS – ACTION INTERNATIONAL BUSINESS COACHING

Sweet business success for Brad Sugars has come on the back of a belief he formed as a child: do the work once and get paid for it forever. 'It has to be fundamentally the core philosophy of running a business,' says the founder of Action International Business Coaching, which operates in 19 countries and is ranked in *Entrepreneur* magazine as the 16th-fastest-growing franchise in the world.

…

For Brisbane-born Sugars – who first started teaching marketing in 1993 at a business school for entrepreneurs in Hawaii – business models are crucial. 'Find the gold rush and sell the pans,' he explains … 'The strategies are relatively the same; the roll-out is similar – it's just a matter of using the localised knowledge in that product or service and adding to that the management, marketing and sales.'

An overriding management approach has served Sugars and Action International well: bosses must lead people and manage resources. Both factors are important, but the former is crucial. According to Sugars, strong leadership calls for:

- *Decisiveness.* If a leader is wishy-washy in decision making, the team feel that.
- *Vision.* Not just that they can see the vision, but that they are able to communicate the vision.
- *Being a 'builder of lieutenants'.* The worst leaders are the ones that are super strong but set the business up for failure because no one else in the company knows what to do.

…

'It's almost impossible to hire people who will do the job as well as you as the owner of the business. You have to understand that that is the case. However, employees do the job to a high level when 'they are following a systematic methodology,' Sugars says.

The author of 15 business books, Sugars views a business as a tree. 'It's either growing or it's dying,' he says. 'A company cannot stand still just as a tree cannot stand still.'

He believes the term 'change management' warrants a review.

'We should look at leading change. We need to plan our change, not manage the changes. If we can plan our changes and keep ahead rather than philosophically trying to manage what is happening to us, we should be at a far better point.

'Too much change is a very bad thing for a company, and too little change' … 'You must allow things time so that any changes you do make do get to a point where they are in rhythm with the company.'

Source: Cameron Cooper, 'Leadership: Part Two: Brad Sugars: Action International Business Coaching', *Management Today*, March 2006.

Critical Thinking Questions: Sugars' quote: 'It's almost impossible to hire people who will do the job as well as you as the owner of the business. You have to understand that that is the case.' Do you agree with this statement? Why or why not?

Comparisons of change models

All three models – Lewin's change model, the action research model and contemporary adaptations to the action research model – describe the phases by which planned change occurs in organisations. As shown in Figure 2.1, the models overlap in that their emphasis on action to implement organisational change is preceded by a preliminary stage (unfreezing, diagnosis or examining positive aspects of the organisation) and is followed by a closing stage (refreezing or evaluation). Moreover, all three approaches emphasise the application of behavioural science knowledge, involve organisation members in the change process and recognise that any interaction between a consultant and an organisation constitutes an intervention that may affect the organisation. However, Lewin's change model differs from the other two in that it focuses on the general process of planned change, rather than on specific OD activities.

Lewin's model and the action research model differ from contemporary approaches in terms of the level of involvement of the participants and the focus of change. The first two models emphasise the role of the consultant with limited member involvement in the change process. Contemporary applications, on the other hand, treat both consultants and participants as co-learners who are heavily involved in planned change. In addition, Lewin's model and action research are more concerned with fixing problems than with focusing on what the organisation does well, and leveraging those strengths.

GENERAL MODEL OF PLANNED CHANGE

The three theories of planned change in organisations described above suggest a general framework for planned change, as shown in Figure 2.2. The framework describes the four basic activities that practitioners and organisation members jointly carry out in organisation development. The arrows connecting the different activities in the model show the typical sequence of events, from entering and contracting, to diagnosing, to planning and implementing change, to evaluating and institutionalising change. The lines connecting the activities emphasise that organisational change is not a straightforward, linear process, but involves considerable overlap and feedback among the activities. Because the model serves to organise the remaining parts of this book, Figure 2.2 also shows which specific chapters apply to the four major change activities.

Entering and contracting

The first set of activities in planned change concerns entering and contracting. They help managers decide whether they want to engage further in a planned change program and commit resources to such a process. Entering an organisation involves gathering initial data to understand the problems or opportunities facing the organisation. Once this information has been collected, the problems are discussed with managers and other organisation members in order to develop a contract or agreement to engage in planned change. The contract spells out future change activities, the resources that will be committed

---

Figure 2.2   General model of planned change

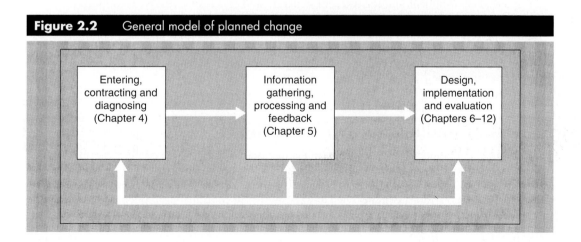

to the process, and how OD practitioners and organisation members will be involved. In many cases, organisations do not get beyond this early stage of planned change, because disagreements about the need for change surface, resource constraints are encountered or other methods for change appear more feasible. When OD is used in non-traditional and international settings, the entering and contracting process must be sensitive to the context in which the change is taking place.

Diagnosing

In this stage of planned change, the client system is carefully studied. Diagnosis can focus on understanding organisational problems, including their causes and consequences, or on identifying the organisation's positive attributes. The diagnostic process is one of the most important activities in OD. It includes choosing an appropriate model for understanding the organisation, and gathering, analysing and feeding back information to managers and organisation members about the problems or opportunities.

Diagnostic models for analysing problems explore three levels of activities. Organisation problems represent the most complex level of analysis and involve the total system. Group-level problems are associated with departmental and group effectiveness, and individual-level problems involve how jobs are designed.

Gathering, analysing and feeding back data are the central change activities in diagnosis. Chapter 5 describes how data can be gathered through interviews, observations, survey instruments or archival sources, such as meeting minutes and organisation charts. It also explains how data can be reviewed and analysed, and the process of feeding back diagnostic data is described. Organisation members, often in collaboration with an OD practitioner, jointly discuss the data and their implications for change.

Planning and implementing change

In this stage, organisation members and practitioners jointly plan and implement OD interventions. They design interventions to improve the organisation and make action plans to implement them. As discussed in Chapter 6, there are several criteria for designing interventions, including the organisation's readiness for change, its current change capability, its culture and power distributions, and the change agent's skills and abilities. Depending on the outcomes of diagnosis, there are four major types of interventions in OD. Chapter 7 describes human process interventions at the individual, group and total system levels. Chapter 8 presents interventions that modify an organisation's structure and technology. Chapter 9 addresses human resource interventions that seek to improve member performance and wellness. Chapter 10 describes strategic interventions. These change programs involve managing the organisation's relationship to its external environment and the internal structure and process necessary to support a business strategy.

Implementing interventions is concerned with managing the change process. As discussed in Chapter 6, it includes motivating change, creating a desired future vision of the organisation, developing political support, managing the transition towards the vision and sustaining momentum for change.

Evaluating and institutionalising change

This last stage in planned change involves an evaluation of the effects of the intervention and management of the institutionalisation of successful change programs. These two activities are described in Chapter 6. Feedback to organisation members about the intervention's results provides information about whether the changes should be continued, modified or suspended. Institutionalising successful changes involves reinforcing them through feedback, rewards and training.

DIFFERENT TYPES OF PLANNED CHANGE

The general model of planned change describes how the OD process typically unfolds in organisations. In actual practice, the different phases are not nearly as orderly as the model implies. OD practitioners tend to modify or adjust the stages to fit the needs of the situation. Steps in planned change can be implemented in a variety of ways that depend on the client's needs and goals, the change agent's skills and values, and the organisation's context. Therefore, it is clear that planned change can vary enormously from one situation to another.

To understand these differences better, planned change can be contrasted across situations on two key dimensions: the magnitude of organisational change and the degree to which the client system is organised.

Magnitude of change

Planned change efforts can be characterised as falling along a continuum, ranging from incremental changes that involve finetuning the organisation to quantum changes that entail fundamentally altering how it operates.[31] Incremental changes tend to involve limited dimensions and levels of the organisation, such as the decision-making processes of work groups. They occur within the context of the organisation's existing business strategy, structure and culture, and are aimed at improving the status quo. Quantum changes, on the other hand, are directed at significantly altering how the organisation operates. They tend to involve several organisational dimensions, including structure, culture, reward systems, information processes and work design. They also involve changing multiple levels of the organisation, from top-level management through departments and work groups to individual jobs.

Planned change has traditionally been applied in situations that involve incremental change. Organisations in the 1960s and 1970s were mainly concerned with finetuning their bureaucratic structures by resolving many of the social problems that emerged with increasing size and complexity. In these situations, planned change involves a relatively bounded set of problem-solving activities. OD practitioners are typically contacted by managers to help solve specific problems in particular organisational systems, such as poor communication among members of a work team or high absenteeism among shop floor employees in a production facility. Diagnostic and change activities tend to be limited to these issues, although additional problems may be uncovered and may need to be addressed. Similarly, the change process tends to focus on those organisational systems that have specific problems, and it generally ends when the problems are resolved. Of course, the change agent may contract to help solve additional problems.

In recent years, OD has increasingly been concerned with quantum change. As described in Chapter 1, the greater competitiveness and uncertainty of today's business environment have led a growing number of organisations to drastically alter the way in which they operate. In these situations, planned change is more complex, extensive and long term than when applied to incremental change.[32] Because quantum change involves most features and levels of the organisation, it is typically driven from the top of the organisation, where corporate strategy and values are set. Change agents help senior managers create a vision of a desired future organisation and energise movement in that direction. They also help executives develop structures for managing the transition from the present to the future organisation. This may include, for example, a variety of overlapping steering committees and redesign teams. Staff experts may also redesign many features of the firm, such as performance measures, rewards, planning processes, work designs and information systems.

Because of the complexity and extensiveness of quantum change, OD professionals often work in teams that consist of members with different yet complementary expertise. The consulting relationship persists over relatively long time periods and includes a great deal of renegotiation and experimentation among consultants and managers. The boundaries of the change effort are more uncertain and diffuse than in incremental change, making diagnosis and change seem more like discovery than problem solving. (Complex strategic and transformational types of change are described in more detail in Chapters 10 and 11.)

It is important to emphasise that quantum change may or may not be developmental in nature. Organisations may drastically alter their strategic direction and way of operating without significantly developing their capacity to solve problems and achieve both high performance and quality of work life. For example, firms may simply change their marketing mix, dropping or adding products, services or customers; they may drastically downsize by cutting out marginal businesses and laying off managers and workers; or they may tighten managerial and financial controls and attempt to squeeze more out of the labour force. On the other hand, organisations may undertake quantum change from a developmental perspective. They may seek to make themselves more competitive by developing their human resources, by getting managers and employees more involved in problem solving and innovation, and by promoting flexibility and direct, open communication. This OD approach to quantum change is particularly relevant in today's rapidly changing and competitive environment. To succeed in this setting, organisations such as Australia Post, the Australian Taxation Office and the Department of Defence are transforming themselves from control-oriented bureaucracies to high-involvement organisations capable of continually changing and improving themselves.

Degree of organisation

Planned change efforts can also vary according to the degree to which the organisation or client system is organised. In overorganised situations, such as in highly mechanistic, bureaucratic organisations, various dimensions, such as leadership styles, job designs, organisation structure, and policies and procedures are too rigid and overly defined for effective task performance. Communication between management and employees is typically suppressed, conflicts are avoided and employees are apathetic. In underorganised organisations, on the other hand, there is too little constraint or regulation for effective task performance. Leadership, structure, job design and policy are ill-defined and fail to control task behaviours effectively. Communication is fragmented, job responsibilities are ambiguous and employees' energies are dissipated because of lack of direction. Underorganised situations are typically found in such areas as product development, project management and community development, where relationships among diverse groups and participants must be co-ordinated around complex, uncertain tasks.

In overorganised situations, where much of OD practice has historically taken place, planned change is generally aimed at loosening constraints on behaviour. Changes in leadership, job design, structure and other features are designed to liberate suppressed energy, to increase the flow of relevant information between employees and managers, and to promote effective conflict resolution. The typical steps of planned change – entry, diagnosis, intervention and evaluation – are intended to penetrate a relatively closed organisation or department and make it increasingly open to self-diagnosis and revitalisation. The relationship between the OD practitioner and the management team attempts to model this loosening process. The consultant shares leadership of the change process with management, encourages open communication and confrontation of conflict, and maintains flexibility when relating to the organisation.

When applied to organisations that face problems because of being underorganised, planned change is aimed at increasing organisation by clarifying leadership roles, structuring communication between managers and employees, and specifying job and departmental responsibilities. These activities require a modification of the traditional phases of planned change and include the following four stages:[33]

1   *Identification.* This step identifies the relevant people or groups that need to be involved in the change program. In many underorganised situations, people and departments can be so disconnected that there is uncertainty about who should be included in the problem-solving process. For example, managers of different departments who have only limited interaction with each other might disagree or be confused about which departments should help to develop a new product or service.

2   *Convention.* In this phase, the relevant people or departments in the company are brought together to begin organising for task performance. For example, department managers might be asked to attend a series of organising meetings to discuss the division of labour and the co-ordination required to introduce a new product.

3   *Organisation.* Different organising mechanisms are created to structure the newly required interactions among people and departments. They might include creating new

leadership positions, establishing communication channels and specifying appropriate plans and policies.

4   *Evaluation.* In this final step the outcomes of the organisation phase are assessed. The evaluation might signal the need for adjustments in the organising process or for further identification, convention and organisation activities.

By carrying out these four stages of planned change in underorganised situations, the relationship between the OD practitioner and the client system attempts to reinforce the organising process. The consultant develops a well-defined leadership role, which might be autocratic during the early stages of the change program. Similarly, the consulting relationship is clearly defined and tightly specified. In effect, the interaction between the consultant and the client system supports the larger process of bringing order to the situation.

Application 2.3 cautions that the costs and stresses of starting a new business are nothing compared with the problems that a lack of experience and knowledge can cause.

APPLICATiON 2.3

THINK AHEAD

The cost and stress of starting a new business [is] nothing compared with the problems that a lack of experience and knowledge can cause.

Ruby Lampard, a designer, and Robin Sinclair, a writer, left senior roles in ad agencies to start their own agency, The Blue Group, in 2002, because they were sick of pointless meetings and the politics of a big agency. Lampard says: 'Our thoughts were to get in there and start a business.' Without thinking about who they wanted as clients or what kind of work they wanted to do, they got started: 'We were accepting any sort of work that was around to keep money in the bank and food in our mouths.'

After a year and a half the business was busy but not profitable. Lampard says, 'We were working zillions of hours and really not making a lot of money.' They did not feel confident enough to hire staff because the work could have dried up at any time, and they were burning out.

...

Something had to change. With the help of an external consultant, they started planning. They aimed for larger clients with long-term potential, and turned work outside their area of expertise. Now they have a more consistent cash flow, they have been able to hire staff. 'The lesson is to plan,' she says. 'Both of us had a look at what our abilities are, and knowing that we are basically creative people we definitely need somebody else to add business knowledge as well.'

...

Andrew Sneddon, a partner at PriceWaterhouseCoopers who worked with high-growth companies, says planning does not have to mean writing a big inflexible document. He says one or two pages containing no more than four to six things to focus on is best: 'The key for a young business is to have milestones and targets and everyone working towards them.'

...

'You need to look hard at each opportunity, and evaluate potential markets, potential margins and partners that are going to help you get that product to market. You have to prioritise opportunities and should really only be focusing on a couple of top priorities.'

...

A cofounder of direct marketing software specialists Impact Data, Kurt Opray, learnt his lesson about planning doing deals with big companies for new software ... Opray could not believe his luck when Coca-Cola and Foster's Group indicated they were interested in selling the product to their pub and restaurant clients. The big companies signed exclusive distribution deals. Impact Data, which had heavily invested in development of the software, sat back and waited for the royalties to flow. They did not.

...

Looking back, Opray says he was star struck by Foster's and Coco-Cola, so he signed the deal without thinking it through, and he should have planned for delays. 'To be perfectly honest we were

▷▷

a little blinded by the fact that we had done a distribution agreement with these big companies. We were so delighted to have them on board that we failed to take into account the fact that they worked differently, and their idea of making things happen is different to ours; theirs is perhaps six months, whereas ours is tomorrow morning.'

Next time he will pay more attention to the detail of how things will work. 'If you are looking to do an agreement with a large company, you need to gear yourself up to the fact that it will take a long time and it will take a significant amount of your resources to do it ... And make sure that what you are going to get out of it represents not the effort of a week but the effort of six months.'

Source: Jacqui Walker, 'Think Ahead', *Business Review Weekly*, Feb–Mar 2006.

Critical Thinking Question: This article promotes planning as the crucial element for successful business relationships between small and large companies. What other considerations or techniques should small companies adopt before engaging in what seems a very prestigious and/or glamorous arrangement?

CRITIQUE OF PLANNED CHANGE

Despite their continued refinement, the models and practice of planned change are still in a formative stage of development, and there is considerable room for improvement. Critics of OD have pointed out several problems with the way planned change has been both conceptualised and practised.

Conceptualisation of planned change

Planned change has typically been characterised as involving a series of activities for carrying out effective change in organisations. Although current models outline a general set of steps that need to be followed, considerably more information is needed to guide how those steps should be performed in specific situations. In an extensive review and critique of planned change theory, Porras and Robertson argued that planned change activities should be guided by information about: (1) the organisational features that can be changed, (2) the intended outcomes from making those changes, (3) the causal mechanisms by which those outcomes are achieved, and (4) the contingencies upon which successful change depends.[34] In particular, they noted that the key to organisational change is change in the behaviour of each member and that the information available about the causal mechanisms that produce individual change is lacking. Overall, Porras and Robertson concluded that the information necessary for guiding change is only partially available and that a good deal more research and thinking are needed to fill the gaps. Chapters 7 to 10 on OD interventions review what is currently known about change features, outcomes, causal mechanisms and contingencies.

A related area where current thinking about planned change is deficient is knowledge about how the stages of planned change differ across situations. Most models specify a general set of steps that are intended to be applicable to most change efforts. The previous section of this chapter showed, however, how change activities can vary, depending on such factors as the magnitude of change and the degree to which the client system is organised. Considerably more effort needs to be expended on identifying situational factors that may require modification of the general stages of planned change. This would probably lead to a rich array of planned change models, each geared to a specific set of situational conditions. Such contingency thinking is sorely needed in planned change.

Planned change also tends to be described as a rationally controlled, orderly process. Critics have argued that, although this view may be comforting, it is seriously misleading.[35] They point out that planned change has a more chaotic quality, often involving shifting goals, discontinuous activities, surprising events and unexpected combinations of changes. For example, managers often initiate changes without clear plans that clarify their strategies and goals. As change unfolds, new stakeholders may emerge and demand modifications that reflect previously unknown or unvoiced needs. These emergent conditions make planned change a far more disorderly and dynamic process than is customarily portrayed, and conceptions need to capture this reality.

Finally, the relationship between planned change and organisational performance and effectiveness is not well understood. OD has traditionally had problems assessing whether interventions are, in fact, producing observed results. The complexity of the change situation, the lack of sophisticated analyses and the long time periods for producing results have all contributed to a weak evaluation of OD efforts. Moreover, managers have often accounted for OD efforts with post-hoc testimonials, reports of possible future benefits and calls to support OD as the right thing to do.

In the absence of rigorous assessment and measurement, it is difficult to make resource-allocation decisions about change programs and to know which interventions are most effective in certain situations.

Practice of planned change

Critics have suggested that there are several problems with the way planned change is carried out.[36] These concerns are not with the planned change model itself, but with how change takes place and with the qualifications and activities of OD practitioners.

A growing number of OD practitioners have acquired skills in specific techniques, such as team building, total quality management, large-group interventions or gain sharing, and have chosen to specialise in those methods. Although such specialisation may be necessary, given the complex array of techniques that make up modern OD, it can lead to a certain myopia. Some OD practitioners favour particular techniques and ignore other OD strategies that might be more appropriate. They tend to interpret organisational problems as requiring the favoured technique. Thus, for example, it is not unusual to see consultants pushing such methods as diversity training, re-engineering, organisation learning or self-managing work teams as solutions to most organisational problems.

Effective change depends on a careful diagnosis of how the organisation is functioning. Diagnosis identifies the underlying causes of organisational problems, such as poor product quality and employee dissatisfaction. It requires both time and money, and some organisations are not willing to make the necessary investment. They rely on preconceptions about what the problem is and hire consultants with appropriate skills for solving it. Managers may think, for example, that work design is the problem and hire an expert in job enrichment to implement a change program. The problem, however, may be caused by other factors, such as poor reward practices, and job enrichment would be inappropriate. Careful diagnosis can help to avoid such mistakes.

In situations that require complex organisational changes, planned change is a long-term process involving considerable innovation and learning on site. It requires a good deal of time and commitment and a willingness to modify and refine changes as the circumstances require. Some organisations demand more rapid solutions to their problems and seek 'quick fixes' from experts. Unfortunately, some OD consultants are more than willing to provide quick solutions. They sell prepackaged programs, which tend to be appealing to managers as they typically include an explicit recipe to be followed, standard training materials and clear time and cost boundaries. The quick fixes, however, have trouble gaining wide organisational support and commitment. They seldom produce the positive results that have been advertised.

Other organisations have not recognised the systemic nature of change. Too often, they believe that intervention into one aspect or unit of the organisation will be sufficient to ameliorate the problems. They are unprepared for the other changes that may be necessary to support a particular intervention. For example, at Mono Pumps in Melbourne the positive benefits of an employee involvement program did not begin to appear until after the organisation had redesigned its reward system to support the cross-functional collaboration necessary for solving highly complex problems. Changing any one part or feature of an organisation often requires adjustments in other parts in order to maintain an appropriate alignment. Thus, although quick fixes and change programs that focus on only one part or aspect of the organisation may resolve some specific problems, they generally do not lead to complex organisational change, or increase members' capacity to carry out change.[37]

Application 2.4 suggests that strategic planning is the basis of business success but sometimes the obsession with planning can distort a company's operations.

APPLiCATiON 2.4

THE FAILURE OF STRATEGY

Strategy may or may not be destiny, but it certainly seems to be cool. Type the word strategy into amazon.com books and some 29 209 entries appear, including 9496 for business strategy. Strategy is big business.

Strategy consulting companies such as Monitor, Bain, Booz Allen Hamilton, McKinsey and Boston Consulting Group charge higher fees, typically have larger total revenues and enjoy higher status among business school graduates seeking jobs than do consulting firms (such as AT & Kearney, Proudfoot and Celerant) that focus on operations and implementation.

…

The justification for the prestige, high prices and attention lavished on strategy seems straightforward: doing the right thing – even if it isn't done perfectly – is more important than doing the wrong thing exceptionally well. This means that it is paramount for companies and organisations of all types to understand what they should be doing to achieve success – to devise a strategy that helps them survive in an increasingly competitive world.

Many strategy consultants and researchers also assert that instituting a disciplined process of decision making – for instance, considering threats and opportunities, communicating assumptions more widely throughout the organisation, and using budgets and plans to set goals and monitor performance – helps to enhance organisational performance.

We have no quarrel with the conclusion that leaders and their people need to know what to do and how to compete. But like many half-truths, a fixation on strategy can obscure as much as it illuminates. The corporate obsession with strategy can cause leaders to overlook other even more crucial and more sustainable avenues for success.

Even corporate successes attributed to great strategy often turn out not to stem from strategy at all, and the empirical evidence shows a surprisingly weak link between the activity of strategic planning and company performance.

Emphasising strategy is only one method of figuring out the right thing to do, and possibly not the best.
Source: Jeffrey Pfeffer & Robert I. Sutton, *Hard Facts: Dangers half-truths & total nonsense*, Harvard Business School Press, 2006. Reproduced by permission of Harvard Business School press.

Critical Thinking Question: If strategic planning and/or strategising are not the best means for guaranteeing the success of a business, then what could be considered more important?

The contingency approach to change management

Australian researchers Dexter Dunphy and Douglas Stace argue that change management should be approached from a situational perspective. Their argument for contingency is as follows:

> [D]ramatically different approaches to change can work in different circumstances … turbulent times create varied circumstances and demand different responses according to the needs of the situation. What is appropriate for one organisation may not be appropriate for another. So we need a model of change … that indicates how to carry change strategies to achieve optimum fit with the changing environment.[38]

As a result of some seven years' research into change management techniques in Australia, Dunphy and Stace have derived a model of change that incorporates both 'soft' and 'hard' approaches. The model is a two-dimensional matrix that categorises the scale of change (from finetuning OD to corporate transformation; CT) and the style of management that needs to be employed to facilitate the change (from collaborative to coercive). Four process change strategies or topologies may be identified from these dimensions.[39] See Figure 2.3.

SCALE OF CHANGE

- *Finetuning.* Organisational change that is an ongoing process characterised by finetuning of the 'fit' or match between the organisation's strategy, structure, people and processes. Such effort is typically manifested at departmental/divisional levels.
- *Incremental adjustment.* Organisational change that is characterised by incremental adjustments to the changing environment. Such change involves distinct modifications (but not radical change) to corporate business strategies, structures and management processes.
- *Modular transformation.* Organisational change that is characterised by major realignment of one or more departments/divisions. The process of radical change is focused on these subparts rather than on the organisation as a whole.
- *Corporate transformation.* Organisational change that is corporation-wide, characterised by radical shifts in business strategy and revolutionary changes throughout the whole organisation.

STYLE OF MANAGEMENT

- *Collaborative.* This involves widespread participation by employees in important decisions about the organisation's future, and about the means of bringing about organisational change.
- *Consultative.* This style of leadership involves consultation with employees, primarily about the means of bringing about organisational change, with their possible limited involvement in goal setting that is relevant to their area of expertise or responsibility.

Figure 2.3 Organisational change strategies

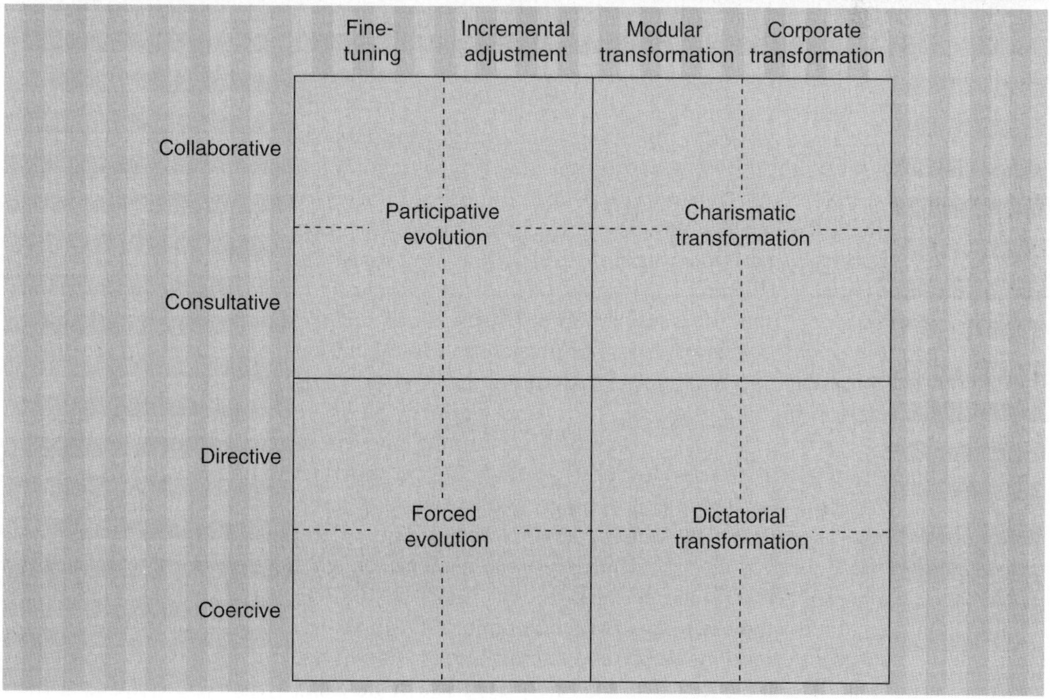

- *Directive*. This style of leadership involves the use of managerial authority and direction as the main form of decision making about the organisation's future, and about the means of bringing about organisational change.
- *Coercive*. This style of leadership involves managers/executives or outside parties forcing or imposing change on key groups in the organisation.

TYPOLOGY OF CHANGE STRATEGIES AND CONDITIONS FOR THEIR USE

- *Participative evolution*. Use when organisation is 'in fit' but needs minor adjustment, or is 'out of fit' but time is available and key interest groups favour change.
- *Charismatic transformation*. Use when organisation is 'out of fit' and there is little time for extensive participation, but there is support for radical change within the organisation.
- *Forced evolution*. Use when organisation is 'in fit' but needs minor adjustment, or is 'out of fit', but time is available. However, key interest groups oppose change.
- *Dictatorial transformation*. Use when organisation is 'out of fit', there is no time for extensive participation and no support within the organisation for radical change, but radical change is vital to organisational survival and fulfilment of the basic mission.

As with any paradigm, Dunphy and Stace's model has created considerable debate. There are certainly positive and negative aspects and issues of resistance, politics, the unpredictability of environment, ethical considerations and the unique characteristics of particular groups.

SUMMARY

Theories of planned change describe the activities that are necessary in order to modify strategies, structures and processes to increase an organisation's effectiveness. Lewin's change model, the action research model and more recent adaptations of action research offer different views of the phases through which planned change occurs in organisations. Lewin's change model views planned change as a three-step process of unfreezing, movement and refreezing. It provides a general description of the process of planned change. The action research model focuses on planned change as a cyclical process involving joint activities between organisation members and OD practitioners. It involves eight sequential steps that overlap and interact in practice: problem identification, consultation with a behavioural science expert, data gathering and preliminary diagnosis, feedback to key client or group, joint diagnosis of the problem, joint action planning, action, and data gathering after action. The action research model places heavy emphasis on data gathering and diagnosis prior to action planning and implementation, as well as on the assessment of results after action has been taken. In addition, change strategies are often modified on the basis of continued diagnosis, and termination of one OD program may lead to further work in other areas of the firm. Recent trends in action research include the movement from smaller to larger systems, from domestic to international applications and from organisational issues to social change. These trends have led to two key adaptations of action research: increased involvement of participants in the change process and a more appreciative approach to organisational change.

These theories can be integrated into a general model of planned change. Four sets of activities – entering and contracting, diagnosing, planning and implementing, and evaluating and institutionalising – can be used to describe how change is accomplished in organisations. These four sets of activities also describe the general structure of the chapters in this book. The general model has broad applicability to planned change: it identifies the steps that an organisation typically moves through in order to implement change and specifies the OD activities necessary for effecting the change.

Although the planned change models describe general stages of how the OD process unfolds, there are different types of change according to the situation. Planned change efforts can vary in terms of the magnitude of the change and the degree to which the client system is organised. When situations differ on these dimensions, planned change can vary greatly. Critics of OD have pointed out several problems with the way planned change has been conceptualised and practised. They point out specific areas where planned change can be improved.

ACTiViTiES

Review questions

① Identify the people generally responsible for carrying out planned change efforts. What factors will influence who is allocated these responsibilities?

② In Lewin's model of change, what brings about the proposed change? Explain why there has to be variations made, over a period of time, to the original model.

③ Describe the three sequential steps in Lewin's change model. Give a current example where Lewin's model is evident.

④ What is action research and what is the 'first step'? What is the relationship between action research and organisation development?

⑤ What happens when an organisation is overorganised? What are the consequences for the change strategy if this were to occur?

⑥ When an action researcher is dealing with an organisation that is underorganised, what are the steps in the change process? What difficulties do you expect in such a circumstance?

⑦ What are the major problems associated with planned change efforts? Are there any problems that are more prevalent than others?

⑧ How useful is the Dunphy and Stace model when considering transformational change? What criticisms or reservations do you have about the model?

Discussion and essay questions

① What is 'planned change' as compared to 'unplanned change'? Give current examples and critically evaluate their appropriateness.

② What are the key features of Lewin's change model? Describe its strengths and weaknesses. Can you design or develop an alternative model that could overcome the weaknesses you described? Why/why not?

③ Describe the major differences between underorganised and overorganised organisations. How would you suggest that these factors be managed?

④ What problems associated with planned change should the OD practitioner be aware of? How might such problems be overcome?

⑤ What are the positive and negative aspects of Dunphy and Stace's model? How does it take into account such things as resistance, politics, dealing with unforeseen circumstances, ethics, particular group characteristics, and so on? Is there an opportunity to modify the model? How may this be done?

⑥ Compare and contrast the various models of planned change. Discuss the advantages and disadvantages of each. Develop and explain your 'ideal' model of planned change.

NOTES

1 W. Bennis, *Changing Organizations* (New York: McGraw-Hill, 1966); J. Porras and P. Robertson, 'Organization development theory: a typology and evaluation', in *Organizational Change and Development*, 1, eds R. Woodman and W. Pasmore (Greenwich, CT: JAI Press, 1987): 1–57.

2 K. Lewin, *Field Theory in Social Science* (New York: Harper and Row, 1951).

3 E. Schein, *Process Consultation*, 1 and 2 (Reading, MA: Addison-Wesley, 1987).

4 R. Lippitt, J. Watson and B. Westley, *The Dynamics of Planned Change* (New York: Harcourt, Brace and World, 1958).

5 R. Benjamin and E. Levinson, 'A framework for managing IT-enabled change', *Sloan Management Review* (Summer 1993): 23–33.

6 A. Shani and G. Bushe, 'Visionary action research: a consultation process perspective', *Consultation*, 6 (Spring 1987): 3–19; G. Sussman and R. Evered, 'An assessment of the scientific merit of action research', *Administrative Science Quarterly*, 12 (1978): 582–603.

7 W. French, 'Organization development: objectives, assumptions, and strategies', *California Management Review*, 12 (1969): 23–34; A. Frohman, M. Sashkin and M. Kavanagh, 'Action research as applied to organization development', *Organization and Administrative Sciences*, 7 (1976): 129–42; E. Schein, *Organizational Psychology*, 3rd edn (Englewood Cliffs, NJ: Prentice-Hall, 1980).

8 N. Tichy, 'Agents of planned change: congruence of values, cognitions, and actions', *Administrative Science Quarterly*, 19 (1974): 163–82.

9 M. Beer, 'The technology of organization development', in *Handbook of Industrial and Organizational Psychology*, ed. M. Dunnette (Chicago: Rand McNally, 1976): 945.

10 E. Schein, *Process Consultation: Its Role in Organization Development* (Reading, MA: Addison-Wesley, 1969): 98.

11 ibid., 6.

12 R. Beckhard and R. Harris, *Organizational Transitions*, 2nd edn (Reading, MA: Addison-Wesley, 1987).

13 M. Elden and R. Chisholm, 'Emerging varieties of action research: introduction to the special issue', *Human Relations*, 46:2 (1993): 121–42.

14 G. Ledford and S. Mohrman, 'Self-design for high involvement', *Human Relations*, 46:2 (1993): 143–68; B. Bunker and B. Alban, 'The large group intervention – a new social innovation?', *Journal of Applied Behavioral Science*, 28:4 (1992): 473–80.

15 R. Marshak, 'Lewin meets Confucius: a review of the OD model of change', *Journal of Applied Behavioral Science*, 29:4 (1993): 393–415; K. Murrell, 'Evaluation as action research: the case of the Management Development Institute in Gambia, West Africa', *International Journal of Public Administration*, 16:3 (1993): 341–56; J. Preston and L. DuToit, 'Endemic violence in South Africa: an OD solution applied to two educational settings', *International Journal of Public Administration*, 16:11 (1993): 1767–91.

16 D. Brown, 'Participatory action research for social change: collective reflections with Asian nongovernmental development organizations', *Human Relations*, 46:2 (1993): 208–27.

17 D. Cooperrider and S. Srivastva, 'Appreciative inquiry in organizational life', in *Organizational Change and Development*, 1, eds R. Woodman and W. Pasmore (Greenwich, CT: JAI Press, 1987): 129–70.

18 D. Cooperrider and W. Pasmore, 'Global social change: a new agenda for social science?', *Human Relations*, 44:10 (1991): 1037–55.

19 W. Burke, *Organization Development: A Normative View* (Reading, MA: Addison-Wesley, 1987).

20 D. Greenwood, W. Whyte and I. Harkavy, 'Participatory action research as process and as goal', *Human Relations*, 46:2 (1993): 175–92.

21 J. Enderby and D. Phelan, 'Action learning groups as the foundation for cultural change', *Asia Pacific Journal of Human Resources*, 32: 1 (1994).

22 C. Argyris, R. Putnam and D. Smith, *Action Science* (San Francisco: Jossey-Bass, 1985).

23 S. Mohrman and T. Cummings, *Self-designing Organizations: Learning How to Create High Performance* (Reading, MA: Addison-Wesley, 1989).

24 P. Senge, *The Fifth Discipline* (New York: Doubleday, 1990).

25 M. Weisbord, *Productive Workplaces* (San Francisco: Jossey-Bass, 1987).

26 D. Cooperrider, 'Positive image, positive action: the affirmative basis for organizing', in *Appreciative Management and Leadership*, eds S. Srivastva, D. Cooperrider and associates (San Francisco, CA: Jossey-Bass, 1990); D. Cooperrider, lecture notes, *Presentation to the MSOD Chi Class*, October 1995, Monterey, CA.

27 Cooperrider and Srivastva, 'Appreciative inquiry in organizational life', op. cit.

28 D. Cooperrider and T. Thachankary, 'Building the global civic culture: making our lives count', in *Global and International Organization Development*, eds P. Sorensen Jr, T. Head, N. Mathys, J. Preston and D. Cooperrider (Champaign, IL: Stipes, 1995): 282–306.

29 D. Eden, 'Creating expectation effects in OD: applying self-fulfilling prophecy', in *Research in Organization Change and Development*, 2, eds W. Pasmore and R. Woodman (Greenwich, CT: JAI Press, 1988); D. Eden, 'OD and self-fulfilling prophesy: boosting productivity by raising expectations', *Journal of Applied Behavioral Science*, 22 (1986): 1–13; Cooperrider, 'Positive image, positive action', op. cit.

30 F. Barrett and D. Cooperrider, 'Generative metaphor intervention: a new approach for working with systems divided by conflict and caught in defensive perception', *Journal of Applied Behavioral Science*, 26 (1990): 219–39.

31 D. Nadler, 'Organizational frame-bending: types of change in the complex organization', in *Corporate Transformation*, eds R. Kilmann and T. Covin (San Francisco: Jossey-Bass, 1988): 66–83; P. Watzlawick, J.

Weakland and R. Fisch, *Change* (New York: WW Norton, 1974); R. Golembiewski, K. Billingsley and S. Yeager, 'Measuring change and persistence in human affairs: types of change generated by OD designs', *Journal of Applied Behavioral Science*, 12 (1975): 133–57; A. Meyer, G. Brooks and J. Goes, 'Environmental jolts and industry revolutions: organizational responses to discontinuous change', *Strategic Management Journal*, 11 (1990): 93–110.

32 A. Mohrman, G. Ledford Jr, S. Mohrman, E. Lawler III and T. Cummings, *Large-Scale Organization Change* (San Francisco: Jossey-Bass, 1989).

33 L. Brown, 'Planned change in underorganised systems', in *Systems Theory for Organisation Development*, ed. T. Cummings (Chichester: John Wiley and Sons, 1980): 181–203.

34 J. Porras and P. Robertson, 'Organization development theory, practice, and research', in *Handbook of Industrial and Organizational Psychology*, 3, 2nd edn, eds M. Dunnette and M. Hough (Palo Alto, CA: Consulting Psychologists Press, 1992).

35 T. Cummings, S. Mohrman, A. Mohrman and G. Ledford, 'Organization design for the future: a collaborative research approach', in *Doing Research That Is Useful for Theory and Practice*, eds E. Lawler III, A. Mohrman, S. Mohrman, G. Ledford and T. Cummings (San Francisco: Jossey-Bass, 1985): 275–305.

36 A. Frohman, M. Sashkin and M. Kavanagh, 'Action research as applied to organization development', *Organization and Administrative Sciences*, 7 (1976): 129–42; S. Mohrman and T. Cummings, *Self-designing Organizations: Learning How to Create High Performance* (Reading, MA: Addison-Wesley, 1989); M. Beer, R. Eisenstat and B. Spector, 'Why change programs don't produce change', *Harvard Business Review*, 6 (November–December 1990): 158–66.

37 Beer, Eisenstat and Spector, 'Why change programs don't produce change', op. cit.

38 D. Dunphy and D. Stace, *Under New Management: Australian Organisations in Transition* (Sydney, McGraw-Hill, 1990): 82.

39 D. Dunphy and D. Stace, 'Strategies for organisational transition', *Centre for Corporate Change*, Paper 002, 1991, AGSM, University of New South Wales.

Online reading

INFOTRAC® COLLEGE EDITION

For additional readings and reviews on planned change, explore **InfoTrac® College Edition**, your online library. Go to **www.infotrac-college.com** and search for any of the InfoTrac key terms listed below:

• **Kurt Lewin**
• **Action research**
• **Magnitude of change**
• **Degree of organisation**
• **Critique of change**
• **Contingency approach**

 INFOTRAC

3

THE ROLE OF THE CHANGE AGENT/ PRACTiTiONER

Chapters 1 and 2 provided an overview of the field of organisation development and a description of the nature of planned change. This chapter extends that introduction by examining the people who perform OD in organisations. A closer look at OD practitioners can provide a more personal perspective on the field, and help us to understand the essential character of OD as a helping profession, involving personal relationships between OD practitioners and organisation members.

Much of the literature about OD practitioners views them as internal or external consultants who provide professional services: diagnosing problems, developing solutions and helping to implement them. More recent perspectives expand the scope of OD practitioners to include professionals in related disciplines, such as industrial psychology and organisation theory, as well as line managers who have learned how to carry out OD in order to change and develop their departments.

A great deal of opinion and some research studies have focused on the necessary skills and knowledge of an effective OD practitioner. Studies provide a comprehensive list of basic skills and knowledge needed by all OD practitioners if they are to be effective.

Most of the relevant literature focuses on people who specialise in OD as a profession and addresses their roles and careers. The OD role can be described in relation to the position of OD practitioners: internal to the organisation, external to it or in a team composed of both internal and external consultants. The OD role can also be examined in terms of its marginality in organisations and of where it fits along a continuum from client-centred to consultant-centred functioning. Finally, organisation development is an emerging profession that provides alternative opportunities for gaining competence and developing a career. The stressful nature of helping professions, however, suggests that OD practitioners must cope with the possibility of professional burnout.

As in other helping professions, values and ethics play an important role in guiding OD practice and minimising the possibility of clients being neglected or abused.

WHO IS THE ORGANISATION DEVELOPMENT PRACTITIONER?

Throughout this text, the term 'organisation development (OD) practitioner' refers to at least three kinds of people. The most obvious group of OD practitioners consists of those people who specialise in OD as a profession. They may be internal or external consultants who offer professional services to organisation clients, including top managers, functional department heads and staff groups. OD professionals have traditionally shared a common set of humanistic values, promoting open communications, employee involvement and personal growth and development. They tend to have common training, skills and experience in the social processes of organisations (for example, group dynamics, decision making and communications). In recent years, OD professionals have expanded those traditional values and expertise to include more concern for organisational effectiveness, competitiveness and bottom-line results, and greater attention to the technical, structural and strategic parts of organisations. This expansion is mainly in response to the highly competitive demands that face modern organisations. It has resulted in a more diverse set of OD professionals geared to helping organisations cope with those pressures.[1]

Second, the term 'OD practitioner' applies to people who specialise in fields related to OD, such as reward systems, organisation design, total quality management, information technology or business strategy. These content-oriented fields are increasingly becoming integrated with OD's process orientation, particularly as OD projects have become more comprehensive, involving multiple features and varying parts of organisations. A growing number of professionals in these related fields are gaining experience and competence in OD, mainly through working with OD professionals on large-scale projects and through attending OD training sessions. For example, Australia's 'Big 5' accounting firms have diversified into management consulting and change management. In most cases, these related professionals do not fully subscribe to traditional OD values, nor do they have extensive training and experience in OD. Rather, they have formal training and experience in their respective specialties, such as industrial relations, management consulting, control systems, health care and work design. They are OD practitioners in the sense that they apply their special competence within an OD-like process, typically by having OD professionals and managers help to design and implement change programs. They also practise OD when they apply their OD competence to their own specialties, thus diffusing an OD perspective into such areas as compensation practices, work design, labour relations and planning and strategy.

Third, the term 'OD practitioner' applies to the increasing number of managers and administrators who have gained competence in OD and who apply it to their own work areas. Various reviewers of change management argue that OD applied by managers, rather than OD professionals, has grown rapidly.[2] It has been suggested that the faster pace of change affecting organisations today is highlighting the centrality of the manager in managing change. Consequently, OD must become a general management skill. Along these lines, the Centre for Corporate Change at the Australian Graduate School of Management has studied a number of firms such as the New South Wales State Library and Woolworths, where managers and employees have become 'change masters'.[3] They have gained the expertise to introduce change and innovation into the organisation.

Managers tend to gain competence in OD by interacting with OD professionals in actual change programs. This on-the-job training is frequently supplemented with more formal OD training, such as the variety of OD workshops offered by the Australian Institute of Management (AIM), Institution of Engineers (IE), Australian Human Resource Institute (AHRI) and others. Line managers are increasingly attending such external programs. Moreover, a growing number of organisations, including Ernst and Young and Ericsson, have instituted in-house training programs for managers to learn how to develop and change their work units. As managers gain OD competence, they become its most basic practitioners.

In practice, the distinction between the three kinds of OD practitioners is becoming blurred. A growing number of managers have moved, either temporarily or permanently, into the OD profession. For example, companies such as Budget trained and rotated managers into full-time OD roles so that they could gain the skills and experience necessary for higher level management positions. Also, it is increasingly common to find managers (for example, David Mallen from MCS Management Consultants and Ann Boland, an independent consultant and psychologist, formerly from Ernst and Young) using their experience in OD to become external consultants, particularly in the employee involvement area. More OD practitioners are gaining professional competence in related specialties, such as business process re-engineering, reward systems, and career planning and development. Conversely, many specialists in these related areas are achieving professional competence in OD. Cross-training and integration are producing a more comprehensive and complex kind of OD practitioner, who has a greater diversity of values, skills and experience than does the traditional OD practitioner.

Application 3.1 presents the case study of an external OD practitioner, Peter O'Donoghue, and his philosophy as a change agent.

APPLICATION 3.1

CHALLENGE OF THE SEA NOW TRANSLATES INTO 'RIPPLE EFFECT' COACHING SKILLS

A round-the-world yacht race and an MBA convinced Peter O'Donoghue that men and women in businesses could benefit from coaching, just as much as any athlete. Here, he explains why he believes the best way to protect your bottom line is to train your frontline staff.

My interest in business coaching took off after I returned from a round-the-world yacht race.

I had an amazing time on that voyage but when I came back I found it very difficult to match my new-found outlook on life with an employer. It made me question how I could use my skills and experience to help others.

That was when I decided the best way forward was to set up business on my own providing business advice and coaching in the SME and corporate workplace.

But it was only after getting professional training as a business adviser and seeing how it works first-hand that I really realised what it is all about and discovered its value to clients.

Instead of simply looking at individual processes within a company and how they can be improved, a business coach will also focus on the individual employees and seek to address their needs.

We find that when we change the behaviour of just one person it can have a positive ripple effect throughout the company.

This is where an outside perspective from a trained coach can prove invaluable. Many companies may question the need to bring in outside help. But when you're in a company you are caught up in the pressure, routines and culture of it and are unable to take an objective view.

There are many reasons for adopting coaching and obviously they do not happen in isolation. But what is important to remember is that no matter what the primary reason for adopting coaching, it will invariably have a significant positive impact on other elements such as improving staff recruitment, staff retention and accelerating organisational change.

Source: David Williamson, 'Challenge of the sea now translates into "ripple effect" coaching skills', *The Western Mail*, 27/5/06.

Critical Thinking Questions: What is the fundamental philosophy of Peter O'Donoghue? Do you agree or disagree? Explain your answer.

COMPETENCIES OF AN EFFECTIVE ORGANISATION DEVELOPMENT PRACTITIONER

Much of the literature about the skills and knowledge of an effective OD practitioner claims that a mixture of personality traits, experiences, kinds of knowledge and skills can be assumed to lead to effective practice. For example, research on the characteristics of successful change practitioners yields the following list of attributes and abilities: diagnostic ability, basic knowledge of behavioural science techniques, empathy, knowledge of the theories and methods within the consultant's own discipline, goal-setting ability, problem-solving ability, ability to do self-assessment, the ability to see things objectively, imagination, flexibility, honesty, consistency and trust.[4] Although these qualities and skills are certainly laudable, there has been relatively little consensus about their importance in effective OD practice.

Many consulting styles or approaches have been suggested, but each style usually varies according to its underlying character – shaped by the kinds of skills and techniques that the consultants use, the values they bring to their clients and the manner in which they carry out their assignments. Other research also examines the degree of emphasis that the consultant places upon two interrelated goals or dimensions of the change process. Application 3.2 describes a classification that involves the consultant's orientation to the two interrelated dimensions:

1   the degree of emphasis upon effectiveness or goal accomplishment
2   the degree of emphasis upon relationships, morale and participant satisfaction.[5]

APPLiCATiON 3.2

Consultant styles matrix

Based upon two dimensions – an emphasis on morale and an emphasis on effectiveness – five different types of consultant styles or roles may be identified.

* *The stabiliser style.* The goal of the stabiliser style consultant is neither effectiveness nor participant satisfaction. Rather, the consultant is trying to refrain from rocking the boat, and to maintain a low profile. The underlying motivation is often survival, or merely following the directives of top management. Such a role is usually found in large organisations where development programs may be part of the staff function and are not highly regarded by top management. This style is usually regarded as having been forced upon the individual by organisation pressures, so that the individual has learned to conform and suppress internal motivations.

* *The cheerleader style.* The cheerleader style places an emphasis on the satisfaction of organisation members and is chiefly concerned with employee motivation and morale. The cheerleader seeks warm working relationships and in general is more comfortable in non-confrontational situations. Effectiveness per se is not emphasised, the assumption being that if member satisfaction is high, effectiveness will also be high. Unfortunately, there is a great deal

Figure 3.1   Consultant styles

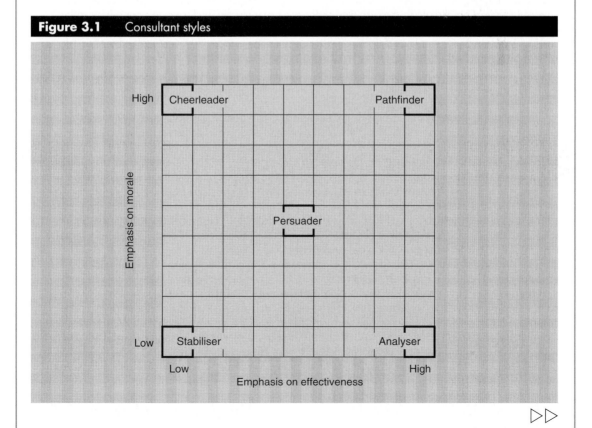

▷▷

of evidence that contradicts this assumption. The cheerleader strongly pushes for improved morale, and open conflict or locking horns is avoided by attempts to smooth over differences and maintain harmony.

- *The analyser style.* The analyser style places the greatest emphasis on efficiency with little emphasis being given to member satisfaction. The analyser feels most comfortable with a rational assessment of problems and assumes that the facts will lead to a solution. This type of consultant may be quite confrontational, usually relying on authority to resolve conflict, and on rational problem-solving processes. The analyser has a background of specialised expertise, knowledge and experience applicable to the solution of specific problems. The client needs to have a problem solved, a service performed or a study made; the analyser consultant takes responsibility for providing these functions. This type of consultant is based on the belief that the client does not need to know, or cannot learn the skills to solve its problems. The success of the consultant is largely dependent on the client having properly diagnosed its problem and having called in the right kind of consultant.
- *The persuader style.* The persuader style focuses on both dimensions, effectiveness and morale, yet optimises neither. Such a style provides a relatively low-risk strategy, yet avoids direct confrontation with other forces. This approach may be used when the consultant's power or leverage is low relative to other participants. This style is motivated primarily by a desire to satisfy; that is, to achieve something that is 'good enough'. A great deal of effort is applied in attempting to satisfy the differing forces, thus gaining a majority bloc of support for prepared changes. The resulting change program may often be watered down or weakened to the point where organisation improvement is unlikely.
- *The pathfinder style.* The pathfinder style seeks both a high degree of effectiveness and a high degree of member satisfaction, believing that greater effectiveness is possible when all members are involved and problem solving is done through teamwork. There is an awareness that confrontation and conflict are often a means to a more effective organisation and to more satisfied individual members. The pathfinder approach uses collaborative problem solving and challenges the underlying patterns of member behaviour.

Most organisation problems are complex situations and may not be neatly solved by any one particular change, but will depend upon the particular consultant, the nature of the problem and the type of organisation climate that exists. The styles are not mutually exclusive. All consultant styles can be effective and are interrelated. A consultant may use different styles at different times to meet changing client system needs and deal with diverse situations. Frequently, some combination of the types may be applied.

Two ongoing projects are attempting to define and categorise the skills and knowledge required of OD practitioners. In the first effort, a broad and growing list of well-known practitioners and researchers annually update a list of professional competencies. The most recent list has grown to 187 statements in nine areas of OD practice, including entry, start-up, assessment and feedback, action planning, intervention, evaluation, adoption, separation and general competencies. The statements range from 'staying centred in the present, focusing on the ongoing process' and 'understanding and explaining how diversity will affect the diagnosis of the culture' to 'basing change on business strategy and business needs' and 'being comfortable with quantum leaps, radical shifts, and paradigm changes'. The discussion is currently considering additional items related to international OD, large-group interventions and transorganisation skills.

The second project, sponsored by the Organisation Development and Change Division of the Academy of Management, seeks to develop a list of competencies to guide curriculum development in graduate OD programs. So far, more than 40 OD practitioners and researchers have worked to develop two competency lists (shown in Table 3.1). First, foundation competencies are oriented towards descriptions of an existing system. They include knowledge from organisation behaviour, psychology, group dynamics, management and organisation theory, research methods and business practices. Second, core competencies are aimed at how systems change over time. They include knowledge of organisation design, organisation research, system dynamics, OD history, and theories and models for change. They also involve the skills needed to: manage the consulting process; analyse and diagnose systems; design and choose interventions; facilitate processes; develop clients' capability to manage their own change; and evaluate organisation change.

Table 3.1	Knowledge and skill requirements of OD practitioners	
	Foundation competencies	Core competencies

Knowledge	1 Organisation behaviour
	  A Organisation culture
	  B Work design
	  C Interpersonal relations
	  D Power and politics
	  E Leadership
	  F Goal setting
	  G Conflict
	  H Ethics
	2 Individual psychology
	  A Learning theory
	  B Motivation theory
	  C Perception theory
	3 Group dynamics
	  A Roles
	  B Communication processes
	  C Decision-making process
	  D Stages of group development
	  E Leadership
	4 Management and organisation theory
	  A Planning, organising, leading, and controlling
	  B Problem solving and decision making
	  C Systems theory
	  D Contingency theory
	  E Organisation structure
	  F Characteristics of environment and technology
	  G Models of organisation and system
	5 Research methods/statistics
	  A Measures of central tendency
	  B Measures of dispersion
	  C Basic sampling theory
	  D Basic experimental design
	  E Sample inferential statistics
	6 Comparative cultural perspectives
	  A Dimensions of natural culture
	  B Dimensions of industry culture
	  C Systems implications
	7 Functional knowledge of business
	  A Interpersonal communication (listening, feedback, and articulation)
	  B Collaboration/working together
	  C Problem solving
	  D Using new technology
	  E Conceptualising
	  F Project management
	  G Present/education/coach
		1 Organisation design: the decision process associated with formulating and aligning the elements of an organisational system, including but not limited to structural systems, human resource systems, information systems, reward systems, work design, political systems, and organisation culture
		  A The concept of fit and alignment
		  B Diagnostic and design model for various subsystems that make up an organisation at any level of analysis, including the structure of work, human resources, information systems, reward systems, work design, political systems, and so on
		  C Key thought leaders in organisation design
		2 Organisation research: field research methods; interviewing; content analysis; design of questionnaires and interview protocol; designing change evaluation processes; longitudinal data collection and analysis; understanding and detecting alpha, beta, and gamma change; and a host of quantitative and qualitative methods
		3 System dynamics: the description and understanding of how systems evolve and develop over time, how systems respond to exogenous and endogenous disruption as well as planned interventions (for example, evolution and revolution, punctuated equilibrium theory, chaos theory, catastrophe theory, incremental vs. quantum change, transformation theory and so on)
		4 History of organisation development and change: an understanding of the social, political, economic, and personal forces that led to the emergence and development of organisation development and change, including the key thought leaders, the values underlying their writings and actions, the key events and writings, and related documentation

(continued)

Table 3.1	Knowledge and skill requirements of OD practitioners *(continued)*	
	Foundation competencies	Core competencies
Knowledge		A Human relations movement B NTL/T-groups/sensitivity training C Survey research D Quality of work life E Tavistock Institute F Key thought leaders G Humanistic values H Statement of ethics 5 Theories and models for change: the basic action research model, participatory action research model, planning model, change typologies (for example, fast, slow, incremental, quantum, revolutionary). Lewin's model, transition models, and so on
Skills		1 Managing the consulting process: the ability to enter, contract, diagnose, design appropriate interventions, implement those interventions, manage unprogrammed events, and evaluate change process
		2 Analysis/diagnosis: the abilities to conduct an inquiry into a system's effectiveness, to see the root cause(s) of a system's current level of effectiveness; the core skill is interpreted to include all systems— individual, group, organisation, and multi-organisation—as well as the ability to understand and inquire into one's self
		3 Designing/choosing appropriate, relevant interventions: understanding how to select, modify, or design effective interventions that will move the organisation from its current state to its desired future state
		4 Facilitation and process consultation: the ability to assist an individual or group towards a goal; the ability to conduct an inquiry into individual and group processes such that the client system maintains ownership of the issue, increases its capacity for reflection on the consequences of its behaviours and actions, and develops a sense of increased control and ability
		5 Developing client capability: the ability to conduct a change process in such a way that the client is better able to plan and implement a successful change process in the future, using technologies of planned change in a values-based and ethical manner
		6 Evaluating organisation change: the ability to design and implement a process to evaluate the impact and effects of change intervention, including control of alternative explanations and interpretation of performance outcomes

The information in Table 3.1 applies primarily to people who specialise in OD as a profession. For those people, the list of skills and knowledge seems reasonable, especially in light of the growing diversity and complexity of interventions in OD. Gaining competence in those areas may take considerable time and effort, and it is questionable whether the other two types of OD practitioners – managers and specialists in related fields – also need this full range of skills and knowledge. It seems more reasonable to suggest that some subset of the items listed in Table 3.1 should apply to all OD practitioners, whether they are OD professionals, managers or related specialists. These items would constitute the basic skills and knowledge of an OD practitioner. Beyond this background, the three types of OD practitioners would probably differ in areas of concentration. OD professionals would extend their breadth of skills across the remaining categories in Table 3.1; managers would focus on the major management knowledge areas; and related specialists would concentrate on skills in their respective areas, such as those included in the major management and collateral knowledge areas.

Based on the data in Table 3.1, as well as on more recent studies of OD skills,[6] all OD practitioners should have the following basic skills and knowledge to be effective:

1   *Intrapersonal skills or 'self-management' competence.* Despite the growing knowledge base and sophistication of the field, organisation development is still a human craft. As the primary instrument of diagnosis and change, practitioners often must process complex, ambiguous information and make informed judgments about its relevance to organisational issues.

The core competency of analysis and diagnosis listed in Table 3.1 includes the ability to inquire into one's self, and it remains one of the cornerstone skills in OD. Practitioners must also have the personal centring to know their own values, feelings and purposes and the integrity to behave responsibly in a helping relationship with others. Bob Tannenbaum, one of the founders of OD, argues that self-knowledge is the most central ingredient in OD practice and suggests that practitioners are becoming too enamoured of skills and techniques.[7] Some recent data support his view. A study of 416 OD practitioners found that 47% agreed with the statement: 'Many of the new entrants into the field have little understanding of or appreciation for the history or values underlying the field'.[8] Because OD is a highly uncertain process that requires constant adjustment and innovation, practitioners need to have active learning skills and a reasonable balance between their rational and emotional sides. Finally, OD practice can be highly stressful and can lead to early burnout, so practitioners need to know how to manage their own stress.

2   *Interpersonal skills.* Practitioners must create and maintain effective relationships with individuals and groups within the organisation to help them gain the competence necessary to solve their own problems. Table 3.1 identifies group dynamics, comparative cultural perspectives and business function as foundation knowledge, plus managing the consulting process and facilitation as core skills. All of these interpersonal competencies promote effective helping relationships. Such relationships start with a grasp of the organisation's perspective and require listening to members' perceptions and feelings to understand how they see themselves and the organisation. This understanding provides a starting point for joint diagnosis and problem solving. Practitioners must establish trust and rapport with organisation members so that they can share pertinent information and work effectively together. This requires being able to converse in the members' own language and to exchange feedback about how the relationship is progressing.

To help members learn new skills and behaviours, practitioners must serve as concrete role models of what is expected. They must act in ways that are credible to organisation members and provide them with the counselling and coaching necessary for development and change. Because the helping relationship is jointly determined, practitioners need to be able to negotiate an acceptable role and to manage changing expectations and demands.

3   *General consultation skills.* Table 3.1 identifies the ability to manage the consulting process and the ability to design interventions as core competencies that all practitioners should possess. OD starts with diagnosing an organisation or department to understand the causes of its problems and to discover areas for further development. OD practitioners need to know how to carry out an effective diagnosis, at least at a rudimentary level. They should know how to engage organisation members in diagnosis,

how to help them ask the right questions and how to collect and analyse information. A manager, for example, should be able to work with subordinates to jointly find out how the organisation or department is functioning. The manager should know basic diagnostic questions, some methods for gathering information (such as interviews or surveys) and some techniques for analysing it, such as force-field analysis or statistical means and distributions.

In addition to diagnosis, OD practitioners should know how to design and execute an intervention. They need to be able to lay out an action plan and to gain commitment to the program. They also need to know how to tailor the intervention to the situation, using information about how the change is progressing in order to guide implementation (see Chapter 6). For example, managers should be able to develop action steps for an intervention with subordinates. They should be able to gain their commitment to the program (usually through participation), sit down with them and assess how it is progressing, and make modifications if necessary.

4   *Organisation development theory.* The final basic tool that OD practitioners should have is a general knowledge of OD, as presented in this book. They should have some appreciation for planned change, the action research model and contemporary approaches to managing change. They should have some familiarity with the range of available interventions and the need for assessing and institutionalising change programs. Perhaps most important is that OD practitioners should understand their own role in the emerging field of organisation development, whether as managers, OD professionals or specialists in related areas.

Application 3.3 describes the skills required for OD.

APPLICATiON 3.3

THE CHANGE AGENTS

A new breed of top female executives are bringing their intellect, strong people skills, vision and drive to Australia's top corporate echelons.

Take a look at the careers of 20 of Australia's most highly regarded female executives. What these women have in common is a motivation to succeed, resilience, sheer capacity for work, intelligence, political savvy and a proven ability to work in senior line management roles with profit-and-loss responsibility.

The defining quality in these women is their ability to turn business around and make change where it is necessary.

...

This crop of executives differs from many of the previous generation of women business leaders in that once they break through the glass ceiling, they do not pull up the ladder behind them and play by the old boy's club rules. They are far more open about the struggle to balance life and work and the need to change the culture in their organisations.

...

Without exception, the women mention the importance of mentors in helping them achieve their professional goals.

...

LIZ CACCIOTTOLO, CHIEF EXECUTIVE, UBS WEALTH MANAGEMENT AUSTRALIA

At 18, Liz Cacciottolo was enrolled in commerce at university and doing work experience at a futures firm in Sydney. 'I was impatient to get on with it,' she says. Cacciottolo went to see a headhunter to find out how she could make a career in finance ... and then went to London where she spent the next 17 years. Cacciottolo joined UBS in 1987, first in the equity division and then in wealth management, where she really made her mark. Between 2000 and 2004, Cacciottolo built the domestic business ... from nothing to £10 billion under management. Having two children has made Cacciottolo rethink the way she does her job. It brought home the importance of measuring the work success of her staff and herself in terms of effect and contribution, not on hours worked. 'You have to focus on the key things.'

CHRISTINE BARTLETT, CHIEF EXECUTIVE, JONES LANG LASALLE

'A lot of people used to think [a client relationship] was like a tool where you install some software and away you go. But it is more than that. It is about bringing change in culture. ... Quite often the best ideas don't come from executives, they come from all areas of the business ... I tend to be passionate about what I do and passion can be infectious. I don't tend to expect from others anything that I don't expect from myself.'

Source: David James & Emily Ross, 'Leadership: The change agents', *Business Review Weekly*, Mar–Apr 2005.

Critical Thinking Questions: What is the importance of mentors in a change process? What problems could occur in such a relationship?

THE PROFESSIONAL ORGANISATION DEVELOPMENT PRACTITIONER

Most of the literature about OD practitioners has focused on people specialising in OD as a profession. In this section, we discuss the role and typical career paths of OD professionals.

The role of organisation development professionals

POSITION

Organisation development professionals have positions that are either internal or external to the organisation. Internal consultants are members of the organisation, and are usually located in the human resources department. They may perform the OD role exclusively, or they may combine it with other tasks, such as compensation practices, training or labour relations.[9] Many large organisations, such as Mayne Nickless, have created specialised OD consulting groups. Their internal consultants typically have a variety of clients within the organisation, serving both line and staff departments.

External consultants are not members of the client organisation; they typically work for a consulting firm, a university or themselves. Organisations generally hire external consultants to provide a particular expertise that is unavailable internally, and to bring a different and potentially more objective perspective into the organisation development process.

Table 3.2 describes the differences between these two roles at each stage of the action research process.

During the entry process, internal consultants have clear advantages. They have ready access to and relationships with clients, know the language of the organisation and have insights about the root cause of many of its problems. This allows internal consultants to save time in identifying the organisation's culture, informal practices and sources of power. They have access to a variety of information, including rumours, company reports and direct observation. In addition, entry is more efficient and congenial, and their pay is not at risk. External consultants, however, have the advantage of being able to select the clients they want to work with according to their own criteria. The contracting phase is less formal for internal consultants and there is less worry about expenses, but there is less choice about whether to complete the assignment. Both types of consultants must address issues of confidentiality, risk project termination (and other negative consequences) by the client, and fill a third-party role.

During the diagnosis process, internal consultants already know most organisation members and enjoy a basic level of rapport and trust. But external consultants often have higher status than internal consultants, which allows them to probe difficult issues and assess the organisation more objectively. In the intervention phase, both types of consultants must rely on valid information, free and informed choice, and internal commitment for their success. However, an internal consultant's strong ties to the organisation may make him or her overly cautious, particularly when powerful others can affect a career. Internal consultants also may lack certain skills and

Table 3.2	The differences between external and internal consulting	
Stage Of Change	External Consultants	Internal Consultants
Entering	• Source clients • Build relationships • Learn company jargon • "Presenting problem" challenge • Time consuming • Stressful phase • Select project/client according to own criteria • Unpredictable outcome	• Ready access to clients • Ready relationships • Knows company jargon • Understands root causes • Time efficient • Congenial phase • Obligated to work with everyone • Steady pay
Contracting	• Formal documents • Can terminate project at will • Guard against out-of-pocket expenses • Information confidential • Loss of contract at stake • Maintain third-party role	• Informal agreements • Must complete projects assigned • No out-of-pocket expenses • Information can be open or confidential • Risk of client retaliation and loss of job at stake • Acts as third party, driver (on behalf of client), or pair of hands
Diagnosing	• Meet most organization members for the first time • Prestige from being external • Build trust quickly • Confidential data can increase political sensitivities	• Has relationships with many organization members • Prestige determined by job rank and client stature • Sustain reputation as trustworthy over time • Data openly shared can reduce political intrigue
Intervening	• Insist on valid information, free and informed choice, and internal commitment • Confine activities within boundaries of client organization	• Insist on valid information, free and informed choice, and internal commitment • Run interference for client across organizational lines to align support
Evaluating	• Rely on repeat business and customer referral as key measures of project success • Seldom see long-term results	• Rely on repeat business, pay raise, and promotion as key measures of success • Can see change become institutionalized • Little recognition for job well done

Source: M. Lacey, 'Internal Consulting: Perspectives on the Process of Planned Change', *Journal of Organizational Change Management*, 8(1995):76. © 1995. Republished with permission, Emerald Group Publishing Limited, www.emeraldinsight.com

experience in facilitating organisational change. Insiders may have some small advantages in being able to move around the system and cross key organisational boundaries. Finally, the measures of success and reward differ from those of the external practitioner in the evaluation process.

A promising approach to having the advantages of both internal and external OD consultants is to include them both as members of an internal–external consulting team.[10] External consultants can combine their special expertise and objectivity with the inside knowledge and acceptance of internal consultants. The two parties can provide complementary consulting skills, while sharing the workload and possibly accomplishing more than either would by operating alone. Internal consultants, for example, can provide almost continuous contact with the client, while their external counterparts can periodically provide specialised services, perhaps on two or three days each month. External consultants can also help train their organisation partners, thus transferring OD skills and knowledge to the organisation.

Although little has been written on internal–external consulting teams, recent studies suggest that the effectiveness of such teams depends on the members developing strong, supportive, collegial relationships. They need to take time to develop the consulting team, confronting individual differences and establishing appropriate roles and exchanges. Members need to provide each other with continuous feedback and to make a commitment to learning from each other. In the absence of these team-building and learning features, internal–external consulting teams can be more troublesome and less effective than consultants working alone.

MARGINALITY

A promising line of research on the professional OD role centres on the issue of marginality.[11] The marginal person is one who successfully straddles the boundary between two or more groups that have differing goals, value systems and behaviour patterns. In the past, the marginal role has always been seen as dysfunctional. Now marginality is seen in a more positive light. There are many examples of marginal roles in organisations: the salesperson, the buyer, the first-line supervisor, the integrator and the project manager.

Evidence is mounting that some people are better at taking marginal roles than others. Those who are good at marginal roles seem to have personal qualities of low dogmatism, neutrality, open-mindedness, objectivity, flexibility and adaptable information-processing ability. Rather than being upset by conflict, ambiguity and stress, they thrive on it. Individuals with marginal orientations are more likely than others to develop integrative decisions that bring together and reconcile viewpoints between opposing organisational groups, and are more likely to remain neutral in controversial situations. Thus, the research suggests that the marginal role can have positive effects when it is filled by a person with a marginal orientation. Such a person can be more objective and better able to perform successfully in linking, integrative or conflict-laden roles.[12]

A study of 89 external OD practitioners and 246 internal practitioners (response rates of 59% and 54%, respectively) showed that external OD professionals were more comfortable with the marginal role than were internal OD professionals. Internal consultants with more years of experience were more marginally oriented than were those with less experience.[13] These findings, combined with other research on marginal roles, suggest the importance of maintaining the OD professional's marginality, with its flexibility, independence and boundary-spanning characteristics.

USE OF KNOWLEDGE AND EXPERIENCE

The professional OD role has been described in terms of a continuum ranging from client-centred (using the client's knowledge and experience) to consultant-centred (using the consultant's knowledge and experience), as shown in Figure 3.2. Traditionally, OD consultants have worked at the client-centred end of the continuum. OD professionals, relying mainly on sensitivity training, process consultation and team building (see Chapter 7), have been expected to remain neutral, refusing to offer expert advice on organisational problems. Rather than contracting to solve specific problems, the consultant has tended to work with organisation members to identify problems and potential solutions, to help them study what they are doing now and to consider alternative behaviours and solutions, and to help them discover whether in fact the consultant and they can learn to do things better. In doing this, the OD professional has generally listened and reflected upon members' perceptions and ideas, and helped to clarify and interpret their communications and behaviours.

With the recent proliferation of OD interventions in the structural, human resource management and strategy areas, this limited definition of the professional OD role has expanded to include the consultant-centred end of the continuum. In many of these newer approaches, the consultant may have to take on a modified role of expert, with the consent and collaboration of organisation members. For example, if a consultant and managers were to try to bring about a major structural redesign (see Chapter 10), managers may not have the appropriate knowledge and expertise to create and manage the change. The consultant's role might be to present the basic concepts and ideas and then to struggle jointly with the managers to select an approach that might be useful to the organisation and decide how it might be best implemented. In this situation, the OD professional recommends or prescribes particular changes and is active in planning how to implement them. However, this expertise is always shared rather than imposed.

With the development of new and varied intervention approaches, the role of the OD professional needs to be seen as falling along the entire continuum from client-centred to consultant-centred. At times, the consultant will rely mainly on organisation members' knowledge and experiences to identify and solve problems. At other times, it may be more appropriate for the OD professional to take on the role of expert, withdrawing from this role as managers gain more knowledge and experience.

CAREERS OF ORGANISATION DEVELOPMENT PROFESSIONALS

Unlike such occupations as medicine and law, OD is an emerging practice. It is still developing the characteristics of an established profession: a common body of knowledge, educational requirements, accrediting procedures, a recognised code of ethics, and rules and methods for governing conduct. This means that people can enter professional OD careers from a variety of educational and work backgrounds. They do not have to follow an established career path,

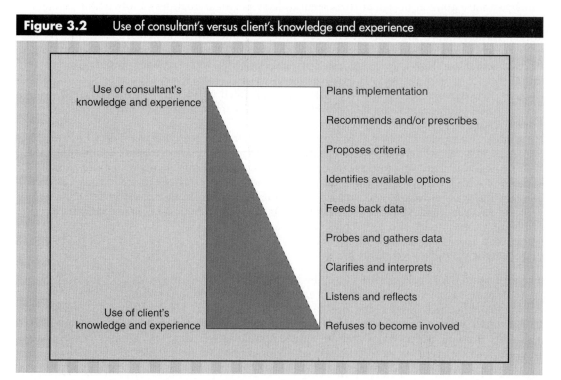

Figure 3.2   Use of consultant's versus client's knowledge and experience

Source: adapted by permission of the authors from W. Schmidt and A. Johnson, 'A continuum of consultancy styles' (unpublished manuscript, July 1970): p. 1.

but rather have some choice about when to enter or leave an OD career and whether to be an internal or external consultant.[14]

Despite the looseness or flexibility of the OD profession, most OD professionals have had specific training in OD. This training can include relatively short courses (one day to two weeks) and programs or workshops conducted within organisations or at outside institutions, such as TAFE's 'Train the Trainer' programs. OD training can also be more formal and lengthy, including master's programs and doctoral training.

As might be expected, career choices widen as people gain training and experience in OD. Those with rudimentary training tend to be internal consultants, often taking on OD roles as temporary assignments on the way to higher managerial or staff positions. Holders of master's degrees are generally evenly split between internal and external consultants. Those with doctorates may join a university faculty and consult part-time, join a consulting firm or seek a position as a relatively high-level internal consultant.

External consultants tend to be older, to have more managerial experience, and to spend more of their time in OD than do internal practitioners. Perhaps the most common career path is to begin as an internal consultant, gain experience and visibility through successful interventions or publishing and then become an external consultant. A field study found that internal consultants acquired greater competence by working with external consultants who deliberately helped to develop them. This development took place through a tutorial arrangement of joint diagnosis and intervention in the organisation, which gave the internal consultants a chance to observe and learn from the model furnished by the external consultants.[15]

There is increasing evidence that an OD career can be stressful, sometimes leading to burnout.[16] Burnout comes from taking on too many jobs, becoming overcommitted and, in general, working too hard. OD work often requires six-day weeks, with some days running up to 14 hours. Consultants may spend a week working with one organisation or department and then spend the weekend preparing for the next client. They may spend 50–75% of their time on the road, living in planes, cars, hotels, meetings and restaurants. Indeed, one practitioner has suggested that the majority of OD consultants would repeat the phrase 'quality of work life for consultants' as follows: 'Quality of work life? For consultants?'[17]

Organisation development professionals are increasingly taking steps to cope with burnout. They may shift jobs, moving from external to internal roles to avoid travel. They may learn to pace themselves better and to avoid taking on too much work. Many are engaging in fitness and health programs and are using stress-management techniques, such as those described in Chapter 9.

PROFESSIONAL VALUES

Values have played an important role in OD from its beginning. Traditionally, OD professionals have promoted a set of humanistic and democratic values. They have sought to build trust and collaboration; to create an open, problem-solving climate; and to increase the self-control of organisation members. More recently, OD practitioners have extended those humanistic values to include a concern for improving organisational effectiveness (for example, to increase productivity or to reduce turnover) and performance (for example, to increase profitability). They have shown an increasing desire to optimise both human benefits and production objectives.[18]

The joint values of humanising organisations and improving their effectiveness have received widespread support in the OD profession, as well as increasing encouragement from managers, employees and union officials. Indeed, it would be difficult not to support these joint concerns. But, increasingly, questions have been raised about the possibility of simultaneously pursuing greater humanism and organisational effectiveness.[19] More practitioners are experiencing situations in which there is conflict between the employees' needs for greater meaning and the organisation's need for more effective and efficient use of its resources. For example, expensive capital equipment may run most efficiently if it is highly programmed and routinised; yet people may not derive satisfaction from working with such technology. Should efficiency be maximised at the expense of people's satisfaction? Can technology be changed to make it more humanly satisfying yet remain efficient? What compromises are possible? These are the value dilemmas often faced when trying to optimise both human benefits and organisational effectiveness.

In addition to value issues within organisations, OD practitioners are dealing more and more with value conflicts with powerful outside groups. Organisations are open systems and exist within increasingly turbulent environments. For example, hospitals are facing complex and changing task environments. Australia has long had privately owned hospitals and now public hospitals are being offered to private operators. This means a proliferation of external stakeholders with interests in the organisation's functioning, including patients, suppliers, health insurance funds, employers, the government, shareholders, unions, the press and various interest groups. These external groups often have different and competing values for judging the organisation's effectiveness. For example, shareholders may judge the firm in terms of price per share, the government in terms of compliance with Equal Employment Opportunity legislation, patients in terms of quality of care, and ecology groups in terms of hazardous waste disposal. Because organisations must rely on these external groups for resources and legitimacy, they cannot simply ignore these competing values: they must somehow respond to them and try to reconcile the different interests.

Recent attempts to help firms manage external relationships suggest the need for new interventions and competence in OD.[20] Practitioners must have not only social skills (like those proposed in Table 3.1) but also political skills. They must understand the distribution of power, conflicts of interest and value dilemmas inherent in managing external relationships and be able to manage their own role and values in respect to those dynamics. Interventions promoting collaboration and system maintenance may be ineffective in this larger arena, especially when there are power and dominance relationships between organisations, plus competition for scarce resources. Under these conditions, OD practitioners may need more power-oriented interventions, such as bargaining, coalition forming and pressure tactics.

For example, firms in the tobacco industry have waged an aggressive campaign against efforts of groups such as the Australian Medical Association, the Royal Australasian College of General Practitioners, the Australian Cancer Society and the federal and state governments, to limit or ban the smoking of tobacco products. They have formed a powerful industry coalition to lobby against anti-smoking legislation, and they have spent enormous sums of money sponsoring leading sporting and culture events, conducting public relations and refuting research that purportedly shows the dangers of smoking. These power-oriented strategies are intended to manage an increasingly hostile environment. They may be necessary for the industry's survival. People practising OD in such settings may need to help organisations implement such strategies if they are to manage their environments effectively. This will require political skills and greater attention to how the OD practitioner's own values fit with those of the organisation.

Application 3.4 describes the value of a positive culture for an organisation.

APPLICATION 3.4

FEEL AT HOME

'What does organisational culture mean to your organisation? How do you ensure that the key features of the culture you want, eg work-life balance, career growth, industrial safety and so on, permeate your organisation?'

Organisations more often than not lapse into a 'default' culture. This is often shaped by a few employees who have managed somehow to claim their share of voice within the office and allowed by the vast majority of employees who give in to this situation. Unfortunately, this 'default' culture may not always be what the organisation needs to succeed in the near future.

...

SAMUEL DAVID – MANAGING DIRECTOR, CBL DATA RECOVERY TECHNOLOGIES

'To CBL, organisational culture is a set of underlying beliefs, principles and values that makes us unique and steers us to success. CBL is in an industry where new technical problems surface every single day. Our objectives are to ensure that our customers' needs are met and surpassed.

'All of CBL's 15 facilities on five continents need to tap on each other's expertise and work as a team to recover data for our customers as quickly as possible so that they can get on with their business. This makes a good culture absolutely essential. We need to be totally synchronised in our values and our behaviour at any one time.

'Our approach is to instil true belief and adoption, among all our employees, of our key corporate value – that it is our business to offer comprehensive and efficient data recovery services to all of our clientele through innovation and creativity. We build this culture through time and results. Every day, as we successfully recover data for someone or some company, we show that it is a realisable value. By communicating these cases through our e-newsletter, *CBL Bits & Bytes*, we have built a powerful culture that anything is possible if we work as a team.

'Another way of building a good culture is by encouraging our people to treat each other as a family member. From sending employees all over the world to our Canada office every year-end to helping single mothers figure out ways to take care of their babies, CBL has developed a culture of genuine care and appreciation among all our people.'

...

ANNIE YAP – MANAGING DIRECTOR, THE GMP GROUP

'The organisational cultures in most companies often reflect the personal values and work ethics of their founders. They are expressed explicitly through the company's core values, vision and mission statements. The culture supports the organisation's goals and is inseparable from the leadership style of the CEO. Though the organisational values do not change, every CEO has his/her own interpretation, thus refreshing the corporate behaviour. At GMP, we believe that organisational culture goes beyond adopting the company's values. It is presenting oneself in a mirror reflection of the company's personality without losing one's identity. It is also important for employees' personal beliefs to be in sync with the company's values. This helps to reduce any personal conflict that the staff might have which can be detrimental to his/her performance and hence, minimising staff turnover.'

...

STEVE RUSSELL – PRESIDENT & CEO, ASIA PACIFIC SALESFORCE.COM

'We strongly believe the value of our corporation should be fully distributed not only to its leadership. Sharing our success with our customers, our people and the communities we work in is, therefore, central to our corporate culture.

'In our experience, making good deeds an organisational priority empowers our employees and is as important to their happiness and career development as the first-rate training and remuneration they receive. In short, we believe philanthropy should be woven into every thread of corporate existence.

'Through the Salesforce.com Foundation, we currently devote 1% of employee time to the community and offer six paid days' community services each year. We currently have a staff participation rate of 85%.

'This approach also has major business benefits as it engages customers and shows the communities in which we operate that we're an organisation worth doing business with or working for.'

Source: Article extracts by courtesy of *SPH/The Business Times*.

Critical Thinking Questions: What is meant by a 'default' culture? What problems does this create? How may it be remedied?

PROFESSIONAL ETHICS

Ethical issues in OD are concerned with how practitioners perform their helping relationship with organisation members. Inherent in any helping relationship is the potential for misconduct and client abuse. OD practitioners can let personal values stand in the way of good practice; they can use the power inherent in their professional role to abuse organisation members (often unintentionally).

Ethical guidelines

To its credit, the field of OD has always shown concern for the ethical conduct of its practitioners. There have been several articles and conferences about ethics in OD. The School of Management, the Australian Business Ethics Network at the Royal Melbourne Institute of Technology (RMIT) and the St James Ethics Centre conducted a successful one-day symposium on teaching and training in business ethics.[21] In addition, statements of ethics governing OD practice have been sponsored by many professional associations; for example, the Australian Association for Professional and Applied Ethics (AAPAE) comprises academics and professionals across a range of disciplines in a non-partisan and non-profit association, while Corporate Ethics is committed to helping business develop a strategic system that incorporates value and ethics.[22] The accounting industry is just one of many professions that has codes of ethics: the Code of Professional Conduct (Chartered Practising Accountants Australia – CPA Australia) and the Rules of Ethical Conduct (the Institute of Chartered Accountants in Australia – ICAA).[23] The ethical guidelines issued by the Real Estate Institute of Australia appears in the appendix to this chapter.

Ethical dilemmas

Although adherence to statements of ethics helps prevent ethical problems from occurring, OD practitioners can still encounter ethical dilemmas. Figure 3.3 is a process model that explains how ethical dilemmas can occur in OD. The antecedent conditions include an OD practitioner and a client system with different goals, values, needs, skills and abilities. During the entry and contracting phase, these differences may or may not be addressed and clarified. If the contracting process is incomplete, the subsequent intervention process or role episode is subject to role conflict and role ambiguity. Neither the client nor the OD practitioner is clear about his or her respective responsibilities. Each is pursuing different goals, and each party is using different skills and values to achieve those goals. The role conflict and ambiguity can lead to five types of ethical dilemmas: (1) misrepresentation, (2) misuse of data, (3) coercion, (4) value and goal conflict, and (5) technical ineptitude.

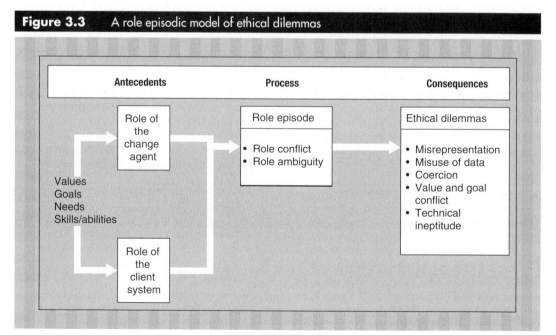

Figure 3.3   A role episodic model of ethical dilemmas

Source: L. White and M. Rhodeback, 'Ethical dilemmas in organization development: a cross-cultural analysis', Figure 1, *Journal of Business Ethics*, 11 (1992): 663–70. With kind permission from Kluwer Academic Publishers.

MISREPRESENTATION

This occurs when OD practitioners claim that an intervention will produce results that are unreasonable for the change program or the situation. The client can contribute to this problem by portraying inaccurate goals and needs. In either case, one or both parties is operating under false pretences and an ethical dilemma exists. For example, in an infamous case called 'The undercover change agent', an attempt was made to use laboratory training in an organisation whose top management did not understand it and was not ready for it. The OD consultant sold 'T-groups' as the intervention that would solve the problems that faced the organisation. After the chairman of the firm made a surprise visit to the site where the training was being held, the consultant was fired. The nature and style of the T-group was in direct contradiction to the chairman's concepts about leadership.[24] Misrepresentation is likely to occur in the entering and contracting phases of planned change when the initial consulting relationship is being established. To prevent misrepresentation, OD practitioners need to be very clear about the goals of the change effort and to explore openly with the client its expected effects, its relevance to the client system and the practitioner's competence in executing the intervention.

MISUSE OF DATA

This occurs when information gathered during the OD process is used punitively. Large amounts of information are invariably obtained during the entry and diagnostic phases of OD; although most OD practitioners value openness and trust, it is important that they be aware of how such data are going to be used. It is a human tendency to use data to enhance a power position. Openness is one thing, but leaking inappropriate information can be harmful to individuals and to the organisation as well. It is easy for a consultant, under the guise of obtaining information, to gather data about whether a particular manager is good or bad. When, how or if this information can be used is an ethical dilemma not easily resolved. To minimise misuse of data, practitioners should agree with organisation members up front about how data collected will be used. This agreement should be reviewed periodically in light of changing circumstances.

COERCION

This ethical dilemma occurs when organisation members are forced to participate in an OD intervention. People should have the freedom to choose whether or not to participate in a change program if they are to gain self-reliance to solve their own problems. In team building, for example, team members should have the option of deciding not to become involved in the intervention. Management should not unilaterally decide that team building is good for members. However, freedom to make a choice implies knowledge about OD. Many organisation members have little information about OD interventions, what they involve and the nature and consequences of becoming involved with them. This makes it imperative for OD practitioners to educate clients about interventions before choices are made as to whether or not to implement them.

Coercion can also pose ethical dilemmas for the helping relationship between OD practitioners and organisation members. Inherent in any helping relationship are possibilities for excessive manipulation and dependency, two facets of coercion. Kelman pointed out that behaviour change 'inevitably involves some degree of manipulation and control, and at least an implicit imposition of the change agent's values on the client or the person he [or she] is influencing'.[25] This places the practitioner on two horns of a dilemma: (1) any attempt to change is in itself a change and thereby a manipulation, no matter how slight; and (2) there exists no formula or method to structure a change situation so that such manipulation can be totally absent. To attack the first aspect of the dilemma, Kelman stressed freedom of choice, seeing any action that limits freedom of choice as being ethically ambiguous or worse. To address the second aspect, Kelman argued that the OD practitioner must remain keenly aware of her or his own value system and alert to the possibility that these values are being imposed upon a client.

In other words, an effective way to resolve this dilemma is to make the change effort as open as possible, with the free consent and knowledge of the individuals involved.

The second facet of coercion that can pose ethical dilemmas for the helping relationship involves dependency. Helping relationships invariably create dependency between those who need help and those who provide it.[26] A major goal in OD is to lessen the clients' dependency on consultants by helping them gain the knowledge and skills to address organisational problems and manage change themselves. In some cases, however, achieving independence from OD practitioners can result in the clients being either counterdependent or overdependent, especially in the early stages of the relationship. To resolve dependency issues, consultants can openly and explicitly discuss with the client how to handle the dependency problem, especially what the client and consultant expect of one another. Another approach is to focus on problem finding. Usually, the client is looking for a solution to a perceived problem. The consultant can redirect the energy to improved joint diagnosis so that both are working on problem identification and problem solving. This moves the energy of the client away from dependency. Finally, dependency can be reduced by changing the client's expectation – from being helped or controlled by the practitioner – to focusing on the need to manage the problem. This helps to reinforce the concept that the consultant is working for the client and offering assistance at the client's discretion.

Value and goal conflict

This ethical dilemma occurs when the purpose of the change effort is not clear or when the client and the practitioner disagree over how to achieve the goals. The important practical issue for OD consultants is whether it is justifiable to unilaterally withhold services from an organisation that does not agree with their values or methods. Lippitt suggested that the real question is the following: Assuming that some kind of change is going to occur anyway, doesn't the consultant have a responsibility to try to guide the change in the most constructive fashion possible?[27] The question may be of greater importance and relevance to an internal consultant or to a consultant who already has an ongoing relationship with the client.

Argyris takes an even stronger stand, maintaining that the responsibilities of professional OD practitioners to clients are comparable to those of lawyers or doctors, who, in principle, are not permitted to refuse their services. He suggests that the very least the consultant can do is provide 'first aid' to the organisation as long as the assistance does not compromise the consultant's values. Argyris suggests that if the Ku Klux Klan were to ask for assistance and the consultant could at least determine that the KKK was genuinely interested in assessing itself and willing to commit itself to all that a valid assessment would entail concerning both itself and other groups, the consultant should be willing to help. If the Klan's objectives later prove to be less than honestly stated, the consultant would be free to withdraw without being compromised.[28]

Technical ineptitude

This final ethical dilemma occurs when OD practitioners attempt to implement interventions for which they are not skilled or when the client attempts a change for which it is not ready. Critical to the success of any OD program is the selection of an appropriate intervention, which depends, in turn, on careful diagnosis of the organisation. Selection of an intervention is closely related to the practitioner's own values, skills and abilities. In solving organisational problems, many OD consultants tend to emphasise a favourite intervention or technique, such as team building, total quality management or self-managed teams. They let their own values and beliefs dictate the change method.[29] Technical ineptitude dilemmas can also occur when interventions do not align with the ability of the organisation to implement them. Again, careful diagnosis can reveal the extent to which the organisation is ready to make a change and possesses the skills and knowledge to implement it.

Application 3.5 gives a short professional biography of John Mulcahy from Suncorp-Metway who joined the company to reinvigorate the staff and improve the performance of the company.

CHANGE MERCHANT

Suncorp-Metway's chief executive, John Mulcahy, has been working on a turnaround program for Australia's sixth-biggest bank since he joined the company in 2003. He says that this year's record $821 million profit was 'planned for, anticipated and delivered'. In the past two financial years, Suncorp-Metway's operating revenue has increased from $4.6 billion to $5.3 billion.

…

Mulcahy's turnaround program was devised and approved by the board within three months of his arrival from Commonwealth Bank. His program was based on changing what he calls the company's under-performing culture. This involved rethinking and redesigning many of the 8400 roles in the company, reorganising management layers and introducing a scorecard that measures the performance of all staff. Many of the top 50 executives in the company felt the effect of the changes. Some were appointed to different positions, some promoted and some left the company. New recruits were added.

One of the hardest aspects of this change was identifying people who were not performing in their roles and were not demonstrating the potential to perform in other roles. 'There was an element of self-selection, people not liking the pace of change, but that will always be the case,' Mulcahy says. 'You lose some people in the process.'

Once Mulcahy and the management team had mapped out a plan, they needed the entire organisation to understand their individual roles in the turnaround. A program of staff surveys was introduced to ensure that employees understood how they fitted into the business plan. Mulcahy wants staff to understand what they are meant to be doing in their roles and to be accountable. The first question on the company's recent 12-question employee engagement survey reads: 'Do you know what is expected of you at work?' For Mulcahy, that is the basis of anyone's performance. 'For me it is a no-brainer,' he says. The scorecards he introduced have individual targets on them that relate to customers, fellow employees, shareholders and the community. Clear goals are set annually with each employee.

…

The real secret to the success of Suncorp-Metway, Mulcahy says, is learning to prioritise by finding what needs to be done and doing it. 'In a lot of organisations there is that idea, "Let's invest a huge amount of money and we'll have a wonderful time in three years". But the reality is, shareholders won't wait that long. Every listed organisation faces that issue and that is why prioritisation is so important.'

Mulcahy came into his role when the stock market was flatter, so an improvement in market conditions was always going to make him look good. But he has not just sat back and enjoyed the ride. 'It's not about keeping staff on their toes, it is about us being in total agreement of where we are going to take the organisation,' he says.

Source: Emily Ross, 'Leadership: Change Merchant', *Business Review Weekly*, 6/10/05.

Critical Thinking Questions: What characteristics of change leadership does Mulcahy exhibit? Would this style work in all situations? Why/why not?

SUMMARY

This chapter examined the role of the OD practitioner. This term applies to three kinds of people: individuals specialising in OD as a profession, people from related fields who have gained some competence in OD and managers who have the OD skills necessary to change and develop their organisations or departments. Comprehensive lists exist of core and advanced skills and knowledge that an effective OD specialist should possess, but a smaller set of basic skills and knowledge is applicable for all practitioners, regardless of whether they are OD professionals, related specialists or managers. These include four kinds of background: intrapersonal skills, interpersonal skills, general consultation skills and knowledge of OD theory.

The professional OD role can apply to internal consultants who belong to the organisation undergoing change, to external consultants who are members of universities and consulting firms or are self-employed, and to members of internal–external consulting teams. The OD role may be aptly described in terms of marginality. People with a tolerance for marginal roles seem especially adapted for OD practice because they are able to maintain neutrality and objectivity, and develop integrative solutions that reconcile viewpoints between opposing organisational departments. Whereas, in the past, the OD role has been described as falling at the client end of the continuum from client-centred to consultant-centred functioning, the development of new and varied interventions has shifted the role of the OD professional to cover the entire range of this continuum.

Although OD is still an emerging profession, most OD professionals have specific training in OD, ranging from short courses and workshops to graduate and doctoral education. No single career path exists, but internal consulting is often a stepping-stone to becoming an external consultant. Because of the hectic pace of OD practice, OD specialists should be prepared to cope with high levels of stress and the possibility of career burnout.

Values have played a key role in OD, and traditional values promoting trust, collaboration and openness have recently been supplemented with concerns for improving organisational effectiveness and productivity. OD specialists may face value dilemmas in trying to jointly optimise human benefits and organisation performance. They may also encounter value conflicts when dealing with powerful external stakeholders, such as the government, stockholders and customers. Dealing with these outside groups may take political skills, as well as the more traditional social skills.

Ethical issues in OD involve how practitioners perform their helping role with clients. OD has always shown a concern for the ethical conduct of practitioners, and several ethical codes for OD practice have been developed by the various professional associations in OD. Ethical dilemmas in OD tend to arise around the following issues: misrepresentation, misuse of data, coercion, value and goal conflict, and technical ineptitude.

ACTIVITIES

Review questions

① Distinguish between an internal and an external change agent. Give examples, or explain particular circumstances, where internal and external change agents have exercised successful change programs.

② What are the core skills of an OD practitioner? How do you think these skills would differ from those of a practitioner who is known to favour organisation transformation (OT)?

③ What are the advantages and disadvantages of an internal change agent? Compare these with the advantages and disadvantages of an external change agent. Give examples that clearly delineate between the two.

④ What is meant by the 'professional ethics' of a change agent? Do you know of any instances where there may be conflict? Explain the circumstances.

Discussion and essay questions

① Discuss the role of the OD practitioner in depth. It would be advisable to interview several change agents to get their varied, or differing, perspectives.

② Which would be more beneficial for an organisation – an external or an internal change agent? What are the factors that need to be considered before such a choice is made? What would be the ideal scenario? Explain your answer.

③ What type of ethical considerations would confront an OD practitioner and how may they be addressed? Investigate instances where there have been contentious situations and the resolution you would recommend.

④ Debate: 'Burnout is prevalent among change agents'.

Notes

1 A. Church and W. Burke, 'Practitioner attitudes about the field of organization development', in *Organization Change and Development*, eds W. Pasmore and R. Woodman (Greenwich, CT: JAI Press, 1995).

2 Centre for Corporate Change in the Australian Graduate School of Management, The University of NSW and The University of Sydney, http://www.ccc.agsm.edu.au.

3 Centre for Corporate Change, Working Papers, Nos 005 and 028.

4 B. Glickman, 'Qualities of change agents' (unpublished manuscript, May 1974); R. Havelock, *The Change Agent's Guide to Innovation in Education* (Englewood Cliffs, NJ: Educational Technology, 1973): 5; R. Lippitt, 'Dimensions of the consultant's job', in *The Planning of Change*, eds W. Bennis, K. Benne and R. Chin (New York: Holt, Rinehart and Winston, 1961): 156–61; C. Rogers, *On Becoming a Person* (Boston: Houghton Mifflin, 1971); N. Paris, 'Some thoughts on the qualifications for a consultant' (unpublished manuscript, 1973); 'OD experts reflect on the major skills needed by consultants: with comments from Edgar Schein', *Academy of Management OD Newsletter* (Spring 1979): 1–4.

5 D. Harvey and D. Brown, *An Experiential Approach to Organization Development*, 5th edn (Englewood Cliffs, NJ: Prentice Hall, 1996): 94–6.

6 J. Esper, 'Core competencies in organization development' (independent study conducted as partial fulfilment of the MBA degree, Graduate School of Business Administration, University of Southern California, June 1987); E. Neilsen, *Becoming an OD Practitioner* (Englewood Cliffs, NJ: Prentice-Hall, 1984); S. Eisen, H. Steele and J. Cherbeneau, 'Developing OD competence for the future', in *Practicing Organization Development*, eds W. Rothwell, R. Sullivan and G. McLean (San Diego: Pfeiffer, 1995).

7 B. Tannenbaum, 'Letter to the editor', Consulting Practice Communique, *Academy of Management Managerial Consultation Division*, 21:3 (1993): 16–17; B. Tannenbaum, 'Self-awareness: an essential element underlying consultant effectiveness', *Journal of Organizational Change Management*, 8:3 (1995): 85–6.

8 A. Church and W. Burke, 'Practitioner attitudes about the field of organization development', in *Organization Change and Development*, eds W. Pasmore and R. Woodman (Greenwich, CT: JAI Press, 1995).

9 M. Lacey, 'Internal consulting: perspectives on the process of planned change', *Journal of Organizational Change Management*, 8:3 (1995): 75–84.

10 E. Kirkhart and T. Isgar, 'Quality of work life for consultants: the internal–external relationship', *Consultation*, 5 (Spring 1986): 5–23; J. Thacker and N. Kulick, 'The use of consultants in joint union/management quality of work life efforts', *Consultation*, 5 (Summer 1986): 116–26.

11 R. Ziller, *The Social Self* (Elmsford, NY: Pergamon, 1973).

12 R. Ziller, B. Stark and H. Pruden, 'Marginality and integrative management positions', *Academy of Management Journal*, 12 (December 1969): 487–95; H. Pruden and B. Stark, 'Marginality associated with interorganizational linking process, productivity and satisfaction', *Academy of Management Journal*, 14 (March 1971): 145–8; W. Liddell, 'Marginality and integrative decisions', *Academy of Management Journal*, 16 (March 1973): 154–6; P. Brown and C. Cotton, 'Marginality, a force for the OD practitioner', *Training and Development Journal*, 29 (April 1975): 14–18; H. Aldrich and D. Gerker, 'Boundary spanning roles and organizational structure', *Academy of Management Review*, 2 (April 1977): 217–30; C. Cotton, 'Marginality – a neglected dimension in the design of work', *Academy of Management Review*, 2 (January 1977): 133–8; N. Margulies, 'Perspectives on the marginality of the consultant's role', in *The Cutting Edge*, ed. W. Burke (La Jolla, CA: University Associates, 1978): 60–79.

13 P. Brown, C. Cotton and R. Golembiewski, 'Marginality and the OD practitioner', *Journal of Applied Behavioural Science*, 13 (1977): 493–506.

14 D. Kegan, 'Organization development as OD network members see it', *Group and Organization Studies*, 7 (March 1982): 5–11.

15 J. Lewis III, 'Growth of internal change agents in organizations', (PhD Dissertation, Case Western Reserve University, 1970).

16 G. Edelwich and A. Brodsky, *Burn-Out Stages of Disillusionment in the Helping Professions* (New York: Human Science, 1980); M. Weisbord, 'The wizard of OD: or, what have magic slippers to do with burnout, evaluation, resistance, planned change, and action research?', *The OD Practitioner*, 10 (Summer 1978): 1–14; M. Mitchell, 'Consultant burnout', in *The 1977 Annual Handbook for Group Facilitators*, eds J. Jones and W. Pfeiffer (La Jolla, CA: University Associates, 1977): 145–56.

17 T. Isgar, 'Quality of work life of consultants', *Academy of Management OD Newsletter* (Winter 1983): 2–4.

18 A. Church and W. Burke, 'Practitioner attitudes about the field of organization development', in *Organization Change and Development*, eds W. Pasmore and R. Woodman (Greenwich, CT: JAI Press, 1995).

19 T. Cummings, 'Designing effective work groups', in *Handbook of Organisational Design*, eds P. Nystrom and W. Starbuck (Oxford: Oxford University Press, 1981): 250–71.

20 J. Schermerhorn, 'Interorganizational development', *Journal of Management*, 5 (1979): 21–38; T. Cummings, 'Interorganisation theory and organisation development', in *Systems Theory for Organisation Development*, ed. T. Cummings (Chichester: John Wiley and Sons, 1980): 323–38.

21 http://www.bf.rmit.edu.au/Aben.

22 http://www.arts.unsw.edu.au/aapae (accessed 1 November 2006); http://corporate-ethos.com.au (accessed 1 November 2006).

23 D. Grace and S. Cohen, *Business Ethics*, Australian Problems and Cases, 2nd edn (Melbourne: Oxford University Press, 1998): 124–6.

24 W. Bennis, *Organization Development: Its Nature, Origins, and Prospects* (Reading, MA: Addison-Wesley, 1969).

25 H. Kelman, 'Manipulation of human behaviour: an ethical dilemma for the social scientist', in *The Planning of Change*, 2nd edn, eds W. Bennis, K. Bennie and R. Chin (New York: Holt, Rinehart and Winston, 1969): 584.

26 R. Beckhard, 'The dependency dilemma', *Consultants' Communique*, 6 (July–August–September 1978): 1–3.

27 G. Lippitt, *Organization Renewal* (Englewood Cliffs, NJ: Prentice-Hall, 1969).

28 C. Argyris, 'Explorations in consulting-client relationships', *Human Organizations*, 20 (Fall 1961): 121–33.

29 J. Slocum, Jr, 'Does cognitive style affect diagnosis and intervention strategies?', *Group and Organization Studies*, 3 (June 1978): 199–210.

Online reading

INFOTRAC® COLLEGE EDITION
For additional readings and reviews on change agents, explore **InfoTrac® College Edition**, your online library. Go to **www.infotrac-college.com** and search for any of the InfoTrac key terms listed below:
- OD practitioner
- Professional values
- Professional ethics
- Code of conduct

APPENDIX

REAL ESTATE INSTITUTE OF AUSTRALIA:

CODE OF CONDUCT FOR MEMBERS[1]

Section 1 – Code Objectives

1.1 This is the model national code of conduct of the Real Estate Institute of Australia ('REIA') as recommended for adoption and implementation by its affiliated bodies and is a public statement of the principles, values and behaviour expected of members of those affiliated bodies.

1.2 The objective of this code of conduct is to promote and encourage a high standard of ethical practice by members and their employees in their dealings with other members, other agents, their employees and members of the public.

1.3 By following this code a member will not engage in conduct that is:

(a) contrary to good estate agency practice; or

(b) detrimental to the reputation or interests of the profession, the Institute or its members.

Section 2 – Professional Standards

2.1 In this Code –
'Agent' means a licensed real estate agent, strata managing agent, stock and station agent, business agent or valuer;
'Client' means a person who retains a member to represent their interests in a real estate transaction;
'Customer' means a person who transacts business with a member but does not retain their services;
'Employee' means a sales person, sales representative, agent's representative, property manager, body corporate manager or any other person in the employ of, or acting on behalf of, a member;
'Fee' includes commission, charges, or other remuneration whether monetary or otherwise;
'Institute' means any affiliated body;
'Member' means any member of an affiliated body, and includes any employee of a member; and
'Estate agents legislation' means legislation in the States and Territories regulating real estate agents, strata managing agents, stock and station agents, business agents and valuers.

DUTIES AND OBLIGATIONS

2.2 A member must have a working knowledge of agency law which sets out the duties and obligations of an agent towards the client.

Knowledge of the Law

2.3   A member must have a working knowledge of:

(a) estate agents legislation and any regulations made under such legislation; and

(b) other statutes and any rules or regulations in force such as fair trading and trade practices legislation to the extent that they are relevant to the conduct of the real estate profession.

Compliance with Legislation

2.4   A member must not, in the conduct of estate agency, contravene or fail to comply with any statute, rule or regulation in force to the extent that it is relevant to the conduct of the real estate profession.

Good Real Estate Agency Practice

2.5   (a) A member must exercise skill, care, and diligence in the conduct of the profession.

(b) A member must complete all work on behalf of the client as soon as is reasonably possible.

2.5.1   A member must act in the best interests of the client except where it would be unreasonable or improper to do so.

2.5.2   A member must not induce or attempt to induce a breach of or an interference with a contract or arrangement of sale, letting, or agency.

2.5.3   A member must not solicit or accept an agency if the member is aware that any other agency is in force which may obligate the client to pay two fees or expose the client to a claim for damages for breach of contract in the event of a sale taking place, unless the member gives a prior written statement to the client that the client may be liable for two fees or for a claim for damages for breach of contract if the client signs a further agency agreement.

2.5.4   A member may act in conjunction with another member if so authorised by a client.

Authorities and Instructions

2.6   A member must not act as agent or represent himself or herself as acting as agent on behalf of a person without authority.

2.6.1   A member must act in accordance with the instructions of a client except where to do so would be unlawful or contrary to good agency practice.

2.6.2   An agent must not:

(a) advertise or offer for sale or lease any real estate or business at a price or on terms different from that authorised by the client; or

(b) advertise or offer to purchase or lease on behalf of a client any real estate or business on terms different from that authorised by the client.

2.6.3   The price at which a member offers a property shall be in accordance with the instructions of the client. However, if the member considers that the price asked by a client is more or less than fair market value, the member shall advise the client accordingly.

Fair Conduct

2.7   A member must act fairly and honestly and to the best of his or her knowledge and ability with all parties in a transaction.

2.7.1   A member must not mislead or deceive any parties in negotiations or a transaction.

2.7.2   A member must not engage in harsh or unconscionable conduct.

SUPERVISION OF EMPLOYEES

2.8 A member or the person in effective or nominal control of the agency must properly supervise the agency business and take reasonable steps to ensure that employees of the agency comply with the provisions of estate agents' legislation, this code of conduct and other relevant statutes, rules and regulations where applicable to them.

2.8.1 If an employee fails to comply with the provisions of estate agents' legislation, this code of conduct or other relevant statutes, rules or regulations where applicable then, for the purposes of section 2.9.1 of this Code, the member or the person in effective or nominal control of the agency business shall have the onus of proving that he or she complied with the requirements of that section.

VERIFYING INFORMATION

2.9 Prior to the execution by the client of any contract relating to the sale or lease of any real estate or business, the member must make all reasonable efforts to ascertain or verify the facts which are material to that transaction which a prudent member would have ascertained in order that the member may avoid error, exaggeration or misrepresentation.

2.9.1 It is the duty of a member to act in a professional manner and to ascertain all available pertinent facts concerning the property for which the member accepts the agency so that in providing the service the member may avoid error, exaggeration or misrepresentation.

2.9.2 When a member receives instructions to offer real estate for sale the member shall take all reasonable steps to verify the ownership of the property and the property description.

ADVICE AS TO MARKET PRICE

2.10 A member engaged to sell, purchase or lease any real estate or business must advise the client as to what the member considers to be the current market price of that real estate or business.

2.10.1 When asked for advice concerning real estate, a member must never offer an unconsidered opinion. A member's counsel constitutes a professional service which a member should not render prior to conducting a full and proper investigation of all the relevant facts and circumstances. A member may, by prior arrangement with a client, make an appropriate professional charge for such advice.

BEST INTERESTS OF THE CLIENT

2.11 A member must not accept an engagement to act, or continue to act, where to do so would place the member's interest in conflict with that of the client.

CONFIDENTIAL INFORMATION

2.12 A member must not, at any time, use or disclose any confidential information obtained while acting on behalf of a client or dealing with a customer, except for information that an agent is required by law to disclose.

2.12.1 A member must communicate all offers to the client as soon as practicable.

COMMISSIONS AND EXPENSES

2.13 A member must not accept or demand any commission from any person, other than the client, in respect of any service performed or to be performed by the member, being a service in respect of which the member receives commission or is entitled to receive commission from the client.

2.13.1 A member must not demand, retain or receive a discount or rebate which relates to a service by a stocktaker or tradesperson, or to advertising, in connection with a transaction or a service provided by the member unless the member has obtained the written consent of the client to the seeking or retaining of the discount or rebate by the member.

2.13.2 A member must not demand, retain or receive a commission for a service or transaction which is:

(a) greater than any prescribed maximum commission; or

(b) greater than the amount agreed with the client.

2.13.3 If a member is entitled to seek reimbursement from a client of any expense which the member has incurred, the member shall promptly supply to the client all relevant information and material which the client may reasonably require as to the amount of the expense, and to be satisfied that the expense was properly incurred by the member.

2.13.4 A member shall not seek or retain reimbursement of an expense which the member has incurred in respect of advertising, signboards, printed material, and promotions unless:

(a) the client has agreed in writing to pay the expense; and

(b) the agreement specifies a maximum amount which the member may seek or retain by way of reimbursement.

TENANCY

2.14 A member must immediately notify the owner when the member becomes aware of a significant breach or repeated breaches of the tenancy agreement.

2.14.1 A member managing a rental property must fully complete an inventory and inspection reports and provide such reports to the owner in accordance with the terms of the property management agreement.

NOTIFYING MANAGING AGENTS

2.15 If a member accepts an engagement to sell any real estate and is or becomes aware that another member is the managing agent of that real estate, the member must immediately give written notice of the appointment to the managing agent, unless otherwise instructed, in writing, by the client.

FRAUD AND MISREPRESENTATION

2.16 It is the duty of every member to protect the public against fraud, misrepresentation or unethical practices in connection with real estate transactions.

MEMBER'S RESPONSIBILITY

2.17 No instructions or inducements from any client or customer will relieve a member from the responsibility of strictly observing this code of conduct.

DISPUTES

2.18 A member must make every effort to minimise disputes with other members, agents, and members of the public and to resolve complaints or disputes that do arise as expeditiously and as fairly as possible. It shall be a breach of this Code for a member, in dispute with a fellow member in relation to this Code, to resort to action at law before submitting the matter to their Institute for adjudication in the first instance.

MEMBER'S EMPLOYEE REPRESENTATIONS

2.19 An employee of a member must not intentionally represent himself or herself as the holder of a real estate agent's licence; or the person in effective control of the estate agency business or a corporation that is the holder of a real estate agent's license.

Section 3 – Complaint Handling and Appeals

...

Section 4 – Code Monitoring

...

Section 5 – Code Review

...

NOTE

1 http://www.reiact.com.au/_upload/pages/2003/4/43/page_content/432.pdf, accessed 10/10/06.

P3

THE PROCESS OF ORGANiSATiON DEVELOPMENT

④ Entering, contracting and diagnosing the organisation

⑤ Information gathering, processing and feedback

⑥ Design, implementation and evaluation of interventions

4

ENTERiNG, CONTRACTiNG AND DiAGNOSiNG THE ORGANiSATiON

The planned change process described in Chapter 2 generally starts when one or more key managers or administrators sense that their organisation, department or group could be improved or has problems that could be alleviated through organisation development. The organisation might be successful, yet have room for improvement. It might be facing impending environmental conditions that necessitate a change in how it operates. The organisation could be experiencing particular problems, such as poor product quality, high rates of absenteeism or dysfunctional conflicts between departments. Conversely, the problems might appear more diffuse and consist simply of feelings that the organisation should be 'more innovative', 'more competitive' or 'more effective'.

ENTERING AND CONTRACTING THE ORGANISATION

Entering and contracting are the initial steps in the OD process. They involve defining in a preliminary manner the organisation's problems or opportunities for development and establishing a collaborative relationship between the OD practitioner and members of the client system about how to work on those issues. Entering and contracting set the initial parameters for carrying out the subsequent phases of OD: diagnosing the organisation, planning and implementing changes, and evaluating and institutionalising them. They help to define what issues will be addressed by those activities, who will carry them out and how they will be accomplished.

Entering and contracting can vary in complexity and formality according to the situation. In those cases where the manager of a work group or department serves as his or her own OD practitioner, entering and contracting typically involve the manager and group members meeting to discuss what issues they should work on and how they will jointly accomplish this. Here, entering and contracting are relatively simple and informal. They involve all relevant members directly in the process without a great deal of formal procedures. In situations where managers and administrators are considering the use of professional OD practitioners, either from inside or outside the organisation, entering and contracting tend to be more complex and formal.[1] Organisation development practitioners may need to collect preliminary information to help define the issues to be worked on. They may need to meet with representatives of the client organisation, rather than with the total membership: they may need to formalise their respective roles as well as how the OD process will unfold.

This section discusses the activities that are involved in entering into, and contracting for, an OD process. The main focus of attention will be the complex processes that involve OD professionals and client organisations. However, similar entering and contracting issues need to be addressed in even the simplest OD efforts, where managers serve as OD practitioners for their own work units. Unless there is clarity and agreement about what issues need to be worked on, who will address them and how this will be accomplished, subsequent stages of the OD process are likely to be confusing and ineffective.

Entering into an OD relationship

An OD process generally starts when a member of an organisation or unit contacts an OD practitioner about potential help in addressing an organisational issue.[2] The organisation member may be a manager, staff specialist or some other key participant, and the practitioner may be an OD professional from inside or outside the organisation. Determining whether the two parties should enter into an OD relationship typically involves clarifying the nature of the organisation's problem, the relevant client system for that issue and the appropriateness of the particular OD practitioner.[3] In helping to assess these issues, the OD practitioner may need to collect preliminary data about the organisation. Similarly, the organisation may need to gather information about the practitioner's competence and experience.[4] This knowledge will help both parties determine whether they should proceed to develop a contract for working together.

This section describes the following activities that are involved in entering an OD relationship: (1) clarifying the organisational issue, (2) determining the relevant client, and (3) selecting an appropriate OD practitioner.

CLARIFYING THE ORGANISATIONAL ISSUE

When seeking help from OD practitioners, organisations typically start with a presenting problem – the issue that has caused them to consider an OD process. It may be specific (decrease in market share, increase in absenteeism) or general ('we're growing too fast', 'we need to prepare for rapid changes'). The presenting problem often has an implied or stated solution. For example, managers may believe that, because members of their teams are in conflict, team building is the obvious answer. They may even state the presenting problem in the form of a solution: 'We need some team building.'

In many cases, however, the presenting problem is only a symptom of an underlying problem. For example, conflict among members of a team may result from several deeper causes, including ineffective reward systems, personality differences, inappropriate structure and poor leadership. The issue facing the organisation or department must be clarified early in the OD process so that subsequent diagnostic and intervention activities are focused on the right issue.[5]

Gaining a clearer perspective on the organisational issue may require the collection of preliminary data.[6] OD practitioners often examine company records and interview a few key members to gain an introductory understanding of the organisation, its context and the nature of the presenting problem. These data are gathered in a relatively short period of time, typically from a few hours to one or two days. They are intended to provide rudimentary knowledge of the organisational issue that will enable the two parties to make informed choices about proceeding with the contracting process.

The diagnostic phase of OD involves a far more extensive assessment of the organisational issue than occurs during the entering and contracting stage. The diagnosis might also discover other issues that need to be addressed, or it might lead to redefining the initial issue that was identified during the entering and contracting stage. This is a prime example of the emergent nature of the OD process, where things may change as new information is gathered and new events occur.

DETERMINING THE RELEVANT CLIENT

A second activity involved in entering an OD relationship is the definition of who is the relevant client for addressing the organisational issue.[7] Generally, the relevant client includes those organisation members who can directly impact on the change issue, whether it be solving a particular problem or improving an already successful organisation or department. Unless these members are identified and included in the entering and contracting process, they may withhold their support for, and commitment to, the OD process. In trying to improve the productivity of a unionised manufacturing plant, for example, the relevant client may need to include union officials as well as managers and staff personnel. It is not unusual for an OD project to fail because the relevant client was inappropriately defined.

Determining the relevant client can vary in complexity according to the situation. In those cases where the organisational issue can be addressed in a particular organisation unit, client definition is relatively straightforward. Members of that unit constitute the relevant client. They or their representatives would need to be included in the entering and contracting process. For example, if a manager asked for help in improving the decision-making process of his or her team, the manager and team members would be the relevant clients. Unless they are actively involved in choosing an OD practitioner and defining the subsequent change process, there is little likelihood that OD will improve team decision making.

Determining the relevant client is more complex when the organisational issue cannot readily be addressed in a single organisation unit. Here, it may be necessary to expand the definition of the client to include members from multiple units, from different hierarchical levels and even from outside the organisation. For example, the manager of a production department may seek help in resolving conflicts between his or her unit and other departments in the organisation. The relevant client would transcend the boundaries of the production department because it alone cannot resolve the organisational issue. The client might include members from all departments involved in the conflict as well as the executive to whom all the departments report. If this interdepartmental conflict also involved key suppliers and customers from outside the firm, the relevant client might also include members of those groups.

In these complex situations, OD practitioners may need to gather additional information about the organisation in order to determine the relevant client. This can be accomplished as part of the preliminary data collection that typically occurs when clarifying the organisational issue. When examining company records or interviewing personnel, practitioners can seek to identify the key members and organisational units that need to be involved in addressing the organisational issue. For example, they can ask organisation members such questions as: 'Who can directly impact the organisational issue?' 'Who has a vested interest in it?' 'Who has the power to approve or reject the OD effort?' Answers to these questions can help determine who is the relevant client for the entering and contracting stage. The relevant client may change, however, during the later stages of the OD process as new data are gathered and changes occur. If so, participants may have to return to this initial stage of the OD effort and modify it.

SELECTING AN OD PRACTITIONER

The last activity involved in entering an OD relationship is selecting an OD practitioner who has the expertise and experience to work with members on the organisational issue. Unfortunately, little systematic advice is available on how to choose a competent OD professional, whether from inside or outside the organisation. Perhaps the best criteria for selecting, evaluating and developing OD practitioners are those suggested by the late Gordon Lippitt, a pioneering practitioner in the field.[8] Lippitt listed areas that managers should consider before selecting a practitioner, including the ability of the consultant to form sound interpersonal relationships, the degree of focus on the problem, the skills of the practitioner relative to the problem, the extent that the consultant clearly informs the client as to his or her role and contribution, and whether the practitioner belongs to a professional association. References from other clients are highly important. A client may not like the consultant's work, but it is critical to know the reasons for both pleasure and displeasure. One important consideration is whether the consultant approaches the organisation with openness and an insistence on diagnosis or whether the practitioner appears to have a fixed program that is applicable to almost any organisation.

Certainly, OD consulting is as much a person specialisation as it is a task specialisation. The OD professional must have not only a repertoire of technical skills but also the personality and interpersonal competence to be able to use himself or herself as an instrument of change. Regardless of technical training, the consultant must be able to maintain a boundary position, co-ordinating various units and departments and mixing disciplines, theories, technology and research findings in an organic rather than a mechanical way. The practitioner is potentially the most important OD technology available.

Thus, in the selection of an OD practitioner, perhaps the most important issue is the fundamental question: 'How effective has the person been in the past, with what kinds of organisations, using what kinds of techniques?' In other words, references must be checked. Interpersonal relationships are tremendously important, but even con artists have excellent interpersonal relationships and skills.

The burden of choosing an effective OD practitioner should not, however, rest entirely with the client organisation.[9] Organisation development practitioners also bear a heavy responsibility for seeking an appropriate match between their skills and knowledge and what the organisation or department needs. Few managers are sophisticated enough to detect or understand subtle differences in expertise among OD professionals. They often do not understand the difference between consultants who specialise in different types of interventions. Thus, practitioners should help to educate potential clients. Consultants should be explicit about their strengths and weaknesses and about their range of competence. If OD professionals realise that a good match does not exist, they should inform managers and help them find more suitable help. Application 4.1 identifies the difficulties that exist in attempting to find the 'right' person for the position.

APPLiCATiON 4.1

MAN AMID CONTROVERSY

When the Melbourne business identity David Edwards landed the job of executive director of the Victorian branch of the Australian Retailers Association (ARA) last month, the trade press crowed: ARA SNAPS UP TOP GUN.

But the appointment has caused controversy, angering some in the business community who claim that he has a poor record of running prestigious organisations and that, although making some important contributions, he had left his last three positions under a cloud.

During the past six years, Edwards, 57, has run the cream of the not-for-profit sector: the Victorian Employers Chamber of Commerce and Industry (VECCI), CPA Australia and the Committee for the Economic Development of Australia (CEDA). He claims to have been successful at these organisations. 'I am a change agent,' he says.

Some people resist change, he says of his critics, and so they run agendas against him. 'I generally work very closely with boards and have had very supportive boards. Management teams that I have been involved in developed very substantially through the period I was there.'

He denies being forced to resign from the three organisations – he says he chose to resign. But some board members and staff at the organisations tell a different story.

When Edwards left VECCI in 1999, after 10 years as chief executive, he left behind an organisation with poor morale, riven with conflict and facing an uncertain financial future, according to some former VECCI executives and staff members. VECCI staff claim that members were neglected under Edward's reign – membership declined from 7700 in 1995 to 7500 in 1997 and net assets fell. A former deputy chairman of VECCI, Peter O'Brien, told *BRW*: 'He [Edwards] held us back for quite a while, although VECCI is stronger than ever now.'

Staff and senior managers also claim Edwards was quickly 'captured' by ambitious and manipulative people, who he then favoured while alienating others.

In 1998, a staff survey was critical of VECCI and Edwards and was the trigger for the board to act. After a long and stormy board meeting, O'Brien says a unanimous decision was reached to declare a vacancy for the chief executive's position. Edwards then resigned and confidentiality agreements were signed. 'He is like a lot of people,' O'Brien says. 'They forget the organisations exist for members and not to pay the CEO.'

By 1999, Edwards had become the executive director of not-for-profit organisation CPA Australia. As one recruiter says: 'The positions are greatly sought-after, as they usually pay between $250 000

▷▷

and $300 000 a year, plus bonuses. And Edwards had the 'wow' factor: an Order of Australia and great references.'

Little more than a year after taking the position, he was gone. Patrick Ponting, who was president of the CPAs in 1999–2000, when Edwards was appointed, says Edwards did a very good job helping CPA Australia build its image and influence, but then the focus moved to governance and administration. 'Perhaps he was not the right man for that job,' he says. A former CPA board member told *BRW*: 'David didn't respond to board requests or directions. He treated the board with disdain. When he left, administration and support were in disarray.'

In 2000, at a long board meeting that stretched into the evening, a vote of no confidence in Edwards was passed. Again, confidentiality agreements were signed and a press release was issued saying Edwards had resigned to pursue his own interests.

In 2002, Edwards became chief executive of the national, not-for-profit economic research organisation CEDA. Its chairman, Ivan Deveson, says Edwards introduced some good reforms, and improved CEDA's financial position. But familiar complaints soon surfaced. A resignation letter from one senior staff member, obtained by *BRW* and dated 15 December 2005, complained that at a time when she should have been celebrating CEDA's success, she and other staff were 'having trouble coping with the culture that was developing', so much so it was affecting her health. She complained that her position was being eroded by another staff member who had Edward's ear, and that behaviour that has occurred may leave CEDA open to litigation.

A source close to the CEDA board says that after certain matters came to the board's attention, there was a performance review. 'It was decided not to renew Edward's contract.'

Deveson refuses to discuss whether Edwards was pushed, citing confidentiality agreements. 'It was time for change. We are looking for different values and a different focus. We felt there was a need for a change of leadership.'

Edwards requested that *BRW* call his referees and others who will speak on his behalf, including Australian Competition & Consumer Commission chairman Graeme Samuel. But Samuel told *BRW* that he did not want to comment, as his dealings with Edwards were 'too far back'.

Edwards says he is looking forward to his new role at ARA. 'The ARA is an organisation that wants to grow and refocus.'

O'Brien, who is now the president of the Australian Chamber of Commerce and Industry, has some advice. 'Hopefully the [ARA] board will reflect on his record and counsel him accordingly,' he says.

Source: Amanda Gome, 'Man amid controversy', *Business Review Weekly*, 9–15 Feb. 2006.

Critical Thinking Questions: What are the considerations that should be made when appointing a 'change' leader in an organisation? Is it possible to have a defined set of characteristics that would be acceptable to all stakeholders in an organisation?

Developing a contract

The activities of entering an OD relationship – clarifying the organisational issue, determining who is the relevant client, and deciding whether the practitioner is appropriate for helping the organisation – are a necessary prelude to developing an OD contract. They define the major focus for contracting, including the relevant parties. Contracting is a natural extension of the entering process and clarifies how the OD process will proceed. It typically establishes the expectations of the parties, the time and resources that will be expended, and the ground rules under which the parties will operate.

The goal of contracting is to make a good decision about how to carry out the OD process.[10] It can be relatively informal and involve only a verbal agreement between the client and OD practitioner. A team leader with OD skills, for example, may voice his or her concerns to members about how the team is functioning. After some discussion, they might agree to devote one hour of future meeting time to diagnosing the team with the help of the leader. Here, entering and contracting are done together in an informal manner. In other cases, contracting can be more protracted and result in a formal document. This typically occurs when organisations employ outside OD practitioners. Government agencies, for example, generally have procurement regulations that apply to contracting with outside consultants.[11]

Regardless of the level of formality, all OD processes require some form of explicit contracting that results in either a verbal or written agreement. Such contracting clarifies the client's and the practitioner's expectations about how the OD process will take place. Unless there is mutual understanding and agreement about the OD process, there is considerable risk that someone's expectations will be unfilled.[12] This can lead to reduced commitment and support, to misplaced action or to premature termination of the process.

The contracting step in OD generally addresses three key areas:[13] (1) what each party expects to gain from the OD process; (2) the time and resources that will be devoted to OD; and (3) the ground rules for working together.

MUTUAL EXPECTATIONS

This part of the contracting process focuses on the expectations of the client and the OD practitioner. The client states the services and outcomes to be provided by the OD practitioner and describes what the organisation expects from the OD process and the consultant. Clients can usually describe the desired outcomes of the OD process, such as decreased turnover or higher job satisfaction. Encouraging them to state their wants in the form of outcomes, working relationships and personal accomplishments can facilitate the development of a good contract.[14]

The OD practitioner should also state what he or she expects to gain from the OD process. This can include the opportunity to try new OD interventions, report the results to other potential clients and receive appropriate compensation or recognition.

TIME AND RESOURCES

To accomplish change, the organisation and the OD practitioner must commit time and resources to the effort. Each must be clear about how much energy and resources will be dedicated to the change process. Failure to make explicit the necessary requirements of a change process can quickly ruin an OD effort. For example, a client may clearly state that the assignment involves diagnosing the causes of poor productivity in a work group. However, the client may expect the practitioner to complete the assignment without talking to the workers. Typically, clients want to know how much time will be necessary to complete the assignment, who needs to be involved, how much it will cost and so on.

Block has suggested that resources can be divided into two parts.[15] Essential requirements are things that are absolutely necessary if the change process is to be successful. From the practitioner's perspective, they can include access to key people or information, enough time to do the job right and commitment from certain people. The organisation's essential requirements might include a speedy diagnosis or assurances that the project will be conducted at the lowest price. Being clear about the constraints on carrying out the assignment will facilitate the contracting process and improve the chances for success. Desirable requirements are the things that would be nice to have but are not absolutely necessary. They may include access to special resources and written (as opposed to verbal) reports.

GROUND RULES

The final part of the contracting process involves specifying how the client and the OD practitioner will work together. This includes such issues as confidentiality, if and how the OD practitioner will become involved in personal or interpersonal issues, how to terminate the relationship and whether the practitioner is supposed to make expert recommendations or help the manager to make decisions. For internal consultants, organisational politics make it especially important to clarify issues of how to handle sensitive information and how to deliver 'bad news'.[16] These process issues are as important as the substantive changes to take place. Failure to address these concerns can mean that the client or the OD practitioner has inappropriate assumptions about how the process will unfold.

DIAGNOSING ORGANISATIONS

Diagnosing organisations is the second major phase in the model of planned change described in Chapter 2 (Figure 2.2). It follows the entering and contracting stage (discussed earlier) and precedes the planning and implementation phase. When it is done well, diagnosis clearly points the organisation and the OD practitioner towards a set of appropriate intervention activities that will improve organisation effectiveness.

Diagnosis is the process of assessing the functioning of the organisation, department, group or job to discover the sources of problems and areas for improvement. It involves collecting pertinent information about current operations, analysing those data and drawing conclusions for potential change and improvement. Effective diagnosis provides the systematic understanding of the organisation necessary for the design of appropriate interventions. Thus, OD interventions derive from diagnosis and include specific actions that are intended to resolve problems and improve organisational functioning. (Chapters 7 to 10 show the major interventions used in OD today.)

Diagnostic models derive from conceptions about how organisations function and tell OD practitioners what to look for when diagnosing organisations, departments, groups or jobs. They represent a road map for discovering current functioning. A general, comprehensive diagnostic model is presented, based on open systems theory.

What is diagnosis?

Diagnosis is the process of understanding how the organisation is currently functioning: it provides the information necessary for designing change interventions. It generally follows from successful entry and contracting. The preliminary activities in planned change set the stage for successful diagnosis. They help OD practitioners and client members jointly determine organisational issues to focus on, show how to collect and analyse data to understand them and how to work together to develop action steps from the diagnosis.

Unfortunately, the term 'diagnosis' can be misleading when applied to organisations. It suggests a model of organisation change analogous to medicine: an organisation (patient) experiencing problems seeks help from an OD practitioner (doctor); the practitioner examines the organisation, finds the causes of the problems and prescribes a solution. Diagnosis in organisation development is, however, much more collaborative than such a medical perspective implies. The values and ethical beliefs that underlie OD suggest that both organisational members and change agents should be jointly involved in discovering the causes of organisational problems. Similarly, both should be actively involved with developing appropriate interventions and implementing them.

For example, a manager might seek OD help to reduce absenteeism in his or her department. The manager and an OD consultant might jointly decide to diagnose the cause of the problem by examining company absenteeism records and by interviewing selected employees about possible reasons for absenteeism. Analysis of these data could uncover causes of absenteeism in the department, thus helping the manager and the practitioner to develop an appropriate intervention for reducing the problem.

The medical view of diagnosis also implies that something is wrong with the patient and that one needs to uncover the cause of the illness. In those cases where organisations do have specific problems, diagnosis is problem-oriented. It seeks reasons for the problems. However, many managers involved with OD are not experiencing specific organisational problems. Rather, they are interested in improving the overall effectiveness of their organisation, department or group. Here, diagnosis is development-oriented. It assesses the current functioning of the organisation to discover areas for future development. For example, a manager might be interested in using OD to improve a department that already seems to be functioning well. Diagnosis might include an overall assessment of both the task-performance capabilities of the department and the impact of the department upon its individual members. This process seeks to uncover specific areas for future development of the department's effectiveness.

In organisation development, diagnosis is used more broadly than a medical definition would suggest. It is a collaborative process between organisation members and the OD consultant to collect pertinent information, analyse it and draw conclusions for action planning and intervention. Diagnosis may be aimed at uncovering the causes of specific problems; or it may be directed at assessing the overall functioning of the organisation or department to discover areas for future development. Diagnosis provides a systematic understanding of organisations so that appropriate interventions may be developed for solving problems and enhancing effectiveness.

The need for diagnostic models

Entry and contracting processes can result in a need to understand a whole system or some part or feature of the organisation. To diagnose an organisation, OD practitioners and organisational members need to have some idea as to what information to collect and analyse, which can be based on intuitive hunches right through to scientific explanations of how the organisations function. Conceptual frameworks that people use to understand organisations are referred to as *diagnostic models*.[17] They describe the relationships between different features of the organisation, its context and its effectiveness. As a result, diagnostic models point out what areas to examine and what questions to ask when assessing how an organisation is functioning.

However, all models represent simplification of reality and therefore choose certain features as critical. Focusing attention on those features, often to the exclusion of others, can result in a biased diagnosis. For example, a diagnostic model that relates team effectiveness to the handling of interpersonal conflict would lead an OD practitioner to ask questions about relationships among members, decision-making processes and conflict-resolution methods. Although relevant, these questions ignore other group issues such as the composition of skills and knowledge, the complexity of the tasks performed by the group and member interdependencies. Thus, diagnostic models must be carefully chosen to address the organisation's presenting problems as well as to ensure comprehensiveness.

Potential diagnostic models are everywhere. Any collection of concepts and relationships that tries to represent a system or explain its effectiveness can potentially qualify as a diagnostic model. Major sources of diagnostic models in OD are the literally thousands of articles and books that discuss, describe and analyse how organisations function. They provide information about how and why certain organisational systems, processes or functions are effective. These studies often concern a specific facet of organisational behaviour, such as employee stress, leadership, motivation, problem solving, group dynamics, job design or career development. They can also involve the larger organisation and its context, including the environment, strategy, structure and culture. Diagnostic models can be derived from that information by noting the dimensions or variables that are associated with organisational effectiveness.

Another source of diagnostic models is the OD practitioner's own experience in organisations. This field knowledge is a wealth of practical information about how organisations operate. Unfortunately, only a small part of this vast experience has been translated into diagnostic models. These more clinical models represent the professional judgements of people with years of experience in organisational diagnosis. They generally link diagnosis with specific organisational processes, such as group problem solving, employee motivation, or communication between managers and employees. The models list specific questions for diagnosing such processes.

This section presents a general framework for diagnosing organisations rather than attempting to cover the diversity of OD diagnostic models. The framework describes the systems perspective prevalent in OD today and integrates several of the more popular diagnostic models. The systems model provides a useful starting point for diagnosing organisations or departments. (Additional diagnostic models that are linked to specific OD interventions are given in Chapters 7 to 10.)

OPEN SYSTEMS MODEL

This section introduces systems theory, a set of concepts and relationships that describes the properties and behaviours of things called *systems* – organisations, groups and people, for example. Systems are viewed as unitary wholes composed of parts or subsystems; they serve to integrate the parts into a functioning unit. For example, organisation systems are composed of departments such as sales, manufacturing and research. The organisation serves to co-ordinate the behaviours of its departments so that they function together. The general diagnostic model based on systems theory that underlies most of OD is called the 'open systems model'.

Systems can vary in how open they are to their outside environments. Open systems, such as organisations and people, exchange information and resources with their environments. They cannot completely control their own behaviour and are influenced in part by external forces. Organisations, for example, are affected by such environmental conditions as the availability of raw material, customer demands and government regulations. Understanding how these external forces affect the organisation can help to explain some of its internal behaviour.

Open systems display a hierarchical ordering. Each higher level of system is composed of lower level systems. Systems at the level of society are composed of organisations; organisations are composed of groups (departments); groups are composed of individuals; and so on. Although systems at different levels vary in many ways – in size and complexity, for example – they have a number of common characteristics by virtue of being open systems. These properties can be applied to systems at any level. The following key properties of open systems are described: (1) inputs, transformations and outputs; (2) boundaries; (3) feedback; (4) equifinality; and (5) alignment.

INPUTS, TRANSFORMATIONS AND OUTPUTS

Any organisational system is composed of three related parts: inputs, transformations and outputs, as shown in Figure 4.1. *Inputs* consist of human or other resources, such as information, energy and materials, coming into the system. They are acquired from the system's external environment. For example, a manufacturing organisation acquires raw materials from an outside supplier. Similarly, a hospital nursing unit acquires information about a patient's condition from the attending doctor. In each case, the system (organisation or nursing unit) obtains resources (raw materials or information) from its external environment.

Transformations are the processes of converting inputs into outputs. In organisations, transformations are generally carried out by a production or operations function that is composed of social and technological components. The social component consists of people and their work relationships, whereas the technological component involves tools, techniques and methods of production or service delivery. Organisations have developed elaborate mechanisms for transforming incoming resources into goods and services. Banks, for example, transform deposits into mortgage loans. Schools attempt to transform students into more educated people. Transformation processes can also take place at the group and individual levels. For example,

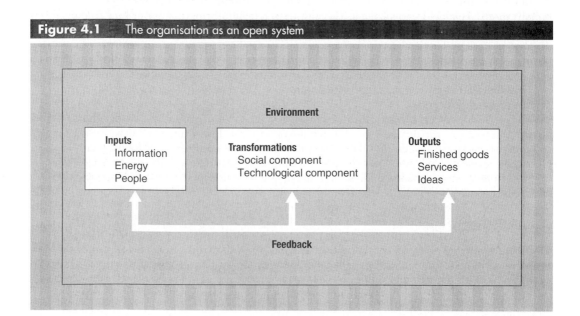

Figure 4.1 The organisation as an open system

research and development departments can transform the latest scientific advances into new product ideas.

Outputs are the result of what is transformed by the system and sent to the environment. Thus, inputs that have been transformed represent outputs ready to leave the system. Health insurance funds, such as HCF and Medibank Private, receive money and medical bills, transform them through the operation of record keeping and export payments to hospitals and doctors.

BOUNDARIES

The idea of boundaries helps to distinguish between systems and environments. Closed systems have relatively rigid and impenetrable boundaries, whereas open systems have far more permeable ones. Boundaries – the borders or limits of the system – are easily seen in many biological and mechanical systems. Defining the boundaries of social systems is more difficult as there is a continuous inflow and outflow through them. For example, where are the organisational boundaries in the following case? Call centres for various companies may be positioned offshore (for example, mail-order services are being centralised and established in India and will be able to service companies based in Australia and elsewhere). The emergence of the information superhighway and worldwide information networks will continue to challenge the notion of boundaries in open systems.

The definition of 'boundary' is arbitrary, as a social system has multiple subsystems and one subsystem's boundary line may not be the same as that of another. As with the system itself, arbitrary boundaries may have to be assigned to any social organisation, depending on the variable to be stressed. The boundaries used for studying or analysing leadership may be quite different from those used to study intergroup dynamics.

Just as systems can be considered to be relatively open or closed, the permeability of boundaries also varies from fixed to diffuse. The boundaries of a community's police force are probably far more rigid and sharply defined than are those of the community's political parties. Conflict over boundaries is always a potential problem within an organisation, just as it is in the world outside the organisation.

FEEDBACK

As shown in Figure 4.1, *feedback* is information about the actual performance or the results of the system. However, not all such information is feedback. Only information used to control the future functioning of the system is considered to be feedback. Feedback can be used to maintain the system in a steady state (for example, keeping an assembly line running at a certain speed) or to help the organisation adapt to changing circumstances. McDonald's, for example, has strict feedback processes for ensuring that a meal in one outlet is as similar as possible to a meal in any other outlet. On the other hand, a salesperson in the field may report that sales are not going well and may suggest some organisational change to improve sales. A market research study may lead the marketing department to recommend a change in the organisation's advertising campaign.

EQUIFINALITY

In closed systems, there is a direct cause-and-effect relationship between the initial condition and the final state of the system. When the 'on' switch on a computer is pushed, the system powers up. Biological and social systems, however, operate quite differently. The idea of equifinality suggests that similar results may be achieved with different initial conditions and in many different ways. This concept suggests that a manager can use varying forms of inputs into the organisation and can transform them in a variety of ways to obtain satisfactory outputs. Thus, the function of management is not to seek a single rigid solution but rather to develop a variety of satisfactory options. Systems and contingency theories suggest that there is no universal best way to design an organisation. Organisations and departments providing routine services, such as Telstra and Optus's long-distance phone services, should be designed differently from pharmaceutical development groups at Mayne Pharma or Glaxo Wellcome Australia.

ALIGNMENT

A system's overall effectiveness is determined by the extent to which the different parts are aligned with each other. This alignment or fit concerns the relationships between inputs and transformations, between transformations and outputs, and among the subsystems of the transformation process. Diagnosticians who view the relationships between the various parts of a system as a whole are taking what is referred to as a 'systemic perspective'. Not all academics are in an agreement and Application 4.2 is just one example of where there may be a differing of opinions.

APPLiCATiON 4.2

IDEAS AND ISSUES: KEEP CLEAR

The professor of organisational behaviour at Stanford University, Jeffrey Pfeffer, is well known for critiquing the misuse of symbols and myths in the workplace.

… Pfeffer suggests that an obsession with individual talent can be hazardous to an organisation's health, especially because talent is hard to measure reliably. He questions the assumption that change has to be difficult and necessarily takes a long time. Strategy, he suggests, may not be important. What is important, he writes, is doing the right thing. Pfeffer's prescription is to be logical and dispassionate about the facts. It is a useful corrective to the proclivity of senior managers to become deluded. But it is an observation also made after the fact, and that is the problem. All evidence can only be collected after the fact. It is the future that matters. Collecting evidence from the past is only useful if it is possible to make reliable projections into the future. Often it is not.

Pfeffer's work stands at the opposite end of the management spectrum to that of gurus such as Tom Peters, who argue that business conditions are becoming so volatile that it is necessary to jettison 'business as usual' (including, presumably, evidence). The advantage of Pfeffer's position is that it imposes a degree of logical rigour on managerial practices. The advantage of Peter's position is that it refers to the fundamental uncertainty that is appearing in industries subject to saturation, industry convergence and rapid technological change. In these sectors, collecting evidence may help managers understand the intensity of the threats they face, but it will not offer them a way out.

It is also wrong to think that speculation lacks rigour. Projections are not based on evidence (because the developments have not happened yet) but they are subject to their own discipline. Brian Anderson, who was a scenario planner for Royal Dutch Shell and formerly managing director of Shell Nigeria, says many managers do not like scenario planning because 'it is too difficult to grab a hold of' – that is, there is no evidence. But he says it is just a way of checking a plan. 'What happens if this project is hit by this scenario or another scenario five years down the road or next year? And we couldn't pass a project through the system if it didn't have some resilience against those scenarios. That is how it was used in a practical sense.'

Anderson concludes that the logical methods do not matter as much as people, especially when handling risk. 'If you have the right people and staff around the world and the right relationships between the people and the outside world, you have covered about what you can do. All the rest stems out of that.'

The same is true of gathering and interpreting evidence. It is the people doing the gathering and interpreting who finally matter the most. Even working out what are half-truths and nonsense finally rests on the quality of the people, not just the quality of the evidence.

Source: David James, 'Ideas and issues: keep clear', *Business Review Weekly*, 11/5/06.

Critical Thinking Questions: How would the ideas of Jeffrey Pfeffer 'fit' with the 'open systems approach'? Read further on what Tom Peters has to write about the subject. Do you agree or disagree with Jeffrey Pfeffer? Explain your answer.

Fit and alignment refer to a characteristic of the relationship between two or more parts. Just as the teeth in two wheels of a watch must mesh perfectly for the watch to keep time, so too do the parts of an organisation need to mesh for it to be effective. For example, Southcorp attempts to achieve its goals through a strategy of diversification, and a divisional structure is used to support that strategy. A functional structure would not be a good fit with the strategy as it is more efficient for one division to focus on one product line than for one manufacturing department to try to make many different products. The systemic perspective suggests that diagnosis is the search for misfits among the various parts and subsystems of an organisation.

Organisation-level diagnosis

When viewed as open systems, organisations can be diagnosed at three levels. The highest level is the overall organisation and includes the design of the company's strategy, structure and processes. Large organisation units, such as divisions, subsidiaries or strategic business units, also can be diagnosed at this level. The next level is the group or department, which includes group design and devices for structuring interactions among members, such as norms and work schedules. The lowest level is the individual position or job. Diagnosis of these includes ways in which jobs are designed in order to elicit required task behaviours.

Diagnosis can occur at all three organisational levels, or it may be limited to problems that occur at a particular level. The key to effective diagnosis is to know what to look for at each level, as well as how the levels affect each other.[18] A basic understanding of organisation-level issues is important in diagnosis at any level of analysis as these issues are important inputs to understanding groups and individuals.

The organisation level of analysis is the broadest systems perspective typically taken in diagnostic activities. The model shown in Figure 4.2 is similar to other popular organisation-level diagnostic models. These include Weisbord's six-box model,[19] Nadler and Tushman's congruency model,[20] and Kotter's organisation dynamics model.[21] Figure 4.2 proposes that an organisation's strategy and organisation design, as well as its design components, represent the way the organisation positions and organises itself within an environment (inputs) to achieve specific outputs. The combination of strategy and organisation design is called a 'strategic orientation'.[22]

INPUTS

To understand how a total organisation functions, it is necessary to examine particular inputs and design components and to examine the alignment of the two sets of dimensions. Figure 4.2 shows that two key inputs affect the way an organisation designs its strategic orientation: the general environment and industry structure.

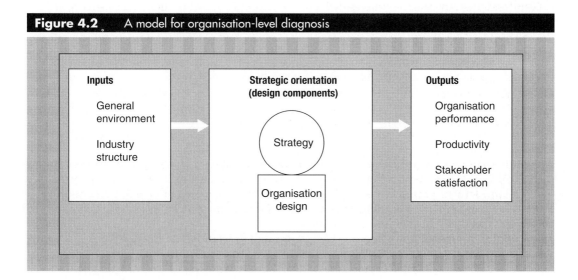

Figure 4.2 A model for organisation-level diagnosis

The general environment represents the external elements and forces that can affect the attainment of organisational objectives.[23] It can be described in terms of the amount of uncertainty present in social, technological, economic, ecological and political forces. The more uncertainty there is in how the environment will affect the organisation, the more difficult it is to design an effective strategic orientation. For example, the technological environment in the watch industry has been highly uncertain over time. The Swiss, who built precision watches with highly skilled craftspeople, were caught off-guard by the mass production and distribution technology of Timex in the 1960s. Similarly, many watch manufacturers were surprised by, and failed to take advantage of, digital technology.

The increased incidence of AIDS in the workplace (social environment) and the implementation of the Equal Opportunity and Anti-Discrimination Acts (political environment) have also forced changes in the strategic orientations of organisations.

An organisation's industry structure or task environment is another important input into strategic orientation. As defined by Michael Porter, an organisation's task environment consists of five forces: suppliers, buyers, threats of entry, threats of substitutes and rivalry among competitors.[24] First, strategic orientations must be sensitive to powerful suppliers who can increase prices (and therefore lower profits) or force the organisation to pay more attention to the supplier's needs than to the organisation's needs. For example, unions represent powerful suppliers of labour that can affect the costs of any organisation within an industry. Second, strategic orientations must be sensitive to powerful buyers. Aeroplane purchasers, such as Qantas Airlines or country governments, can force Airbus, McDonnell-Douglas or Boeing to lower prices or appoint the planes in particular ways. Third, strategic orientations must be sensitive to the threat of new firms entering into competition. Profits in the restaurant business tend to be low because of the ease of starting a new restaurant. Fourth, strategic orientations must be sensitive to the threat of new products or services that can replace existing offerings. Ice-cream producers must carefully monitor their costs and prices because it is easy for a consumer to purchase frozen yoghurt or other types of dessert. Finally, strategic orientations must be sensitive to rivalry among existing competitors. If many organisations are competing for the same customers, for example, the strategic orientation must monitor product offerings, costs and structures carefully if the organisation is to survive and prosper. Together, these forces play an important role in determining the success of an organisation, whether it be a manufacturing firm, a non-profit organisation or a government agency.

General environments and industry structures both change over time. This makes the process of designing a strategic orientation all the more difficult.

DESIGN COMPONENTS

Figure 4.3 shows that an organisation's strategic orientation is composed of two primary elements: strategy and organisation design.

Strategy

A strategy represents the way an organisation uses its resources (human, economic or technical) to gain and sustain a competitive advantage.[25] It can be described by the organisation's mission, goals and objectives, strategic intent and functional policies. A mission statement describes the long-term purpose of the organisation, the range of products or services offered, the markets to be served and the social needs served by the organisation's existence. Goals and objectives are statements that provide explicit direction, set organisational priorities, provide guidelines for management decisions and serve as the cornerstone for organising activities, designing jobs and setting standards of achievement. Goals and objectives should set a target of achievement such as 50% gross margins, an average employee satisfaction score of four on a five-point scale or some level of productivity. They should also provide a means or system for measuring achievement; and provide a deadline or time frame for accomplishment.[26] A strategic intent is a succinct label that describes how the organisation intends to achieve its goals and objectives. For example, an organisation can achieve goals through differentiation of its product or service, by achieving the lowest costs in the industry or by growing the organisation. Finally, functional policies are the methods, procedures, rules or administrative practices that guide decision

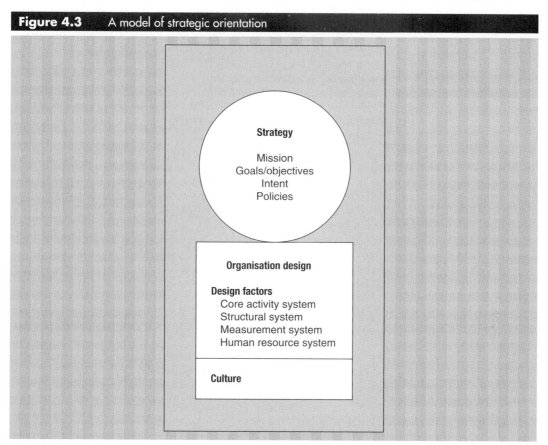

Figure 4.3   A model of strategic orientation

making and convert plans into actions. In the semiconductor business, for example, Intel has a policy of allocating about 30% of revenues to research and development in order to maintain its lead in microprocessors.[27]

Organisation design

The organisation's design comprises four design factors and culture. *Design factors* are organisational subsystems or change levers that support the business strategy. To implement a strategy successfully, the design factors must be aligned with the strategic intent and with each other. The four design factors are the core activity system, the structural system, the measurement system and the human resource system.

The core activity system is concerned with the way in which an organisation converts inputs into products and services. It represents the heart of the transformation function and includes production methods, work flow and equipment. For example, the automobile industry has traditionally used an assembly-line technology to build cars and trucks. Two features of the technological core have been shown to influence other design components: interdependence and uncertainty.[28] Technical interdependence involves ways in which the different parts of a technological system are related. High interdependence requires considerable co-ordination between tasks, such as might occur when departments must work together to bring out a new product. Technical uncertainty refers to the amount of information processing and decision making required during task performance. Generally, when tasks require high amounts of information processing and decision making, they are difficult to plan and create routines for. The technology of car manufacturing is relatively certain and moderately interdependent. As a result, car manufacturers specify in advance the tasks that workers should perform and how their work should be co-ordinated.

The structural system describes how attention and resources are focused on task accomplishment. It represents the basic organising mode chosen to: (1) divide the overall work of an organisation into sub-units that can assign tasks to individuals or groups, and (2) co-ordinate these sub-units for completion of the overall work.[29] Structure, therefore, needs to be closely aligned with the organisation's core activity systems.

Two ways of determining how an organisation divides work are to examine its formal structure and to examine its level of differentiation and integration. Formal structures divide work by function (accounting, sales or production), by product or service (Fairlane, LTD or Falcon) or by some combination of both (a matrix composed of functional departments and product groupings). The second way to describe how work is divided is to specify the amount of differentiation and integration in a structure. Applied to the total organisation, differentiation refers to the degree of similarity or difference in the design of two or more sub-units or departments.[30] In a highly differentiated organisation, there are major differences in design between the departments. Some departments are highly formalised with many rules and regulations, others have few rules and regulations, and still others are moderately formal or flexible.

The way an organisation co-ordinates the work across sub-units is called integration. Integration can be achieved in a variety of ways: for example, by using plans and schedules; using budgets; assigning special roles, such as project managers, liaison positions or integrators; or creating cross-departmental task forces and teams. The amount of integration required in a structure is a function of: (1) the amount of uncertainty in the environment, (2) the level of differentiation in the structure, and (3) the amount of interdependence between departments. As uncertainty, differentiation and interdependence increase, more sophisticated integration devices are required.

Measurement systems are methods of gathering, assessing and disseminating information on the activities of groups and individuals in organisations. Such data tell how well the organisation is performing and are used to detect and control deviations from goals. Closely related to structural integration, measurement systems monitor organisational operations and feed data about work activities to managers and organisational members so that they can better understand current performance and co-ordinate work. Effective information and control systems are clearly linked to strategic objectives. They also provide accurate, understandable and timely information; are accepted as legitimate by organisational members; and produce benefits in excess of their cost.

Human resource systems include mechanisms for selecting, developing, appraising and rewarding organisation members. These influence the mix of skills, personalities and behaviours of organisation members. The organisation's strategy and core activities provide important information about the required skills and knowledge that need to be present if the organisation is to be successful. Appraisal processes identify whether those skills and knowledge are being applied to the work, while reward systems complete the cycle by recognising performance that contributes to goal achievement. Reward systems may be tied to measurement systems so that rewards are allocated on the basis of measured results.

Organisation *culture* is the final element in an organisation's design. It represents the basic assumptions, values and norms shared by organisation members.[31] These cultural elements are generally taken for granted and serve to guide members' perceptions, thoughts and actions. For example, McDonald's culture emphasises 'efficiency', 'speed' and 'consistency'. It orients employees to company goals and suggests the kinds of behaviours necessary for success. In Figure 4.3, culture is separated from, and beneath, the design factors as it represents both an outcome of prior choices made about the strategy and the design factors, and a foundation that can either hinder or facilitate change. In diagnosis, the focus is on understanding the current culture well enough to determine its alignment with the other design factors. Such information may partly explain current outcomes, such as performance or effectiveness.

OUTPUTS

The outputs of a strategic orientation can be classified into three components. First, organisation performance refers to financial outputs such as profits, return on investment and earnings per share. For non-profit and governmental agencies, performance often refers to the extent to which costs were lowered or budgets met as well as other performance measures. Second, productivity concerns the internal measurements of efficiency such as sales per employee, waste, error rates, quality or units produced per hour. Third, stakeholder satisfaction reflects how well the organisation has met the expectations of different groups. Customer satisfaction can be measured in terms of market share or focus group data; employee satisfaction can be measured in terms of an opinion survey; and investor satisfaction can be measured in terms of share price.

ALIGNMENT

Assessing the effectiveness of an organisation's current strategic orientation requires that knowledge of the above information be acquired in order to determine the alignment among the different elements.

1   Does the organisation's strategic orientation fit with the inputs?
2   Do the elements of the strategy fit with each other?
3   Do the elements of the organisation design fit with each other?
4   Do the elements of the organisation design support the strategy?

    For example, if the elements of the external environment (inputs) are fairly similar in their degree of certainty, then an effective organisation structure (design factor) should have a low degree of differentiation. Its departments should be designed similarly because each faces similar environmental demands. On the other hand, if the environment is complex and each element presents different amounts of uncertainty, a more differentiated structure is warranted. Esso's regulatory, ecological, technological and social environments differ greatly in their amount of uncertainty. The regulatory environment is relatively slow-paced and detail-oriented. Accordingly, the regulatory affairs function within Esso is formal and bound by protocol. In the technological environment, on the other hand, new methods for discovering, refining and distributing oil and oil products are changing at a rapid pace. These departments are much more flexible and adaptive, very different from the regulatory affairs function.

ANALYSIS

Application 4.3 describes the Nike organisation and provides an opportunity to perform an organisation-level analysis.

APPLICATiON 4.3

NIKE'S STRATEGIC ORIENTATION

In 1993, Nike was the leader in US domestic-brand athletic footwear with more than 30% market share. It also produced sports apparel, hiking boots and upmarket men's shoes. But after six years of solid growth, international sales were falling, sales of basketball shoes were down and the firm's stock price had dropped 41% since November 1992. Analysts were projecting declines in both total revenues and profits for the next fiscal year. In addition, Nike had been the focus of attack from several stakeholder groups. Organised labour believed that Nike exploited foreign labour, the African-American sector noted the lack of diversity in Nike's work force, and the general public was getting tired of sensationalising athletes.

    Nike's traditional strategy was built around high-performance, innovative athletic shoes, aggressive marketing and low-cost manufacturing. Using input from athletes, Nike developed a strong competence in producing high-quality athletic shoes, first for running, then for basketball and other sports. By contracting with well-known and outspoken athletes to endorse the product, a Nike image of renegade excellence and high performance emerged. Other consumers who wanted to associate with the Nike image could do so by purchasing their shoes. Thus, a large market of weekend warriors, people pursuing a more active lifestyle, serious runners and anyone wanting to project a more athletic image became potential customers. Nike contracted with low-cost, foreign manufacturing plants to produce its shoes.

▷▷

An athletic shoe retailer places orders with Nike representatives, who are not employees of Nike but contract with Nike to sell its shoes, for delivery in six to eight months. The Futures program, as it is called, offers the retailer 10% off the wholesale price for making these advance orders. The orders are then compiled and production-scheduled with one of Nike's Asian manufacturing partners. Nike doesn't actually make shoes. Instead, it develops contract relationships with Taiwanese, Korean, Japanese and other low-cost sources. On-site Nike employees guarantee that the shoes meet the Nike standards of quality.

Nike's culture is distinctive. The organisation – built by athletes, for athletes – is very entrepreneurial, and the 'Just Do It' marketing campaign aptly describes the way things are done at Nike. As one senior executive put it, 'It's fine to develop structures and plans and policies, if they are viewed, and used, as tools. But it is so easy for them to become substitutes for good thinking, alibis for not taking responsibility, reasons to not become involved. And then we'd no longer be Nike.'

What emerged, by the mid-1980s, was a way of working that involved setting direction, dividing up the work, pulling things together, and providing rewards.

Although Phil Knight, founder and chairman of Nike, sets the general direction for Nike, he rarely sets clear goals. For example, Knight views Nike as a growth company. The athletic drive pushes employers to achieve bigger sales and put more shoes on more feet than anyone else. Others are concerned that the decision to go public in the early 1980s produced pressures for profitability that sometimes work against growth. Implementation of the general direction depends on people being tuned into the day-to-day operations. 'You tune into what other people are doing and, if you're receptive, you start to see the need for something to be done,' Knight says.

Nike changed from a functional organisation in 1985 to a product division structure in 1987. In addition, 1993 brought additional structural change. The new president, Tom Clark, was busy implementing stronger communication and collaboration among manufacturing, marketing and sales. This description, however, belies the informality of the organisation. In essence, the aim of the Nike structure is to fit the pieces together in ways that best meet the needs of the product, the customers and the market.

In pulling things together, Nike relies on meetings as the primary method for co-ordination. The word 'meeting' connotes more formality than is really intended. Meetings, which occur at all levels and in all parts of the organisation, range from an informal gathering in the hallway to a three-day off-site conference or formal reviews of a product line. Membership in a meeting is equally fluid – only those people who need to be involved are invited. Although more formal systems have emerged over the years, their use is often localised to the people or groups who invented them and is met with resistance by others. Thus, with the exception of Futures, there is little in the way of formal information systems.

Finally, Knight favours an annual performance review system with annual pay increases tied to performance. In actuality, however, the system is fairly unstructured and some managers take time to do the reviews well while others do not. And although no formal compensation policy exists, most employees and managers believe that Nike is a 'great place to work'. For most people, rewards come in the form of growth opportunities, autonomy and responsibility.

Source: adapted from material in G. Willigan, 'High performance marketing: an interview with Nike's Phil Knight', *Harvard Business Review* (July–August 1992); D. Yang and M. Oneal, 'Can Nike just do it?' *Business Week* (18 April 1994): 86–90; D. Rikert and C. Christensen, 'Nike (A)' 9-395-025 (Boston: Harvard Business School, 1984); D. Rikert and C.Christensen, 'Nike (B)' 9-385-027 (Boston: Harvard Business School, 1984).

Critical Thinking Question: This application has been used in previous editions of the book to typify what organisations should do. Much has happened since this compilation, particularly with the documentary, *The Big One*, by Michael Moore. What is the status of Nike today?

Organisation-level dimensions and relationships may be applied to the diagnosis of Nike, as an example. A useful starting point is to ask how well the organisation is currently functioning – to examine the organisation's outputs, yields, measures of market share, financial performance and stakeholder satisfaction. Nike's string of solid annual increases over six years was followed by real or predicted declines. Discovering the underlying causes of these problems begins with an assessment of the inputs and strategic orientation and then proceeds to an evaluation of the alignments among the different parts. In diagnosing the inputs, two questions are important:

1   *What is the company's general environment?* Nike's environment is uncertain and complex. Technologically, Nike is dependent on the latest breakthroughs in shoe design and materials to keep its high-performance image. Socially and politically, Nike's international manufacturing and marketing operations require that it be aware of a variety of stakeholder demands from several countries, cultures and governments, including the US government, which might view Nike's foreign manufacturing strategy with some concern about US jobs. Other stakeholders are pressuring Nike for changes to its human resource practices.

2   *What is the company's industry structure?* Nike's industry is highly competitive and places considerable pressure on profits. First, the threat of entry is high. It is not difficult or expensive to enter the athletic shoe market. Many shoe manufacturers could easily offer an athletic shoe if they wanted. The threat of substitute products is also high. Nike's image and franchise depend on people wanting to be athletic. If fitness trends were to change, then other footwear could easily fill the need. This possibility clearly exists because Nike's marketing has sensationalised professional athletes and sports, rather than emphasising fitness for the average person. The bargaining power of suppliers – such as providers of labour, shoe materials and manufacturing – is generally low because the resources are readily available and there are many sources. The bargaining power of buyers is moderate. At the high-performance end, buyers are willing to pay more for high quality, whereas at the casual end, price is important and the purchasing power of large accounts can bid down Nike's price. Finally, rivalry among firms is severe. A number of international and domestic competitors exist, such as Reebok, Adidas, New Balance, Puma, Converse and Tiger. Many of them have adopted similar marketing and promotion tactics to Nike and are competing for the same customers. Thus, the likelihood of new competition, the threat of new substitute products and the rivalry among existing competitors are the primary forces creating uncertainty in the environment and squeezing profits in the athletic shoe industry.

The following two questions are important in assessing Nike's strategic orientation:

1   *What is the company's strategy?* Nike's strategy is clear on some points and nebulous on others. First, although the company has no formal mission statement, it has a clear sense about its initial purpose in producing high-quality, high-performance athletic footwear. That focus has blurred somewhat as Nike has ventured into apparel, hiking boots and casual shoes. Its goals are also nebulous because Phil Knight does not set specific goals, only general directions. The tension between growth and profits is a potential source of problems for the organisation. On the other hand, its strategic intent is fairly clear. It is attempting to achieve its growth and profitability goals by offering a differentiated product – a high-quality, high-performance shoe. Informal policies dominate the Nike organisation.

2   *What is the company's organisation design?* First, the core activities of Nike are moderately uncertain and interdependent. For example, developing high-quality, state-of-the-art shoes is uncertain, but there is no evidence that research and development is tightly linked to production. In addition, the Futures program creates low interdependence between manufacturing and distribution, both of which are fairly routine processes. Second, Nike's product division structure appears moderately differentiated, but the new president's emphasis on communication and co-ordination suggests that it is not highly integrated. Moreover, although Nike appears to have a divisional structure, its contract relationships with manufacturing plants and sales representatives give it a fluid, network-like structure. Third, human resource and measurement systems are underdeveloped. There is no compensation policy, for example, and formal control systems are generally resisted. The one exception to this is the Futures program that tracks orders (which are really advance revenues). Finally, Nike's culture is a dominant feature of the organisation design. The organisation appears driven by typical athletic norms of winning, competition, achievement and performance.

Now that the organisation outputs, inputs and throughputs have been assessed, it is time to ask the crucial question about how well they fit together. The first concern is the fit between inputs and strategic orientation. The complex and uncertain environment suits Nike's focus on differentiation and a generally flexible organisation design, which explains its incredible success during the 1970s, 1980s and into the 1990s. The alignment between its strategic orientation and its environment appears sound.

The second concern is the alignment of the elements within strategy and organisation design. The elements of Nike's strategy are not aligned. It clearly intends to differentiate its product by serving the high-end athlete with high-performance shoes. However, this small group of athletes may have trouble communicating its needs to a large, diversified organisation. Growth goals and a diversified mission quite obviously do not align with Nike's differentiation intent. This hypothesis is supported by the lack of clear goals in general, and policies that support neither growth nor profitability.

Within the organisation design, the core activity systems appear to be well supported and aligned with the structure. Product development, market development and manufacturing development are inherently unprogrammable tasks that require flexibility and adaptability from the organisation. Although a product structure overlays most of Nike's activities, the structure is not rigid and there appears to be a willingness to create structure as and when it is required to complete a task. In addition, the Futures program is important for two reasons. First, it reduces uncertainty from the market by getting retailers to take the risk that a shoe will not do well. For the retailer, this risk is mitigated by Nike's tremendous reputation and marketing clout. Second, knowing in advance what will be ordered provides Nike with the ability to schedule production and distribution far in advance. This is a powerful device for integrating Nike's activities. Finally, the lack of a formal human resources system supports the fluid and flexible design, but creates problems in that there is no direction for hiring and development, a point noted by the various stakeholders at the beginning of the application.

Obviously, any discussion of Nike's organisation design has to recognise the powerful role its culture plays. More than any design factor, the culture promotes co-ordination of a variety of tasks, serves as a method for socialising and developing people, and establishes methods for moving information around the organisation. Clearly, any change effort at Nike will have to acknowledge this role, and design an intervention accordingly. The strong culture will either sabotage or facilitate change, depending on how the change process aligns with the culture's impact on individual behaviour.

The last element of alignment is the extent to which the organisation design supports the strategy. In this case, there appears to be a good fit. The differentiated strategic intent requires an organisation design that focuses on the creation of new ideas in products, marketing and manufacturing. The flexible structure, informal systems and driving culture would seem well suited for that purpose.

Based on this diagnosis of the Nike organisation, at least two intervention possibilities are suggested. First, the OD practitioner could suggest increasing Nike's clarity about its strategy. In this intervention, the practitioner would want to avoid talking about formalising Nike's strategy because the culture would resist such an attempt. However, there are some distinct advantages to be gained from a clearer sense of Nike's future, its businesses and the relationship between them. Second, Nike could focus on increasing the integration and co-ordination of its organisation design. Although the culture provides a considerable amount of social control, the lack of any human resource systems and the relatively underdeveloped integration mechanisms suggest that finding ways to co-ordinate activities without increasing formalisation would be a value-added intervention.

Group-level diagnosis

After the organisation level, the next two levels of diagnosis are the group and job. Many large organisations have groups or departments that are themselves relatively large, such as the operating divisions at BHP Billiton and Pacific Dunlop. Diagnosis of large groups can follow the dimensions and relational fits applicable to organisation-level diagnosis, because large groups or departments essentially operate much like organisations, and diagnosing them as organisations can assess their functioning.

However, small departments and groups can behave differently from large organisations. Therefore, they need their own diagnostic models to reflect these differences. Previously we discussed the diagnosis of work groups. Such groups generally consist of a relatively small number of people working face to face on a shared task. Work groups are prevalent in all sizes of organisations. They can be relatively permanent and perform an ongoing task, or they can be temporary and exist only to perform one particular task or to make a specific decision.

Figure 4.4 shows the inputs, design components, outputs and relational fits for group-level diagnosis.[32] The model is similar to other popular group-level diagnostic models, such as Hackman and Morris's task group design model[33] and Ledford, Lawler and Mohrman's participation group design model.[34]

INPUTS

Organisation design is clearly the major input in group design. It consists of the design components that characterise the larger organisation within which the group is embedded. These include core activity, structural, measurement and human resource systems, as well as organisational culture. Core activity systems can determine the characteristics of the group's task; structural systems can specify the level of co-ordination required between groups. The human resource and measurement systems, such as performance appraisal and reward systems, play an important role in determining team functioning.[35] For example, individually based performance appraisal and reward systems tend to interfere with team functioning as the members may be more concerned with maximising their individual performance to the detriment of team performance. Collecting information about the group's organisation design context can greatly improve the accuracy of diagnosis.

DESIGN COMPONENTS

Figure 4.4 shows that groups have five major components: (1) goal clarity, (2) task structure, (3) group composition, (4) group functioning, and (5) performance norms.

Goal clarity involves how well the group understands its objectives. In general, goals should: be moderately challenging; include a method for measuring, monitoring and feeding back information about goal achievement; and be clearly understood by all members.

Task structure is concerned with how the group's work is designed. Task structures can vary along two key dimensions: co-ordination of members' efforts and regulation of their task behaviours.[36] The co-ordination dimension involves the degree to which group tasks are

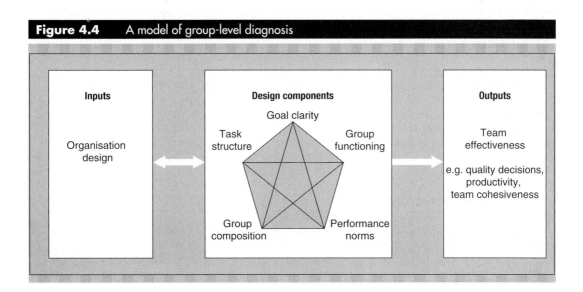

Figure 4.4   A model of group-level diagnosis

structured to promote effective interaction among group members. Co-ordination is important in groups who perform interdependent tasks, such as surgical teams and problem-solving groups. It is relatively unimportant, however, in groups composed of members performing independent tasks, such as a group of telephone operators or salespeople. The regulation dimension involves the degree to which members can control their own task behaviours and be relatively free from external controls, such as supervision, plans and programs. Self-regulation generally occurs when members can decide on such issues as task assignments, work methods, production goals and membership. (Interventions for designing group task structure are discussed in Chapter 8.)

Composition concerns the membership of groups. Members can differ on a number of dimensions that have relevance to group behaviour. Demographic variables, such as age, education, experience, and skills and abilities, can affect how people behave and relate to each other in groups. Demographics can determine whether the group is composed of people who have task-relevant skills and knowledge, including interpersonal skills. People's internal needs can also influence group behaviours. Individual differences in social needs can determine whether group membership is likely to be satisfying or stressful.[37]

Group functioning is the underlying basis of group life. How members relate to each other is important in work groups as the quality of relationships can affect task performance. In some groups, for example, interpersonal competition and conflict between members result in their providing little support and help for each other. Conversely, groups may become too concerned about sharing good feelings and support, and spend too little time on task performance. In organisation development, considerable effort has been invested to help work groups develop healthy interpersonal relations, including an ability and willingness to openly share feelings and perceptions about the members' behaviours so that interpersonal problems and task difficulties can be worked through and resolved.[38] Group functioning therefore involves: (1) task-related activities, such as giving and seeking information, and elaborating, co-ordinating and evaluating activities; and (2) the group-maintenance function, which is directed towards holding the group together as a cohesive team and includes encouraging, harmonising, compromising, setting standards and observing.[39] (Interpersonal interventions are discussed in Chapter 7.)

Application 4.4 describes how insurance company Axa has utilised group dynamics as a positive and constructive medium for change.

APPLICATION 4.4

TRAINING: A RELEASE OF POSITIVE ENERGY

When Axa wanted to up the ante on its performance, it called in the experts to unlock the energy bank. Simon Walsh investigates how they went about it and what effect it has had.

Ten years ago, workplaces focused more on the individual, insists David Aiston, regional director (North) of Axa Commercial. 'Views were quite constrained then but business leadership mindsets are now more attuned to the positive dynamics of teamwork,' he adds.

Axa Commercial engaged directed energy specialist Attiva to help formulate their approach in developing and progressing the way their teams interact with each other. Attiva has so far completed two projects for Axa: the first assisted in the merging of three teams into one; the other looked to improve communications and work interrelations between different UK teams in the north and south.

Mr Aiston [states]: 'It's about taking the raw energy of people and working with it to refine and enhance performance. World-class teams produce world-class results, but that's difficult to keep up. It needs attention and support.'

Axa clearly had the right people in the right places but needed to ensure the formula for the overall mix was the best possible. 'A team in which people understand and intuit each other is a better team,' says Mr Aiston.

Attiva looked to challenge the insurance teams. They were taken up a mountain and invited to reassess their views in an inspirational environment – the Peak District provided the setting for the northern team, and Bedford for those in the south. They were then encouraged to review their behaviour and motivation as a team in a cooking workshop where the challenge was to create and produce a meal together. Attiva helped the group draw important lessons from this exercise, including the impact on each other of their personal styles and their potential to coach and support each other.

One of the key factors in ensuring such work will bear fruit is the initial understanding of the participants and their individual challenges. 'We call every participant beforehand and go over our objectives,' explains Mr Robertson. 'We involve them in designing the workshop or process so they have a stake and an interest in the outcome from the outset.'

…

The belief that organisational development happens best through the personal, to truly succeeding in the plural, has been grasped quickly by the business world. High-performing teams such as those at Axa recognise and exploit the power of the collective spirit and effort.

Source: 'Training: a release of positive energy', *Insurance Age*, 1/1/06.

Critical Thinking Questions: Search the internet for the website of Axa. How has the company benefited from this approach to 'group functioning'? Is it possible for other organisations to replicate their strategy? Why/why not?

Performance norms are member beliefs about how the group should perform its task and include acceptable levels of performance.[40] Norms derive from interactions among members and serve as guides to group behaviour. Once members agree on performance norms, either implicitly or explicitly, then members routinely perform tasks according to those norms. For example, members of problem-solving groups often decide early in the life of the group that decisions will be made through voting; voting then becomes a routine part of group task behaviour. (Interventions aimed at helping groups develop appropriate performance norms are discussed in Chapter 7.)

OUTPUTS

Group effectiveness has two dimensions: performance and quality of work life. Performance is measured in terms of the group's ability to successfully control or reduce costs, increase productivity or improve quality. This is a 'hard' measure of effectiveness. In addition, effectiveness is indicated by the group member's quality of work life. It concerns work satisfaction, team cohesion and organisational commitment.

FITS

The diagnostic model in Figure 4.4 shows that group design components must fit inputs if groups are to be effective in terms of performance and the quality of work life. Research suggests the following fits between the inputs and design dimensions:

1   Group design should be congruent with the larger organisation design. Organisation structures with low differentiation and high integration should have work groups that are composed of highly skilled and experienced members performing highly interdependent tasks. Organisations with differentiated structures and formalised human resource and information systems should spawn groups that have clear, quantitative goals and support standardised behaviours. Although there is little direct research on these fits, the underlying rationale is that congruence between organisation and group designs supports overall integration within the company. When group designs are not compatible with organisation designs, groups often conflict with the organisation.[41] They may develop norms that run counter to organisational effectiveness, such as happens in groups that are supportive of horseplay, mockery and other counterproductive behaviours.

2   When the core activity system of organisation design results in interdependent tasks, co-ordination among members should be promoted by task structures, composition, performance norms and group functioning. Conversely, when technology permits independent tasks, the design components should promote individual task performance.[42] For example, when co-ordination is needed: task structure might physically locate related

tasks together; composition might include members with similar interpersonal skills and social needs; performance norms would support task-relevant interactions; and healthy interpersonal relations would be developed.

3   When the core activity system is relatively uncertain and requires high amounts of information processing and decision making, group task structure, composition, performance norms and group functioning should promote self-regulation. Members should have the necessary freedom, information and skills to assign members to tasks, to decide on production methods and to set performance goals.[43] When technology is relatively certain, group designs should promote standardisation of behaviour, and groups should be externally controlled by supervisors, schedules and plans.[44] For example, when self-regulation is needed: task structure might be relatively flexible and allow the interchange of members across group tasks; composition might include members with multiple skills, interpersonal competencies and social needs; performance norms would support complex problem solving; and efforts would be made to develop healthy interpersonal relations.

ANALYSIS

The key issue in diagnosing group inputs is the design of the larger organisation within which groups were embedded. Petroleum giant BP's design is relatively differentiated. Each plant, such as Kwinana in Western Australia, is allowed to set up its own organisation design. Similarly, although no specific data are given, the company's technology, structure, measurement systems, human resource systems and culture appear to promote flexible and innovative behaviours at the plant level. Indeed, freedom to innovate in the manufacturing plants is probably an outgrowth of the firm's OD activities and participative culture.

In the case of decision-making groups, such as Occupational Health and Safety, organisation design also affects the nature of the issues that are worked on. A single Refinery Safety and Health Committee (RS&HC) was established as 'an independent body accountable to the refinery manager'. Only the chief fire and safety officer and a safety inspector are ex-officio members: all of the 14 other representatives are elected by work groups that cover the whole of the refinery. The committee exists to 'ensure that arrangements exist for joint consultation with all employees on health and safety matters and to encourage effective participation by employees in accident prevention, consistent with policies laid down by the RS&HC'. Although the committee's terms of reference are not as explicit as the union's draft document that formed part of its claim in the negotiations, the essential elements of establishing an effective joint approach to safety are present, reflecting the common ground between management and unions on this issue.

The issue of health and safety can be addressed in three broad areas: policy formulation, plant design and the operation of the plant. In essence, the committee has been concerned with correctly channelling the information made available by management, but which had not been getting through to where it was needed, when it was needed.

There are determinants of safe performance, such as design, the level of training, work pressures, management commitment and so on. The joint approach adopted by management, employees and unions at BP is part of achieving a safe working environment at the refinery. Management commitment is evident. Employee involvement takes place in a variety of ways, including the development of work procedures and in the activity of the committee itself. Employee control, rather than just participation in decision making, is at two levels. First is at the point of production, where for example, any BP refinery employee has the authority to shut down a process if he or she considers that it is becoming unsafe. Second, control can be exercised collectively where the union membership is prepared to make safety an industrial issue. It is the integration of all these aspects that will determine the long-term success of the safety program at BP.

Diagnosis of the team's design components answers the following questions:

1   How clear are the group's goals?
2   What is the group's task structure?
3   What is the composition of the group?

4   What are the group's performance norms?
5   What is the nature of team functioning in the group?

The issues that the team deals with are highly interdependent and often uncertain. The meetings are intended to resolve plant-wide problems that affect the various functional departments. Those problems are generally complex and require the members to process considerable information and create innovative solutions. The team's task structure and composition appear to fit the nature of team issues. The face-to-face meetings help to co-ordinate problem solving among the department managers. Team members seem to have the necessary task-relevant skills and experience, apart from the interpersonal skills, that could help the problem-solving process. However, there may be a conflict in the priority between the problems chosen by the team to be solved and the problems facing individual managers.

The key difficulty seems to be a mismatch between the team's performance norms and interpersonal relations and the demands of the problem-solving task. Complex, interdependent problems require performance norms that support the sharing of diverse and often conflicting kinds of information. The norms must encourage members to generate novel solutions and assess the relevance of problem-solving strategies in the light of new issues. Members need to explicitly address how they are using their knowledge and skills and how they are weighing and combining members' individual contributions.

A team's performance norms may fail to support complex problem solving; in fact, it may promote a problem-solving method that is often superficial, haphazard and subject to external disruptions. Members' interpersonal relations reinforce adherence to the ineffective norms. Members do not confront personal differences or dissatisfaction with the group process. They fail to examine the very norms that contribute to their problems. In this case, diagnosis suggests the need for group interventions aimed at improving performance norms and developing healthy interpersonal relations.

Individual-level diagnosis

The lowest level of organisational diagnosis is the individual job or position. An organisation consists of numerous groups; a group, in turn, is composed of several individual jobs. This section discusses the inputs, design components and relational fits for diagnosing jobs. The model shown in Figure 4.5 is similar to other popular job diagnostic frameworks, such as Hackman and Oldham's job diagnostic survey and Herzberg's job-enrichment model.[45]

INPUTS

Three major inputs affect job design: (1) organisation design, (2) group design, and (3) the personal characteristics of job holders.

Organisation design is concerned with the larger organisation within which the individual job is the smallest unit. Organisation design is a key part of the larger context surrounding jobs. Core activity systems, structure, measurement systems, human resource systems and culture can have a powerful impact on the way jobs are designed and on people's experiences in jobs. For example, company reward systems can orient employees to particular job behaviours and influence whether people see job performance as fairly rewarded. In general, core activity systems composed of relatively uncertain tasks and low interdependency are likely to support job designs that allow employees flexibility and discretion in performing tasks. Conversely, low-uncertainty work systems are likely to promote standardised job designs requiring routinised task behaviours.[46]

Group design concerns the larger group or department containing the individual job. Like organisation design, group design is an essential part of the job context. Group task structure, goal clarity, composition, performance norms and group functioning serve as inputs to job design. They typically have a more immediate impact on jobs than the larger, organisation-design components. For example, group task structure can determine how individual jobs are grouped together – as in groups that require co-ordination among jobs or in ones comprising

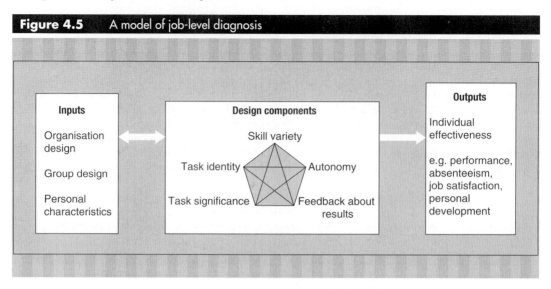

Figure 4.5   A model of job-level diagnosis

collections of independent jobs. Group composition can influence the kinds of people that are available to fill jobs. Group performance norms can affect the kinds of job designs that are considered acceptable, including the level of job-holders' performances. Goal clarity helps members to prioritise work, and group functioning can affect how powerfully the group influences job behaviours. When members maintain close relationships and the group is cohesive, group norms are more likely to be enforced and followed.[47]

Personal characteristics of individuals occupying jobs include their age, education, experience, and skills and abilities. All of these can affect job performance as well as how people react to job designs. Individual needs and expectations can also affect employee job responses. For example, individual differences in growth need – the need for self-direction, learning and personal accomplishment – can determine how much people are motivated and satisfied by jobs with high levels of skill variety, autonomy and feedback about results.[48] Similarly, work motivation can be influenced by people's expectations that they can perform a job well, and that good job performance will result in valued outcomes.[49]

DESIGN COMPONENTS

Figure 4.5 shows that individual jobs have five key dimensions: (1) skill variety, (2) task identity, (3) task significance, (4) autonomy, and (5) feedback about results.[50]

Skill variety identifies the degree to which a job requires a range of activities and abilities to perform the work. Assembly-line jobs, for example, generally have limited skill variety because employees perform a small number of repetitive activities. Most professional jobs, on the other hand, include a great deal of skill variety because people engage in diverse activities and employ several different skills in performing their work.

Task identity measures the degree to which a job requires the completion of a relatively whole, identifiable piece of work. Skilled craftspeople, such as tool-and-die makers and carpenters, generally have jobs with high levels of task identity. They are able to see a job through from beginning to end. Assembly-line jobs involve only a limited piece of work and score low on task identity.

Task significance identifies the degree to which a job has a significant impact on other people's lives. Custodial jobs in a hospital are likely to have more task significance than similar jobs in a toy factory. Hospital custodians are likely to see their jobs as affecting someone else's health and welfare.

Autonomy indicates the degree to which a job provides freedom and discretion in scheduling the work and determining work methods. Assembly-line jobs generally have little autonomy: the work pace is scheduled and rigid, and the workers perform preprogrammed tasks. University teaching positions have more autonomy: academic staff can usually determine how a course is taught, even though they may have limited say over class scheduling.

Feedback about results involves the degree to which a job provides employees with direct and clear information about the effectiveness of task performance. Assembly-line jobs often provide high levels of feedback about results, whereas academics must often contend with indirect and ambiguous feedback about how they are performing in the classroom.

The five job dimensions can be combined into an overall measure of *job enrichment*. Enriched jobs have high levels of skill variety, task identity, task significance, autonomy and feedback about results. They provide opportunities for self-direction, learning and personal accomplishment at work. Many people find enriched jobs internally motivating and satisfying. (Job enrichment is discussed more fully in Chapter 8.)

FITS

The diagnostic model in Figure 4.5 suggests that job design must fit job inputs to produce effective job outputs, such as high quality and quantity of individual performance, low absenteeism and high job satisfaction. Research reveals the following fits between job inputs and job design:

1   Job design should be congruent with the larger organisation and group designs within which the job is embedded.[51] Both the organisation and the group serve as a powerful context for individual jobs or positions. They tend to support and reinforce particular job designs. Highly differentiated and integrated organisations and groups that permit members to self-regulate their behaviour fit enriched jobs. These larger organisations and groups promote autonomy, flexibility and innovation at the individual job level. Conversely, bureaucratic organisations and groups relying on external controls are congruent with job designs that score low on the five key dimensions. Both organisations and groups reinforce standardised, routine jobs. As suggested earlier, congruence across different levels of organisation design promotes integration of the organisation, group and job levels. Whenever the levels do not fit each other, conflict is likely to emerge.

2   Job design should fit the personal characteristics of the job holders if they are to perform effectively and derive satisfaction from work. Generally, enriched jobs fit people with strong growth needs.[52] These people derive satisfaction and accomplishment from performing jobs that involve skill variety, autonomy and feedback about results. Enriched jobs also fit people possessing moderate to high levels of task-relevant skills, abilities and knowledge. Enriched jobs generally require complex information processing and decision making; people must have comparable skills and abilities in order to perform effectively. Jobs scoring low on the five job dimensions generally fit people with rudimentary skills and abilities and with low growth needs. Simpler, more routine jobs require limited skills and experience; they fit better with people who place a low value on opportunities for self-direction and learning. In addition, because people grow through education, training and experience, job design must be monitored and adjusted from time to time.

ANALYSIS

The most positive thing that can occur with award restructuring is that it causes people to become more interested in their jobs. It provides more interesting work with more input from everyone on the way they perform. However, it is also two-sided. It benefits the workers because jobs are more interesting and this will benefit an organisation because it is creating a more productive workforce. Creating the climate for change has set the scene. Establishing the JCC and the working parties, and holding courses such as the RMIT industrial participation workshop and job redesign seminars, have created an air of enthusiasm. Developing a training program is seen as a priority in two areas: personal development and job skills. The training program includes:
•   identifying the skills required for each job and assessing the value of skills
•   upgrading workers' skills, rather than deskilling

- holding developmental courses, such as presentation skills, facilitator skills, supervisory courses, meeting procedures courses, communication skills, team building, job redesign and participation courses
- developing language courses for non-English speakers
- introducing a familiarisation tour of Groote Eylandt, the mine and the township for employees and their families so that families learn about the mine.

Having a plan for restructuring and what needs to be done has given the company employees an idea of how restructuring will work. It has also given employees a goal on which to focus.

Examination of inputs and job design features, and how the two fit, can help explain the causes of these problems and anticipate their remedy. Diagnosis of individual-level inputs answers the following questions:

1   What is the design of the larger organisation within which the individual jobs are embedded?
2   What is the design of the group containing the individual jobs?
3   What are the personal characteristics of job holders?

Diagnosis of individual jobs involves the following job dimensions:

1   How much skill variety is included in the jobs?
2   How much task identity do the jobs contain?
3   How much task significance is involved in the jobs?
4   How much autonomy is included in the jobs?
5   How much feedback about results do the jobs contain?

SUMMARY

The first half of the chapter explains how the entering and contracting processes constitute the initial activities of the OD process. They set the initial parameters for the phases of planned change that follow: diagnosing, planning and implementing change, and evaluating and institutionalising it. Organisational entry involves clarifying the organisational issue or presenting problem, determining the relevant client and selecting an OD practitioner. Developing an OD contract focuses on making a good decision about whether or not to proceed, and allows both the client and the OD practitioner to clarify expectations about how the change process will unfold. Contracting involves setting mutual expectations, negotiating time and resources, and developing ground rules for working together.

The remainder of the chapter gives an explanation of the diagnosis of an organisation, which is a collaborative process involving both managers and consultants in collecting pertinent data, analysing them and drawing conclusions for action planning and intervention. Diagnosis may be aimed at discovering the causes of specific problems, or it may be directed at assessing the organisation or department to find areas for future development. Diagnosis provides the practical understanding that is necessary in order to devise interventions for solving problems and improving organisation effectiveness.

Diagnosis is based on conceptual frameworks about how organisations function. Such diagnostic models serve as road maps in that they identify areas to examine and questions to ask when determining how an organisation or department is operating.

The comprehensive model presented here views organisations as open systems. The organisation serves to co-ordinate the behaviours of its departments. It is open to exchanges with the larger environment and is influenced by external forces. As open systems, organisations are hierarchically ordered – they are composed of groups, which in turn are composed of individual jobs. Organisations also display five key systems properties: (1) inputs, transformations and outputs; (2) boundaries; (3) feedback; (4) equifinality; and (5) alignment.

An organisation-level diagnostic model is described and applied. It consists of environmental inputs, a set of design components called a strategic orientation and a variety of outputs, such as performance, productivity and stakeholder satisfaction. Diagnosis involves understanding each part in the model and then assessing how the elements of the strategic orientation align with each other and with the inputs. Organisation effectiveness is likely to be high when there is good alignment.

Finally, diagnostic models associated with groups and individuals were described and applied. Each of the models derive from the open systems view of organisations developed in this chapter. Diagnostic models include the input, design component and output dimensions necessary for understanding groups and individual jobs.

Group diagnostic models take the organisation's design as the primary input; examine goal clarity, task structure, group composition, performance norms and group functioning as the key design components; and list group performance and member quality of work life as the outputs. As with any open systems model, the alignment of these parts is the key to understanding effectiveness.

At the individual job level, organisation design, group design and characteristics of each job are the salient inputs. Task variety, task significance, task identity, autonomy and feedback work together to produce outputs of work satisfaction and work quality.

ACTIViTiES

ENTERING AND CONTRACTING THE ORGANISATION

Review questions

① What is the process of entering a client system?

② What problems may be encountered when entering a client system? What are your recommendations to resolve these problems?

③ Who has the burden of responsibility for selecting an OD consultant? Can you think of instances where this would be inappropriate?

④ What is the goal of the contracting process and what are the steps involved? Give current business examples of where these processes have been successful and unsuccessful.

Discussion and essay questions

① Describe the process of entering an organisational system from an internal OD practitioner's perspective. How does this differ if it is an external change agent? Use business examples to fully explain your understanding of the ramifications.

② How would you explain the contracting process to someone who had never heard of OD? Why is it important? Contrast this to the contracting process for organisation transformation.

DIAGNOSING ORGANISATIONS

Review questions

① What are the possible symptoms of an organisational problem? What strategies would you use to detect and distinguish between symptoms and problems? Why is this important?

② What is diagnosis? Explain its multifaceted aspects giving examples to reinforce your understanding.

③ What does proper diagnosis involve? How could the process be evaluated?

▷▷

(④) When is it appropriate to seek an organisation-level diagnosis? What are the important aspects to consider when doing an organisation-level diagnosis?

(⑤) Identify the people generally responsible for carrying out planned change efforts. What does 'group-level' diagnosis examine? Why would this be used and under what circumstances?

Discussion and essay questions

(①) Outline some of the key issues in open systems theory. What is your opinion of the theory and can you suggest any modifications? Why/why not?

(②) Describe an effective diagnostic model at the organisation level. Discuss its major inputs, outputs and strategic orientation. What were the anticipated problems and how did they 'prepare' the organisation to prevent a negative impact on the change process?

(③) Discuss the similarities and differences among the organisation, group and individual levels in open systems theory. Identify needs for improvement in this open systems theory.

(④) What are the key components of group-level diagnosis? Discuss how the absence of any one of these components can impact on outputs. What should a change agent do to remedy any inadequacies?

NOTES

1   M. Lacey, 'Internal consulting: perspectives on the process of planned change', *Journal of Organization Change Management*, 8:3 (1995): 75–84; J. Geirland and M. Maniker-Leiter, 'Five lessons for internal organization development consultants', *OD Practitioner*, 27 (1995): 44–8.

2   C. Margerison, 'Consulting activities in organizational change', *Journal of Organizational Change Management*, 1 (1988): 60–7; P. Block, *Flawless Consulting: A Guide to Getting Your Expertise Used* (Austin, TX: Learning Concepts, 1981); R. Harrison, 'Choosing the depth of organizational intervention', *Journal of Applied Behavioural Science*, 6:11 (1970): 182–202.

3   M. Beer, *Organization Change and Development: A Systems View* (Santa Monica, CA: Goodyear, 1980); G. Lippitt and R. Lippitt, *The Consulting Process in Action*, 2nd edn (San Diego: University Associates, 1986).

4   L. Greiner and R. Metzger, *Consulting to Management* (Englewood Cliffs, NJ: Prentice-Hall, 1983): 251–8; Beer, *Organization Change and Development*, op. cit., 81–3.

5   Block, *Flawless Consulting*, op. cit.

6   J. Fordyce and R. Weil, *Managing WITH People*, 2nd edn (Reading, MA: Addison-Wesley, 1979).

7   Beer, *Organization Change and Development*, op. cit.; Fordyce and Weil, *Managing WITH People*, op. cit.

8   G. Lippitt, 'Criteria for selecting, evaluating, and developing consultants', *Training and Development Journal*, 28 (August 1972): 10–15.

9   Greiner and Metzger, *Consulting to Management*, op. cit.

10 Block, *Flawless Consulting*, op. cit.; Beer, *Organization Change and Development*, op. cit.

11 T. Cody, *Management Consulting: A Game Without Chips* (Fitzwilliam, NH: Kennedy and Kennedy, 1986): 108–16; H. Holtz, *How to Succeed as an Independent Consultant*, 2nd edn (New York: John Wiley and Sons, 1988): 145–61.

12 G. Bellman, *The Consultant's Calling* (San Francisco: Jossey-Bass, 1990).

13 M. Weisbord, 'The organization development contract', *Organization Development Practitioner*, 5:11 (1973): 1–4; M. Weisbord, 'The organization contract revisited', *Consultation*, 4 (Winter 1985): 305–15; D. Nadler, *Feedback and Organization Development: Using Data Based Methods* (Reading, MA: Addison-Wesley, 1977): 110–14.

14 Block, *Flawless Consulting*, op. cit.

15 ibid.

16 Lacey, 'Internal consulting', op. cit.

17 D. Nadler, 'Role of models in organizational assessment', in *Organizational Assessment*, eds E. Lawler III, D. Nadler and C. Cammann (New York: John Wiley and Sons, 1980): 119–31; R. Keidel, *Seeing Organizational Patterns* (San Francisco: Berrett-Koehler, 1995); M. Harrison, *Diagnosing Organizations*, 2nd edn (Thousand Oaks, CA: Sage Publications, 1994).

18 D. Coghlan, 'Organization development through interlevel dynamics', *The International Journal of Organizational Analysis*, 2 (1994): 264–79.

19 M. Weisbord, 'Organizational diagnosis: six places to look for trouble with or without a theory', *Group and Organizational Studies*, 1 (1976): 430–7.

20 D. Nadler and M. Tushman, 'A diagnostic model for organization behaviour', in *Perspectives on Behaviour in Organizations*, eds J. Hackman, E. Lawler III and L. Porter (New York: McGraw-Hill, 1977): 85–100.

21 J. Kotter, *Organizational Dynamics: Diagnosis and Intervention* (Reading, MA: Addison-Wesley, 1978).

22 M. Tushman and E. Romanelli, 'Organization evolution: a metamorphosis model of convergence and reorientation', in *Research in Organization Behaviour*, 7, eds L. Cummings and B. Staw (Greenwich, CT: JAI Press, 1985); C. Worley, D. Hitchin and W. Ross, *Integrated Strategic Change: How OD Builds Competitive Advantage* (Reading, MA: Addison-Wesley, 1996).

23 F. Emery and E. Trist, 'The causal texture of organizational environments', *Human Relations*, 18 (1965): 21–32; H. Aldrich, *Organizations and Environments* (Englewood Cliffs, NJ: Prentice-Hall, 1979).

24 M. Porter, *Competitive Strategy* (New York: Free Press, 1980).

25 M. Porter, *Competitive Advantage* (New York: Free Press, 1985); C. Hill and G. Jones, *Strategic Management*, 3rd edn (Boston: Houghton Mifflin, 1995).

26 C. Hofer and D. Schendel, *Strategy Formulation: Analytical Concepts* (St Paul, MN: West Publishing Company, 1978).

27 R. Hoff, 'Inside Intel', *Business Week* (1 June 1992): 86–94.

28 J. Thompson, *Organizations in Action* (New York: McGraw-Hill, 1967); D. Gerwin, 'Relationships between structure and technology', in *Handbook of Organisational Design*, 2, eds P. Nystrom and W. Starbuck (Oxford: Oxford University Press, 1981): 3–38.

29 J. Galbraith, *Organization Design* (Reading, MA: Addison-Wesley, 1977); D. Robey and C. Sales, *Designing Organizations*, 4th edn (Homewood, IL: Irwin, 1994).

30 P. Lawrence and J. Lorsch, *Organization and Environment* (Cambridge: Harvard University Press, 1967).

31 V. Sathe, 'Implications of corporate culture: a manager's guide to acting', *Organizational Dynamics* (Autumn 1983): 5–23; E. Schein, *Organizational Culture and Leadership*, 2nd edn (San Francisco: Jossey-Bass, 1990).

32 S. Cohen, 'Designing effective self-managing work teams', in *Advances in Interdisciplinary Studies of Work Teams*, 1, ed. M. Beyerlein (Greenwich, CT: JAI Press, 1995).

33 J. Hackman and C. Morris, 'Group tasks, group interaction process, and group performance effectiveness: a review and proposed integration', in *Advances in Experimental Social Psychology*, 9, ed. L. Berkowitz (New York: Academic Press, 1975): 45–99; J. Hackman, ed., *Groups That Work (And Those That Don't): Creating Conditions for Effective Teamwork* (San Francisco: Jossey-Bass, 1989).

34 G. Ledford, E. Lawler and S. Mohrman, 'The quality circle and its variations', in *Productivity in Organizations: New Perspectives from Industrial and Organizational Psychology*, eds J. Campbell, R. Campbell and associates (San Francisco: Jossey-Bass, 1988): 255–94.

35 D. Ancona and D. Caldwell, 'Bridging the boundary: external activity and performance in organizational teams', *Administrative Science Quarterly*, 37 (1992): 634–65; Cohen, 'Designing effective self-managing work teams', op. cit.; S. Mohrman, S. Cohen and A. Mohrman, *Designing Team-Based Organizations* (San Francisco: Jossey-Bass, 1995).

36 G. Susman, *Autonomy at Work* (New York: Praeger, 1976); T. Cummings, 'Self-regulating work groups: a socio-technical synthesis', *Academy of Management Review*, 3 (1978): 625–34; J. Slocum and H. Sims, 'A typology for integrating technology, organization, and job design', *Human Relations*, 33 (1980): 193–212.

37 J. Hackman and G. Oldham, *Work Redesign* (Reading, MA: Addison-Wesley, 1980).

38 E. Schein, *Process Consultation*, I–II (Reading, MA: Addison-Wesley, 1987).

39 W. Dyer, *Team Building*, 3rd edn (Reading, MA: Addison-Wesley, 1994).

40 Hackman and Morris, 'Group tasks, group interaction process, and group performance effectiveness', op. cit.; T. Cummings, 'Designing effective work groups', in *Handbook of Organisational Design*, 2, eds P. Nystrom and W. Starbuck (Oxford: Oxford University Press, 1981): 250–71.

41 Cummings, 'Designing effective work groups', op. cit.

42 Susman, *Autonomy at Work*, op. cit.; Cummings, 'Self-regulating work groups', op. cit.; Slocum and Sims, 'A typology for integrating technology, organization, and job design', op. cit.

43 Cummings, 'Self-regulating work groups', op. cit.; Slocum and Sims, 'A typology for integrating technology, organization, and job design', op. cit.

44 ibid.

45 Hackman and Oldham, *Work Redesign*, op. cit.; F. Herzberg, 'One more time: how do you motivate employees?', *Harvard Business Review*, 46 (1968): 53–62.

46 J. Pierce, R. Dunham and R. Blackburn, 'Social systems structure, job design, and growth need strength: a test of a congruence model', *Academy of Management Journal*, 22 (1979): 223–40.

47 Susman, *Autonomy at Work*, op. cit.; Cummings, 'Self-regulating work groups', op. cit.; Slocum and Sims, 'A typology for integrating technology, organization, and job design', op. cit.

48 Hackman and Oldham, *Work Redesign*, op. cit.; Pierce, Dunham and Blackburn, 'Social systems structure, job design, and growth need strength: a test of a congruence model', op. cit.

104 | The process of organisation development

49 E. Lawler III, *Motivation in Work Organizations* (Monterey, CA: Brooks/Cole, 1973).
50 Hackman and Oldham, *Work Redesign*, op. cit.
51 Pierce, Dunham and Blackburn, 'Social systems structure, job design, and growth need strength: a test of a congruence model', op. cit.; Susman, *Autonomy at Work*, op. cit.; Cummings, 'Self-regulating work groups', op. cit.; Slocum and Sims, 'A typology for integrating technology, organization, and job design', op. cit.
52 Hackman and Oldham, *Work Redesign*, op. cit.; Pierce, Dunham and Blackburn, 'Social systems structure, job design, and growth need strength: a test of a congruence model', op. cit.

Online reading

INFOTRAC® COLLEGE EDITION
For additional readings and reviews on entering, contracting and diagnosing, explore **InfoTrac® College Edition**, your online library. Go to **www.infotrac-college.com** and search for any of the InfoTrac key terms listed below:
• Contracting change agents
• Diagnosing organisations
• Open systems
• Strategic orientation
• Design components

INFOTRAC

iNFORMATiON GATHERiNG, PROCESSiNG AND FEEDBACK

Organisation development is vitally dependent on organisation diagnosis: the process of collecting information that will be shared with the client when jointly assessing how the organisation is functioning and determining the best change intervention. The quality of the information gathered is, therefore, a key part of the OD process. But perhaps the most important step in the diagnostic process – and often 'forgotten' – is feeding back diagnostic information to the client organisation. Although the data may have been collected with the client's help, the OD practitioner is usually responsible for organising and presenting the data to the client. Properly analysed and meaningful data can have an impact on organisational change only if organisation members can use the information to devise appropriate action plans. A key objective of the feedback process is to be sure that the client has ownership of the data. This chapter introduces some basic methods of gathering data and emphasises the importance of gaining accurate and honest feedback before proceeding with the design, implementation and evaluation of change interventions.

COLLECTING AND ANALYSING DIAGNOSTIC INFORMATION

Data collection involves gathering information on specific organisational features, such as the inputs, design components and outputs presented in Chapter 4. The process begins by establishing an effective relationship between the OD practitioner and those from whom data will be collected, and then choosing data-collection techniques. Four methods can be used to collect data: questionnaires, interviews, observations and unobtrusive measures. Data analysis organises and examines the information to make clear the underlying causes of an organisational problem or to identify areas for future development. The next step in the cyclical OD process is the feeding back of data to the client system. The overall process of data collection, analysis and feedback is shown in Figure 5.1.

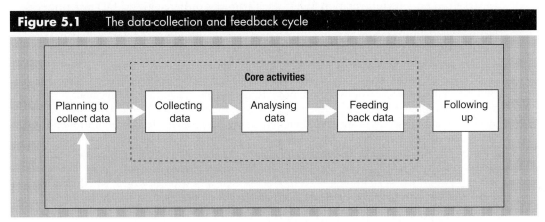

Figure 5.1 The data-collection and feedback cycle

Source: D. Nadler, *Feedback and Organization Development* © 1977 by Addison-Wesley Publishing Company, Inc.: 43.

The diagnostic relationship

In most cases of planned change, OD practitioners play an active role in gathering data from organisation members for diagnostic purposes. For example, they might interview members of a work team about causes of conflict among members, or they might survey employees at a large industrial plant about factors that contribute to poor product quality. Before collecting diagnostic information, practitioners need to establish a relationship with those who will provide and subsequently use it. Because the nature of that relationship affects the quality and usefulness of the data collected, it is vital that OD practitioners provide organisation members with a clear idea of who they are, why the data are being collected, what the data gathering will involve and how the data will be used.[1] Answers to these questions can help to allay people's natural fears that the data might be used against them. Such answers also help to gain members' participation and support, which is essential for developing successful interventions.

Establishing the diagnostic relationship between the consultant and relevant organisation members is similar to forming a contract. It is meant to clarify expectations and to specify the conditions of the relationship. In those cases where members have been directly involved in the entering and contracting process (described in Chapter 4), the diagnostic contract will typically be part of the initial contracting step. However, in situations where data will be collected from members who have not been directly involved in entering and contracting, OD practitioners will need to establish a diagnostic contract as a prelude to diagnosis. The answers to the following questions provide the substance of the diagnostic contract:[2]

1   *Who am I?* The answer to this question introduces the OD practitioner to the organisation, particularly to those members who do not know the consultant, but who will be asked to provide diagnostic data.

2   *Why am I here, and what am I doing?* These answers are aimed at defining the goals of the diagnosis and data-gathering activities. The consultant needs to present the objectives of the action research process and to describe how the diagnostic activities fit into the overall developmental strategy.

3   *Who do I work for?* This answer clarifies who has hired the consultant, whether it be a manager, a group of managers or a group of employees and managers. One way to build trust and support for the diagnosis is to have such persons directly involved in establishing the diagnostic contract. Thus, for example, if the consultant works for a joint labour–management committee, representatives from both sides of that group could help the consultant build the proper relationship with those from whom data will be gathered.

4   *What do I want from you, and why?* Here the consultant needs to specify how much time and effort people will need to give in order to provide valid data, and subsequently to work with these data in solving problems. Because some people may not want to participate in the diagnosis, it is important to specify that such involvement is voluntary.

5   *How will I protect your confidentiality?* This answer addresses member concerns about who will see their responses and in what form. This is especially critical when employees are asked to provide information about their attitudes or perceptions. OD practitioners can either assure confidentiality or state that full participation in the change process requires open information sharing. In the first case, employees are frequently concerned about privacy and the possibility of being punished for their responses. To alleviate concern and to increase the likelihood of getting honest responses, the consultant may need to assure employees of the confidentiality of their information. This may require explicit guarantees of response anonymity. In the second case, full involvement of the participants in their own diagnosis may be a vital ingredient in the change process. If sensitive issues arise, assurances of confidentiality can restrict the OD practitioner and thwart meaningful diagnosis. The consultant is bound to keep confidential the issues that are most critical for the group or organisation to understand.[3] OD practitioners must think carefully about how they want to handle confidentiality issues.

6   *Who will have access to the data?* Respondents typically want to know whether or not they will have access to their data and who else in the organisation will have similar access. The OD practitioner needs to clarify access issues and, in most cases, should agree to provide respondents with their own results. Indeed, the collaborative nature of

diagnosis means that organisation members will work with their own data to discover causes of problems and to devise relevant interventions.

7   *What's in it for you?* This answer is aimed at providing organisation members with a clear assessment of the benefits they can expect from the diagnosis. This usually entails describing the feedback process and how they can use the data to improve the organisation.

8   *Can I be trusted?* The diagnostic relationship ultimately rests on the trust that is established between the consultant and those providing the data. An open and honest exchange of information depends on such trust, and the practitioner should provide ample time and face-to-face contact during the contracting process in order to build this trust. This requires the consultant to actively listen and openly discuss all questions raised by respondents.

Careful attention to establishing the diagnostic relationship helps to promote the three goals of data collection.[4] The first and most immediate objective is to obtain valid information about organisational functioning. Building a data-collection contract can ensure that organisation members provide information that is honest, reliable and complete.

Data collection can also rally energy for constructive organisational change. A good diagnostic relationship helps organisation members to start thinking about issues that concern them, and it creates expectations that change is possible. When members trust the consultant, they are likely to participate in the diagnostic process and to generate energy and commitment for organisational change. In Application 5.1, Harry Onsman identifies why change programs fail and suggests means by which organisations improve their diagnostic process.

APPLiCATiON 5.1

BUSTED: THE MORE THINGS CHANGE

The new field of behavioural economics has found that people don't always behave as rational beings and will often settle for a satisfactory outcome rather than an optimal one. Much of this research is driven by the notion of 'bounded rationality' (developed by the Nobel Prize winner Herbert Simon). This suggests that the decisions people make are constrained by particular factors such as access to limited information, complexity, a reliance on simple 'rules-of-thumb' and other inherent limitations in our thinking. As a result we tend to search for a satisfactory solution (rather than the best) and then promptly stop thinking about the problem. Research is now showing that when we herd together in organisational groups we do much the same thing collectively as we do individually.

Our collective decisions are as 'bounded' as our individual ones. And just as this upset the apple-cart of the 'rational consumer' so beloved of the economists, so it is starting to provide an explanation as to why so many organisational change efforts fail so predictably.

The fact that change management is one of the flops of modern management is well documented. Failures rates for TQM projects, business re-engineering, empowerment programs and mergers and acquisitions are all around the 60–70% mark.

Just as individual decision making is difficult, organisational decision making is complicated by information explosion, time compression, proliferation of choices and rapid changes in the operating environment. But this does not explain why so many change programs fail; it merely suggests the barriers that have to be overcome.

MANAGING LARGE-SCALE CHANGE SUCCESSFULLY

It seems the cognitive restraints built into us all are preventing us from managing large-scale change successfully. In our attempts to handle the complexity of organisational decision making, we tend to use three strategies:

• Factored decision making, which involves breaking big goals into sub-goals until we get a manageable chunk of work.

• Using partial but certain information, which involves reducing the level of complexity by only considering those aspects of the problem about which we have known information.

▷▷

- Employing standard ways of operating, which rely on mental shortcuts based on 'rule-of-thumb' thinking.

Unfortunately, each of these strategies is constrained in ways that lead to sub-optimal outcomes. Hierarchical structures multiply the impact of bounded rationality in that we now have lots of sub-groups deciding things sub-optimally, leading to the well-known situation that everyone in the organisation works really hard but the organisation still fails.

Preferring information that is certain over the challenge of considering ambiguous data leads to ineffective decisions. This factor sits behind the problem of organisations doing what they have always done even when circumstances have changed. Researchers have identified a major risk in organisational decision making. Because we do understand risk management, many organisations have exceptionally effective systems and processes in place to mitigate risks in special areas such as financial investment, safety, key-person loss and environmental risk. The need now is to do something similar in general decision making.

There are some suggestions for how to systematically double-check organisational decisions, including the use of review systems to get a second opinion, obtaining impact statements, using experts, seeking out contrary opinions, doing scenario planning, favouring individual opinions over group reports, using decision post-mortems and encouraging group diversity.

But it's early days, and few organisations have pulled all this together into the sort of cohesive system that we rely on in other areas of operation. We don't fly planes, commission new computer systems or construct large mines without doing proper risk analysis. It's time for the same rigour to be applied to organisational change and renewal projects.

Source: Harry Onsman, 'Busted: the more things change', *Boss Magazine, Australian Financial Review*, 2002.

Critical Thinking Questions: Are you surprised at the failure rate of organisations as stated by the article? Investigate further and determine if you can verify the statement. Also, downsizing has received varying reports of its success or otherwise. What is the current attitude of businesses towards downsizing?

Finally, data collection helps to develop the collaborative relationship necessary for effecting organisational change. The diagnostic stage of action research is probably the first time that most organisation members meet the OD practitioner. It can provide the basis for building a longer-term relationship. The data-collection contract and the subsequent data-gathering and feedback activities provide members with opportunities for seeing the consultant in action and for getting to know her or him personally. If the consultant can show employees that she or he is trustworthy, is willing to work with them and is able to help improve the organisation, then the data-collection process will contribute to the longer-term collaborative relationship so necessary for carrying out organisational changes.

Methods for collecting data

The four major techniques for gathering diagnostic data are questionnaires, interviews, observations and unobtrusive methods. Table 5.1 briefly compares the methods and lists their major advantages and problems. No single method can fully measure the kinds of variables important to OD; each has certain strengths and weaknesses.[5] For example, perceptual measures, such as questionnaires and surveys, are open to self-report biases, such as the respondents' tendency to give socially desirable answers rather than honest opinions. Observations, on the other hand, are susceptible to observer biases, such as seeing what one wants to see rather than what is really there. Because of the biases inherent in any data-collection method, we recommend that more than one method be used when collecting diagnostic data. The data from the different methods can be compared and, if they are consistent, it is likely that the variables are being validly measured. For example, questionnaire measures of job discretion could be supplemented with observations of the number and kinds of decisions that the employees are making. If the two kinds of data support one another, job discretion is probably being accurately assessed. If the two kinds of data conflict, then the validity of the measures should be examined further – perhaps by employing a third method, such as interviews.

Table 5.1	Different methods of data collection	
Method	Major advantages	Major potential problems
Questionnaires	1 Responses can be quantified and easily summarised 2 Easy to use with large samples 3 Relatively inexpensive 4 Can obtain large volume of data	1 Non-empathy 2 Pre-determined questions missing issues 3 Over-interpretation of data 4 Response bias
Interviews	1 Adaptive – allows data collection on a range of possible subjects 2 Source of 'rich' data 3 Empathic 4 Process of interviewing can build rapport	1 Expense 2 Bias in interviewer responses 3 Coding and interpretation difficulties 4 Self-report bias
Observations	1 Collects data on behaviour, rather than reports of behaviour 2 Real time, not retrospective 3 Adaptive	1 Coding and interpretation difficulties 2 Sampling inconsistencies 3 Observer bias and questionable reliability 4 Expense
Unobtrusive measures	1 Non-reactive – no response bias 2 High face validity 3 Easily quantified interviews	1 Access and retrieval difficulties 2 Validity concerns 3 Coding and interpretation difficulties

Source: D. Nadler, *Feedback and Organization Development* ©1977 by Addison-Wesley Publishing Company Inc.: 119.

QUESTIONNAIRES

One of the most efficient ways of collecting data is through questionnaires. Because they typically contain fixed-response questions about various features of an organisation, these paper-and-pencil measures can be administered to large numbers of people simultaneously. Also, they can be analysed quickly, especially with the use of computers, thus permitting quantitative comparison and evaluation. As a result, data can easily be fed back to employees. Numerous basic resource books on survey methodology and questionnaire development are available.[6]

Questionnaires can vary in scope: some measuring selected aspects of organisations and others assessing more comprehensive organisational characteristics. They can also vary in the extent to which they are either standardised or tailored to a specific organisation. Standardised instruments are generally based on an explicit model of organisation, group or individual effectiveness. These questionnaires usually contain a predetermined set of questions that have been developed and refined over time. For example, Table 5.2 presents a standardised questionnaire for measuring the job design dimensions identified in Chapter 6: skill variety, task identity, task significance, autonomy and feedback about results. The questionnaire includes three items or questions for each dimension; a total score for each job dimension is computed simply by adding the responses for the three relevant items and arriving at a total score from 3 (low) to 21 (high). The questionnaire has wide applicability. It has been used in a variety of organisations with employees in both blue-collar and white-collar jobs.

Several research organisations have been highly instrumental in developing and refining surveys. The Australian Council for Educational Research is a prominent example. Two of the council's most popular measures of organisational dimensions are 'Changing your management style' and 'Team climate inventory'.[7] Other examples include 'Organization change: orientation scale' available from the Australian Institute of Management.[8] In fact, so many questionnaires are available that rarely would an organisation have to create a totally new one. However, because every organisation has unique problems and special jargon for referring to them, almost any standardised instrument will need to have organisation-specific additions, modifications or omissions.

Table 5.2   Job design questionnaire

Here are some statements about your job. How much do you agree or disagree with each?

My job:	Strongly disagree	Disagree	Slightly disagree	Undecided	Slightly agree	Agree	Strongly agree
1 provides much variety	[1]	[2]	[3]	[4]	[5]	[6]	[7]
2 permits me to be left on my own to do my own work	[1]	[2]	[3]	[4]	[5]	[6]	[7]
3 is arranged so that I often have the opportunity to see jobs or projects through to completion	[1]	[2]	[3]	[4]	[5]	[6]	[7]
4 provides feedback on how well I am doing as I am working	[1]	[2]	[3]	[4]	[5]	[6]	[7]
5 is relatively significant in our organisation	[1]	[2]	[3]	[4]	[5]	[6]	[7]
6 gives me considerable opportunity for independence and freedom in how I do my work	[1]	[2]	[3]	[4]	[5]	[6]	[7]
7 gives me the opportunity to do a number of different things	[1]	[2]	[3]	[4]	[5]	[6]	[7]
8 provides me with an opportunity to find out how well I am doing	[1]	[2]	[3]	[4]	[5]	[6]	[7]
9 is very significant or important in the broader scheme of things	[1]	[2]	[3]	[4]	[5]	[6]	[7]
10 provides an opportunity for independent thought and action	[1]	[2]	[3]	[4]	[5]	[6]	[7]

Table 5.2	Job design questionnaire *(continued)*							
11	provides me with a great deal of variety at work	[1]	[2]	[3]	[4]	[5]	[6]	[7]
12	is arranged so that I have the opportunity to complete the work I start	[1]	[2]	[3]	[4]	[5]	[6]	[7]
13	provides me with the feeling that I know whether I am performing well or poorly	[1]	[2]	[3]	[4]	[5]	[6]	[7]
14	is arranged so that I have the chance to do a job from the beginning to the end (that is, a chance to do the whole job)	[1]	[2]	[3]	[4]	[5]	[6]	[7]
15	is one where a lot of other people can be affected by how well the work gets done	[1]	[2]	[3]	[4]	[5]	[6]	[7]

Scoring:

Skill variety	questions 1, 7, 11
Task identity	questions 3, 12, 14
Task significance	questions 5, 9, 15
Autonomy	questions 2, 6, 10
Feedback about results	questions 4, 8, 13

Source: reproduced by permission of E. Lawler, S. Mohrman and T. Cummings, Center for Effective Organizations, University of Southern California.

Customised questionnaires, on the other hand, are tailored to the needs of a particular client. Typically, they include questions composed by consultants or organisation members, receive limited use and do not undergo longer-term development. Customised questionnaires can be combined with standardised instruments to provide valid and reliable data focused on the particular issues that face an organisation.

Questionnaires, however, have a number of drawbacks that need to be taken into account when choosing whether to employ them for data collection. First, responses are limited to the questions asked in the instrument. They provide little opportunity to probe for additional data or ask for points of clarification. Second, questionnaires tend to be impersonal, and employees may not be willing to provide honest answers. Third, questionnaires often elicit response biases, such as the tendency to answer questions in a socially acceptable manner. This makes it difficult to draw valid conclusions from employees' self-reports.

INTERVIEWS

A second important measurement technique is the individual or group interview. These probably represent the most widely used technique for collecting data in OD. They permit the interviewer to ask the respondent direct questions, and further probing and clarification is possible as the interview proceeds. This flexibility is invaluable for gaining private views and feelings about the organisation and for exploring new issues that emerge during the interview.

Interviews may be highly structured, resembling questionnaires, or highly unstructured, starting with general questions that allow the respondent to lead the way. Structured interviews typically derive from a conceptual model of organisation functioning; the model guides the types of questions that are asked. For example, a structured interview based on the organisation-level design components identified in Chapter 4 would ask managers specific questions about organisation structure, measurement systems, human resource systems and organisation culture.

Unstructured interviews are more general and include broad questions about organisational functioning, such as:

- What are the major goals or objectives of the organisation or department?
- How does the organisation currently perform with respect to these purposes?
- What are the strengths and weaknesses of the organisation or department?
- What barriers stand in the way of good performance?

Although interviewing typically involves one-to-one interaction between an OD practitioner and an employee, it can be carried out in a group context. Group interviews save time and allow people to build on others' responses. A major drawback, however, is that group settings may inhibit some people from responding freely.

A popular type of group interview is the focus group or sensing meeting.[9] These are unstructured meetings conducted by a manager or a consultant. A small group of 10 to 15 employees is selected, representing either a cross-section of functional areas and hierarchical levels or a homogeneous grouping, such as minorities or engineers. Group discussion is frequently started by asking general questions about organisational features and functioning, an intervention's progress or current performance. Group members are then encouraged to discuss their answers in some depth. Consequently, focus groups and sensing meetings are an economical way of obtaining interview data and are especially effective in understanding particular issues in some depth. The richness and validity of that information will depend on the extent to which the manager or consultant develops a trust relationship with the group and listens to member opinions.

Another popular unstructured group interview involves assessing the current state of an intact work group. The manager or consultant generally directs a question to the group, calling its attention to some part of group functioning. For example, group members may be asked how they feel the group is progressing on its stated task. The group might respond and then come up with its own series of questions about barriers to task performance. This unstructured interview is a fast, simple way of collecting data about group behaviour. It allows members to discuss issues of immediate concern and to engage actively in the questioning-and-answering process. This technique is, however, limited to relatively small groups and to settings where there is trust among employees and managers, and a commitment to assessing group processes.

Interviews are an effective method of collecting data in OD. They are adaptive, allowing the interviewer to modify questions and to probe emergent issues during the interview process. They also permit the interviewer to develop an empathetic relationship with employees, frequently resulting in frank disclosure of pertinent information. Such interviews can only be successful if both parties are prepared to listen. Application 5.2 discusses two forms of listening that can test their understanding of what is being communicated.

APPLICATION 5.2

SHUT UP AND LISTEN

Sneaky listening is what corporations do best. They have all manner of sophisticated ways to find out what consumers want: market research, surveys, polling and interactive websites. Unfortunately, while they may like what they 'hear' there's a good chance it is wrong. According to American futurist Steven Ames, public listening is where the action is, but finding a management team with the courage to engage on that level is extremely rare.

He came to community planning from the public sector in the US, where he worked as a futurist and strategic planner. While both community planning – or 'visioning' as it is called in the US – and the public sector may seem a world away from corporate life, Ames says companies can learn a lot from the work done on cities and towns where corporate, social and environmental elements have to be integrated.

…

He cites Rio Tinto's backing away from the Jabiluka uranium mine as a recent example of the impact of stakeholders on corporations. 'Here's a company that has read the community sentiment about this and chosen not to proceed. [Royal] Dutch Shell would be another example. In this tightly knit, media-lit world it's no longer possible for corporations to separate themselves from the community.'

…

Prove it

In Australia's pre-election climate, 'listening' has taken on political overtones. Everyone from the prime minister to pollsters and shock jocks are 'listening' to the community/mainstream/average Australians. However, as Ames points out, listening shouldn't be confused with hearing, and the most useful advice may come from those normally excluded from the discussion.

'There are two kinds of listening that I use,' he says. The first is the most sophisticated, and that is private listening. This is the form most corporations are quite good at. You can do this through polling, surveys and marketing research. It's very useful but it also has a potential downside.' That downside is the increasing tendency for organisations to ask the questions in ways that guarantee they get the answers they want, as opposed to the answers that may reflect the truth. 'This private listening can easily be skewed when an organisation lets their own agenda inform the research,' Ames says. 'Genuine intent is vital. Most organisations fall into the trap of using this approach to gain strategic advantage, to find out who's going to buy what, etc. That is, they don't have a genuine intent on discovering what the stakeholders think and feel about certain things. They miss out on learning things that would be advantageous for them.'

The second kind of listening is what Ames calls 'public listening'. This too can have its pitfalls. 'Public listening is where we get groups of people together – and they're often groups of very angry people – and we ask them to have their say,' he says. 'This can be frightening, especially if the facilitator is not comfortable with anger.' While public listening can contain the alchemical ingredients for gold, it also demands those in charge – be it politicians or executives – surrender control. 'This is the kind of listening corporations are not good at and they don't do it very often. It can be particularly frightening for people used to the old command and control structure. To be effective, an organisation needs to be open about what the outcome will be. Trying to impose control over what gets said and how it gets said is a disaster.'

This kind of listening is increasingly important. 'The world is changing and either they're hip to that or they soon will be,' Ames says. 'The paradigm has changed and new technologies guarantee that companies that don't listen to stakeholders won't be viable in the long term.'

Source: Julie Macken, 'Shut up and listen', *Boss Magazine, Australian Financial Review*, 2002.

Critical Thinking Questions: What do you understand to be the difference between 'listening' and 'hearing'? Is Ames's theory just a new fad, a reinvention of previous constructs or a revolutionary approach to collecting data? Use examples where appropriate to support your response.

A major drawback of interviews is the amount of time required to conduct and analyse them. They can consume a great deal of time, especially if the interviewers take full advantage of the opportunity to hear respondents out, and change their questions accordingly. Personal biases can also distort the data. Like questionnaires, interviews are subject to the self-report biases of respondents and, perhaps more importantly, to the biases of the interviewer. For example, the nature of the questions and the interactions between the interviewer and the respondent may discourage or encourage certain kinds of responses. These problems suggest that interviewing takes considerable skill to gather valid data. Interviewers must be able to understand their own biases, to listen and establish empathy with respondents and to change questions to pursue issues that develop during the course of the interview.

OBSERVATIONS

One of the more direct ways of collecting data is simply to observe organisational behaviours in their functional settings. The OD practitioner may do this by casually walking through a work area and looking around or by simply counting the occurrences of specific kinds of behaviours (for example, the number of times a phone call is answered after three rings in a service department). Observation can range from complete participant observation, in which the OD practitioner becomes a member of the group under study, to more detached observation, in which the observer is clearly not part of the group or situation itself and may use film, videotape or other methods to record behaviours.

Observations have a number of advantages. They are free of the biases inherent in self-report data. They put the practitioner directly in touch with the behaviours in question, without having to rely on others' perceptions. Observations also involve real-time data, describing behaviour that is occurring in the present rather than the past. This avoids the distortions that invariably arise when people are asked to recollect their behaviours. Finally, observations are adaptive in that the consultant can modify what she or he is observing according to the circumstances.

Among the problems with observations are difficulties in interpreting the meaning that underlies the observations. Practitioners may need to code the observations to make sense of them, and this can be expensive, take time and introduce bias into the data. Because the observer is the data-collection instrument, personal bias and subjectivity can distort data unless the observer is trained and skilled in knowing what to look for, how to observe, where and when to observe, and how to record data systematically. Another problem concerns sampling. Observers must not only decide which people to observe but also choose the time periods, territory and events in which observations will be made. Failure to attend to these sampling issues can result in highly biased samples of observational data.

When used correctly, observations provide insightful data about organisation and group functioning, intervention success and performance. For example, observations are particularly helpful in diagnosing the interpersonal relations of members of work groups. As discussed in Chapter 4, interpersonal relations are a key component of work groups; observing member interactions in a group setting can provide direct information about the nature of those relationships.

UNOBTRUSIVE MEASURES

Unobtrusive data are not collected directly from respondents but from secondary sources, such as company records and archives. These data are generally available in organisations and include records of absenteeism or tardiness, grievances, quantity and quality of production or service, financial performance and correspondence with key customers, suppliers or governmental agencies.

Unobtrusive measures are especially helpful in diagnosing the organisation, group and individual outputs presented in Chapter 4. At the organisation level, for example, market share and return on investment can usually be obtained from company reports. Similarly, organisations typically measure the quantity and quality of the outputs of work groups and individual employees. Unobtrusive measures can also help to diagnose organisation-level design components – structure, work systems, control systems and human resource systems. A company's organisation chart, for example, can provide useful information about organisation structure. Information about control systems can usually be obtained by examining the firm's management information system, operating procedures and accounting practices. Data about human resource systems are often included in a company's personnel manual.

Unobtrusive measures provide a relatively objective view of organisational functioning. They are free from respondent and consultant biases and are perceived by many organisation members as being real. Moreover, unobtrusive measures tend to be quantified and reported at periodic intervals, permitting statistical analysis of behaviours occurring over time. Examination of monthly absenteeism rates, for example, might reveal trends in employee withdrawal behaviour.

The major problems with unobtrusive measures occur when collecting such information and drawing valid conclusions from it. Company records may not include data in a form that is usable by the consultant. If, for example, individual performance data are needed, the consultant may find that many firms only record production information at the group or departmental level. Unobtrusive data may also have their own built-in biases. Changes in accounting procedures and in methods of recording data are common in organisations; such changes can affect company records independently of what is actually happening in the organisation. For example, observed changes in productivity over time might be caused by modifications in methods of recording production, rather than by actual changes in organisational functioning.

Despite these drawbacks, unobtrusive data serve as a valuable adjunct to other diagnostic measures, such as interviews and questionnaires. Archival data can be used in preliminary diagnosis, indicating those organisational units that have absenteeism, grievance or production problems. Interviews can then be conducted or observations made in those units to discover the underlying causes of the problems. Conversely, unobtrusive data can be used to cross-check other forms of information. For example, if questionnaires reveal that employees in a department are dissatisfied with their jobs, company records might show whether that discontent is manifested in heightened withdrawal behaviours, in lowered quality of work or in similar counterproductive behaviours.

Application 5.3 presents one of many innovative tools to predict future organisational needs. In this instance it is discussing human resource management but it could equally apply to other functional areas of an organisation.

APPLiCATiON 5.3

SOFTWARE REPLACES CRYSTAL BALL

The discipline of workforce planning has never been a more complex challenge for human resources (HR) executives, nor has it been such a critical element in the formulation of corporate strategy. Many companies find the task of accurately predicting their future labour needs so daunting that they simply ignore it or, at best, approach workforce planning on an ad hoc, short-term basis.

But such companies should be encouraged by the recent emergence of innovative workforce planning tools that promise to substantially reduce the complexity of the discipline. HR professionals agree that organisations that continue to regard workforce planning as either too hard or unnecessary are taking a large commercial risk.

…
A report last year by the Australian National Audit Office into workforce planning in the public sector said almost a quarter of all public service employees will be eligible for retirement by 2010, and that situation will worsen within the next 10 years. HR professionals say the position in the private sector is similar, and add that the very fact the audit office conducted a survey into workforce planning in the public service shows how critical the labour market situation has become.

[Rilla Moore, executive general manager, Stocklands] says Australian organisations are only just 'waking up' to workforce planning. 'We have been reading about it for the past five years, but people haven' known how to do it properly. It's becoming a very complex challenge.' That challenge arises from a dearth of talent available, an ageing workforce and the dramatic difference in work attitudes between baby boomers and generations X and Y – the latter generations being comfortable with 'shopping around' for an employer.

…
Moore points to a young Australian company called Aruspex as leading the field in the development of new workforce planning tools. Formed in December 2003 by two HR executives, Tess Walton and Stacey Chapman, Aruspex has produced a new software program, CAPTure, designed to allow organisations to examine their workforce needs up to a decade into the future. Moore says: 'It's an exciting piece of software. It removes the need to do manual scenario planning, which is quite a nightmare.'

CAPTure enables HR executives and chief executives to make quantitative and qualitative decisions about their future workforce. Walton says: 'It used to be the case that workforce planning

▷▷

was just maths, just about numbers. But you can't just talk about workforce planning by saying, 'I'm going to need X number of people to finish this project'. You need to have a look at your own organisational culture, to think about what types of people available in the market are right for you to fulfil your goals. A lot of money is spent on workforce programs, but it's fired into darkness because companies don't have an accurate, overarching view of exactly which types of employees they should be going after.'

Source: Simon Lloyd, 'Software replaces crystal ball', *Business Review Weekly*, 20/4/2006.

Critical Thinking Questions: Do you think that the emergence of China and India as new economic powers will tighten the global demand for skilled labour, creating an even more critical shortage in Australia? Is there a role in change management for an effective process for forecasting and evaluating current and future workforce capacity? What type of programs should be implemented to ensure that their organisations can attract and retain a quality workforce?

Sampling

Before discussing how to analyse data, the issue of sampling needs to be emphasised. Application of the different data-collection techniques invariably raises the following questions: 'How many people should be interviewed and who should they be?' 'What events should be observed and how many?' and 'How many records should be inspected and which ones?'[10]

In many OD cases, sampling is not an issue. Practitioners simply collect interview or questionnaire data from all members of the organisation or department in question, and so do not have to worry about whether the information is representative of the organisation or unit because all members of the population are included in the sample.

Sampling becomes an issue in OD, however, when data are collected from selected members, behaviours or records. This is often the case when diagnosing organisation-level issues or large systems. In these cases, it may be important to ensure that the sample of people, behaviours or records adequately represents the characteristics of the total population. For example, a sample of 50 employees might be used to assess the perceptions of all 300 members of a department, or a sample of production data might be used to evaluate the total production of a work group. OD practitioners often find that it is more economical and quicker to gather a sampling of diagnostic data than to collect all possible information. If done correctly, the sample can provide useful and valid information about the entire organisation or unit.

Sampling design involves considerable technical detail, and consultants may need to become familiar with basic references in this area or to obtain professional help.[11] The first issue to address is *sample size*, or how many people, events or records are needed to carry out the diagnosis or evaluation. This question has no simple answer: the necessary sample size is a function of size of the population, the confidence desired in the quality of the data and the resources (money and time) available for data collection.

First, the larger the population (for example, the number of organisation members or total number of work outcomes) or the more complex the client system (for example, the number of salary levels that must be sampled or the number of different functions), the more difficult it is to establish a 'right' sample size. As the population increases in size and complexity, the less meaning one can attach to simple measures, such as an overall average score on a questionnaire item. Because the population is composed of such different types of people or events, more data are needed to ensure an accurate representation of the potentially different subgroups. Second, the larger the proportion of the population that is selected, the more confidence one can have about the quality of the sample. If the diagnosis concerns an issue of great importance to the organisation, then extreme confidence may be needed, indicative of a larger sample size. Third, limited resources constrain sample size. If resources are limited but the required confidence is high, then questionnaires will be preferred to interviews because more information can be collected per member per dollar.

The second issue to address is sample selection. Probably the most common approach to sampling diagnostic data in OD is a simple random sample in which each member, behaviour or record has an equal chance of being selected. For example, assume that an OD practitioner would like to randomly select 50 people out of the 300 employees at a manufacturing plant. Using a complete list of all 300 employees, the consultant can generate a random sample in one of two ways. The first method would be to use a random number table in the back of almost any statistics text; the consultant would pick out the employees corresponding to the first 50 numbers under 300 beginning anywhere in the table. The second method would be to pick every sixth name (300 ÷ 50 = 6) starting anywhere in the list.

If the population is complex, or many subgroups need to be represented in the sample, a *stratified sample* may be more appropriate than a random one. In a stratified sample, the population of members, events or records is segregated into a number of mutually exclusive subpopulations. Then, a random sample is taken from each subpopulation. For example, members of an organisation might be divided into three groups: managers, white-collar workers and blue-collar workers. A random sample of members, behaviours or records could be selected from each grouping in order to make diagnostic conclusions about each of the groups.

Adequate sampling is critical when gathering valid diagnostic data, and the OD literature has tended to pay little attention to this issue. OD practitioners should gain rudimentary knowledge in this area and use professional help if necessary.

Techniques for analysing data

Data analysis techniques fall into two broad classes: qualitative and quantitative. Qualitative techniques are generally easier to use because they do not rely on numerical data. This also makes them easier to understand and interpret. Quantitative techniques, on the other hand, can provide more accurate readings of the organisational problem.

QUALITATIVE TOOLS

Of the several methods for summarising diagnostic data in qualitative terms, two of the most important are content analysis and force-field analysis.

Content analysis

A popular technique for assessing qualitative data, especially interview data, is content analysis. Content analysis attempts to summarise comments into meaningful categories. When done well, a content analysis can reduce hundreds of interview comments into a few themes that effectively summarise the issues or attitudes of a group of respondents. The process of content analysis can be quite formal, and specialised references describe this technique in detail.[12] In general, however, the process can be broken down into three major steps. First, responses to a particular question are read to gain familiarity with the range of comments made and to assess whether some answers are occurring over and over again. Second, based on this sampling of comments, themes are generated that capture these recurring comments. Themes consolidate different responses that say essentially the same thing. For example, in answering the question 'What do you like most about your job?' different respondents might list their co-workers, their supervisors, the new machinery and a good supply of tools. The first two answers concern the social aspects of work, and the second two address the resources available for doing the work. Third, the respondents' answers to a question are then placed into one of the categories. The categories with the most responses represent those themes that are most often mentioned.

Force-field analysis

A second method of analysing qualitative data in OD derives from Kurt Lewin's three-step model of change. Called 'force-field analysis', this method organises information pertaining to organisational change into two major categories: forces for change and forces for maintaining the status quo or resisting change.[13] Using data collected through interviews, observation or unobtrusive measures, the first step in conducting a force-field analysis is to develop a list of all the forces that promote change and all those that resist change. Then, based on either personal belief or perhaps on input from several members of the client organisation, a determination is made of which of the positive and which of the negative forces are most powerful. One can either rank the order or rate the strength of the different forces.

Figure 5.2 illustrates a force-field analysis of the performance of a work group. The arrows represent the forces, and the length of the arrows corresponds to the strength of the forces. The information could have been collected in a group interview in which members were asked to list those factors maintaining the current level of group performance and those factors pushing for a higher level. Members could also have been asked to judge the strength of each force, with the average judgement shown by the length of the arrows.

This analysis reveals two strong forces pushing for higher performance: pressures from the supervisor of the group and competition from other work groups performing similar work. These forces for change are offset by two strong forces for maintaining the status quo: group norms supporting present levels of performance and well-learned skills that are resistant to change. According to Lewin, efforts to change to a higher level of group performance, shown by the darker band in Figure 5.2, should focus on reducing the forces that maintain the status quo. This might entail changing the group's performance norms and helping members to learn new skills. The reduction of forces maintaining the status quo is likely to result in organisational change with little of the tension or conflict that typically accompanies change caused by increasing the forces for change.

QUANTITATIVE TOOLS

Methods for analysing quantitative data range from simple descriptive statistics of items or scales from standard instruments to more sophisticated, multivariate analysis of the underlying instrument properties and relationships among measured variables.[14] The most common quantitative tools are means, standard deviations, frequency distributions, scattergrams, correlation coefficients and

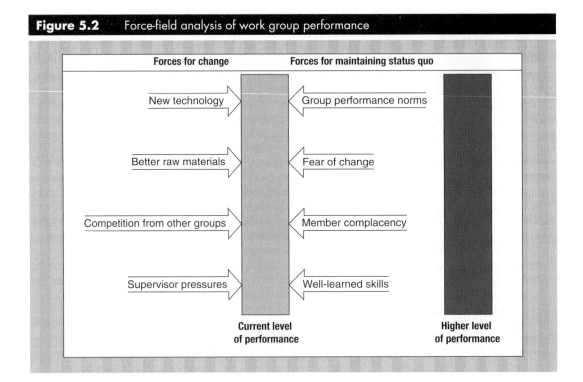

Figure 5.2 Force-field analysis of work group performance

Forces for change | Forces for maintaining status quo

New technology → ← Group performance norms

Better raw materials → ← Fear of change

Competition from other groups → ← Member complacency

Supervisor pressures → ← Well-learned skills

Current level of performance   **Higher level of performance**

difference tests. These measures are routinely produced by most statistical computer software packages. Therefore, mathematical calculations are not discussed here.

Means, standard deviations and frequency distributions

One of the most economical and straightforward ways of summarising quantitative data is to compute a mean and standard deviation for each item or variable measured. These represent the respondents' average score and the spread or variability of the responses, respectively. These two numbers can easily be compared across different measures or subgroups. For example, Table 5.3 shows the means and standard deviations for six questions asked of 100 employees about the value of different kinds of organisational rewards. Based on the five-point scale ranging from one (very low value) to five (very high value), the data suggest that challenging work and respect from peers are the two most highly valued rewards. Monetary rewards, such as pay and fringe benefits, are not as highly valued.

Table 5.3	Descriptive statistics of value of organisational rewards	
Organisational rewards	Mean	Standard deviation
Challenging work	4.6	0.76
Respect from peers	4.4	0.81
Pay	4.0	0.71
Praise from supervisor	4.0	1.55
Promotion	3.3	0.95
Fringe benefits	2.7	1.14

Number of respondents = 100
1 = very low value; 5 = very high value

Table 5.4	Frequency distribution of responses to 'Pay' and 'Praise from supervisor' items	
Pay (mean = 4.0) response	Number checking each response	Graph*
1 Very low value	0	
2 Low value	0	
3 Moderate value	25	XXXXX
4 High value	50	XXXXXXXXXX
5 Very high value	25	XXXXX
Praise from supervisor (mean = 4.0) response	Number checking each response	Graph*
1 Very low value	15	XXX
2 Low value	10	XX
3 Moderate value	0	
4 High value	10	XX
5 Very high value	65	XXXXXXXXXXXXX

*Each X = 5 people checking the response

But the mean can be a misleading statistic. It only describes the average value and so provides no information on the distribution of the responses. Different patterns of responses can produce the same mean score. Therefore, it is important to use the standard deviation along with the frequency distribution to gain a clearer understanding of the data. The frequency distribution is a graphical method for displaying data that shows the number of times a particular response was given. For example, the data in Table 5.3 suggest that both pay and praise from the supervisor are equally valued with a mean of 4.0. However, the standard deviations for these two measures are very different at 0.71 and 1.55, respectively. Table 5.4 shows the frequency distributions of the responses to the questions about pay and praise from the supervisor. Employees' responses to the value of pay are distributed towards the higher end of the scale, with no one rating it as being of low or very low value. In contrast, responses about the value of praise from the supervisor fall into two distinct groupings: 25 employees felt that supervisor praise has a low or very low value, whereas 75 people rated it high or very high. Although both rewards have the same mean value, their standard deviations and frequency distributions suggest different interpretations of the data.

In general, when the standard deviation for a set of data is high, there is considerable disagreement over the issue posed by the question. If the standard deviation is small, the data are similar on a particular measure. In the example described above, there is disagreement over the value of supervisory praise (some people think it is important but others do not), but there is fairly good agreement that pay is a reward with high value.

Scattergrams and correlation coefficients

In addition to describing data, quantitative techniques also permit OD consultants to make inferences about the relationships between variables. Scattergrams and correlation coefficients are measures of the strength of a relationship between two variables. For example, suppose the problem being faced by an organisation is increased conflict between the Manufacturing and the Engineering Design departments. During the data-collection phase, information about the number of conflicts and change orders per month over the past year is collected. The data are shown in Table 5.5 and plotted in a scattergram in Figure 5.3.

A scattergram is a diagram that visually displays the relationship between two variables. It is constructed by locating each case (person or event) at the intersection of its value for each of the two variables being compared. For example, in the month of August, there were eight change orders and three conflicts, and their intersection is shown on Figure 5.3 as an X.

Table 5.5	Relationship between change orders and conflicts	
Month	Number of change orders	Number of conflicts
April	5	2
May	12	4
June	14	3
July	6	2
August	8	3
September	20	5
October	10	2
November	2	1
December	15	4
January	8	3
February	18	4
March	10	5

Figure 5.3 ∘ Scattergram of change order versus conflict

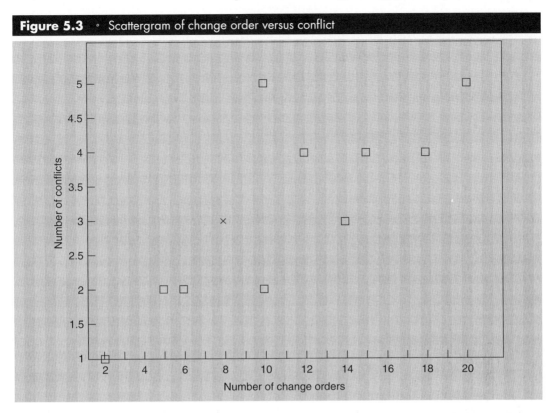

Three basic patterns can emerge from a scattergram, as shown in Figure 5.4. The first pattern is called a positive relationship, because as the values of *x* increase so do the values of *y*. The second pattern is called a negative relationship, because as the values of *x* increase the values of *y* decrease. Finally, there is the 'shotgun' pattern. Here, no relationship between the two variables is apparent. In the example shown in Figure 5.3, an apparently strong positive relationship exists between the number of change orders and the number of conflicts between the Engineering Design and the Manufacturing departments. This suggests that change orders may contribute to the observed conflict between the two departments.

The correlation coefficient is simply a number that summarises data in a scattergram. Its value ranges between +1.0 and −1.0. A correlation coefficient of +1.0 means that there is a perfect, positive relationship between two variables, whereas a correlation of −1.0 signifies a perfectly negative relationship. A correlation of 0 implies a 'shotgun' scattergram where there is no relationship between two variables.

Figure 5.4 Basic scattergram patterns ∘

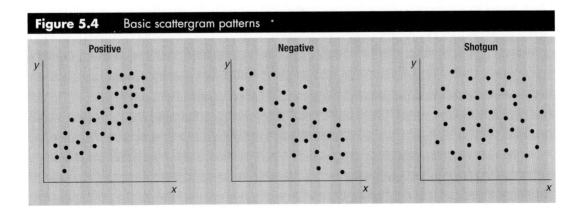

Difference tests

The final technique for analysing quantitative data is the difference test. It can be used to compare a sample group against some standard or norm to determine whether the group is above or below this standard. It can also be used to determine whether two samples are significantly different from each other. In the first case, such comparisons provide a broader context for understanding the meaning of diagnostic data. They serve as a basis for determining 'how good is good or how bad is bad'.[15] Many standardised questionnaires have standardised scores based on the responses of large groups of people. It is critical, however, to choose a comparison group that is similar to the organisation being diagnosed. For example, if 100 engineers take a standardised attitude survey, it makes little sense to compare their scores against standard scores representing married males from across the country. On the other hand, if industry-specific data are available, a comparison of sales per employee (as a measure of productivity) against the industry average would be valid and useful.

The second use of difference tests involves assessing whether two (or more) groups differ from one another on a particular variable, such as job satisfaction or absenteeism. For example, job satisfaction differences between an accounting department and a sales department can be determined with this tool. Given that each group took the same questionnaire, their means and standard deviations can be used to compute a difference score (t-score or z-score) indicating whether the two groups are statistically different. The larger the difference score relative to the sample size and standard deviation for each group, the more likely that one group is more satisfied than the other.

Difference tests can also be used to determine whether a group has changed its score on job satisfaction or some other variable over time. The same questionnaire can be given to the same group at two points in time. Based on the group's means and standard deviations at each point in time, a difference score can be calculated. The larger the score, the more likely that the group actually changed its job satisfaction level.

The calculation of difference scores can be very helpful for diagnosis but requires the OD practitioner to make certain assumptions about how the data were collected. These assumptions are discussed in most standard statistical texts, and OD practitioners should consult them before calculating difference scores for the purposes of diagnosis or evaluation.[16]

FEEDING BACK DIAGNOSTIC INFORMATION

As shown in Figure 5.5, the success of data feedback depends largely on its ability to arouse organisational action and to direct energy towards organisational problem solving. Whether or not feedback helps to energise the organisation depends on the content of the feedback data and on the process by which they are fed back to organisation members.

Determining the content of the feedback

Large amounts of data are collected in the course of diagnosing the organisation. In fact, there is often more information than the client needs or could interpret in a realistic period of time. If too many data are fed back, the client may decide that changing is impossible. Therefore, OD practitioners need to summarise the data in ways that are useful for clients, so that they can both understand the information and draw action implications from it.

Several characteristics of effective feedback data have been described in the literature.[17] They include the following nine properties:

1   *Relevant.* Organisation members are more likely to use feedback data for problem solving if they find the information meaningful. Including managers and employees in the initial data-collection activities can increase the relevance of the data.

2   *Understandable.* Data must be presented to organisation members in a form that is readily interpreted. Statistical data, for example, can be made understandable through the use of graphs and charts.

Figure 5.5   Possible effects of feedback

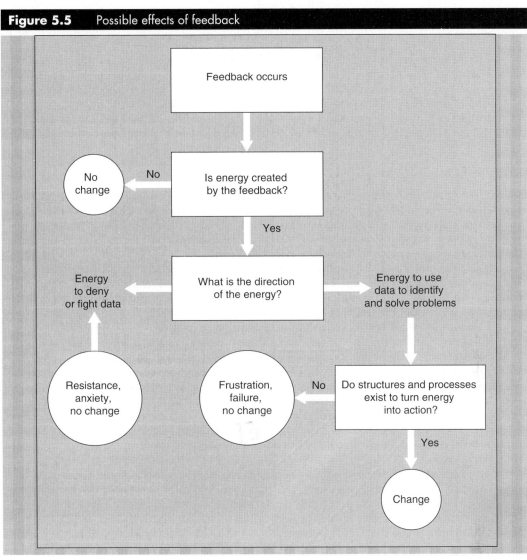

Source: D. Nadler, *Feedback and Organization Development*, p. 146, © 1977 by Addison-Wesley
Publishing Company, Inc.

3   *Descriptive.* Feedback data need to be linked to real organisational behaviours if they
    are to arouse and direct energy. The use of examples and detailed illustrations can help
    employees gain a better feel for the data.

4   *Verifiable.* Feedback data should be valid and accurate if they are to guide action. Thus,
    the information should allow organisation members to verify whether the findings really
    describe the organisation. For example, questionnaire data might include information
    about the sample of respondents as well as frequency distributions for each item or
    measure. This kind of information can help members verify whether the feedback data
    accurately represent organisational events or attitudes.

5   *Timely.* Data should be fed back to members as quickly as possible after being collected
    and analysed. This will help ensure that the information is still valid and is linked to
    members' motivations to examine it.

6   *Limited.* Because people can easily become overloaded with too much information, feedback
    data should be limited to what employees can realistically process at any one time.

7   *Significant.* Feedback should be limited to those problems that organisation members can do something about. This will help energise them and direct their efforts towards realistic changes.

8   *Comparative.* Feedback data without some benchmark as a reference can be ambiguous. Whenever possible, data from comparative groups should be provided in order to give organisation members a better idea of how their group fits into a broader context.

9   *Unfinalised.* Feedback is primarily a stimulus for action and should, therefore, spur further diagnosis and problem solving. Members should be encouraged, for example, to use the data as a starting point for more in-depth discussion of organisational issues.

Characteristics of the feedback process

In addition to providing effective feedback data, it is equally important to attend to the process by which that information is fed back to people. Typically, data are provided to organisation members in a meeting or series of meetings. Feedback meetings provide a forum for discussing the data, drawing relevant conclusions and devising preliminary action plans. Because the data might include sensitive material and evaluations of organisation members' behaviours, people may come to the meeting with considerable anxiety and fear about receiving the feedback. This anxiety can result in defensive behaviours aimed at denying the information or providing rationales. More positively, people can be stimulated by the feedback and the hope that desired changes will result from the feedback meeting.

Because people are likely to come to feedback meetings with anxiety, fear and hope, OD practitioners need to manage the feedback process so that constructive discussion and problem solving will occur. The most important objective of the feedback process is to ensure that organisation members own the data. Ownership is the opposite of resistance to change and refers to people's willingness to take responsibility for the data, its meaning and the consequences of using the data to devise a change strategy.[18] If the feedback session results in organisation members rejecting the data as invalid or useless, then the motivation to change is lost and members will have difficulty in engaging in a meaningful process of change.

Ownership of the feedback data is facilitated by the following five features of successful feedback processes:[19]

1   *Motivation to work with the data.* People need to feel that working on the feedback data will have beneficial outcomes. This may require explicit sanction and support from powerful groups so that people feel free to raise issues and identify concerns during the feedback sessions. If they have little motivation to work with the data or feel that there is little chance to use the data for change, the information will not be owned by the client system.

2   *Structure for the meeting.* Feedback meetings need some structure, or they may degenerate into chaos or aimless discussion. An agenda or outline and a discussion leader can usually provide the necessary direction. If the meeting is not kept on track, especially when the data are negative, ownership can be lost in conversations that become too general. When this happens, the energy gained from dealing directly with the problem is lost.

3   *Appropriate membership.* Generally, people who have common problems and can benefit from working together should be included in the feedback meeting. This may involve a fully intact work team, or groups made up of members from different functional areas or hierarchical levels. Without proper representation in the meeting, ownership of the data is lost because the participants cannot address the problem(s) suggested by the feedback.

4   *Appropriate power.* It is important to clarify the power possessed by the group. Members need to know to which issues they can make necessary changes, on which they can only recommend changes and on which they have no control. Unless there are clear boundaries, members are likely to have some hesitation about using the feedback data for generating action plans. Moreover, if the group has no power to make changes, the feedback meeting will become an empty exercise rather than a real problem-solving session. Without the power to address change, there will be little ownership of the data.

5   *Process help.* People in feedback meetings need help to work together as a group. When the data are negative, there is a natural tendency to resist the implications, deflect the conversation onto safer subjects and the like. An OD practitioner with group process skills can help members stay focused on the subject and improve feedback discussion, problem solving and ownership.

When combined with effective feedback data, these features of successful feedback meetings enhance member ownership of the data. They help to ensure that organisation members fully discuss the implications of the diagnostic information and that their conclusions are directed towards organisational changes that are relevant and feasible.

Survey feedback

Survey feedback is a process of collecting data from an organisation or department through the use of a questionnaire or survey. The data are analysed, fed back to organisation members and used by them to diagnose the organisation and to develop interventions to improve it. Because questionnaires are often used in organisation diagnosis, particularly in OD efforts that involve large numbers of participants, survey feedback is discussed here as a special case of data feedback. It is both an integral part of diagnostic feedback and a powerful intervention in its own right.

As discussed in Chapter 1, survey feedback is a major technique in the history and development of OD. Originally, this intervention included only data from questionnaires about members' attitudes. However, attitudinal data can be supplemented with interview data and more objective measures, such as productivity, turnover and absenteeism.[20] Another trend has been to combine survey feedback with other OD interventions, including work design, structural change and intergroup relations. These change methods are the outcome of the planning and implementation phase that follows on from survey feedback, and are fully described in Chapters 7 to 10.

WHAT ARE THE STEPS?

Survey feedback generally involves the following five steps:[21]

1   Members of the organisation, including those at the top, are involved in preliminary planning of the survey. In this step, it is important that all parties are clear about the level of analysis (organisation, department or small group) and the objectives of the survey itself. Because most surveys derive from a model about organisational or group functioning, organisation members must, in effect, approve that diagnostic framework. This is an important initial step in gaining ownership of the data and in ensuring that the right problems and issues are addressed by the survey.

Once the objectives have been determined, the organisation can use one of the standardised questionnaires, or it can develop its own survey instrument. If the survey is developed internally, pre-testing the questionnaire is important in order to be certain that it has been constructed properly. In either case, the survey items need to reflect the objectives established for the survey and the diagnostic issues being addressed.

2   The survey instrument is administered to members of the organisation or department. Ideally, the survey could be administered to all members; however, because of cost or time constraints, it may be necessary to administer it to a sample of members. If so, the size of the sample should be as large as possible to improve the motivational basis for participation in the feedback sessions.

3   The OD consultant usually analyses the survey data, tabulates the results, suggests approaches to diagnosis and trains client members to lead the feedback process.

4   Data feedback usually begins at the top of the organisation and cascades downward to groups reporting to managers at successively lower levels. This waterfall approach ensures that all groups at all organisational levels involved in the survey receive appropriate feedback. Most often, members of each organisation group at each level

discuss and deal with only that portion of the data that involves their particular group. They, in turn, prepare to introduce data to groups at the next lower organisational level, if appropriate.

Data feedback can also occur in a 'bottom-up' approach. Initially, the data for specific work groups or departments are fed back and action items proposed. At this point, the group addresses problems and issues within its control. The group notes any issues that are beyond its authority and suggests actions. This information is combined with information from groups that report to the same manager. These combined data are then fed back to the managers who review the data and the recommended actions. Problems that can be solved at this level are addressed. In turn, their analyses and suggestions about problems of a broader nature are combined, and feedback and action sessions proceed up the hierarchy. In this way, the people who are the most likely to carry out recommended action get the first chance to propose suggestions.

5   Feedback meetings provide an opportunity to work with the data. At each meeting, members discuss and interpret their data, diagnose problem areas and develop action plans. OD practitioners can play an important role during these meetings.[22] They can facilitate group discussion to produce accurate understanding, focus the group on its strengths and weaknesses, and help to develop effective action plans.

Application 5.4 describes how Blackmores, a health care company, has proactively structured a means by which employees are encouraged to contribute suggestions. Such tools as 'climate surveys' have dramatically improved its organisational culture and employees' commitment to change.

APPLiCATiON 5.4

SMALL TALK

Creating a corporate environment that nurtures innovation is tough, particularly when rigid management structures, fear of failure and inflexible policies work to stifle initiative. But Australian businesses are starting to recognise that the first step to creative thinking can be found in strong communication and staff commitment.

...

The complementary health-care company Blackmores says an open culture of employee dialogue is crucial to its success. Blackmores' chief operating officer, Jennifer Tait, says employees must feel valued by a company if they are expected to care about its future. At Blackmores, new employees are given a bottle of champagne, and receive a bottle each year to celebrate the anniversary of their employment.

Staff have been forthcoming with ideas for innovation. One production employee noticed that shrink-wrapped export lines were taking longer to package. A subsequent redesign cleared a backlog and saved costs. An engineering employee also stepped forward to redesign bottle-cap machinery. Tait has received numerous design suggestions for Blackmores' new factory, and says it is these 'small' innovations that help enhance the company's performance. (In 2004–05, Blackmores had net profit growth of 26%, and a 16% increase in sales, to $134 million.) Blackmores also has a central lunch room, which encourages the sharing of ideas. Tait says: 'Staff have to be engaged – they need to know where the company is headed so they are feeding ideas about what we can do to head in that direction'.

...

When the complementary health sector was tarnished by a mass drug recall triggered by the Pan Pharmaceuticals scare in 2003, Blackmores staff rallied. Tait says: 'It was like we were absolutely under siege, and everyone pulled together. We were constantly confronting bad stories, and couldn't get enough stock out – sales were going through the roof because 60% of our competitors were off the market, so staff were working weekends for weeks on end.' A few months into the crisis, staff were each given 100 company shares as recognition of their commitment.

...

Tait says companies cannot take employee engagement for granted. Three years ago, Blackmores started an annual 'climate survey', which acts as a barometer for staff morale and seeks opinions on executive management. 'When we first started, the executive committee didn't get a great rap. We've worked on speeding up responsiveness, and changed executive membership so we have several new people.'

Tait says executives and staff are presented with survey results, and asked for suggestions. 'All our measures have steadily improved, and the executive committee leadership score has improved significantly,' she says.

Source: Jane Searle, 'Small Talk', *Business Review Weekly*, Oct 27–Nov 2 2005.

Critical Thinking Questions: How is Blackmores an example of both 'top-down' and 'bottom-up' approaches to information gathering? Which do you think is more effective and why? There are many forms of surveys – for example, you are often approached in shopping centres – but what is different about a survey in an 'organisation development' context?

SURVEY FEEDBACK AND ORGANISATIONAL DEPENDENCIES

Traditionally, the steps of survey feedback have been applied to work groups and organisational units with little attention to dependencies among them. Recent studies, however, suggest that the design of survey feedback should vary according to how closely linked the participating units are with one another.[23] When the units are relatively independent and have little need to interact, survey feedback can focus on the dynamics that occur within each group and can be applied to the groups separately. When there is greater dependency among units and they need to co-ordinate their efforts, survey feedback must take into account relationships among the units, paying particular attention to the possibility of intergroup conflict. In these situations, the survey-feedback process needs to be co-ordinated across the interdependent groups. Special committees and task forces representing the groups will typically manage the process. They will facilitate the intergroup confrontation and conflict resolution generally needed when relations across groups are diagnosed.

LIMITATIONS OF SURVEY FEEDBACK

Although the use of survey feedback is widespread in contemporary organisations, the following limits and risks have been identified:[24]

1   *Ambiguity of purpose.* Managers and staff groups responsible for the survey-feedback process may have difficulty reaching sufficient consensus about the purposes of the survey, its content and how it will be fed back to participants. This confusion can lead to considerable disagreement over the data collected and the probability that nothing will be done with it.

2   *Distrust.* High levels of distrust in the organisation can render the survey feedback ineffective. Employees need to trust that their responses will remain anonymous and that management is serious about sharing the data and solving problems jointly.

3   *Unacceptable topics.* Most organisations have certain topics that they do not want examined. This can severely constrain the scope of the survey process, particularly if the neglected topics are important to employees.

4   *Organisational disturbance.* The survey-feedback process can unduly disturb organisational functioning. Data collection and feedback typically infringe on employee work time. Moreover, administration of a survey can call attention to issues with which management is unwilling to deal. It can create unrealistic expectations about organisational improvement.

RESULTS OF SURVEY FEEDBACK

Survey feedback has been used widely in business organisations, schools, hospitals, federal and state governments, and branches of the military. The United States Navy used survey feedback in more than 500 navy commands. More than 150 000 individual surveys were given, and a large bank of computerised research data was generated. Promising results were noted between survey indices and non-judicial punishment rates, incidence of drug abuse reports and the performance of ships undergoing refresher training (a post-overhaul training and evaluation period).[25] Positive results have been reported in such diverse areas as an industrial organisation in Sweden and the Israeli Army.[26]

One of the most important studies of survey feedback was done by Bowers, who conducted a five-year longitudinal study (the Inter-company Longitudinal Study) of 23 organisations in 15 companies, involving more than 14 000 people in both white- and blue-collar positions.[27] In each of the 23 organisations studied, repeat measurements were taken. The study compared survey feedback with three other OD interventions: interpersonal process consultation, task process consultation and laboratory training. The study reported that survey feedback was the most effective of the four treatments and the only one 'associated with large across-the-board positive changes in organisation climate'.[28]

These findings have been questioned on a number of methodological grounds and, since then, a more critical and comprehensive study has provided alternative explanations for the findings of the original study.[29] Although pointing to the original study as a seminal piece, the critique discovered methodological problems in the research itself. It did not question the original conclusion that survey feedback is effective in achieving organisational change, but it did question the fairness of the procedure employed for the evaluation of the other intervention techniques. It suggested that any conclusions to be drawn from action research studies should be based, at least in part, on objective operating data.

Comprehensive reviews of the literature present differing perspectives on the effects of survey feedback. In one review, survey feedback's biggest impact was on attitudes and perceptions of the work situation. The study suggests that survey feedback might best be viewed as a bridge between the diagnosis of organisational problems and the implementation of problem-solving methods, because there is little evidence to suggest that survey feedback alone will result in changes in individual behaviour or organisational output.[30] Another study suggests that survey feedback has positive effects on both outcome variables (for example, productivity, costs and absenteeism) and process variables (for example, employee openness, decision making and motivation) in 53% and 48%, respectively, of the studies measuring those variables.[31] When compared with other OD approaches, survey feedback was only bettered by interventions that used several approaches together; for example, change programs involving a combination of survey feedback, process consultation and team building. On the other hand, another review found that, in contrast to laboratory training and team building, survey feedback was least effective, with only 33% of the studies that measured hard outcomes reporting success.[32] The success rate increased to 45%, however, when survey feedback was combined with team building. Finally, a meta-analysis of OD process interventions and individual attitudes suggested that survey feedback was not significantly associated with overall satisfaction or attitudes about co-workers, the job or the organisation. Survey feedback was only able to account for about 11% of the variance in satisfaction and other attitudes.[33]

Studies of specific survey-feedback interventions in the US have suggested conditions that improve the success of this technique. One study in an urban school district reported difficulties with survey feedback and suggested that its effectiveness depends partly on the quality of those leading the change effort, members' understanding of the process, the extent to which the survey focuses on issues important to participants and the degree to which the values expressed by the survey are congruent with those of the respondents.[34] Another study in the military concluded that survey feedback works best when supervisors play an active role in feeding data back to employees and helping them to work with it.[35] Similarly, a field study of funeral co-operative societies concluded that the use and dissemination of survey results increased when organisation members were closely involved in developing and carrying out the project and when the consultant provided technical assistance in the form of data analysis and interpretation.[36] Finally, a long-term study of survey feedback in an underground mining operation suggests that continued periodic use of survey feedback can produce significant changes in organisations.[37] The feedback process can guide the change program.

Survey feedback is widely used in OD. It enables practitioners to collect diagnostic data from a large number of organisation members and to feed that information back to them for the purposes of problem solving. Organisations can use any of several predesigned surveys or they can develop their own. Evidence supporting the effectiveness of survey feedback is mixed, in part because it is difficult to separate the effects of collecting and feeding back information from the subsequent problem-solving interventions based on those data. The available evidence also suggests that survey feedback is most effective when used in combination with other OD techniques. More systematic and rigorous research is needed to assess the impact of survey feedback.

SUMMARY

This chapter has described several different methods of collecting and analysing diagnostic data. Because diagnosis is an important step that occurs frequently in the planned change process, a working familiarity with these techniques is essential. Methods of data collection include questionnaires, interviews, observation and unobtrusive measures. Methods of analysis include qualitative techniques, such as content and force-field analysis, and quantitative techniques, such as the mean, standard deviation, correlation coefficient and difference tests.

This chapter has also described the process of feeding back data to a client system. It is concerned with identifying the content of the data to be fed back and designing a process of feedback that ensures ownership of the data. Feeding back data is a central activity in almost any OD program. If members own the data, they will be motivated to solve organisational problems. A special application of the data-collection and feedback process is called survey feedback, and is one of the most accepted processes in organisation development. Survey feedback highlights the importance of contracting appropriately with the client system, establishing relevant categories for data collection, and feeding back the data as necessary steps for diagnosing organisational problems and developing interventions for resolving them.

ACTIVITIES

COLLECTING AND ANALYSING DIAGNOSTIC INFORMATION

Review questions

1. What is the meaning, and basis, of a 'diagnostic relationship'?

2. Why is it important to define objectives before collecting data?

3. What are the goals of data collection and what significant factors should be considered?

4. Under what circumstances would a questionnaire be used? How does a survey in an OD context differ from a survey distributed for any other purpose?

5. What value is 'observation' when diagnosing? What are the inherent dangers and pitfalls of such an approach?

6. Which method of gathering data is the most objective and why? Under what circumstances would purely objective data gathering be ineffectual?

Discussion and essay questions

1. Describe the advantages and disadvantages of the various methods of data collection. Also consider the situations in which they would be used.

▷▷

(2) Under what conditions are quantitative and/or qualitative tools useful in analysing data? Discuss which is better.

FEEDING BACK DIAGNOSTIC INFORMATION

Review questions

(1) What does 'implementation feedback' try to measure? What would happen if these feedback mechanisms were absent?

(2) When should you identify the measurement variables to be used for evaluation and feedback? How would such measurement be inculcated into OD process?

(3) What do homemade surveys typically have? What are their advantages and disadvantages?

(4) Which data collection method accurately measures all the variables important to OD? Is there a need to modify or adapt data collection methods? Why/why not?

(5) List the outcomes that OD consultants should measure. What limitations should an OD consultant consider?

Discussion and essay questions

(1) What are the two kinds of feedback involved in evaluation and what do they tell us? Debate the value of each.

(2) What are the issues involved in measurement? Consider the implication/s of the way change agents function in an OD process.

(3) Discuss setting up valid research designs and consider the contexts in which they will be used.

(4) Define institutionalisation and discuss specific institutionalisation processes. In your answer, discuss the ethical ramifications of institutionalisation.

NOTES

1 S. Mohrman, T. Cummings and E. Lawler III, 'Creating useful knowledge with organizations: relationship and process issues', in *Producing Useful Knowledge for Organizations*, eds R. Kilmann and K. Thomas (New York: Praeger, 1983): 613–24; C. Argyris, R. Putnam and D. Smith, eds, *Action Science* (San Francisco: Jossey-Bass, 1985); E. Lawler III, A. Mohrman, S. Mohrman, G. Ledford, Jr and T. Cummings, *Doing Research That Is Useful for Theory and Practice* (San Francisco: Jossey-Bass, 1985).
2 D. Nadler, *Feedback and Organization Development: Using Data-Based Methods* (Reading, MA: Addison-Wesley, 1977): 110–14.
3 W. Nielsen, N. Nykodym and D. Brown, 'Ethics and organizational change', *Asia Pacific Journal of Human Resources*, 29 (1991).
4 Nadler, *Feedback and Organization Development*, op. cit., 105–7.
5 W. Wymer and J. Carsten, 'Alternative ways to gather opinion', *HR Magazine* (April 1992): 71–8.
6 Examples of basic resource books on survey methodology include: S. Seashore, E. Lawler III, P. Mirvis and C. Cammann, *Assessing Organizational Change* (New York: Wiley Interscience, 1983); J. Van Mannen and J. Dabbs, *Varieties of Qualitative Research* (Beverly Hills, CA: Sage Publications, 1983); E. Lawler III, D. Nadler and C. Cammann, *Organizational Assessment: Perspectives on the Measurement of Organizational Behaviour and the Quality of Worklife* (New York: Wiley Interscience, 1980); R. Golembiewski and R. Hilles, *Toward the Responsive Organization: The Theory and Practice of Survey/Feedback* (Salt Lake City: Brighton Publishing, 1979); Nadler, *Feedback and Organization Development*, op. cit.; S. Sudman and N. Bradburn, *Asking Questions* (San Francisco: Jossey-Bass, 1983).
7 http://www.acer.edu.au/index3.html/ (accessed 1 November 2006).

8   J. Jones and W. Bearley, 'Organization change: orientation scale', *HRDQ* (King of Prussia, Pennsylvania, 1986).
9   J. Fordyce and R. Weil, *Managing WITH People*, 2nd edn (Reading, MA: Addison-Wesley, 1979); W. Wells, 'Group interviewing', in *Handbook of Marketing Research*, ed. R. Ferder (New York: McGraw-Hill, 1977); R. Krueger, *Focus Groups: A Practical Guide for Applied Research*, 2nd edn (Thousand Oaks, CA: Sage Publications, 1994).
10 C. Emory, *Business Research Methods* (Homewood, IL: Richard D. Irwin, 1980): 146.
11 W. Deming, *Sampling Design* (New York: John Wiley, 1960); L. Kish, *Survey Sampling* (New York: John Wiley, 1965); S. Sudman, *Applied Sampling* (New York: Academic Press, 1976).
12 B. Berelson, 'Content analysis', in *Handbook of Social Psychology*, ed. G. Lindzey (Reading, MA: Addison-Wesley, 1954); O. Holsti, 'Content analysis', *Handbook of Social Psychology*, 2nd edn, eds G. Lindzey and E. Aronson (Reading, MA: Addison-Wesley, 1968).
13 K. Lewin, *Field Theory in Social Science* (New York: Harper and Row, 1951).
14 More sophisticated methods of quantitative analysis are found in the following: W. Hays, *Statistics* (New York: Holt, Rinehart and Winston, 1963); J. Nunnally, *Psychometric Theory*, 2nd edn (New York: McGraw-Hill, 1978); F. Kerlinger, *Foundations of Behavioral Research*, 2nd edn (New York: Holt, Rinehart and Winston, 1973); J. Cohen and P. Cohen, *Applied Multiple Regression/Correlation Analysis for the Behavioral Sciences*, 2nd edn (Hillsdale, NJ: Lawrence Erlbaum Associates, 1983).
15 A. Armenakis and H. Field, 'The development of organizational diagnostic norms: an application of client involvement', *Consultation*, 6 (Spring 1987): 20–31.
16 Cohen and Cohen, *Applied Multiple Regression/Correlation Analysis for the Behavioral Sciences*, op. cit.
17 S. Mohrman, T. Cummings and E. Lawler III, 'Creating useful knowledge with organizations: relationship and process issues', in *Producing Useful Knowledge for Organizations*, eds R. Kilmann and K. Thomas (New York: Praeger, 1983): 61–124.
18 C. Argyris, *Intervention Theory and Method: A Behavioral Science View* (Reading, MA: Addison-Wesley, 1970); P. Block, *Flawless Consulting* (Austin, TX: Learning Concepts, 1981).
19 D. Nadler, *Feedback and Organization Development: Using Data-Based Methods* (Reading, MA: Addison-Wesley, 1977): 156–8.
20 D. Nadler, P. Mirvis and C. Cammann, 'The ongoing feedback system: experimenting with a new managerial tool', *Organizational Dynamics*, 4 (Spring 1976): 63–80.
21 F. Mann, 'Studying and creating change', in *The Planning of Change*, eds W. Bennis, K. Benne and R. Chin (New York: Holt, Rinehart and Winston, 1964): 605–15; R. Golembiewski and R. Hilles, *Toward the Responsive Organization: The Theory and Practice of Survey/Feedback* (Salt Lake City: Brighton, 1979); Nadler, *Feedback and Organization Development*, op. cit.; J. Wiley, 'Making the most of survey feedback as a strategy for organization development', *OD Practitioner*, 23 (1991): 1–5.
22 G. Ledford and C. Worley, 'Some guidelines for effective survey feedback' (unpublished working paper, Center for Effective Organizations, University of Southern California, 1987).
23 M. Sashkin and R. Cooke, 'Organizational structure as a moderator of the effects of data-based change programs' (Paper delivered at the Thirty-sixth Annual Meeting of the Academy of Management, Kansas City, 1976); D. Nadler, 'Alternative data-feedback designs for organizational intervention', in *The 1979 Annual Handbook for Group Facilitators*, eds J. Jones and J. Pfeiffer (LaJolla, CA: University Associates, 1979): 78–92.
24 S. Seashore, 'Surveys in organizations', in *Handbook of Organizational Behavior*, ed. J. Lorsch (Englewood Cliff, NJ: Prentice-Hall, 1987): 142.
25 R. Forbes, 'Quo Vadis: the Navy and organization development' (paper delivered at the Fifth Psychology in the Air Force Symposium, United States Air Force Academy, Colorado Springs, CO, 8 April 1976).
26 S. Rubenowitz, Goteborg, Sweden: Goteborg Universitet, private communication; D. Eden and S. Shlomo, 'Survey-based OD in the Israel Defense Forces: a field experiment' (unpublished and undated manuscript, Tel Aviv University).
27 D. Bowers, 'OD techniques and their results in 23 organizations: the Michigan ICL Study', *Journal of Applied Behavioral Science*, 9 (January–February–March 1973): 21–43.
28 ibid: 42.
29 W. Pasmore, 'Backfeed, the Michigan ICL Study revisited: an alternative explanation of the results', *Journal of Applied Behavioral Science*, 12 (April–May–June 1976): 245–51; W. Pasmore and D. King, 'The Michigan ICL Study revisited: a critical review' (Working Paper 548, Krannert Graduate School of Industrial Administration, West Lafayette, IN, 1976).
30 F. Friedlander and L. Brown, 'Organization development', in *Annual Review of Psychology*, eds M. Rosenzweig and L. Porter (Palo Alto, CA: Annual Reviews, 1974).
31 J. Porras and P. Berg, 'The impact of organization development', *Academy of Management Review*, 3 (April 1978): 249–66.
32 J. Nicholas, 'The comparative impact of organization development interventions on hard criteria measures', *Academy of Management Review*, 7 (October 1982): 531–42.
33 G. Neuman, J. Edwards and N. Raju, 'Organizational development interventions: a meta-analysis of their effects on satisfaction and other attitudes', *Personnel Psychology*, 42 (1989): 461–83.

34 S. Mohrman, A. Mohrman, R. Cooke and R. Duncan, 'Survey feedback and problem-solving intervention in a school district: "we'll take the survey but you can keep the feedback"', in *Failures in Organization Development and Change*, eds P. Mirvis and D. Berg (New York: John Wiley and Sons, 1977): 149–90.

35 F. Conlon and L. Short, 'An empirical examination of survey feedback as an organizational change device', *Academy of Management Proceedings* (1983): 225–9.

36 R. Sommer, 'An experimental investigation of the action research approach', *Journal of Applied Behavioral Science*, 23 (1987): 185–99.

37 J. Gavin, 'Observation from a long-term survey-guided consultation with a mining company', *Journal of Applied Behavioral Science*, 21 (1985): 201–20.

Online reading

INFOTRAC® COLLEGE EDITION

For additional readings and reviews on information processing, explore **InfoTrac® College Edition**, your online library. Go to **www.infotrac-college.com** and search for any of the InfoTrac key terms listed below:

* Data collection
* Feedback cycles
* Diagnostic relationship
* Force-field analysis

6

DESiGN, iMPLEMENTATiON AND EVALUATiON OF iNTERVENTiONS

An organisation development intervention is a sequence of activities, actions and events intended to help an organisation improve its performance and effectiveness. Intervention design, or action planning, derives from careful diagnosis and is meant to resolve specific problems and to improve particular areas of organisational functioning identified in the diagnosis. OD interventions vary from standardised programs that have been developed and used in many organisations to unique programs tailored to a specific organisation or department.

Once diagnosis has revealed the causes of problems or opportunities for development, organisation members can begin planning, and subsequently implementing, the changes necessary for improving organisation effectiveness and performance. A large part of OD is concerned with interventions for improving organisations.

This chapter finishes with the final stage of the OD cycle – evaluation and institutionalisation. Evaluation is concerned with providing feedback to practitioners and organisation members about the progress and impact of interventions. Such information may suggest the need for further diagnosis and modification of the change program, or it may show that the intervention is successful. Institutionalisation involves making OD interventions a permanent part of the organisation's normal functioning. It ensures that the results of successful change programs persist over time.

DESIGNING INTERVENTIONS

This section describes criteria that define effective OD interventions and then identifies contingencies that guide successful intervention design. Finally, the various types of OD interventions presented in this book are reviewed. Chapters 7–10 of this book describe fully the major interventions used in OD today.

What are effective interventions?

The term 'intervention' refers to a set of sequenced planned actions or events that are intended to help an organisation increase its effectiveness. Interventions purposely disrupt the status quo; they are a deliberate attempt to move an organisation or sub-unit towards a different and more effective state. In OD, three major criteria define an effective intervention: (1) the extent to which it fits the needs of the organisation, (2) the degree to which it is based on causal knowledge of intended outcomes, and (3) the extent to which it transfers competence to manage change to organisation members.

The first criterion concerns the extent to which the intervention is relevant to the organisation and its members. Effective interventions are based on valid information about the organisation's functioning. They provide organisation members with opportunities to make free and informed choices; and they gain members' internal commitment to those choices.[1]

Valid information is the result of an accurate diagnosis of the organisation's functioning. It must fairly reflect what organisation members perceive and feel about their primary concerns and issues. Free and informed choice suggests that members are actively involved in making decisions about the changes that will affect them. It means that they can choose not to participate and that interventions will not be imposed upon them. Internal commitment means that organisation members will accept ownership of the intervention and take responsibility for implementing it. If interventions are to result in meaningful changes, management, staff and other relevant members must be committed to implementing them.

The second criterion of an effective intervention involves knowledge of outcomes. Because interventions are intended to produce specific results, they must be based on valid knowledge that those outcomes can actually be produced. Otherwise there is no scientific basis for designing an effective OD intervention. Unfortunately, and in contrast to other applied disciplines, such as medicine and engineering, knowledge of intervention effects is in a rudimentary stage of development in OD. Much of the evaluation research lacks sufficient rigour to make strong causal inferences about the success or failure of change programs. (Chapter 11 discusses how to evaluate OD programs rigorously.) Moreover, few attempts have been made to examine the comparative impacts of different OD techniques. This makes knowing whether one method is more effective than another difficult.

Despite these problems, more attempts are being made to systematically assess the strengths and weaknesses of OD interventions and to compare the impact of different techniques on organisation effectiveness.[2] Many of the OD interventions that will be discussed in this book have been subjected to evaluative research. This research is explored in the appropriate chapters, along with respective change programs.

The third criterion of an effective intervention involves the extent to which it enhances the organisation's capacity to manage change. The values underlying OD suggest that organisation members should be better able to carry out planned change activities on their own after an intervention. They should gain knowledge and skill in managing change from active participation in designing and implementing the intervention. Competence in change management is essential in today's environment, where technological, social, economic and political changes are rapid and persistent.

How to design effective interventions

Designing OD interventions requires careful attention to the needs and dynamics of the change situation and to crafting a change program that will be consistent with the criteria of the effective interventions outlined above. Current knowledge of OD interventions provides only general prescriptions for change. There is little precise information or research about how to design interventions or how they can be expected to interact with organisational conditions to achieve specific results.[3] Moreover, the ability to implement most OD interventions is highly dependent on the skills and knowledge of the change agent. Thus, the design of an intervention will depend to some extent on the expertise of the practitioner.

Two major sets of contingencies that can affect intervention success have been discussed in the OD literature: those having to do with the change situation (including the practitioner) and those related to the target of change. Both kinds of contingencies need to be considered when designing interventions.

CONTINGENCIES RELATED TO THE CHANGE SITUATION

Researchers have identified a number of contingencies present in the change situation that can affect intervention success. These include individual differences among organisation members (for example, needs for autonomy), organisational factors (for example, management style and technical uncertainty) and dimensions of the change process itself (for example, the degree of top-management support). Unless these factors are taken into account when designing an intervention, the intervention will have little impact on organisational functioning, or, worse, it might even produce negative results. For example, if you are seeking to resolve motivational problems among blue-collar workers in an oil refinery, it is important that you know whether interventions intended to improve motivation (for example, job enrichment) will succeed with the kinds of people who work there. In many cases, having knowledge of these contingencies might result in modifying or adjusting the change program to fit the setting. In applying a reward-system intervention to an organisation, the changes might have to be modified according to whether the firm wants to reinforce individual or team performance.

Although knowledge of contingencies is still in a rudimentary stage of development in OD, researchers have discovered several situational factors that can affect intervention success.[4] These include contingencies for many of the interventions reviewed in this book, and they will be discussed in the relevant chapters that describe the change programs. More generic contingencies that apply to all OD interventions follow, including the situational factors that must be considered when designing any intervention: the organisation's readiness for change, its change capability, its cultural context and the change agent's skills and abilities.

Readiness for change

Intervention success depends heavily on the organisation being ready for planned change. Indicators of readiness for change include sensitivity to pressures for change, dissatisfaction with the status quo, availability of resources to support change, and commitment of significant management time. When these conditions are present, interventions can be designed to address the organisational issues uncovered during diagnosis. When readiness for change is low, however, interventions need to focus on increasing the organisation's willingness to change.[5]

Application 6.1 draws an analogy with a hive wherein bees know the business integration game backwards and are prepared for every eventuality.

APPLiCATiON 6.1

LISTEN TO THE VOICE OF THE HIVE

Sometimes from disaster comes inspiration. Russell O'Brien was involved in an IT overhaul project that was scrapped at a cost of £19 million. Soon after, he founded a company to help others avoid the same fate.

As chief executive officer of Sydney-based Bluescribe, Mr O'Brien creates 'integration blueprints' to steer his clients safely along the often perilous path of technological integration, in which disparate modes and practices are brought together into one whole, working system. This can involve such things as hardware and software upgrades, changes to work practices and improved management techniques.

'Integration blueprinting is about risk prevention for IT projects,' he says. 'It stops IT projects from becoming major headaches, financial black holes.'

It's no secret that IT integration projects are prone to failure of varying degrees. A 2005 survey of 87 Australian chief information officers by InterSystems found 51% of such projects they had worked on failed to come in on time, and 46% failed to deliver the targeted return on investment.

Integration blueprinting tackles this problem by guiding every step of a project. It is not a form of technology; rather, it is a detailed methodology for bringing together technology using business intelligence.

Bluescribe's blueprints are a three-stage process. They begin with an all-inclusive snapshot of a business – how it is run, what its goals are, where the IT fits in – then map the best route to achieving its aims.

▷▷

The probable financial return that integration will generate is also calculated, and if everything goes to plan the blueprint should form the basis for similar projects in the company for years to come.

…

The amateur apiarist says bees have plenty to teach people about working single-mindedly.

'Bees are very organised. They know what the rules are and they stick to them. It's all in for the hive. They will gladly give up their lives for the hive, and there's no miscommunication inside the hive,' he says.

Poor communication between the IT department and the rest of the business is the most common cause of failure for integration projects – and indeed a lot of other problems in industry.

'IT would say the business don't know what they want and business would say IT don't give them what they ask for,' Mr O'Brien says. He has seen many poorly planned integration projects result in millions of dollars and countless hours' work wasted.

'There are quite a few well-known failures in the industry. Sydney Water tried to rationalise their billing system and lost something like $60 million over it,' he says (the exact figure was $61 million).

A 2003 report by the NSW Auditor-General into Sydney Water's attempt to rationalise its customer information and billing system found it was crippled from the start by 'poor communication between the project team and the customer services division'.

It also found that Sydney Water approved the project without an IT strategy, and that once it developed one it found the technology architecture was incompatible.

But perhaps the key finding of the report was the one that stated: 'Sydney Water recognised that it needed a business improvement process, but during the project it reverted to only implementing a computer system.'

Mr O'Brien has to fight a misconception that IT is somehow separate from the rest of the business. His blueprints avoid the kind of acronym-laden language that can alienate the less technologically literate. Instead they use diagrams that describe the technological architecture and use plain language to relate it to business needs.

'There is no keeping the business in the dark any more. They can see what progress is being made, and all in a language they can understand. One thing I learned a long time ago – the business loves to read about itself. One compliment I was paid by a manager was that it was something he felt he could read and take to bed at night,' he says.

…

Integration blueprinting is a relatively new methodology so there are few proven examples of its effectiveness. The first person to put his trust in Mr O'Brien's blueprinting methodology was Allan Marshall, when he was chief of operations and technology director at Associated Newspapers in Britain in 2003.

…

Mr Marshall believes the greatest impact it had on the company was not financial but cultural, with managers and IT staff finally working in harmony. 'I think the biggest benefit of the blueprint was that it helped to involve the business and get them positive about what we were doing, rather than wanting never-ending quick fixes to what they were doing,' he says.

…

Bluescribe seeks to patent its particular methodology of integration blueprinting, but others in the industry perform comparable services under a different name.

'Enterprise architect' Joe McCormick takes a business-focused approach to his work as a strategic planner of IT architecture and integration projects. Now a consultant with Deloitte, Mr McCormick previously worked for Sensis, where he was approached by Bluescribe to discuss a blueprint for integration.

…

Mr McCormick believes technology solutions should only be considered once business goals have been clearly defined. 'I've seen many great technologies implemented so badly,' he says.

Mr McCormick's business-first approach has found favour at Deloitte. 'Traditionally the technologists get together and they look at a technology solution,' says Adam Powick, a partner in government services at the international accountancy firm. 'They might put some middleware in place and just try to integrate the systems as tactically and quickly as they can, but that's very much a short-term solution. The more robust approach is actually looking at the end business and defining the key functions or capabilities that business needs to support.'

Mr Powick is working with a federal government agency as it overhauls its legacy system, which handles about 80% of operations. He says the agency had started out searching for a technical solution, such as rebuilding the architecture or buying an entirely new system.

'We didn't even look at technology probably for eight weeks. We defined the business functions they were trying to support – information flows, data requirements – then we mapped what they had today against that, which identified the gaps and where it did support the business functions quite well,' he says.

The legacy environment was broken down into components. 'All of a sudden it became much clearer that we could migrate this environment in an incremental fashion at a much lower risk than taking a really big bang approach,' he says.

Source: Adam Carey, 'Listen to the voice of the hive', *The Age*, 3/10/2006.

Critical Thinking Question: This application identifies the need to prepare an organisation for a significant change, particularly in information technology. What interventions do you think may assist with the design and implementation of an IT change strategy?

Capability to change

Managing planned change requires particular knowledge and skills, as outlined in Chapter 10. These include the ability to motivate change, to lead change, to develop political support, to manage the transition and to sustain momentum. If organisation members do not have these capabilities, then a preliminary training intervention may be needed before members can meaningfully engage in intervention design.

Cultural context

The national culture within which the organisation is embedded can have a powerful influence on members' reactions to change. Thus, intervention design needs to account for the cultural values and assumptions held by organisation members. Interventions may need to be modified to fit the local culture, particularly when OD practices developed in one culture are applied to organisations in another culture.[6] For example, a team-building intervention designed for top managers at an Australian firm may need to be modified when applied to the company's foreign subsidiaries.

Capabilities of the change agent

Many failures in OD result when change agents apply interventions beyond their competence. In designing interventions, OD practitioners should assess their experience and expertise against the requirements needed to implement the intervention effectively. When a mismatch is discovered, practitioners can explore whether the intervention can be modified to fit their talents better, whether another intervention more suited to their skills can satisfy the organisation's needs or whether they should enlist the assistance of another change agent who can guide the process more effectively. The ethical guidelines under which OD practitioners operate require full disclosure of the applicability of their knowledge and expertise to the client situation. Practitioners are expected to intervene within their capabilities or to recommend someone more suited to the client's needs.

CONTINGENCIES RELATED TO THE TARGET OF CHANGE

OD interventions seek to change specific features or parts of organisations. These targets of change are the main focus of interventions, and researchers have identified two key contingencies related to change targets that can affect intervention success: the organisational issues that the intervention is intended to resolve and the level of organisational system at which the intervention is expected to have a primary impact.

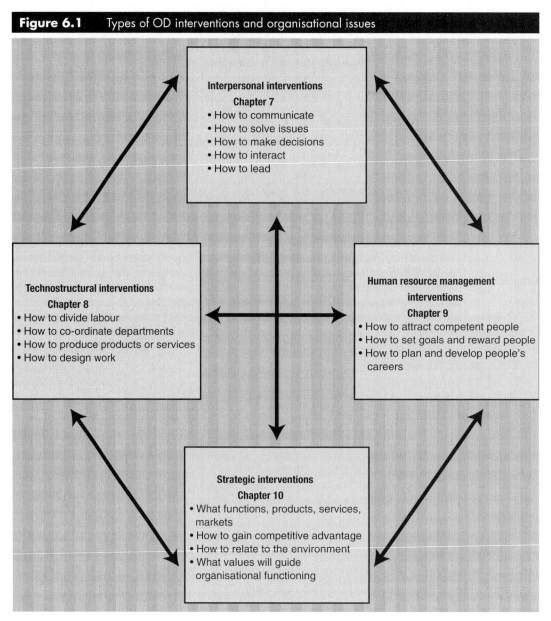

Figure 6.1   Types of OD interventions and organisational issues

Interpersonal interventions
Chapter 7
- How to communicate
- How to solve issues
- How to make decisions
- How to interact
- How to lead

Technostructural interventions
Chapter 8
- How to divide labour
- How to co-ordinate departments
- How to produce products or services
- How to design work

Human resource management interventions
Chapter 9
- How to attract competent people
- How to set goals and reward people
- How to plan and develop people's careers

Strategic interventions
Chapter 10
- What functions, products, services, markets
- How to gain competitive advantage
- How to relate to the environment
- What values will guide organisational functioning

Organisational issues

Organisations need to address certain issues to operate effectively. Figure 6.1 lists these issues along with the OD interventions that are intended to resolve them. (The parts and chapters of this book that describe the specific interventions are also identified in the figure.) It shows four interrelated issues that are key targets of OD interventions:

1   *Strategic issues*. Organisations need to decide what products or services they will provide and the markets in which they will compete, as well as how to relate to their environments and how to transform themselves to keep pace with changing conditions. These strategic issues are among the most critical facing organisations in today's changing and highly competitive environments. OD methods aimed at these issues are called 'strategic interventions'. They are among the most recent additions to OD and include integrated strategic change, transorganisational development and organisation transformation.

2   *Technology and structure issues.* Organisations must decide how to divide work into departments and then how to co-ordinate them to support strategic directions. They must also make decisions about how to produce products or services and how to link people with tasks. OD methods for dealing with these structural and technological issues are called 'technostructural interventions'. They include OD activities relating to organisation design, employee involvement and work design.

3   *Human resource issues.* These issues are concerned with attracting competent people to the organisation, setting goals for them, appraising and rewarding their performance and ensuring that they develop their careers and manage stress. OD techniques aimed at these issues are called 'human resource management interventions'.

4   *Interpersonal issues.* These issues have to do with social processes occurring among organisation members, such as communication, decision making, leadership and group dynamics. OD methods focusing on these kinds of issues are called 'human process interventions'; included among them are some of the most common OD techniques, such as conflict resolution and team building.

Consistent with systems theory as described in Chapter 4, these organisational issues are interrelated and need to be integrated with each other. The double-headed arrows connecting the different issues in Figure 6.1 represent the fits or linkages among them. Organisations need to match answers to one set of questions with answers to other sets of questions to achieve high levels of effectiveness. For example, decisions about gaining competitive advantage need to fit with choices about organisation structure, setting goals for people, rewarding people, communication and problem solving.

The interventions presented in this book are intended to resolve these different concerns. As shown in Figure 6.1, particular OD interventions apply to specific issues. Thus, intervention design must create change methods appropriate to the organisational issues identified in diagnosis. Moreover, because the organisational issues are themselves linked, OD interventions need to be similarly integrated with one another. For example, a goal-setting intervention that attempts to establish motivating goals may need to be integrated with supporting interventions, such as a reward system that links pay to goal achievement. The key point is to think systematically. Interventions that are aimed at one kind of organisational issue will invariably have repercussions on other kinds of issues. This requires careful thinking about how OD interventions affect the different kinds of issues and how different change programs might be integrated to bring about a broader and more coherent impact on organisational functioning.

Organisational levels

In addition to facing interrelated issues, organisations function at different levels – individual, group and organisation. Thus, organisational levels are targets of change in OD. Table 6.1 lists OD interventions in terms of the level of organisation they mainly affect. For example, some technostructural interventions affect mainly individuals and groups (for example, work design), whereas others impact primarily on the total organisation (for example, structural design).

It is important to emphasise that only the primary level affected by the intervention is identified in Table 6.1. Many OD interventions also have a secondary impact on other levels. For example, structural design affects mainly the organisation level but can have an indirect impact on groups and individuals. It sets the broad parameters for designing work groups and individual jobs. Again, practitioners need to think systematically. They must design interventions to apply to specific organisational levels. Moreover, they need to address the possibility of cross-level effects and may need to integrate interventions that affect different levels to achieve overall success.[7] For example, an intervention to create self-managed work teams may need to be linked to organisation-level changes in measurement and reward systems to promote team-based work.

Overview of interventions

The OD interventions discussed in Chapters 7 to 10 of this book are briefly described below. They represent the major organisational change methods used in OD today.

Table 6.1 Types of OD interventions and organisational levels			
	Primary organisational level affected		
	Individual	Group	Organisation
Interpersonal interventions (Chapter 7)			
T-groups	x	x	
Process consultation		x	
Third-party intervention	x	x	
Team building		x	
Organisation confrontation meeting		x	x
Intergroup relations		x	x
Large-group interventions			x
Grid organisation development		x	x
Technostructural interventions (Chapter 8)			
Structural design			x
Downsizing			x
Re-engineering		x	x
Parallel structures		x	x
High-involvement organisations	x	x	x
TQM		x	x
Work design	x	x	
Human resource management interventions (Chapter 9)			
Goal setting	x	x	
Performance appraisal	x	x	
Reward systems	x	x	x
Career planning and development	x		
Managing workforce diversity	x	x	
Employee wellness	x		
Strategic interventions (Chapter 10)			
Open systems planning		x	x
Integrated strategic change			x
Transorganisation development			x
Culture change			
Self-designing organisations		x	x
Organisation learning		x	x

INTERPERSONAL INTERVENTIONS

Chapter 7 of the book presents interventions that focus on people within organisations and the processes through which they accomplish organisational goals. These processes include communication, problem solving, group decision making and leadership. This type of intervention is deeply rooted in the history of OD. It represents the earliest change programs characterising OD, including the T-group and the organisational confrontation meeting. Human process interventions derive mainly from the disciplines of psychology and social psychology, and the applied fields of group dynamics and human relations. Practitioners applying these interventions generally value human fulfilment and expect that organisational effectiveness follows from improved functioning of people and organisational processes.[8]

Chapter 9 discusses human process interventions that are related to interpersonal relations and group dynamics. These include the following four interventions:

1   *T-group.* This traditional change method is designed to provide members with experiential learning about group dynamics, leadership and interpersonal relations. The basic T-group consists of about 10 to 15 strangers who meet with a professional trainer to examine the social dynamics that emerge from their interactions. Members gain feedback on the impact of their own behaviours on each other in addition to learning about group dynamics.

2   *Process consultation.* This intervention focuses on the interpersonal relations and social dynamics that occur in work groups. Typically, a process consultant helps group members to diagnose group functioning and to devise appropriate solutions to process problems, such as dysfunctional conflict, poor communication and ineffective norms. The aim is to help members to gain the skills and understanding necessary to identify and solve problems themselves.

3   *Third-party intervention.* This change method is a form of process consultation aimed at dysfunctional interpersonal relations in organisations. Interpersonal conflict may derive from substantive issues, such as disputes over work methods, or from interpersonal issues, such as miscommunication. The third-party intervener helps people resolve conflicts through such methods as problem solving, bargaining and conciliation.

4   *Team building.* This intervention is concerned with helping work groups to more effectively accomplish tasks. Like process consultation, team building helps members to diagnose their group processes and to devise solutions to problems. It goes beyond group processes, however, to include an examination of the group's task, member roles and strategies for performing tasks. The consultant may also function as a resource person who can offer expertise that is related to the group's task.

Interpersonal interventions that are system-wide typically focus on the total organisation or an entire department, as well as on relations between groups. These include the following four change programs:

1   *Organisation confrontation meeting.* This change method is intended to mobilise organisation members to identify problems, to set action targets and to begin working on problems. It is usually applied when organisations are experiencing stress and when management needs to organise resources for immediate problem solving. The intervention generally includes various groupings of employees in identifying and solving problems.

2   *Intergroup relations.* These interventions are designed to improve interactions between different groups or departments in organisations. The microcosm group intervention involves a small group that is made up of people whose backgrounds closely match the organisational problems being addressed. This group then addresses the problem and develops the means to solve it. The intergroup conflict model typically involves a consultant helping two groups to understand the causes of the conflict and to choose appropriate solutions.

3   *Large-group interventions.* These interventions involve a meeting of a broad variety of stakeholders to clarify important values, develop new ways of working and articulate a new vision for the organisation or to solve pressing organisational problems. It is a powerful tool for creating awareness of organisational problems and opportunities and for specifying valued directions for future action.

4   *Grid organisation development.* This intervention specifies a particular way of managing an organisation. It is a packaged OD program that includes standardised instruments for measuring organisational practices as well as specific procedures for helping organisations to achieve the prescribed approach.

TECHNOSTRUCTURAL INTERVENTIONS

Chapter 8 of the book presents interventions that focus on the technology (for example, task methods and job design) and structure (for example, division of labour and hierarchy) of organisations. These change methods are receiving increasing attention in OD, especially in view of current concerns about productivity and organisational effectiveness. They include approaches to employee involvement, as well as methods for designing organisations, groups and jobs. Technostructural interventions are rooted in the disciplines of engineering, sociology and psychology, and in the applied fields of sociotechnical systems and organisation design. Practitioners generally stress both productivity and human fulfilment and expect that organisation effectiveness will result from appropriate work designs and organisation structures.[9]

In Chapter 8 we discuss technostructural interventions that are concerned with restructuring organisations. These include the following three change programs:

1   *Structural design.* This process concerns the organisation's division of labour: how to specialise task performances. Interventions aimed at structural design include moving from more traditional ways of dividing the organisation's overall work, such as functional, self-contained-unit and matrix structures, to more integrative and flexible forms, such as process-based and network-based structures. Diagnostic guidelines exist to help determine which structure is appropriate for particular organisational environments, technologies and conditions.

2   *Downsizing.* This intervention seeks to reduce costs and bureaucracy by decreasing the size of the organisation. This reduction in personnel can be accomplished through lay-offs, organisation redesign and outsourcing. Each of these downsizing methods must be planned with a clear understanding of the organisation's strategy.

3   *Re-engineering.* This recent intervention radically redesigns the organisation's core work processes to create tighter linkage and co-ordination among the different tasks. This work flow integration results in faster, more responsive task performance. Re-engineering is often accomplished with new information technology that permits employees to control and co-ordinate work processes more effectively. Re-engineering often fails if it ignores basic principles and processes of OD.

Chapter 8 is also concerned with employee involvement (EI). This broad category of interventions is aimed at improving employee well-being and organisational effectiveness. It generally attempts to move knowledge, power, information and rewards downward in the organisation. EI includes parallel structures (such as co-operative union–management projects and quality circles), high-involvement plants and total quality management.

It also discusses work design. These change programs are concerned with designing work for work groups and individual jobs. It includes the engineering, motivational and sociotechnical systems approaches. These approaches produce: traditionally designed jobs and work groups; enriched jobs that provide employees with greater task variety, autonomy and feedback about results; and self-managing teams that can govern their own task behaviours with limited external control.

HUMAN RESOURCE MANAGEMENT INTERVENTIONS

This book focuses on personnel practices used to integrate people into organisations. These practices include career planning, reward systems, goal setting and performance appraisal. These change methods have traditionally been associated with the personnel function in organisations. In recent years, interest has grown in integrating human resource management with organisation development. Human resource management interventions are rooted in the disciplines of economics and labour relations and in the applied personnel practices of wages and compensation, employee selection and placement, performance appraisal and career development. Practitioners in this area typically focus on the people in organisations, believing that organisational effectiveness results from improved practices for integrating employees into organisations.

Chapter 9 deals with interventions concerning performance management. These include the following change programs:

1   *Goal setting.* This change program involves setting clear and challenging goals. It attempts to improve organisation effectiveness by establishing a better fit between personal and organisational objectives. Managers and subordinates periodically meet to plan work, review accomplishments and solve problems in achieving goals.

2   *Performance appraisal.* This intervention is a systematic process of jointly assessing work-related achievements, strengths and weaknesses. It is the primary human resource management intervention for providing performance feedback to individuals and work groups. Performance appraisal represents an important link between goal setting and reward systems.

3   *Reward systems.* This intervention involves the design of organisational rewards to improve employee satisfaction and performance. It includes innovative approaches to pay, promotions and fringe benefits.

Chapter 9 also focuses on three change methods that are associated with developing and assisting organisation members:

1   *Career planning and development.* This intervention involves helping people choose organisations and career paths, and attain career objectives. It generally focuses on managers and professional staff and is seen as a way of improving their quality of work life.

2   *Managing workforce diversity.* This change program seeks to make human resource practices more responsive to a variety of individual needs. Important trends, such as the increasing number of women, ethnic minorities, and physically and mentally challenged workers in the workforce, require a more flexible set of policies and practices.

3   *Employee wellness.* These interventions include employee assistance programs (EAPs) and stress management. EAPs are counselling programs that help employees deal with substance abuse and mental health, marital and financial problems often associated with poor work performance. Stress management programs help organisation members cope with the negative consequences of stress at work. They help managers to reduce specific sources of stress, such as role conflict and ambiguity, and provide methods for reducing stress symptoms, such as hypertension and anxiety.

STRATEGIC INTERVENTIONS

Chapter 10 of the book presents interventions that link the internal functioning of the organisation to the larger environment and transform the organisation to keep pace with changing conditions. These change programs are new additions to OD. They are organisation-wide and bring about a fit between business strategy, structure, culture and the larger environment. The interventions derive from the disciplines of strategic management, organisation theory, open systems theory and cultural anthropology.

In Chapter 10, we discuss three major interventions for managing organisation and environment relationships:

1   *Open systems planning.* This change method helps organisations and departments to systematically assess their environmental relationships and to plan for improvements in interactions. It is intended to help organisations become more active in relating to their environment.

2   *Integrated strategic change.* This comprehensive OD intervention suggests that the principles of planned change can make a value-added contribution to strategic management. It argues that business strategies and organisational systems must be changed together in response to external and internal disruptions. A strategic change plan helps members to manage the transition from a current strategy and organisation design to the desired future strategic orientation.

3   *Transorganisational development.* This intervention is concerned with helping organisations to form partnerships with other organisations to perform tasks or to solve problems that are too complex for single organisations to resolve. It helps organisations to recognise the need for partnerships and develop appropriate structures for implementing them.

Chapter 11 presents three major interventions for transforming organisations:

1 *Culture change.* This intervention is aimed at helping organisations to develop cultures (behaviours, values, beliefs and norms) appropriate to their strategies and environments. It focuses on developing a strong organisation culture to keep organisation members pulling in the same direction.

2 *Self-designing organisations.* This change program involves helping organisations gain the capacity to fundamentally alter themselves. It is a highly participative process that involves multiple stakeholders in setting strategic directions and designing and implementing appropriate structures and processes. Organisations learn how to design and implement their own strategic changes.

3 *Organisation learning.* This intervention involves a process where the organisation systematically examines the way it operates to uncover the patterns in its actions, the assumptions underlying those patterns and the alteration of those patterns. Distinct from individual learning, this intervention helps the organisation move beyond solving existing problems and gain the capability to improve continuously. An organisation that engages in learning over a sustained period of time creates a learning organisation.

IMPLEMENTING CHANGE

Change can vary in complexity from the introduction of relatively simple processes into a small work group to transforming the strategies and organisation design features of the whole organisation.

Overview of change activities

The OD literature has directed considerable attention to managing change. Much of this material is highly prescriptive, offering advice to managers about how to plan and implement organisational changes. Traditionally, change management has focused on identifying sources of resistance to change and offering ways of overcoming them.[10] Recent contributions have been aimed at creating visions and desired futures, gaining political support for them and managing the transition of the organisation towards them.[11]

The diversity of practical advice for managing change can be organised into five major activities, as shown in Figure 6.2. The activities contribute to effective change management and are listed in roughly the order in which they are typically performed. The first activity involves motivating change and includes creating a readiness for change among organisation members and helping them to manage resistance to change. This involves creating an environment in which people accept the need for change and commit physical and psychological energy to it. Motivation is a critical issue in starting change, and there is ample evidence to show that people and organisations seek to preserve the status quo and are willing to change only when there are compelling reasons to do so. The second activity is concerned with creating a vision. The vision provides a purpose and reason for change and describes the desired future state. Together, they provide the 'why' and 'what' of planned change. The third activity involves the development of political support for change. Organisations are made up of powerful individuals and groups that can either block or promote change, and change agents need to gain their support to implement changes. The fourth activity is concerned with managing the transition from the current state to the desired future state. It involves creating a plan for managing the change activities as well as planning special management structures for operating the organisation during the transition. The fifth activity involves sustaining momentum for change so that it will be carried to completion. This includes providing resources for implementing the changes, building a support system for change agents, developing new competencies and skills, and reinforcing the new behaviours necessary for implementing the changes.

Each of the activities shown in Figure 6.2 is important for managing change. Although little research on their relative contributions to change has been conducted, they all seem to

Figure 6.2   Activities contributing to effective change

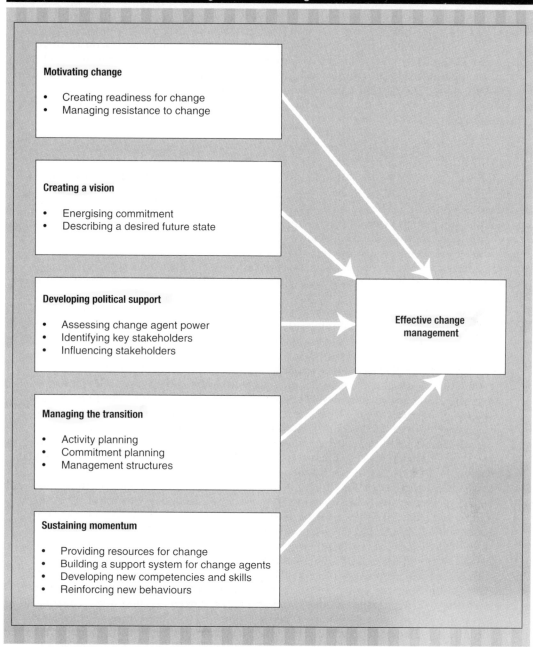

demand careful attention when planning and implementing organisational change. Unless individuals are motivated and committed to change, unfreezing the status quo will be extremely difficult. In the absence of vision, change is likely to be disorganised and diffuse. Without the support of powerful individuals and groups, change is likely to be blocked and possibly sabotaged. Unless the transition process is carefully managed, the organisation will have difficulty functioning while it is moving from the current state to the future state. Without efforts to sustain the momentum for change, the organisation will have problems carrying the changes through to completion. Thus, all five activities must be managed effectively if organisational change is to be successful.

Motivating change

Organisational change involves moving from the known to the unknown. Because the future is uncertain and may adversely affect people's competencies, worth and coping abilities, organisation members do not generally support change unless compelling reasons convince them to do so. Similarly, organisations tend to be heavily invested in the status quo, and they resist changing it in the face of uncertain future benefits. Consequently, a key issue in planning for action is how to motivate commitment to organisational change. As shown in Figure 6.2, this requires attention to two related tasks: creating readiness for change and managing resistance to change.

CREATING READINESS FOR CHANGE

One of the more fundamental axioms of OD is that people's readiness for change depends on creating a felt need for change. This involves making people so dissatisfied with the status quo that they are motivated to try new things and ways of behaving. Creating such dissatisfaction can be rather difficult, as evidenced by anyone who has tried to lose weight, to stop smoking or to change some other habitual behaviour. Generally, people and organisations need to experience deep levels of hurt before they will seriously undertake meaningful change. For example, IBM experienced threats to its very survival before it undertook significant change programs. The following three methods can help generate sufficient dissatisfaction that change will be produced:

1   *Sensitise organisations to pressures for change.* Innumerable pressures for change operate both externally and internally to organisations. As described in Chapter 1, modern organisations are facing unprecedented environmental pressures to change themselves, including heavy foreign competition, rapidly changing technology and global markets. Internal pressures to change include poor product quality, high production costs, and excessive employee absenteeism and turnover. Before these pressures can serve as triggers for change, however, organisations must be sensitive to them. The pressures must pass beyond an organisation's threshold of awareness if managers are to respond to them. Many organisations set their thresholds of awareness too high, thus neglecting pressures for change until they reach disastrous levels.[12] Organisations can make themselves more sensitive to pressures for change by encouraging leaders to surround themselves with devil's advocates;[13] by cultivating external networks made up of people or organisations with different perspectives and views; by visiting other organisations to gain exposure to new ideas and methods; and by using external standards of performance, such as competitors' progress or benchmarks, rather than the organisation's own past standards of performance. A study by Monash University reported that 65% of Australia's top 500 companies believe they will have to benchmark to survive.[14]

2   *Reveal discrepancies between current and desired states.* In this approach to generating a felt need for change, information about the organisation's current functioning is gathered and compared with desired states of operation. (See the later section titled 'Creating a vision' for more information about desired future states.) These desired states may include organisational goals and standards, as well as a general vision of a more desirable future state.[15] Significant discrepancies between actual and ideal states can motivate organisation members to initiate corrective changes, particularly when members are committed to achieving those ideals. A major goal of diagnosis, as described in Chapter 4, is to provide members with feedback about current organisational functioning so that this information can be compared with goals or with desired future states. Such feedback can energise action to improve the organisation. At Honeywell, Chrysler and Imperial Chemical Industries, for example, balance sheets had reached the point at which it was painfully obvious that drastic renewal was needed.

3   *Convey credible positive expectations for the change.* Organisation members invariably have expectations about the results of organisational changes, and those expectations can play an important role in generating motivation for change.[16] The expectations can serve as a self-fulfilling prophecy, leading members to invest energy

in change programs that they expect will succeed. When members expect success, they are likely to develop greater commitment to the change process and to direct more energy into the kinds of constructive behaviour needed to implement change.[17] The key to achieving these positive effects is to communicate realistic, positive expectations about the organisational changes. Organisation members can also be taught about the benefits of positive expectations and can be encouraged to set credible positive expectations for the change program.

MANAGING RESISTANCE TO CHANGE

Change can generate deep resistance in people and in organisations, making it difficult, if not impossible, to implement organisational improvements.[18] At a personal level, change can arouse considerable anxiety about letting go of the known and moving to an uncertain future. Individuals may be unsure whether their existing skills and contributions will be valued in the future. They may have significant questions about whether they can learn to function effectively and to achieve benefits in the new situation. At the organisation level, resistance to change can come from three sources.[19] Technical resistance comes from the habit of following common procedures and the investment cost of resources invested in the status quo. Political resistance can arise when organisational changes threaten powerful stakeholders, such as top executive or staff personnel, and may call into question the past decisions of leaders. Organisation change often implies a different allocation of already scarce resources, such as capital, training budgets and good people. Finally, cultural resistance takes the form of systems and procedures that reinforce the status quo, promoting conformity to existing values, norms and assumptions about how things should operate.

There are at least three major strategies for dealing with resistance to change:[20]

1   *Empathy and support.* A first step in overcoming resistance is to know how people are experiencing change. This can help to identify those who are having trouble accepting the changes, the nature of their resistance and possible ways of overcoming it. Understanding how people experience change requires a great deal of empathy and support. It demands a willingness to suspend judgement and to try to see the situation from another's perspective, a process called 'active listening'. When people feel that those managing change are genuinely interested in their feelings and perceptions, they are likely to be less defensive and more willing to share their concerns and fears. This more open relationship not only provides useful information about resistance but also helps to establish the basis for the kind of joint problem solving that is necessary for overcoming barriers to change.

2   *Communication.* People tend to resist change when they are uncertain about its consequences. Lack of adequate information fuels rumours and gossip, and adds to the anxiety generally associated with change. Effective communication about changes and their likely consequences can reduce this speculation and allay unfounded fears. It can help members realistically prepare for change.

     However, communication is also one of the most frustrating aspects of managing change. Organisation members are constantly receiving data about current operations and future plans as well as informal rumours about people, changes and politics. Managers and OD practitioners must think seriously about how to break through this stream of information. One strategy is to make change information more salient by communicating through a new or different channel. If most information is delivered through memos and letters, then change information can be sent through meetings and presentations. Another method that can be effective during large-scale change is to deliberately substitute change information for normal operating information. This sends a message that changing one's activities is a critical part of a member's job.

3   *Participation and involvement.* One of the oldest and most effective strategies for overcoming resistance is to involve organisation members directly in planning and implementing change. Participation can lead both to designing high-quality changes and to overcoming resistance to implementing them.[21] Members can provide a diversity of information and ideas, which can contribute to making the innovations

effective and appropriate to the situation. They can also identify pitfalls and barriers to implementation. Involvement in planning the changes increases the likelihood that members' interests and needs will be accounted for during the intervention. Consequently, participants will be committed to implementing the changes as it is in their best interests to do so. Implementing the changes will contribute to meeting their needs. Moreover, for people who have strong needs for involvement, the very act of participation can be motivating, leading to greater effort to make the changes work.[22]

Application 6.2 is about the debate concerning the involvement of women in combat zones and the various types of resistance that it has met.

APPLICATiON 6.2

LET WOMEN FIGHT: SENATOR JOINS RECRUITMENT DEBATE

Women should have the right to fill combat jobs in the Australian Defence Force if they meet the standards needed, Victorian Liberal senator Mitch Fifield says.

Now the armed forces are lowering their entry criteria to attract more recruits, women should be given access to all jobs, he has argued in the Liberal magazine, *The PartyRoom*.

'Soon overweight, asthmatic, tattooed, former cannabis smoking men may be eligible for ADF service, while qualified women (including those who already serve) will remain ineligible for combat roles,' he writes.

ADF rules prevent women taking direct combat roles such as clearance divers, airfield defence guards, artillery, armour, combat engineers and infantry, Senator Fifield says, adding that liberalising the rules should be a decision for the government rather than the ADF.

His view ran into some resistance and scepticism. Defence Minister Brendan Nelson said neither he nor the ADF leadership supported women in all frontline combat roles.

Sex Discrimination Commissioner Pru Goward said: 'In theory, yes; in practice, you would have to heavily qualify it by what would work and how you would manage a male culture that has been designed for combat.'

Shadow defence minister Robert McClelland said there was 'a wide range of frontline roles women can and should be permitted to perform. My personal view is the community is not at a stage that it would like to see women in hand-to-hand combat.'

But Liberal senator Marise Payne, a member of the parliamentary Joint Standing Committee on Foreign Affairs, Defence and Trade, said in the context of the current recruitment debate all options should be examined.

Senator Fifield says a 1998 review expanded employment for women to include 87% of categories. He says ADF roles should be entirely competency-based with the only criterion being merit.

'It is not the lack of women in combat roles that should be troubling, but the denial of opportunity,' he writes.

The ADF said yesterday the government had last year altered its policy on women in support roles in previously exempted employment categories – infantry, armoured and artillery units. Women were eligible to serve in about 90% of employment categories across the ADF, up from 73% in 2003.

Australia needs a cultural change in the family like the one it is having in the workforce, so that more women pursue their careers and more men share the child-rearing, says Ms Goward.

...

To change that, she said, men, women and employers needed to change their attitudes to how families worked – giving more support to men who became carers, and to women who put careers first.

Source: Michelle Grattan & Tim Colebatch, 'Let women fight: Call goes out Senator joins recruitment debate', *The Age*, 2/10/2006.

Critical Thinking Questions: This suggestion will create considerable debate. What are the arguments for and against this proposal? How would you change attitudes on both sides of the argument?

Creating a vision

The second activity for managing change involves creating a vision of what members want the organisation to look like or become. Generally, the vision describes the desired future, towards which change is directed. It provides a valued direction for designing, implementing and assessing organisational changes. The vision can also energise commitment to change by providing a compelling rationale as to why change is necessary and worth the effort. It can provide members with a common goal and challenge. However, if the vision is seen as impossible or promotes changes that the organisation cannot implement, it can actually depress member motivation. For example, Bob Hawke's unfulfilled vision that 'no child will live in poverty' was emotionally appealing, but impossible to achieve. In contrast, John Kennedy's vision of 'putting a man on the moon and returning him safely to the earth' was only just beyond current engineering and technical feasibility. In the context of the 1960s, it was bold, alluring and vivid; it not only provided a purpose, but a valued direction as well.[23]

Creating a vision is considered a key element in most leadership frameworks.[24] Those leading the organisation or unit are responsible for its effectiveness, and they must take an active role in describing a desired future, and energising commitment to it. In many cases, leaders encourage participation in developing the vision in order to gain wider input and support. For example, they may involve subordinates and others who have a stake in the changes. The popular media include numerous accounts of executives who have helped to mobilise and direct organisational change, including Richard Pratt (Visy).[25] Although these people are at the senior executive level, providing a description of a desired future is no less important for those who lead change in small departments and work groups. At these lower organisational levels, ample opportunities exist to get employees directly involved in the visioning process.

People's values and preferences for what the organisation should look like, and how it should function, heavily drive the process of developing a vision. The vision represents people's ideals, fantasies or dreams of what they would like the organisation to look like or become.

Unfortunately, dreaming about the future is discouraged in most organisations.[26] It requires creative and intuitive thought processes that tend to conflict with the rational, analytical methods prevalent in organisations. Consequently, leaders may need to create special conditions for describing a desired future, such as off-site workshops or exercises that stimulate creative thinking.

To be effective in managing change, creating a vision addresses two key aspects of organisation change: (1) describing the desired future, and (2) energising commitment to moving towards it.

DESCRIBING THE DESIRED FUTURE

The visioning process is future-oriented. It generally results in a vision statement that describes the organisation's desired future state. Although the vision statement may be detailed, it does not generally specify how the changes will occur. These details are part of the subsequent activity planning that occurs when managing the transition towards the desired future.

A vision statement may include all or some of the following elements that can be communicated to organisation members:

1   *Mission.* Participants often define the mission of their organisation or sub-unit as a prelude to describing the desired future state. The mission includes the organisation's major strategic purpose or reason for existing. It may include specification of the following: target customers and markets, principal products or services, geographic domain, core technologies, strategic objectives and desired public image. A study of the mission statements from 218 Fortune 500 companies showed that the higher financial performers prepared written mission statements for public dissemination.[27] The statements included the firms' basic beliefs, values, priorities, competitive strengths and desired public images. Defining the mission can provide a sound starting point for envisioning what the organisation should look like and how it should operate. In some cases, members may have conflicting views about the mission, and surfacing and resolving those conflicts can help to mobilise and direct energy for the process.

2   *Valued outcomes.* Descriptions of desired futures often include specific performance and human outcomes that the organisation or unit would like to achieve. These valued outcomes can serve as goals for the change process and standards for assessing progress. Valued performance outcomes might include high levels of product innovation, manufacturing efficiency and customer service. Valued human outcomes could include high levels of employee satisfaction, development, safety and job security. These outcomes specify the kinds of values that the organisation would like to promote in the future.

ENERGISING COMMITMENT

In addition to describing a desired future, creating a vision includes energising the commitment to change. This aspect of the visioning process is exciting, connected to the past and present, and compelling. It seeks to create a vision that is emotionally powerful to organisation members and which motivates them to change. To achieve excitement for change, organisations often create a slogan or metaphor that captures the essence of the changes. For example, part of Disneyland's return to prominence was guided by the motto, 'Creating a place where people can feel like kids again'. The metaphor of feeling like a kid provided an important emotional appeal to Disney's change effort.

A vision that is clearly linked to the organisation's past and present can also energise commitment to change. It can provide a realistic context for moving towards the future and can enable members to develop realistic goals and maintain a temporal perspective of the 'big picture'. Apple's original vision of 'changing the way people do their work' provides a good example. Many employees had experienced the drudgery of a boring job, an uninspired boss or an alienating workplace. The notion that they could be a part of an organisation that is changing work into something more challenging, creative or satisfying was naturally alluring to many of them.

Finally, a compelling vision can energise commitment to change. By identifying a powerful reason or purpose for the change, the vision can provide meaning to the change activities that members will need to undertake during the transition. Thus, the words used in the vision can encourage behaviour towards the desired future as well as generate feelings of inclusiveness. Conversely, words can constrain people and leave them feeling controlled or manipulated. For example, 'shrewd' and 'creative' both imply innovative behaviour but have different connotations.

Developing political support

From a political perspective, organisations can be seen as loosely structured coalitions of individuals and groups with different preferences and interests.[28] For example, shop-floor workers may want secure, high-paying jobs, while top executives may be interested in diversifying the organisation into new businesses. The marketing department might be interested in developing new products and markets, and the production department may want to manufacture standard products in the most efficient way. These different groups or coalitions compete with one another for scarce resources and influence. They act to preserve or enhance their self-interest while managing to arrive at a sufficient balance of power to sustain commitment to the organisation and to achieve overall effectiveness.

Given this political view, attempts to change the organisation may threaten the balance of power among groups, resulting in political conflicts and struggles.[29] Individuals and groups will be concerned with how the changes affect their own power and influence, and they will act accordingly. Some groups will become less powerful, while others will gain influence. Those whose power is threatened by the change will act defensively and seek to preserve the status quo; for example, they might attempt to present compelling evidence that change is unnecessary or that only minor modifications are needed. On the other hand, those participants who will gain power from the changes will tend to push heavily for them. They may bring in seemingly impartial consultants to legitimise the need for change. Consequently, conflicting interests, distorted information and political turmoil frequently accompany significant organisational changes.

Methods for managing the political dynamics of organisational change are relatively recent additions to OD. Traditionally, OD has tended to neglect political issues, mainly because its humanistic roots promoted collaboration and power sharing among individuals and groups.[30] Today, change agents are increasingly paying attention to power and political activity, particularly as they engage in strategic change that involves most parts and features of organisations. Some practitioners are concerned, however, about whether power and OD are compatible. A growing number of advocates suggest that OD practitioners can use power in positive ways.[31] They can build their own power base to gain access to other power holders within the organisation. Without such access, those who influence or make decisions may not have the advantage of an OD perspective. OD practitioners can use power strategies that are open and above board to get those in power to consider OD applications. They can facilitate processes for examining the uses of power in organisations and can help power holders devise more creative and positive strategies than political bargaining, deceit and the like. They can help power holders to confront the need for change and can help to ensure that the interests and concerns of those with less power are considered. Although OD professionals can use power constructively in organisations, they will probably always be ambivalent and tense about whether such uses promote OD values and ethics or whether they represent the destructive, negative side of power. This tension seems healthy, and it is hoped that it will guide the wise use of power in OD.

As shown in Figure 6.3, managing the political dynamics of change includes the following activities:

1   *Assessing change agent power*. The first task is to evaluate the change agent's own sources of power. The change agent might be the leader of the organisation or department undergoing change, or he or she might be the OD consultant, if professional help is being used. By assessing their own power base, change agents can determine how to use it to influence others to support changes. They can also identify areas in which they might need to enhance their sources of power.

Greiner and Schein, in the first OD book written entirely from a power perspective, identified three key sources of personal power in organisations (in addition to one's formal position): knowledge, personality and others' support.[32] Knowledge bases of power include having expertise that is valued by others and controlling important information. OD professionals typically gain power through their expertise in

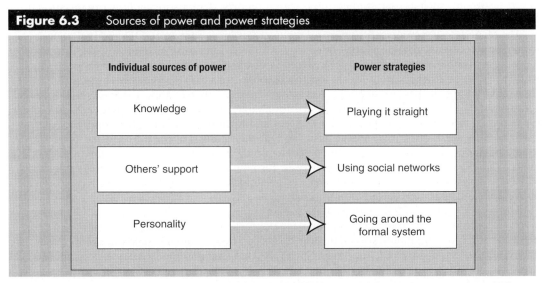

Figure 6.3   Sources of power and power strategies

Source: L. Greiner and V. Schein, *Power and Organization Development: Mobilizing Power to Implement Change*: 52; copyright © 1988 by Addison-Wesley Publishing Co.

organisational change. Personality sources of power can derive from change agents' charisma, reputation and professional credibility. Charismatic leaders can inspire devotion and enthusiasm for change from subordinates. OD consultants with strong reputations and professional credibility can wield considerable power during organisational change. Others' support can contribute to individual power by providing access to information and resource networks. Others may also use their power on behalf of the change agent. For example, leaders in organisational units undergoing change can call on their informal networks for resources and support. They can encourage subordinates to exercise power in support of the change.

2   *Identifying key stakeholders.* Once change agents have assessed their own power bases, they can identify powerful individuals and groups who have an interest in the changes, such as staff groups, unions, departmental managers and top-level executives. These stakeholders can either thwart or support change, and it is important to gain broad-based support to minimise the risk that a single interest group will block the changes. Identifying key stakeholders can start from the simple question: 'Who stands to gain or lose from the changes?' Once stakeholders have been identified, creating a map of their influence may be useful.[33] The map could show relationships among the stakeholders in terms of who influences whom and what the stakes are for each party. This would provide change agents with information about which individuals and groups need to be influenced to accept and support the changes.

3   *Influencing stakeholders.* This activity involves gaining the support of key stakeholders to motivate a critical mass for change. There are at least three major strategies for using power to influence others in OD: playing it straight, using social networks and going around the formal system.[34] Figure 6.3 links these strategies to the individual sources of power discussed above.

The strategy of *playing it straight* is very consistent with an OD perspective, and so is the most widely used power strategy in OD. It involves determining the needs of particular stakeholders and presenting information as to how the changes can benefit them. This relatively straightforward approach is based on the premise that information and knowledge can persuade people about the need and direction for change. The success of this strategy relies heavily on the change agent's knowledge base. He or she must have the expertise and information necessary for persuading stakeholders that the changes are a logical way to meet their needs. For example, a change agent might present diagnostic data, such as company reports on productivity and absenteeism or surveys of members' perceptions of problems, to generate a felt need for change among specific stakeholders. Other persuasive evidence might include educational material and expert testimony, such as case studies and research reports, demonstrating how organisational changes can address pertinent issues.

The second power strategy, *using social networks*, is more foreign to OD and includes forming alliances and coalitions with other powerful individuals and groups, dealing directly with key decision makers and using formal and informal contacts to gain information. In this strategy, change agents try to use their social relationships to gain support for changes. As shown in Figure 6.3, they use the individual power base of others' support to gain the resources, commitment and political momentum needed for change. This social networking might include, for example, meeting with other powerful groups and forming an alliance to support specific changes. This would probably involve ensuring that the interests of the different parties – for example, labour and management– are considered in the change process. Many union and management quality-of-work-life efforts involve forming such alliances. This strategy might also include using informal contacts to discover key roadblocks to change and gain access to major decision makers that need to sanction the changes.

The power strategy of *going around the formal system* is probably least used in OD and involves deliberately circumventing organisational structures and procedures to get the changes implemented. Existing organisational arrangements can be roadblocks to change, and, rather than taking the time and energy to remove them, working around the barriers may be more expedient and effective. As shown in Figure 6.3, this strategy relies on a strong personality base of power. The change agent's charisma, reputation or professional credibility lend legitimacy to going around the system and can reduce the likelihood of negative reprisals. For example, managers with reputations as 'winners' can often bend the rules to implement organisational changes. Those needing to support change trust their judgement. This power strategy is relatively easy to abuse, however, and OD practitioners should carefully consider the ethical issues and possible unintended consequences of circumventing formal policies and practices.

Managing the transition

Implementing organisational change involves moving from the existing organisation state to the desired future state. This movement does not occur immediately but, as shown in Figure 6.4, requires a transition state during which the organisation learns how to implement the conditions needed to reach the desired future. Beckhard and Harris pointed out that the transition state may be quite different from the present state of the organisation and consequently may require special management structures and activities.[36] They identified three major activities and structures to facilitate organisational transition:

1   *Activity planning.* This involves making a road map for change, citing specific activities and events that must occur if the transition is to be successful. Activity planning should clearly identify, temporally orient and integrate discrete change tasks and should link these tasks to the organisation's change goals and priorities. Activity planning should also gain top-management approval, be cost-effective and remain adaptable as feedback is received during the change process.

    An important feature of activity planning is that visions and desired future states can be quite general when compared with the realities of actually implementing change. As a result, it may be necessary to supplement them with midpoint goals as part of the activity plan.[37] These represent desirable organisational conditions between the current state and the desired future state. Midpoint goals are clearer and more detailed than desired future states, and so provide more concrete and manageable steps and benchmarks for change. Activity plans can use midpoint goals to successfully provide members with the direction and security for embarkation towards the desired future.

2   *Commitment planning.* This activity involves identifying key people and groups whose commitment is needed for change to occur and deciding how to gain their support. Although commitment planning is generally a part of developing political support (discussed above), specific plans for identifying key stakeholders and obtaining their commitment to change need to be made early in the change process.

3   *Management structures.* Because organisational transitions tend to be ambiguous and to need direction, special structures for managing the change process need to be created. These management structures should include people who have the power to mobilise resources to promote change, the respect of the existing leadership and advocates of change, and the interpersonal and political skills to guide the change process. Alternative management structures include the following:[38]

    - The chief executive or head person manages the change effort.

    - A project manager is given the temporary assignment of co-ordinating the transition.

    - The formal organisation manages the change effort in addition to supervising normal operations.

Figure 6.4   Organisation change as a transition state

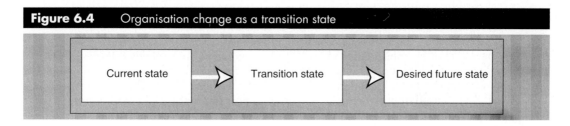

- Representatives of the major constituencies involved in the change jointly manage the project.

- Natural leaders who have the confidence and trust of large numbers of affected employees are selected to manage the transition.

- A cross-section of people representing different organisational functions and levels manages the change.

- A kitchen cabinet representing people whom the chief executive consults and confides in manages the change effort.

Sustaining momentum

Once organisational changes are under way, explicit attention must be directed at sustaining energy and commitment for implementing them. Often, the initial excitement and activity of changing dissipate in the face of the practical problems of trying to learn new ways of operating. A strong tendency exists among organisation members to return to what is well known and learned, unless they receive sustained support and reinforcement for carrying the changes through to completion.

The following four activities can help to sustain momentum for carrying change through to completion:

1   *Providing resources for change.* Implementing organisation change generally requires additional financial and human resources, particularly if the organisation continues day-to-day operations while trying to change itself. These extra resources are needed for such change activities as training, consultation, data collection and feedback, and special meetings. Extra resources are also helpful to provide a buffer as performance drops during the transition period. Organisations can seriously underestimate the need for special resources devoted to the change process. Significant organisational change invariably requires considerable management time and energy, as well as the help of consultants. A separate 'change budget' that exists along with capital and operating budgets can help to identify the resources needed for training members in how to behave differently and for assessing progress and making necessary modifications in the change program.[39] Unless these extra resources are planned for and provided, meaningful change is not as likely to occur.

2   *Building a support system for change agents.* Organisation change can be difficult and filled with tension, not only for participants but also for change agents.[40] Change agents must often provide members with emotional support, yet they may receive little support themselves. They must often maintain 'psychological distance' from others in order to gain the perspective needed to lead the change process. This can produce considerable tension and isolation, and change agents may need to create their own support system to help them cope with these problems. This typically consists of a network of people with whom the change agent has close personal relationships. These people can provide emotional support and can serve as a sounding board for ideas and problems. They can challenge untested assumptions. For example, OD professionals often use trusted colleagues as 'shadow consultants' to help them think through difficult issues with clients and to offer conceptual and emotional support. Similarly, a growing number of companies, such as Fisher & Paykel and Heinz-Wattie, are forming internal networks of change agents to provide mutual learning and support.[41]

3   *Developing new competencies and skills.* Organisational changes frequently demand new knowledge, skills and behaviours from organisation members. In many cases, the changes cannot be implemented unless members gain new competencies. For example, employee-involvement programs often require managers to learn new leadership styles and new approaches to problem solving. Change agents need to ensure that such learning occurs. They need to provide multiple learning opportunities, such as traditional training programs, on-the-job counselling and coaching, and experiential simulations. This learning should cover both technical and social skills. Because it is easy to overlook

the social component, change agents may need to devote special time and resources to helping members gain the social skills needed to implement changes.

4   *Reinforcing new behaviours.* People in organisations generally do those things that bring them rewards. Consequently, one of the most effective ways of sustaining momentum for change is to reinforce the kinds of behaviours needed to implement the changes. This can be accomplished by linking formal rewards directly to the desired behaviours. Desired behaviours can also be reinforced through recognition, encouragement and praise. These can usually be given more frequently than formal rewards, and change agents should take advantage of the myriad of informal opportunities available to recognise and praise changed behaviours in a timely fashion. Perhaps equally important are the intrinsic rewards that people can experience through early success in the change effort. Achieving identifiable, early successes can make participants feel good about themselves and their behaviours, thus reinforcing the drive to change.

EVALUATING ORGANISATION DEVELOPMENT INTERVENTIONS

Evaluation processes consider both the implementation success of the intended intervention and the long-term results it produces. Two key aspects of effective evaluation are measurement and research design. The institutionalisation or long-term persistence of intervention effects is examined in a framework that shows the organisation characteristics, intervention dimensions and processes that contribute to institutionalisation of OD interventions in organisations.

Evaluating OD interventions

Assessing OD interventions involves judgements about whether an intervention has been implemented as intended and, if so, whether it is having desired results. Managers investing resources in OD efforts are increasingly being held accountable for the results. They are being asked to justify the expenditures in terms of hard, bottom-line outcomes. More and more, managers are asking for rigorous assessment of OD interventions and are using the results to make important resource allocation decisions about OD, such as whether to continue to support the change program, whether to modify or alter it, or whether to terminate it altogether and perhaps try something else.

Traditionally, OD evaluation has been discussed as something that occurs after the intervention. Chapters 7 to 10, for example, present evaluative research about the interventions after discussing the respective change programs. This view can be misleading. Decisions about the measurement of relevant variables and the design of the evaluation process should be made early in the OD cycle so that evaluation choices can be integrated with intervention decisions.

There are two distinct types of OD evaluation: one intended to guide the implementation of interventions and the other to assess their overall impact. The key issues in evaluation are measurement and research design.

IMPLEMENTATION AND EVALUATION FEEDBACK

Most discussions and applications of OD evaluation imply that evaluation is something done after intervention. It is typically argued that, once the intervention has been implemented, it should be evaluated to discover whether it is producing the intended effects. For example, it might reasonably be expected that a job-enrichment program would lead to higher employee satisfaction and performance. After implementing job enrichment, evaluation would involve assessing whether or not it did actually lead to positive results.

This after-implementation view of evaluation is only partially correct. It assumes that interventions have actually been implemented as intended and that the key problem of evaluation is to assess their effects. In many, if not most, OD programs, however, implementing interventions cannot be taken for granted.[42] Most OD interventions require significant changes

Figure 6.5 Implementation and evaluation feedback

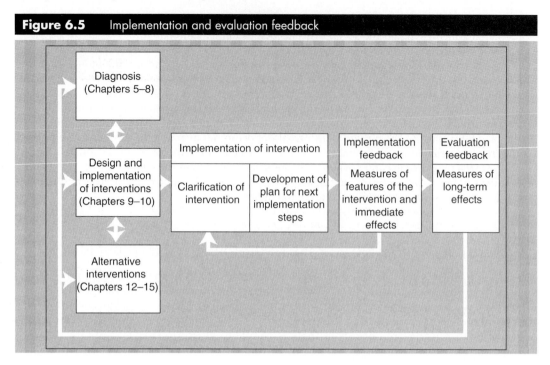

in people's behaviours and ways of thinking about organisations, yet interventions typically offer only broad prescriptions for how such changes are to occur. For example, job enrichment calls for adding discretion (freedom of judgement), variety and meaningful feedback to people's jobs. Implementing such changes requires considerable learning and experimentation as employees and managers discover how to translate these general prescriptions into specific behaviours and procedures. This learning process involves much trial and error and needs to be guided by information about whether behaviours and procedures are being changed as intended.[43] Consequently, we should expand our view of evaluation to include both during-implementation assessment of whether interventions are actually being implemented and after-implementation evaluation of whether they are producing expected results.

Both kinds of evaluation provide organisation members with feedback about interventions. Evaluation aimed at guiding implementation may be called *implementation feedback*, and assessment intended to discover intervention outcomes might be called *evaluation feedback*[44]. Figure 6.5 shows how the two kinds of feedback fit with the diagnostic and intervention stages of OD. The application of OD to a particular organisation starts with a thorough diagnosis of the situation (Chapters 4 to 5), which helps to identify particular organisational problems or areas for improvement, as well as likely causes underlying them. Next, from an array of possible interventions (Chapters 7 to 10), one or more sets are chosen as a means of improving the organisation. This choice is based on knowledge that links interventions to diagnosis and change management.

Application 6.3 describes an integrative approach to change management where Kotter's 'Eight Steps to Transforming Your Organisation' was utilised by the World Bank.

APPLiCATiON 6.3

EVALUATING CHANGE AND CHANGE MANAGEMENT AT THE WORLD BANK

In the mid-'90s the World Bank, an international agency with a mission to help reduce poverty worldwide, was facing criticism and declining support from many of its key constituencies.

The concerns included arrogance, insularity, slowness, cost and a lack of client focus. Moreover, stakeholders believed the quality and relevance of funded projects and the advice the Bank provided were deteriorating.

To stem its slide toward irrelevance, the Bank undertook a massive change program affecting every dimension of the organisation and every principle behind its way of doing business. The culmination of this effort was reached in 1997 with the conclusion – shortly after the arrival of a new president at the Bank – of a Strategic Compact between the Bank and its shareholders. In exchange for a one-time injection of $250 million, the Bank committed to delivering a substantially transformed institution within 3 years.

The Compact was ambitious in both its timetable and scope and focused on the implementation of four priority change programs: refueling the current business activity; refocusing the development agenda; retooling the knowledge base; and revamping institutional capabilities.

A large number of task forces and other parallel structures were deployed to implement the resulting agenda, with senior management assuming an active role.

In early 2001, an evaluation of the Compact's transformation effort and a report to the Board were begun. An evaluation team, assembled to look at each change program, was expected to address both the content and effectiveness of the change and also how the change was managed. This application focuses on the evaluation of the change management process.

The sub-team responsible for evaluating change management settled early on an evaluation framework and on a variety of methodologies to collect, integrate and validate evaluation data. The framework was based on Kotter's 'Eight Steps to Transforming Your Organization'; a widely recognised set of best practices that were well known within the Bank, and expanded to include classic change management principles advocated by Richard Beckhard. The headings of the framework are shown below:

1 Establish a Sense of Urgency
2 Form a Powerful Guiding Coalition
3 Create a Vision
4 Communicate the Vision
5 Manage the Transition
6 Build Change Capacity/Readiness
7 Empower Others to Act on the Vision
8 Plan for and Create Short-term Wins
9 Consolidate Improvements, Sustain Momentum, Produce More Change
10 Institutionalise New Approaches

Multiple sources of data were used: *Written materials* were collected documenting statements and events associated with the Compact; *Numeric data,* such as surveys or organisational data, were collected to supplement and validate other data; *Interviews* were conducted with key change actors to generate data about what happened, and to gather perspectives on how to interpret data and events; *Focus groups* gathered additional data and diverse perspectives to validate, compare and confront different assessments; and *The Assessment* team's own perspectives from researching each main element of the Compact.

The reliability and the completeness of the data were ensured in several ways. First, focus group questions were framed to elicit positive evidence before eliciting critical assessments, so as to counteract well-documented natural tendencies to be overly negative toward the past. Second, discordant data were surfaced with the interviewees or the groups to ensure any discordance was understood and reconciled wherever possible. Third, the process was carried to the point where further interviews and focus groups were deemed not to be necessary as the later ones added little new data or perspectives to the data produced earlier, thus suggesting the data were reasonably complete. Finally, the resulting assessments were submitted to all interviewees and focus group participants for validation purposes.

Overall, the Compact process was seen as quite successful from a change management perspective. In many ways, the Bank emerged from the Compact a changed institution. Based on focus group findings, the evaluation found that the Bank's culture had shifted. The most pronounced change was a movement from being inward-looking to being client focused.

Source: From *Organization Development and Change* (ISE), 8e, by Cummings/Worley, 2005. Reprinted with permission of South-Wester, a division of Thomson Learning: www.thomsonrights.com, pp. 156–7.

Critical Thinking Question: This article identifies a 'culture shift' within the organisation. What type of culture shift was described and how could this be managed? Research Kotter's 'Eight Steps' and critically analyse his recommendations. Would it be suitable in all circumstances?

In most cases, the chosen intervention provides only general guidelines for organisational change, leaving managers and employees with the task of translating them into specific behaviours and procedures. Implementation feedback guides this process. It consists of two types of information: data about the different features of the intervention itself and data about the immediate effects of the intervention. These data are collected repeatedly and at short intervals. They provide a series of snapshots about how the intervention is progressing. Organisation members can use this information first to gain a clearer understanding of the intervention (the kinds of behaviours and procedures required to implement it) and, second, to plan for the next implementation steps. This feedback cycle might proceed for several rounds, with each round providing members with knowledge about the intervention and ideas for the next stage of implementation.

Once implementation feedback has informed organisation members that the intervention is sufficiently in place, evaluation feedback begins. In contrast to implementation feedback, it is concerned with the overall impact of the intervention and whether resources should continue to be allocated to it or to other possible interventions. Evaluation feedback takes longer to gather and interpret than implementation feedback. It typically includes a broad array of outcome measures, such as performance, job satisfaction, absenteeism and turnover. Negative results on these measures tell members that either the initial diagnosis was seriously flawed or that the choice of intervention was wrong. Such feedback might prompt additional diagnosis and a search for a more effective intervention. Positive results, on the other hand, tell members that the intervention produced the expected outcomes and might prompt a search for ways of institutionalising the changes, making them a permanent part of the organisation's normal functioning.

An example of a job-enrichment intervention helps to clarify the OD stages and feedback linkages shown in Figure 6.5. Suppose the initial diagnosis reveals that employee performance and satisfaction are low and that an underlying cause of this problem lies with jobs that are overly structured and routinised. An inspection of alternative interventions to improve productivity and satisfaction suggests that job enrichment might be applicable for this situation. Existing job-enrichment theory proposes that increasing employee discretion, task variety and feedback can lead to improvements in work quality and attitudes, and that this job design and outcome linkage are especially strong for employees with growth needs – needs for challenge, autonomy and development. Initial diagnosis suggests that most employees have high growth needs and that the existing job design prevents the fulfilment of these needs. Therefore, job enrichment seems particularly suited to this situation.

Managers and employees now start to translate the general prescriptions offered by job-enrichment theory into specific behaviours and procedures. At this stage, the intervention is relatively broad and needs to be tailored to fit the specific situation. To implement the intervention, employees might decide on the following organisational changes: job discretion can be increased through more participatory styles of supervision; task variety can be enhanced by allowing employees to inspect their job outputs; and feedback can be made more meaningful by providing employees with quicker and more specific information about their performances.

After three months of trying to implement these changes, the members use implementation feedback to see how the intervention is progressing. Questionnaires and interviews (similar to those used in diagnosis) are administered in order to measure the different features of job enrichment (discretion, variety and feedback) and to assess employees' reactions to the changes. Company records are analysed to show the short-term effects on productivity of the intervention. The data reveal that productivity and satisfaction have changed very little since the initial diagnosis. Employee perceptions of job discretion and feedback have also shown negligible change, but perceptions of task variety have shown significant improvement. In-depth discussion and analysis of this first round of implementation feedback help the supervisors gain a better feel for the kinds of behaviours needed to move towards a participatory leadership style. This greater clarification of one feature of the intervention leads to a decision to involve the supervisors in leadership training and so help them to develop the skills and knowledge needed to lead participatively. A decision is also made to make job feedback more meaningful by translating such data into simple bar graphs, rather than continuing to provide voluminous statistical reports.

After these modifications have been in effect for about three months, members institute a second round of implementation feedback to see how the intervention is progressing. The data now show that productivity and satisfaction have moved moderately higher than in the first round of feedback and that employee perceptions of task variety and feedback are both high. Employee perceptions of discretion, however, remain relatively low. Members conclude that the variety and feedback dimensions of job enrichment are sufficiently implemented but that the discretion component needs improvement. They decide to put more effort into supervisory training and to ask OD practitioners to provide on-line counselling and coaching to supervisors about their leadership styles.

After four more months, a third round of implementation feedback occurs. The data now show that satisfaction and performance are significantly higher than in the first round of feedback and moderately higher than in the second round. The data also show that discretion, variety and feedback are all high, suggesting that the job-enrichment interventions have been successfully implemented. Now evaluation feedback is used to assess the overall effectiveness of the program.

The evaluation feedback includes all the data from the satisfaction and performance measures used in the implementation feedback. Because both the immediate and broader effects of the intervention are being evaluated, additional outcomes are examined, such as employee absenteeism, maintenance costs and reactions of other organisational units not included in job enrichment. The full array of evaluation data might suggest that one year after the start of implementation, the job-enrichment program is having the expected effects and so should be continued and made more permanent.

Measurement

Providing useful implementation and evaluation feedback involves two activities: selecting the appropriate variables and designing good measures.

Selecting variables

Ideally, the variables measured in OD evaluation should derive from the theory or conceptual model that underlies the intervention. The model should incorporate the key features of the intervention as well as its expected results. The general diagnostic models described in Chapter 4 met this criterion, as do the more specific models introduced in Chapters 6 to 10. For example, the job-level diagnostic model described in Chapter 6 proposes several major features of work: task variety, feedback and autonomy. The theory argues that high levels of these elements can be expected to result in high levels of work quality and satisfaction.

The job-level diagnostic model suggests a number of measurement variables for implementation and evaluation feedback. Whether or not the intervention is being implemented could be assessed either by determining how many job descriptions have been rewritten to include more responsibility, or how many organisation members have received cross-training in other job skills. Evaluation of the immediate and long-term impact of job enrichment would include measures of employee performance and satisfaction over time. Again, these measures would probably be included in the initial diagnosis, when the company's problems or areas for improvement are discovered.

The measurement of both intervention and outcome variables is necessary for implementation and evaluation feedback. Unfortunately, there has been a tendency in OD to measure only outcome variables while neglecting intervention variables altogether.[45] It is generally assumed that the intervention has been implemented, and attention is directed to its impact on organisational outcomes, such as performance, absenteeism and satisfaction. As argued earlier, implementing OD interventions generally takes considerable time and learning. It must be empirically determined that the intervention has been implemented; it cannot simply be assumed. Implementation feedback serves this purpose, guiding the implementation process and helping to interpret outcome data. Outcome measures are ambiguous unless it is known how well the intervention has been implemented. For example, a negligible change in measures of performance and satisfaction could mean that the wrong intervention has been chosen, that the correct intervention has not been implemented effectively or that the wrong variables have been measured. Measurement of the intervention variables helps to determine the correct interpretation of outcome measures.

As suggested above, the choice of what intervention variables to measure should derive from the conceptual framework that underlies the OD intervention. Organisation development research and theory have increasingly come to identify the specific organisational changes that are necessary for the implementation of particular interventions. Much of that information is discussed in Chapters 7 to 10; these variables should guide not only the implementation of the intervention but also choices about what change variables to measure for evaluative purposes. Additional sources of knowledge about intervention variables can be found in the numerous references at the end of each of the intervention chapters in this book and in several of the books in the Wiley Series on Organisational Assessment and Change.[46]

The choice of what outcome variables to measure should also be dictated by intervention theory, which specifies the kinds of results that can be expected from particular change programs. Again, the material in this book and elsewhere identifies numerous outcome measures, such as job satisfaction, intrinsic motivation, organisational commitment, absenteeism, turnover and productivity.

Historically, OD assessment has tended to focus on attitudinal outcomes, such as job satisfaction, while neglecting hard measures, such as performance. There has been a growing number of calls from both managers and researchers, however, for the development of behavioural measures of OD outcomes. Managers are primarily interested in applying OD to change work-related behaviours that have to do with joining, remaining and producing at work. They are increasingly assessing OD in terms of such bottom-line results. Macy and Mirvis have done extensive research to develop a standardised set of behavioural outcomes that can be used to assess and compare the results of OD interventions.[47] Table 6.2 lists these 11 outcomes, including their behavioural definitions and recording categories. The outcomes are in two broad categories: *participation-membership*, including absenteeism, tardiness, turnover, internal employment stability, and strikes and work stoppages; and *performance on the job*, including productivity, production quality, grievances, accidents, unscheduled machine down time and repair, material and supply overuse, and inventory shrinkage. These outcomes should be important to most managers, and they represent generic descriptions that can be adapted to both industrial and service organisations.

Table 6.2   Behavioural outcomes for OD interventions: recording categories

Behavioural definitions	Recording categories
Absenteeism: Each absence or illness over four hours	*Voluntary*: Short-term illness (less than three consecutive days), personal business, family illness *Involuntary*: Long-term illness (more than three consecutive days), funerals, out-of-plant accidents, lack of work (temporary lay-off), pre-sanctioned days off *Leaves*: Medical, personal, maternity, military and other (for example, jury duty)
Tardiness: Each absence or illness under four hours	*Voluntary*: Same as absenteeism *Involuntary*: Same as absenteeism
Turnover: Each movement beyond the organisational	*Voluntary*: Resignation *Involuntary*: Termination, disqualification, requested resignation, permanent lay-off, retirement, disability, death
Internal employment stability: Each movement within the organisational boundary	*Internal movement*: Transfer, promotion, promotion with transfer *Internal stability*: New hires, lay-offs, rehires
Strikes and work stoppages: Each day lost due to strike or work stoppage	*Sanctioned*: Union authorised strike, company authorised lockout *Unsanctioned*: Work slowdown, walkout, strike

(continued)

Table 6.2	Behavioural outcomes for OD interventions: recording categories *(continued)*
Accidents and work-related illness: Each recordable injury, illness or death from a work-related accident or from exposure to the work environment	*Major*: OH&S accident, illness, or death that results in medical treatment by a medical practitioner or registered professional person under standing orders from a medical practitioner *Minor*: Non-OH&S accident or illness that results in one-time treatment and subsequent observation not requiring professional care *Revisits*: OH&S and non-OH&S accident or illness that requires subsequent treatment and observation
Grievances: Written grievance in accordance with labour-management contract	*Stage*: Recorded by step (first through arbitration)
Productivity:* Resources used in production of acceptable outputs (comparison of inputs with outputs)	*Output*: Product or service quantity (units or $) *Input*: Direct and/or indirect (labour in hours or $)
Production quality: Resources used in production of unacceptable output	*Resource utilised*: Scrap (unacceptable in-plant products in units or $) *Customer returns*: Unacceptable out-of-plant products in units or $ *Recoveries*: Salvageable products in units *Rework*: Additional direct and/or indirect labour in hours or $
Down time: Unscheduled breakdown of machinery	*Down time*: Duration of breakdown (hours or $) *Machine repair*: Non-preventative maintenance ($)
Inventory, material, and supply variance: Unscheduled resource utilisation	*Variance*: Over- or under-utilisation of supplies, materials, inventory (due to theft, inefficiency, and so on)

* Reports only labour inputs.

Source: From *EVALUATION REVIEW* by MACY & MERVIS. Copyright 1982 by SAGE PUBLICATIONS INC JOURNALS. Reproduced with permission of SAGE PUBLICATIONS INC JOURNALS in the format Textbook via Copyright Clearance Center.

Designing good measures

Each of the measurement methods described in Chapter 7 has advantages and disadvantages. Many of these characteristics are linked to the extent to which a measurement is operationally defined, reliable and valid. These characteristics are discussed below.

1   *Operational definition.* A good measure is operationally defined. That is, it specifies the empirical data needed, how it will be collected and, most importantly, how it will be converted from data to information. For example, Macy and Mirvis developed operational definitions for the behavioural outcomes listed in Table 6.2 (see Table 6.3).[48] They consist of specific computational rules that can be used to construct measures for each of the behaviours. Most of the behaviours are reported as rates adjusted for the number of employees in the organisation and for the possible incidents of behaviour. These adjustments make it possible to compare the measures across different situations and time periods. These operational definitions should have wide applicability across both industrial and service organisations, although some modifications, deletions and additions may be necessary for a particular application.

Operational definitions are extremely important in measurement as they provide precise guides as to what characteristics of the situation are to be observed and how they are to be used. They tell OD practitioners and the client system exactly how diagnostic, intervention and outcome variables will be measured.

Table 6.3   Behavioural outcomes for OD interventions: computational formulae

Behavioural measures	Computational formula
Absenteeism rate** (monthly)	$\dfrac{\Sigma \text{ Absence days}}{\text{Average workforce size} \times \text{working days}}$
Tardiness rate** (monthly)	$\dfrac{\Sigma \text{ Tardiness incidents}}{\text{Average workforce size} \times \text{working days}}$
Turnover rate (monthly)	$\dfrac{\Sigma \text{ Turnover incidents}}{\text{Average workforce size}}$
Internal stability rate (monthly)	$\dfrac{\Sigma \text{ Internal movement incidents}}{\text{Average workforce size}}$
Strike rate (yearly)	$\dfrac{\Sigma \text{ Striking workers} \times \text{strike days}}{\text{Average workforce size} \times \text{working days}}$
Accident rate (yearly)	$\dfrac{\Sigma \text{ of accidents, illnesses} \times 200\,000{***}}{\text{Total yearly hours worked}}$
Grievance rate (yearly)	Plant: $\dfrac{\Sigma \text{ Grievance incidents}}{\text{Average workforce size}}$ Individual: $\dfrac{\Sigma \text{ Aggrieved individuals}}{\text{Average workforce size}}$
Productivity**** Total Below standard Below budget Variance Per employee	$\dfrac{\text{Output of goods or services (units or \$)}}{\text{Direct and/or indirect labour (hours or \$)}}$ Actual versus engineered standard Actual versus budgeted standard Actual versus budgeted variance $\dfrac{\text{Output}}{\text{Average workforce size}}$
Quality**** Total	Scrap + customer returns + rework – recoveries ($, units, or hours)
Below standard	Actual versus engineered standard
Below budget	Actual versus budgeted standard
Variance	Actual versus budgeted variance
Per employee	$\dfrac{\text{Total workforce size}}{\text{Average}}$
Down time	Labour ($) + repair costs or dollar value of replaced equipment ($)
Inventory, supply and material usage	Variance (actual versus standard utilisation) ($)

*All measures reflect the number of incidents divided by an exposure factor that represents the number of employees in the organisation and the possible incidence of behaviour (for example, for absenteeism, the average workforce size x the number of working days). Mean monthly rates (that is, absences per workday) are computed and averaged for absenteeism, leaves and tardiness for a yearly figure and summed for turnover, grievances and internal employment stability for a yearly figure. The term rate refers to the number of incidents per unit of employee exposure to the risk of such incidences during the analysis interval.
**Sometimes combined as number of hours missing/average workforce size x working days.
***Base for 100 full-time equivalent workers (40 hours x 50 weeks).
****Monetary valuations can be expressed in labour dollars, actual dollar costs, sales dollars; overtime dollar valuations can be adjusted to base year dollars to control for salary, raw material and price increases.

2   *Reliability.* Reliability concerns the extent to which a measure represents the 'true' value of a variable; that is, how accurately the operational definition translates data into information. For example, there is little doubt about the accuracy of the number of cars

leaving an assembly line as a measure of plant productivity. Although it is possible to miscount, there can be a high degree of confidence in the measurement. On the other hand, when people are asked about their level of job satisfaction on a scale of 1 to 5, there is considerable room for variation in their response. They may have just had an argument with their supervisor, suffered an accident on the job, been rewarded for high levels of productivity or given new responsibilities. Each of these events can sway the response to the question on a given day. The individual's 'true' satisfaction score from this one question is difficult to discern, and the measure lacks reliability.[49]

Organisation development practitioners can improve the reliability of their measures in four ways. First, rigorously and operationally define the chosen variables. Clearly specified operational definitions contribute to reliability by explicitly describing how collected data will be converted into information about a variable. This explicit description helps to allay the client's concerns about how the information was collected and coded.

Second, use multiple methods to measure a particular variable. As discussed in Chapter 5, the use of questionnaires, interviews, observations and unobtrusive measures can improve reliability and result in more comprehensive understanding of the organisation. Because each method contains inherent biases, several different methods can be used to triangulate on dimensions of organisational problems. If the independent measures converge or show consistent results, the dimensions or problems have probably been accurately diagnosed.[50]

Third, use multiple items to measure the same variable on a questionnaire. For example, in Hackman and Oldham's Job Diagnostic Survey for measuring job characteristics (Chapter 8), the intervention variable 'autonomy' has the following operational definition – the average of respondents' answers to the following three questions (measured on a seven-point scale):[51]

- The job permits me to decide on my own how to go about doing the work.

- The job denies me any chance of using my personal initiative or judgement when carrying out the work (reverse scored).

- The job gives me considerable opportunity for independence and freedom in how I do the work.

By asking more than one question about 'autonomy', the survey increases the accuracy of its measurement of this variable. Statistical analyses (called psychometric tests) are readily available for assessing the reliability of perceptual measures, and OD practitioners should apply these methods or seek assistance from those who can.[52] Similarly, there are methods for analysing the content of interview and observational data, and OD evaluators can use these methods to categorise such information so that it can be understood and replicated.[53]

Fourth, use standardised instruments. A growing number of standardised questionnaires are available for measuring OD intervention and outcome variables. For example, the Center for Effective Organizations at the University of Southern California and the Institute for Survey Research at the University of Michigan have developed comprehensive survey instruments to measure the features of many of the OD interventions described in this book, as well as their attitudinal outcomes.[54] Considerable research and testing have gone into establishing measures that are reliable and valid. These survey instruments can be used for initial diagnosis, for guiding implementation of interventions, and for evaluating immediate and long-term outcomes.

3 *Validity.* Validity concerns the extent to which a measure actually reflects the variable it is intended to reflect. For example, the number of cars leaving an assembly line might be a reliable measure of plant productivity, but it may not be a valid measure. The number of cars is only one aspect of productivity; they may have been produced at an unacceptably high cost. Because the number of cars does not account for cost, it is not a completely valid measure of plant productivity.

OD practitioners can increase the validity of their measures in several ways. First, ask colleagues and clients if a proposed measure actually represents a particular variable. This is called 'face validity' or 'content validity'. If experts and clients agree that the measure reflects the variable of interest, then there is increased confidence in the measure's validity. Second, use multiple measures of the same variable, as described in the previous section about reliability. In this way, preliminary assessments can be made about the measure's criterion or convergent validity; that is, if several different measures of the same variable correlate highly with each other, especially if one or more of the other measures has been validated in prior research, then there is increased confidence in the measure's validity. A special case of criterion validity, called 'discriminant validity', exists when the proposed measure does not correlate with measures that it is not supposed to correlate with. For example, there is no good reason for daily measures of assembly-line productivity to correlate with daily air temperature. The lack of a correlation would be one indicator that the number of cars is measuring productivity and not some other variable. Finally, predictive validity is demonstrated when the variable of interest accurately forecasts another variable over time. For example, a measure of team cohesion can be said to be valid if it accurately predicts improvements in team performance in the future.

However, it is difficult to establish the validity of a measure until after it has been used. To address this concern, OD practitioners should make heavy use of content validity processes and use measures that have already been validated. For example, presenting proposed measures to colleagues and clients for evaluation prior to measurement has several positive effects. It builds ownership and commitment to the data-collection process and improves the likelihood that the client system will find the data meaningful. In addition, using measures that have been validated through prior research improves confidence in the results and provides a standard that can be used to validate any new measures used in the data-collection process.

RESEARCH DESIGN

In addition to measurement, OD practitioners need to make choices about how to design the evaluation to achieve valid results. The key issue is how to design the assessment to show whether the intervention did, in fact, produce the observed results. This is called 'internal validity'; the secondary question of whether the intervention would work similarly in other situations is referred to as 'external validity'. External validity is irrelevant without first establishing an intervention's primary effectiveness. Thus, internal validity is the essential minimum requirement for assessing OD interventions. Unless managers can have confidence that the outcomes are the result of the intervention, they have no rational basis for making decisions about accountability and resource allocation.

Assessing the internal validity of an intervention is, in effect, testing a hypothesis – namely, that specific organisational changes lead to certain outcomes. Moreover, testing the validity of an intervention hypothesis means that alternative hypotheses or explanations of the results must be rejected; that is, to claim that an intervention is successful, it is necessary to demonstrate that other explanations – in the form of rival hypotheses – do not account for the observed results. For example, if a job-enrichment program appears to increase employee performance, other possible explanations, such as the introduction of new technology, improved raw materials or new employees, must be eliminated.

Accounting for these rival explanations is not a precise, controlled experimental process such as might be found in a research laboratory.[55] Organisation development interventions tend to have a number of features that make it difficult to determine whether they produced observed results. They are complex and often involve several interrelated changes, obscuring whether individual features or combinations of features are accounting for the results. Many OD interventions are long-term projects and take considerable time to produce desired outcomes. The longer the time period of the change program, the greater are the chances that other factors, such as technology improvements, will emerge to affect the results. Finally, OD interventions are almost always applied to existing work units rather than to randomised groups of organisation members. In the absence of randomly selected intervention and comparison groups, ruling out alternative explanations for the results is difficult.

Given the problems inherent in assessing OD interventions, practitioners have turned to *quasi-experimental* research designs,[56] which are not as rigorous and controlled as randomised experimental designs, yet still allow evaluators to rule out many rival explanations for OD results other than the intervention itself. Although several quasi-experimental designs are available, those with the following three features are particularly powerful for assessing OD changes:[57]

1   *Longitudinal measurement.* This means measuring results repeatedly over relatively long time periods. Ideally, the data collection should start before the implementation of the change program and should continue for a period that is considered reasonable for producing the expected results.

2   *Comparison unit.* It is always desirable to compare results in the intervention situation with those in another situation where no such change has taken place. Although it is never possible to get a matching group that is identical to the intervention group, most organisations include a number of similar work units that can be used for comparison purposes.

3   *Statistical analysis.* Whenever possible, statistical methods should be used to rule out the possibility that the results are caused by random error or chance. There are a variety of statistical techniques applicable to quasi-experimental designs, and OD practitioners should apply these methods or seek help from those who can.[58]

Table 6.4 provides an example of a quasi-experimental design that has these three features. The intervention is intended to reduce employee absenteeism. Measures of absenteeism are taken from company monthly records for both the intervention and comparison groups. The two groups are similar, yet geographically separate, subsidiaries of a multiplant company. Table 6.4 shows each plant's monthly absenteeism rate for four consecutive months both before and after the start of the intervention. The plant receiving the intervention shows a marked decrease in absenteeism in the months after the intervention, whereas the control plant shows comparable levels of absenteeism in both time periods. Statistical analyses of these data suggest that the abrupt downward shift in absenteeism following the intervention was not attributable to chance variation. This research design and the data provide relatively strong evidence that the intervention was successful.

Quasi-experimental research designs that use longitudinal data, comparison groups and statistical analysis permit reasonable assessments of intervention effectiveness. Repeated measures can often be collected from company records without directly involving members of the experimental and comparison groups. These unobtrusive measures are especially useful in OD assessment as they do not interact with the intervention and affect the results. More obtrusive measures, such as questionnaires and interviews, are reactive and can sensitise people to the intervention. When this happens, it is difficult to know whether the observed findings are the result of the intervention, the measuring methods or some combination of both.

Multiple measures of intervention and outcome variables should be applied to minimise measurement and intervention interactions. For example, obtrusive measures such as questionnaires could be used sparingly, perhaps once before and once after the intervention. Unobtrusive measures, such as the behavioural outcomes shown in Tables 6.2 and 6.3, could be used repeatedly. These provide a more extensive time series than the questionnaires. When used together, the two kinds of measures should produce accurate and non-reactive evaluations of the intervention.

The use of multiple measures is also important in assessing perceptual changes resulting from interventions. Considerable research has identified three types of change – alpha, beta and gamma – that occur when using self-report, perceptual measures.[59]

Table 6.4	Quasi-experimental research design								
Monthly absenteeism (%)									
	Sep	Oct	Nov	Dec		Jan	Feb	Mar	Apr
Intervention group	5.1	5.3	5.0	5.1	Start of intervention	4.6	4.0	3.9	3.5
Comparison group	2.5	2.6	2.4	2.5		2.6	2.4	2.5	2.5

Alpha change refers to movement along a measure that reflects stable dimensions of reality. For example, comparative measures of perceived employee discretion might show an increase after a job-enrichment program. If this increase represents alpha change, it can be assumed that the job-enrichment program actually increased employee perceptions of discretion.

Beta change involves the recalibration of the intervals along some constant measure of reality. For example, before-and-after measures of perceived employee discretion can decrease after a job-enrichment program. If beta change is involved, it can explain this apparent failure of the intervention to increase discretion. The first measure of discretion may accurately reflect the individual's belief about the ability to move around and talk to fellow workers in the immediate work area. During the implementation of the job-enrichment intervention, however, the employee may learn that the ability to move around is not limited to the immediate work area. At a second measurement of discretion, the employee, using this new and recalibrated understanding, may rate the current level of discretion as lower than before.

Gamma change involves fundamentally redefining the measure as a result of an OD intervention. In essence, the framework within which a phenomenon is viewed changes. For example, the presence of gamma change would make it difficult to compare measures of employee discretion taken before and after a job-enrichment program. The measure taken after the intervention might use the same words, but they would represent an entirely different concept. As described above, the term 'discretion' might originally have referred to the ability to move about the department and interact with other workers. After the intervention, discretion might be defined in terms of the ability to make decisions about work rules, work schedules and productivity levels. In sum, the job-enrichment intervention changed the way in which discretion is perceived and how it is evaluated.

These three types of change apply to perceptual measures. When other than alpha changes occur, the interpretation of measurement changes becomes far more difficult. Potent OD interventions may produce both beta and gamma changes, which severely complicate interpretations of findings that report change and no change. Further, the distinctions among the three different types of change suggest that the heavy reliance on questionnaires, so often cited in the literature, should be balanced by using other measures, such as interviews and unobtrusive records. Analytical methods have been developed to assess the three kinds of change, and OD practitioners should gain familiarity with these recent techniques.[60]

Institutionalising interventions

Once it has been determined that an intervention has been implemented and is effective, attention is directed at institutionalising the changes: making them a permanent part of the organisation's normal functioning. Lewin described change as occurring in three stages: unfreezing, moving and refreezing (see Chapter 2). Institutionalising an OD intervention concerns refreezing. It involves the long-term persistence of organisational changes. To the extent that changes persist, they can be said to be institutionalised. Such changes are not dependent on any one person but exist as part of the culture of an organisation: numerous others share norms about the appropriateness of the changes. Application 6.4 describes where a Western Australian company is testing the idea that good management systems can be used successfully and institutionalised in any business.

APPLiCATiON 6.4

THEORY MEETS REALITY

Advantage Air could be making anything. Its founders, the husband-and-wife team of David and Margaret Devoy, believe that the real value in their business is a management system that gets the best out of everyone involved, from the owners to those on the factory floor.

'We really have taken the theories of workforce empowerment, flat management structures and core competencies and applied them rigorously,' David Devoy says. 'The aim has been to make every employee feel that he or she is part of the total process, to eliminate hierarchies, to keep everyone informed about our financial performance, and to maximise productivity and creativity.'

Listening to Devoy during a walk through the Advantage Air factory in the outer Perth suburb of Bentley is like hearing a management lecture. The difference is that this is where theory is being applied. David chats with workers on the walkabout, and Margaret supervises fabrication and packing electronic switching consoles.

It would not be immediately apparent to an outsider that they own 70% of the business, which in just 10 years has grown to employ almost 200 people. It is on track to have a turnover of $27 million and, assuming a 15% margin on sales, post a profit of about $4 million. As well as its base in Perth and sales outlets across Australia, Advantage Air has a subsidiary in South Africa, producing items ranging from plastic ducting to 'smart' electronic systems that micro-manage air-conditioning units made by companies such as Fujitsu, Hitachi and Carrier.

Their key to success has not just been to identify a niche opportunity. It has also been in the way that management has been able to harness workforce loyalty. This was put to the test on 1 September when a fire destroyed the company's head office, call centre and warehouse. Just eight days after that event, which would have destroyed other companies, Advantage Air was back in business.

Survival instinct was a factor, but this was also a case of everyone pitching in, salvaging the handful of computers not damaged, and reconstructing the head office and call centre in spare rooms adjacent to the factory.

Source: Tim Treadgold, 'Theory meets reality', *Business Review Weekly*, 24–30 Nov. 2005.

Critical Thinking Questions: Various factors that have not been mentioned could also have improved the likelihood of success of this company. What do you think they may be? What leadership style is David Devoy exhibiting and is this style transferable to other individuals? Research where this company is now and determine whether it is still successful.

How planned changes become institutionalised has not received much attention in recent years. Rapidly changing environments have led to admonitions from consultants and practitioners to 'change constantly', to 'change before you have to' and 'if it's not broke, fix it anyway'. Such a context has challenged the utility of the institutionalisation concept. Why endeavour to make any change permanent, given that it may require changing again soon? However, the admonitions have also resulted in institutionalisation concepts being applied in new ways. Change itself has become the focus of institutionalisation. Total quality management, organisation learning, integrated strategic change and self-design interventions are all aimed at enhancing the organisation's capability for change.[61] In this vein, processes of institutionalisation take on increased utility. This section presents a framework that identifies factors and processes contributing to the institutionalisation of OD interventions, including the process of change itself.

INSTITUTIONALISATION FRAMEWORK

Figure 6.6 presents a framework that identifies organisation and intervention characteristics and institutionalisation processes affecting the degree to which change programs are institutionalised.[62] The model shows that two key antecedents – organisation and intervention characteristics – affect different institutionalisation processes operating in organisations. These processes in turn affect various indicators of institutionalisation. The model also shows that organisation characteristics can influence intervention characteristics. For example, organisations with powerful unions may have trouble gaining internal support for OD interventions.

ORGANISATION CHARACTERISTICS

Figure 6.6 shows that three key dimensions of an organisation can affect intervention characteristics and institutionalisation processes.

1   *Congruence*. This is the degree to which an intervention is perceived as being in harmony with the organisation's managerial philosophy, strategy and structure; its current environment; and other changes taking place.[63] When an intervention is congruent

Figure 6.6   Institutional framework

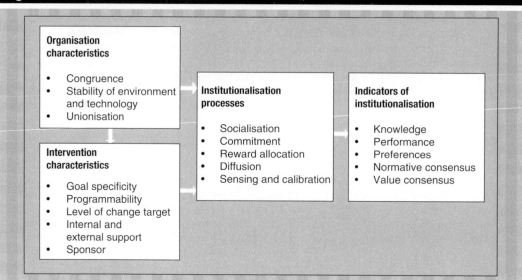

with these dimensions, the probability is improved that it will be institutionalised. Congruence can facilitate persistence by making it easier to gain member commitment to the intervention and to diffuse it to wider segments of the organisation. The converse is also true. Many OD interventions promote employee participation and growth. When applied in highly bureaucratic organisations with formalised structures and autocratic managerial styles, participative interventions are not perceived as being congruent with the organisation's managerial philosophy.

2   *Stability of environment and technology.* This involves the degree to which the organisation's environment and technology are changing. Unless the change target is buffered from these changes or unless the changes are directly dealt with by the change program, it may be difficult to achieve long-term stability of the intervention.[64] For example, decreased demand for the firm's products or services can lead to reductions in personnel, which may change the composition of the groups involved in the intervention. Conversely, increased product demand can curtail institutionalisation by bringing new members on board at a rate faster than they can be effectively socialised.

3   *Unionisation.* Diffusion of interventions may be more difficult in unionised settings, especially if the changes affect union contract issues, such as salary and fringe benefits, job design and employee flexibility. For example, a rigid union contract can make it difficult to merge several job classifications into one, as might be required to increase task variety in a job-enrichment program. It is important to emphasise, however, that unions can be a powerful force for promoting change, especially when a good relationship exists between union and management.

INTERVENTION CHARACTERISTICS

Figure 6.6 shows that five major features of OD interventions can affect institutionalisation processes:

1   *Goal specificity.* This involves the extent to which intervention goals are specific rather than broad. Specificity of goals helps to direct socialising activities (for example, training and orienting new members) to particular behaviours required to implement the intervention. It also facilitates operationalising the new behaviours so that rewards can be clearly linked to them. For example, an intervention aimed only at the goal of increasing product quality is likely to be more focused and readily put into operation than a change program intended to improve quality, quantity, safety, absenteeism and employee development.

2   *Programmability.* This involves the degree to which the changes can be programmed. This means that the different characteristics of the intervention are clearly specified in advance, thus facilitating socialisation, commitment and reward allocation.[65] For example, job enrichment specifies three targets of change: employee discretion, task variety and feedback. The change program can be planned and designed to promote these specific features.

3   *Level of change target.* This concerns the extent to which the change target is the total organisation, rather than a department or small work group. Each level possesses facilitators and inhibitors to persistence. Departmental and group change are susceptible to countervailing forces from others in the organisation, which can reduce the diffusion of the intervention, thus lowering its ability to improve organisation effectiveness. However, this does not necessarily preclude institutionalising the change within a department that successfully insulates itself from the rest of the organisation. This often manifests itself as a subculture within the organisation.[66]

Targeting the intervention to wider segments of the organisation, on the other hand, can also help or hinder change persistence. It can facilitate institutionalisation by promoting a consensus across organisational departments exposed to the change. A shared belief about the intervention's value can be a powerful incentive to maintain the change. But targeting the larger system can also inhibit institutionalisation. The intervention can become mired in political resistance because of the 'not invented here' syndrome, or because powerful constituencies oppose it.

4   *Internal and external support.* Internal support refers to the degree to which there is an internal support system to guide the change process. Internal support, typically provided by an internal consultant, can help to gain commitment to the changes and help organisation members to implement them. External consultants can also provide support, especially on a temporary basis during the early stages of implementation. For example, in many interventions aimed at implementing high-involvement organisations (see Chapter 8), both external and internal consultants provide support for the changes. The external consultant typically provides expertise on organisational design and trains members to implement the design. The internal consultant generally helps members to relate to other organisational units, to resolve conflicts and to legitimise the change activities within the organisation.

5   *Sponsor.* This concerns the presence of a powerful sponsor who can initiate, allocate and legitimise resources for the intervention. Sponsors must come from levels in the organisation high enough to control appropriate resources. They must have the visibility and power to nurture the intervention and see that it remains viable in the organisation. There are many examples of OD interventions that persisted for several years and then collapsed abruptly when the sponsor, usually a top administrator, left. There are also numerous examples of middle managers withdrawing support for interventions because top management did not include them in the change program.

INSTITUTIONALISATION PROCESSES

The framework depicted in Figure 6.6 shows five institutionalisation processes operating in organisations that can directly affect the degree to which OD interventions are institutionalised:

1   *Socialisation.* This concerns the transmission of information about beliefs, preferences, norms and values with respect to the intervention. Because implementation of OD interventions generally involves considerable learning and experimentation, a continual process of socialisation is necessary to promote persistence of the change program. Organisation members must focus attention on the evolving nature of the intervention and its ongoing meaning. They must communicate this information to other employees, especially new members. Transmission of information about the intervention helps to bring new members on board and allows participants to reaffirm the beliefs, norms and values that underlie the intervention.[67] For example, employee-involvement programs often include an initial transmission of information about the intervention, as well as the retraining of existing participants and training of new members. These processes are intended to encourage persistence with the program, as both new behaviours are learned and new members introduced.

2   *Commitment.* This binds people to behaviours associated with the intervention. It includes initial commitment to the program, as well as recommitment over time. Opportunities for commitment should allow people to select the necessary behaviours freely, explicitly and publicly. These conditions favour high commitment and can promote stability of the new behaviours. Commitment should derive from several organisational levels, including the employees directly involved and the middle and upper managers who can support or thwart the intervention. In many early employee-involvement programs, for example, attention was directed at gaining the workers' commitment to such programs. Unfortunately, middle managers were often ignored, resulting in considerable management resistance to the interventions.

3   *Reward allocation.* This involves linking rewards to the new behaviours required by an intervention. Organisational rewards can enhance the persistence of interventions in at least two ways. First, a combination of intrinsic and extrinsic rewards can reinforce new behaviours. Intrinsic rewards are internal and derive from the opportunities for challenge, development and accomplishment found in the work. When interventions provide these opportunities, motivation to perform should persist. Providing extrinsic rewards, such as money, for increased contributions can further reinforce this behaviour. Because the value of extrinsic rewards tends to diminish over time, it may be necessary to revise the reward system to maintain high levels of desired behaviours.

    Second, new behaviours should persist to the extent that employees perceive rewards as equitable. When new behaviours are fairly compensated, people are likely to develop preferences for those behaviours. Over time, those preferences should lead to normative and value consensus about the appropriateness of the intervention. For example, many employee-involvement programs fail to persist because the employees feel that their increased contributions to organisational improvements are unfairly rewarded. This is especially true for interventions that rely exclusively on intrinsic rewards. People argue that an intervention that provides opportunities for intrinsic rewards should also provide greater pay or extrinsic rewards for higher levels of contribution to the organisation.

4   *Diffusion.* This refers to the process of transferring interventions from one system to another. Diffusion facilitates institutionalisation by providing a wider organisational base to support the new behaviours. Many interventions fail to persist because they run counter to the values and norms of the larger organisation. Rather than support the intervention, the larger organisation rejects the changes and often puts pressure on the change target to revert to old behaviours. Diffusion of the intervention to other organisational units reduces this counter-implementation strategy. It tends to lock in behaviours by providing normative consensus from other parts of the organisation. Moreover, the very act of transmitting institutionalised behaviours to other systems reinforces commitment to the changes.

5   *Sensing and calibration.* This involves detecting deviations from desired intervention behaviours and taking corrective action. Institutionalised behaviours invariably encounter destabilising forces, such as changes in the environment, new technologies and pressures from other departments to nullify changes. These factors cause some variation in performances, preferences, norms and values. To detect this variation and take corrective actions, organisations must have some sensing mechanism. Sensing mechanisms, such as implementation feedback, provide information about the occurrence of deviations. This knowledge can then initiate corrective actions to ensure that behaviours are more in line with the intervention. For example, the high level of job discretion associated with job enrichment might fail to persist. Information about this problem might initiate corrective actions, such as renewed attempts to socialise people or to gain commitment to the intervention.

INDICATORS OF INSTITUTIONALISATION

Institutionalisation is not an all-or-nothing concept, but it does reflect degrees of persistence of an intervention. Figure 6.6 shows five indicators that can be used to determine the extent of an intervention's persistence. The extent to which these factors are present or absent indicates the degree of institutionalisation.

1   *Knowledge.* This involves the extent to which organisation members have knowledge of the behaviours associated with an intervention. It is concerned with whether members know enough to perform the behaviours and to recognise the consequences of that performance. For example, job enrichment includes a number of new behaviours, such as performing a greater variety of tasks, analysing information about task performance and making decisions about work methods and plans.

2   *Performance.* This is concerned with the degree to which intervention behaviours are actually performed. It may be measured by counting the proportion of relevant people performing the behaviours. For example, 60% of the employees in a particular work unit might be performing the job-enrichment behaviours described above. Another measure of performance is the frequency with which the new behaviours are performed. In assessing frequency, it is important to account for different variations of the same essential behaviour, as well as highly institutionalised behaviours that only need to be performed infrequently.

3   *Preferences.* This involves the degree to which organisation members privately accept the organisational changes. This contrasts with acceptance that is based primarily on organisational sanctions or group pressures. Private acceptance is usually reflected in people's positive attitudes towards the changes, and can be measured by the direction and intensity of these attitudes across the members of the work unit receiving the intervention. For example, a questionnaire that assesses members' perceptions of a job-enrichment program might show that most employees have a strong positive attitude towards making decisions, analysing feedback and performing a variety of tasks.

4   *Normative consensus.* This focuses on the extent to which people agree on the appropriateness of the organisational changes. This indicator of institutionalisation reflects the extent to which organisational changes have become part of the normative structure of the organisation. Changes persist to the degree that members feel they should support them. For example, a job-enrichment program would become institutionalised to the extent that employees support it and see it as appropriate to organisational functioning.

5   *Value consensus.* This is concerned with social consensus on values that are relevant to the organisational changes. Values are beliefs about how people ought or ought not to behave. They are abstractions from more specific norms. Job enrichment, for example, is based on values promoting employee self-control and responsibility. Different behaviours associated with job enrichment, such as making decisions and performing a variety of tasks, would persist to the extent that employees widely share values of self-control and responsibility.

These five indicators can be used to assess the level of institutionalisation of an OD intervention. The more the indicators are present in a situation, the higher will be the degree of institutionalisation. Further, these factors seem to follow a specific development order: knowledge, performance, preferences, norms and values. People must first understand new behaviours or changes before they can perform them effectively. Such performance generates rewards and punishments, which in time affect people's preferences. As many individuals come to prefer the changes, normative consensus about their appropriateness develops. Finally, if there is normative agreement about the changes reflected in a particular set of values, over time there should be some consensus on those values among organisation members. This developmental view of institutionalisation implies that, whenever one of the last indicators is present, all the previous ones are automatically included as well; for example, if employees normatively agree with the behaviours that are associated with job enrichment, then they also have knowledge about the behaviours, can perform them effectively and prefer them. An OD intervention is fully institutionalised only when all five factors are present.

SUMMARY

This chapter presented an overview of the design, implementation and evaluation of interventions currently used in OD. An intervention is a set of planned activities intended to help an organisation improve its performance and effectiveness. Effective interventions are designed to fit the needs of the organisation, are based on causal knowledge of intended outcomes and transfer competence to manage change to organisation members.

The chapter's first section, Designing OD Interventions, discussed the selection of the most appropriate intervention, or series of interventions, which is an extremely difficult and sometimes risky venture. It is not only common to use more than one intervention but also tempting often to choose the most familiar, thereby ignoring alternatives that may be more aligned with the needs of the organisation.

It is important to ask two primary questions when considering the multifaceted approach to change management. First, what is the type of change required? Is it behavioural (including people and process), structural, technical or a combination of these? Second, what is the impact of the change process? Will the impact be on individuals, groups or the organisation as a whole? By determining a response to these questions, it is possible to limit the choices and reduce the confusion that may occur.

Table 6.5 is a matrix representation that considers the interventions mentioned in this book. This is not to suggest that the choice is limited to these options. In fact there are many interventions – too many to consider in detail; this is just a sample. What is important to remember is that intervention design involves understanding situational contingencies such as individual differences among organisation members and dimensions of the change process itself. Four key organisational factors – readiness for change, capability to change, cultural context and the capabilities of the change agent – affect the design and implementation of almost any intervention.

In addition, OD interventions seek to change specific features or parts of organisations. Classification of these targets of change can be based on the organisational issues that the intervention is intended to resolve, and the level of organisational system at which the intervention is expected to have a primary impact. Four types of OD interventions are addressed in this book: (1) human process programs aimed at people within organisations and their interaction processes; (2) technostructural methods directed at organisation technology and structures for linking people and technology; (3) human resource management interventions aimed at successfully integrating people into the organisation; and (4) strategic programs directed at how the organisation uses its resources to gain a competitive advantage in the larger environment.

This chapter's middle section, Implementing Change, described five kinds of activities that change agents must carry out when planning and implementing changes. The first activity is

Table 6.5	OD interventions			
	Individual	Team	Intergroup	Organisational
Behavioural	Career planning Managerial grid Goal setting Stress management QWL	Team building Process consultation Quality control Grid OD (Phase 2) Goal setting Third-party intervention	Intergroup development Third-party intervention Process consultation Grid OD (Phase 3) TQM	Goal setting Grid OD (phases 4, 5, 6) Survey feedback Action research QWL TQM
Structural	Stress management QWL Job enrichment	Team building Self-managed work teams Job enrichment Grid OD (Phase 2)	Job enrichment Goal setting TQM	Grid OD (phases 4, 5, 6) Survey feedback Action research QWL TQM Restructuring
Technical	Job design	Job design Quality control Grid OD (Phase 3)	Job design Grid OD (Phase 3) TQM	Grid OD (phases 4, 5, 6) Survey feedback Action research TQM Re-engineering

motivating change, which involves creating a readiness for change among organisation members and managing their resistance. The second activity is about describing the desired future state, which may include the organisation's mission, valued performance and human outcomes, and valued organisational conditions to achieve those results, and creating a vision by articulating a compelling reason for implementing change. The third task for change agents is developing political support for the changes. Change agents must first assess their own sources of power, then identify key stakeholders whose support is needed for change, and then devise strategies for gaining their support. The fourth activity concerns managing the transition of the organisation from its current state to the desired future state. This calls for planning a road map for the change activities, as well as planning how to gain commitment for the changes. It may also involve creating special management structures for managing the transition. The fifth change task is sustaining momentum for the changes so that they are carried to completion. This includes providing resources for the change program, creating a support system for change agents, developing new competencies and skills, and reinforcing the new behaviours required to implement the changes.

The final section, Evaluating OD Interventions, discussed the final two stages of planned change – evaluating interventions and institutionalising them. Evaluation was discussed in terms of two kinds of necessary feedback. Implementation feedback is concerned with whether the intervention is being implemented as intended, and evaluation feedback indicates whether the intervention is producing expected results. The former is collected data about features of the intervention and its immediate effects, which are fed back repeatedly and at short intervals. The latter is data about the long-term effects of the intervention, which are fed back at long intervals.

Evaluation of interventions also involves decisions about measurement and research design. Measurement issues focus on selecting variables and designing good measures. Ideally, measurement decisions should derive from the theory that underlies the intervention and should include measures of the features of the intervention and its immediate and long-term consequences. Further, these measures should be operationally defined, valid and reliable and should involve multiple methods, such as a combination of questionnaires, interviews and company records.

Research design focuses on setting up the conditions for making valid assessments of an intervention's effects. This involves ruling out explanations for the observed results other than the intervention. Although randomised experimental designs are rarely feasible in OD, quasi-experimental designs exist for eliminating alternative explanations.

Organisation development interventions are institutionalised when the change program persists and becomes part of the organisation's normal functioning. A framework for understanding and improving the institutionalisation of interventions identified organisation characteristics (congruence, stability of environment and technology, and unionisation) and intervention characteristics (goal specificity, programmability, level of change target, internal support and sponsor) affecting institutionalisation processes. It also described specific institutionalisation processes (socialisation, commitment, reward allocation, diffusion and sensing and calibration) that directly affect indicators of intervention persistence (knowledge, performance, preferences, normative consensus and value consensus).

ACTiViTiES

DESIGNING OD INTERVENTIONS

Review questions

① What is meant by the term 'intervention'? Identify and give examples of interventions for various situations.

② Compare and contrast different types of interventions.

③ What/who are the primary targets of change programs? Why is it important that the identification of the primary target be accurate? What could occur if a mistake is made?

▷▷

④ What does 'interpersonal' refer to? Compare and contrast the interventions that could facilitate interpersonal development.

Discussion and essay questions

① Compare and contrast employee involvement (EI) and quality of work life (QWL) with OD. Under what circumstances are these best used?

② Explain what an 'intervention' is and how it fits into the OD process. What are the key considerations when deciding on an intervention? What are the inherent dangers in selecting the most appropriate interventions?

IMPLEMENTING CHANGE

Review questions

① Why do people resist change? In your opinion, is this acceptable? Give reasons.

② List the means by which resistance may be managed. Should managers consider the ethical component of such management?

③ Which power strategy is most closely aligned with OD's traditional humanistic values? What is the relationship between power and politics?

④ How may you develop political support for the change process? Was Machiavelli the first OD practitioner? Give reasons.

Discussion and essay questions

① If you were developing a change program, how would you create readiness for change? Where would be the 'hidden' dangers?

② 'Resistance is bad: it should be suppressed at all costs.' Discuss.

EVALUATING OD INTERVENTIONS

Review questions

① What does 'implementation feedback' try to measure? Is it likely to cover all aspects? Why/why not?

② When should you identify the measurement variables to be used for evaluation and feedback? Is there a different perspective that you should consider?

③ Which indicator represents the highest degree of institutionalisation? Is this a good or a bad thing for an organisation?

④ Whose ultimate responsibility is it to measure the outcomes of an OD process?

Discussion and essay questions

① 'The process of evaluating OD interventions are often ignored.' Why would this be the case? Consider the consequences of this occurring.

② Some would say that the word 'institutionalising' is an emotive term and should not be used when describing OD. Why is this so? Do you agree? Why/why not?

NOTES

1 C. Argyris, *Intervention Theory and Method: A Behavioral Science View* (Reading, MA: Addison-Wesley, 1970).

2 T. Cummings, E. Molloy and R. Glen, 'A methodological critique of 58 selected work experiments', *Human Relations*, 30 (1977): 675–708; T. Cummings, E. Molloy and R. Glen, 'Intervention strategies for improving productivity and the quality of work life', *Organizational Dynamics*, 4 (Summer 1975): 59–60; J. Porras and P. Berg, 'The impact of organization development', *Academy of Management Review*, 3 (1978): 249–66; J. Nicholas, 'The comparative impact of organization development interventions on hard criteria measures', *Academy of Management Review*, 7 (1982): 531–42; R. Golembiewski, C. Proehl and D. Sink, 'Estimating the success of OD applications', *Training and Development Journal*, 72 (April 1982): 86–95.

3 D. Warrick, 'Action planning', in *Practicing Organization Development*, eds W. Rothwell, R. Sullivan and G. McClean (San Diego: Pfeiffer and Co., 1995).

4 Nicholas, 'The comparative impact of organization development interventions', op. cit.; J. Porras and P. Robertson, 'Organization development theory: a typology and evaluation', in *Research in Organizational Change and Development*, 1, eds R. Woodman and W. Pasmore (Greenwich, CT: JAI Press, 1987): 1–57.

5 T. Stewart, 'Rate your readiness for change', *Fortune* (7 February 1994): 106–10.

6 G. Hofstede, *Culture's Consequences* (Beverly Hills, CA: Sage, 1980); K. Johnson, 'Estimating national culture and OD values', in *Global and International Organization Development*, eds P. Sorensfen Jr, T. Head, K. Johnson, N. Mathys, J. Preston and D. Cooperrider (Champaign, IL: Stipes, 1995): 266–81.

7 D. Coghlan, 'Rediscovering organizational levels for OD interventions', *Organization Development Journal*, 13 (1995): 19–27.

8 F. Friedlander and L. Brown, 'Organization development', *Annual Review of Psychology*, 25 (1974): 313–41.

9 E. Lawler III, *The Ultimate Advantage* (San Francisco: Jossey-Bass, 1992).

10 J. Kotter and L. Schlesinger, 'Choosing strategies for change', *Harvard Business Review*, 57 (1979): 106–14; R. Ricardo, 'Overcoming resistance to change', *National Productivity Review*, 14 (1995): 28–39.

11 M. Weisbord, *Productive Work Places* (San Francisco: Jossey-Bass, 1987); R. Beckhard and R. Harris, *Organizational Transitions: Managing Complex Change*, 2nd edn (Reading, MA: Addison-Wesley, 1987); R. Beckhard and W. Pritchard, *Changing the Essence* (San Francisco: Jossey-Bass, 1991).

12 N. Tichy and M. Devanna, *The Transformational Leader* (New York: John Wiley and Sons, 1986).

13 R. Cosier and C. Schwenk, 'Agreement and thinking alike: ingredients for poor decisions', *Academy of Management Executive*, 4 (1990): 69–74.

14 Reported in 'Briefing', *Business Review Weekly*, 15:7 (26 February 1993): 12.

15 W. Burke, *Organization Development: A Normative View* (Reading, MA: Addison-Wesley, 1987).

16 D. Eden, 'OD and self-fulfilling prophesy: boosting productivity by raising expectations', *Journal of Applied Behavioral Science*, 22 (1986): 1–13.

17 ibid: 8.

18 Kotter and Schlesinger, 'Choosing strategies', op. cit.; P. Block, *Flawless Consulting: A Guide to Getting Your Expertise Used* (Austin, TX: Learning Concepts, 1981).

19 N. Tichy, 'Revolutionize your company', *Fortune* (13 December 1993): 114–18.

20 D. Kirkpatrick, ed., *How to Manage Change Effectively* (San Francisco: Jossey-Bass, 1985).

21 V. Vroom and P. Yetton, *Leadership and Decision Making* (Pittsburgh: University of Pittsburgh Press, 1973).

22 T. Cummings and E. Molloy, *Improving Productivity and the Quality of Work Life* (New York: Praeger, 1977).

23 P. Senge, *The Fifth Discipline* (New York: Doubleday, 1990).

24 J. Kotter, *Leading Change* (Boston, MA: Harvard Business School Press, 1994); W. Bennis and B. Nanus, *Leadership* (New York: Harper and Row, 1985); J. O'Toole, *Leading Change: Overcoming the Ideology of Comfort and the Tyranny of Custom* (San Francisco: Jossey-Bass, 1995); F. Hesselbein, M. Goldsmith and R. Beckhard, eds, *The Leader of the Future* (San Francisco: Jossey-Bass, 1995).

25 J. Kirby, 'Nothing appeals like success', *Business Review Weekly* (20 July 1998): 48.

26 Tichy and Devanna, *The Transformational Leader*, op. cit.

27 J. Pearce II and F. David, 'Corporate mission statements: the bottom line', *Academy of Management Executive* 1 (1987): 109–15.

28 J. Pfeffer, *Power in Organizations* (New York: Pitman, 1982).

29 D. Nadler, 'The effective management of change', in *Handbook of Organizational Behavior*, ed. J. Lorsch (Englewood Cliffs, NJ: Prentice–Hall, 1987): 358–69.

30 C. Alderfer, 'Organization development', *Annual Review of Psychology*, 28 (1977): 197–223.

31 T. Bateman, 'Organizational change and the politics of success', *Group and Organization Studies*, 5 (June 1980): 198–209; A. Cobb and N. Margulies, 'Organization development: a political perspective', *Academy of Management Review*, 6 (1981): 49–59; A. Cobb, 'Political diagnosis: applications in organization development', *Academy of Management Review*, 11 (1986): 482–96; L. Greiner and V. Schein, *Power and Organization Development: Mobilizing Power to Implement Change* (Reading, MA: Addison-Wesley, 1988).

32 Greiner and Schein, *Power and Organization Development*, op. cit.

33 Nadler, 'The effective management of change', op. cit; Beckhard and Pritchard, *Changing the Essence*, op. cit.

34 Greiner and Schein, *Power and Organization Development*, op. cit.

35 ibid: 48.

36 Beckhard and Harris, *Organizational Transitions*, op. cit.

37 ibid.

38 ibid.

39 C. Worley, D. Hitchin and W. Ross, *Integrated Strategic Change: How OD Helps to Build Competitive Advantage* (Reading, MA: Addison-Wesley, 1996).

40 M. Beer, *Organization Change and Development: A Systems View* (Santa Monica, CA: Goodyear, 1980).

41 R. Hill, T. Bullard, P. Capper, K. Hawes and K. Wilson, 'Learning about learning organisations: case studies of skill formation in five New Zealand organisations', *The Learning Organisation*, 5:4 (1998): 184–92.

42 T. Cummings and E. Molloy, *Strategies for Improving Productivity and the Quality of Work Life* (New York: Praeger, 1977); J. Whitfield, W. Anthony and K. Kacmar, 'Evaluation of team-based management: a case study', *Journal of Organizational Change Management*, 8:2 (1995): 17–28.

43 S. Mohrman and T. Cummings, 'Implementing quality-of-work-life programs by managers', in *The NTL Manager's Handbook*, eds R. Ritvo and A. Sargent (Arlington, VA: NTL Institute, 1983): 320–8; T. Cummings and S. Mohrman, 'Self-designing organizations: towards implementing quality-of-work-life innovations', in *Research in Organizational Change and Development*, 1, eds R. Woodman and W. Pasmore (Greenwich, CT: JAI Press, 1987): 275–310.

44 T. Cummings, 'Institutionalising quality-of-work-life programs: the case for self-design' (paper delivered at the Annual Meeting of the Academy of Management, Dallas, TX, August 1983).

45 Cummings and Molloy, *Strategies for Improving Productivity and the Quality of Work Life*, op. cit.

46 P. Goodman, *Assessing Organizational Change: The Rushton Quality of Work Experiment* (New York: John Wiley, 1979); A. Van de Ven and D. Ferry, eds, *Measuring and Assessing Organizations* (New York: John Wiley, 1985); E. Lawler III, D. Nadler and C. Cammann, eds, *Organizational Assessment: Perspectives on the Measurement of Organizational Behavior and Quality of Work Life* (New York: John Wiley, 1980); A. Van de Ven and W. Joyce, eds, *Perspectives on Organizational Design and Behavior* (New York: John Wiley, 1981); S. Seashore, E. Lawler III, P. Mirvis and C. Cammann, eds, *Assessing Organizational Change: A Guide to Methods, Measures, and Practices* (New York: John Wiley, 1983).

47 B. Macy and P. Mirvis, 'Organizational change efforts: methodologies for assessing organizational effectiveness and program costs versus benefits', *Evaluation Review*, 6 (1982): 301–72.

48 Macy and Mirvis, 'Organizational change efforts: methodologies for assessing organizational effectiveness and program costs versus benefits', op. cit.

49 J. Nunnally, *Psychometric Theory*, 2nd edn (New York: McGraw-Hill, 1978); J. Kirk and M. Miller, *Reliability and Validity in Qualitative Research* (Beverly Hills, CA: Sage Publications, 1985).

50 D. Miller, *Handbook of Research Design and Social Measurement* (Thousand Oaks, CA: Sage Publications, 1991); N. Denzin and Y. Lincoln, eds, *Handbook of Qualitative Research* (Thousand Oaks, CA: Sage Publications, 1994).

51 R. Hackman and G. Oldham, *Word Redesign* (Reading, MA: Addison-Wesley, 1980): 275–306.

52 Nunnally, *Psychometric Theory*, op. cit.

53 C. Selltiz, M. Jahoda, M. Deutsch and S. Cook, *Research Methods in Social Relations*, rev. edn (New York: Holt, Rinehart and Winston, 1966): 385–440.

54 J. Taylor and D. Bowers, *Survey of Organizations: A Machine-Scored Standardized Questionnaire Instrument* (Ann Arbor: Institute for Social Research, University of Michigan, 1972); *Comprehensive Quality-of-Work-Life Survey* (Los Angeles: Center for Effective Organizations, University of Southern California, 1981); C. Cammann, M. Fichman, G. Jenkins and J. Klesh, 'Assessing the attitudes and perceptions of organizational members', in *Assessing Organization Change: A Guide to Methods, Measures, and Practices*, eds S. Seashore, E. Lawler III, P. Mirvis and C. Cammann (New York: Wiley-Interscience, 1983): 71–119.

55 R. Bullock and D. Svyantek, 'The impossibility of using random strategies to study the organization development process', *Journal of Applied Behavioral Science*, 23 (1987): 255–62.

56 D. Campbell and J. Stanley, *Experimental and Quasi-Experimental Design for Research* (Chicago: Rand McNally, 1966); T. Cook and D. Campbell, *Quasi-Experimentation: Design and Analysis Issues for Field Settings* (Chicago: Rand McNally, 1979).

57 E. Lawler III, D. Nadler and P. Mirvis, 'Organizational change and the conduct of assessment research', in *Assessing Organizational Change: A Guide to Methods, Measures and Practices*, eds S. Seashore, E. Lawler III, P. Mirvis and C. Cammann (New York: Wiley-Interscience, 1983): 19–47.

58 Cook and Campbell, *Quasi-Experimentation: Design and Analysis Issues for Field Settings*, op. cit.

59 R. Golembiewski and R. Munzenrider, 'Measuring change by OD designs', *Journal of Applied Behavioral Science*, 12 (April–May–June 1976): 133–57.

60 A. Bedeian, A. Armenakis and R. Gilson, 'On the measurement and control of beta change', *Academy of Management Review*, 5 (1980): 561–6; W. Randolph and R. Edwards, 'Assessment of alpha, beta and gamma changes in a university-setting OD intervention', *Academy of Management Proceedings* (1978): 313–17; J.

Terborg, G. Howard and S. Maxwell, 'Evaluating planned organizational change: a method for assessing alpha, beta, and gamma change', *Academy of Management Review*, 7 (1982): 292–5; M. Buckley and A. Armenakis, 'Detecting scale recalibration in survey research', *Group and Organization Studies*, 12 (1987): 464–81; R. Millsap and S. Hartog, 'Alpha, beta, and gamma change in evaluation research: a structural equation approach', *Journal of Applied Psychology*, 73 (1988): 574–84.

61 D. Ciampa, *Total Quality: A User's Guide for Implementation* (Reading, MA: Addison-Wesley, 1992); P. Senge, *The Fifth Discipline* (New York: Doubleday, 1990); Cummings and Mohrman, 'Self-designing organizations: towards implementing quality-of-work-life innovations', op. cit.; C. Worley, D. Hitchin and W. Ross, *Integrated Strategic Change* (Reading, MA: Addison-Wesley, 1996).

62 This section is based on the work of P. Goodman and J. Dean, 'Creating long-term organizational change', in *Change in Organizations*, ed. P. Goodman (San Francisco: Jossey-Bass, 1982): 226–79. To date, the framework is largely untested and unchallenged. Ledford's process model of persistence (see note 63) is the only other model proposed to explain institutionalisation. The empirical support for either model, however, is nil.

63 G. Ledford, 'The persistence of planned organizational change: a process theory perspective' (PhD dissertation, University of Michigan, 1984).

64 L. Zucker, 'Normal change or risky business: institutional effects on the "hazard" of change in hospital organizations, 1959–1979', *Journal of Management Studies*, 24 (1987): 671–700.

65 S. Mohrman and T. Cummings, *Self-Designing Organizations: Learning How to Create High Performance* (Reading, MA: Addison-Wesley, 1989).

66 J. Martin and C. Siehl, 'Organizational cultures and counterculture: an uneasy symbiosis', *Organizational Dynamics* (1983): 52–64; D. Meyerson and J. Martin, 'Cultural change: an integration of three different views', *Journal of Management Studies*, 24 (1987): 623–47.

67 L. Zucker, 'The role of institutionalization in cultural persistence', *American Sociological Review*, 42 (1977): 726–43.

Online reading

INFOTRAC® COLLEGE EDITION

For additional readings and reviews on design, implementation and evaluation, explore **InfoTrac® College Edition**, your online library. Go to **www.infotrac-college.com** and search for any of the InfoTrac key terms listed below:

- Design
- Implementation
- Evaluation
- Contingencies
- Readiness for change
- Resistance
- Power
- Research design
- Institutionalisation

INFOTRAC

iNTERVENTiON STRATEGiES

7

iNTERPERSONAL iNTERVENTiONS

This chapter discusses change programs relating to interpersonal relations and group dynamics. These change programs are among the earliest in organisation development and represent attempts to improve people's working relationships with one another. The interventions are aimed at helping group members to assess their interactions and to devise more effective ways of working together. These interventions represent a basic skill requirement for an OD practitioner.

INTERPERSONAL PROCESS APPROACH

There are many OD interventions that are aimed at enhancing the development and empowerment of individuals within organisations. T-groups and team building are the techniques most often used to improve employees' communication ability, performance and interpersonal skills in an organisational context, although process consultation and third-party intervention can be used under particular circumstances.

* *T-groups*, derived from the early laboratory training stem of OD, are mainly used today to help managers learn about the effects of their behaviour on others.
* *Process consultation* is another OD technique for helping group members to understand, diagnose and improve their behaviour. Through process consultation, the group should become better able to use its own resources to identify and solve interpersonal problems, which often block the solving of work-related problems.
* *Third-party intervention* focuses directly on dysfunctional interpersonal conflict. This approach is used only in special circumstances and only when both parties are willing to engage in the process of direct confrontation.
* *Team building* is aimed both at helping a team to perform its tasks better and at satisfying individual needs. Through team-building activities, group goals and norms become clearer. In addition, team members become better able to confront difficulties and problems and to understand the roles of individuals within the team. Among the specialised team-building approaches presented are interventions associated with ongoing teams as well as temporary teams, such as project teams and task forces.

T-groups

As discussed in Chapter 1, sensitivity training, or the T-group, is an early forerunner of modern OD interventions. Its direct use in OD has lessened considerably, but OD practitioners often attend T-groups to improve their own functioning. For example, T-groups can help OD practitioners become more aware of how others perceive them and thus increase their effectiveness with client systems. In addition, OD practitioners often recommend that organisation members attend a T-group to learn how their behaviours affect others, and to develop more effective ways of relating to people.

WHAT ARE THE GOALS?

T-groups are traditionally designed to provide members with experiential learning about group dynamics, leadership and interpersonal relations. The basic T-group consists of about 10 to 15 strangers who meet with a professional trainer to explore the social dynamics that emerge from their interactions. Modifications of this basic design have generally moved in two directions. The first path has used T-group methods to help individuals gain deeper personal understanding and development. This intrapersonal focus is typically called an encounter group or a personal-growth group. It is generally considered outside the boundaries of OD and should be conducted only by professionally trained clinicians. The second direction uses T-group techniques to explore group dynamics and member relationships within an intact work group. Considerable training in T-group methods and group dynamics should be acquired before attempting these interventions.

After an extensive review of the literature, Campbell and Dunnette listed six overall objectives common to most T-groups, although not every practitioner need accomplish every objective in every T-group.[1] These objectives are:

1   increased understanding, insight and awareness of one's own behaviour and its impact on others
2   increased understanding and sensitivity about the behaviour of others
3   better understanding and awareness of group and intergroup processes
4   increased diagnostic skills in interpersonal and intergroup situations
5   increased ability to transform learning into action
6   improvement in individuals' ability to analyse their own interpersonal behaviour.

These goals seem to meet many T-group applications, although any one training program may emphasise one goal more than the others.

THE RESULTS OF T-GROUPS

T-groups have been among the most controversial topics in organisation development, and probably more has been written about them than any other single topic in OD. A major issue of concern relates to the effectiveness of T-groups, and their impact on both the individual and the organisation. Campbell and Dunnette reviewed a large number of published articles on T-groups and criticised them for their lack of scientific rigour.[2] Argyris, on the other hand, criticised Campbell and Dunnette, arguing that a different kind of scientific rigour is necessary for evaluating T-groups.[3] Although there are obvious methodological problems, the studies generally support the notion that T-group training does bring about change in the individual back in his or her work situation.[4] Among the most frequently found changes are increased flexibility in role behaviour; more openness, receptivity and awareness; and more open communication, with better listening skills and less dependence on others. However, because the goals of many T-group designs are not carefully spelled out, because there are so many variations in design, and particularly because many of the research designs do not carefully measure an individual's real work climate and culture, the findings are not highly predictable. Further, some individuals do not attend T-group sessions voluntarily, and little knowledge is available about the differences between those who want to attend and those who are forced to attend.

In considering the value of T-groups for organisations, the evidence is even more mixed. One comparative study of different human process interventions showed that T-groups had the least impact on measures of process (for example, openness and decision making) and outcome (for example, productivity and costs).[5] Another comparative study showed, however, that structured T-groups had the most impact on hard measures, such as productivity and absenteeism.[6] The T-groups in this study were structured so that learning could be explicitly transferred back to the work setting. A third comparative study showed that, although T-groups improved group process, they failed to improve the organisational culture surrounding the groups and to gain peer and managerial support in the organisation.[7] Finally, in a meta-analysis of 16 studies, researchers concluded that laboratory training interventions had significant positive effects on overall employee satisfaction and other attitudes.[8]

In his review of the T-group literature, Kaplan concluded that, despite their tarnished reputation, such interventions 'can continue to serve a purpose they are uniquely suited for, to provide an emotional education and to promote awareness of relationships and group process'.[9]

Process consultation

Process consultation (PC) is a general model for carrying out helping relationships in groups.[10] It is oriented to helping managers, employees and groups to assess and improve processes, such as communication, interpersonal relations, group performance and leadership. Schein argues that effective consultants and managers are good helpers, aiding others to get things done and achieve the goals they have set.[11] Process consultation is an approach to performing this helping relationship. It is aimed at ensuring that those who are receiving the help own their problems and gain the skills and expertise to diagnose and solve them themselves. Thus, it is an approach to helping people and groups to help themselves. Schein defines process consultation as 'a set of activities on the part of the consultant that helps the client to perceive, understand and act upon the process events which occur in the client's environment'.[12] The process consultant does not offer expert help in the sense of providing solutions to problems as in the doctor–patient model. Rather, the process consultant observes groups and people in action, helps them to diagnose the nature and extent of their problems, and helps them to learn to solve their own problems.

The stages of process consultation follow closely those described for planned change in Chapter 2: entering, defining the relationship, selecting an approach, gathering data and making a diagnosis, intervening, reducing the involvement and terminating the relationship. However, when used in process consultation, these stages are not so clear-cut, because any one of the steps constitutes an intervention. For example, the process consultant has intervened merely by conducting some preliminary interviews with group members. By being interviewed, the members may begin to see the situation in a new light.

GROUP PROCESS

Process consultation deals primarily with five important group processes:
1   communications
2   the functional roles of group members
3   the ways in which the group solves problems and makes decisions
4   the development and growth of group norms
5   the use of leadership and authority.

Communications

One of the process consultant's areas of interest is the nature and style of communication among group members, at both the overt and covert levels. At the overt level, communication issues involve who talks to whom, for how long and how often. By keeping a time log, the consultant can also note who talks and who interrupts. Watching body language and other non-verbal behaviour can also be a highly informative way of understanding communication processes.[13]

At the covert or hidden level of communication, sometimes one thing is said but another meant, thus giving a double message. Luft has described this phenomenon in what is called the Johari window.[14] Figure 7.1, a diagram of the Johari window, shows that some personal issues are perceived by both the individual and others (cell 1). Other people are aware of their own issues, but they conceal them from others (cell 2). In this situation, persons may have certain feelings about themselves or about others in the work group that they do not share with others unless they feel safe and protected; by not revealing reactions that they feel might be hurtful or impolite, they lessen the degree of communication.

Cell 3 comprises personal issues that are unknown to the individual but that are communicated clearly to others. Cell 4 of the Johari window represents those personal aspects that are unknown to either the individual or others. Because such areas are outside the realm of the consultant and the group, focus is typically on the other three cells. The consultant can help

Figure 7.1 Johari window

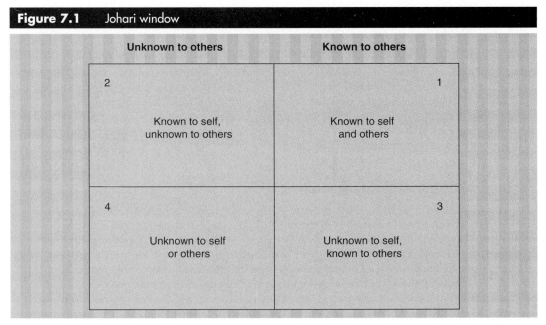

Source: Adapted from J. Luft, 'The Johari Window', *Human Relations Training News*, 5 (1961): 6–7.

people to learn about how others experience them, thus reducing cell 3. Further, the consultant can help individuals to give feedback to others, thus reducing cell 2. Reducing the size of these two cells helps to improve the communication process by enlarging cell 1, the 'self that is open to both the individual and others'.

The climate of the work group can have a great impact on the size of the quadrants in the Johari window, particularly cell 2. Gibb has outlined two basic types of climate: supportive and threatening.[15] Threatening climates (those that put the receiver on the defensive) can be of several types, and for each there is a corresponding supportive climate.

- *Evaluative versus descriptive.* A listener who perceives a statement as evaluative is put on guard. If, on the other hand, the comment is perceived as descriptive and factual, the receiver is more likely to accept the communication.
- *Control versus problem orientation.* One person's attempt to control another increases the latter's defensiveness. Problem orientation, by contrast, is supportive, as it does not imply that the receiver is somehow inferior.
- *Strategy versus spontaneity.* Strategy implies manipulation, whereas spontaneity reduces defensive behaviour.
- *Superiority versus equality.* To the extent that a person assumes a superior role, he or she arouses defensiveness in the other person. Equality is much more likely to result in joint problem solving.
- *Certainty versus provisionalism.* The more dogmatic a person is, the more that defensiveness will be aroused in others. Provisionalism, on the other hand, allows the other person to have some control over the situation and increases the likelihood of collaboration.

Functional roles of group members

The process consultant must be keenly aware of the different roles that individual members take on within a group. Both upon entering and while remaining in a group, the individual must determine a self-identity, influence and power that will satisfy personal needs while working to accomplish group goals. Preoccupation with individual needs or power struggles can severely reduce the effectiveness of a group, and unless the individual can, to some degree, expose and share those personal needs, the group is unlikely to be productive. Therefore, the process consultant must help the group confront and work through these needs.

Two other functions that need to be performed if a group is to be effective are: (1) task-related activities, such as giving and seeking information and elaborating, co-ordinating and evaluating activities; and (2) the group-maintenance function, which is directed towards holding the group together as a cohesive team and includes encouraging, harmonising, compromising, setting standards and observing. Most ineffective groups do little group maintenance. This is a primary reason for bringing in a process observer. The process consultant can help by suggesting that some part of each meeting be reserved for examining these functions and periodically assessing the feelings of the group's members. The consultant's role is to make comments and to assist with diagnosis, but the emphasis should be on facilitating the group's understanding and articulation of its own processes.

Problem solving and decision making

To be effective, a group must be able to identify problems, examine alternatives and make decisions. The first part of this process is the most important. Groups often fail to distinguish between problems (either task-related or interpersonal) and symptoms. Once the group has identified the problem, an OD consultant can help the group analyse its approach, restrain the group from reacting too quickly and making a premature diagnosis, or suggest additional options. The process consultant can help the group understand how it makes decisions and the consequences of each decision process, as well as help diagnose which type of decision process may be most effective in the given situation. Decision by unanimous consent, for example, may sometimes be ideal, but too time-consuming or costly at other times.

Group norms and growth

If a group of people works together over a period of time, it often develops group norms or standards of behaviour about what is good or bad, allowed or forbidden, and right or wrong. There may be an explicit norm that group members are free to express their ideas and feelings, whereas the implicit norm is that one does not contradict the ideas or suggestions of certain members (usually the more powerful ones) of the group. The process consultant can be very helpful in assisting the group to understand and articulate its own norms and to determine whether those norms are helpful or dysfunctional. By understanding its norms and recognising which ones are helpful, the group can grow and deal realistically with its environment, make optimum use of its own resources and learn from its own experiences.[16]

Leadership and authority

A process consultant needs to understand the processes of leadership and how different leadership styles can help or hinder a group's functioning. In addition, the consultant can help the leader to adjust his or her style to fit the situation. An important step in that process is for the leader to gain a better understanding of his or her own behaviour and the group's reaction to that behaviour. It is also important that the leader become aware of alternative behaviours.

BASIC PROCESS INTERVENTIONS

For each of the five group processes described above, a variety of interventions may be used. In broad terms, these interventions may be of the following types:[17]

1   Process interventions, including:

- questions that direct attention to interpersonal issues

- process-analysis periods

- agenda review and testing procedures

- meetings devoted to interpersonal processes

- conceptual inputs on interpersonal-process topics.

Process interventions are designed to make the group sensitive to its own internal processes and to generate interest in analysing these processes.

2 Diagnostic and feedback interventions, including:

- diagnostic questions and probes

- forcing historical reconstruction, concretisation and process emphasis

- feedback to groups during process analysis or regular work time

- feedback to individuals after meetings or data-gathering sessions.

To give feedback to a group, the consultant must first observe relevant events, ask the proper questions, and make certain that the feedback is given to the client system in a usable manner. The process consultant's feedback must be specific, timely and descriptive.

3 Coaching or counselling of individuals or groups to help them learn to observe and process their own data, accept and learn from the feedback process, and become active in identifying and solving their own problems.

4 Structural suggestions pertaining to the following:

- group membership

- communication or interaction patterns

- allocation of work, assignments of responsibility or lines of authority.

WHEN IS PROCESS CONSULTATION APPROPRIATE?

Process consultation is a general model for helping relationships, and so has wide applicability in organisations. Because process consultation helps people and groups to own their problems and learn how to diagnose and resolve them, it is most applicable when:[18]

1 the client has a problem but does not know its source or how to resolve it
2 the client is unsure of what kind of help or consultation is available
3 the nature of the problem is such that the client would benefit from involvement in its diagnosis
4 the client is motivated by goals that the consultant can accept and has some capacity to enter into a helping relationship
5 the client ultimately knows what interventions are most applicable
6 the client is capable of learning how to assess and resolve his or her own problem.

RESULTS OF PROCESS CONSULTATION

A number of difficulties arise when trying to measure performance improvements as a result of process consultation. One problem is that most process consultation is conducted with groups that perform mental tasks (for example, decision making) – the outcomes of such tasks are difficult to evaluate. A second difficulty with measuring its effects occurs because, in many cases, process consultation is combined with other interventions in an ongoing OD program. Isolating the impact of process consultation from other interventions is difficult. A third problem with assessing the performance effects of process consultation is that much of the relevant research has used people's perceptions as the index of success, rather than hard performance measures. Much of this research shows positive results, including studies in which the success of process consultation was measured by questionnaires.

Third-party intervention

Third-party intervention focuses on conflicts arising between two or more people within the same organisation. Conflict is inherent in groups and organisations and can arise from a variety of sources, including differences in personality, task orientation and perceptions among group members, as well as competition over scarce resources. To emphasise that conflict is neither good nor bad *per se* is important. It can enhance motivation and innovation and lead to greater understanding of ideas and views. On the other hand, conflict can prevent people from working together constructively; it can destroy necessary task interactions among group members. Consequently, third-party intervention is used primarily in situations in which conflict significantly disrupts necessary task interactions and work relationships among members.

Third-party intervention varies considerably according to the kind of issues that underlies the conflict. Conflict can arise over substantive issues, such as work methods, pay rates and conditions of employment; or it can emerge from interpersonal issues, such as personality conflicts and misperceptions. When applied to substantive issues, conflict resolution interventions traditionally involve resolving labour–management disputes through arbitration and mediation. These methods require considerable training and expertise in law and labour relations and are not generally considered to be part of OD practice. When conflict involves interpersonal issues, however, OD has developed approaches that help to control and to resolve it. These third-party interventions help the parties to directly interact with each other, facilitating their diagnosis of the conflict and how to resolve it. That ability to facilitate conflict resolution is a basic skill in OD and applies to all of the process interventions discussed in this chapter. Consultants, for example, frequently help organisation members to resolve the interpersonal conflicts that invariably arise during process consultation and team building.

Third-party consultation interventions cannot resolve all interpersonal conflicts in organisations, and nor should they. Interpersonal conflicts are frequently not severe or disruptive enough to warrant attention. At other times, they may simply burn themselves out without any intervention.

AN EPISODIC MODEL OF CONFLICT

Interpersonal conflict often occurs in iterative, cyclical stages known as 'episodes'. An episodic model is shown in Figure 7.2. At times, the issues underlying the conflict are latent and do not present any manifest problems for the parties. Something triggers the conflict, however, and brings it into the open. For example, a violent disagreement or frank confrontation can unleash conflict behaviour. Because of the negative consequences of conflict behaviour, the disagreement usually becomes latent again, even though it is still unresolved. Once again, something triggers the conflict, making it overt, and so the cycle continues with the next conflict episode. Conflict has both costs and benefits for the antagonists and for those in contact with them. Unresolved conflict can proliferate and expand. An interpersonal conflict may be concealed under a cause or issue, serving to make the conflict more legitimate. Frequently, the overt conflict is only a symptom of a deeper problem.

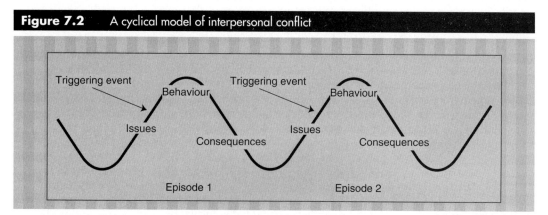

Figure 7.2 A cyclical model of interpersonal conflict

Source: R. G. Walton, *Managing Conflict*, 2nd edn, copyright © 1987 by Addison-Wesley Publishing Company Inc.

The episode model identifies four strategies for conflict resolution. The first three attempt to control the conflict, and only the last approach tries to change the basic issues that underlie it.[19] The first strategy is to prevent the ignition of conflict by arriving at a clear understanding of the triggering factors and thereafter avoiding or blunting them when the symptoms occur. This may not always be functional and may merely drive the conflict underground until it explodes. As a control strategy, though, this method may help to achieve a temporary cooling-off period.

The second control strategy is to set limits on the form of the conflict. Conflict can be constrained by informal gatherings before a formal meeting or by exploration of other options. It can also be limited by setting rules and procedures that specify the conditions under which the parties can interact.

The third control strategy is to help the parties cope differently with the consequences of the conflict. The third-party consultant may work with the individuals involved to help them to devise coping techniques, such as reducing their dependence on the relationship, airing their feelings to friends and developing additional sources of emotional support. These methods can reduce the costs of the conflict without resolving the underlying issues.

The fourth method is an attempt to eliminate or resolve the basic issues causing the conflict.

FACILITATING THE CONFLICT-RESOLUTION PROCESS

Walton has identified a number of factors and tactical choices that can facilitate the use of the episode model in resolving the underlying causes of conflict.[20] The following ingredients can help third-party consultants achieve productive dialogue between the disputants so that they examine their differences and change their perceptions and behaviours: mutual motivation to resolve the conflict; equality of power between the parties; co-ordinated attempts to confront the conflict; relevant phasing of the stages of identifying differences and of searching for integrative solutions; and open and clear forms of communication and productive levels of tension and stress.

Among the tactical choices identified by Walton are those that have to do with diagnosis, the context of the third-party intervention and the role of the consultant. One of the tactics in third-party intervention is the gathering of data, usually through preliminary interviewing. Group-process observations can also be used. Data gathering provides some understanding of the nature and type of conflict, the personality and conflict styles of the individuals involved, the issues and attendant pressures, and the participants' readiness to work together to resolve the conflict.

The context in which the intervention occurs is also important. Consideration of the neutrality of the meeting area, the formality of the setting, the appropriateness of the time for the meeting (that is, a meeting should not be started until a time has been agreed upon to conclude or adjourn) and the careful selection of those who should attend the meeting are all elements of this context. In addition, the third-party consultant must decide on an appropriate role to assume in resolving conflict. The specific tactic chosen will depend on the diagnosis of the situation.

The third-party consultant must develop considerable skill at diagnosis, intervention and follow-up. The third-party intervener must be highly sensitive to his or her own feelings and to those of others. He or she must also recognise that some tension and conflict are inevitable and that, although there can be an optimum amount and degree of conflict, too much conflict can be dysfunctional for both the individuals involved and the larger organisation. The third-party consultant must be sensitive to the situation and able to use a number of different intervention strategies and tactics when intervention appears to be useful. Finally, he or she must have professional expertise in third-party intervention and must be seen by the parties as neutral or unbiased regarding the issues and outcomes of the conflict resolution.

Team building

Team building refers to a broad range of planned activities that help groups to improve the way they accomplish tasks and help group members to enhance their interpersonal and problem-solving skills.

Organisations consist of many permanent and temporary groups. Team building is an effective approach to improving teamwork and task accomplishment in these situations. It can help problem-solving groups make maximum use of members' resources and contributions. It can help members to develop a high level of motivation to carry out group decisions. Team building can also help groups overcome specific problems, such as: apathy and general lack of interest among members; loss of productivity; increasing complaints within the group; confusion about assignments; low participation in meetings; lack of innovation and initiation; increasing complaints from those outside the group about the quality, timeliness and effectiveness of services and products; and hostility or conflict among members.

Equally importantly, team building can facilitate other OD interventions, such as employee involvement, work design, restructuring and strategic change. These change programs are typically designed by management teams and implemented by various committees and work groups. Team building can help these groups design high-quality change programs. It can ensure that the programs are accepted and implemented by organisation members. Indeed, most technostructural, human resource management and strategic interventions depend on some form of team building for effective implementation.

Team building is not clearly differentiated from process consultation in the OD literature. This confusion stems mainly from the fact that most team building includes process consultation: helping the group to diagnose and to understand its own internal processes. However, process consultation is a more general approach to helping relationships than team building. Team building focuses explicitly on helping groups to perform tasks and to solve problems more effectively. Process consultation, on the other hand, is concerned with establishing effective helping relationships in organisations. It is seen as being essential for effective management and consultation, and can be applied to any helping relationship, from subordinate development to interpersonal relationships to group development. Thus, team building consists of process consultation plus other, more task-oriented, interventions.

Dyer has developed a checklist for identifying whether a team-building program is needed and whether the organisation is ready to start such a program (Table 7.1).[21] If the problem is a structural or technical one, an intergroup issue, an administrative mistake or a conflict between only two people, team building would not be an appropriate change strategy.

TEAM-BUILDING ACTIVITIES

A team is a group of interdependent individuals who share a common purpose, have common work methods and hold each other accountable.[22] The nature of that interdependence varies, creating the following types of teams:

- groups reporting to the same supervisor, manager or executive
- groups involving people with common organisational goals
- temporary groups formed to do a specific, one-time task
- groups consisting of people whose work roles are interdependent
- groups whose members have no formal links in the organisation but whose collective purpose is to achieve tasks they cannot accomplish as individuals.

Just as there are various types of teams, so there are a number of factors that affect the outcomes of a specific team-building activity: the length of time allocated to the activity; the team's willingness to look at the way in which it operates; the length of time the team has been working together; and the permanence of the team. Consequently, the results of team-building activities can range from comparatively modest changes in the team's operating mechanisms (for example, meeting more frequently or gathering agenda items from more sources) to much deeper changes (for example, modifying team members' behaviour patterns or the nature and style of the group's management, or developing greater openness and trust).

In general, team-building activities can be classified as follows:

- activities relevant to one or more individuals
- activities specific to the group's operation and behaviour
- activities that affect the group's relationship with the rest of the organisation.

| **Table 7.1** | Team-building checklist |

| **I** | Problem identification: To what extent is there evidence of the following problems in your work unit? |

		Low evidence		Some evidence		High evidence
1	Loss of production or work-unit output	1	2	3	4	5
2	Grievances or complaints within the work unit	1	2	3	4	5
3	Conflicts or hostility between unit members	1	2	3	4	5
4	Confusion about assignments or unclear relationships between people	1	2	3	4	5
5	Lack of clear goals or low commitment to goals	1	2	3	4	5
6	Apathy or general lack of interest or involvement of unit members	1	2	3	4	5
7	Lack of innovation, risk taking, imagination or taking initiative	1	2	3	4	5
8	Ineffective staff meetings	1	2	3	4	5
9	Problems in working with the boss	1	2	3	4	5
10	Poor communications: people afraid to speak up, not listening to each other or not talking together	1	2	3	4	5
11	Lack of trust between boss and members or between members	1	2	3	4	5
12	Decisions made that people do not understand or agree with	1	2	3	4	5
13	People feel that good work is not recognised or rewarded	1	2	3	4	5
14	People are not encouraged to work together in a better team effort	1	2	3	4	5

Scoring: Add the score for the 14 items. If your score is between 14 and 28, there is little evidence that your unit needs team building. If your score is between 29 and 42, there is some evidence but no immediate pressure, unless two or three items are very high. If your score is between 43 and 56, you should seriously think about planning the team-building program. If your score is over 56, then team building should be the top priority for your work unit.

| **II** | Are you (or your manager) prepared to start a team-building program? Consider the following statements. To what extent do they apply to you or your department? |

		Low		Medium		High
1	You are comfortable in sharing organisational leadership and decision making with subordinates and prefer to work in a participative atmosphere	1	2	3	4	5
2	You see a high degree of interdependence as necessary among functions and workers in order to achieve your goals	1	2	3	4	5
3	The external environment is highly variable or changing rapidly and you need the best thinking of all your staff to plan for these conditions	1	2	3	4	5
4	You feel you need the input of your staff to plan major changes or develop new operating policies and procedures	1	2	3	4	5
5	You feel that broad consultation among your people as a group in goals, decisions and problems is necessary on a continuing basis	1	2	3	4	5
6	Members of your management team are (or can become) compatible with each other and are able to create a collaborative rather than a competitive environment	1	2	3	4	5
7	Members of your team are located close enough to meet together as needed	1	2	3	4	5

(continued)

Table 7.1	Team-building checklist *(continued)*									

II Are you (or your manager) prepared to start a team-building program? Consider the following statements. To what extent do they apply to you or your department?

		Low		Medium		High	
8	You feel you need to rely on the ability and willingness of subordinates to resolve critical operating problems directly and in the best interest of the company or organisation	1	2	3	4	5
9	Formal communication channels are not sufficient for the timely exchange of essential information, views and decisions among your team members	1	2	3	4	5
10	Organisation adaptation requires the use of such devices as project management, task forces or ad hoc problem-solving groups to augment conventional organisation structure	1	2	3	4	5
11	You feel it is important to bring out and deal with critical, albeit sensitive, issues that exist in your team	1	2	3	4	5
12	You are prepared to look at your own role and performance with your team	1	2	3	4	5
13	You feel there are operating or interpersonal problems that have remained unsolved too long and need the input from all group members	1	2	3	4	5
14	You need an opportunity to meet with your people to set goals and develop commitment to these goals	1	2	3	4	5

Scoring: If your total score is between 50 and 70, you are probably ready to go ahead with the team-building program. If your score is between 35 and 49, you should probably talk the situation over with your team and others to see what would need to be done to get ready for team building. If your score is between 14 and 34, you are probably not prepared to start team building.

Source: W. Dyer, *Team Building*, 2nd edn, copyright © 1987 by Addison-Wesley Publishing Company, Inc.

Usually, a specific team-building activity will overlap these three categories. On occasion, a change in one area may lead to negative results in other areas. Nevertheless, the development of a team-building strategy can be essential to the cohesion and effectiveness of the team, as illustrated in Application 7.1

APPLICATION 7.1

BUILDING A TEAM ESSENTIAL

Businesses have been urged to make team building an essential part of their daily routine. Greater demands on workers' time means social aspects of their work are being neglected to the detriment of employee performances, a human resources company has warned. Locher Human Resources says relationships between staff members are also suffering. 'Effective teamwork springs from the members of the team sharing an understanding about how their fellow workers think and operate,' Locher Human Resources director of organisational development Danielle Jiranek says. 'When the members of a team know each other well, they naturally play to the strengths of each member,' she says. 'If a colleague works in isolation, it is harder to maximise their potential in the broader context of the office.'

She says an increasing number of women with children who have returned to work also contribute to the issue, as they are often under pressure to collect children from care at the end of the day. As a result they often miss out on social moments in workplace life. Employers need to build team-based activities into work time if they want to achieve an effective team environment.

Source: Nhada Larkin, 'Building a team essential', Money & You, The Courier-Mail, 8/2/06.

Critical Thinking Question: How important do you think it is to include social activities in a team-building strategy?

THE MANAGER ROLE

Ultimately, the manager is responsible for team functioning, even though the team itself must obviously share this responsibility. Therefore, the development of a team group that can regularly stop to analyse and diagnose its own effectiveness and work process is management's task. The manager has the responsibility of diagnosing (with the team) the effectiveness of the team and taking appropriate action if the work unit shows signs of operating difficulty or stress. Strategies for managers include those listed in Application 7.2.

APPLiCATiON 7.2

NEW LEADER TIPS

Here's some tips for new leaders and managers seeking to gain the respect of their teams, from Margaret Locke, General Manager, Management Recruiters Australia:

- Early in your tenure make small improvements to procedures that will make life easier for the team. This may be anything from a small tweak of internal procedure to flexible hours to help strike a better work/life balance for members of the team.
- Establish key performance indicators (KPIs) if there are none.
- Re-establish KPIs if these are unrealistic. Many dictatorial managers will fail to break down large targets into 'bit size' KPIs. Doing so will often improve morale as a result of working to achievable goals.
- Get the team involved in decision making. This is never so more important than when a manager has been promoted from their peer group. Recognition of the team's skills and 'empowerment' of team members will certainly help the new manager establish vital personal relationships following their new appointment.
- Be a facilitator and mentor rather than a manager.

Source: 'New Leader Tips', *Management Today*, May 2004.

Critical Thinking Question: Why do you think the author sees the establishment of realistic KPIs as being so important in efforts by a newly appointed leader to establish an effective team?

However, many managers have not been trained to perform the data gathering, diagnosis, planning and action necessary for them to continually maintain and improve their teams. Thus, the issue of who should lead a team-building session is a function of managerial capability. The initial use of a consultant is usually advisable if a manager is aware of problems, feels that she or he may be part of the problem and believes that some positive action is needed to improve the operation of the unit, but is not exactly sure how to go about it. Dyer has provided a checklist for assessing the need for a consultant (Table 7.2). Some of the questions ask the manager to examine problems and to establish the degree to which the manager feels comfortable in trying out new and different things, the degree of knowledge about team building, whether the boss might be a major source of difficulty, and the openness of group members.

Basically, the role of the consultant is to work closely with the manager (and members of the unit) to a point at which the manager is capable of actively engaging in team-development activities as a regular and ongoing part of overall managerial responsibilities. Assuming that the manager wants and needs a consultant, the two should work together as a team in developing the initial program, keeping in mind that: (1) the manager is ultimately responsible for all team-building activities, even though the consultant's resources are available; and (2) the goal of the consultant's presence is to help the manager to learn to continue team-development processes with minimum consultant help or without the ongoing help of the consultant. Thus, in the first stages, the consultant might be much more active in data gathering, diagnosis and action planning, particularly if a one- to three-day off-site workshop is considered. In later stages, the consultant takes a much less active role, with the manager becoming more active and taking on the role of both manager and team developer.

Table 7.2	Addressing the need for a consultant			
Should you use an outside consultant to help in team building?				
		Circle the appropriate response		
1	Does the manager feel comfortable in trying out something new and different with the staff?	Yes	No	?
2	Is the staff used to spending time in an outside location working on issues of concern to the work unit?	Yes	No	?
3	Will group members speak up and give honest data?	Yes	No	?
4	Does your group generally work together without a lot of conflict or apathy?	Yes	No	?
5	Are you reasonably sure that the boss is not a major source of difficulty?	Yes	No	?
6	Is there a high commitment by the boss and unit members to achieving more effective team functioning?	Yes	No	?
7	Is the personal style of the boss and his or her management philosophy consistent with a team approach?	Yes	No	?
8	Do you feel you know enough about team building to begin a program without help?	Yes	No	?
9	Would your staff feel confident enough to begin a team-building program without outside help?	Yes	No	?

Scoring: If you have circled six or more 'yes' responses, you probably do not need an outside consultant. If you have four or more 'no' responses, you probably do need a consultant. If you have a mixture of 'yes', 'no' and '?' responses, you should probably invite a consultant to talk over the situation and make a joint decision.

Source: W. Dyer, *Team Building*, 2nd edn, © 1987 by Addison-Wesley Publishing Co., Inc.

WHEN IS TEAM BUILDING APPLICABLE?

Team building is applicable to a large number of team situations, from starting a new team and resolving conflicts among members to revitalising a complacent team. Lewis has identified the following conditions as best suited to team building:[23]

1   Patterns of communication and interaction are inadequate for good group functioning.
2   Group leaders desire an integrated team.
3   The group's task requires interaction among members.
4   The team leader will behave differently as the result of team building, and members will respond to the new behaviour.
5   The benefits outweigh the costs of team building.
6   Team building must be congruent with the leader's personal style and philosophy.

THE RESULTS OF TEAM BUILDING

The research on team building has a number of problems. First, it focuses mainly on the feelings and attitudes of group members. There is little evidence to support the notion that group performance improves as a result of team-building experiences. One study, for example, found that team building was a smashing success in the eyes of the participants.[24] However, a rigorous field test of the results over time showed no appreciable effects on either the team's or the larger organisation's functioning and efficiency. Second, the positive effects of team building are typically measured over relatively short periods. Evidence suggests that the positive effects of off-site team building are short-lived and tend to fade after the group returns to the organisation. Third, team building rarely occurs in isolation. It is usually carried out in conjunction with other interventions that lead to, or result from, team building itself. For this reason, it is difficult to separate the effects of team building from those of the other interventions.[25]

Studies of the empirical literature present a mixed picture of the impact of team building on group performance. One review shows that team building improves process measures (such as employee openness and decision making) about 45% of the time; it improves outcome measures (such as productivity and costs) about 53% of the time.[26] Another review reveals that team building positively affects hard measures of productivity, employee withdrawal and costs about 50% of the time.[27] Still another review concludes that team building cannot be convincingly linked to improved performance. Of the 30 studies reviewed, only 10 attempted to measure changes in performance. Although these changes were generally positive, the studies' research designs were relatively weak, reducing confidence in the findings.[28] One review concluded that process interventions, such as team building and process consultation, are most likely to improve process variables, such as decision making, communication and problem solving.[29]

Boss has conducted extensive research on arresting the potential 'fade-out effects' of off-site team building.[30] He proposes that the tendency for the positive behaviours developed at off-site team building to regress once the group is back in the organisation can be checked by conducting a follow-up intervention called 'personal management interview' (PMI). This is done soon after the off-site team building and involves the team leader – who first negotiates roles with each member and then holds weekly or biweekly meetings with each member to improve communication – to resolve problems and to increase personal accountability.

Buller and Bell have attempted to differentiate the effects of team building from the effects of other interventions that occur along with team building.[31] Specifically, they tried to separate the effects of team building from the effects of goal setting, an intervention aimed at setting realistic performance goals and developing action plans for achieving them. In a rigorous field experiment, Buller and Bell examined the differential effects of team building and goal setting on productivity measures of underground miners. The results show that team building affects the quality of performance, while goal setting affects the quantity of performance. This differential impact was explained in terms of the nature of the mining task. The task of improving the quality of performance was more complex, unstructured and interdependent than the task of achieving quantity. This suggests that team building can improve group performance, particularly on tasks that are complex, unstructured and interdependent.

ORGANISATION PROCESS APPROACHES

This second section of the chapter describes four system-wide process interventions – change programs directed at improving such processes as organisational problem solving, leadership, visioning and task accomplishment between groups – for a major subsystem or for an entire organisation.

- The first type of intervention, the *organisation confrontation meeting*, is among the earliest organisation-wide process approaches. It helps to mobilise the problem-solving resources of a major subsystem or an entire organisation by encouraging members to identify and confront pressing issues.
- The second organisation process approach is called *intergroup relations*. It consists of two interventions: the intergroup conflict resolution meeting and microcosm groups. Both interventions are aimed at diagnosing and addressing important organisation-level processes, such as conflict, the co-ordination of organisational units and diversity. The intergroup conflict intervention is specifically oriented towards conflict processes, whereas the microcosm group is a more generic system-wide change strategy.
- A third organisation-wide process approach, the *large-group intervention*, has received considerable attention recently and is one of the fastest-growing areas in OD. Large-group interventions get a 'whole system into the room'[32] and create processes that allow a variety of stakeholders to interact simultaneously. A large-group intervention can be used to clarify important organisational values, develop new ways of looking at problems,

articulate a new vision for the organisation, solve cross-functional problems, restructure operations or devise an organisational strategy. It is a powerful tool for addressing organisational problems and opportunities and for accelerating the pace of organisational change.

• The final section of this chapter describes a normative approach to OD: Blake and Mouton's Grid® Organization Development. This is a popular intervention, particularly in large organisations. Grid® Organization Development is a packaged program that organisations can purchase and train members to use. In contrast to modern contingency approaches, the Grid proposes that there is one best way of managing organisations. Consequently, OD practitioners have increasingly questioned its applicability and effectiveness in contemporary organisations.

Organisation confrontation meeting

The confrontation meeting is an intervention designed to mobilise the resources of the entire organisation to identify problems, set priorities and action targets, and begin working on identified problems. Originally developed by Beckhard,[33] the intervention can be used at any time, but is particularly useful when the organisation is in stress and when there is a gap between the top and the rest of the organisation (such as a new top manager). General Electric's 'WorkOut' program is a recent example of how the confrontation meeting has been adapted to fit today's organisations.[34]

WHAT ARE THE STEPS?

The organisation confrontation meeting typically involves the following steps:

1   A group meeting of all involved is scheduled and held in an appropriate place. Usually the task is to identify problems about the work environment and the effectiveness of the organisation.

2   Groups are appointed, with representatives from all departments of the organisation. For example, each group might have one or more members from sales, purchasing, finance, manufacturing and quality assurance.

3   It must be stressed that the groups are to be open and honest and must work hard at identifying problems they see in the organisation. No one will be criticised for bringing up problems and, in fact, the groups will be judged on their ability to do so.

4   The groups are given an hour or two to identify organisation problems. Generally, an OD practitioner goes from group to group, encouraging openness and assisting the groups with their tasks.

5   The groups then reconvene in a central meeting place. Each group reports the problems it has identified and sometimes offers solutions. Because each group hears the reports of all the others, a maximum amount of information is shared.

6   Either then or later, the master list of problems is broken down into categories. This process eliminates duplication and overlap, and allows the problems to be separated according to functional or other appropriate areas.

7   Following problem categorisation, participants are divided into problem-solving groups, whose composition may (and usually does) differ from that of the original problem-identification groups.

8   Each group ranks the problems, develops a tactical action plan and determines an appropriate timetable for completing this phase of the process.

9   Each group then periodically reports its list of priorities and tactical plans of action to management or to the larger group.

10 Schedules for periodic (often monthly) follow-up meetings are established. The formal establishment of such follow-up meetings ensures both continuing action and the modification of priorities and timetables as needed.

RESULTS OF CONFRONTATION MEETINGS

Because organisation confrontation meetings are often combined with other approaches, such as survey feedback, determining specific results is difficult. In many cases, the results appear dramatic in mobilising the total resources of the organisation for problem identification and solution. Alec Bashinsky's use of 'tiger teams', described in Application 7.3, is one innovative application of the confrontation meeting approach.

APPLiCATiON 7.3

HUMAN RESOURCE INNOVATION

Alec Bashinsky describes himself as an extremely persistent person. His success at Deloitte as the accounting firm's national partner, People and Performance, has led to several awards for human-resources practice, the latest being the JML Australia Human Capital Leadership Award. He has led initiatives such as a staff-referral recruitment program, which is estimated to have saved Deloitte $1.2 million in recruitment fees in the past year.

With adequate resources and a pro-change chief executive, Giam Swiegers, behind him, Bashinsky has been able to orchestrate a new three-year graduate development program. It simply uses the budget previously spent on entertaining prospective graduates. Other learning programs have been introduced – lunchtime seminars have been popular – as well as programs to promote more women into senior ranks.

To make these changes, Bashinsky had to move human-resources staff away from their spreadsheets and other mundane tasks to concentrate on more strategic work that will improve the business. 'It is about changing the mandate and structure around HR,' he says. 'The company has to change or we will be left behind.'

Bashinsky's next great challenge is centred on developing the leadership capabilities of the firm's partners. Deloitte will invest more in partner development over the next year than it has in the past five. Tips on leading organisational change include:
* Communicate to the whole group about the desired changes for the business and why they need to be made.
* Rather than thinking of the process of change management as an entire project, break it down into smaller pieces and work on specific areas. Publicise changes as they happen, and then move on to the next stage of the project.
* Bashinsky has had success with what he calls 'tiger teams' within Deloitte. Groups of staff from different walks of life are set up to challenge the ways things are done. 'The group takes something that is existing and tears it to shreds,' he says.

Source: Emily Ross, 'Ideas & Issues: The meetings divide', *Business Review Weekly*, 27/4/06.

Critical Thinking Question: Do you think the use of 'tiger teams' might create difficulties for management rather than successes?

Beckhard cites a number of specific examples in such varying organisations as a food-products manufacturer, a military-products manufacturer and a hotel.[35] Positive results were also found in a confrontation meeting with 40 professionals in a research and development firm.[36] The organisation confrontation meeting is a promising approach for mobilising organisational problem solving, especially in times of low performance.

Intergroup relations interventions

The ability to diagnose and understand intergroup relations is important for OD practitioners as:
* groups must often work with and through other groups to accomplish their goals
* groups within the organisation often create problems and demands on each other

- the quality of the relationships between groups can affect the degree of organisational effectiveness.

Two OD interventions – microcosm groups and intergroup conflict resolution – are described here. A microcosm group uses members from several groups to help solve organisation-wide problems. Intergroup issues are explored in this context, and then solutions are implemented in the larger organisation. Intergroup conflict resolution helps two groups work out dysfunctional relationships. Together, these approaches help to improve intergroup processes and lead to organisational effectiveness.

MICROCOSM GROUPS

A microcosm group consists of a small number of individuals who reflect the issue being addressed.[37] For example, a microcosm group made up of members who represent a spectrum of ethnic backgrounds, cultures and races can be created to address diversity issues in the organisation. This group, with the assistance of OD practitioners, can create programs and processes targeted to specific problems. In addition to addressing diversity problems, microcosm groups have been used to carry out organisation diagnoses, solve communications problems, integrate two cultures, smooth the transition to a new structure and address dysfunctional political processes.

Microcosm groups work through 'parallel processes', which are the unconscious changes that take place in individuals when two or more groups interact.[38] After two or more groups have interacted, members often find that their characteristic patterns of roles and interactions change to reflect the roles and dynamics of the group with whom they were relating. Put simply, one group seems to 'infect' and become 'infected' by the other groups.

What are the steps?

The process of using a microcosm group to address organisation-wide issues involves the following five steps:

1. *Identify an issue.* This step involves finding a system-wide problem to be addressed. This may result from an organisational diagnosis or may be an idea generated by an organisation member or task force.

2. *Convene the group.* Once an issue has been identified, the microcosm group can be formed. The most important convening principle is that group membership needs to reflect the appropriate mix of stakeholders related to the issue. For example, if the issue is organisational communication, then the group should contain people from all hierarchical levels and functions, including staff groups and unions, if applicable. Following the initial set-up, the group itself becomes responsible for determining its membership. It will decide whether to add new members and how to fill vacant positions. Convening the group also draws attention to the issue and gives the group status. Members also need to be perceived as credible representatives of the problem. This will increase the likelihood that organisation members will listen to, and follow, the suggestions they make.

3. *Provide group training.* Group training focuses on establishing a group mission or charter, working relationships between members, group decision-making norms and definitions of the problem to be addressed. Team-building interventions may also be appropriate. From a group-process perspective, OD practitioners may need to observe and comment on how the group develops. Because the group is a microcosm of the organisation, it will tend, through its behaviour and attitudes, to reflect the problem in the larger organisation.

4. *Address the issue.* This step involves solving the problem and implementing solutions. OD practitioners may help the group to diagnose, design, implement and evaluate changes. A key issue is gaining wider organisation commitment to implementing the group's solutions. The following factors can facilitate such ownership. First, a communication plan should link group activities to the organisation. Second, group members need to

be visible and accessible to management and labour. Third, problem-solving processes should include an appropriate level of participation by organisation members.

5   *Dissolve the group*. The microcosm group can be disbanded after the successful implementation of changes. This typically involves writing a final report or holding a final meeting.

The microcosm group intervention derives from an intergroup relations theory developed by Alderfer[39] and has been applied by him to communications and race-relations problems. A dearth of research exists on microcosm groups. This is partly due to the difficulty of measuring parallel processes and associating them with measures of organisational processes.

RESOLVING INTERGROUP CONFLICT

This intervention is specifically designed to help two groups or departments within an organisation resolve dysfunctional conflicts. Intergroup conflict is neither good nor bad in itself. In some cases, conflict among departments is necessary and productive for organisations. This applies in organisations where there is little interdependence among departments. Here, departments are independent, and conflict or competition among them can lead to higher levels of productivity. In other organisations, especially those with very interdependent departments, conflict may become dysfunctional.[40] Two or more groups may become polarised, and continued conflict may result in the development of defensiveness and negative stereotypes of the other group. It is particularly the case that, when intergroup communication is necessary, the amount and quality of communication usually drops off. Groups become defensive and begin seeing the others as 'the enemy', rather than in either positive or neutral terms. As the amount of communication decreases, the amount of mutual problem solving also falls off. The tendency increases for one group to sabotage the efforts of the other group, either consciously or unconsciously.

What are the steps? — tut wk 8

A basic strategy for improving interdepartmental or intergroup relationships is to change the perceptions (perhaps, more accurately, misperceptions) that the two groups have of each other. One formal approach for accomplishing this consists of a 10-step procedure, originally described by Blake and his associates.[41]

1   A consultant external to the two groups obtains their agreement to work directly on improving intergroup relationships. (The use of an outside consultant is highly recommended because without the moderating influence of such a neutral third party, it is almost impossible for the two groups to interact without becoming deadlocked and polarised in a defensive position.)

2   A time is set for the two groups to meet; preferably away from normal work situations.

3   The consultant, together with the managers of the two groups, describes the purpose and objectives of the meeting: the development of better mutual relationships, the exploration of the perceptions the groups have of each other and the development of plans for improving the relationship. The two groups are asked the following or similar questions: 'What qualities or attributes best describe our group?', 'What qualities or attributes best describe the other group?' and 'How do we think the other group will describe us?' Then the two groups are encouraged to establish norms of openness for feedback and discussion.

4   The two groups are then placed in separate rooms and asked to write their answers to the three questions. Usually, an outside consultant works with each group to help the members become more open and to encourage them to develop lists that accurately reflect their perceptions of their own image and of the other group.

5   After completing their lists, the two groups come together again. A representative from each group presents the written statements. Only the two representatives are allowed to speak. The primary objective at this stage is to make certain that the images, perceptions and attitudes are presented as accurately as possible and to avoid the arguments that

might arise if the two groups openly confronted each other. Questions, however, are allowed to ensure that both groups clearly understand the written lists. Justifications, accusations or other statements are not permitted.

6   When it is clear that the two groups thoroughly understand the content of the lists, they again separate. By this time, a great number of misperceptions and discrepancies have already been brought to light.

7   The task of the two groups (almost always with a consultant as a process observer) is to analyse and review the reasons for the discrepancies. The emphasis is on solving the problems and reducing the misperceptions.

8   When the two groups have worked through the discrepancies, as well as the areas of common agreement, they meet to share both the identified discrepancies and their problem-solving approaches to those discrepancies.

9   The two groups are then asked to develop specific plans of action for solving specific problems and for improving their relationships.

10   When the two groups have gone as far as possible in formulating action plans, at least one follow-up meeting is scheduled so that the two groups can report on actions that have been implemented, identify any further problems that have emerged and, where necessary, formulate additional action plans.

In addition to this formal approach to improving interdepartmental or intergroup relationships, there are a number of more informal procedures. Beckhard asks each of the two groups to develop a list of what irritates or exasperates them about the other group and to predict what they think the other group will say about them.[42]

Different approaches to resolving intergroup conflict form a continuum varying from behavioural solutions to attitudinal change solutions.[43] Behavioural methods are oriented to keeping the relevant parties physically separate and specifying the limited conditions under which interaction will occur. Little attempt is made to understand or to change how members of each group see the other. Conversely, attitudinal methods – such as exchanging group members or requiring intense interaction with important rewards or opportunities clearly tied to co-ordination – are directed at changing how each group perceives the other. Here, it is assumed that perceptual distortions and stereotyping underlie the conflict and need to be changed to resolve it.

Intergroup conflict may, to an extent, be the result of office politics. As illustrated in Application 7.4, effective managers need to be able to understand and mitigate any negative impact of office politics.

APPLICATION 7.4

POLITICAL ANIMALS

Politics in the workplace is unavoidable, because work involves basic human interactions, says Jim Grant from the coaching firm Dattner Grant. But there are ways to counteract the negative influences of politics and deal with people who refuse to play fair.

Grant teaches executives to first become aware of office politics and take simple steps to become 'transparent' in work situations. Grant uses animal metaphors to explain the types of people within a social or work group. 'We are all political animals,' he says. 'We are just different kinds.'

A mule has low political awareness and is focused on completing set tasks. A sheep is intelligent but follows the pack on big decisions and is unaware of the finer details. A fox is astute at networking for their own individual goals. Finally, the owl is the ideal model: he or she is aware of political plays but is aligned with the organisation's goals.

Grant tells executives to use the water-cooler test: what would you think if you stepped up to the office water cooler and the three people standing there stopped talking? Mules may think nothing is wrong; foxes may be instantly suspicious that the three people were talking about them.

He says executives should try to be owls because being a good role model is the most effective way to encourage openness and reduce selfish behaviour in a team. But leading by example will never eliminate all fox behaviour, Grant says. The first step in counteracting destructive politics is to make sure you have your facts right and that the other person is wrong. A confident executive can then use the organisation's overall strategy and vision to question the distrusted person on details. 'I call it going meta, because a fox cannot operate at that higher level,' Grant says. He recommends executives use open questions about how the suspect viewpoint will affect the product or customer service. Closed statements may be construed as a counterattack.

The wise owl:

- *Be open.* Share information freely. But if you cannot, then tell the team that you are uncomfortable or unable to provide details.
- *Be an active* listener. Stop thinking of the next question you are going to ask and reinforce important points made in the meeting by repeating them. Maintain eye contact.
- *Celebrate success appropriately.* Align your own success with that of the organisation. Inform colleagues of your achievements without bragging.
- *Avoid sending two messages.* Be certain to send the same message to everyone so there is no room for ambiguity about your meaning.
- *Stop using jargon.* Executives who use specialist language can confuse their colleagues and appear arrogant. Be careful not to divide the team.

Source: Amita Tandukar, 'Knowhow: Political animals', *Business Review Weekly*, 25/5/06.

Critical Thinking Question: Open communication is emphasised as a strategy for success by 'wise owls'. Requests for what types of information might make a manager uncomfortable?

Most of the OD solutions to intergroup conflict reviewed in this section favour attitudinal change strategies. However, these interventions typically require considerably more skill and time than the behavioural solutions. Changing attitudes can be quite difficult in conflict situations, especially if the attitudes are deep-seated and form an integral part of people's personalities. Attitudinal change interventions should be reserved for those situations in which behavioural solutions might not work.

Results of intergroup conflict interventions

Several studies have been done on the effects of intergroup conflict resolution. In his original study, Blake reported vastly improved relationships between the union and management.[44] In a later study, Bennis used Blake's basic design to improve relationships between two groups of State Department officials: high-level administrative officers and officers in the Foreign Service.[45] Initially, there was much mutual distrust, negative stereotyping, blocked communication and hostility between the two groups: 'Each side perceived the other as more threatening than any realistic overseas enemy.'[46] Although no hard data were obtained, the intervention seemed to improve relationships so that the two groups 'at least understood the other side's point of view'.

Golembiewski and Blumberg used a modification of the Blake design that involved an exchange of 'images' among both organisational units and individuals in the marketing division of a large firm.[47] An attitude questionnaire was used to make before-and-after comparisons. The results were found to be different for more or less 'deeply involved' individuals or units. In general, the more deeply involved individuals or units (promotion, regions and divisions, and sales) reflected more positive attitudes towards collaboration and had greater feelings of commitment to the success of the entire organisation. Less deeply involved positions or units (such areas as sales training, hospital sales and trade relations) did not show any particular trends in attitudinal changes, either positive or negative.

French and Bell, who used a somewhat similar design, reported that they were able to work successfully with three groups simultaneously.[48] They obtained positive results in their work with key groups in an Indian tribal organisation: the tribal council, the tribal staff and the Community Action Program (CAP). The researchers asked each group to develop perceptions of the other two, as well as of itself, and to share those perceptions in the larger group. The tribal council developed four lists: both favourable and unfavourable items about the tribal staff, a similar list about the CAP, and predictions as to what the staff and CAP, respectively, would say about the council. Once each group had developed its lists, the results were shared in a three-group meeting, and the similarities and dissimilarities in the various lists worked through.

According to the researchers, the use of this method reduces intergroup problems and friction while increasing communications and interactions.

Huse and Beer have described positive results arising from periodic cross-departmental meetings, whereby personnel within one department would meet, in sequence, with those from other departments to discuss perceptions, expectations and strong and weak points about one another.[49] In another study, Huse found that bringing representatives of different groups together to work on common work-related problems had a marked effect, not only on relationships among a number of different manufacturing groups but also on the quality of the product, which increased by 62%.[50] The basic tactic in this study was to ensure that representatives of two or more groups worked jointly on each work-related problem.

Based on their experience at TRW Systems, Fordyce and Weil developed a modified approach whereby each group builds three lists: one containing 'positive feedback' items (those things the group values and likes about the other group), a 'bug' list (those things the group dislikes about the other group) and an 'empathy' list (predictions about what the other group's list would contain).[51] When the groups come together, they build a master list of major concerns and unresolved problems, which are assigned priorities and developed into an agenda. When they have completed the task, the subgroups report the results of their discussions to the total group, which then develops a series of action steps for improving the relations between the groups and commits itself to following through. For each action step, specific responsibilities are assigned and an overall schedule developed for prompt completion of the action steps.

In conclusion, the technology for improving intergroup relations is promising. A greater distinction between attitudinal and behavioural changes needs to be made in planning effective intergroup interventions. A greater variety of interventions that address the practical difficulties of bringing two groups together is also necessary. Finally, a better background of knowledge must be developed as to when perceptions and behaviour need to be diverse and when they need to be brought more closely together. Growing knowledge and theory suggest that conflict can be either functional or dysfunctional, depending on the circumstances.[52]

Large-group interventions

System-wide process interventions in the third group are called large-group interventions. These change programs have been variously referred to as 'search conferences', 'open space meetings' and 'future searches'.[53] They focus on issues that affect the whole organisation or large segments of it, such as budget cuts, introduction of new technology and changes in senior leadership. The defining feature of large-group interventions is bringing together large numbers of organisation members (often more than 100) for a two- to four-day meeting or conference. Here, members work together to identify and resolve organisation-wide problems, design new approaches to structuring and managing the firm or propose future directions for the organisation.

Large-group interventions are among the fastest-growing OD applications. Large-group interventions can vary on several dimensions including purpose, size, length, structure and number. The purpose of these change methods can range from solving particular organisational problems to envisioning future strategic directions. Large-group interventions have been run with groups of fewer than 50 to more than 2000 participants and have lasted between one and five days. Some large-group processes are relatively planned and structured, although others are more informal.[54] Some interventions involve a single large-group meeting, and others include a succession of meetings to accomplish system-wide change in a short period of time.[55]

Despite these differences, large-group interventions have similar conceptual foundations and methods. Large-group interventions have evolved over the past 25 years and represent a combination of open systems applications and 'futuring' and 'visioning' exercises. Open systems approaches direct attention to how organisations interact with, and are shaped by, their environments. A popular method used in large-group interventions is called 'environmental scanning', which involves mapping the pressures placed on the organisation by external stakeholders, such as regulatory agencies, customers and competitors.[56] This analysis helps members devise new ways of responding to, and influencing, the environment. Futuring and visioning exercises guide members in creating 'images of potential' towards which the organisation can grow and develop.[57] Focusing on the organisation's potential rather than on its problems can increase members' energy for change.

WHAT ARE THE STEPS?

Conducting a large-group intervention generally involves the following three steps:

1   *Preparing for the large-group meeting.* A design team consisting of OD practitioners and several members from the organisation is convened to organise the event. The team generally addresses three key ingredients for successful large-group meetings: a compelling meeting theme, appropriate members to participate, and relevant tasks to address the theme. First, large-group interventions require a compelling reason or focal point for change. Although 'people problems' can be an important focus, more powerful reasons for large-group efforts include impending mergers or reorganisations, responding to environmental threats and opportunities, or proposing radical organisational changes.

A second issue in preparing for a large-group meeting includes inviting relevant people to participate. A fundamental goal of large-group interventions is to 'get the whole system in the room'. This involves inviting as many people as possible who have a stake in the conference theme, and who are energised and committed to conceiving and initiating change. The third ingredient for successful large-group meetings is to have a range of task activities that enable the participants to fully address the conference theme.

2   *Conducting the meeting.* The flow of events in a large-group meeting can vary greatly according to its purpose and the framework adopted. These gatherings, however, tend to involve three sequential activities: developing common ground among participants, discussing the issues and creating an agenda for change. First, participants develop sufficient common ground among themselves to permit joint problem solving. This generally involves team-building activities. One exercise for creating teamwork is called 'appreciating the past'. It asks participants to examine the significant events, milestones and highlights of the organisation's previous 20 years.[58]

Second, members discuss the system-wide issue or theme. To promote widespread participation, members are typically organised into subgroups of eight to 10 people, representing as many stakeholder viewpoints as possible. The subgroups may be asked to address a general question. Subgroup members brainstorm answers to these questions, record them on flipchart paper, and share them with the larger group. The responses from the different subgroups are compared, and common themes identified. The final task of large-group meetings is creating an agenda for change. Participants are asked to reflect on what they have learned at the meeting and to suggest changes for themselves, their department and the whole organisation. Members from the same department are often grouped together to discuss their proposals and to decide on action plans, timetables and accountabilities.

Action items for the total organisation are referred to a steering committee that addresses organisation-wide policy issues and action plans. At the conclusion of the large-group meeting, the departmental subgroups and the steering committee report their conclusions to all participants and seek initial commitment for change.

3   *Follow-up on the meeting outcomes.* Follow-up efforts are vital if the action plans from large-scale interventions are to be implemented. These activities involve communicating the results of the meeting to the rest of the organisation, gaining wider commitment to the changes, and structuring the change process.

RESULTS OF LARGE-GROUP INTERVENTIONS

In the past 10 years, the number of case studies describing the methods and results of large-group interventions has increased dramatically. Large-group interventions have been conducted in a variety of organisations (including Hewlett-Packard and Rockport); around a variety of themes or issues, including natural resource conservation, community development and strategic change; and in a variety of countries, including Pakistan, England and India.[59]

Despite this proliferation of practice, however, little systematic research has been done on the effects of large-group interventions. Because these change efforts often set the stage for subsequent OD interventions, it is difficult to isolate their specific results from those of the other changes. Anecdotal evidence from practitioners suggests the following benefits from large-group interventions: increased energy towards organisational change, improved feelings of 'community', ability to see 'outside the boxes' and improved relationships with stakeholders. Clearly, systematic research is needed on this important system-wide process intervention.

Grid® Organization Development: a normative approach

Normative approaches to system-wide process intervention suggest that there is one best way of managing all organisations. This contrasts sharply with modern contingency theory, which proposes that managerial practices should vary according to the organisation's environment, technology and member needs and values. Two interventions represent the primary normative approaches. Likert's System 4 model was discussed in Chapter 1 as an important element in the history of OD, but its application in current organisations has declined substantially.

Blake and Mouton's Grid® Organization Development, however, has been extensively applied in organisations and is still used today. Both approaches originated from research about managerial and organisational effectiveness. Over time, instruments for measuring managerial practices, as well as procedures for helping organisations achieve the prescribed objectives, were developed. These instruments and methods evolved into packaged programs for OD, which are purchased by organisations or practitioners who become trained exclusively in their use. Probably the most structured intervention in OD, the Grid derives from research on corporate excellence[60] and consists of six phases that are designed to analyse an entire business and increase its overall effectiveness.

Blake and Mouton gathered data on organisational excellence from 198 organisations located in the United States, Japan and the United Kingdom.[61] They found that the two foremost barriers to excellence were planning and communication. Rather than accept these barriers at face value, the researchers treated them as symptoms of deeper problems. For Blake and Mouton, 'planning as a barrier' is a symptom of a deeper problem that results from either organisational strategy based on faulty logic or the absence of a strategy as such.[62] To achieve excellence, the organisation should systematically develop an overall strategic model that contains explicit descriptions of the nature of the organisation and its client or market, clear specifications for the optimum organisational structure and clear descriptions of 20 to 35 major goals or policies that can serve as guidelines for immediate and future decisions and actions. Organisational planning is sound when the properties of the model have been clearly expressed and are well understood throughout the organisation. A primary objective of Grid® Organization Development is to improve planning by developing a strategy for organisational excellence based on clear logic.

Like planning as a barrier, 'communications as a barrier' is only a symptom; the cause itself lies deeper. Blake and Mouton believe that the underlying cause of communications difficulties is the character of supervision, which in turn is highly influenced by knowledge (or lack of knowledge) about explicit theories of human behaviour. Although technically competent, a supervisor who does not have a good understanding of human motivation and group dynamics will not be able to generate the best results. Such a supervisor will not be able to establish or work within a climate that provides clear objectives, full commitment and the closeness of co-operation that results from the sound utilisation of people. Consequently, a second primary objective of Grid® Organization Development is to help managers gain the necessary knowledge and skills to supervise effectively.

Blake and Mouton developed a grid to help supervisors understand their managerial style and possibly to improve it. The Leadership Grid® postulates two basic assumptions about managerial behaviour: (1) concern for production (the emphasis on accomplishing productive tasks), and (2) concern for people, for those who get the work done (compare this with the 'Consultant styles matrix' in Application 3.2). According to Blake and Mouton, concern for production covers a wide range of considerations, such as the number of creative ideas developed, the quality of policy decisions, the thoroughness and quality of staff services, efficiency and workload measurements, and the number of accounts processed or units of output. Concern for production is not limited to things but also may involve human accomplishment within the organisation, whatever the assigned tasks or activities. Concern for people encompasses a diversity of issues, including concern for the individual's personal worth, good working conditions, a degree of involvement or commitment to completing the job, security, a fair salary structure and fringe benefits, and good social and other relationships. The relationship between concern for production and concern for people is shown in Figure 7.3, which shows 81 possible variations of the two aspects of management: concern for people and concern for production. Blake and Mouton focus on the four extreme positions, as well as on the middle 5,5 style.[63] These five managerial styles are described below.[64]

THE 1,1 MANAGERIAL STYLE

The manager who has a 1,1 orientation to jobs and people demonstrates little concern for either people or production. The approach is to stay out of trouble. In a sense, the manager has accepted defeat and is primarily concerned with job security and not making waves.

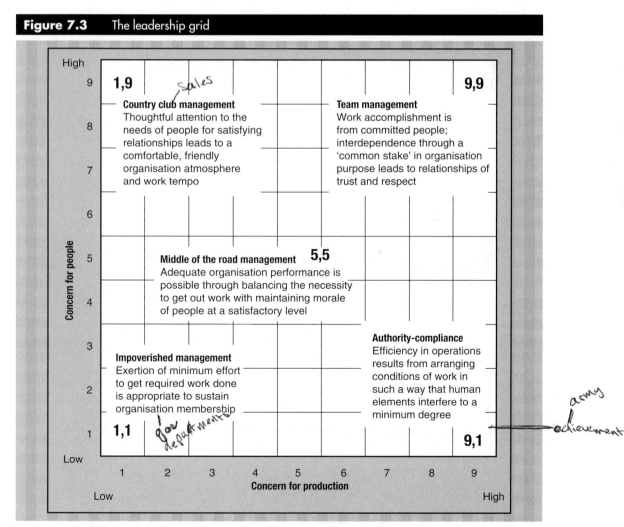

Figure 7.3   The leadership grid

Source: R. Blake and A. Adams McCanse, *Leadership Dilemmas – Grid Solutions* (formerly *The Managerial Grid* by R. Blake and J. Mouton). Houston: Gulf Publishing Co., 29, copyright © 1991, Scientific Methods, Inc.

Tut WK 8

THE 1,9 MANAGERIAL STYLE

The 1,9 manager exhibits a low concern for production but a high concern for people. To the 1,9 manager, people's feelings, attitudes and needs are valuable in their own right, and this type of manager strives to provide subordinates with work conditions that provide ease, security and comfort.

THE 9,1 MANAGERIAL STYLE

This style, which falls in the lower right-hand corner of the grid, is characterised by low concern for people, together with a high concern for production. The 9,1 manager assumes that there must be a conflict between personal needs and the organisation's needs for production. Because it is impossible to satisfy both, the 9,1 manager reduces the dilemma by minimising the attitudes and feelings of subordinates, primarily by arranging work conditions. As a result, little attention is given to individual creativity, conflict and commitment, and the focus is on the work organisation.

THE 5,5 MANAGERIAL STYLE

The 5,5 managerial style, in the middle of the grid, indicates intermediate concern for people and for production. The 5,5 manager assumes conflict between organisational goals and the needs of people in much the same way as the 9,1 or the 1,9 manager. However, the mode of conflict resolution is different. The 5,5 manager seeks compromise among these 'inevitable' conflicts of organisational and personal needs. He or she assumes that practical people know they have to work to get the job done and that compromise, trading and paying attention to both job demands and personal needs will allow subordinates to be relatively satisfied.

THE 9,9 MANAGERIAL STYLE

The 9,9 managerial style is located in the upper right-hand corner of the grid. The basic assumptions behind this managerial style are qualitatively and quantitatively different from those underlying the other managerial styles, which assume that there is an inherent conflict between the needs of the organisation and the needs of people. The 9,9 manager, by contrast, believes that the needs of both the organisation and its members can be integrated by involving people in making decisions about the strategies and conditions of work. Therefore, the basic aim of the 9,9 manager is to develop cohesive work teams that can achieve both high productivity and high morale.

Blake and Mouton propose that the 9,9 managerial style is the most effective in overcoming the communications barrier to corporate excellence. By showing a high concern for both people and production, managers allow employees to think and influence the organisation. This results in active support for organisational plans. Employee participation means that better communication is critical; therefore, necessary information is shared by all relevant parties. Moreover, better communication means self-direction and self-control, rather than unquestioning, blind obedience. Organisational commitment arises out of discussion, deliberation and debate over major organisational issues.

APPLYING THE GRID

The application of Grid® Organization Development occurs in the following six phases, which are aimed at overcoming the planning and communications barriers to corporate excellence.

Phase 1: the Grid seminar

In this one-week program, participants analyse their managerial style and learn team methods of problem solving. First, top management attends the seminar and then returns and takes the next level of management through a similar experience. In addition to assessing themselves through the use of questionnaires and case studies, participants receive feedback on their styles from other group members.

Phase 2: teamwork development

In this phase of the Grid program, managers are expected to do team development in at least two different groups – with their own boss and with their immediate subordinates. As with the Grid seminar itself, the team-building phase is usually conducted in an off-the-job setting so that team members can work without interruption. Usually, as in the seminar, team building starts with top management: the manager and the corporate staff or the manager and the department, division or plant staff. There is usually a steering committee or OD co-ordinator to ensure that the team-building efforts are co-ordinated throughout the organisation, to provide materials and to establish overall priorities.

Phase 3: intergroup development

Although an organisation may have various sections or units, each with specialised tasks and different goals, it must still work as a whole if it is to achieve organisational excellence. In most organisations, a fair amount of intergroup or interdepartmental conflict is present. Each group begins to build negative stereotypes of the other groups, which can easily escalate into subtle or not-so-subtle power struggles that result in win–lose situations. Improving intergroup relations involves the following steps:

1   Before the sessions, each person involved prepares a written description of the actual working relationship as contrasted with the ideal relationship.
2   Each group isolates itself for several days to summarise its perceptions of the actual and ideal relationships.
3   The two groups meet and, using a spokesperson, limit their interaction to comparing their perceptions.
4   The two groups then work on making the relationship more productive. This action phase is completed when both groups have a clear understanding of the specific actions that each group will take and how the actions will be followed up.[65]

Phase 4: developing an ideal strategic organisation model

In Phase 4, the top managers in the organisation work towards achieving a model of organisational excellence, following six basic rules:

1   clear definitions of minimum and optimum organisational financial objectives
2   clear, explicit definitions of the character and nature of organisational activities
3   clear operational definitions of the character and scope of markets, customers or clients
4   an organisational structure that integrates operations for synergistic results
5   basic policies for organisational decision making
6   approaches to implementing growth capacity and avoiding stagnation or obsolescence.

Phase 5: implementing the ideal strategic model

Blake and Mouton point out that if the first four phases have been successfully completed, many of the barriers to implementation will already have been remodelled or reduced, managers will have a good understanding of Grid theories, and communication blocks will have been identified and (one would hope) resolved. Implementing the ideal strategic model thus becomes a matter of keeping certain considerations in mind. First, the nature of the organisation and its market or environment defines business segments that are contained within the ideal organisational strategic model. Second, specific organisational units, such as cost centres or profit centres, are identified. Third, planning teams are appointed for each autonomous unit. The planning team is responsible for preparing and testing the unit's operation in accordance with the specifics of the ideal strategic model for the larger organisation. Fourth, because the units cannot be completely autonomous, an overall headquarters organisation must be established. This organisation must have, at a minimum, the ability to develop executive talent, develop investment capital and provide service to the entire organisation more cheaply or efficiently than can be done by the local decision centres or autonomous units. Finally, the planning co-ordinator and the corporate strategy-implementation committee need to ensure that the implementation strategy is clearly understood while it is in progress, so that enthusiasm for the change can be maintained and resistance to the development and to implementation of the ideal strategic model kept to a minimum.

Phase 6: systematic critique

The final phase in achieving ideal organisational excellence is the systematic effort to examine the organisation's progress towards that goal, including formal and informal measurement and evaluation of direction, rate, quality and quantity of progress. Phase 6 also allows for the systematic planning of future development activities. Because communication and planning are the greatest barriers to organisational excellence, this critique becomes more important as an organisation goes through the Grid process.[66]

Grid® Organization Development has been adopted in whole or in part by many organisations, with phases 1, 2 and 3 (which apply mainly to communication barriers) especially popular.[67] Research about the effectiveness of the Grid is mixed, however. On the positive side, Blake and Mouton collected data on two similar organisations; the one that went through the six Grid phases improved profitability significantly, while the control organisation did not.[68] An example of a Grid failure, on the other hand, is a study that examined the impact of Grid® Organization Development in six geographic districts of a large federal agency. The researchers assessed the organisational climate of each district to determine the extent to which the organisation was moving towards 9,9 management. The results showed no significant climate changes in any of the six districts. The failure of the Grid program was attributed mainly to the lack of support for the program by top management.[69]

In conclusion, like Likert's System 4 Management, Blake and Mouton's Grid® Organization Development is a normative intervention, proposing one most effective way to manage organisations: 9,9 management.

SUMMARY

In this chapter, we presented human process interventions aimed at interpersonal relations and group dynamics. Among the earliest interventions in OD, these change programs help people to gain interpersonal skills, work through interpersonal conflicts and develop effective groups. The first intervention discussed was the T-group, the forerunner of modern OD change programs. T-groups typically consist of a small number of strangers who meet with a professional trainer to explore the social dynamics that emerge from their interactions. OD practitioners often attend T-groups themselves to improve their interpersonal skills, or recommend that managers attend a T-group to learn more about how their behaviours affect others.

Process consultation is used not only as a way of helping groups become effective but also as a process whereby groups can learn to diagnose and solve their own problems and to continue to develop their competence and maturity. Important areas of activity include communications, roles of group members, difficulties with problem-solving and decision-making norms, and leadership and authority. The basic difference between process consultation and third-party intervention is that the latter focuses on interpersonal dysfunction in social relationships between two or more individuals within the same organisation, and is directed more towards resolving direct conflict between those individuals.

Team building is directed towards improving group effectiveness and the ways in which members of teams work together. These teams may be permanent or temporary, but their members have either common organisational aims or work activities. The general process of team building, like process consultation, attempts to equip a group to handle its own ongoing problem solving. Selected aspects of team building include the family group diagnostic meeting and family group team-building meeting.

This chapter also described four types of system-wide process interventions: confrontation meetings, intergroup interventions, large-group interventions and Grid® Organization Development. Grid® Organization Development is a normative program that proposes a single best way to manage organisations. Although its authors claim that it can be successful in all situations, research assessing normative models is mixed. This suggests that the Grid can be successful under certain conditions and that more research is needed to pinpoint what these conditions are.

The other organisation process interventions do not claim universal success; they work best only in certain situations. The organisation confrontation meeting is a way of mobilising resources for organisational problem solving and seems especially relevant for organisations undergoing stress. The intergroup relations approaches are designed to help solve a variety of organisational problems. Microcosm groups can be formed to address particular issues and use parallel processes to diffuse group solutions to the organisation. The intergroup conflict resolution approach involves a method for mitigating dysfunctional conflicts between groups or departments. Conflict can be dysfunctional in situations in which groups must work together. It may, however, promote organisational effectiveness when departments are relatively independent of each other. Large-group interventions are designed to focus the energy and attention of a 'whole system' around organisational processes such as a vision, strategy or culture. It is best used when the organisation is about to begin a large-scale change effort or is facing a new situation.

ACTiViTiES

Review questions

① How can you best describe a 'process consultant'?

② Describe the two major components of group problem solving.

③ What are the basic implications of the model for conflict resolution?

④ In a third party consultation, what skill must the third party develop in order to be successful?

⑤ The results of team building can be classified into three main areas. What are they?

⑥ What are the characteristics of a system-wide process intervention?

⑦ Identify the characteristics of intergroup conflict resolution methods.

⑧ What are the two basic assumptions about managerial behaviour in the management grid?

Discussion and essay questions

① What is a T-group? Discuss the basic objectives of T-groups. What are their strengths and weaknesses?

② Describe the similarities and differences between a normative approach, such as Grid® Organization Development, and an organisation confrontation meeting.

③ Discuss the similarities and differences between an organisation confrontation meeting and an intergroup conflict resolution intervention.

NOTES

1 J. Campbell and M. Dunnette, 'Effectiveness of T-group experiences in managerial training and development', *Psychological Bulletin*, 70 (August 1968): 73–103.

2 ibid.

3 M. Dunnette, J. Campbell and C. Argyris, 'A symposium: laboratory training', *Industrial Relations*, 8 (October 1968): 1–45.

4 Campbell and Dunnette, 'Effectiveness of T-Group experiences', op. cit.; R. House, 'T-group education and leadership effectiveness: a review of the empirical literature and a critical evaluation', *Personnel Psychology*, 20 (Spring 1967): 1–32; J. Campbell, M. Dunnette, E. Lawler III and K. Weick, *Managerial Behavior, Performance, and Effectiveness* (New York: McGraw-Hill, 1970): 292–8.

5 J. Porras and P. Berg, 'The impact of organization development', *Academy of Management Review*, 3 (April 1978): 249–66.

6 J. Nicholas, 'The comparative impact of organization development interventions on hard criteria measures', *Academy of Management Review*, 7 (October 1982): 531–42.

7 D. Bowers, 'OD techniques and their results in 23 organizations: the Michigan IGL Study', *Journal of Applied Behavioral Science*, 9 (January–February 1973): 21–43.

8 G. Neuman, J. Edwards and N. Raju, 'Organizational development interventions: a meta-analysis of their effects on satisfaction and other attitudes', *Personnel Psychology*, 42 (1989): 461–83.

9 R. Kaplan, 'Is openness passe?', *Human Relations*, 39 (November 1986): 242.

10 E. Schein, *Process Consultation II: Lessons for Managers and Consultants* (Reading, MA: Addison-Wesley, 1987).

11 ibid., 5–17.

12 ibid., 34.

13 J. Fast, *Body Language* (Philadelphia: Lippincott, M. Evans, 1970).

14 J. Luft, 'The Johari window', *Human Relations Training News*, 5 (1961): 6–7.

15 J. Gibb, 'Defensive communication', *Journal of Communication*, 11 (1961): 141–8.

16 N. Clapp, 'Work group norms: leverage for organizational change, theory and application', working paper (Plainfield, NJ: Block Petrella Weisbord, no date); R. Allen and S. Pilnick, 'Confronting the shadow organization: how to detect and defeat negative norms', *Organizational Dynamics* (Spring 1973): 3–18.

17 Schein, *Process Consultation; Process Consultation II*, op. cit.

18 ibid., 32–4.

19 R. Walton, *Managing Conflict: Interpersonal Dialogue and Third-Party Roles*, 2nd edn (Reading, MA: Addison-Wesley, 1987).

20 ibid., 83–110.

21 W. Dyer, *Team Building: Issues and Alternatives*, 2nd edn (Reading, MA: Addison-Wesley, 1987).

22 J. Katzenbach and D. Smith, *The Wisdom of Teams* (Boston: Harvard Business School Press, 1993).

23 J. Lewis III, 'Management team development: will it work for you?', *Personnel* (July/August 1975): 14–25.

24 D. Eden, 'Team development: a true field experiment at three levels of rigor', *Journal of Applied Psychology*, 70 (1985): 94–100.

25 R. Woodman and J .Sherwood, 'The role of team development in organizational effectiveness: a critical review', *Psychological Bulletin*, 88 (July–November 1980): 166–86.

26 Porras and Berg, 'Impact of organization development', op. cit.

27 Nicholas, 'Comparative impact', op. cit.

28 Woodman and Sherwood, 'The role of team development', op. cit.

29 R. Woodman and S. Wayne, 'An investigation of positive-finding bias in evaluation of organization development interventions', *Academy of Management Journal*, 28 (December 1985): 889–913.

30 R. Boss, 'Team building and the problem of regression: the personal management interview as an intervention', *Journal of Applied Behavioral Science*, 19 (1983): 67–83.

31 R. Buller and C. Bell Jr, 'Effects of team building and goal setting: a field experiment', *Academy of Management Journal*, 29 (1986): 305–28.

32 M. Weisbord, *Productive Workplaces* (San Francisco: Jossey-Bass, 1987).

33 R. Beckhard, 'The confrontation meeting', *Harvard Business Review*, 4 (1967): 149–55.

34 B. Benedict Bunker and B. Alban, 'What makes large-group interventions effective?', *Journal of Applied Behavioral Science*, 28 (4, 1992): 579–91; N. Tichy and S. Sherman, *Control Your Destiny or Someone Else Will* (New York: HarperCollins Publishers, 1993).

35 R. Beckhard, *Organization Development: Strategies and Models* (Reading, MA: Addison-Wesley, 1969).

36 W. Bennis, *Organization Development: Its Nature, Origins, and Prospects* (Reading, MA: Addison-Wesley, 1969): 7.

37 C. Alderfer, 'An intergroup perspective on group dynamics', in *Handbook of Organizational Behavior*, ed. J. Lorsch (Englewood Cliffs, NJ: Prentice-Hall, 1987): 190–222; C. Alderfer, 'Improving organizational communication through long-term intergroup intervention', *Journal of Applied Behavioral Science*, 13 (1977): 193–210; C. Alderfer, R. Tucker, C. Alderfer and L. Tucker, 'The Race Relations Advisory Group: An intergroup

intervention', in *Organizational Change and Development*, 2, eds W. Pasmore and R. Woodman (Greenwich, CT: JAI Press, 1988): 269–321.

38 Alderfer, 'An intergroup perspective on group dynamics', op. cit.
39 Alderfer, 'Improving organizational communication', op. cit.
40 D. Tjosvold, 'Cooperation theory and organizations', *Human Relations*, 37 (1984): 743–67.
41 R. Blake, H. Shepard and J. Mouton, *Managing Intergroup Conflict in Industry* (Houston: Gulf, 1954).
42 Beckhard, *Organization Development*, op. cit.
43 E. Neilson, 'Understanding and managing intergroup conflict', in *Organizational Behavior and Administration*, eds P. Lawrence, L. Barnes and J. Lorsch (Homewood, IL: Richard Irwin, 1976): 291–305.
44 Blake, Shepard and Mouton, *Managing Intergroup Conflict*, op. cit.
45 Bennis, *Organization Development*, op. cit.
46 ibid., 4.
47 R. Golembiewski and A. Blumberg, 'Confrontation as a training design in complex organizations: attitudinal changes in a diversified population of managers', *Journal of Applied Behavioral Science*, 3 (1967): 525–47.
48 W. French and C. Bell, *Organization Development: Behavioral Science Interventions for Organization Improvement* (Englewood Cliffs, NJ: Prentice-Hall, 1978).
49 E. Huse and M. Beer, 'Eclectic approach to organizational development', *Harvard Business Review*, 49 (1971): 103–13.
50 E. Huse, 'The behavioral scientist in the shop', *Personnel*, 44 (May–June 1965): 8–16.
51 J. Fordyce and R. Weil, *Managing WITH People* (Reading, MA: Addison-Wesley, 1971).
52 K. Thomas, 'Conflict and conflict management', in *Handbook of Industrial and Organizational Psychology*, ed. M. Dunnette (Chicago: Rand McNally, 1976): 889–936.
53 Weisbord, *Productive Workplaces*, op. cit.; M. Weisbord, *Discovering Common Ground* (San Francisco: Berrett Koehler, 1993); B. Benedict Bunker and B. Alban, eds, 'Special issue: large-group interventions', *Journal of Applied Behavioral Science*, 28:4 (1992); H. Owen, *Open Space Technology: A User's Guide* (Potomac, MD: Abbott, 1992).
54 H. Owen, *Open Space Technology*, ibid.
55 D. Axelrod, 'Getting everyone involved', *Journal of Applied Behavioral Science*, 28:4 (1992): 499–509.
56 F. Emery and E. Trist, *Towards a Social Ecology* (New York: Plenum Publishing, 1973); R. Beckhard and R. Harris, *Organizational Transitions: Managing Complex Change*, 2nd edn (Reading, MA: Addison-Wesley, 1987).
57 R. Lippitt, 'Future before you plan', in *NTL Manager's Handbook* (Arlington, VA: NTL Institute, 1983): 38–41.
58 Weisbord, *Productive Workplaces*, op. cit.
59 Weisbord, *Discovering Common Ground*, op. cit.
60 R. Blake and J. Mouton, *The Managerial Grid* (Houston: Gulf, 1964); R. Blake, J. Mouton, L. Barnes and L. Greiner, 'Breakthrough in organization development', *Harvard Business Review*, 42 (1964): 133–55; R. Blake and J. Mouton, *Corporate Excellence Through Grid Organization Development: A Systems Approach* (Houston: Gulf, 1968); R. Blake and J. Mouton, *Building a Dynamic Corporation Through Grid Organization Development* (Reading, MA: Addison-Wesley, 1969).
61 Blake and Mouton, *Corporate Excellence*, op. cit.
62 ibid.
63 R. Blake and A. McCanse, *Leadership Dilemmas – Grid Solutions* (Houston: Gulf, 1991).
64 This discussion is based primarily on Blake and Mouton, *Corporate Excellence*, op. cit.
65 ibid.
66 ibid.
67 'Using the managerial grid to ensure MBO', *Organizational Dynamics*, 2 (Spring 1974): 55.
68 Blake and Mouton, *The Managerial Grid*, op. cit., 178–9. A more complete description is given in R. Blake and J. Mouton, *Organizational Change by Design* (Austin, TX: Scientific Methods, 1976): 1–16.
69 L. Greiner, D. Leitch and L. Barnes, 'The simple complexity of organisation climate in a government agency', undated manuscript.

Online reading

INFOTRAC® COLLEGE EDITION
For additional readings and reviews on interpersonal interventions, explore **InfoTrac® College Edition**, your online library. Go to **www.infotrac-college.com** and search for any of the InfoTrac key terms listed below:

- T-groups
- Process consultation
- Johari window
- Third-party intervention
- Conflict
- Team-building
- Grid® Organization Development

8

TECHNOSTRUCTURAL iNTERVENTiONS

In this chapter, we begin to examine technostructural interventions: change programs that focus on the technology and structure of organisations.

The first section explains how increasing global competition and rapid technological and environmental changes are forcing organisations to restructure themselves from rigid bureaucracies to leaner, more flexible structures. These new forms of organisation are highly adaptive and cost efficient. They often result in fewer managers and employees, and streamlined work flows that break down functional barriers.

The second section presents OD interventions that are aimed at moving decision making downward in the organisation, closer to where the actual work takes place. This increased employee involvement (EI) can lead to quicker, more responsive decisions, continuous performance improvement, and greater employee flexibility, commitment and satisfaction.

The final section is concerned with work design: creating jobs and work groups that generate high levels of employee fulfilment and productivity. This technostructural intervention can be part of a larger employee involvement application, or it can be an independent change program. Work design has been extensively researched and applied in organisations. Recently, organisations have tended to combine work design with formal structure and the support of changes in goal setting, reward systems, work environment and other performance management practices. These organisational factors can help to structure and reinforce the kinds of work behaviours associated with specific work designs.

RESTRUCTURING ORGANISATIONS

Interventions aimed at structural design include moving from more traditional ways of dividing the organisation's overall work – such as functional, self-contained unit and matrix structures – to more integrative and flexible forms, such as process- and network-based structures. Diagnostic guidelines help determine which structure is appropriate for particular organisational environments, technologies and conditions.

Downsizing seeks to reduce costs and bureaucracy by decreasing the size of the organisation. This reduction in personnel can be accomplished by lay-offs, organisation redesign and outsourcing, which involves moving functions that are not part of the organisation's core competence to outside contractors. Successful downsizing is closely aligned with the organisation's strategy.

Re-engineering radically redesigns the organisation's core work processes to give tighter linkage and co-ordination among the different tasks. This work-flow integration results in faster, more responsive task performance. Business process management is often accomplished with new information technology that permits employees to control and co-ordinate work processes more effectively.

Structural design

Organisation structure describes how the overall work of the organisation is divided into sub-units and how these sub-units are co-ordinated for task completion. It is a key feature of an

Figure 8.1   Contingencies that influence structural design

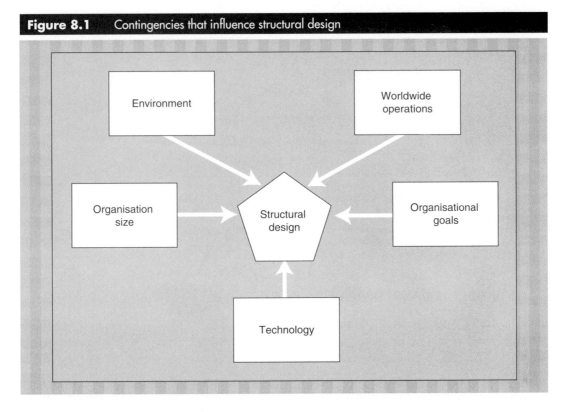

organisation's strategic orientation.[1] Based on a contingency perspective shown in Figure 8.1, organisation structures should be designed to fit with at least five factors:

- the environment
- organisation size
- technology
- organisation strategy
- worldwide operations.

Organisation effectiveness depends on the extent to which organisation structures are responsive to these contingencies.[2] Organisations have traditionally structured themselves into three forms:

- functional departments that are task specialised
- self-contained units that are oriented to specific products, customers or regions
- matrix structures that combine both functional specialisation and self-containment.

Faced with accelerating changes in competitive environments and technologies, however, organisations have increasingly redesigned their structures into more integrative and flexible forms. These more recent innovations include process-based structures that design sub-units around the organisation's core work processes and network-based structures that link the organisation to other, interdependent organisations. The advantages, disadvantages and contingencies of the different structures are described next.

THE FUNCTIONAL ORGANISATION

Perhaps the most widely used organisational structure in the world today is the basic hierarchical structure, shown in Figure 8.2. This is the standard pyramid, with senior management at the top, middle and lower managers spread out directly below and workers at the bottom. The organisation is usually subdivided into different functional units, such as engineering, research, operations, human resources, finance and marketing. This organisational structure is based on early management theories regarding specialisation, line and staff relations, span of control, authority and responsibility.[3] The major functional sub-units are staffed by specialists in such disciplines as engineering and accounting. It is considered easier to manage

Figure 8.2 The functional organisation

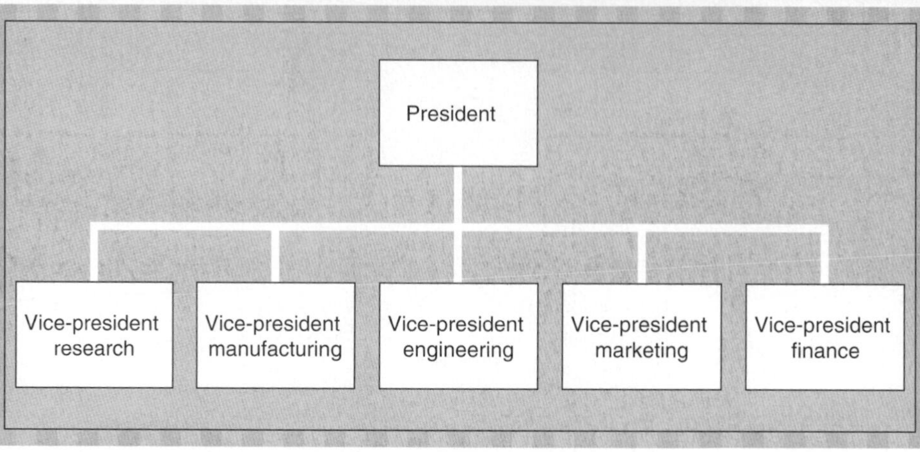

specialists if they are grouped together under the same head and if the head of the department has training and experience in that particular discipline.

Table 8.1 lists the advantages and disadvantages of functional structures. On the positive side, functional structures promote specialisation of skills and resources. People who perform

Table 8.1 Advantages, disadvantages and contingencies of the functional form

Advantages

- Promotes skill specialisation
- Reduces duplication of scarce resources and uses resources full time
- Enhances career development for specialists within large departments
- Facilitates communication and performance because superiors share expertise with their subordinates
- Exposes specialists to others within the same speciality

Disadvantages

- Emphasises routine tasks, which encourages short time horizons
- Fosters parochial perspectives by managers, which limit their capacities for top-management positions
- Reduces communication and co-operation between departments
- Multiplies the interdepartmental dependencies, which can make co-ordination and scheduling difficult
- Obscures accountability for overall outcomes

Contingencies

- Stable and certain environment
- Small to medium size
- Routine technology, interdependence within functions
- Goals of efficiency and technical quality

Source: adapted from J. McCann and J. Galbraith, 'Interdepartmental relations', in *Handbook of Organizational Design: Remodelling Organizations and Their Environment*, eds P. Nystrom and W. Starbuck, 2 vols. (New York: Oxford University Press, 1981) 2: 61.

similar work and face similar problems are grouped together. On the negative side, functional structures tend to promote routine tasks with a limited orientation. Departmental members focus on their own tasks, rather than on the organisation's total task.

The functional structure tends to work best in small to medium-sized firms that face relatively stable and certain environments. These organisations typically have a small number of products or services, and co-ordination across specialised units is relatively easy. This structure is also best suited to routine technologies in which there is interdependence within functions, and to organisational goals that emphasise efficiency and technical quality.

THE SELF-CONTAINED UNIT ORGANISATION

The self-contained unit structure represents a fundamentally different way of organising. Also known as a product or divisional structure, it was developed at about the same time by General Motors, Exxon and DuPont.[4] It groups organisational activities on the basis of products, services, customers or geography. All or most of the resources necessary for the accomplishment of specific objectives are set up as self-contained units headed by product or division managers. For example, Southcorp has plants that specialise in manufacturing packaging and others that specialise in wine producing. Each plant manager reports to a particular division or product vice-president, rather than a manufacturing vice-president. In effect, a large organisation may set up smaller (sometimes temporary) special-purpose organisations, each geared to a specific product, service, customer or region. A typical product structure is shown in Figure 8.3. Interestingly, the formal structure within a self-contained unit is often functional in nature.

Table 8.2 provides a list of the advantages and disadvantages of self-contained unit structures. These organisations recognise key interdependencies and promote the co-ordination of resources towards an overall outcome. This strong outcome orientation ensures departmental accountability and promotes cohesion among those contributing to the product.

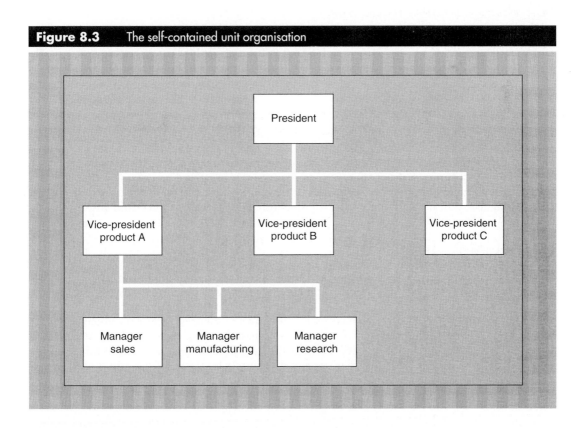

Figure 8.3   The self-contained unit organisation

Table 8.2 Advantages, disadvantages and contingencies of the self-contained unit form

Advantages

- Recognises sources of interdepartmental interdependencies
- Fosters an orientation towards overall outcomes and clients
- Allows diversification and expansion of skills and training
- Ensures accountability by departmental managers and so promotes delegation of authority and responsibility
- Heightens departmental cohesion and involvement in work

Disadvantages

- May use skills and resources inefficiently
- Limits career advancement by specialists to movements out of their departments
- Impedes specialists' exposure to others within the same specialities
- Puts multiple-role demands upon people and so creates stress
- May promote departmental objectives, as opposed to overall organisational objectives

Contingencies

- Unstable and uncertain environments
- Large size
- Technological interdependence across functions
- Goals of product specialisation and innovation

Source: adapted from J. McCann and J. Galbraith, 'Interdepartmental relations', in *Handbook of Organizational Design: Remodelling Organizations and Their Environment*, eds P. Nystrom and W. Starbuck, 2 vols. (New York: Oxford University Press, 1981) 2: 61.

Self-contained unit organisations do, however, have certain problems. There may not be enough specialised work to fully utilise people's skills and abilities. Specialists may feel isolated from their professional colleagues and may fail to advance in their career speciality. The self-contained unit structure works best in conditions that are almost the opposite of those favouring a functional organisation, as shown in Table 8.2. The organisation needs to be relatively large to support the duplication of resources assigned to the units. Because each unit is designed to fit a particular niche, the structure adapts well to uncertain conditions.

THE MATRIX ORGANISATION

Some OD practitioners have focused on maximising the strengths and minimising the weaknesses of both the functional and the self-contained unit structures. This has resulted in the matrix organisation.[5] It superimposes the lateral structure of a product or project co-ordinator on the vertical functional structure, as shown in Figure 8.4. Matrix organisational designs originally evolved in the aerospace industry, where changing customer demands and technological conditions caused managers to focus on lateral relationships between functions in order to develop a flexible and adaptable system of resources and procedures, and to achieve a series of project objectives. Matrix organisations are now widely used in manufacturing, service, non-profit, governmental and professional organisations, such as Monsanto Corporation.[6]

Figure 8.4   The matrix organisation.

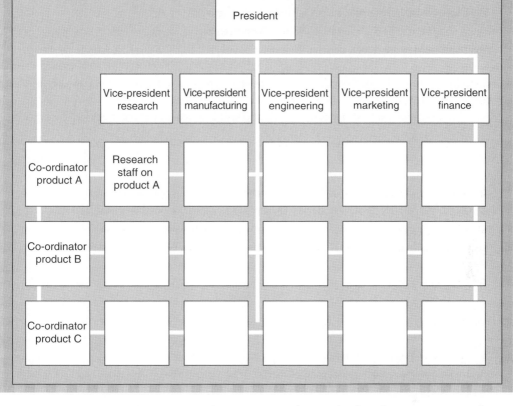

Every matrix organisation contains three unique and critical roles: the top manager who heads and balances the dual chains of command; the matrix bosses (functional, product or area) who share subordinates; and the two-boss managers who report to two different matrix bosses. Each of these roles has its own unique requirements. For example, functional matrix bosses are expected to maximise their respective technical expertise within constraints posed by market realities. Two-boss managers, however, must accomplish work within the demands of supervisors who want to achieve technical sophistication on the one hand and meet customer expectations on the other. Thus, a matrix organisation is more than matrix structure. It must also be reinforced by matrix processes, such as performance management systems that get input from both functional and project bosses; by matrix leadership behaviour that operates comfortably with lateral decision making; and by a matrix culture that fosters open conflict management and a balance of power.[7]

Matrix organisations, like all organisation structures, have both advantages and disadvantages, as shown in Table 8.3. On the positive side, matrix structures allow multiple orientations. Specialised, functional knowledge can be applied to all projects. On the negative side, matrix organisations can be difficult to manage. To implement and maintain them requires heavy managerial costs and support. When people are assigned to more than one department, there may be role ambiguity and conflict.

As shown in Table 8.3, matrix structures are appropriate under three important conditions.[8] First, there must be outside pressures for a dual focus: a matrix structure works best when there are many customers with unique demands on the one hand, and strong requirements for technical sophistication on the other hand. Second, there must be pressures for high information-processing capacity. A matrix organisation is appropriate when the organisation must process a large amount of information. Third, there must be pressure for shared resources. When customer demands vary greatly and technological requirements are strict, valuable human and physical

Table 8.3 Advantages, disadvantages and contingencies of the matrix form

Advantages

- Makes specialised, functional knowledge available to all projects
- Uses people flexibly, since departments maintain reservoirs of specialists
- Maintains consistency between different departments and projects by forcing communication between managers
- Recognises and provides mechanisms for dealing with legitimate, multiple sources of power in the organisation
- Can adapt to environmental changes by shifting emphasis between project and functional aspects

Disadvantages

- Can be very difficult to introduce without a pre-existing supportive management climate
- Increases role ambiguity, stress and anxiety by assigning people to more than one department
- Without power balancing between product and functional forms, lowers overall performance
- Makes inconsistent demands, which may result in unproductive conflicts and short-term crisis management
- May reward political skills as opposed to technical skills

Contingencies

- Dual focus on unique product demands and technical specialisation
- Pressure for high information-processing capacity
- Pressure for shared resources

Source: adapted from J. McCann and J. Galbraith, 'Interdepartmental relations', in *Handbook of Organizational Design: Remodelling Organizations and Their Environment*, eds P. Nystrom and W. Starbuck, 2 vols. (New York: Oxford University Press, 1981) 2: 61.

resources are likely to be scarce. If any of these conditions are not met, a matrix organisation is likely to fail.

PROCESS-BASED STRUCTURES

A radical new logic for structuring organisations is to form multidisciplinary teams around core processes, such as product development, sales generation and customer support.[9] As shown in Figure 8.5, process-based structures emphasise lateral rather than vertical relationships.[10] They group all related functions that are necessary to produce a product or service into a common unit, usually managed by someone called a 'process owner'. There are few hierarchical levels, and the senior executive team is relatively small: typically consisting of the chairperson, the chief operating officer and the heads of a few key support services, such as strategic planning, human resources and finance. Process-based structures eliminate many of the hierarchical and departmental boundaries that can impede task co-ordination, and slow decision making and task performance. They reduce the enormous costs of managing across departments and up and down the hierarchy. Process-based structures enable organisations to focus most of their resources on serving customers, both inside and outside the firm.

The application of process-based structures is growing rapidly in a variety of manufacturing and service companies. Typically referred to as 'horizontal', 'boundaryless' or 'team-based' organisations, they are used to enhance customer service at such firms as Motorola, Hewlett-Packard, Xerox and

Figure 8.5 The process-based structure

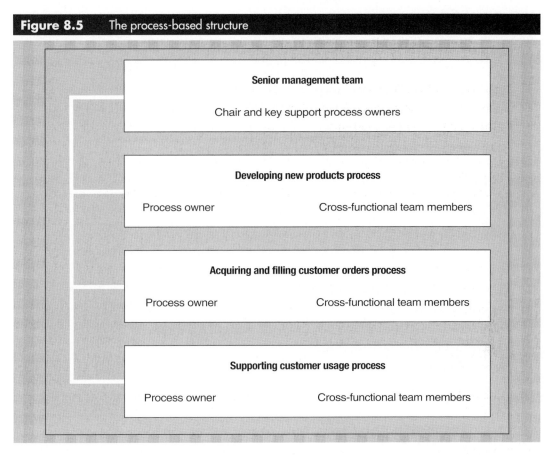

Varian Technologies (Australia). Although there is no one right way of designing process-based structures, the following features characterise this new form of organising:[11]

- Processes drive structure.
- Work adds value.
- Teams are fundamental.
- Customers define performance.
- Teams are rewarded for performance.
- Teams are tightly linked to suppliers and customers.
- Team members are well informed and trained.

Table 8.4 lists the advantages and disadvantages of process-based structures. The most frequently mentioned advantage is the intense focus on meeting customer needs, which can result in dramatic improvements in speed, efficiency and customer satisfaction. Process-based structures remove layers of management, and consequently information flows more quickly and accurately throughout the organisation.

A major disadvantage of process-based structures is the difficulty of changing to this new organisational form. Process-based structures typically require radical shifts in mindsets, skills and managerial roles. These changes involve considerable time and resources and can be resisted by functional managers and staff specialists. Moreover, process-based structures may result in expensive duplication of scarce resources and, if team skills are not present, in slower decision making as teams struggle to define and reach consensus. Finally, implementation of process-based structures relies on the proper identification of key processes needed to satisfy customer needs. If critical processes are misidentified or ignored altogether, performance and customer satisfaction are likely to suffer.

Table 8.4 shows that process-based structures are particularly appropriate for highly uncertain environments where customer demands and market conditions are changing rapidly. They enable organisations to manage non-routine technologies and to co-ordinate work flows that are highly interdependent.

Table 8.4	Advantages, disadvantages and contingencies of the process-based form

Advantages

- Focuses resources on customer satisfaction
- Improves speed and efficiency, often dramatically
- Adapts to environmental change rapidly
- Reduces boundaries between departments
- Increases ability to see total work flow
- Enhances employee involvement
- Lowers costs because of lower overhead structure

Disadvantages

- Can threaten middle managers and staff specialists
- Requires changes in command-and-control mindsets
- Duplicates scarce resources
- Requires new skills and knowledge to manage lateral relationships and teams
- May take longer to make decisions in teams
- Can be ineffective if wrong processes are identified

Contingencies

- Uncertain and changing environments
- Moderate to large size
- Non-routine and highly interdependent technologies
- Customer-oriented goals

NETWORK-BASED STRUCTURES

A network-based structure manages the diverse, complex and dynamic relationships among multiple organisations, each specialising in a particular function or task.[12] As shown in Figure 8.6, the network structure redraws organisational boundaries and links separate organisations to facilitate task interaction. The essence of networks is the relationship between organisations that perform different aspects of work. In this way, organisations do the things that they do well; for example, manufacturing expertise is applied to production and logistical expertise is applied to distribution.

Network-based structures are called by a variety of names, including 'virtual corporations', 'modular corporations' or 'Shamrock organisations'.[13] Less formally, they have been described as 'pizza' structures, spider webs, starbursts and cluster organisations. Organisations such as Apple Computers and Benetton have implemented fairly sophisticated network structures. They are also found in the construction, fashion and entertainment industries, as well as in the public sector.[14]

Network structures typically have the following characteristics:
- *Vertical disaggregation.* Different network members perform different business functions – such as production, marketing and distribution – that are traditionally performed within a single organisation.
- *Brokers.* Networks are often managed by broker organisations that locate and assemble member organisations.
- *Co-ordinating mechanisms.*

Figure 8.6 The network organisation

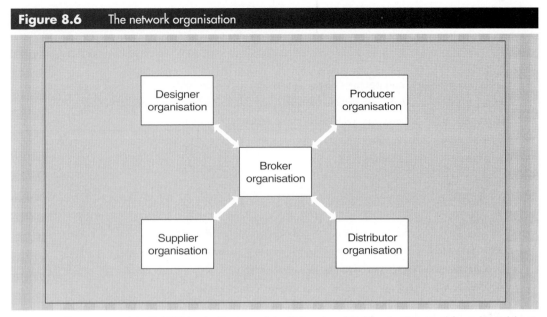

Network structures have a number of advantages and disadvantages, as shown in Table 8.5.[15] They are highly flexible and adaptable to changing conditions. Their ability to form partnerships with different organisations permits the creation of a 'best of the best' company that is better able to exploit opportunities, which may often be global in nature. They allow each member to exploit its distinctive competence. They can enable sufficient resources and expertise to be applied to large, complex tasks in a way that a single organisation could not. Perhaps most important is the fact that network organisations can have synergistic effects, allowing members to build on each other's strengths and competencies.

The major problems with network organisations lie in managing such complex structures. Galbraith and Kazanjian describe network structures as matrix organisations that extend beyond the boundaries of single firms but lack the ability to appeal to a higher authority to resolve conflicts.[16] Thus, matrix skills of managing lateral relations across organisational boundaries are critical to administering network structures.

Downsizing

Downsizing refers to interventions that are aimed at reducing the size of the organisation.[17] This is typically accomplished by decreasing the number of employees through lay-offs, attrition, redeployment or early retirement, or by reducing the number of organisational units or managerial levels through divestiture, outsourcing, reorganisation or delayering. An important consequence of downsizing has been the rise of the contingent workforce. These less expensive temporary or permanent part-time workers are often hired by the organisations that just laid off thousands of their employees. In many cases, terminated employees become independent contractors or consultants to the organisation that just terminated them. Overall cost reduction is achieved by replacing expensive permanent workers with a contingent workforce.

Over the past decade, many major corporations and government agencies have engaged in downsizing activities. Among the biggest job-shedders since 1990 are Telstra, which has reduced staff by 15 000 to 66 000; Foster's Brewing Group, down 13 000 to 8304; Westpac Bank, down 33 000 to 45 000; and Mayne Nickless, down 11 000 to 29 000.[18] According to the recruitment/outplacement firm DBM, 30 000 banking jobs were abolished between 1991 and

Table 8.5	Advantages, disadvantages and contingencies of the network-based form

Advantages

- Enables highly flexible and adaptive response to dynamic environments
- Creates a 'best of the best' organisation to focus resources on customer and market needs
- Each organisation can leverage a distinctive competency
- Permits rapid global expansion
- Can produce synergistic results

Disadvantages

- Managing lateral relations across autonomous organisations is difficult
- Motivating members to relinquish autonomy to join the network is troublesome
- Sustaining membership and benefits can be problematic
- May give partners access to proprietary knowledge/technology

Contingencies

- Highly complex and uncertain environments
- All sizes of organisations
- Highly uncertain technologies
- Goals of organisational specialisation and innovation
- Worldwide operations

1997. A 1995 study of 1450 organisations in Australia and New Zealand showed that 36% of the surveyed organisations reported permanent reductions in their workforce.[19]

Downsizing is generally a response to several factors, including product or service demand, pressure to focus on short-term profits or budget goals, a major change in organisational strategy and the belief that the slimmer the organisation the better.[20] John Corrigan, the Technical Support Consultant at Chartered Practising Accountants Australia Management Accounting Centre of Excellence, states that cutting costs has been the mantra of business for the past decade, but that there is evidence to suggest that the decimation of middle management ranks in organisations has caused a loss of valuable experience and knowledge.[21] This view is supported by Professor Collins of the Australian Graduate School of Management, who says that downsizing in Australia has very negative connotations and that, through downsizing, companies have lost a lot of skills that were really needed.

Where downsizing is necessary, how it is handled by management is of tremendous importance to the organisation involved, as discussed in Application 8.1.

APPLICATION 8.1

ETHICS OF THE AXE

Suddenly Telstra staff are nervous again. The telco's American chief executive Solomon Trujillo is coming in to overhaul Telstra's culture and cut costs ahead of the $30 billion-plus final tranche of the telecommunications behemoth's privatisation. Everyone knows that jobs are on the line.

The moment of truth is expected to come after Telstra is unshackled from government control – it's easier to get rid of people when there are no political constraints – and analysts are talking of $2 billion worth of cost cuts and as many as 10 000 jobs; around a quarter of the headcount.

Similarly, many Southcorp employees are tipped to be out of work following Foster's Group's $3.2 billion takeover of what was Australia's biggest wine producer. But how many? For now, Foster's is saying nothing. All will be revealed following a two-month review of the combined entity. Still, the cuts might go deep to make the debt-funded acquisition pay. How deep? Analysts say that to meet its cost of capital, Foster's will need to more than double Southcorp's profitability.

The stakes are high. Underlining market concerns about whether Foster's can actually achieve this, ratings agency Standard & Poor's has downgraded the drinks company to just one notch above junk status, from BBB to BBB-, the lowest investment grade.

At other companies, employees have already learned how many are to be 'restructured'; that is, sacked. Reeling from last year's $360 million foreign exchange currency fiasco and board upheaval, National Australia Bank will cut 4200 jobs worldwide, 2000 of them in Australia. Up to 600 employees at WMC Resources – pretty much the entire management and corporate team – will lose their jobs as the miner is absorbed into BHP Billiton's global operations following its $9.2 billion takeover.

In a desperate move to regain its position in the US car market, General Motors is cutting 25 000 jobs: more than 22% of its blue-collar workforce in the US. Dairy Farmers, the maker of Coon and Cracker Barrel cheese and Ski yoghurt, is slashing 460 jobs, or 20% of its workforce, in preparation for a float. At Nestle, 147 workers will lose their jobs in September when the company winds up milk powder production at its Tongala factory, southeast of Echuca.

Roll out the packages, it's time again for redundancies. The axe is back. From one end, companies flush with cash and desperate for quick growth are chasing acquisitions. From the other side, a slowdown in the global economy combined with hyper-competition and deregulating markets has forced businesses to restructure. Employees are caught in the middle.

No business in the world has a moral obligation to keep an employee in a job. Managers have every right to hire and fire depending on circumstances. But in an age of skills shortages and workforce mobility, smarter companies are using a cushion and not an axe. Marching orders can be delivered with career opportunities outside the company.

Katherine Teh-White, managing director of sustainability strategists and change agents FutureEye, said: 'There are a number of issues the organisation has to think about. What does it say about the workplace you operate? Are you, as an employee, treated with respect and dignity, or are you just treated as an FTE, or full-time equivalent, as described by chief financial officers? Companies that treat employees with respect and dignity when letting them go will have greater loyalty from the ones left behind, and they will be better able to attract new staff in the future.'

WMC employees are feeling the heat right now. 'We feel like we are living in the Big Brother house and there is a live eviction every night,' is how one put it this week. 'It has been ugly and traumatic; a lot of angst in what has been a very difficult time,' she said. 'It hasn't helped that depending on your situation, there have been some different outcomes. Some people have been told they will be hanging around for 15 months. Some go at the end of this week. Others have six weeks to go and others are still waiting to get some clarity.'

Another WMC staffer is more sanguine. Because of the department he is in, he knew straight-up that, on BHP taking control, he would fall into a 'duplicated function area'. That means he knew his job was gone because it was already done by someone at BHP's Lonsdale Street head office in Melbourne's Greek quarter. Although only in his early 30s, he has been through it all before: a two-time victim of a job loss caused by the wave of consolidation that has washed over the resources industry in the past five years. He plans to take a holiday with his young family, and tells himself that the challenge of setting himself up again in a well-paid corporate position could bring some excitement.

Certainly, it didn't take him long to realise that it was time to move again. BHP officially collected the keys to WMC's offices on Monday, less than 60 hours after moving to outright control under the terms of its $7.85-a-share home-town bid. But to many at WMC's Southbank head office, BHP's presence in the corporate centre has been all-pervasive ever since the bid was announced on March 8, coming as it did with a warm welcome from the WMC board.

Like the Swiss-based Xstrata with its failed WMC tilt before it, BHP made clear from day one of its bid that as many as 600 white-collar jobs would go once it got control and set about extracting $120 million in annual cost savings.

▷▷

WMC's board was the first to go and, in the days since, there has been a steady flow of staff briefings at which the deferred pain of the job cuts has become a reality. Getting rid of 600 jobs from an establishment company such as WMC was always going to be difficult. But even critics of the process agree that both WMC and BHP have done just about all they can to make it as painless as possible.

Working in their favour was the early endorsement of the BHP bid by the WMC board. That meant the planning and preparation for the inevitable job losses could start early. Preserving commercial-in-confidence considerations pending BHP's move to a control position, the human resources departments of the two companies were able to liaise on planning and implementation.

Given it was their people who were to be left without jobs, WMC was keen to offer what counsel and services it could. A weekly email offering all sorts of support and services was central to WMC's aim to be as open as possible with its staff about what lay ahead. 'From my perspective, it was really well thought out,' another WMC staffer said. All of the standard offerings to people facing job loss have been in place for the past two months. Access to an out-placement service for 12 months, training on how to prepare a CV, and advice sessions with chartered accountants on financial planning were all part of what was made available. Neck and shoulder massages to help with the stress of it all were made available, as was counselling for those showing signs of denial.

However, unwitting acts of arrogance, no matter how small, can undermine the best of intentions. And so it was with the replacement of the @wmc.com staff email address lines with ones containing @bhpbilliton.com shortly after BHP took control. For many in the proud WMC workforce, there was no need for the reminder that BHP had taken control, particularly as they were not going to be part of its future.

Staff at Southcorp might have a longer wait. Foster's has sent in a 25-member team to meet staff and look at the merged businesses. As part of the restructure, Foster's has merged its Carlton & United Beverages (CUB) division and the Australian division of Beringer Blass Wine Estates, which will become one business, operating as Foster's Australia. Foster's Wine Estates managing director Jamie Odell said this had sent just as big a signal to CUB and Beringer staff as it had to those at Southcorp. 'We either all win this or all lose it,' Mr Odell said.

Questioned last month about the restructure following the takeover, Foster's chief executive officer Trevor O'Hoy said changes were inevitable. But handling it well, he said, was about talking straight. For Mr O'Hoy, there's no sense giving people false hope. 'Quite clearly you have got to be honest and up front with people,' Mr O'Hoy said. 'You've got to be quite clear about the strategy and the vision for the company and give people a chance and time to decide whether they want to buy into that strategy. We'll put the flag pole or the goal post in the ground. Then you've got to be very open and tell people how we will make changes. There's no doubt there will be significant change . . . so quite clearly it's best to flag that and be honest and up front.'

In the case of NAB, there could be a fight over one particular rule. Under clause 8.1.2 of the enterprise bargaining agreement between the bank and Finance Sector Union, NAB can 'only reduce existing staff levels in a particular workplace following a reduction in workloads as a result of restructuring, re-engineering or the introduction of new process of technology.'

FSU national secretary Paul Schroder said the head of NAB's Australian operations, Ahmed Fahour, had told him that NAB would stick to that commitment. But he said it meant the bank could not do anything until it had shown the union exactly how the workloads had been reduced, and that's a bridge they still had to cross. 'If they want to go crunch with us, we're happy to take it further,' Mr Schroder said.

Global outplacement specialists Right Management Consultants say redundancies come in three contexts: acquisitions, industry-wide changes and a short-term earnings squeeze. Right's executive vice-president in the Asia-Pacific region, Ted Davies, said: 'You actually need to look at circumstances and consequences of each downsizing. Look at the context and those three scenarios may give rise to different options.' But whatever the context, he said, there were rules: 'You need to treat people with dignity and respect. There is some self-interest there, too, because it impacts on those left behind and on the company's reputation in the community. Number two is you need to give people as much control over their exit as is reasonable and possible.' As for redeployment, it has to be fair dinkum: 'There has to be a sincere intention to redeploy and not just do it for the sake of appearance.'

Simon Longstaff, executive director of the St James Ethics Centre, said that companies had no obligation to maintain people in their jobs. But if they had to lay off staff, they had to take into account the 'human dimension'. 'It exists partly as a matter of ethical obligation and partly as enlightened self-interest and, if it's done badly, returns to haunt them,' he said.

Still there's no escaping the fact that in the event of a merger, there has to be duplication and people have to go. Stuff happens. And what if the company suddenly falls on hard times and has to restructure? What if there's no time or resources to consider the impact on people? That's just a sign of bad management, said Mr Longstaff. Good managers are able to forecast market trends and are therefore in a position to prepare staff for what's ahead.

Redundancy packages went together with retraining and outplacement, which involve career counselling and assessment, financial counselling and job search, even helping them to establish their own business. 'It's not unreasonable to assume that care and concern is in the minds of management when preparing employees for outplacing and retraining,' Mr Longstaff said.

Source: Leon Gettler and Barry Fitzgerald, 'Ethics of the axe', *The Age*, 11/6/05.

Critical Thinking Question: How far do you agree that having insufficient time and/or resources to consider the impact on people would be a sign of bad management?

APPLICATION STAGES

Successful downsizing interventions tend to proceed in the following steps:[22]

1   *Clarify the organisation's strategy.* In this initial stage, organisation leaders specify corporate strategy and clearly communicate how downsizing relates to it.
2   *Assess downsizing options and make relevant choices.* Once corporate strategy is clear, the full range of downsizing options can be identified and assessed. Table 8.6 describes three primary downsizing methods: workforce reduction, organisation redesign and systemic changes. A specific downsizing strategy may use elements of all three approaches.

From around the mid-1980s to today, it has become common for both private and public sector organisations to announce the elimination of thousands of jobs in the quest for quick productivity improvement. For example, in recent years Telstra and the Australian Public Service have each undergone major downsizing efforts involving thousands of employees. Organisations going through such downsizing have to be concerned about managing the effects of these cutbacks, not only for those who are being made redundant, but also for those who 'survive' – albeit with a reduced level of job security.

Table 8.6   Three types of downsizing tactics

Downsizing tactic	Characteristics	Examples
Workforce reduction	Aimed at headcount reduction Short-term implementation Fosters a transition	Attrition Transfer and outplacement Retirement incentives Buyout packages Lay-offs
Organisation redesign	Aimed at organisation change Moderate-term implementation Fosters transition and, potentially, transformation	Eliminate functions Merge units Eliminate layers Eliminate products Redesign tasks
Systemic	Aimed at culture change Long-term implementation Fosters transformation	Change responsibility Involve all constituents Fosters continuous improvement and innovation Simplification Downsizing: a way of life

Source: From *ACADEMY OF MANAGEMENT EXECUTIVE: THE THINKING MANAGER'S SOURCE* by K. CAMERON, S. FREEMAN AND A. MISHRA. Copyright 1991 by ACADEMY OF MANAGEMENT (NY). Reproduced with permission of ACADEMY OF MANAGEMENT (NY) in the format Textbook via Copyright Clearance Center.

Unfortunately, organisations often choose obvious solutions for downsizing, such as lay-offs, that can be quickly implemented. This can produce a climate of fear and defensiveness as members focus on identifying who will be separated from the organisation. It is important to examine a broad range of options and to consider the entire organisation rather than certain areas. This can help to allay fears that favouritism and politics are the basis for downsizing decisions. Moreover, the participation of organisation members in such decisions can have positive benefits. It can create a sense of urgency for identifying and implementing options to downsizing other than lay-offs.

3   *Implement the changes.* This stage involves implementing methods for reducing the size of the organisation. Several practices characterise successful implementation. First, understand that downsizing is best controlled from the top down. Second, identify and target specific areas of inefficiency and high cost. Third, link specific actions to the organisation's strategy. Finally, communicate frequently, using a variety of media.

4   *Address the needs of survivors and those who leave.* When lay-offs occur, employees are generally asked to take on additional responsibilities and to learn new jobs, often with little or no increase in compensation. This added workload can be stressful, and when combined with anxiety over past lay-offs and possible future ones, it can lead to what researchers have labelled the 'survivor syndrome'.[23] This involves a narrow set of self-absorbed and risk-averse behaviours that can threaten the organisation's survival. Organisations can address these survivor problems with communication processes that increase the amount and frequency of information provided. Communication should shift from explanations about who left (or why) to clarification of where the company is going, including its visions, strategies and goals.

Given the negative consequences typically associated with job loss, organisations have developed a number of methods to help employees who have been laid off. These include outplacement counselling, personal and family counselling, severance packages, office support for job searches, relocation services and job retraining. Each of these services is intended to help employees in their transition to another work situation.

5   *Follow through with growth plans.* Failure to move quickly to implement growth plans is a key determinant of ineffective downsizing.[24] For example, a 1992 study of 1020 human resource directors reported that only 44% of the companies that had downsized in the previous five years had shared details of their growth plans with employees; only 34% had told employees how they would fit into the company's new strategy.[25] These findings suggest that organisations need to ensure that employees understand the renewal strategy.

RESULTS OF DOWNSIZING

Research on the effects of downsizing has shown mixed results. Many studies have indicated that downsizing may not meet its intended goals, and there is mounting evidence that workforce reduction efforts were carried out in piecemeal fashion and failed to meet the objectives of the organisation.[26] Craig Littler studied 3500 companies across Australia and monitored downsizing patterns: in more than 60% of those companies, the practice of downsizing had not led to any improvement in productivity.[27]

These research findings paint a rather bleak picture of the success of downsizing. The results must be interpreted cautiously, however, as they are subject to at least two major flaws. First, many of the surveys were sent to human resource specialists who might have been naturally inclined to view downsizing in a negative light. Second, the studies of financial performance may have included a biased sample of firms. If the companies selected for analysis had been poorly managed, then downsizing alone would have been unlikely to improve financial performance.

On the positive side, a number of organisations – such as Telstra, General Electric, Motorola, Texas Instruments, Boeing, Chrysler and Hewlett-Packard – have posted solid financial returns after downsizing. Although this evidence contradicts the negative findings described above, recent research suggests that the way in which downsizing is conducted may explain these divergent outcomes. A study of 30 downsized firms in the automobile industry showed that those companies that had effectively implemented the application stages described above scored significantly higher on several performance measures than had firms that had no downsizing strategy or that had implemented the steps poorly.[28] Anecdotal evidence from case studies of downsized firms also shows that organisations that effectively apply the application stages are more satisfied with the process and outcomes of downsizing than are firms that do not. Thus, the success of downsizing efforts may depend as much on how effectively this intervention is applied as on the size of the lay-offs or the amount of delayering.

Re-engineering

The final restructuring intervention is re-engineering: the fundamental rethinking and radical redesign of business processes in order to achieve dramatic improvements in performance.[29] Re-engineering seeks to transform how organisations produce and deliver goods and services. Beginning with the Industrial Revolution, organisations have increasingly fragmented work into specialised units, each focusing on a limited part of the overall production process. Although this division of labour has enabled organisations to mass-produce standardised products and services efficiently, it can be overly complicated and difficult to manage, as well as being slow to respond to the rapid and unpredictable changes experienced by many organisations today. Re-engineering addresses these problems by breaking down specialised work units into more integrated, cross-functional work processes. This streamlines work processes and makes them faster and more flexible; consequently, they are more responsive to changes in competitive conditions, customer demands, product life cycles and technologies.[30] As might be expected, re-engineering requires an almost revolutionary change in how organisations design and think about work. It addresses fundamental issues about why organisations do what they do, and why they do it in a particular way.

In radically changing business processes, re-engineering frequently takes advantage of new information technology. Modern information technologies – such as teleconferencing, expert systems, shared databases and wireless communication – can enable organisations to re-engineer. They can help organisations to break out of traditional ways of thinking about work and can permit entirely new ways of producing and delivering products. Amcor is nearing completion of a major restructuring plan that has been under way for two years. According to Amcor's managing director, Russell Jones, the company felt it had to carry out the re-engineering program if it was going to achieve the financial and strategic objectives that the management had set for the group. Amcor has focused closely on changes designed to improve profitability and help the group regain its corporate credibility through improved earnings. Having embarked on the process to identify core and non-core businesses, and then taken the decision to sell off non-core assets, Amcor now has a far leaner operation. Jones believes that the real benefit to customers and shareholders is that the company is more focused in what it is delivering and will continue to be more efficient in both the short and long term.[31]

Whereas new information technology can enable organisations to re-engineer themselves, existing technology can thwart such efforts. Many re-engineering projects fail because existing information systems do not provide the information needed to operate integrated business processes. The systems do not allow interdependent departments to interface with each other; they often require new information to be entered by hand into separate computer systems before people in different work areas can access it.

Re-engineering is also associated with interventions that have to do with downsizing and work design. Although these interventions have different conceptual and applied backgrounds, they overlap considerably in practice. Re-engineering can result in production and delivery processes that require fewer people and layers of management. Conversely, downsizing may require subsequent re-engineering interventions. When downsizing occurs without fundamental changes in how work is performed, the same tasks are simply being performed by a smaller number of people. Thus, expected cost savings may not be realised because lower productivity offsets lower salaries and fewer benefits.

Re-engineering invariably involves aspects of work design, where tasks are assigned to jobs or teams. It identifies and assesses core business processes and redesigns work to account for key task interdependencies running through them. This typically results in new jobs or teams that emphasise multifunctional tasks, results-oriented feedback and employee empowerment – characteristics associated with motivational and sociotechnical approaches to work design. Regrettably, re-engineering has failed to apply to its own work-design prescriptions these approaches' attention to differences in individual people's reactions to work. It advocates enriched work and teams, without consideration for the considerable research that shows that not all people are motivated to perform such work.

One example of information technology enhancing the opportunity for re-engineering is with the insurance industry, as illustrated in Application 8.2.

APPLiCATiON 8.2

INSURERS PLAY CATCH-UP

The insurance industry has taken a long time to dump the paperwork. Now technology is helping to create efficiencies and more innovative products.

Innovation is not a word generally associated with the insurance industry, but pressure on operating margins and the growing complexity of insurance products is forcing insurers to renew their systems and rethink the paper-intensive insurance claim process.

The chief executive of CommInsure, Simon Swanson, says insurance used to be a straightforward business of signing someone on to a contract and, as long as they paid their premiums, the insurer paid out a defined amount when the event occurred. But the modern world is not so simple.

Swanson says that because of consumer demand, life insurers such as CommInsure have now moved from simply selling mortality products, which are triggered when someone dies, to morbidity products – a range of products that protect income when someone is incapacitated. The shift to managing incapacitated clients, along with the need to be aware of new medical research, is increasing the need for smarter processes.

In general insurance, insurers are being challenged to underwrite or price a multitude of new liabilities. For example, they are trying to understand how emerging threats to property (such as climate) and to employees covered by workers' compensation policies (such as the long-term health effects of mobile phones) will change product innovation and pricing.

Insurers are moving away from paper-based processes that mean settling claims often takes a long time because of delays in lodgement, assessment and payment.

The research vice-president for insurance at the consultants Gartner, Todd Eyler, says that in the past two years insurers around the world have been rethinking the way they hold information, process claims and market products to consumers to overcome their long-term business model problems. The insurance industry was an early adopter of technology; it was one of the first to adopt computers in the late 1960s. But the large investments devoted to mainframe computers and data systems meant that insurers were reluctant to approve spending on new technology. Eyler says that as the systems aged, the small technology budgets were skewed towards maintenance. Insurers typically spend 3% of their budgets on technology, a low level compared with banks, which spend 5–6%.

Although 20% of insurers are aggressively replacing systems, most are upgrading and introducing new technology and work processes. 'The interesting thing is that because they have lagged for so long they now often leapfrog others to adopt the newest products,' Eyler says.

Swanson says insurers must provide consistent service to customers if they are to be successful, irrespective of whether policies become more complex than in the past. Income-protection products have led to more complications for underwriters in assessing the correct premium. For example, underwriters are now able to rate the risks of illness associated with different types of age groups and occupations, such as shift workers. Only 20% of CommInsure's life insurance applications are approved without investigation; the rest require individual assessment.

Swanson, who has worked overseas and most recently for Sovereign Insurance based in Auckland, introduced a mobile service that originated in New Zealand to reduce long approval processes that were slowed by drawn-out decision making. He sends underwriters, who base their pricing decisions on detailed global actuarial research, into the field with advisers to talk to consumers face to face. Swanson says six or seven are available in each Australian state and the service has substantially cut approval time.

Gartner's Eyler predicts insurers will be much more diligent about examining where they can find efficiencies in their business processes with the help of new software that tracks work flow. A fast and accurate claims process is the best way to retain existing customers and attract new ones.

REDUCING THE PAPERWORK

Freemans is Australia's largest loss-adjusting firm, employing 320 people in 50 offices. It is a specialist that assesses damage in large or complex property claims such as the property and business interruption claims associated with Cyclone Larry, which hit north Queensland in March 2006.

The chief executive of Freemans, Martin Hartcher, was hired two years ago to manage a new strategy incorporating innovation because of his experience in managing the listed online procurement business, Market-boomer. He says moving to a paperless claims management system through a secure internet connection has improved efficiency enormously. Adjusters in remote locations can now use laptops to send information and photographs through a web connection directly to underwriters, who make a final decision on the claim. Previously, faxes were used. Hartcher says tablets are being tested to make the process even faster.

Freemans is also using new technology to improve the accuracy of insurance assessments. The firm, which specialises in agriculture claims, is working with the University of South Queensland to improve ways to assess damage to crops from insects or storms.

Hartcher says it is difficult to assess damage to crops such as wheat, where only sections of a field are damaged. 'Adjusters used to stand on the top of their utes and work it out that way,' he says. Now, a new infrared photography technique called leaf reflexology compares light intensity.

In a similar way, Freemans is using global positioning system devices to more accurately measure distances on large properties and satellite images to pinpoint the timing and scope of damage. Hartcher says these images also help to quickly identify neighbouring claimants who may want to join a liability claim; after a bushfire, for example.

The Australian insurance industry is dominated by large insurers such as the Insurance Australia Group (IAG), Suncorp Metway, QBE and Promina. The money and planning needed to push innovations through the entire organisation are sometimes difficult to manage. IAG recently replaced the computer systems it inherited from various insurers it acquired, to provide one central database.

IAG and Promina are managed as a house of brands. Promina is using a strategy that is specific to each brand to reinvigorate its focus on innovation, promising that any change will originate and be controlled within the individual brands such as AAMI, the workers' compensation insurer Vero and the Australian Pensioners' Insurance Agency (APIA).

The chief executive of APIA, Kevin Pattison, says that a focus on consumers is important. Although introducing a paperless system in applications and claims would make any insurer more efficient, there are product and service features that are aimed at the APIA demographic: people aged over 55 who do not work full-time.

APIA staff offer consumers an extra level of financial advice that office and call-centre staff in general insurers typically do not. Pattison says that means banning computerised answering services on all phones so that a person will always answer a sales or customer inquiry. Standard call times are longer, too, because the staff are trained and authorised by the Australian Securities and Investments Commission to give legal advice on insurance policies.

An example of an extra feature is that APIA offers flood cover across all its policies to reassure policyholders that they will be covered in disasters such as Cyclone Larry. General insurers usually only offer limited flood cover with certain property policies because flood risk is difficult to assess. 'We don't want to buy into that because at that time, consumers are at their most distressed,' Pattison says.

Not all innovations will be adopted by consumers straight away, he warns. APIA had a claims lodgement facility on its web site from 1999, but it is only now being used regularly.

INSURERS' TO-DO LIST

- *Partnerships.* Form research partnerships to assess future risks such as climate change and design appropriately priced products.
- *Technology.* Explore the use of web-based technology for claims processing to give underwriters and claims assessors instant access to information.

- *Efficiencies.* Track the time spent on administrative tasks using new advanced software to reduce claims processing time.
- *Data.* Access new sources of data, such as satellite photography, to improve the assessment of complex claims.
- *Outsourcing.* Form long-term relationships with outsourcing agencies to reduce claims processing time but maintain quality control.

Source: Amita Tandukar, 'Innovation: Insurers play catch-up', *Business Review Weekly*, 13/4/06.

Critical Thinking Question: In introducing new technology as the insurance industry has done, what barriers, internal and/or external, might a company face?

WHAT ARE THE STEPS?

Re-engineering is a relatively new intervention and is still developing applied methods. Early applications emphasised the identification of which business processes to re-engineer and technical assessment of the work flow. More recent efforts have extended re-engineering practice to address issues of managing change, such as how to manage resistance to change and how to manage the transition to new work processes.[32] The following application steps are included in re-engineering efforts, although the order may change slightly from one application to another.[33]

1   *Prepare the organisation.* Re-engineering begins with clarification and assessment of the organisation's strategic context, including its competitive environment, strategy and objectives.

2   *Fundamentally rethink the way work gets done.* This step lies at the heart of business process management and involves these activities:

- identifying and analysing core business processes

- defining their key performance objectives

- designing new processes.

These tasks are the real work of business process management and are typically performed by a cross-functional team that is given considerable time and resources to accomplish them.[34]

3   *Restructure the organisation around the new business processes.* An important element of this restructuring is the implementation of new information and measurement systems. They must reinforce a shift from measuring behaviours, such as absenteeism and grievances, to assessing outcomes, such as productivity, customer satisfaction and cost savings. Moreover, information technology is one of the key drivers of business process management because it can drastically reduce the cost and time associated with integrating and co-ordinating business processes.

Re-engineered organisations typically have the following characteristics:[35]

- Work units change from functional departments to process teams.

- Jobs change from simple tasks to multidimensional work.

- People's roles change from controlled to empowered.

- The focus of performance measures and compensation shifts from activities to results.

- Organisation structures change from hierarchical to flat.

- Managers change from supervisors to coaches; executives change from score-keepers to leaders.

RESULTS FROM RE-ENGINEERING

The results from re-engineering vary widely. Industry journals and the business press regularly contain accounts of dramatic business results attributable to re-engineering. On the other hand, a best-selling book on re-engineering reported that as many as 70% of the efforts failed to meet their cost, cycle time or productivity objectives.[36] Despite its popularity, re-engineering is only beginning to be evaluated systematically, and there is little research to help unravel the disparate results.[37]

One evaluation of business process re-engineering examined more than 100 companies' efforts.[38] In-depth analysis of 20 re-engineering projects found that 11 cases had total business unit cost reductions of less than 5% while six cases had total cost reductions averaging 18%. The primary difference was the scope of the business process selected. Re-engineering key value-added processes significantly affected total business unit costs; re-engineering narrow business processes did not. Similarly, performance improvements in particular processes were strongly associated with changes in six key levers of behaviour, including structure, skills, information systems, roles, incentives and shared values. Efforts that addressed all six levers produced average cost reductions in specific processes by 35%; efforts that affected only one or two change levers reduced costs by 19%. Finally, the percentage reduction in total unit costs was associated with committed leadership.

EMPLOYEE INVOLVEMENT

Employee involvement is a broad term that has been variously referred to as 'empowerment', 'participative management', 'work design', 'industrial democracy' and 'quality of work life'. It covers a diversity of approaches to gaining greater participation in relevant workplace decisions. Some organisations, such as Intel, have enhanced worker involvement through enriched forms of work, while others, such as Ford, have increased participation by forming employee involvement teams that develop suggestions for improving productivity and quality. Chrysler and Shell Oil have sought greater participation through union–management co-operation on performance and quality-of-work–life issues, while Texas Instruments, Glaxo and Motorola have improved employee involvement by emphasising participation in total quality management.

Current EI approaches have evolved from earlier quality-of-work–life efforts in Europe (particularly Scandinavia) and the United States. Although the terms 'employee involvement' and 'empowerment' have gradually replaced the designation 'quality of work life', reviewing this historical background provides a clearer understanding of what EI means today. A current definition of EI includes four elements that can promote meaningful involvement in workplace decisions: power, information, knowledge and skills, and rewards. These components of EI can combine to have powerful effects on productivity and employee well-being.

The following major EI applications are discussed in this chapter:
- parallel structures, including co-operative union–management projects and quality circles
- high-involvement organisations
- total quality management.

Employee involvement: what is it?

Employee involvement can be understood against its background in the quality-of-work-life (QWL) movement started in the late 1950s. The phrase 'quality of work life' was used to stress the prevailing poor quality of life at the workplace.[39] Over the past 40 years, both the term 'QWL' and the meaning attributed to it have undergone considerable change and development, giving rise to the current emphasis on EI. In this section, the history of QWL and its influence on employee involvement are reviewed. In addition, the important and often misunderstood relationship between EI and productivity is clarified.

EVOLUTION OF THE QUALITY-OF-WORK-LIFE MOVEMENT

The present concern with employee involvement can be traced to the 1950s, when Eric Trist and his co-workers at the Tavistock Institute of Human Relations in London conducted a series of studies on work and its human and technical outcomes. This research became the foundation for sociotechnical systems theory: a set of principles that optimises both the social and the technical components of work systems. In the United States in the 1950s, Davis and his associates began working on ways of changing assembly lines to make them more productive and satisfying places to work.[40] The decade also saw a great deal of research on the causes and consequences of job satisfaction and the beginning of systematic employee attitude surveys.

In the 1960s, the rising concern for civil rights and social responsibility led to a number of US governmental actions, including the *Equal Pay Act (Fair Labor Standards Act*, 1963), the *Civil Rights Act* (1964) and the development of equal opportunity guidelines. From these activist roots sprang two distinct phases of QWL activity. From 1969 to 1974, a widespread interest emerged in improving the quality of experiences that people have at work. The major impetus was the growing concern of a generally affluent society for the health, safety and satisfaction of workers. At the same time, the United States was becoming increasingly aware of European efforts to enhance QWL that basically followed a sociotechnical systems perspective.

Two definitions of 'QWL' emerged during this first major phase of activity.[41] QWL was first defined in terms of people's reaction to work, particularly individuals' job satisfaction and mental health. Using this definition, QWL focused primarily on the personal consequences of the work experience and how to improve work to satisfy personal needs. The following criteria for QWL characterise this individual outcome orientation:[42]

1   adequate and fair compensation
2   safe and healthy environment
3   development of human capacities
4   growth and security
5   social integration
6   constitutionalism
7   the total life space
8   social relevance.

A second, later conception of QWL from this period defined it as an approach or method.[43] People defined QWL in terms of specific techniques and approaches used for improving work. It was viewed as synonymous with methods such as job enrichment, self-managed teams and labour–management committees. This technique orientation derived mainly from the growing publicity surrounding QWL projects, such as the General Motors–United Auto Workers project at Tarrytown and the Gaines Pet Food plant. These pioneering projects drew attention to specific approaches for improving work.

United States corporations became fascinated with these alternative management styles and with catching up with management developments abroad. Books extolling the virtues of Japanese management practices, such as Ouchi's *Theory Z*,[44] made best-seller lists, and the adoption of Japan's quality circle concept became widespread almost overnight. At the same time, many of the QWL programs started in the early 1970s were achieving success, including those of highly visible corporations such as General Motors, Ford and Honeywell, and unions such as the United Automobile Workers.

Today, this second phase of QWL activity continues primarily under the banner of 'employee involvement', rather than of QWL. For many OD practitioners, the term 'EI' signifies (more than the name 'QWL') the growing emphasis on how employees can contribute more to running the organisation so that it can be more flexible, productive and competitive. Recently, the term 'employee empowerment' has been used interchangeably with the name 'employee involvement' – the former suggesting the power inherent in moving decision making downward in the organisation.[45] The term 'employee empowerment' may be too restrictive, however. Because it draws attention to the power aspects of these interventions, it may lead practitioners to neglect other important elements necessary for success, such as information, skills and rewards. Consequently, employee involvement seems a broader and less restrictive banner for these approaches to organisational improvement than employee empowerment.

There is increasing international concern with productivity and with discovering new approaches for enhancing employee involvement in the workplace. For example, at the annual Ecology of Work Conference, co-sponsored by the National Training Laboratories (NTL) Institute and the OD Network, an increasing number of public and private organisations are sharing their EI experiences. In the 1980s, some of the initial fascination with Japanese methods waned, and Americans looked at home for solutions, as evidenced by Peters and Waterman's *In Search of Excellence*[46] and Peters and Austin's *A Passion for Excellence*,[47] both of which topped the *New York Times* non-fiction best-seller list. Extensive plant redesign was undertaken in such well-known companies as Procter and Gamble and Johnson & Johnson, as well as in many smaller organisations.

Although there are major differences among approaches in different countries, EI has also clearly prospered outside the United States, including in Australia. Countries using EI in Western Europe include France, Germany, Denmark, Sweden, Norway, the Netherlands, Italy and the United Kingdom.[48] Although the tremendous changes currently taking place in countries such as Russia, the Czech Republic, Slovakia, Hungary and Bulgaria may have dampened EI efforts, several programs are actively under way.[49] Canada, Mexico, India and Japan are also using EI. Internationally, EI may be considered a set of processes directed at changing the structure of the work situation within a particular cultural environment and under the influence of particular values and philosophies. As a result, in some instances EI has been promoted by unions; in others by management. In some cases, EI has been part of a pragmatic approach to increasing productivity; in other cases, it has been driven by socialist values.[50]

A WORKING DEFINITION OF EMPLOYEE INVOLVEMENT

Employee involvement seeks to increase members' input into decisions that affect organisation performance and employee well-being.[51] It can be described in terms of four key elements that promote worker involvement:[52]

- *Power*. This element of EI includes providing people with sufficient authority to make decisions. Such empowerment can cover a diversity of work-related decisions that involve such things as work methods, task assignments, performance outcomes, customer service and employee selection.
- *Information*. Timely access to relevant information is vital to making effective decisions. Organisations can promote EI by ensuring that necessary information flows freely to those empowered to make decisions.
- *Knowledge and skills*. Employee involvement contributes to organisational effectiveness only to the extent that employees have the requisite skills and knowledge to make good decisions. Organisations can facilitate EI by providing training and development programs for improving members' knowledge and skills.
- *Rewards*. Meaningful opportunities for involvement can provide employees with internal rewards, such as feelings of self-worth and accomplishment. External rewards, such as pay and promotions, can reinforce EI when they are linked directly to performance outcomes that result from participation in decision making.

These four elements – power, information, knowledge and skills, and rewards – contribute to EI success. They determine how much participation in decision making is possible in organisations. The further that all four elements are moved downward throughout the organisation, the greater the employee involvement in decision making. Moreover, because the four elements of EI are interdependent, they must be changed together to obtain positive results. For example, if organisation members are given more power and authority to make decisions but do not have the information or knowledge and skill necessary to make good decisions, then the value of involvement is likely to be negligible. The EI methods that will be described in this section vary in how much involvement is afforded employees.

One manager with a reputation for effective employee involvement is Ralph Norris, chief executive of the Commonwealth Bank of Australia (CBA), profiled in Application 8.3.

APPLiCATiON 8.3

NORRIS READY TO RISE TO THE CHALLENGE

Commonwealth Bank chief executive-elect Ralph Norris is keen to get a few things straight. He is not a union buster, double-digit earnings growth is an 'aspirational target', not a promise, and he is happy to support the Wallabies rugby team. Just not when they are playing the All Blacks.

Much has been said about the 56-year-old Aucklander since he was appointed to one of the biggest jobs in corporate Australia. . . . His track record at Auckland Savings Bank and Air New Zealand has been widely praised, as has his ability to overcome the onset of diabetes late in life and re-enter the workforce in a high-profile CEO position.

Norris, who will start with a potential remuneration package of $7.6 million, is conscious of setting realistic expectations. 'I'm not underestimating the challenge,' he said. . . . 'I realise I'm going to have to work very hard and develop strategies that will enhance Commonwealth's strong position and that's against a market that is already slowing. I never said that I vowed double-digit growth. I said my objective would be double-digit growth but I think all objectives should have a degree of stretch and aspiration about them. We need to be aiming for CBA to grow a little bit faster than the market.'

Norris's personal views have also been dragged into the spotlight as questions re-emerged about a letter he and his wife signed late last year opposing legal recognition for same-sex couples. The letter was private, he said, and not signed in his capacity as a business leader. He did not expect it to be made public. 'I'm very much of the view that organisations are made up of diverse groups of people and that from diversity comes strength. I want to make sure that people understand I respect people regardless of their race, creed, sexual orientation or whatever.'

On the banking front, Norris has his work cut out for him. Analysts are starting to downgrade their recommendations on the sector because of the slowing economy. Competition from foreign players such as HBOS and Citigroup is gnawing away at CBA's $76 billion retail deposit base. And the bank is fighting a legal battle with the Finance Sector Union over the 3700 job cuts involved in the 'Which New Bank' restructure. 'As I've always said, I'm not anti-union, I'm pro-staff,' Norris said. 'Air New Zealand was a highly unionised organisation and there were huge fears that I was going to come into Air NZ and potentially try and de-unionise the organisation. That wasn't the case; I spent a lot of time trying to engage the unions.'

He is not about to overhaul his management team either, subject to their performance and commitment. 'If people perform well, want to be part of the team and operate in the best interests of the company, then nobody should have any fears. I'm not going into the job as an axe wielder.'

Some analysts still predict there will be executive departures as part of the regime change. But Norris disagrees. He said he has already had conversations with internal candidates who missed out on the job, rumoured to include head of business banking Michael Katz and head of wealth management Stuart Grimshaw. 'They were good conversations. We're talking about very competent, professional executives who by their very nature are not going to make knee-jerk reactions. All I can do is give people an insight into the way that I operate. People have to be comfortable working for a chief executive.'

It is difficult to find any major failings in Norris's career so far. ASB's market share grew from 10% to 16% during his 10-year reign, which ended in 2001 when he decided to get his health back on track. The bank was a pioneer in online and telephone banking and its business model was used as the framework for CBA's 'Which New Bank' overhaul. 'ASB was ahead of its time in how they used technology, and in their customer-focused approach,' Telecom New Zealand chief executive Theresa Gattung said, adding that Norris was 'incredibly well-regarded and well-liked' by his peers.

Air NZ's former deputy chief executive, Andrew Miller, said one key feature of Norris's management style was his accessibility. 'His door's always open. At Air New Zealand he set up a lot of communication channels directly to the front line,' said Mr Miller, who now heads the consulting arm of the Sydney-based Centre for Asia Pacific Aviation. 'He'd give out his telephone number, email address and anybody could write to him. So if you had a problem or an issue and you felt it wasn't being addressed you could send him a note about it,' Mr Miller said. He said anyone within the airline, from an engineer, crew member to executive, was encouraged to give feedback.

Source: Lisa Murray and Scott Rochfort, 'Norris ready to rise to the challenge', *Sydney Morning Herald*, 21/6/05.

Critical Thinking Question: Having an open door policy might be a popular management strategy, but to what extent do you think it would be feasible for the CEO of one of Australia's biggest companies?

HOW EMPLOYEE INVOLVEMENT AFFECTS PRODUCTIVITY

Attempts to explain this positive linkage between EI and productivity have traditionally followed the idea that by giving people more involvement in work decisions, they will become more satisfied with their work. Satisfaction, in turn, should improve productivity. There is growing evidence that this satisfaction-causes-productivity premise is too simplistic and sometimes wrong.

A more realistic explanation for how EI interventions can affect productivity is shown in Figure 8.7. EI practices, such as participation in workplace decisions, can improve productivity in at least three ways.[53] First, such interventions can improve communication and co-ordination among employees and organisational departments. This can increase productivity by helping to integrate different jobs or departments contributing to an overall task. Second, EI interventions can improve employee motivation, particularly when they satisfy important individual needs. Motivation is translated into improved performance when people have the necessary skills and knowledge to perform well and when the technology and work situation allow people to affect productivity. Third, EI practices can improve the capabilities of employees, thus enabling them to perform better. For example, attempts at increasing employee participation in decision making generally include skill training in group problem solving and communication.

The secondary effects of EI are shown in Figure 8.8. EI practices can increase employee well-being and satisfaction by providing a better work environment and a more fulfilling job. Improved productivity can also increase satisfaction, particularly when it leads to greater rewards. Increased employee satisfaction, deriving from EI interventions and increased productivity, can ultimately have a still greater impact on productivity by attracting good employees to join and remain with the organisation.

In sum, EI interventions are expected to increase productivity by improving communication and co-ordination, employee motivation and individual capabilities. They can also influence productivity by means of the secondary effects of increased employee well-being and satisfaction. Although a growing body of research supports these relationships,[54] there is considerable debate over the strength of the association between EI and productivity.[55] So far, organisations have tended to implement only relatively modest levels of EI, with correspondingly moderate improvements in performance and satisfaction.

Figure 8.7 How employee involvement affects productivity

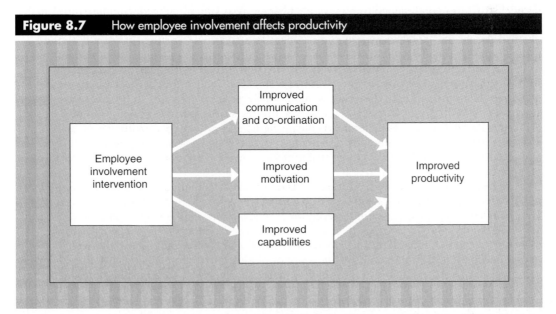

Source: From 'Productivity and the quality of work life', Edward E. Lawler, III, and Gerald E. Ledford, Jr., *National Productivity Review,* Winter 1981–82, pp. 23–36. Reproduced by permission of John Wiley & Sons.

Figure 8.8 Secondary effects on productivity

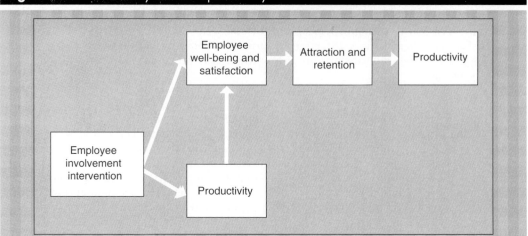

Source: From 'Productivity and the quality of work life', Edward E. Lawler, III, and Gerald E. Ledford, Jr., *National Productivity Review,* Winter 1981–82, pp. 23–36. Reproduced by permission of John Wiley & Sons.

Employee involvement applications

This section describes examples of three major EI applications that vary in the amount of power, information, knowledge and skills, and rewards that are moved downward throughout the organisation (from least to most involvement):
- parallel structures, including co-operative union–management projects and quality circles
- high-involvement organisations
- total quality management.

PARALLEL STRUCTURES

Parallel structures are designed to involve members in resolving ill-defined, complex problems and to build adaptability into bureaucratic organisations.[56] Also known as 'collateral structures', 'dualistic structures' or 'shadow structures',[57] parallel structures operate in tandem with the formal organisation. They provide members with an alternative setting in which to address problems and to propose innovative solutions free from formal work demands. For example, members may attend periodic off-site meetings where they can explore ways of improving quality in their work area; or they may be temporarily assigned to a special project or facility, such as Lockheed's 'skunkworks', to devise new products or solutions to organisational problems. Parallel structures facilitate problem solving and change by providing time and resources for members to think, talk and act in completely new ways. Consequently, norms and procedures for working in parallel structures are entirely different from those of the formal organisation.

Parallel structures fall at the lower end of the EI scale. Member participation is typically restricted to making proposals and to offering suggestions for change. Subsequent decisions about implementing proposals are reserved for management. Membership in parallel structures also tends to be limited, primarily to volunteers and to the numbers of employees for which there are adequate resources. Management heavily influences the conditions under which parallel structures operate. It controls the amount of authority that members have in making recommendations, the amount of information that is shared with them, the amount of training they receive to increase their knowledge and skills, and the amount of monetary rewards for participation. Because parallel structures offer limited amounts of EI, they are most appropriate for organisations with little or no history of employee participation, plus top-down management styles and bureaucratic cultures.

A parallel structure typically consists of a steering committee that provides overall direction and authority, and a number of small groups with norms and operating procedures that promote a climate conducive to innovation, learning and group problem solving. Zand describes these structures as having the following three characteristics:[58]

- All information channels are open so that managers and others can communicate directly, without using formal communication channels.
- A major norm is that individuals operating within the collateral structure can get problem-solving assistance from anyone in the formal organisation.
- As both organisations remain intact, inputs to the formal organisation are outputs from the parallel organisation. The final decisions occur within the formal structure.

Parallel learning structures are typically implemented in the following six steps:[59]

1 *Define the parallel structure's purpose and scope.* Organisational diagnosis can help to clarify how a parallel structure can address specific problems and issues, such as productivity, absenteeism or service quality. In addition, management training in the use of parallel structures can include: discussions about the commitment and resources necessary to implement them; the openness needed to examine organisational practices, operations and policies; and the willingness to experiment and learn.

2 *Form a steering committee.* This committee performs the following six tasks:

   - refining the scope and purpose of the parallel structure

   - developing a vision for the effort

   - guiding the creation and implementation of the structure

   - establishing the linkage mechanisms between the parallel structure and the formal organisation

   - creating problem-solving groups and activities

   - ensuring the support of senior management.

   OD practitioners can play an important role in the formation of the steering committee. First, they can help to develop and maintain group norms of learning and innovation. These set the tone for problem solving throughout the parallel structure. Second, practitioners can help the committee create a vision statement that refines the structure's purpose and promotes ownership of it. Third, OD practitioners can help committee members develop and specify objectives and strategies, organisational expectations, and required resources and potential rewards for participating in the parallel structure.

3 *Communicate with organisation members.* Communicating the purpose, procedures and rewards from participation in the parallel structure can help to gain that involvement. Moreover, employee participation in the development of the vision and purpose for the parallel structure can increase ownership and visibly demonstrate the 'new way' of working.

4 *Form employee problem-solving groups.* Their formation involves selecting and training group members, establishing problems for the groups to work on and providing appropriate facilitation. Selecting group members is important as success is often a function of group membership.[60] Members need to represent the appropriate hierarchical levels, expertise, functions and constituencies that have relevance to the problems at hand. This allows the parallel structure to identify and communicate with the formal structure. It also provides the necessary resources for solving the problems. Once formed, the groups need appropriate training. This may include discussions about the vision of the parallel structure, the specific problems to be addressed and the way they will be solved.

   Another key resource for parallel structures is facilitation for the problem-solving groups. Although this can be expensive, it can yield important benefits in problem-solving efficiency and quality. Group members are asked to solve problems by cutting through traditional hierarchical and functional boundaries. Facilitators can pay special attention to processes that require disparate groups to co-operate. They can help members identify and resolve problem-solving issues within and between groups.

5   *Address the problems and issues.* Generally, groups in parallel structures solve problems by using an action research process. They diagnose specific problems, plan appropriate solutions, and implement and evaluate them. Problem solving can be facilitated when the groups and the steering committee relate effectively to each other.

6   *Implement and evaluate the changes.* Change proposals need to have the support of the steering committee and the formal authority structure. As changes are implemented, the organisation needs information about their effects. This lets members know how successful the changes have been and whether or not they need to be modified.

Parallel structures create a source of involvement beyond that found in most bureaucratic organisations. For many people, especially lower-level employees, this opportunity to influence the formal organisation leads to increased work satisfaction and task effectiveness.[61] Parallel structures can also improve organisational functioning. Although parallel structures promise to free up organisations and their members for innovative problem solving and personal development, little controlled research on the approach has been published. The evidence is primarily case study and anecdotal. A recent study of parallel structures composed of employee-involvement teams suggests that unless these structures are carefully integrated with the formal organisation, they are unlikely to have much impact on the organisation and are likely to be abandoned.[62]

Co-operative union–management projects

Co-operative union–management projects are one of the oldest EI interventions. Typically, these projects seek to improve both worker satisfaction and organisational effectiveness through a parallel organisation. They are mostly associated with the original QWL movement and its focus on workplace change. As a result, only moderate increases in power, information, knowledge and skills, and rewards are achieved. Essentially they have the same structural characteristics:

•   *Quality-of-working life committee.* This committee is a top-level joint union–management committee that serves as the basic centre for planning.

•   *External consultants.* The consultant provides QWL training for all participants. In most projects the co-operative union–management project committee selects the consultant or consultant group.[63]

•   *External researchers.* Separate roles are created for the change agent and the evaluation researcher. It is assumed that keeping these functions separate would allow the consultant to be concerned with client needs and development, and would also permit a more objective assessment of change. Therefore, each QWL program has a separate research team that uses a partially standardised package of measurement instruments.[64]

As experience has increased and the number of projects has grown, the general design has evolved to include the following additional steps:

•   *Multiple-level committees.* It is frequently necessary to establish more than one labour–management committee at a number of selected levels in the organisation to reflect the differing interests and knowledge. These are permanent working committees in departments, plants or work units that deal with day-to-day project activities.

•   *Ad hoc committees.* In many instances, the labour–management committee initiates a particular project that involves workers and managers in a specific part of the organisation. At the same time, employees themselves frequently initiate action towards a particular goal. In such cases, an ad hoc committee is established to bring about change. Such committees have a specific task and a limited lifetime.

The 1983 Accord between the ruling Australian Labor Party and the Australian Council of Trade Unions created a favourable framework for employee participation, further strengthened by National Wage Decisions. However, the Workplace Industrial Relations Survey of 1991 revealed that management–employee consultation remained sporadic on most issues. Although some firms – such as Australia Post, Ford, Lend Lease, Telecom and Woodlawn Mining Co. – demonstrated a commitment to information sharing, consultation and a measure of employee participation, they were exceptions rather than the rule. A crucial factor in the extension of employee participation and industrial democracy in the 1990s was the restructuring and development of unions as well as managerial attitudes and approaches.[65]

A few studies raise caution about co-operative union–management programs. In a study of five plant-level projects, only two of the five plants reported improvements in productivity and union–management relationships. In three of the five plants, relations among managers improved and grievance levels decreased. However, contrary to expectations, the more successful plants had neither clear agreement on the goals of the EI program nor a jointly developed statement of philosophy, and both union and management leadership tried to subvert the process.[66] Another study covering 25 manufacturing plants showed that involvement in joint union–management programs had no impact on economic performance.[67]

Studies of unionists' attitudes towards union–management co-operative programs found a generally positive stance among those directly involved in such programs.[68] The researchers cautioned, however, that the positive findings may reflect self-justification processes, where respondents assess programs positively because of the time and effort they have invested. In a study of nine union and nine non-union EI projects, union involvement improved the program's design and implementation, but there were no differences in the outcomes between the union and non-union efforts.[69] On the other hand, in a longitudinal study of three union–management projects, the union increased its influence over both traditional decisions, such as scheduling and vacations, and non-traditional decisions, such as the implementation of new technology and helping to improve customer service. In addition, when attitudes regarding the program's success were positive, both management and unionists were viewed as positively contributing to the outcomes. However, when the EI program was perceived as unsuccessful, management was viewed as the reason for poor performance. The authors concluded that supporting a co-operative union–management effort is a no-lose situation for the union.[70] Still another study suggests that joint EI programs can inadvertently benefit low-seniority workers at the expense of high-seniority participants.[71] The programs studied provided easier access to management for junior employees, thus upsetting the time-honoured, benefits-accrue-to-seniority-first tradition of unionised settings.

HIGH-INVOLVEMENT ORGANISATIONS

Over the past few years, an increasing number of EI projects have been aimed at creating high-involvement organisations. Typically applied to new industrial plants, this EI intervention attempts to create organisational conditions that support high levels of employee participation. What makes these interventions unique is the comprehensive nature of the design process. Unlike parallel structures that do not alter the formal organisation, almost all organisation features are designed jointly by management and workers to promote high levels of involvement and performance, including structure, work design, information and control systems, physical layout, personnel policies and reward systems.

Design features for a participative system

High-involvement organisations are designed to have features that are congruent with one other. For example, in high-involvement organisations, employees have considerable influence over decisions. To support this decentralised philosophy, employees are given extensive training in problem-solving techniques, plant operation and organisational policies. In addition, both operational and issue-oriented information is shared widely and is easily obtained by employees. Finally, rewards are closely tied to unit performance, as well as to knowledge and skill levels. These different aspects of the organisation are mutually reinforcing and form a coherent pattern that contributes to employee involvement. Table 8.7 presents a list of compatible design elements characterising a high-involvement organisation.[72]

Most such organisations include several, if not all, of these features.

- *Flat, lean organisation structures* contribute to involvement by pushing the scheduling, planning and controlling functions typically performed by management and staff groups towards the shop floor.

Table 8.7   Definitions of organisation development

- Organisation structure
  1 Flat
  2 Lean
  3 Mini-enterprise-oriented
  4 Team-based
  5 Participative council or structure
- Job design
  1 Individually enriched
  2 Self-managing teams
- Information system
  1 Open
  2 Inclusive
  3 Tied to jobs
  4 Decentralised; team-based
  5 Participatively set goals and standards
- Career system
  1 Tracks and counselling available
  2 Open job posting
- Selection
  1 Realistic job preview
  2 Team-based
  3 Potential and process-skill oriented

- Training
  1 Heavy commitment
  2 Peer training
  3 Economic education
  4 Interpersonal skills
- Reward system
  1 Open
  2 Skill-based
  3 Gain sharing or ownership
  4 Flexible benefits
  5 All salary
  6 Egalitarian perquisites
- Personnel policies
  1 Stability of employment
  2 Participatively established through representative group
- Physical layout
  1 Around organisational structure
  2 Egalitarian
  3 Safe and pleasant

Source: Reproduced by permission of the publisher from Edward Lawler III, 'Increasing worker involvement to enhance organizational effectiveness: Design features for a participation system'; in P. Goodman and associates, *Change in Organizations*, San Francisco, Jossey-Bass, 1982.

- *Job designs* that provide employees with high levels of discretion, task variety and meaningful feedback can enhance involvement.
- *Open information systems* that are tied to jobs or work teams provide the necessary information for employees to participate meaningfully in decision making.
- *Career systems* that provide different tracks for advancement, and counselling to help people choose appropriate paths can help employees to plan and prepare for long-term development in the organisation.
- *Selection of employees* for high-involvement organisations can be improved through a realistic job preview that provides information about what it will be like to work in such situations.
- *Training employees* to gain the necessary knowledge and skills to participate effectively in decision making is a heavy commitment at high-involvement organisations.
- *Reward systems* that can contribute to employee involvement when information about them is open and rewards are based on acquiring new skills, as well as on sharing gains from improved performance.
- *Personnel policies* that are participatively set and encourage stability of employment provide employees with a strong sense of commitment to the organisation.
- *Physical layouts of organisations* can also enhance employee involvement.

These different design features of high-involvement organisations are mutually reinforcing. Moreover, these design components tend to motivate and focus organisational behaviour in a strategic direction and thus can lead to superior effectiveness and competitive advantage, particularly in contrast to more traditionally designed organisations.[73] A survey of 98 high-involvement organisations showed that about 75% of them perceived their performance, relative to that of competitors, as better than average on quality of work life, customer service, productivity, quality and grievance rates.[74] For the high-involvement organisations, voluntary turnover was 2%, substantially below the national average of 13.2%; return on investment was almost four times greater than industry averages; and return on sales was more than five times greater. In Australia, the management at the Burswood Resort Hotel in Western Australia recognised that they wanted to develop problem-solving competencies in their employees and embarked on an empowerment program, acknowledging that achieving an empowered workplace was a long-term initiative that required continued management commitment. Their approach was based on management theory and practice, yet remained flexible to the needs of the hotel's employees and customers. A program was designed and tailored to the hotel's culture and work environment. An empowerment survey was conducted prior to the program and again 18 months after its completion.[75]

These results cannot be expected in all situations, of course. The following situational contingencies seem to favour high-involvement organisations: interdependent technologies, small organisation size, new plant start-ups and conditions under which quality is an important determinant of operating effectiveness.

At present, there is no universally accepted approach to implementing the high-involvement features described here. The actual implementation process is often specific to the situation, and little systematic research has been devoted to understanding the change process itself.[76] Nevertheless, at least two distinct factors seem to characterise how high-involvement organisations are created. First, implementation is generally guided by an explicit statement of values that members want the new organisation to support. A second feature of the implementation process is its participative nature. Managers and employees take active roles in both choosing and implementing the design features. They may be helped by OD practitioners, but the locus of control for the change process resides clearly within the organisation.

WORK DESIGN

This section examines three approaches to work design:

- The engineering approach focuses on efficiency and simplification, and results in traditional job and work group designs.
- A second approach to work design rests on motivational theories and attempts to enrich the work experience. Job enrichment involves designing jobs with high levels of meaning, discretion and knowledge of results.
- The third and most recent approach to work design derives from sociotechnical systems methods. This perspective seeks to optimise both the social and the technical aspects of work systems. It has led to the development of a popular form of work design called 'self-managed teams'.

The section describes each of these perspectives. Then, a contingency framework for integrating the approaches is presented, based on personal and technical factors in the workplace. When work is designed to fit these factors, it is both satisfying and productive.

The engineering approach

The oldest and most prevalent approach to work design is based on engineering concepts and methods. It proposes that the most efficient work designs can be determined by specifying the tasks to be performed, the work methods to be used and the work flow between individuals. The engineering approach is based on the pioneering work of Frederick Taylor, the father of scientific management. He developed ways of analysing and designing work and laid the groundwork for the professional field of industrial engineering.[77]

The engineering approach seeks to scientifically analyse the tasks performed by workers so as to discover those procedures that produce the maximum output with the minimum input of energies and resources.[78] This generally results in work designs with high levels of specialisation and specification. Such designs have several benefits: they allow workers to learn tasks rapidly, they permit short work cycles so that performance can take place with little or no mental effort, and they reduce costs as lower-skilled people can be hired and trained easily and paid relatively low wages.

The engineering approach produces two kinds of work design: traditional jobs and traditional work groups. When one person can complete the work, as is the case with bank tellers and telephone operators, traditional jobs are created. They tend to be simplified, with routine and repetitive tasks having clear specifications concerning time and motion. When the work requires co-ordination between people, such as automobile assembly lines, traditional work groups are developed. They are composed of members who perform relatively routine, yet related, tasks. The overall group task is typically broken into simpler, discrete parts (often called jobs). The tasks and work methods are specified for each part, and the different parts are assigned to group members. Each member performs a routine and repetitive part of the group task. Members' separate task contributions are co-ordinated for overall task achievement through external controls, such as schedules, rigid work flows and supervisors.[79] In the 1950s and 1960s, this method of work design was popularised by the assembly lines of Australian automobile manufacturers, such as GM Holden, and was an important reason for the growth of Australian industry after the Second World War.

The engineering approach to job design is less an OD intervention than a benchmark in history. Critics of the approach argue that the method ignores the social and psychological needs of workers. They suggest that the increasing educational level of the workforce and the substitution of automation for menial labour point to the need for more enriched forms of work, where people have greater discretion and challenge. Moreover, current competitive challenges require a more committed and involved workforce that is able to make on-line decisions and develop performance innovations. Work designed with the employee in mind is more humanly fulfilling and productive than that designed in traditional ways. However, it is important to recognise the strengths of the engineering approach. It remains an important work design intervention as its immediate cost savings and efficiency can easily be measured. It is also well understood and easily implemented and managed.

The motivational approach

The motivational approach to work design views the effectiveness of organisational activities primarily as a function of member needs and satisfaction. It seeks to improve employee performance and satisfaction by enriching jobs. This provides people with opportunities for autonomy, responsibility, closure (doing a complete job) and feedback about performance. Enriched jobs can be found in Australia at such companies as Queensland Golden Circle Limited and Rupnorth Co-operative Limited, among others.

The motivational approach is usually associated with the research of Herzberg, as well as that of Hackman and Oldham. Herzberg's two-factor theory of motivation proposed that certain attributes of work (such as opportunities for advancement and recognition, which he called 'motivators') help to increase job satisfaction.[80] Other attributes (called 'hygiene' factors, such as company policies, working conditions, pay and supervision) do not produce satisfaction but prevent dissatisfaction. Only satisfied workers are motivated to produce.

Although Herzberg's motivational factors sound appealing, increasing doubt has been cast on the underlying theory. For example, motivation and hygiene factors are difficult to put into operation and measure, making implementation and evaluation of the theory difficult. Important worker characteristics that can affect whether or not people will respond favourably to job enrichment were also not included in the theory. Finally, Herzberg's failure to involve employees in the job enrichment process itself does not sit well with most current OD practitioners. Consequently, a second, well-researched approach to job enrichment has been favoured. It focuses on the attributes of the work itself and has resulted in a more scientifically acceptable theory of job enrichment than Herzberg's model. The research of Hackman and Oldham represents this more recent trend in job enrichment.[81]

A large company may have scope to offer employees motivation through the opportunity to take on different positions, and therefore different challenges, as illustrated in Application 8.4.

A PAST MASTER AT LOGISTICS

A change of career must also mean a change of company. That is a common perception but is not necessarily true – especially if you work for FedEx Express, which has more than 138 000 positions in 220 countries. The logistics company has a global network that delivers about 3.2 million packages every day, and employment opportunities arise regularly, especially as it develops new markets and systems.

John Allison, vice-president of human resources for FedEx, never imagined that he would enter the field of logistics, let alone forge a career in human resources. 'My ambition was to become a university professor or an attorney. As a 15 year old, I did not think transport would be my life,' he said.

Mr Allison majored in political science and was studying industrial engineering at Riverside City College in California when he began looking for part-time work in 1984. He found an opening with FedEx and was soon offered a service engineer's job in southern California with the rapidly expanding logistics company. 'The next thing I knew, I was caught up in it,' he said.

Mr Allison, who hailed from San Antonio in Texas, moved to Detroit at the company's request. He moved up to a senior management position in a year and went on to take charge of FedEx's operations in Minnesota. However, the cold troubled him – Minnesota receives an average annual snowfall of 1.77 metres. 'I told my boss I wanted to go south,' Mr Allison said. 'I was looking for a warmer climate and the company offered me the opportunity to open an office in Sydney.'

Soon, Mr Allison began overseeing the acquisition of Rainers Transport and the merger of the Australian and New Zealand branches of Flying Tigers. He was the managing director for three years and became an expert in international operations. That gave him good experience for his next assignment – in Hong Kong. 'We are a flat organisation and tend to move people around a lot,' Mr Allison said.

FedEx saw no reason why a service engineer turned operations specialist should not become vice-president of human resources. 'My first reaction was surprise,' Mr Allison said. 'I used to think the salary cheque came automatically, and then I found out there was a whole apparatus and a team of people to make it all work.' Mr Allison deals with 3000 employees in the Asia–Pacific region.

He found that every new job required the development of new skills and also realised how important it was for human resource professionals to understand the rest of the company's operations. 'Too often, HR is relegated to an administrative function. I do not think this is appropriate in any company. HR ought to have a seat at the table for strategic planning, organisational development and guiding the entire company,' he said.

He has taken to heart the company's philosophy that every line manager also has to be an HR manager. The business depends on managing people. To reinforce this concept, FedEx has come up with ways to praise and reward the contributions of star employees. There is a 'Bravo Zulu' award for outstanding performance, another to recognise concern for human welfare, and the highest – a five-star award – for improving service, profitability and team spirit.

'People issues are never secondary; they are an integral part of our business,' Mr Allison said. 'Lots of companies talk about people being their greatest asset and then lay them off as soon as the economy slows down. We try to run a lean organisation so that we do not put ourselves in trouble in those situations.' About half of the company's recurrent expenditure goes towards salaries and benefits.

The system seems to be working and FedEx has won many accolades for implementing it. It has been one of the '100 Best Companies to Work for in America' for eight years. Last year, it was nominated among the best employers in Hong Kong by Hewitt Associates and was also ranked eighth on Fortune magazine's 'World's Most Admired Companies' list.

Despite this reputation, FedEx has had its share of criticism. In fact, a few dissatisfied customers have posted messages on websites about logistical foul-ups and other service failures. Mr Allison constantly monitors what the blogger community says and is serious about setting right any perceived wrongs. 'Customers are usually very forgiving,' he said. 'But if you make a mistake and do not correct it, then it remains a mistake forever.'

▷▷

To increase its share in the mainland market, FedEx plans to transfer its Asian hub from the Philippines to a new US$150 million facility in Guangzhou. The objective is to expand its service network from 206 mainland cities to 290 cities in four years. The expansion of services will require a well-planned recruitment strategy. Mr Allison plans to move people from Hong Kong to Guangzhou and initiate training programs. 'I am very lucky to have worked in so many countries and done different things,' he said. The experience made it easier to anticipate needs and co-ordinate new developments, Mr Allison said.

Source: Angie Wong, 'A past master at logistics', *South China Morning Post*, 4/2/06.

Critical Thinking Question: The article focuses on the benefits to the individual staff member of position change within a single organisation. What might the benefits, and difficulties, be for the organisation itself?

THE CORE DIMENSIONS OF JOBS

Considerable research has been devoted to defining and understanding core job dimensions.[82] Figure 8.9 summarises the Hackman and Oldham model of job design. Five core dimensions of work affect three critical psychological states, which in turn produce personal and job outcomes. These outcomes include high internal work motivation, high-quality work performance, satisfaction with the work, and low absenteeism and turnover.

Figure 8.9 The relationships among the core job dimensions – the critical individual differences

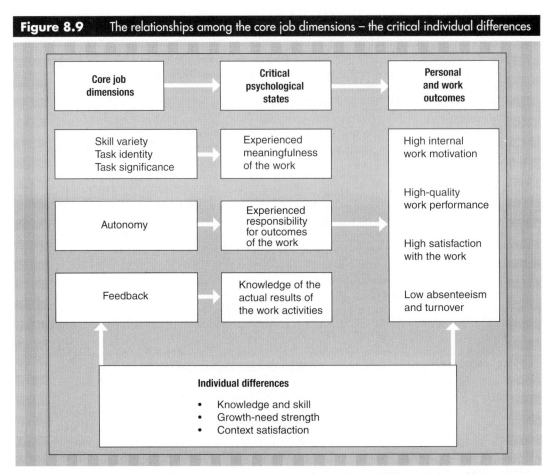

Source: J. Hackman and G. Oldham, *Work Redesign*, copyright © 1980 by Addison-Wesley Publishing Co. Inc.

Not all people react in similar ways to job enrichment interventions. Individual differences – such as a worker's knowledge and skill levels, growth-need strength and satisfaction with contextual factors – moderate the relationships between core dimensions, psychological states and outcomes. 'Worker knowledge and skill' refers to the education and experience levels that characterise the workforce. If employees lack the appropriate skills, for example, increasing skill variety may not improve a job's meaningfulness. Similarly, if workers lack the intrinsic motivation to grow and develop personally, attempts to provide them with increased autonomy may be resisted. (We discuss growth needs more fully in the last section of this chapter.) Finally, contextual factors include reward systems, supervisory style and co-worker satisfaction. When the employee is unhappy with the work context, attempts to enrich the work itself may be unsuccessful.

BARRIERS TO JOB ENRICHMENT

As the application of job enrichment has spread, several obstacles to significant job restructuring have been identified. Most of these barriers exist in the organisational context within which the job design is executed. Other organisational systems and practices, whether technical, managerial or personnel, can affect both the implementation of job enrichment and the life span of whatever changes are made. At least four organisational systems can constrain the implementation of job enrichment:[83]

1   *The technical system.* The technology of an organisation can limit job enrichment by constraining the number of ways in which jobs can be changed. Technology may also set an 'enrichment ceiling'. Some types of work, such as continuous process production systems, may be naturally enriched, so there is little more that can be gained from a job enrichment intervention.

2   *The personnel system.* Personnel systems can constrain job enrichment by creating formalised job descriptions that are rigidly defined and that limit flexibility in changing people's job duties.

3   *The control system.* Control systems, such as budgets, production reports and accounting practices, can limit the complexity and challenge of jobs within the system.

4   *The supervisory system.* Supervisors determine to a large extent the amount of autonomy and feedback that subordinates can experience. To the extent that supervisors use autocratic methods and control work-related feedback, jobs will be difficult, if not impossible, to enrich.

Once these implementation constraints have been overcome, other factors determine whether the effects of job enrichment are strong and lasting.[84] Consistent with the contingency approach to OD, the staying power of job enrichment depends largely on how well it fits and is supported by other organisational practices, such as those associated with training, career development, compensation and supervision. These practices need to be congruent with, and to reinforce, jobs that have high amounts of discretion, skill variety and meaningful feedback.

RESULTS OF JOB ENRICHMENT

Hackman and Oldham reported on more than 1000 people in about 100 different jobs in more than a dozen organisations.[85] In general, they found that employees whose jobs were high on the core dimensions were more satisfied and motivated than those whose jobs were low on the dimensions. The core dimensions were also related to such behaviours as absenteeism and performance, although the relationship was not strong for performance. In addition, they found that responses were more positive for people with high growth needs than for those with weaker ones. Similarly, recent research has shown that enriched jobs are strongly correlated with mental ability.[86] Enriching the jobs of workers with low growth needs or with low knowledge and skills is more likely to produce frustration than satisfaction.

An impressive amount of research has been done on Hackman and Oldham's approach to job enrichment. In addition, several studies have extended and refined Hackman and Oldham's approach to both produce more reliable data[87] and incorporate other moderators, such as the need for achievement and job longevity.[88] In general, research has supported the proposed relationships between job characteristics and outcomes, including the moderating effects of growth needs, knowledge and skills, and context satisfaction.[89] In regard to context satisfaction, for example, research indicates that employee turnover, dissatisfaction and withdrawal are associated with dark offices, a lack of privacy and high worker densities.[90]

Reviews of the job enrichment research also report positive effects. An analysis of 28 studies concluded that the job characteristics are positively related to job satisfaction, particularly for people with high growth needs.[91] Another review concluded that job enrichment is effective at reducing employee turnover.[92] A different examination of 28 job enrichment studies reported overwhelming positive results.[93] Improvements in quality and cost measures were reported slightly more frequently than improvements in employee attitudes and quantity of production. However, the studies suffered from methodological weaknesses that suggest that the positive findings should be viewed with some caution. Another review of 16 job enrichment studies showed mixed results.[94] Thirteen of the programs were developed and implemented solely by management. These studies showed significant reduction in absenteeism, turnover and grievances, and improvements in quality of production in only about half of the cases where these variables were measured. The three studies with high levels of employee participation in the change program showed improvements in these variables in all cases where they were measured. Although it is difficult to generalise from such a small number of studies, employee participation in the job enrichment program appears to enhance the success of such interventions.

The sociotechnical systems approach

The sociotechnical systems (STS) approach is the most extensive body of scientific and applied work underlying employee involvement and innovative work designs today. Its techniques and design principles derive from extensive action research in both public and private organisations across a diversity of national cultures. This section reviews the conceptual foundations of the STS approach and then describes its most popular application: self-managed work teams.

CONCEPTUAL BACKGROUND

Sociotechnical systems theory was originally developed at the Tavistock Institute of Human Relations in London and has spread to most industrialised nations in a little more than 45 years. In Europe, and particularly Scandinavia, STS interventions are almost synonymous with work design and employee involvement. In Canada and the United States, STS concepts and methods underlie many of the innovative work designs and team-based structures that are so prevalent in today's organisations. Intel and Procter and Gamble are among the many organisations applying the STS approach to transform how work is designed and performed. Sociotechnical systems theory is based on two fundamental premises:
- that an organisation or work unit is a combined, social-plus-technical system
- that this system is open in relation to its environment.[95]

Sociotechnical system

The first assumption suggests that whenever human beings are organised to perform tasks, a joint system is operating – a sociotechnical system. This system consists of two independent, yet related, parts: a social part that includes the people performing the tasks and the relationships among them, and a technical part consisting of the tools, techniques and methods for task performance. These two parts are independent of each other by virtue of each following a different set of behavioural laws. The social part operates according to biological and psychosocial laws, whereas the technical part functions according to mechanical and physical laws. Nevertheless, the two parts are related because they must act together to accomplish tasks.

Hence, the term 'sociotechnical' signifies the joint relationship that must occur between the social and technical parts, and the word 'system' communicates that this connection results in a unified whole.

Because a sociotechnical system is composed of social and technical parts, it follows that it will produce two kinds of outcomes: products, such as goods and services, and social and psychological consequences, such as job satisfaction and commitment. The key issue is how to design the relationship between the two parts so that these outcomes are both positive (referred to as 'joint optimisation').

Sociotechnical practitioners design work and organisations so that the social and technical parts work well together, producing high levels of product and human satisfaction. This contrasts with the engineering approach to designing work, which tends to focus on the technical component and worries about fitting in people later. This often leads to mediocre performance at high social costs. This also contrasts with the motivation approach that views work design in terms of human fulfilment. This approach can lead to satisfied employees, but inefficient work processes.

Environmental relationship

The second major premise underlying STS theory concerns the fact that such systems are open to their environments. As discussed in Chapter 5, open systems need to interact with their environments to survive and develop. The environment provides the STS with necessary inputs of energy, raw materials and information, while the STS, in turn, provides the environment with products and services. The key issue here is how to design the interface between the STS and its environment so that the system has sufficient freedom to function while exchanging effectively with the environment. In what is typically referred to as boundary management, STS practitioners attempt to structure environmental relationships to both protect the system from external disruptions and to facilitate the exchange of necessary resources and information. This enables the STS to adapt to changing conditions and to influence the environment in favourable directions.

In summary, sociotechnical systems theory suggests that effective work systems jointly optimise the relationship between their social and technical parts. Moreover, such systems effectively manage the boundary that separates them from, while relating them to, the environment. This allows them to exchange with the environment while protecting themselves from external disruptions.

SELF-MANAGED WORK TEAMS

The most prevalent application of the STS approach is self-managed work teams.[96] Alternatively referred to as 'self-directed work teams', 'self-regulating work teams' or 'high-performance work teams', these work designs consist of members performing interrelated tasks.[97] Self-managed work teams are typically responsible for a whole product or service, or a major part of a larger production process. They control members' task behaviours and make decisions about task assignments and work methods. In many cases, the team sets its own production goals, within broader organisational limits, and may be responsible for support services, such as maintenance, purchasing and quality control. Team members are generally expected to learn many, if not all, of the jobs within the team's control and frequently are paid on the basis of knowledge and skills rather than seniority. When pay is based on performance, team rather than individual performance is used.

Figure 8.10 is a model explaining how self-managed work teams perform. It summarises current STS research and shows how teams can be designed for high performance. Although the model is mainly based on experience with teams that perform the daily work of the organisation (work teams), it also has relevance to other team designs, such as problem-solving teams, management teams, cross-functional integrating teams and employee involvement teams.[98]

The model shows that team performance and member satisfaction follow directly from how well the team functions. This includes how well members communicate and co-ordinate with

Figure 8.10 · Model of self-managed work teams

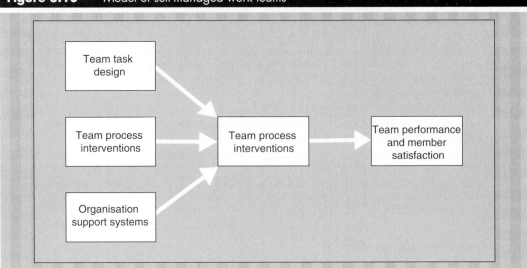

each other, resolve conflicts and problems, and make and implement task-relevant decisions. Team functioning, in turn, is influenced by three major inputs:

* team task design
* team process interventions
* organisation support systems.

Because these inputs affect how well teams function and subsequently perform, they are key intervention targets for designing and implementing self-managed work teams.

APPLICATION STEPS

Sociotechnical systems work designs have been implemented in a variety of settings, including manufacturing firms, hospitals, schools and government agencies. Although the specific implementation strategy is tailored to the situation, a common method of change underlies many of these applications. It generally involves high worker participation in the work design and implementation process. Such participative work design allows employees to translate their special knowledge of the work situation into relevant work designs. Because employees have ownership over the design process, they tend to be highly committed to implementing the work designs.[99] STS applications generally proceed in six steps:[100]

1   *Sanctioning the design effort.* In this stage, workers are provided with the necessary protection and support to diagnose their work system and to design an appropriate work design.
2   *Diagnosing the work system.* Knowledge of existing operations (or of intended operations, in the case of a new work system) is the basis for designing an appropriate work design. Sociotechnical systems practitioners have devised diagnostic models applicable to work systems making products or delivering services.
3   *Generating appropriate designs.* Although this typically results in self-managed work teams, it is important to emphasise that, in some cases, the diagnosis may reveal that tasks are not very interdependent and that an individual-job work design, such as an enriched job, might be more appropriate.

      The output of this design step specifies the new work design. In the case of self-managed work teams, this would include the team's mission and goals, an ideal work flow, the skills and knowledge required of team members, a plan for training members to meet those requirements and a list of the decisions the team will make now, as well as the ones it should make over time as members develop greater skills and knowledge.
4   *Specifying support systems.* When self-managed work teams are designed, for example, the basis for pay and measurement systems may need to be changed from individual to team performance to facilitate necessary task interaction among workers.

5   *Implementing and evaluating the work designs.* For self-managing work teams, implementation generally requires considerable training to enable workers to gain the necessary technical and social skills to perform multiple tasks, and to control members' task behaviours. Organisation development consultants often help team members carry out these tasks with a major emphasis on helping them gain competence in this area. Evaluation of the work design is necessary both to guide the implementation process and to assess the overall effectiveness of the design. In some cases, the evaluation information suggests the need for further diagnosis and redesign efforts.

6   *Continual change and improvement.* The ability to continually design and redesign work needs to be built into existing work designs. Members must have the skills and knowledge to continually assess their work unit and to make necessary changes and improvements.

Results of self-managed teams

Research on sociotechnical systems design efforts is extensive. For example, a 1994 bibliography by researchers at Eindhoven University of Technology in the Netherlands found 3082 English-language studies.[101] And, as with reports on job enrichment, most of the published reports on self-managed teams show favourable results.[102]

A series of famous case studies at General Foods' Gaines Pet Food/Topeka plant, the Saab-Scania engine assembly plant and Volvo's Kalmar and Udevalla plants provides one set of positive findings. The Gaines Pet Food plant operated at an overhead rate some 33% below that of traditional plants.[103] It reported annual variable cost savings of US$600 000, one of the best safety records in the company, turnover rates far below average and high levels of job satisfaction. A long-term, external evaluation of the groups at the Gaines plant[104] attributed savings related to work innovation at about US$1 million a year, and, despite a variety of problems, productivity increased in every year but one over a decade of operation. The plant has maintained one of the highest product quality ratings at General Foods since its opening.

Extensive research on self-managing groups has been done by Saab-Scania.[105] The first group was established in 1969, and four years later there were 130 production groups. These groups have generally shown improvements in production and employee attitudes and decreases in unplanned work stoppages and turnover rates. Interestingly, when workers from the United States visited Saab's engine assembly plant, they reported that work was too fast and that lunch breaks were too short.[106] A Saab executive commented that the visitors had not stayed long enough to become completely proficient, causing their complaint that the pace was too fast.

The widely publicised use of self-managing groups at Volvo's automotive plant in Kalmar, Sweden, has also shown positive results.[107] The Kalmar factory opened in July 1974, and by the following year it was operating at 100% efficiency. As a reference point, highly productive automobile plants normally operate at about 80% of engineering standards. Interviews with workers and union officials indicated that the quality of work life was considerably better than in assembly jobs that they had had in the past. In addition, Volvo's Udevalla plant reported significant quality improvements and higher productivity than in comparable plants.[108]

A second set of studies supporting the positive impact of sociotechnical design teams comes from research comparing self-managed teams with other interventions. For example, probably one of the most thorough assessments of self-managing groups is a longitudinal study conducted in a food-processing plant in the midwest of the United States.[109] Self-managing groups were created as part of an overall revamping of a major part of the plant's production facilities. The effects of the intervention were extremely positive. One year after start-up, production was 133% higher than originally planned, while start-up costs were 7.7% lower than planned. Employee attitudes were extremely positive towards the group design. These positive effects, however, did not result solely from the self-managing design. The intervention also included survey feedback for diagnostic purposes and changes in technology, the physical work setting and management. These kinds of changes are common in self-managing group projects. They suggest that such designs may require supporting changes in other organisational dimensions, such as technology, management style and physical setting, in order to facilitate the development of self-managed teams.

This study also permitted a comparison of self-managing groups with job enrichment, which occurred in another department of the company. Both interventions included survey feedback. The self-managing project involved technological changes, whereas the job enrichment program did not. The results showed that both interventions had similar positive effects in terms of employee attitudes. However, only the self-managing project had significant improvements in productivity and costs. Again, the productivity improvements cannot be totally attributed to the self-managed teams, but were also the result of the technological changes. Although the majority of studies report positive effects of self-managing groups, some research suggests a more mixed assessment.

Designing work for technical and personal needs

This section has described three approaches to work design: engineering, motivational and sociotechnical. However, trade-offs and conflicts among the approaches must be recognised. The engineering approach produces traditional jobs and work groups, and focuses on efficient performance. This approach tends to downplay employee needs and emphasise economic outcomes. The motivational approach strives to design jobs that are stimulating and demanding, and highlights the importance of employee need satisfaction. Research suggests, however, that increased satisfaction does not necessarily produce improvements in productivity. Finally, the sociotechnical systems approach attempts to optimise both social and technical aspects. Despite this integrative goal, STS has not produced consistent research results.

In this final section, we attempt to integrate the three perspectives by providing a contingency framework that suggests all three approaches can be effective when applied in the appropriate circumstances. Work design involves creating jobs and work groups for high levels of employee satisfaction and productivity. Considerable research shows that achieving such results depends on designing work to match specific factors that operate in the work setting. These factors have to do with the technology for producing goods and services and the personal needs of employees. When work is designed to fit or match these factors, it is most likely to be both productive and humanly satisfying.

TECHNICAL FACTORS

Two key dimensions can affect change on the shop floor: technical interdependence, or the extent to which co-operation among workers is required to produce a product or service; and technical uncertainty, or the amount of information processing and decision making that employees must do in order to complete a task.[110] In general, the degree of technical interdependence determines whether work should be designed for individual jobs or work groups. With low technical interdependence and little need for worker co-operation – as, for example, in field sales and data entry – work can be designed for individual jobs. Conversely, when technical interdependence is high and employees must co-operate – as in production processes such as coal mining, assembly lines and software writing – work should be designed for groups composed of people who perform interacting tasks.

The second dimension, technical uncertainty, determines whether work should be designed for external forms of control, such as supervision, scheduling or standardisation, or for worker self-control. When technical uncertainty is low and little information has to be processed by employees, work can be designed for external control, such as might be found on assembly lines and in other forms of repetitive work. On the other hand, when technical uncertainty is high and people must process information and make decisions, work should be designed for high levels of employee self-control, such as might be found in professional work and troubleshooting tasks.

Figure 8.11 shows the different types of work designs that are most effective, from a purely technical perspective, for different combinations of interdependence and uncertainty. In quadrant 1, where technical interdependence and uncertainty are both low, such as might be found in data entry, jobs should be designed traditionally with limited amounts of employee interaction and self-control. When task interdependence is high yet uncertainty is low (quadrant 2), such as work occurring on assembly lines, work should be designed for traditional work groups in which employee interaction is scheduled and self-control is limited. In quadrant 3, where technical interdependence is low but uncertainty is high, as in field sales, work should be structured for individual jobs with internal forms of control, as in enriched jobs. Finally, when

Figure 8.11   Work designs that optimise technology

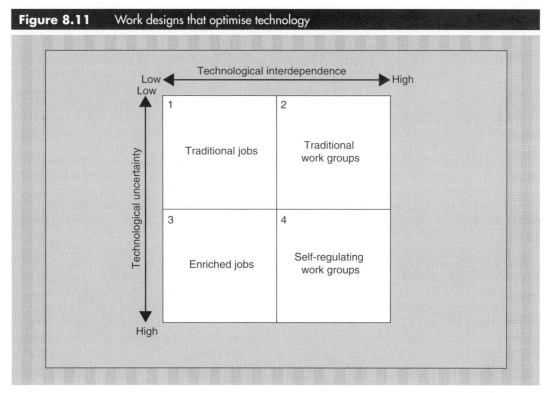

Source: reproduced from T. Cummings, 'Designing work for productivity and quality of work life',
Outlook, 6 (1982): 39.

both technical interdependence and uncertainty are high (quadrant 4), such as might be found in a continuous-process chemical plant, work should be designed for self-managed teams in which members have the multiple skills, discretion and information necessary to control their interactions around the shared tasks.

PERSONAL-NEED FACTORS

Most of the research identifying individual differences in work design has focused on selected personal traits. Two types of personal needs can influence the kinds of work designs that are most effective: social needs, or the desire for significant social relationships; and growth needs, or the desire for personal accomplishment, learning and development.[111] In general, the degree of social needs determines whether work should be designed for individual jobs or work groups. People with low needs for social relationships are more likely to be satisfied working on individualised jobs than in interacting groups. Conversely, people with high social needs are more likely to be attracted to group forms of work than to individualised forms.

The second individual difference, growth needs, determines whether work designs should be routine and repetitive or complex and challenging. People with low growth needs are generally not attracted to jobs that offer complexity and challenge (that is, enriched jobs). They are more satisfied performing routine forms of work that do not require high levels of decision making. On the other hand, people with high growth needs are satisfied with work offering high levels of discretion, skill variety and meaningful feedback. Performing enriched jobs allows them to experience personal accomplishment and development.

That some people have low social and growth needs is often difficult for OD practitioners to accept, particularly in view of the growth and social values that underlie much OD practice. It is important to recognise that individual differences do exist, however. Assuming that all people have high growth needs or want high levels of social interaction can lead to inappropriate work designs. For example, a new manager of a clerical support unit was astonished to find the six members using typewriters when a significant portion of the work consisted of retyping memos and reports that were produced frequently, but changed very little from month to month. In addition, the unit had a terrible record for quality and on-time production. The manager quickly ordered new word processors and redesigned the work flow to increase interaction among members. Worker satisfaction declined, interpersonal conflicts increased and work quality and on-time performance remained poor. An assessment of the effort revealed that all six of the staff members had low growth needs and low needs for inclusion in group efforts. In the words of one worker: 'All I want is to come into work, do my job and get my pay cheque.'

It is important to emphasise that people who have low growth or social needs are not inferior to those placing a higher value on these factors. They are simply different. It is also necessary to recognise that people can change their needs through personal growth and experience. OD practitioners need to be sensitive to individual differences in work design and careful not to force their own values on others. Many consultants, eager to be seen on the cutting edge of practice, tend to recommend self-managed teams in all situations, without careful attention to technological and personal considerations.

Figure 8.12 shows the different types of work designs that are most effective for the various combinations of social and growth needs. When employees have relatively low social and growth needs (quadrant 1), traditional jobs are most effective. In quadrant 2, where employees have high social needs but low growth needs, traditional work groups, such as might be found on an assembly line, are most appropriate. These allow for some social interaction but limited amounts of challenge and discretion. When employees have low social needs but high growth needs (quadrant 3), enriched jobs are most satisfying. Here, work is designed for individual jobs that have high levels of task variety, discretion and feedback about results. A research scientist's job is likely to be an enriched one, as is that of a skilled craftsperson. Finally, in quadrant 4, where employees have high social and growth needs, work should be specifically designed for self-managed teams. Such groups offer opportunities for significant social interaction around

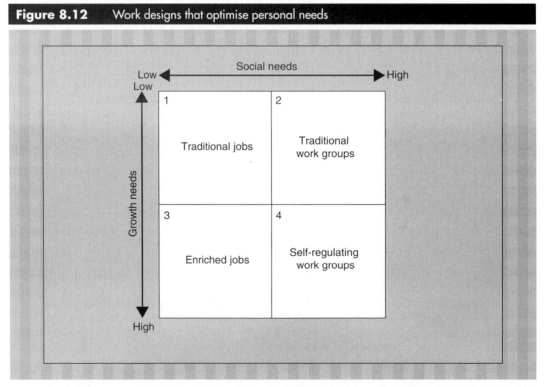

Figure 8.12   Work designs that optimise personal needs

Source: reproduced from T. Cummings, 'Designing work for productivity and quality of work life', *Outlook*, 6 (1982): 40.

tasks that are both complex and challenging. A team of astronauts in a space shuttle resembles a self-managing work group, as does a group managing the control room of an oil refinery or a group of nurses in a hospital unit.

MEETING BOTH TECHNICAL AND PERSONAL NEEDS

Satisfying both technical and human needs to achieve work-design success is likely to occur only in limited circumstances. When the technical conditions of a company's production processes (as shown in Figure 8.11) are compatible with the personal needs of its employees (as shown in Figure 8.12), the respective work designs combine readily and can satisfy both. On General Motors' assembly lines, for example, the technology is highly interdependent, yet low in uncertainty (quadrant 2 in Figure 8.11). Much of the work is designed around traditional work groups in which task behaviours are standardised, and interactions among workers are scheduled. Such work is likely to be productive and fulfilling to the extent that General Motors' production workers have high social needs and low growth needs (quadrant 2 in Figure 8.12).

When technology and people are incompatible – for example, when an organisation has quadrant 1 technology and quadrant 4 worker needs – at least two kinds of changes can be made to design work to satisfy both requirements.[112] One strategy is to change technology or people to bring them more into line with each other. This is a key point underlying sociotechnical systems approaches. For example, technical interdependence can be reduced by breaking long assembly lines into more discrete groups. In Sweden, Volvo redesigned the physical layout and technology for assembling automobiles and trucks to promote self-managed teams. Modifying people's needs is more complex, and begins by matching new or existing workers to available work designs. For example, companies can assess workers' needs through standardised paper-and-pencil tests. The information from these can be used to counsel employees and to help them locate jobs that are compatible with their needs. Similarly, employees can be allowed to volunteer for specific work designs, a common practice in sociotechnical systems projects. This matching process is likely to require high levels of trust and co-operation between management and workers, as well as a shared commitment to designing work for high performance and employee satisfaction.

A second strategy for accommodating both technical and human requirements is to leave the two components alone and to design compromise work designs that only partially fulfil the demands of either. The key issue is to decide to what extent one contingency will be satisfied at the expense of the other. For example, when capital costs are high relative to labour costs (such as is found in highly automated plants) work design is likely to favour the technology. Conversely, in many service jobs where labour is expensive relative to capital, organisations may design work for employee motivation and satisfaction at the risk of short-changing their technology. These examples suggest a range of possible compromises based on different weightings of technical and human demands. Careful assessment of both types of contingencies and of the cost–benefit trade-offs is necessary to design an appropriate compromise work design.

Clearly, the strategy of designing work to bring technology and people more into line with each other is preferable to compromise work designs. Although the latter approach seems necessary when there are heavy constraints on changing the contingencies, in many cases those constraints are more imagined than real. The important thing is to understand the technical and personal factors that exist in a particular situation and to design work accordingly. Traditional jobs and traditional work groups are likely to be successful in certain situations (as shown in Figures 8.11 and 8.12); in other settings, enriched jobs and self-managed teams are likely to be more effective.

SUMMARY

The first section of this chapter presented interventions aimed at restructuring organisations. Several basic structures, such as the functional structure, the self-contained unit and the matrix configuration, dominate most organisations. Two newer forms, process-based and network structures, were also described. Each of these structures has corresponding strengths and weaknesses, and contingency guidelines must be used to determine which structure is an appropriate fit with the organisation's environment.

Two restructuring interventions were described: downsizing and re-engineering. Downsizing decreases the size of the organisation through workforce reduction or organisational redesign. It is generally associated with lay-offs where a certain number or class of organisation member is no longer employed by the organisation. Downsizing can contribute to organisation development by focusing on the organisation's strategy, using a variety of downsizing tactics, addressing the needs of all organisation members and following through with growth plans.

Re-engineering is the fundamental rethinking and radical redesign of business processes to achieve dramatic improvements in performance. It seeks to transform how organisations traditionally produce and deliver goods and services. A typical re-engineering project prepares the organisation, rethinks how work gets done and finally restructures the organisation around the newly designed core processes.

The second section of this chapter described employee involvement (EI) interventions. These technostructural change programs are aimed at moving organisation decision making downward to improve responsiveness and performance, and to increase employee flexibility, commitment and satisfaction. Different approaches to EI can be described by the extent to which power, information, knowledge and skills, and rewards are shared with employees. The relationship between EI and productivity can be oversimplified. Productivity can be increased through improved employee communication, motivation, and skills and abilities. It can also be effected through increased worker satisfaction, which in turn results in productive employees joining and remaining with the organisation.

Major EI interventions include:
- parallel structures, including co-operative union–management projects and quality circles
- high-involvement designs.

The results of these approaches tend to be positive, and the quality of research supporting these interventions is increasing.

In the final section we discussed three different approaches to work design. In addition, a contingency framework was described to determine the approach most likely to result in high productivity and worker satisfaction, given certain workplace characteristics. The contingency framework reconciles the strengths and weaknesses of each approach. The engineering approach produces traditional jobs and traditional work groups. Traditional jobs are highly simplified and involve routine and repetitive forms of work. They do not require co-ordination among people to produce a product or service. Traditional jobs achieve high productivity and worker satisfaction in situations that are characterised by low technical uncertainty and interdependence, and low growth and social needs.

Traditional work groups are composed of members performing routine yet interrelated tasks. Member interactions are controlled externally, usually by rigid work flows, schedules and supervisors. Traditional work groups are best suited to conditions of low technical uncertainty, but high technical interdependence. They fit people with low growth needs but high social needs.

The motivational approach produces enriched jobs that involve high levels of skill variety, task identity, task significance, autonomy and feedback from the work itself. Enriched jobs achieve good results when the technology is uncertain but does not require high levels of co-ordination, and when employees have high growth needs and low social needs.

Finally, the sociotechnical systems approach is associated with self-managed teams. These groups are composed of members performing interrelated tasks. Members are given the multiple skills, autonomy and information necessary to control their own task behaviours with relatively little external control. Many organisation development practitioners argue that self-managed teams represent the work design of the 1990s. This is because high levels of technical uncertainty and interdependence are prevalent in today's workplaces and because today's workers often have high growth and social needs.

ACTiViTiES

RESTRUCTURING ORGANISATIONS

Review questions

① What types of strategies are included in interventions aimed at structural design?

② What should be considered when determining the appropriate technostructural intervention?

③ How would you describe successful downsizing and what are the key success factors?

④ What are the characteristics of re-engineering?

Discussion and essay questions

① Compare and contrast the two primary technostructural interventions – downsizing and re-engineering.

② Describe a functional, self-contained or matrix structure and discuss its advantages and disadvantages.

EMPLOYEE INVOLVEMENT

Review questions

① What characteristics are encompassed in a working definition of EI?

② How may QWL improve productivity?

③ What are the major applications of EI?

④ What is the value of co-operative union–management projects?

⑤ Identify some of the limiting factors of quality circles.

⑥ What are the distinguishing features of the total quality management approach?

Discussion and essay questions

① Discuss parallel structures and the type of organisation that would benefit most from this structure.

WORK DESIGN

Review questions

① Under what conditions would you recommend self-managed work groups?

② When the technology and the needs of the employees are incompatible, which changes should be made?

▷▷

③ What are the constraints on job enrichment interventions?

④ List the principles of sociotechnical systems design.

Discussion and essay questions

① Describe the motivational approach to job design. What are the key dimensions that lead to high work quality and internal motivation?

② Describe self-managed work groups and the best-suited environments for implementation.

NOTES

1 M. Tushman and E. Romanelli, 'Organizational evolution: a metamorphosis model of convergence and reorientation', in *Research in Organization Behavior*, 7, eds L. Cummings and B. Staw (Greenwich, CT: JAI Press, 1985); C. Worley, D. Hitchin and W. Ross, *Integrated Strategic Change* (Reading, MA: Addison-Wesley, 1996).

2 P. Lawrence and J. Lorsch, *Organization and Environment: Managing Differentiation and Integration* (Cambridge: Harvard Graduate School of Business, Administration Division of Research, 1967); J. Galbraith, *Organization Design* (Reading, MA: Addison-Wesley, 1977): 5.

3 L. Gulick and L. Urwick, eds, *Papers on the Science of Administration* (New York: Institute of Public Administration, Columbia University, 1937); M. Weber, *The Theory of Social and Economic Organization*, eds A. Henderson and T. Parsons (Glencoe, IL: Free Press, 1947).

4 A. Chandler, *Strategy and Structure: Chapters in the History of the Industrial Enterprise* (Cambridge: MIT Press, 1962).

5 S. Davis and P. Lawrence, *Matrix* (Reading, MA: Addison-Wesley, 1977); H. Kolodny, 'Managing in a matrix', *Business Horizons*, 24 (March–April 1981): 17–35.

6 Davis and Lawrence, *Matrix*, op. cit.

7 W. Joyce, 'Matrix organization: a social experiment', *Academy of Management Journal*, 29 (1986): 536–61; C. Worley and C. Teplitz, 'The use of "expert power" as an emerging influence style within successful US Matrix organizations', *Project Management Journal* (1993): 31–6.

8 Davis and Lawrence, *Matrix*, op. cit.

9 J. Byrne, 'The horizontal corporation', *Business Week* (20 December 1993): 76–81; S. Mohrman, S. Cohen and A. Mohrman, *Designing Team-Based Organizations* (San Francisco: Jossey-Bass, 1995); R. Ashkenas, D. Ulrich, T. Jick and S. Kerr, *The Boundaryless Organization* (San Francisco: Jossey-Bass, 1995).

10 J. Galbraith, E. Lawler and associates, *Organising for the Future: The New Logic for Managing Complex Organizations* (San Francisco: Jossey-Bass, 1993).

11 Byrne, 'The horizontal corporation', op. cit.

12 W. Halal, 'From hierarchy to enterprise: internal markets are the new foundation of management', *Academy of Management Executive*, 8:4 (1994): 69–83; C. Snow, R. Miles and H. Coleman Jr, 'Managing 21st century network organizations', *Organizational Dynamics*, 20 (1992): 5–19; S. Tully, 'The modular corporation', *Fortune* (8 February 1993): 106–14.

13 W. Davidow and M. Malone, *The Virtual Corporation: Structuring and Revitalizing the Corporation of the 21st Century* (New York: Harper Business, 1992); J. Bryne, R. Brandt and O. Port, 'The virtual corporation', *Business Week* (8 February 1993); Tully, 'The modular corporation', op. cit.; R. Keidel, 'Rethinking organizational design', *The Academy of Management Executive*, 8 (1994): 12–30; C. Handy, *The Age of Unreason* (Cambridge: Harvard Business School Press, 1989).

14 W. Powell, 'Neither market nor hierarchy: network forms of organization', in *Research in Organizational Behavior*, 12, eds B. Staw and L. Cummings (Greenwich, CT: JAI Press, 1990): 295–336; M. Lawless and R. Moore, 'Interorganizational systems in public service delivery: a new application of the dynamic network framework', *Human Relations*, 42 (1989): 1167–84; M. Gerstein, 'From machine bureaucracies to networked organizations: an architectural journey', in *Organizational Architecture*, eds D. Nadler, M. Gerstein, R. Shaw and associates (San Francisco: Jossey-Bass, 1992): 11–38.

15 Bryne, Brandt and Port, 'The virtual corporation', op. cit.; G. Dess, A. Rasheed, K. McLaughlin and R. Priem, 'The new corporate architecture', *Academy of Management Executive*, 9 (1995): 7–20.

16 J. Galbraith and R. Kazanjian, *Strategy Implementation: Structure, Systems and Process*, 2nd edn (St. Paul: West Publishing Company, 1986): 159–60.

17 W. Cascio, 'Downsizing: what do we know? what have we learned?', *The Academy of Management Executive*, 7 (1993): 95–104.

18 J. Kirby, 'Downsizing gets the push', *Business Review Weekly*, 21:10 (22 March 1999).
19 T. Wagar and C. Gilson, 'Workforce reduction in Australia and New Zealand: a research note', *Human Resource Management Journal*, 6:2 (1996): 88–98.
20 ibid.
21 J. Corrigan, 'Corporate anorexia?', *Australian Accountant*, 67:8 (1997): 50–1.
22 Adapted from Cameron, Freeman and Mishra, 'Best practices in white-collar downsizing: managing contradictions', op. cit.; and R. Marshall and L. Lyles, 'Planning for a restructured, revitalized organization', *Sloan Management Review*, 35 (1994): 81–91.
23 J. Brockner, 'The effects of work layoffs on survivors: research, theory and practice', in *Research in Organization Behavior*, 10, eds B. Staw and L. Cummings (Greenwich, CT: JAI Press, 1989): 213–55.
24 Marshall and Lyles, 'Planning for a restructured, revitalized organization', op. cit.
25 J. Rogdon, 'Lack of communication burdens restructurings', *The Wall Street Journal* (2 November 1992): B1.
26 Kirby, 'Downsizing gets the push', op. cit.
27 ibid.
28 Cameron, Freeman and Mishra, 'Best practices in white-collar downsizing: managing contradictions', op. cit.
29 M. Hammer and J. Champy, *Reengineering the Corporation* (New York: HarperCollins, 1993); T. Stewart, 'Reengineering: the hot new managing tool', *Fortune* (23 August 1993): 41–8; J. Champy, *Reengineering Management* (New York: HarperCollins, 1994).
30 R. Kaplan and L. Murdock, 'Core process redesign', *The McKinsey Quarterly*, 2 (1991): 27–43.
31 J. Potter, 'Amcor comes in for an overhaul', *PPI*, 41:6: 69–71, ISSN: 0033409X.
32 M. Miller, 'Customer service drives reengineering effort', *Personnel Journal*, 73 (1994): 87–93.
33 Kaplan and Murdock, 'Core process redesign', op. cit.; R. Manganelli and M. Klein, *The Reengineering Handbook* (New York: AMACOM, 1994).
34 J. Katzenbach and D. Smith, 'The rules for managing cross-functional reengineering teams', *Planning Review* (March–April 1993): 12–13; A. Nahavandi and E. Aranda, 'Restructuring teams for the reengineered organization', *The Academy of Management Executive*, 8 (1994): 58–68.
35 ibid.
36 Hammer and Champy, *Reengineering the Corporation*, op. cit.
37 Champy, *Reengineering Management*, op. cit.; K. Jensen, 'The effects of business process management on injury frequency', unpublished Master's thesis (Culver City, CA: Pepperdine University, 1993).
38 G. Hall, J. Rosenthal and J. Wade, 'How to make reengineering really work', *Harvard Business Review* (November–December 1993): 119–31.
39 L. Davis, 'Enhancing the quality of work life: developments in the United States', *International Labor Review*, 116 (July–August 1977): 53–65.
40 L. Davis, 'Job design and productivity: a new approach', *Personnel*, 33 (1957): 418–30.
41 D. Nadler and E. Lawler III, 'Quality of work life: perspectives and directions' (working paper, Center for Effective Organizations, University of Southern California, 1982).
42 R. Walton, 'Improving the quality of work life', *Harvard Business Review*, 52 (May–June 1974): 12; C. McNichols, T. Stanley and M. Stahl, 'Quality of life in the US Air Force: 1977 vs. 1975' (paper delivered at the Military Testing Association Conference, San Antonio, TX, October 1978); *Organizational Research and Development, The Quality of Your Work Life in General Motors* (Detroit, MI: General Motors, 1976); L. Davis and A. Cherns, eds, *The Quality of Working Life*, 2 vols. (New York: Free Press, 1975).
43 Nadler and Lawler, 'Quality of work life', op. cit.
44 W. Ouchi, *Theory Z* (Reading, MA: Addison-Wesley, 1981).
45 J. Vogt and K. Murrell, *Empowerment in Organizations* (San Diego: University Associates, 1990).
46 T. Peters and R. Waterman, *In Search of Excellence* (New York: Harper & Row, 1985).
47 T. Peters and N. Austin, *A Passion for Excellence* (New York: Random House, 1985).
48 M. Marchington, A. Wilkinson and P. Ackers, 'Understanding the meaning of participation: views from the work place', *Human Relations*, 47:8 (1994): 867–94; C. Goulden, 'Supervisory management and quality circle performance: an empirical study', *Journal of Management Development*, 14:7 (1995): 15–27.
49 D. Welsh, F. Luthans and S. Sommer, 'Managing Russian factory workers: the impact of US-based behavioral and participative techniques', *Academy of Management Journal*, 36:1 (1993): 58–79; D. Jones, 'Employee participation during the early stages of transition: evidence from Bulgaria', *Economic and Industrial Democracy*, 16:1 (1995): 111–35.
50 C. Cooper and E. Mumford, *The Quality of Working Life in Western and Eastern Europe* (Westport, CT: Greenwood Press, 1979); P. Sorenson, T. Head, N. Mathys, J. Preston and D. Cooperrider, *Global and Organizational Development* (Champaign, IL: Stipes, 1995).
51 D. Glew, A. O'Leary-Kelly, R. Griffin and D. Van Fleet, 'Participation in organizations: a preview of the issues and proposed framework for future analysis', *Journal of Management*, 21:3 (1995): 395–421.
52 E. Lawler III, *High Involvement Management* (San Francisco: Jossey-Bass, 1986).
53 E. Lawler III and G. Ledford, 'Productivity and the quality of work life', *National Productivity Review*, 2 (Winter 1981–82): 23–36.

54 Glew, O'Leary-Kelly, Griffin and Van Fleet, 'Participation in organizations', op. cit.; J. Wagner, 'Participation's effects on performance and satisfaction: a reconsideration of research evidence', *Academy of Management Review*, 19:2 (1994): 312–30.

55 G. Ledford and E. Lawler, 'Research on employee participation: beating a dead horse?', *Academy of Management Review*, 19:4 (1994): 633–6.

56 G. Bushe and A. Shani, 'Parallel learning structure interventions in bureaucratic organisations', in *Research in Organisation Change and Development*, 4, eds W. Pasmore and R. Woodman (Greenwich, CT: JAI Press, 1990): 167–94.

57 D. Zand, 'Collateral organization: a new change strategy', *Journal of Applied Behavioral Science*, 10 (1974): 63–89; S. Goldstein, 'Organisational dualism and quality circles', *Academy of Management Review*, 10 (1985): 504–17; V. Schein and L. Greiner, 'Can organization development be fine tuned to bureaucracies?', *Organizational Dynamics* (Winter 1977): 48–61.

58 Zand, 'Collateral organization', op. cit.; D. Zand, *Information, Organization and Power: Effective Management in the Knowledge Society* (New York: McGraw-Hill, 1981): 57–88; G. Bushe and A. Shani, *Parallel Learning Structures: Increasing Innovation in Bureaucracies* (Reading, MA: Addison-Wesley, 1991).

59 Bushe and Shani, *Parallel Learning Structures*, op. cit., 123–37.

60 C. Worley and G. Ledford, 'The relative impact of group process and group structure on group effectiveness' (paper presented at the Western Academy of Management, Spokane, WA, April 1992).

61 Zand, 'Collateral organization', op. cit.

62 E. Lawler III and S. Mohrman, 'Quality circles after the fad', *Harvard Business Review*, 85 (1985): 64–71; S. Mohrman and G. Ledford Jr, 'The design and use of effective employee participation groups: implications for human resource management', *Human Resource Management*, 24 (Winter 1985): 413–28.

63 M. Duckles, R. Duckles and M. Maccoby, 'The process of change at Bolivar', *Journal of Applied Behavioral Science*, 13 (1977): 387–499.

64 D. Nadler, G. Jenkins, P. Mirvis and B. Macy, 'A research design and measurement package for the assessment of quality of work interventions', *Proceedings of the Academy of Management* (New Orleans: Thirty-Fifth Annual Meeting, 1975): 87–102.

65 R. Lansbury and E. Davis, 'Employee participation: some Australian cases', *International Labour Review*, 131:2 (1992), 231.

66 G. Bushe, 'Developing cooperative labor–management relations in unionised factories: a multiple case study of quality circles and parallel organizations within joint quality of work life projects', *Journal of Applied Behavioral Science*, 24 (1988): 129–50.

67 H. Katz, T. Kochan and M. Weber, 'Assessing the effects of industrial relations systems and efforts to improve the quality of working life on organizational effectiveness', *Academy of Management Journal*, 28 (1985): 509–26.

68 M. Hanlon and D. Nadler, 'Unionists' attitudes toward joint union–management quality of work life programs', *Journal of Occupational Behavior*, 7 (1986): 53–9; D. Collins, 'Self-interests and group interests in employee involvement programs: a case study', *Journal of Labor Research*, 16 (1995): 57–79.

69 J. Thacker and M. Fields, 'Union involvement in quality-of-work life efforts: a longitudinal investigation', *Personnel Psychology*, 40 (1987): 97–111.

70 B. Gilbert, 'The impact of union involvement on the design and introduction of quality of working life', *Human Relations*, 42 (1989): 1057–78.

71 G. Bocialetti, 'Quality of work life: some unintended effects on the seniority tradition of an industrial union', *Group and Organizational Studies*, 12 (1987): 386–410.

72 Lawler, *High Involvement Management*, op. cit.

73 Lawler, *High Involvement Management*, op. cit.; E. Lawler, *The Ultimate Advantage* (San Francisco: Jossey-Bass, 1992).

74 G. Ledford, 'High involvement organizations', working paper (Center for Effective Organizations, University of Southern California, 1992).

75 R. Cacioppe, 'Structured empowerment: an award-winning program at the Burswood Resort Hotel', *Leadership & Organization Development Journal*, 19:5 (1998): 264–74.

76 Glew, O'Leary-Kelly, Griffin and Van Fleet, 'Participation in organizations', op. cit.

77 F. Taylor, *The Principles of Scientific Management* (New York: Harper and Row, 1911).

78 ibid.

79 T. Cummings, 'Self-regulating work groups: a socio-technical synthesis', *Academy of Management Review*, 3 (1978): 625–34; G. Susman, *Autonomy at Work* (New York: Praeger, 1976); J. Slocum and H. Sims, 'A typology of technology and job redesign', *Human Relations*, 33 (1983): 193–212.

80 F. Herzberg, B. Mausner and B. Snyderman, *The Motivation to Work* (New York: John Wiley and Sons, 1959); F. Herzberg, 'The wise old Turk', *Harvard Business Review*, 52 (September–October 1974): 70–80; F. Herzberg and Z. Zautra, 'Orthodox job enrichment: measuring true quality in job satisfaction', *Personnel*, 53 (September–October 1976): 54–68.

81 J. Hackman and G. Oldham, *Work Redesign* (Reading, MA: Addison-Wesley, 1980).

82 A. Turner and P. Lawrence, *Industrial Jobs and the Worker* (Cambridge: Harvard Graduate School of Business Administration, Division of Research, 1965); J. Hackman and G. Oldham, 'Development of the job diagnostic survey', *Journal of Applied Psychology*, 60 (April 1975): 159–70; H. Sims, A. Szilagyi and R. Keller, 'The measurement of job characteristics', *Academy of Management Journal*, 19 (1976): 195–212.

83 G. Oldham and J. Hackman, 'Work design in the organizational context', in *Research in Organizational Behavior*, 2, eds B. Staw and L. Cummings (Greenwich, CT: JAI Press, 1980): 247–78; J. Cordery and T. Wall, 'Work design and supervisory practice: a model', *Human Relations*, 38 (1985): 425–41.

84 Hackman and Oldham, *Work Redesign*, op. cit.

85 ibid.

86 M. Campion, 'Interdisciplinary approaches to job design: a constructive replication with extensions', *Journal of Applied Psychology*, 73 (1988): 467–81.

87 C. Kulik, G. Oldham and P. Langner, 'Measurement of job characteristics: comparison of the original and the revised job diagnostic survey', *Journal of Applied Psychology*, 73 (1988): 426–66; J. Idaszak and F. Drasgow, 'A revision of the job diagnostic survey: elimination of a measurement artifact', *Journal of Applied Psychology*, 72 (1987): 69–74.

88 R. Steers and D. Spencer, 'The role of achievement motivation in job design', *Journal of Applied Psychology*, 62 (1977): 472–9; J. Champoux, 'A three sample test of some extensions to the job characteristics model', *Academy of Management Journal*, 23 (1980): 466–78; R. Katz, 'The influence of job longevity on employee reactions to task characteristics', *Human Relation*, 31 (1978): 703–25.

89 R. Zeffane, 'Correlates of job satisfaction and their implications for work redesign', *Public Personnel Management*, 23 (1994): 61–76.

90 G. Oldham and Y. Fried, 'Employee reactions to workspace characteristics', *Journal of Applied Psychology*, 72 (1987): 75–80.

91 B. Loher, R. Noe, N. Moeller and M. Fitzgerald, 'A meta-analysis of the relation of job characteristics to job satisfaction', *Journal of Applied Psychology*, 70 (1985): 280–9.

92 B. McEvoy and W. Cascio, 'Strategies for reducing employee turnover: a meta-analysis', *Journal of Applied Psychology*, 70 (1985): 342–53.

93 T. Cummings and E. Molloy, *Improving Productivity and the Quality of Work Life* (New York: Praeger, 1977).

94 J. Nicholas, 'The comparative impact of organization development interventions on hard criteria measures', *Academy of Management Review*, 7 (1982): 531–42.

95 E. Trist, B. Higgin, H. Murray and A. Pollock, *Organizational Choice* (London: Tavistock, 1963); T. Cummings and B. Srivastva, *Management of Work: A Socio-Technical Systems Approach* (San Diego: University Associates, 1977); A. Cherns, 'Principles of sociotechnical design revisited', *Human Relations*, 40 (1987): 153–62.

96 Cummings, 'Self-regulating work groups', op. cit., 625–34; J. Hackman, *The Design of Self-Managing Work Groups*, Technical Report No. 11 (New Haven: Yale University, School of Organization and Management, 1976); Cummings and Srivastva, *Management of Work*, op. cit.; Susman, *Autonomy at Work*, op. cit.; H. Sims and C. Manz, 'Conversations within self-managed work groups', *National Productivity Review*, 1 (Summer 1982): 261–9; T. Cummings, 'Designing effective work groups', in *Handbook of Organizational Design: Remodeling Organizations and Their Environments*, 2, eds P. Nystrom and W. Starbuck (New York: Oxford University Press, 1981): 250–71.

97 C. Manz, 'Beyond self-managing teams: toward self-leading teams in the work place', in *Research in Organizational Change and Development*, 4, eds W. Pasmore and R. Woodman (Greenwich, CT: JAI Press, 1990): 273–99; C. Manz and H. Sims Jr, 'Leading workers to lead themselves: the external leadership of self-managed work teams', *Administrative Science Quarterly*, 32 (1987): 106–28.

98 Dumaine, 'The trouble with teams', *Fortune* (5 September 1994): 86–92.

99 Weisbord, 'Participative work design: a personal odyssey', *Organizational Dynamics* (1984): 5–20.

100 T. Cummings, 'Socio-technical systems: an intervention strategy', in *New Techniques in Organization Development*, ed. W. Burke (New York: Basic Books, 1975): 228–49; Cummings and Srivastva, *Management of Work*, op. cit.; Cummings and Molloy, *Improving Productivity and the Quality of Work Life*, op. cit.

101 F. van Eijnatten, S. Eggermont, G. de Goffau and I. Mankoe, 'The socio-technical systems design paradigm' (Eindhoven, The Netherlands: Eindhoven University of Technology, 1994).

102 P. Goodman, R. Devadas and T. Hughson, 'Groups and productivity: analysing the effectiveness of self-managing teams', in *Productivity in Organizations*, eds J. Campbell, R. Campbell and associates (San Francisco: Jossey-Bass, 1988): 295–325.

103 R. Walton, 'How to counter alienation in the plant', *Harvard Business Review*, 12 (November–December 1972): 70–81.

104 R. Schrank, 'On ending worker alienation: the Gaines Pet Food plant', in *Humanizing the Workplace*, ed. R. Fairfield (Buffalo, NY: Prometheus Books, 1974): 119–20, 126; R. Walton, 'Teaching an old dog food new tricks', *The Wharton Magazine*, 4 (Winter 1978): 42; L. Ketchum, *Innovating Plant Managers Are Talking About . . .* (International Conference on the Quality of Working Life, Toronto, Canada, 30 August–3 September 1981): 2–3; H. Simon et al., *General Foods Topeka: Ten Years Young* (International Conference on the Quality of Working Life, Toronto, Canada, 30 August–3 September 1981): 5–7.

105 J. Norsted and S. Aguren, *The Saab-Scania Report* (Stockholm: Swedish Employer's Confederation, 1975).

106 'Doubting Sweden's way', *Time* (10 March 1975): 40.

107 P. Gyllenhammär, *People at Work* (Reading, MA: Addison-Wesley, 1977): 15–17, 43, 52–3; B. Jönsson, *Corporate Strategy for People at Work – The Volvo Experience* (International Conference on the Quality of Working Life, Toronto, Canada, 30 August–3 September 1981); N. Tichy and J. Nisberg, 'When does work restructuring work? Organizational innovations at Volvo and GM', *Organizational Dynamics*, 5 (Summer 1976): 73.

108 J. Kapstein and J. Hoerr, 'Volvo's radical new plant: the death of the assembly line?', *Business Week* (28 August 1989): 92–3.

109 W. Pasmore, 'The comparative impacts of sociotechnical system, job-redesign and survey–feedback interventions', in *Sociotechnical Systems: A Source Book*, eds W. Pasmore and J. Sherwood (San Diego, University Associates, 1978): 291–300.

110 T. Cummings, 'Self-regulating work groups: a socio-technical synthesis', *Academy of Management Review*, 3 (1978): 625–34; G. Susman, *Autonomy at Work* (New York: Praeger, 1976); J. Slocum and H. Sims, 'A typology of technology and job redesign', *Human Relations*, 33 (1983): 193–212; M. Kiggundu, 'Task interdependence and job design: test of a theory', *Organizational Behavior and Human Performance*, 31 (1983): 145–72.

111 Hackman and Oldham, *Work Redesign*, op. cit.; K. Brousseau, 'Toward a dynamic model of job–person relationships: findings, research questions and implications for work system design', *Academy of Management Review*, 8 (1983): 33–45; G. Graen, T. Scandura and M. Graen, 'A field experimental test of the moderating effects of growth needs strength on productivity', *Journal of Applied Psychology*, 71 (1986): 484–91.

112 T. Cummings, 'Designing work for productivity and quality of work life', *Outlook*, 6 (1982): 35–9.

Online reading

INFOTRAC® COLLEGE EDITION

For additional readings and reviews on technostructural interventions, explore **InfoTrac® College Edition**, your online library. Go to **www.infotrac-college.com** and search for any of the InfoTrac key terms listed below:

- Restructuring
- Matrix
- Downsizing
- Re-engineering
- Quality of work life
- Work design

INFOTRAC

HUMAN RESOURCE MANAGEMENT iNTERVENTiONS

In this chapter, we initially discuss human resource management interventions that are concerned with the management of individual and group performance: goal setting, performance appraisal and reward systems. Later in the chapter we look at three interventions that are concerned with developing and assisting the well-being of organisation members: career planning, workforce diversity and employee wellness.

INDIVIDUAL AND GROUP PERFORMANCE

Performance management involves goal setting, performance appraisal and reward systems that align member work behaviour with business strategy, employee involvement and workplace technology.

- *Goal setting* describes the interaction between managers and employees in jointly defining member work behaviours and outcomes. Orienting employees to the appropriate kinds of work outcomes can reinforce the work designs and can support the organisation's strategic objectives. Goal setting can clarify the duties and responsibilities that are associated with a particular job or work group. When applied to jobs, goal setting can focus on individual goals and reinforce individual contributions and work outcomes. When applied to work groups, goal setting can be directed at group objectives and reinforce members' joint actions, as well as overall group outcomes. One popular approach to goal setting is called 'management by objectives'.
- *Performance appraisal* involves collecting and disseminating performance data to improve work outcomes. It is the primary human resource management intervention for providing performance feedback to individuals and work groups. Performance appraisal is a systematic process of jointly assessing work-related achievements, strengths and weaknesses, but it can also facilitate career development counselling, provide information about the strength and diversity of human resources in the company, and link employee performance with rewards.
- *Reward systems* are concerned with eliciting and reinforcing desired behaviours and work outcomes. They can support goal-setting and feedback systems by rewarding the kinds of behaviours required, implementing a particular work design or supporting a business strategy. Like goal setting, rewards systems can be oriented to individual jobs and goals or to group functions and objectives. Moreover, they can be geared to traditional work designs that require external forms of control or to enriched, self-regulating work designs requiring employee self-control. Several innovative and effective reward systems are in use in organisations today.

The personnel or human resource departments of organisations traditionally implement performance management interventions, and personnel practitioners have special training in these areas. Because of the diversity and depth of knowledge required to successfully carry out these kinds of change programs, practitioners tend to specialise in one part of the personnel function, such as performance appraisal or compensation.

A model of performance management

Performance management is an integrated process of defining, assessing and reinforcing employee work behaviours and outcomes.[1] Organisations with a well-developed performance management process tend to outperform organisations that don't have this element of organisation design.[2] As shown in Figure 9.1, performance management includes practices and methods for goal setting, performance appraisal and reward systems, all of which work together to influence the performance of individuals and work groups.

Goal setting specifies the kinds of performances that are desired; performance appraisal assesses those outcomes; and reward systems provide the reinforcers that ensure that desired outcomes are repeated. Because performance management occurs in a larger organisational context, at least three contextual factors determine how these practices affect work performance: business strategy, workplace technology and employee involvement.[3] High levels of work performance tend to occur when goal setting, performance appraisal and reward systems are jointly aligned with these organisational factors.

- *Business strategy*. This defines the goals and objectives that are needed if an organisation is to compete successfully. Performance management needs to focus, assess and reinforce member work behaviours towards those objectives, thus ensuring that work behaviours are strategically driven.
- *Workplace technology*. This affects the decision as to whether performance management practices should be based on the individual or the group. When technology is low in

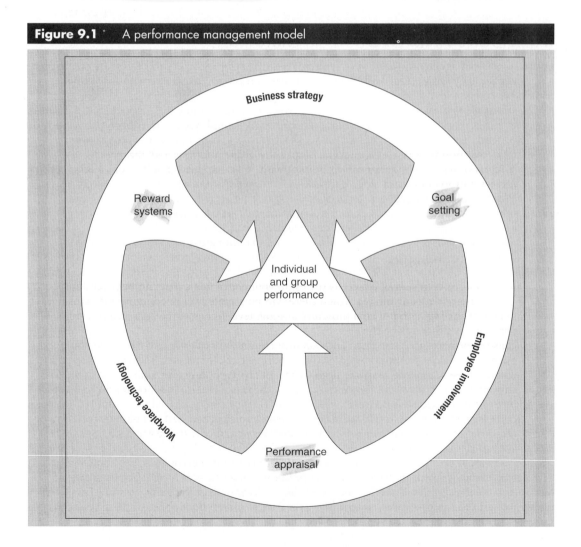

Figure 9.1 A performance management model

interdependence and work is designed for individual jobs, goal setting, performance appraisal and reward systems should be aimed at individual work behaviours. Conversely, when technology is highly interdependent and work is designed for groups, performance management should be aimed at group behaviours.[4]

- *Employee involvement.* Finally, the level of employee involvement in an organisation should determine the nature of performance management practices. When organisations are highly bureaucratic with low levels of participation, goal setting, performance appraisal and reward systems should be formalised and administered by management and staff personnel. In high-involvement situations, on the other hand, performance management should be heavily participative, with both management and employees setting goals and appraising and rewarding performance. In high-involvement plants, for example, employees tend to participate in all stages of performance management. They are heavily involved in both designing and administering performance management practices.

Goal setting

Goal setting involves managers and subordinates in jointly establishing and clarifying employee goals. In some cases, such as management by objectives, it can also facilitate employee counselling and support. The process of establishing challenging goals involves management in the level of participation and goal difficulty. Once goals have been established, how they are measured is an important determinant of member performance.[5] Goal setting can affect performance in at least three ways: it influences what people think and do as it focuses behaviour in the direction of the goals, rather than elsewhere; goals energise behaviour, motivating people to make an effort to reach difficult goals that are accepted; and, finally, goal setting leads to persistence in effort over time when goals are difficult but achievable.

CHARACTERISTICS OF GOAL SETTING

An impressive amount of research underlies goal-setting interventions and practices.[6] This research has resulted in the identification of two major processes that affect positive outcomes:
1   the establishment of challenging goals
2   the clarification of goal measurement.
   Goal setting appears to work equally well in both individual and group settings.[7]

Establishing challenging goals

The first element of goal setting concerns the establishment of goals that can be perceived as challenging, but are realistic and for which there will be a high level of commitment. This can be accomplished by varying goal difficulty and the level of employee participation in the goal-setting process. Increasing the difficulty of employee goals, also known as 'stretch goals', can increase their perceived challenge and enhance the amount of effort necessary for their achievement.[8] Thus, more difficult goals tend to lead to increased effort and performance, as long as they can be seen to be feasible. If goals are set too high, however, they may lose their motivating potential, and employees will give up when they fail to achieve them. Another aspect of establishing challenging goals is to vary the amount of participation in the goal-setting process. Having employees participate can increase motivation and performance, but only to the extent that members set higher goals than those that are typically assigned to them.

   All three contextual factors play an important role in the establishment of challenging goals. First, there must be a clear 'line of sight' between the business strategy goals and the goals established for individuals or groups. Second, employee participation in goal setting is more likely to be effective if employee involvement policies in the organisation support it. Third, when tasks are highly interdependent and work is designed for groups, group-oriented participative goal setting tends to increase commitment.[9]

Clarifying goal measurement

The second element in the goal-setting process involves the specification and clarification of the goals. When employees are given specific goals, they tend to perform higher than when they are simply told to 'do their best', or when they receive no guidance at all. Specific goals reduce ambiguity about what is expected, and focus the search for appropriate behaviours.

To clarify goal measurement, objectives should be operationally defined. For example, a group of employees may agree to increase productivity by 5%, a challenging and specific goal. Clarifying goal measurement also requires that employees and supervisors negotiate the resources necessary for their achievement. These resources may include time, equipment, raw materials or access to information.

Contextual factors also play an important role in the clarifying process. Goal specification and clarity can be difficult in high-technology settings. The work is often uncertain and highly interdependent. Increasing employee participation in the clarification of goal measurement can give employees ownership of a non-specific but challenging goal. Finally, the process of specifying and clarifying goals is extremely difficult if the business strategy is itself unclear. Under these conditions, attempting to gain consensus on the measurement and importance of goals can lead to frustration and resistance to change.

APPLICATION STEPS

Based on these features of the goal-setting process, OD practitioners have developed specific approaches to goal setting. The following steps characterise those applications:

1   *Diagnosis.* This provides information about the nature and difficulty of specific goals, the appropriate types and levels of participation and the necessary support systems.
2   *Preparing for goal setting.* This typically involves increased interaction and communication between managers and employees, as well as formal training in goal-setting methods.
3   *Setting goals.* In this step, challenging goals are established and goal measurement clarified. Employees participate in the process to the extent that contextual factors support such involvement, and because employees are likely to set higher goals than those assigned by management.
4   *Review.* The goal attributes are evaluated to see whether the goals are energising and challenging, and whether they support the business strategy and can be influenced by the employees.

MANAGEMENT BY OBJECTIVES

A common form of goal setting used in organisations is management by objectives (MBO). This method is mainly an attempt to align personal goals with business strategy by increasing communications and shared perceptions between the manager and subordinates, either individually or as a group, or by reconciling conflict where it exists.

All organisations have goals and objectives, and all managers have goals and objectives. In many instances, however, those goals are not clearly stated, and managers and subordinates have different perceptions as to what those objectives are. MBO is an approach to resolving these differences in perceptions and goals. Management by objectives can be defined as systematic and periodic manager–subordinate meetings that are designed to accomplish organisational goals by mutual planning of the work, periodic reviewing of accomplishments and mutual solving of problems that arise in the course of getting the job done.

MBO has its origin in two different backgrounds: organisational and developmental. The organisational root of MBO was developed by Drucker, who emphasised that organisations need to establish objectives in eight key areas: 'market standing; innovation; productivity; physical and financial resources; profitability; manager performance and development; worker performance and attitude; and public responsibility'.[10] Drucker's work was expanded by Odiorne, whose first book on MBO stressed the need for quantitative measurement.[11]

According to Levinson,[12] MBO's second root is found in the work of McGregor, who stressed its qualitative nature, and its use for development and growth on the job.[13] McGregor attempted to shift the emphasis from identifying weaknesses to analysing performance in order to define strengths and potentials. He believed that this shift could be accomplished by having subordinates reach agreement with their boss on major job responsibilities, after which they could develop short-term performance goals and action plans for their achievement, thus allowing them to appraise their own performance. Subordinates would then discuss the results of this self-appraisal with their supervisors, thus developing a new set of performance goals and plans. This emphasis on mutual understanding and performance, rather than on personality, would change the supervisor's role from that of judge to helper, thereby reducing both role conflict and ambiguity. The second root of MBO reduces role ambiguity by making goal setting more participative and transactional as it increases communication between role incumbents, and by ensuring that both individual and organisational goals are identified and achieved.

An MBO program often goes beyond the one-on-one, manager–subordinate relationship to focus on problem-solving discussions that also involve work teams. Setting goals and reviewing individual performance are considered within the larger context of the job. In addition to organisational goals, the MBO process gives attention to individuals' personal and career goals, and tries to make these and organisational goals more complementary. The target-setting procedure allows real (rather than simulated) subordinate participation in goal setting, with open, problem-centred discussions among team members, supervisors and subordinates.

EFFECTS OF GOAL SETTING

Goal setting appears to produce positive results over a wide range of jobs and organisations. It has been tested on keypunch operators, logging crews, clerical workers, engineers and truck drivers, and has produced performance improvements of between 11% and 27%.[14] Moreover, four meta-analyses of the extensive empirical evidence that support goal setting conclude that the proposed effects of goal difficulty, goal specificity and participation in goal setting are generally substantiated across studies and with both groups and individuals.[15] Longitudinal analyses support the conclusion that the profits in performance are not short-lived.[16] A recent field study of the goal-setting process, however, failed to replicate the typical positive linear relationship between goal difficulty and performance, raising some concern about the generalisability of the method from the laboratory to practice.[17] Additional research has tried to identify potential factors that might moderate the results of goal setting, including task uncertainty, amount and quality of planning, need for achievement, education, past goal successes and supervisory style.[18] Some support for the moderators has been found. For example, when the technical context is uncertain, goals tend to be less specific and people need to engage in more search behaviour to establish meaningful goals.

Performance appraisal

Performance appraisal is a feedback system that involves the direct evaluation of individual or work group performance by a supervisor, manager or peers. Most organisations have some kind of evaluation system that is used for performance feedback, pay administration and, in some cases, counselling and developing employees.[19] Thus, performance appraisal represents an important link between goal-setting processes and reward systems. One survey of more than 500 firms found that 90% used performance appraisal to determine merit pay increases, 87% used it to review performance and 79% used it as the opportunity to set goals for the next period.[20]

Abundant evidence, however, indicates that organisations do a poor job in appraising employees.[21] A recent study found that 32% of managers surveyed rated their performance appraisal process as very ineffective.[22] Application 9.1 comments on particular difficulties for many managers in appraising underperforming staff members, a process that demands particular managerial skills.

APPLiCATiON 9.1

Lift performance

Poor performance-management systems corrupt the whole organisation by alienating the company's best staff, according to the managing director of the Hay Group in the Pacific region, Richard Hardwick.

Research using the Hay Group's global database, which has 1.2 million employees in 400 organisations registered, found that less than 50% of the employees in the manufacturing, telecommunications, health care and technology industries believed their companies had adequate systems to deal with poor performers. The pharmaceutical, retail and insurance industries fared better: more than 50% of employees were satisfied with performance systems. Hardwick says the result is the same in Australian companies that he knows of – and there is much room for improvement by employers.

Hardwick says managers often tell him they have difficulty carrying out performance reviews but, rather than confront underperformers, they choose the path of least resistance and distribute pay rises evenly. Hardwick says the risk is that morale will drop when top performers realise that their colleagues are being paid the same amount for less work; discretionary effort may be withdrawn or the top performers may leave. He suggests managers should:

- Move the performance focus from results to how employees achieved the results.
- Provide evidence on employee behaviour by giving 360-degree feedback (from managers, co-workers and customers).
- Redefine the job with each performance review. More freedom and autonomy for employees can lead to less accountability if the job role changes.
- Set employees clear goals and objectives. Explain how the employee's goals are linked to the organisation's goals to encourage greater commitment.
- Practise tough conversations by role-playing.

Source: Amita Tandukar, 'Lift Performance', *Business Review Weekly,* 17/11/05.

Critical Thinking Question: What would be examples of the 'tough conversations' mentioned at the end of the article, and how might you role-play them?

As a consequence of the problems associated with performance appraisal, a growing number of firms have sought ways of improving the process. Some innovations have been made in enhancing employee involvement, balancing organisational and employee needs, and increasing the number of raters.[23] These newer forms of appraisal are being used in such organisations as Levi-Strauss, Intel and Monsanto.

The performance appraisal process

Table 9.1 summarises several common elements of performance appraisal systems.[24] For each element, two contrasting features – representing traditional bureaucratic approaches and newer, high-involvement approaches – are presented. Performance appraisals are conducted for a variety of purposes, including affirmative action, pay and promotion decisions, as well as human resource planning and development.[25] Because each purpose defines what performances are relevant and how they should be measured, separate appraisal systems are often used. For example, appraisal methods for pay purposes are often different from systems that assess employee development or promotability. Employees also have a variety of reasons for wanting appraisal, such as receiving feedback for career decisions, getting a raise and being promoted. Rather than trying to meet these multiple purposes with a few standard appraisal systems, the new appraisal approaches are more tailored to balance the multiple organisational and employee needs. This is accomplished by actively involving the appraised, their co-workers and their managers in assessing the purposes of the appraisal at the time it takes place, and adjusting the process to fit that purpose. Thus, at one time the appraisal process might focus on pay decisions, another time on employee development and still another on employee promotability. Actively involving all relevant participants can increase the chances that the purpose of the appraisal will be correctly identified and understood, and that the appropriate appraisal methods will be applied.

Table 9.1	Performance appraisal elements	
Elements	Traditional approaches	Newer approaches
Purpose	Organisational, legal Fragmented	Developmental Integrative
Appraiser	Supervisor, managers	Appraised, co-workers and others
Role of appraised	Passive recipient	Active participant
Measurement	Subjective Concerned with validity	Objective and subjective
Timing	Periodic, fixed and administratively driven	Dynamic, timely and employee- or work-driven

The new methods tend to expand the appraiser role beyond managers to include multiple raters, such as the appraised, co-workers and others having direct exposure to the employee's performance. Also known as 360-degree feedback, it is used more for member development than for compensation purposes.[26] This wider involvement provides a number of different views of the appraisee's performance. It can lead to a more comprehensive assessment of the employee's performance and can increase the likelihood that both organisational and personal needs will be taken into account. The key task is to find an overall view of the employee's performance that incorporates all the different appraisals. Thus, the process of working out differences and arriving at an overall assessment is an important aspect of the appraisal process. This improves the appraisal's acceptance, the accuracy of the information and its focus on activities that are critical to the business strategy.

The newer methods also expand the role of the appraised. Traditionally, the employee is simply a receiver of feedback. The supervisor unilaterally completes a form about performance on predetermined dimensions – usually personality traits, such as initiative or concern for quality. The newer approaches actively involve the appraisee in all phases of the appraisal process. The appraisee joins with superiors and staff personnel in gathering data on performance, and on identifying training needs. This active involvement increases the likelihood that the content of the performance appraisal will include the employee's views, needs and criteria, along with those of the organisation. This newer role for employees increases their acceptance and understanding of the feedback process.

Performance measurement is typically the source of many problems in appraisal as it is seen as subjective. Traditionally, performance evaluation focuses on the consistent use of prespecified traits or behaviours. To improve consistency and validity of measurement, considerable training is used to help raters (supervisors) make valid assessments. This concern for validity stems largely from legal tests of performance appraisal systems and leads organisations to develop measurement approaches, such as the behaviourally anchored rating scale (BARS) and its variants. In newer approaches, validity is not only a legal or methodological issue but also a social issue, and all appropriate participants are involved in negotiating acceptable ways of measuring and assessing performance. Increased participation in goal setting is a part of this new approach. Rather than simply training the supervisor, all participants are trained in methods of measuring and assessing performance. By focusing on both objective and subjective measures of performance, the appraisal process is better understood, accepted and accurate.

The timing of performance appraisals is traditionally fixed by managers or staff personnel and is based on administrative criteria, such as annual pay decisions. Newer approaches now being used increase the frequency of feedback. Although it may not be practical to increase the number of formal appraisals, the frequency of informal feedback can increase, especially when the strategic objectives change or when the technology is highly uncertain. In these situations, frequent performance feedback is often necessary in order to ensure appropriate adaptations in work behaviour. The newer approaches to appraisal increase the timeliness of feedback and allow employees to have more control over their work.

EFFECTS OF PERFORMANCE APPRAISAL

Research strongly supports the role of feedback on performance. One study concluded that objective feedback as a means for improving individual and group performance has been 'impressively effective'[27] and has been supported by a large number of literature reviews over the years.[28] Another researcher concluded that 'objective feedback does not usually work, it virtually always works'.[29] In field studies where performance feedback contained behaviour-specific information, median performance improvements were more than 47%, and when the feedback concerned less specific information, median performance improvements were over 33%. In a meta-analysis of performance appraisal interventions, feedback was found to have a consistently positive effect across studies.[30] In addition, although most appraisal research has focused on the relationship between performance and individuals, several studies have demonstrated a positive relationship between group performance and feedback.[31]

Reward systems

Organisational rewards are powerful incentives for improving employee and work group performance. OD has traditionally relied on intrinsic rewards, such as enriched jobs and opportunities for decision making, to motivate employee performance. Early quality-of-work-life interventions were mainly based on the intrinsic satisfaction to be derived from performing challenging, meaningful types of work. More recently, OD practitioners have expanded their focus to include extrinsic rewards, such as pay, along with various incentives, such as stock options, bonuses and profit sharing, promotions and benefits. They have discovered that both intrinsic and extrinsic rewards can enhance performance and satisfaction.[32]

OD practitioners are increasingly attending to the design and implementation of reward systems. This recent attention to rewards has derived in part from research into organisation design and employee involvement. These perspectives treat rewards as an integral part of organisations. They hold that rewards should be congruent with other organisational systems and practices, such as the organisation structure, top-management's human-relations philosophy and work designs. Many features of reward systems contribute to both employee fulfilment and organisational effectiveness.

HOW REWARDS AFFECT PERFORMANCE

Considerable research has been done on how rewards affect individual and group performance. The most popular model to describe this relationship is the value expectancy theory. In addition to explaining how performance and rewards are related, it suggests requirements for designing and evaluating reward systems.

The value expectancy model[33] posits that employees will expend effort to achieve performance goals that they believe will lead to outcomes that they value. This effort will result in the desired performance goals as long as the goals are realistic, the employees fully understand what is expected of them, and that they have the necessary skills and resources. Ongoing motivation depends on the extent to which attaining the desired performance goals actually results in valued outcomes. Consequently, key objectives of reward-systems interventions are to identify the intrinsic and extrinsic outcomes (rewards) that are highly valued and to link them to the achievement of desired performance goals.

Based on value expectancy theory, the ability of rewards to motivate desired behaviour depends on six factors:

1   *Availability*. For rewards to reinforce desired performance, they must be not only desired but also available. Too little of a desired reward is no reward at all.

2   *Timeliness*. A reward's motivating potential is reduced to the extent that it is separated in time from the performance that it is intended to reinforce.

3   *Performance contingency*. Rewards should be closely linked with particular performances. If the employees succeed in meeting the goal, the reward must be given; if the target is missed, the reward must be reduced or not given. The clearer the linkage between performance and rewards, the better rewards are able to motivate desired behaviour.

4   *Durability*. Some rewards last longer than others. Intrinsic rewards, such as increased autonomy and pride in workmanship, tend to last longer than extrinsic rewards.

5   *Equity*. Satisfaction and motivation can be improved when employees believe that the pay policies of the organisation are equitable or fair. Internal equity concerns a comparison of personal rewards to those holding similar jobs or performing similarly in the organisation. External equity concerns a comparison of rewards with those of other organisations in the same labour market.

6   *Visibility*. Organisation members must be able to see who is getting the rewards. Visible rewards – such as placement on a high-status project, promotion to a new job or increased authority – send signals to employees that rewards are available, timely and performance-contingent.

Reward-systems interventions are used to elicit and maintain desired levels of performance. To the extent that rewards are available, durable, equitable, timely, visible and performance-contingent, they can support and reinforce organisational goals, work designs and employee involvement.

REWARD-SYSTEM PROCESS ISSUES

Process refers to how rewards are typically administered in the organisation. At least two process issues affect employees' perceptions of the reward system:
*   who should be involved in designing and administering the reward system
*   what kind of communication should exist with respect to rewards.[34]

Traditionally, reward systems are designed by top managers and compensation specialists and then simply imposed on employees. Although this top-down process may result in a good system, it cannot ensure that employees will understand and trust it. In the absence of trust, workers are likely to have negative perceptions of the reward system. There is growing evidence that employee participation in the design and administration of a reward system can increase employee understanding and can contribute to feelings of control over, and commitment to, the plan.

Lawler and Jenkins described a small manufacturing plant where a committee of workers and managers designed a pay system.[35] The committee studied alternative plans and collected salary survey data. This resulted in a plan that gave control over salaries to members of work groups. Team members behaved responsibly in setting wage rates. They gave themselves 8% raises, which fell at the fiftieth percentile in the local labour market. Moreover, the results of a survey administered six months after the start of the new pay plan showed significant improvements in turnover, job satisfaction and satisfaction with pay and its administration. Lawler attributed these improvements to employees having greater information about the pay system. Participation led to employee ownership of the plan and feelings that it was fair and trustworthy.

Communication about reward systems can also have a powerful impact on employee perceptions of pay equity and on motivation. Most organisations maintain secrecy about pay rates, especially in the managerial ranks. Managers typically argue that employees prefer secrecy. It also gives managers freedom in administering pay as they do not have to defend their judgements. There is evidence to suggest, however, that pay secrecy can lead to dissatisfaction with pay and to reduced motivation. Dissatisfaction derives mainly from people's misperceptions about their pay relative to the pay of others. Research shows that managers tend to overestimate the pay of peers and of people below them in the organisation, and that they tend to underestimate the pay of superiors. These misperceptions contribute to dissatisfaction with pay because, regardless of the pay level of a manager, it will seem small in comparison to the perceived pay level of subordinates and peers. Perhaps worse, potential promotions will appear less valuable than they actually are.

Secrecy can reduce motivation by obscuring the relationship between pay and performance. For organisations that have a performance-based pay plan, secrecy prevents employees from testing whether the organisation is actually paying for performance, so employees come to mistrust the pay system, fearing that the company has something to hide. Secrecy can also reduce the beneficial impact of accurate performance feedback. Pay provides people with feedback about how they are performing in relation to some standard. Because managers tend to overestimate the pay of peers and subordinates, they will consider their own pay low and thus perceive performance feedback more negatively than it really is. Such misperceptions about performance discourage those managers who are actually performing effectively.

It is important to emphasise that both the amount of participation in designing reward systems and the amount of frankness in communicating about rewards should fit the rest of the organisation design and managerial philosophy. Clearly, high levels of participation and openness are congruent with democratic organisations. It is questionable whether authoritarian organisations would tolerate either one.

DEVELOPING AND ASSISTING MEMBERS

This section looks at three human resource management interventions that are concerned with developing and assisting the well-being of organisation members. First, organisations have had to adapt their career planning and development processes to a variety of trends. For example, there are the different needs and concerns of individuals as they progress through various career stages. In addition, technological changes have dramatically altered organisational structures and systems, and global competition has forced organisations to rethink how work gets done. These processes and concerns have forced individuals and organisations to re-examine the social contract that binds them together. Career planning and development interventions can help to deal effectively with these issues. Second, increasing workforce diversity provides an especially challenging environment for human resource management. The mix of genders, ages, value orientations, thinking styles and ethnic backgrounds that make up the modern workforce is increasingly varied. Flexible human resource interventions can help to satisfy the variety of needs posed by this diversity. Finally, wellness interventions, such as employee assistance and stress management programs, are addressing several important social trends, such as fitness and health consciousness, drug and alcohol abuse and work–life balance.

Career planning and development interventions

Career planning and development have been receiving increased attention in organisations. Growing numbers of managers and professional staff are seeking more control over their work lives. As organisations downsize and restructure, there is less trust in the organisation to provide job security. Employees are not willing to have their careers 'just happen' and are taking an active role in planning and managing them. This is particularly true for women, employees in mid-career and university recruits, who are increasingly asking for career planning assistance.[36] On the other hand, organisations are becoming more and more reliant on their 'intellectual capital'. Providing career planning and development opportunities for organisation members helps to recruit and retain skilled and knowledgeable workers. Many talented job candidates, especially minorities and women, are showing a preference for employers who offer career advancement opportunities.

Many organisations, such as 3M, Ford and Westpac, have adopted career planning and development programs.[37] These programs have attempted to improve the quality of work life of managers and professionals, improve their performance, reduce unwanted turnover and respond to equal employment and affirmative action legislation. Companies have discovered that organisational growth and effectiveness require career development programs if they are to ensure that needed talent will be available. Competent managers are often the scarcest resource. Many companies have also experienced the high costs of turnover among recent university graduates, including those with a Master of Business Administration (MBA) degree, which can reach 50% after five years. Career planning and development helps to attract and hold such highly talented employees, and can increase the chances that their skills and knowledge will be fully utilised. Application 9.2 shows the danger to any company of failing to develop and retain their human resources in an era of high labour mobility is great.

APPLICATiON 9.2

THE HUMAN FACTOR

The days of managing a workforce with an impersonal attitude to staff are coming to an end.

They litter annual reports like confetti: those throw-away lines at the end of the chief executive's three- or four-page report where he sings the praises of staff – 'our most valuable resource'. Typically, so valuable are staff they merit one or two lines; the insult to staff could not be more calculated if the words were preceded by a PS.

What these few words so poignantly symbolise is how management in many companies still only pays lip service to maximising their staff's potential; despite the rhetoric, employees are seen as a cost – not an asset. The need to maximise shareholder returns makes any serious investment in their employees' skills a low priority. Anyone who doubts the veracity of this statement need only cast their mind back to how employers bitterly complained about – and, in some instances, rorted – the Labor Government's 0.75% training levy. Its abolition was one of the Howard Government's first initiatives after winning office in 1996.

But will employers be able to maintain this short-sighted approach into the future? Will inept human resource management flow to the bottom line as visibly as a bad acquisition? Will a stockmarket that has, until now, largely equated good human resource management with cost cutting and a 'hard line' towards staff and unions begin to appreciate that highly trained and motivated employees enhance companies' earnings?

There are no clear-cut answers. But one thing that does seem to be changing is that the conventional ratio – whereby about three-quarters of productivity improvements typically come from investment in capital, and only a quarter from investment in people – will be re-aligned. A report by the Boston Consulting Group, titled *2020 Vision – the Manager of the 21st Century*, for Innovation and Business Skills Australia (it is one of 10 federal government–sponsored national industry skills councils), argues that employers that fail to invest in their employees will pay the price in the marketplace: in terms of earnings and share price.

The problem is that investment in people is more dangerous than investment in capital. People can walk; plant and equipment cannot. If the emphasis in management is becoming more about getting and retaining skilled knowledge workers, then it will involve very different leadership skills from those normally exhibited by Australian managers. Possessing the ability to understand the motivation and aims of a more mobile, potentially cynical workforce will be paramount. And it will need to be applied to individual workers and the collective workforce, a level of understanding that is largely foreign to the conventional Australian manager.

It is also a foreign way of thinking in the political sphere. When the Howard Government won a Senate majority in 2004, it wasted no time in pushing through the radical WorkChoices legislation, which increased the authority of employers in the workplace. But in many respects it dealt with the issues of yesterday: a heavily regulated system designed for the hierarchical, union-dominated workplaces that were characterised by an us-and-them attitude. The emphasis is on productivity and incremental improvements.

It is a far cry from the workplace relations described in *2020 Vision*: 'The tools, methodologies and approaches used … are increasingly sophisticated and are rapidly evolving. Current best practice may be viewed in a decade as barely scratching the surface. In a period that may involve ongoing labour shortages, managing and improving the performance of people is likely to demand the same level of attention and rigour that financial processes do today.' It would be the ultimate

▷▷

irony if employers, having lobbied long and hard for WorkChoices, find the legislation is not the solution to their human resources needs in the coming years.

The report, by Boston Consulting Group's senior vice-president Jon Nicholson and manager Amanda Nairn, says: 'The workplace will increasingly focus on the performance of people as the core company asset … Greater attention will be given to measuring the performance of people, not just physical and financial assets, and also to developing new techniques for improving performance. Problem-solving and creativity skills will become increasingly important.'

The demands on managers will not end there, according to Nicholson and Nairn. They say: 'Executives will need to master a range of new management tools and will be expected to operate efficiently in a highly dynamic environment. They will find themselves assessed on a new range of metrics and will rely much more on output measures to assess their staff. They will require new skills to create more flexible work environments that better accommodate the needs of their employees, including greater numbers of contractors and part-time workers.' If this was not enough, the authors argue that today's shareholder focus will shift towards a wider view of whose opinion matters. 'This will create closer scrutiny of the way in which companies and executives behave.'

It has all been said before, of course: the dawning of the age of the highly valued skilled worker. Unfortunately, in recent years, it seems most managers have confused shortage of supply, which increases pressure to pay higher wages, with the greater long-term requirement: the need for a sophisticated approach to hiring, training and retaining valued employees.

The director of the Centre for R&D Leadership at Melbourne University, Leon Mann, says the notion of nurturing the skilled worker does not slot easily into Australia's management culture: 'Ours is a pragmatic business culture. We like to be able to put a dollar value on something, especially with today's emphasis on creating shareholder wealth. It fits in neatly with our can-do approach. Certainly managers are not, in my opinion, long-range thinkers in these areas. They tend to go with what works.'

Mann's opinion is just that – an opinion. But there is considerable research and anecdotal evidence to suggest it has validity. And if he is right, managers, especially senior managers, face enormous challenges in the years ahead. Employers simply will not be able to hire the skilled labour they need. *2020 Vision* puts it bluntly: 'Australia is likely to experience a long period of prolonged skill shortage.'

Compounding the problem for employers are two other factors operating in the labour market, and both are related to the characteristics that define what demographers call Generation Y – those born after 1981. First, and most importantly, Gen Ys are entering the workforce at a time of unprecedented prosperity; the last recession, in 1990–01, is simply not on their radar screen. They therefore think and act as if they can always get work. In addition, many are still not married and are living at home. Without the burden of children, a mortgage and, in many instances, even rent, they have the luxury to pick and choose where they work – especially if they are skilled.

Generation Y workers tend to possess economic security and have an optimistic view of life; they are more prepared to start their own business. Australian Bureau of Statistics figures show that there were 720 000 companies registered in Australia in 1975; today there are 2.5 million. And if you include those turning over less than $50 000, the number jumps to 3.75 million. People working as independent contractors comprise nearly 30% of the private-sector workforce. The chairman of IBISWorld, Phil Ruthven, says this trend reflects, in part, a Generation Y that is more assertive, with a 'can-do attitude'. They have also seen their parents retrenched and have no illusions about employer loyalty. What this means for employers is that the competition for labour will not be restricted to the company next door; it will be the contractor working out of the nearby garage.

Nicholson argues that companies' need for different skill sets, an ageing workforce and the different attitudinal approach of younger workers mean employers will have no option but to take a more enlightened view towards their human resource management.

Source: Nicholas Way, 'The human factor', *Business Review Weekly*, 4/5/06.

Critical Thinking Question: Why do you think members of Generation Y are more willing than their parents to start their own companies?

Recent legislation and court actions have motivated many firms to set up career planning and development programs for minority and female employees, who are in short supply at the middle- and upper-management levels. Organisations are discovering that the career development needs of women and minorities often require special programs and the use of non-traditional methods, such as integrated systems for recruitment, placement and development. The restructuring of employment – notably the growth in non-standard employment forms, the implementation of affirmative action and equal employment opportunity legislation, and the development of enterprise-based decentralised bargaining – have created a scenario where the central issue is whether or not the employment conditions of women workers have been enhanced, unaffected or regressed by these developments.[38] Similarly, age-discrimination laws have led many organisations to set up career programs aimed at older managers and professionals. Thus, career planning and development are increasingly being applied to people at various ages and stages of development: from new recruits to those nearing retirement age.

Finally, career planning and development interventions have been increasingly applied to cases of 'career halt', where lay-offs and job losses have resulted from organisation decline, downsizing, re-engineering and restructuring. These abrupt halts to career progress can have severe human consequences, and human resource practices have been developed for helping to cope with these problems.

Career planning is concerned with individuals who are choosing occupations, organisations and positions at each stage of their careers. Career development involves helping employees to attain their career objectives.[39] Although both of these interventions are generally aimed at managerial and professional employees, a growing number of programs are including lower level employees, particularly those in white-collar jobs.

CAREER STAGES

A career is the sequence of work-related positions occupied by a person during the course of a lifetime.[40] Traditionally, careers have been judged in terms of advancement and upward promotion in the organisational hierarchy. Today, they are defined in more holistic ways to include an individual's attitudes and experiences. For example, a person can remain in the same job, acquiring and developing new skills and having a successful career without ever getting promoted. Similarly, people may move horizontally through a series of jobs in different functional areas of the firm. Although they may not be promoted upward in the hierarchy, their broadened job experiences would constitute a successful career.

Considerable research has been devoted to understanding how ageing and experience affect people's careers. This research has drawn on the extensive work done on adult growth and development[41] and has adapted that developmental perspective to include work experience.[42] Results suggest that employees progress through at least four distinct career stages as they mature and gain experience. Each stage has unique concerns, needs and challenges.

1   *The establishment stage* (age 21–26). This phase is the outset of a career when people are generally uncertain about their competence and potential. They are dependent on others – especially bosses and more experienced employees – for guidance, support and feedback.

2   *The advancement stage* (age 26–40). During this phase, employees become independent contributors who are concerned with achieving and advancing in their chosen careers. They have typically learned to perform autonomously and need less guidance from bosses and closer ties with colleagues.

3   *The maintenance stage* (age 40–60). This phase involves levelling off and holding on to career successes. For those who are dissatisfied with their career progress, this period can be conflictual and depressing, as characterised by the term 'mid-life crisis'. People often reappraise their circumstances, search for alternatives and redirect their career efforts. Success in these endeavours can lead to continuing growth, whereas failure can lead to early decline.

4   *The withdrawal stage* (age 60 and above). This final stage is concerned with leaving a career. It involves letting go of organisational attachments, and the employee's major contributions are imparting knowledge and experience to others.

The different career stages represent a broad developmental perspective on people's jobs. They provide insight about the personal and career issues that people are likely to face at different career phases. These issues can be potential sources of stress. Employees are likely to go through the phases at different rates, and they are likely to experience personal and career issues differently at each stage.

CAREER PLANNING

Career planning involves setting individual career objectives. It is highly personalised and generally includes: assessing one's interests, capabilities, values and goals; examining alternative careers; making decisions that may affect the current job; and planning how to progress in the desired direction. This process results in people choosing occupations, organisations and jobs. It determines, for example, whether individuals will accept or decline promotions and transfers, and whether they will stay in the company or leave it for another job or retirement.

The four career stages can be used to make career planning more effective. Table 9.2 shows the different career stages and the career planning issues relevant at each phase. Applying the table to a particular employee involves first diagnosing the person's career stage: establishment, advancement, maintenance or withdrawal. Next, available career planning resources are used to help the employee address pertinent issues. Career planning programs include some or all of the following resources:

- communication regarding career opportunities and resources within the organisation and available to employees
- workshops to encourage employees to assess their interests, abilities and job situations and to formulate career development plans
- career counselling by managers or human resource department personnel
- self-development materials, such as books, videotapes and other media, directed towards identifying life and career issues
- assessment programs that provide various tests on vocational interests, aptitudes and abilities relevant to setting career goals.

Table 9.2	Career stages and career planning
Stage	Career-planning issues
Establishment	What are alternative occupations, organisations and jobs? What are my interests and capabilities? How do I get the work accomplished? Am I performing as expected? Am I developing the necessary skills for advancement?
Advancement	Am I advancing as expected? How can I advance more effectively? What long-term options are available? How do I get more exposure and visibility? How do I develop more effective peer relationships? How do I better integrate career choices with my personal life?
Maintenance	How do I help others to become established and advance? Should I reassess myself and my career? Should I redirect my actions?
Withdrawal	What are my interests outside work? What post-retirement work options are available to me? How can I be financially secure? How can I continue to help others?

According to Table 9.2, employees who are just becoming established in careers can be stressed by concerns for identifying alternatives, assessing their interests and capabilities, learning how to perform effectively and finding out how they are doing. At this stage, the company should provide individuals with considerable communication and counselling about available career paths and the skills and abilities needed to progress in them. Workshops, self-development materials and assessment techniques should be aimed at helping employees to assess their interests, aptitudes and capabilities, and at linking that information to possible careers and jobs. Considerable attention should be directed at giving employees continual feedback about job performance and at counselling them about how to improve performances. The supervisor–subordinate relationship is especially important for these feedback and development activities.

People at the advancement stage are mainly concerned with getting ahead, discovering long-term career options and integrating career choices, such as transfers or promotions, with their personal lives. Here, the company should provide employees with communication and counselling about challenging assignments and possibilities for more exposure and demonstration of skills. It should help to clarify the range of possible long-term career options and provide individuals with some idea about where they stand in achieving them. Workshops, developmental materials and assessment methods should be aimed at helping employees to develop wider collegial relationships, join with effective mentors and sponsors, and develop more creativity and innovation. These activities should also help people to assess both career and personal life spheres and to integrate them more successfully.

At the maintenance stage, individuals are concerned with helping newer employees to become established and grow in their careers. This phase may also involve a reassessment of self and career, and a possible redirection to something more rewarding. The firm should provide individuals with communications about the broader organisation and how their roles fit into it. Workshops, developmental materials, counselling and assessment techniques should be aimed at helping employees to assess and develop skills in order to train and coach others. For those experiencing a mid-life crisis, career planning activities should be directed at helping them to reassess their circumstances and to develop in new directions. Mid-life crises are generally caused by perceived threats to people's career or family identities.[43] Career planning should help people to deal effectively with identity issues, especially in the context of an ongoing career. This may include workshops and close interpersonal counselling to help people confront identity issues and reorient their thinking about themselves in relation to work and family. These activities might also help employees to deal with the emotions evoked by a mid-life crisis and develop the skills and confidence to try something new.

Employees who are at the withdrawal stage can experience stress about disengaging from work and establishing a secure leisure life. Here, the company should provide communications and counselling about options for post-retirement work and financial security, and it should convey the message that the employee's experience in the organisation is still valued. Retirement planning workshops and materials can help employees gain the skills and information necessary for making a successful transition from work to non-work life. They can prepare individuals for shifting their attention away from the organisation to other interests and activities.

Effective career planning and development requires a comprehensive program that integrates both corporate business objectives and employee career needs. This is accomplished through human resource planning, as shown in Figure 9.2.

Human resource planning is aimed at developing and maintaining a workforce to meet business objectives. It includes recruiting new talent, matching people to jobs, helping them develop careers and perform effectively, and preparing them for satisfactory retirement. Career planning activities feed into and support career development and human resource planning activities.

CAREER DEVELOPMENT

Career development helps individuals to achieve career objectives. It follows closely from career planning and includes organisational practices that help employees to implement those plans. These may include skill training, performance feedback and coaching, planned job rotation, mentoring and continuing education.

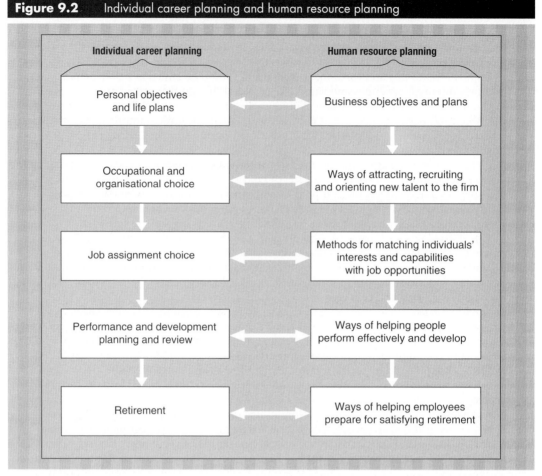

Figure 9.2 Individual career planning and human resource planning

Source: Reprinted from *Business Horizons*, Vol. 16. Copyright 1973, with permission from Elsevier.

Career development can be integrated with people's career needs by linking it to different career stages. As described earlier, employees progress through distinct career stages, each with unique issues relevant to career planning: establishment, advancement, maintenance and withdrawal. Career development interventions help employees to implement these plans. Table 9.3 identifies career development interventions, lists the career stages to which they are most relevant, and defines their key purposes and intended outcomes. It shows that career development practices may apply to one or more career stages. Performance feedback and coaching, for example, are relevant to both the establishment and advancement stages. Career development interventions can also serve a variety of purposes, such as helping members to identify a career path or providing feedback on career progress and work-effectiveness. They can contribute to different organisational outcomes such as lowering turnover and costs, and enhancing member satisfaction.

Career development interventions have traditionally been applied to younger employees who have a longer time to contribute to the firm than older members. Managers often stereotype older employees as being less creative, alert and productive than younger workers and consequently provide them with less career development support.[44] Similarly, Table 9.3 suggests that the OD field has been relatively lax in developing methods for helping older members cope with the withdrawal stage. Only two of the 11 interventions presented in Table 9.3 apply to the withdrawal stage: consultative roles and phased retirement. This relative neglect can be expected to change in the near future, however, as the Australian workforce continues to age. To sustain a highly committed and motivated workforce,

Table 9.3	Career development interventions		
Intervention	Career stage	Purpose	Intended outcome
Realistic job preview	Establishment Advancement	To provide members with an accurate expectation of work requirements	Reduce turnover Reduce training costs Increase commitment Increase job satisfaction
Job pathing	Establishment Advancement	To provide members with a sequence of work assignments leading to a career objective	Reduce turnover Build organisational knowledge
Performance feedback and coaching	Establishment Advancement	To provide members with knowledge about their career progress and work effectiveness	Increase productivity Increase job satisfaction Monitor human resource development
Assessment centres	Establishment Advancement	To select and develop members for managerial and technical jobs	Increase person–job fit Identify high-potential candidates
Mentoring	Establishment Advancement Maintenance	To link a less-experienced member with a more-experienced member for member development	Increase job satisfaction Increase member motivation
Developmental training	Establishment Advancement Maintenance	To provide education and training opportunities that help members to achieve career goals	Increase organisational capacity
Work–life balance planning	Establishment Advancement Maintenance	To help members balance work and personal goals	Improve quality of life Increase productivity
Job rotation and challenging assignments	Advancement Maintenance	To provide members with interesting work	Increase job satisfaction Maintain member motivation
Dual-career accommodations	Advancement Maintenance	To assist members with significant others to find satisfying work assignments	Attract and retain high-quality members Increase job satisfaction
Consultative roles	Maintenance Withdrawal	To help members fill productive roles later in their careers	Increase problem-solving capacity Increase job satisfaction
Phased retirement	Withdrawal	To assist members in moving into retirement	Increase job satisfaction Lower stress during transition

organisations will increasingly need to address the career needs of older employees. They will need to recognise and reward the contributions that older workers make to the company. Workforce diversity interventions, discussed later in this chapter, are a positive step in this direction.

Realistic job preview

This intervention provides individuals with realistic expectations about the job during the recruitment process. It provides recruits with information about whether the job is likely to be consistent with their needs and career plans. Such knowledge is especially useful during the establishment stage, when people are most in need of realistic information about organisations and jobs. It can also help employees during the advancement stage, when promotion is likely to cause job changes.

Job pathing

This intervention provides members with a carefully developed sequence of work assignments leading to a career objective. It helps members in the establishment and advancement stages of their careers. Job pathing helps employees develop skills, knowledge and competencies by performing jobs that require new skills and abilities. Research suggests that employees who receive challenging job assignments early in their careers do better in later jobs.[45] Career pathing allows for a gradual stretching of people's talents by moving them through selected jobs of increasing challenge and responsibility. As the person gains experience and demonstrates competence in the job, he or she is moved to another job with more advanced skills and knowledge. Performing well on one job increases the chance of being assigned to a more demanding job.

Performance feedback and coaching

One of the most effective interventions during the establishment and advancement phases includes feedback about job performance and coaching to improve performance. As was suggested earlier when discussing goal setting and performance appraisal interventions, employees need continual feedback about goal achievement as well as the necessary support and coaching to improve their performances. Feedback and coaching are particularly relevant when employees are establishing careers. They have concerns about how to perform the work, whether they are performing up to expectations and whether they are gaining the necessary skills for advancement.

Mentoring

One of the most useful ways of helping employees advance in their careers is sponsorship.[46] This involves establishing a close link between a manager or someone more experienced and another organisation member who is less experienced. Mentoring is a powerful intervention that assists members in the establishment, advancement and maintenance stages of their careers. For those in the establishment stage, a sponsor or mentor takes a personal interest in the employee's career, and guides and sponsors it. This helps to ensure that an individual's hard work and skill are translated into actual opportunities for promotion and advancement.[47] For older employees in the maintenance stage, mentoring provides opportunities to share knowledge and experience with others who are less experienced. Older managers can be given the responsibility of mentoring younger employees who are in the establishment and advancement career stages. Mentors do not have to be the direct supervisors of the younger employees, but can be hierarchically or functionally distant from them. In Australia, James Packer went through extensive mentoring processes. On the death of his late father, media billionaire Kerry Packer, he took over the running of one of Australia's largest corporations.

In both Australia and New Zealand, the use of mentors for new advisers is increasing and the companies using this development technique usually compensate mentors. But it is still only a minority of companies that have formal mentoring programs, with many companies leaving this role to sales managers.

Developmental training

This intervention helps employees to gain the skills and knowledge for training and coaching others. It may include workshops and training materials that are oriented to human relations, communications, active listening and mentoring. It can also involve substantial investments in education, such as tuition reimbursement programs that assist members in achieving advanced degrees. Developmental training interventions are generally aimed at increasing the organisation's reservoir of skills and knowledge, which enhances the organisational capability to implement personal and organisational strategies.

A large number of organisations offer developmental training programs, including Honeywell, Procter & Gamble, Alcoa and IBM. Many of these efforts are directed at mid-career managers who generally have good technical skills but only rudimentary experience in coaching others. In-house developmental training typically involves preparatory reading, short lectures, experiential exercises and case studies on such topics as active listening, defensive communication, personal problem solving and supportive relationships.

Work–life balance planning

This relatively new OD intervention helps employees better integrate and balance work and home life. Restructuring, downsizing and increased global competition have contributed to longer work hours and more stress. Organisations, such as Dow Chemical, are responding to these concerns so that they can attract, retain and motivate the best workforce. A more balanced work and family life can benefit both employees and the company through increased creativity, morale and effectiveness, and lower turnover.

Work–life balance planning involves a variety of programs to help members better manage the interface between work and family. These include such organisational practices as flexible hours, job sharing and day care, as well as interventions to help employees identify and achieve both career and family goals. A popular program is called 'mid-laning', a metaphor for a legitimate, alternative career track that acknowledges choices about living life in the 'fast lane'.[48]

Mid-laning helps people redesign their work and income-generating activities so that more time and energy are available for family and personal needs. It involves education in work addiction, guilt, anxiety and perfectionism; skill development in work contract negotiation; examination of alternatives such as changing careers, freelancing and entrepreneuring; and the exploration of options for controlling financial pressures by improving income–expense ratios, limiting 'black hole' worries such as education fees for children and retirement expenses, and replacing financial worrying with financial planning. Because concerns about work–life balance are unlikely to abate and may even increase in the near future, we can expect requisite OD interventions, such as mid-laning, to proliferate throughout the public and private sectors.

Work–life balance can be a more important factor for women than men, but there are other significant differences between the genders in their approaches to career development within an organisation, as illustrated in Application 9.3.

APPLICATiON 9.3

Dᴉꜰꜰᴇʀᴇɴᴛ ᴀᴍʙɪᴛɪᴏɴs

Companies can get into trouble by assuming that men and women have the same ideas about success. Forget career ladders or pay rises. What most professional women want in business is training, coaching, flexibility and mentoring. In fact, a successful 'promotion' for many senior professional women may well be a move sideways to more interesting work. Coming to terms with what women want (and not what their male managers think they want) is emerging as a big problem for male-dominated companies grappling with looming skills shortages, an ageing workforce and worldwide competition for workers.

The findings of a new survey by Perspectives Coaching of 556 professional women, including entrepreneurs, chief executives, consultants and managers, will not help. In fact, it may make the conventional male manager – and feminists – groan in unison. The survey concludes that most women judge success differently from the way men do. This changes the way they operate in the workplace, and they have a different perspective that managers need to understand if they want to attract and retain women.

Unlike men, who typically make decisions as isolated individuals, women consider their relationships with their immediate circle (family and friends), the company, broader social networks

▷▷

and even society itself as an integral part of their multiple paths to success. They seek to balance their lives with the needs of others, and of society, rather than believing they have arrived when they reach a certain rung on the ladder.

The founder and principal of Perspectives Coaching, Pollyanna Lenkic, says this means that when offered a promotion, a woman might reject the move up the career ladder as not being in the best interests of her family, her community, her colleagues or the company. In fact, 91% of respondents report feeling successful and say the top factors leading to a feeling of success in their lives are good relationships and work–life balance. Many women also base their self-esteem on a broad definition of success and not a narrow definition of career position and salary package, and are hungry to learn, according to the survey.

The findings are consistent with surveys in Britain and Canada that show that most women consider multiple factors to be crucial in achieving success for themselves and the organisations they work for. In an article in Career Development International, a researcher writes: 'Men build careers, while women compose lives.'

The American journal, *The Academy of Management Executive*, calls the career histories of women 'relational'. It says: 'Their career decisions are normally part of a larger and intricate web of interconnected people, issues and aspects that had to come together in a delicately balanced package.'

The result is that few women in a conventional hierarchical work culture make it to board and executives roles or can seize the opportunity to change company cultures. Lenkic, who founded a large IT recruitment company then sold it in 2000, says many women leave organisations to run their own businesses. But that may not provide the flexibility and interconnectedness that women seek, because developing a business brings different constraints.

The survey finds that women are more likely to move between self-employment and different organisations over their working lives. 'It's fine to say, "I am going to leave this organisation or position to look for a more flexible job that interests me and makes a difference",' Lenkic says. 'But sometimes you might be better off sticking to what you have and then reaching a point where you can have more say and dictate your own flexibility.'

A sociologist and workplace-change consultant, Mark Bahnisch, says the challenge for business is to understand the different perspective of most women and make changes. 'Companies also have to think about what the career ladder means and widen its definition to include more challenging work instead of just a pay increase. The career ladder in the future could well become a climbing frame. If people are to be promoted sideways, there needs to be a more lateral development of the career ladder.'

In the long run, Bahnisch says, companies will be forced to accept the female perspective: 'Look at the law firms. Many women prefer to work part-time but are leaving because they are expected to say until 10 in the evening. Law firms won't have the luxury of continuing to hold those views because they won't have enough staff. Managers not thinking creatively about how to keep their women are in trouble.'

And they are receiving help from an unexpected quarter. Bahnisch says his research shows that Generation-Y men share many of these perspectives.

WHAT WOMEN WANT

- Management skills training (45%)
- Business networks (40%)
- Coaching (42%)
- Mentoring programs (39%)
- Flexible working conditions (41%)
- Child-care facilities (11%)

Source: Amanda Gome, 'Different ambition', *Business Review Weekly,* Feb. 2–8, 2006.

Critical Thinking Question: The table above lists six things that female managers want from their organisations:

- How do you think these would differ from what male managers would want?
- Rank these items in terms of the cost to the organisation, including financial, time and resource costs.

Job rotation and challenging assignments

The purpose of these interventions is to provide employees with the experience and visibility needed for career advancement, or with the challenge necessary for revitalising a stagnant career at the maintenance stage. Unlike job pathing that specifies a sequence of jobs to reach a career objective, job rotation and challenging assignments are less planned and may not be as oriented to promotion opportunities.

Members in the advancement stage may be moved into new job areas once they have demonstrated competence in a particular job speciality. Companies such as Corning Glass Works and Hewlett-Packard identify 'comers' (managers under 40 years old with potential for assuming top-management positions) and 'hipos' (high potential candidates), and provide them with cross-divisional job experiences during the advancement stage. These job transfers provide managers with a broader range of skills and knowledge as well as opportunities to display their managerial talent to a wider audience of corporate executives.

In the maintenance stage, challenging assignments can help to revitalise veteran employees by providing them with new challenges and opportunities for learning and contribution. Research on enriched jobs suggests that people are most responsive to them during the first one to three years on a job, when enriched jobs are likely to be seen as challenging and motivating.[49] People who have levelled off and remain on enriched jobs for three years or more tend to become unresponsive to them. They are no longer motivated and satisfied by jobs that have ceased to seem enriched. One way of preventing this loss of job motivation, especially among mid-career employees who are likely to remain on jobs for longer periods of time than people in the establishment and advancement phases, is to rotate people to new, more challenging jobs at about three-year intervals. An alternative is to redesign their jobs at these times. Such job changes would keep employees responsive to challenging jobs, and sustain motivation and satisfaction during the maintenance phase.[50]

Dual-career accommodations

These are practices for helping employees cope with the problems inherent in 'dual careers'; that is, where both the employee and a spouse or significant other pursue full-time careers. Dual careers are becoming more prevalent as women increasingly enter the workforce. It has been estimated that 58% of Australian married couples now have both partners in the labour force; by contrast, only 14% of families conform to the traditional family stereotype of male breadwinner with a stay-at-home wife.[51] Although these interventions can apply to all career stages, they are especially relevant during advancement. One of the biggest problems created by dual careers is job transfers, which are likely to occur during the advancement stage. Transfer to another location usually means that the working partner must also relocate. In many cases, the company employing the partner must either lose the employee or arrange a transfer to the same location. Similar problems can occur in recruiting employees. A recruit may not join an organisation if its location does not provide career opportunities for the partner.

Some companies have also established co-operative arrangements with other firms to provide sources of employment for the other partner.[52] General Electric, for example, has created a network of other firms to share information about job opportunities for dual-career couples.

Consultative roles

These provide late-career employees with opportunities to apply their wisdom and knowledge to helping others develop and solve organisational problems. Such roles can be structured around specific projects or problems and they involve offering advice and expertise to those responsible for resolving the issues.

In contrast to mentoring roles, consultative roles are not focused directly on guiding or sponsoring younger employees' careers. They are directed at helping others deal with complex problems or projects. Similarly, in contrast to managerial positions, consultative roles do not include the performance evaluation and control inherent in being a manager. They are based more on wisdom and experience than on managerial authority. Consequently, consultative roles provide an effective transition for moving pre-retirement managers into more support-staff positions. They free up managerial positions for younger employees while allowing older managers to apply their experience and skills in a more supportive and less threatening way than might be possible from a strictly managerial role.

Phased retirement

This provides older employees with an effective way of withdrawing from the organisation and establishing a productive leisure life. It includes various forms of part-time work. Employees gradually devote less of their time to the organisation and more time to leisure pursuits (which to some might include developing a new career). Phased retirement allows employees to make a gradual transition from organisational to leisure life. It enables them to continue to contribute to the firm while having the necessary time to establish themselves outside work. For example, people may use the extra time off work to take courses, to gain new skills and knowledge, and to create opportunities for productive leisure. IBM, for example, offers tuition rebates for courses on any topic taken within three years of retirement.[53] Many IBM pre-retirees have used this program to prepare for second careers. Equally importantly, phased retirement lessens the reality shock often experienced by those who retire all at once. It helps employees to grow accustomed to leisure life and to withdraw emotionally from the organisation. A growing number of companies have some form of phased retirement.

ORGANISATIONAL DECLINE AND CAREER HALT

In recent years, Australia has experienced an enormous amount of organisation decline, downsizing and restructuring across a variety of smokestack, service, government and high-technology industries. A decreasing and uneven demand for products and services; growing numbers of mergers, acquisitions, divestitures and failures; and increasing restructuring to operate leaner and more efficiently have resulted in lay-offs, reduced job opportunities and severe career disruptions for a large number of managers and employees.[54] An example in Australia is the ongoing restructuring of the financial services sector that saw one in two banking jobs eliminated by the year 2000 and is still continuing. Some 30 000 banking jobs were abolished between 1991 and 1997.[55]

Organisations have also developed human resource practices for managing decline in those situations where lay-offs are unavoidable, such as plant closings, divestitures and business failures. The following methods can help people to deal more effectively with lay-offs and premature career halts:[56]

- spreading equitable lay-off policies throughout organisational ranks, rather than focusing on specific levels of employees, such as shop-floor workers or middle managers
- having generous relocation and transfer policies that help people to make the transition to a new work situation
- helping people to find new jobs, including outplacement services and help in retraining
- treating people with dignity and respect, rather than belittling or humiliating them because they are unfortunate enough to be in a declining business that can no longer afford to employ them
- keeping people informed about organisational problems and possibilities of lay-offs so that they can reduce ambiguity and prepare themselves for job changes
- setting realistic expectations, rather than offering excessive hope and promises, so that employees can plan for the organisation's future and for their own.

In today's environment, organisation decline, downsizing and restructuring can be expected to continue. OD practitioners are likely to become increasingly involved in helping people to manage career dislocation and halt. The methods described above can help organisations manage the human resource consequences of decline. However, considerably more research is needed to assess the effects of these strategies and to identify factors that contribute to their success. Because career disruption and halt can be extremely stressful, the interventions described in the section on employee wellness can play an important role in managing the human consequences of organisation decline.

Workforce diversity interventions

Several important trends are profoundly shaping the labour markets of modern organisations. Researchers suggest that workforce characteristics are radically different from what they were just 20 years ago. Workforce diversity is more than a euphemism for cultural or ethnic differences. Such a definition is too narrow and focuses attention away from the broad range of issues that a diverse workforce causes. Diversity results from a mix of people who bring different resources and perspectives to the workplace and who have distinctive needs, preferences, expectations and lifestyles.[57] Organisations need to design human resource systems that account for these differences if they are to attract and retain a productive workforce and if they want to turn diversity into a competitive advantage.[58]

North American organisations have tended to address workforce diversity issues in a piecemeal fashion: only 5% of more than 1400 companies surveyed in the United States thought they were doing a 'very good job' of managing diversity.[59] As each trend makes itself felt, the organisation influences appropriate practices and activities. However, in Australia, the encouragement of more diverse workforces is part of major policy documents such as the Karpin Report and a range of state and federal statutes. The composition of the workforce will continue to change dramatically in the next 10 years; specifically, it will continue to become more diverse as women and older workers play greater roles in the workplace.

Workforce diversity interventions are growing rapidly in OD. The number of training experts specialising in diversity quadrupled between 1990 and 1993,[60] and a national survey reveals that 75% of firms either have, or plan to begin, diversity efforts.[61] Research suggests that diversity interventions are especially prevalent in large organisations with diversity-friendly senior management and human resource policies.[62] Although existing evidence shows that diversity interventions are growing in popularity, there is still ambiguity about the depth of organisational commitment to such practices and their personal and organisational consequences.

Many of the OD interventions described in this book can be applied to managing workforce diversity, as shown in Table 9.4, which summarises different dimensions of workforce diversity, including age, gender, disability, culture, values and sexual orientation.[63] The table also reports the major trends characterising those dimensions, organisational implications and workforce needs, and specific OD interventions that can be used to address those implications.

Employee wellness interventions

In the past decade, organisations have become increasingly aware of the relationship between employee wellness and productivity.[64] The estimated cost for medical treatment and loss of worker productivity for all diseases is more than $150 billion per year.[65] Employee assistance programs (EAPs) and stress management interventions have grown as organisations take more responsibility for the welfare of their employees. Companies such as Yahoo! and FAI Home Security are sponsoring a wide variety of fitness and wellness programs.[66]

In this section, we discuss two important wellness interventions: EAPs and stress management. EAPs are primarily reactive programs. They identify, refer and treat employee problems – such as drug abuse, marital difficulties or depression – that impact on worker performance. Stress management is both proactive and reactive. It is concerned with helping employees alleviate or cope with the negative consequences of stress at work.

EMPLOYEE ASSISTANCE PROGRAMS

Forces affecting psychological and physical problems at the workplace are increasing. In 1985, 8% of mayors, governors and CEOs of the *Fortune* 1000 said that substance abuse was a very significant problem. By 1989, that percentage had risen to 22%. More recently, a study suggested that one out of 10 workers abuse drugs or alcohol and that each of those workers costs an employer about one-quarter of the worker's salary in lost productivity.[67] Britain's Royal College of Psychiatrists suggested that up to 30% of employees in British companies would experience mental health problems and that 115 million work days were lost each year due to depression.[68] Other factors, too, have contributed to increased problems. Altered family

Table 9.4	Workforce diversity dimensions and interventions		
Workforce differences	Trends	Implications and needs	Interventions
Age	Median age up Distribution of ages changing	Health care Mobility Security	Wellness program Job design Career planning and development Reward systems Job design
Gender	Percentage of women increasing Dual-income families	Child care Maternity/paternity leaves Single parents	Fringe benefit rewards
Disability	The number of people with disabilities entering the workforce is increasing	Job challenge Job skills Physical space Respect and dignity	Performance management Job design Career planning and development
Culture and values	Rising proportion of immigrant and minority-group workers Shift in rewards	Flexible organisational policies Autonomy Affirmation Respect	Career planning and development Employee involvement Reward systems
Sexual orientation	Number of single-sex households up More liberal attitudes towards sexual preference	Discrimination	Equal employment opportunities Fringe benefits Education and training

structures, the growth of single-parent households, the increase in divorce, greater mobility and changing modes of child rearing are all fairly recent phenomena that have added to the stress experienced by employees. These trends indicate that an increasing number of employees need assistance for a variety of personal problems.

Employee assistance programs help to identify, refer and treat employees whose personal problems affect their performance.[69] Initially started in the 1940s to combat alcoholism, these programs have expanded to deal with emotional, family, marital and financial problems and, more recently, drug abuse. EAPs can be either broad programs that address a full range of issues, or they can focus on specific problems, such as drug or alcohol abuse.

Central to the philosophy underlying EAPs is the belief that, although the organisation has no right to interfere in the private lives of its employees, it does have a right to impose certain standards of work performance and to establish sanctions when these are not met. Anyone whose work performance is impaired because of a personal problem is eligible for admission into an EAP program. Successful EAPs have been implemented at General Motors, Johnson & Johnson, Motorola, BHP, Lend Lease and Qantas.

The employee assistance program model

Figure 9.3 displays the components of a typical EAP program, including the identification and referral of employees into the program, the management of the EAP process, and diagnosis and treatment.

1   *Identification and referral*. This can occur through formal or informal referral. In the case of formal referrals, the process involves the identification of those employees who

Figure 9.3   An employee assistance program (EAP)

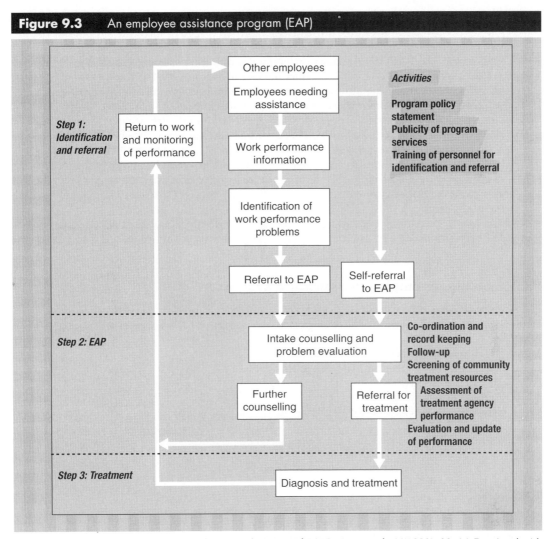

Source: S. Appelbaum and B. Shapiro, 'The ABCs of EAPS', Personnel, 66(1989): 39–46. Reprinted with permission, *Workforce*, 1989 Copyright Crain Communications Inc. www.workforce.com

are having work performance problems and getting them to consider entering the EAP. Identification of problem employees is closely related to the performance management process mentioned earlier. Performance records need to be maintained and corrective action taken whenever performance falls below an acceptable standard. During action planning to improve performance, managers can point out the existence of support services, such as the EAP. A formal referral takes place if the performance of an employee continues to deteriorate and the manager decides that EAP services are required. An informal referral occurs when an employee initiates admission to an EAP program, even though performance problems may not exist or may not have been detected.

As shown in Figure 9.3, several organisational activities support this first step in the EAP process. First, a written policy with clear procedures regarding the EAP is necessary. Second, top management and the human resources department must publicly support the EAP, and publicity about the program should be well distributed throughout the organisation. Third, training and development programs should help supervisors to effectively identify and document performance problems, to carry out performance improvement action planning, and to develop appropriate methods for suggesting and referring employees to the EAP. Finally, the confidentiality of employees using the program must be safeguarded if it is to have the support of the workforce.

2   *EAP office.* The EAP office accepts the employee into the program, provides problem evaluation and initial counselling, refers the employee to treatment resources and agencies, monitors the employee's progress during treatment, and reintegrates the employee into the workforce. The EAP program itself needs to be managed if it is to be effective. For example, the program's relationship to disciplinary procedures must be clear. In some organisations, corrective actions are suspended if the employee seeks EAP help. In others, the two processes are not connected. Maintaining confidential records and treatment information is also essential. In-house resources have the disadvantage of appearing to compromise this important program element but may offer some cost savings. If external treatment resources are used, care must be taken to screen and qualify these resources.

3   *Treatment.* Potential resources include in-patient and out-patient care, social services and self-help groups. The resources tapped by EAPs will vary from program to program.

Implementing an employee assistance program

EAPs can be flexible and customised to fit with a variety of organisational philosophies and employee problems. Practitioners have suggested seven steps to follow when establishing an EAP.[70]

1   Develop an EAP policy and procedure.
2   Select and train a program co-ordinator.
3   Obtain employee/union support for the EAP.
4   Publicise the program.
5   Establish relationships with health care providers and insurers.
6   Schedule EAP training.
7   Establish administrative planning and management.

STRESS MANAGEMENT PROGRAMS

Concern has been growing in organisations about managing the dysfunction caused by stress. There is increasing evidence that work-related stress can contribute to a variety of ailments, such as tension headaches, backaches, high blood pressure, cardiovascular disease and mental illness. It can also lead to alcoholism and drug abuse: two problems that are reaching epidemic proportions in organisations and society. For organisations, these personal effects can result in costly health benefits, absenteeism, turnover and low performance. A recent study reported that one in three workers said they have thought about quitting because of stress; one in two workers said job stress reduces their productivity; and one in five workers said they had taken sick leave in the past month because of stress.[71] Another study estimates that each employee who suffers from a stress-related illness loses an average of 16 days of work per year.[72] Finally, the Research Triangle Institute estimated the cost to the US economy from stress-related disorders at US$87 billion per year. Other estimates are more conservative, but they invariably run into the billions of dollars.[73]

Like the other human resource management interventions, stress management is often carried out by practitioners who have special skills and knowledge in this area. These typically include psychologists, doctors and other health professionals specialising in work stress. Recently, some OD practitioners have gained competence in this area and there has been a growing tendency to include stress management as part of larger OD efforts. The concept of stress is best understood in terms of a model that describes the organisational and personal conditions contributing to the dysfunctional consequences of stress. Two key types of stress-management interventions may be employed: those aimed at the diagnosis or awareness of stress and its causes, and those directed at changing the causes and helping people to cope with stress.

Definition and model

Stress refers to the reaction of people to their environments. It involves both physiological and psychological responses to environmental conditions, causing people to change or adjust their behaviours. Stress is generally viewed in terms of the fit between people's needs, abilities and expectations, and environmental demands, changes and opportunities.[74] A good person–environment fit results in positive reactions to stress, whereas a poor fit leads to the negative consequences already described. Stress is generally positive when it occurs at moderate levels and contributes to effective motivation, innovation and learning. For example, a promotion is a stressful event that is experienced positively by most employees. On the other hand, stress can be dysfunctional when it is excessively high (or low) or persists over a long period of time. It can overpower people's coping abilities and exhaust them physically and emotionally. For example, a boss who is excessively demanding and unsupportive can cause subordinates undue tension, anxiety and dissatisfaction. These factors, in turn, can lead to: withdrawal behaviours, such as absenteeism and turnover; ailments, such as headaches and high blood pressure; and lowered performance. Situations like this one, where there is a poor fit between employees and the organisation, produce negative stress consequences.

A tremendous amount of research has been conducted on the causes and consequences of work stress. Figure 9.4 presents a model that summarises stress relationships. It identifies specific occupational stresses that may result in dysfunctional consequences. The individual differences among people determine the extent to which the stresses are perceived negatively. For example, people who have strong social support experience the stresses as less stressful than those who do not have such support. This greater perceived stress can lead to such negative consequences as anxiety, poor decision making, increased blood pressure and low productivity.

The stress model shows that almost any dimension of the organisation (for example, working conditions, structure, role or relationships) can cause negative stress. This suggests that much of the material covered so far in this book provides knowledge about work-related stresses. Moreover, it implies that virtually all of the OD interventions included in the book can play a role in stress management. For example, process consultation, third-party intervention, survey feedback, intergroup relations, structural design, employee involvement, work design, goal setting, reward systems, and career planning and development can all help to alleviate stressful working conditions. Thus, to some degree, stress management has been under discussion throughout this book. Here, the focus is upon those occupational stresses and stress-management techniques that are unique to the stress field and that have received the most systematic attention from stress researchers.

1   *Occupational stresses.* Figure 9.4 identifies several organisational sources of stress, including structure, role on the job, physical environment and relationships. Extensive research has been done on three key organisational sources of stress: the individual items related to work overload, role conflict and role ambiguity.

Work overload can be a persistent source of stress, especially among managers and white-collar employees who have to process complex information and make difficult decisions. Quantitative overload consists of having too much to do in a given period. Qualitative overload refers to having work that is too difficult for one's abilities and knowledge. A review of the research suggests that work overload is highly related to managers' needs for achievement, suggesting that it may be partly self-inflicted.[75] Research relating workload to stress outcomes reveals that either too much or too little work can have negative consequences. Apparently, when the amount of work is in balance with people's abilities and knowledge, stress has a positive impact on performance and satisfaction. However, when workload either exceeds employees' abilities (overload) or fails to challenge them (underload), people experience stress negatively. This can lead to lowered self-esteem and job dissatisfaction, nervous symptoms, increased absenteeism and lowered participation in organisational activities.[76]

People's roles at work can also be a source of stress. A role can be defined as the sum total of expectations that the individual and significant others have about how the person should perform a specific job. The employee's relationships with peers, supervisors, vendors, customers and others can result in a diversity of expectations about how a particular role should be performed. The employee must be able to integrate these

Figure 9.4 Stress and work: a working mode

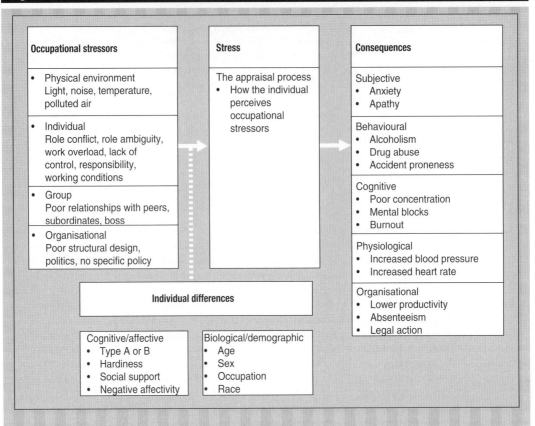

Source: J. Gibson, J. Ivancevich and J. Donnelly Jr, *Organizations: Behaviours, Structure, Processes*, 8e, Plano, TX, Business Publications, 1994. Reproduced by permission of the McGraw-Hill Companies.

expectations into a meaningful whole in order to perform the role effectively. Problems arise, however, when there is role ambiguity and the person does not clearly understand what others expect of him or her, or when there is role conflict and the employee receives contradictory expectations and cannot satisfy the different role demands.[77]

Extensive studies of role ambiguity and conflict suggest that both conditions are prevalent in organisations, especially among managerial jobs where clarity is often lacking and job demands are often contradictory.[78] For example, managerial job descriptions are typically so general that it is difficult to know precisely what is expected on the job. Similarly, managers tend to spend most of their time interacting with people from other departments. Opportunities for conflicting demands abound in these lateral relationships. Role ambiguity and conflict can cause severe stress, resulting in increased tension, dissatisfaction and withdrawal, and reduced commitment and trust in others. Some evidence suggests that role ambiguity has a more negative impact on managers than role conflict. In terms of individual differences, people with a low tolerance for ambiguity respond more negatively to role ambiguity than others; introverts and individuals who are more flexible react more negatively to role conflict than do others.[79]

2   *Individual differences.* Figure 9.4 identifies several individual differences that affect how people respond to occupational stresses. These include hardiness, social support, age, education, occupation, race, negative affectivity and Type A behaviour pattern. Much research has been devoted to the Type A behaviour pattern, which is characterised by impatience, competitiveness and hostility. Type A personalities (in contrast to Type Bs) tend to invest long hours working under tight deadlines. They put themselves under extreme time pressure by trying to do more and more work in less and less time. Type

B personalities, on the other hand, are less hurried, aggressive and hostile than Type As. Considerable research shows that Type A people are especially prone to stress. For example, a longitudinal study of 3500 men found that Type As had twice as much heart disease, five times as many second heart attacks and twice as many fatal heart attacks as Type Bs.[80] Researchers explain Type A susceptibility to stress in terms of an inability to deal with uncertainty, such as might occur with qualitative overload and role ambiguity. To work rapidly and meet pressing deadlines, Type As need to be in control of the situation. They do not allocate enough time for unforeseen disturbances and consequently experience extreme tension and anxiety when faced with unexpected events.[81]

Diagnosis and awareness of stress and its causes

Stress management is directed at preventing negative stress outcomes by either changing the organisational conditions that cause stress or by enhancing employees' abilities to cope with them. This preventive approach starts from a diagnosis of the current situation, including the employees' self-awareness of their own stress and its sources. This provides the information necessary to develop an appropriate stress-management program.[82] Two methods for diagnosing stress are the following:

1   *Charting stresses.* This involves identifying organisational and personal stresses that operate in a particular situation. It is guided by a conceptual model like that shown in Figure 9.4 and measures potential stresses that affect employees negatively. Data can be collected through questionnaires and interviews about environmental and personal stresses. It is important to obtain perceptual measures, as people's cognitive appraisal of the situation makes a stressor stressful. Most organisational surveys measure dimensions that are potentially stressful to employees, such as work overload, role conflict and ambiguity, promotional issues, opportunities for participation, managerial support and communication. Similarly, there are specific instruments for measuring the individual differences, such as hardiness, social support and Type A or B behaviour pattern. In addition to perceptions of stresses, it is necessary to measure stress consequences, such as subjective moods, performance, job satisfaction, absenteeism, blood pressure and cholesterol level. Various instruments and checklists have been developed for obtaining people's perceptions of negative consequences, and these can be supplemented with empirical data taken from company records, medical reports and physical examinations. Once measures of the stresses and consequences have been obtained, it is necessary to relate the two sets of data. This will reveal which stresses contribute most to negative stress in the situation under study. For example, a relational analysis might show that qualitative overload and role ambiguity are highly related to employee fatigue, absenteeism and poor performance, especially for Type A employees. This kind of information points to specific organisational conditions that need to be improved to reduce stress. Moreover, it identifies the kinds of employees who may need special counselling and training in stress management.

2   *Health profiling.* This method is aimed at identifying stress symptoms so that corrective action can be taken. It starts with a questionnaire asking people for their medical history, personal habits, current health and vital signs, such as blood pressure, cholesterol and triglyceride levels. It may also include a physical examination if some of the information is not readily available. Information from the questionnaire and physical examination is then analysed, usually by a computer that calculates a person's health profile. This compares the individual's characteristics with those of an average person of the same sex, age and race. The profile identifies the person's future health prospect, typically by placing her or him in a health-risk category with a known probability of fatal disease, such as cardiovascular. The health profile also indicates how the health risks can be reduced by personal and environmental changes, such as dieting, exercising or travelling.

   Many firms cannot afford to do their own health profiling and contract with health firms to do it on a fee basis per employee. Other firms have extensive in-house health and stress-management programs. At one program, health profiling was an initial diagnostic step. Each participant first went through a rigorous physical and medical history examination, which determined their health risks and was used to prescribe an individualised health program. Company officials reported that the program had positive results: 'It has generated good public interest, helped recruiting efforts and provided better all-around fitness for participants in the program. Individual health screening has uncovered six cases of early-stage cancer and a number of cases of high blood pressure and heart disease.'[83]

Alleviating stresses and coping with stress

After diagnosing the presence and causes of stress, the next stage of stress management is to do something about it. Interventions for reducing negative stress tend to fall into two groups: those aimed at changing the organisational conditions that cause stress and those directed at helping people to cope better with stress. Because stress results from the interaction between people and the environment, both strategies are necessary for effective stress management.

This section first presents two methods for alleviating stressful organisational conditions: role clarification and supportive relationships. These are aimed at decreasing role ambiguity and conflict, and improving poor relationships – key sources of managerial stress. Then, two interventions aimed at helping people to better cope with stress are discussed: stress inoculation training and health facilities. These can help employees alleviate stress symptoms and prepare themselves for handling stressful situations.

1   *Role clarification*. This involves helping employees better understand the demands of their work roles. A manager's role is embedded in a network of relationships with other managers, and each has specific expectations about how the manager should perform the role. Role clarification is a systematic process for finding out others' expectations and arriving at a consensus about the activities constituting a particular role. There are a variety of role-clarification methods, such as job-expectation (JET)[84] and role-analysis techniques (RAT).[85] They follow a similar strategy. First, the people relevant to defining a particular role are identified (for example, members of a managerial team: a boss, a subordinate and members of other departments relating to the role holder) and brought together at a meeting, usually away from the organisation.

Second, the role holder is given the opportunity to discuss his or her perceived job duties and responsibilities. The other participants are encouraged to comment and to agree or disagree with the perceptions. An OD practitioner may be present and may act as a process consultant to facilitate interaction and reduce defensiveness. Third, when everyone has reached consensus on defining the role, the role holder is responsible for writing a description of the activities that are now seen as constituting the role. A copy of the role description is distributed to the participants to ensure that they fully understand and agree with the role definition. Fourth, the participants periodically check to see whether the role is being performed as intended and make modifications if necessary.

Role clarification can be used for defining a single role or the roles of members of a group. It has been used in such companies as Alcoa, Johnson & Johnson and Honeywell to help management teams arrive at agreed-upon roles for members. The process is generally included as part of initial team-building meetings for new management teams starting high-involvement plants. Managers share perceptions and negotiate about one another's roles as a means of determining areas of discretion and responsibility. Role clarity is particularly important in new plant situations where managers are trying to implement participative methods. The ambiguity of such settings can be extremely stressful and role clarification can reduce stress by helping managers translate such ambiguous concepts as 'involvement' and 'participation' into concrete role behaviours.

Research on role clarification supports these benefits. One study found that it reduced stress and role ambiguity, and increased job satisfaction.[86] Another study reported that it improved interpersonal relations among group members and contributed to improved production and quality.[87] These findings should be interpreted carefully, however, as both studies had weak research designs and used only perceptual measures.

2   *Supportive relations*. This involves establishing trusting and genuinely positive relations among employees, including bosses, subordinates and peers. Supportive relations have been a hallmark of organisation development and are a major part of such interventions as team building, intergroup relations, employee involvement, work design, goal setting, and career planning and development. Considerable research shows that supportive relations can buffer people from stress.[88] When people feel that relevant others really care about what happens to them and are willing to help, they can better cope with stressful

conditions. The pioneering coal-mining studies that gave rise to the sociotechnical systems theory found that miners needed the support from a cohesive work group to deal effectively with the stresses of underground mining.

Recent research on the boss–subordinate relationship suggests that a supportive boss can provide subordinates with a crucial defence against stress. This research suggests that organisations need to become more aware of the positive value of supportive relationships in helping employees to cope with stress. They may need to build supportive, cohesive work groups in situations that are particularly stressful, such as the introduction of new products, solving emergency problems and handling customer complaints. For example, firms such as Procter & Gamble and Alcoa have recognised that internal OD consultation can be extremely stressful and they have encouraged internal OD practitioners to form support teams to help each other better cope with the demands of the role. Equally importantly, organisations need to direct more attention to ensuring that managers provide the support and encouragement necessary to help subordinates cope with stress.

3   *Stress inoculation training.* Companies have developed programs to help employees gain the skills and knowledge to better cope with stresses. Participants are first taught to understand stress-warning signals, such as difficulty in making decisions, disruption in sleeping and eating habits, and a greater frequency of headaches and backaches. Then they are encouraged to admit that they are overstressed (or understressed) and to develop a concrete plan for coping with the situation. One strategy is to develop and use a coping self-statement procedure. Participants verbalise a series of questions or statements each time they experience negative stress. The following sample questions or statements address the four stages of the stress-coping cycle: preparation ('What am I going to do about these stresses?'), confrontation ('I must relax and stay in control'), coping ('I must focus on the present set of stresses') and self-reinforcement ('I handled it well').[89]

Stress inoculation training is aimed at helping employees cope with stress, rather than at changing the stresses themselves. Its major value is sensitising people to stress and preparing them to take personal action. Self-appraisal and self-regulation of stress can free employees from total reliance on others for stress management. Given the multitude of organisational conditions that can cause stress, such self-control is a valuable adjunct to interventions that are aimed at changing the conditions themselves.

4   *Health facilities.* A growing number of organisations are providing facilities for helping employees cope with stress. Before starting such programs, employees are required to take an exercise tolerance test and to have the approval of either a private or a company doctor. Each participant is then assigned a safe level of heart response to the various parts of the fitness program. Preliminary evidence suggests that fitness programs can reduce absenteeism and coronary risk factors, such as high blood pressure, body weight, percentage of body fat and triglyceride levels.[90]

Application 9.4 illustrates the practical steps an employer can take to assist a worker suffering from stress, and prevent the future recurrence of stress.

APPLICATION 9.4

STRESS: COPING STRATEGIES FOR EMPLOYERS

Picture the scene: a senior employee who regularly works long hours is signed off for two weeks; his sick note says he's suffering from stress. He returns, apparently fully recovered and carries on working as usual. A month later he is signed off with severe depression, never to return. Too ill to work again, he successfully claims several hundred thousand pounds in compensation against your company because his illness was caused by stress at work. This is not as unlikely as it may seem. [Britain's Health and Safety Executive; HSE] surveys found that in 2003–04 over half a million people in Britain believed work-related stress was making them ill.

An employee will not win a stress claim if you did not (and could not have been expected to) predict that work was likely to make him ill. Just because an employee is in a job which many people

▷▷

would think of as stressful, does not automatically mean he or she is likely to become ill. As a general rule, you are entitled to assume that staff can cope with normal job pressures, unless you have reason to believe otherwise. Signs that might alert you to dangerous stress levels include workload higher than normal for a particular job; uncharacteristic behaviour (for example, irritability or carelessness); and abnormal levels of sickness/absenteeism in a particular job or department. Be alert; simply claiming you didn't realise there was a problem doesn't get you off the hook. If you have reason to believe that stress at work is threatening an employee's health, you must take reasonable steps to protect him or her – such as redistributing work or arranging extra help, such as temporary cover. The lengths you're expected to go to depend on factors such as how ill the employee is likely to become, the size of your business, and your financial and other resources. The interests of other employees are also relevant; it may not be reasonable to expect you to rearrange the work to help one employee if this could make others ill. You have to strike a balance between your business needs and the employee's interests.

Information gathering is important. You should consult the employee about the cause of the stress and what might be done to improve things. If the employee is already ill, or has had a previous stress-related illness, it may be helpful to obtain information from the GP, and possibly a report from an independent doctor, to assess appropriate action. If there really are no changes that you can make – you may be a small employer with limited resources – it's up to the employee to decide whether to carry on in the same job (and risk becoming ill) or leave. You are not expected to dismiss an employee to protect his or her health, only to take whatever steps you reasonably can to reduce stress.

What if you get it wrong? Compensation for stress claims is unlimited, and depends on the impact of the illness on the employee and his or her ability to work in future. This could be several years' pay, if the employee is very ill, and much more if the employee will be unable to work again. The best course is to avoid excessive stress in the first place. The HSE has produced *Management Standards*: voluntary guidelines to help employees eliminate the most common causes of stress. These identify six stress factors, and the benchmarks employers should target in relation to each one. There are practical steps that should help you to meet these standards. Regular and open appraisals help to identify problems with workload or role, allowing them to be addressed early. The employee should be assessed objectively against realistic targets, and be clear on the standards required. Upward appraisals, where employees give feedback about managers, allows them to raise any problems they might be experiencing; for example, a lack of support. Regular team meetings also help, enabling managers to monitor workloads and ensure appropriate distribution of work. These meetings should also help employees feel supported, and assist them in understanding their precise roles and responsibilities.

Change is a common causes of stress identified by the HSE. This is not limited to organisational change (often undertaken with employees' involvement). Equally relevant is a gradual change of role; for example, where someone leaves without being replaced and responsibilities are reallocated.

Again, team meetings can assist to ensure the employee is involved in the changes, and this should be coupled with regular reviews of job descriptions and mandates. Since stress is very often caused by how a person copes in the job, rather than the job itself, it is important to make sure that at the recruitment stage an individual's skills are accurately matched to the demands of the job. Although training during employment might be helpful, if the person really is not suited to the role, there is a limit to what can be done. Increasing the control an employee has over the work may help to reduce stress. How much this is possible will partly depend on seniority, but even for junior employees, the employer might have scope for more flexibility over how the work is done; for example, in terms of hours and breaks.

It may be helpful to include a stress policy in your staff handbook, explaining how stress is managed and stating whom employees could speak to if they have any concerns. This should assist in identifying any issues early on. With all of these steps, the real key is having an open atmosphere in which employees can raise concerns and discuss them, and where the employer is prepared to address the issues. A workplace in which an admission of difficulty coping is seen as a weakness will be vulnerable to stress claims.

Source: 'Management: Stress: coping strategies for employers', *Metalworking Production*, 22/5/06, www.metalworkingproduction.co.uk.

Critical Thinking Question: The final paragraph of the article suggests developing an organisational policy on stress. Write a simple stress policy for an organisation with which you are familiar. What do you consider to be the most important information to include in such a policy?

SUMMARY

The first part of this chapter presented three types of human resource management interventions: goal setting, performance appraisal and rewards systems. Although all three change programs are relatively new to organisation development, they offer powerful methods for managing employee and work group performance. They also help to enhance worker satisfaction and support work design, business strategy and employee involvement practices.

Principles contributing to the success of goal setting include the establishment of challenging goals and the clarification of measurement. These are accomplished by setting difficult but feasible goals, managing participation in the goal-setting process and being sure that the goals can be measured and influenced by the employee or work group. The most common form of goal setting – management by objectives – depends upon top-management support and participative planning to be effective.

Performance appraisals represent an important link between goal setting and reward systems. As part of an organisation's feedback and control system, they provide employees and work groups with information that they can use to improve work outcomes. Appraisals are becoming more participative and developmental. An increasing number of people are involved in collecting performance data, evaluating an employee's performance and determining how the appraised can improve.

Reward-systems interventions attempt to elicit and maintain desired performance. They can be oriented to both individual jobs or work groups and affect both performance and employee well-being. Three major kinds of reward-systems interventions are the design of pay, promotions and benefits.

The critical process of implementing a reward system involves decisions about who should be involved in designing and administering it and how much information about pay should be communicated.

The second part of the chapter presented three major human resource interventions: career planning and development, workforce diversity interventions and employee wellness programs. Although these kinds of change programs are generally carried out by human resource specialists, a growing number of OD practitioners are gaining competence in these areas and the interventions are increasingly being included in OD programs.

Career planning involves helping people choose occupations, organisations and jobs at different stages of their careers. Employees typically pass through four different career stages – establishment, advancement, maintenance and withdrawal – with different career planning issues relevant to each stage. Major career planning practices include communication, counselling, workshops, self-development materials and assessment programs. Career planning is a highly personalised process that includes assessing one's interests, values and capabilities; examining alternative careers; and making relevant decisions.

Career development helps employees achieve career objectives. Effective career development includes linking corporate business objectives, human resource needs and the personal needs of employees. Different career development needs and practices exist, and are relevant to each of the four stages of people's careers.

Workforce diversity interventions are designed to adapt human resource practices to an increasingly diverse workforce. Demographic, gender, disability, and culture and values trends all point to a more complex set of human resource demands. Within this context, OD interventions such as job design, performance management and employee involvement practices have to be adapted to a diverse set of personal preferences, needs and lifestyles.

Employee wellness interventions, such as employee assistance programs and stress management, recognise the important link between worker health and organisational productivity. EAPs identify, refer and treat employees and their families for a variety of problems. These include marital problems, drug and alcohol abuse, emotional disturbances and financial difficulties. EAPs preserve the dignity of the individual, but also recognise the organisations' right to expect certain work behaviours. EAPs typically include these activities:

- identifying and referring an employee to the program
- accepting the employee into the program, monitoring the employee's progress in treatment and reintegrating the employee into the workforce
- diagnosis and treatment.

Stress management is concerned with helping employees to cope with the negative consequences of stress at work. The concept of stress involves the fit between people's needs, abilities and expectations, and environmental demands, changes and opportunities. A good person–environment fit results in positive reactions to stress, such as motivation and innovation, whereas a poor fit results in negative effects, such as headaches, backache and cardiovascular disease. A model for understanding work-related stress includes occupational stresses; individual differences that affect how people respond to the stresses; and negative stress outcomes. Occupational stresses include work overload and role ambiguity and conflict. People with a Type A behaviour pattern, which is characterised by impatience, competitiveness and hostility, are especially prone to stress. The two main stages of stress management are diagnosing stress and its causes, and alleviating stresses and helping people to cope with stress. Two methods for diagnosing stress are charting stresses and health profiling. Techniques for alleviating stressful conditions include role clarification and supportive relationships; stress inoculation training and health facilities are ways of helping employees better cope with stress.

ACTiViTiES

Review questions

1. What parts does the performance management model include?
2. What does the goal-setting process involve and how does it work?
3. What are the design criteria for performance appraisal?
4. Which model relates work performance to rewards?
5. Implementing a career planning program includes what strategies?
6. What are the trends indicative of increasing workforce diversity?
7. What is the underpinning philosophy of EAPs, and what are the key steps in implementation?
8. What is (are) the characteristic(s) of stress? Explain the organisational sources of stress.
9. What are the strategies for role clarification?

Discussion and essay questions

1. Discuss the performance management model. How does performance management relate to employee involvement and work design?
2. Contrast the effects of various reward systems. Which are most effective?
3. Compare and contrast career development and career planning.

NOTES

1 A. Mohrman, S. Mohrman and C. Worley, 'High technology performance management', in *Managing Complexity in High Technology Organisations*, eds M. Von Glinow and S. Mohrman (New York: Oxford University Press, 1990): 216–36.

2 D. McDonald and A. Smith, 'A proven connection: performance management and business results', *Compensation and Benefits Review*, 27 (1995): 59–64.

3 J. Riedel, D. Nebeker and B. Cooper, 'The influence of monetary incentives on goal choice, goal commitment and task performance', *Organisational Behaviour and Human Decision Processes*, 42 (1988): 155–80; P. Earley, T. Connolly and G. Ekegren, 'Goals, strategy development and task performance: some limits on the efficacy of goal setting', *Journal of Applied Psychology*, 74 (1989): 24–33; N. Perry, 'Here come richer, riskier pay plans', *Fortune* (19 December 1988): 50–8; E. Lawler III, *High Involvement Management* (San Francisco: Jossey-Bass, 1986); A. Mohrman, S. Resnick-West and E. Lawler III, *Designing Performance Appraisal Systems* (San Francisco: Jossey-Bass, 1990).

4 Mohrman, Mohrman and Worley, 'High technology performance management', op. cit.

5 E. Locke and G. Latham, *A Theory of Goal Setting and Task Performance* (Englewood Cliffs, NJ: Prentice-Hall, 1990).

6 Locke and Latham, *A Theory of Goal Setting*, op. cit.; E. Locke, R. Shaw, L. Saari and G. Latham, 'Goal setting and task performance: 1969–1980', *Psychological Bulletin*, 97 (1981): 125–52; M. Tubbs, 'Goal setting: a meta-analytic examination of the empirical evidence', *Journal of Applied Psychology*, 71 (1986): 474–83.

7 A. O'Leary-Kelly, J. Martocchio and D. Frink, 'A review of the influence of group goals on group performance', *Academy of Management Journal*, 37:5 (1994): 1285–301.

8 S. Tully, 'Why to go for stretch targets', *Fortune* (14 November 1994): 145–58.

9 D. Crown and J. Rosse, 'Yours, mine and ours: facilitating group productivity through the integration of individual and group goals', *Organisation Behaviour and Human Decision Processes*, 64:2 (1995): 138–50.

10 P. Drucker, *The Practice of Management* (New York: Harper and Row, 1954): 63.

11 G. Odiorne, *Management by Objectives* (New York: Pitman, 1965).

12 H. Levinson, 'Management by objectives: a critique', *Training and Development Journal*, 26 (1972): 410–25.

13 D. McGregor, 'An uneasy look at performance appraisal', *Harvard Business Review*, 35 (May–June 1957): 89–94.

14 Locke and Latham, *A Theory of Goal Setting*, op. cit.

15 Tubbs, 'Goal setting', op. cit.; R. Guzzo, R. Jette and R. Katzell, 'The effects of psychologically based intervention programs on worker productivity: a meta-analysis', *Personal Psychology*, 38 (1985): 275–91; A. Mento, R. Steel and R. Karren, 'A meta-analytic study of the effects of goal setting on task performance: 1966–84', *Organisational Behaviour and Human Decision Processes*, 39 (1987): 52–83; O'Leary-Kelly, Martocchio and Frink, 'A review of the influence of group goals on group performance', op. cit.

16 C. Pearson, 'Participative goal setting as a strategy for improving performance and job satisfaction: a longitudinal evaluation with railway track maintenance gangs', *Human Relations*, 40 (1987): 473–88; R. Pritchard, S. Jones, P. Roth, K. Stuebing and S. Ekeberg, 'Effects of group feedback, goal setting and incentives on organisational productivity', *Journal of Applied Psychology*, 73 (1988): 337–58.

17 S. Yearta, S. Maitlis and R. Briner, 'An exploratory study of goal setting in theory and practice: a motivational technique that works?', *Journal of Occupational and Organisational Psychology*, 68 (1995): 237–52.

18 R. Steers, 'Task-goal attributes: achievement and supervisory performance', *Organisational Behaviour and Human Performance*, 13 (1975): 392–403; G. Latham and G. Yukl, 'A review of research on the application of goal setting in organisations', *Academy of Management Journal*, 18 (1975): 824–45; R. Steers and L. Porter, 'The role of task-goal attributes in employee performance', *Psychological Bulletin*, 81 (1974): 434–51; Early, Connolly and Ekegren, 'Goals, strategy development and task performance', op. cit.; J. Hollenbeck and A. Brief, 'The effects of individual differences and goal origin on goal setting and performance', *Organisational Behaviour and Human Decision Processes*, 40 (1987): 392–414.

19 G. Latham and R. Wexley, *Increasing Productivity Through Performance Appraisal* (Reading, MA: Addison-Wesley, 1981).

20 C. Peck, 'Pay and performance: the interaction of compensation and performance appraisal', *Research Bulletin*, 155 (New York: Conference Board, 1984).

21 E. Lawler III, *Pay and Organisation Development* (Reading, MA: Addison-Wesley, 1981): 113; Mohrman, Resnick-West and Lawler, *Designing Performance Appraisal Systems*, op. cit.

22 D. Antonioni, 'Improve the performance management process before discounting performance appraisals', *Compensation and Benefits Review*, 26:3 (1994): 29–37.

23 S. Mohrman, G. Ledford Jr, E. Lawler III and A. Mohrman, 'Quality of work life and employee involvement', in *International Review of Industrial and Organisational Psychology*, eds C. Cooper and I. Robertson (New York: John Wiley, 1986); G. Yukl and R. Lepsinger, 'How to get the most out of 360 degree feedback', *Training*, 32:12 (1995): 45–50.

24 Mohrman, Ledford, Lawler and Mohrman, 'Quality of work life and employee involvement', op. cit.

25 E. Huse, 'Performance appraisal – a new look', *Personnel Administration*, 30 (March–April 1967): 3–18.

26 S. Gebelein, 'Employee development: multi-rater feedback goes strategic', *HR Focus*, 73:1 (1996): 1, 4; B. O'Reilly, '360 degree feedback can change your life', *Fortune* (17 October 1994): 93–100.

27 J. Fairbank and D. Prue, 'Developing performance feedback systems', in *Handbook of Organisational Behaviour Management*, ed. L. Frederiksen (New York: John Wiley & Sons, 1982).

28 R. Ammons, *Knowledge of Performance: Survey of Literature, Some Possible Applications and Suggested Experimentation*, USAF WADC technical report 5414 (Wright Patterson Air Force Base, Ohio: Wright Air Development Center, Aero Medical Laboratory, 1954); J. Adams, 'Response feedback and learning', *Psychology Bulletin*, 70 (1968): 486–504; J. Annett, *Feedback and Human Behaviour* (Baltimore, MD: Penguin, 1969); J. Sassenrath, 'Theory and results on feedback and retention', *Journal of Educational Psychology*, 67 (1975): 894–9; F. Luthans and T. Davis, 'Behavioural management in service organisations', in *Service Management Effectiveness*, eds D. Bowen, R. Chase and T. Cummings (San Francisco: Jossey-Bass, 1989): 177–210.

29 R. Kopelman, *Managing Productivity in Organisations* (New York: McGraw-Hill, 1986).

30 Guzzo, Jette and Katzell, 'The effects of psychologically based intervention programs', op. cit.

31 D. Nadler, 'The effects of feedback on task group behaviour: a review of the experimental research', *Organisational Behaviour and Human Performance*, 23 (1979): 309–38; D. Nadler, C. Cammann and P. Mirvis, 'Developing a feedback system for work units: a field experiment in structural change', *Journal of Applied Behavioural Science*, 16 (1980): 41–62; J. Chobbar and J. Wallin, 'A field study on the effect of feedback frequency on performance', *Journal of Applied Psychology*, 69 (1984): 524–30.

32 W. Scott, J. Farh and P. Podsakoff, 'The effects of "intrinsic" and "extrinsic" reinforcement contingencies on task behaviour', *Organisational Behaviour and Human Decision Processes*, 41 (1988): 405–25; E. Lawler III, *Strategic Pay* (San Francisco: Jossey-Bass, 1990).

33 J. Campbell, M. Dunnette, E. Lawler III and K. Weick, *Managerial Behaviour, Performance and Effectiveness* (New York: McGraw-Hill, 1970).

34 Lawler, *Pay and Organisation Development*, op. cit., 101–11.

35 E. Lawler III and G. Jenkins, *Employee Participation in Pay Plan Development* (unpublished technical report to US Department of Labor, Ann Arbor, MI: Institute for Social Research, University of Michigan, 1976).

36 J. Fierman, 'Beating the mid-life career crisis', *Fortune* (6 September 1993): 52–62; L. Richman, 'How to get ahead in America', *Fortune* (16 May 1994): 46–54.

37 'Catalysts for career development: four case studies', *Training & Development*, 47:11 (1993): 26.

38 G. Strachan and J. Burgess, 'Towards a new deal for women workers in Australia? Growing employment share, enterprise bargaining and the "family friendly" workplace', *Equal Opportunity International*, 17:8 (1998): 1–13.

39 D. Hall and J. Goodale, *Human Resource Management: Strategy, Design and Implementation* (Glenview, IL: Scott, Foresman, 1986): 392.

40 D. Feldman, *Managing Careers in Organisations* (Glenview, IL: Scott Foresman, 1988).

41 E. Erikson, *Childhood and Society* (New York: Norton, 1963); G. Sheehy, *Passages: Predictable Crises of Adult Life* (New York: E.P. Dutton, 1974); D. Levinson, *Seasons of a Man's Life* (New York: Alfred A. Knopf, 1978); R. Gould, *Transformations: Growth and Change in Adult Life* (New York: Simon and Schuster, 1978).

42 D. Super, *The Psychology of Careers* (New York: Harper and Row, 1957); D. Hall, *Careers in Organisations* (Santa Monica, CA: Goodyear, 1976); E. Schein, *Career Dynamics: Matching Individual and Organisational Needs* (Reading, MA: Addison-Wesley, 1978); L. Baird and K. Kram, 'Career dynamics: the superior/subordinate relationship', *Organisational Dynamics*, 11 (Spring 1983): 46–64; J. Slocum and W. Cron, 'Job attitudes and performance during three career stages' (working paper, Edwin L. Cox School of Business, Southern Methodist University, Dallas, 1984).

43 M. McGill, 'Facing the mid-life crisis', *Business Horizons*, 16 (November 1977): 5–13.

44 B. Rosen and T. Jeered, 'Too old or not too old', *Harvard Business Review*, 55 (November–December 1977): 97–106.

45 D. Bray, R. Campbell and D. Grant, *Formative Years in Business: A Long Term AT&T Study of Managerial Lives* (New York: John Wiley and Sons, 1974).

46 J. Clawson, 'Mentoring in managerial careers', in *Family and Career*, ed. C. Derr (New York: Praeger, 1980); K. Kram, *Mentoring at Work* (Glenview, IL: Scott, Foresman, 1984); A. Geiger–DuMond and S. Boyle, 'Mentoring: a practitioner's guide', *Training and Development* (March 1995): 51–4.

47 E. Collins and P. Scott, 'Everyone who makes it has a mentor', *Harvard Business Review*, 56 (July–August 1978): 100.

48 D. Hitchin, 'Midlaning: a method for work–life balance planning' (working paper, Pepperdine University, Culver City, CA, 1996).

49 R. Katz, 'Time and work: towards an integrative perspective', in *Research in Organisational Behaviour*, 2, eds B. Staw and L. Cummings (New York: JAI Press, 1979): 81–127.

50 K. Brousseau, 'Toward a dynamic model of job–person relationships: findings, research questions and implications for work system design', *Academy of Management Review*, 8 (January 1983): 33–45.

51 J. Pierce and B. Delahaye, 'Human resource management implications of dual-career couples', *The International Journal of Human Resource Management*, 7:4 (1996), 905–23.

52 M. Bekas, 'Dual-career couples – a corporate challenge', *Personnel Administrator* (April 1984): 37–44.

53 J. Ivancevich and W. Glueck, *Foundations of Personnel/Human Resource Management*, 3rd edn (Plano, TX: Business Publications, 1986): 541.

54 J. Nocera, 'Living with lay-offs', *Fortune* (1 April 1996): 69–71.

55 'Job pressure for finance sector executives continues', *Australian Accountant*, 68:11 (1998): 13.

56 D. Cook and G. Ferris, 'Strategic human resource management and firm effectiveness in industries experiencing decline', *Human Resource Management*, 25 (Fall 1986): 441–58; R. Sutton, K. Eisenhardt and J. Jucker, 'Managing organisational decline: lessons from Atari', *Organisational Dynamics*, 14 (Spring 1986): 17–29; K. Cameron, S. Freeman and A. Mishra, 'Best practices in white-collar downsizing: managing contradictions', *The Academy of Management Executive*, 5 (1991): 57–73; K. Cameron, 'Strategies for successful organisational downsizing', *Human Resource Management*, 33 (1994): 189–212.

57 D. Jamieson and J. O'Mara, *Managing Workforce 2000: Gaining the Diversity Advantage* (San Francisco: Jossey-Bass).

58 F. Rice, 'How to make diversity pay', *Fortune* (8 August 1994): 78–86; R. Thomas Jr, 'From affirmative action to affirming diversity', *Harvard Business Review* (March–April 1990): 107–17.

59 Rice, 'How to make diversity pay', op. cit., 79.

60 K. Murray, 'The unfortunate side effects of diversity training', *The New York Times* (1 August 1993): Section 3, 5.

61 P. Towers, *Workforce 2000 Today: A Bottom-line Concern – Revisiting Corporate Views on Workforce Change* (New York: Author, 1992).

62 S. Rynes and B. Rosen, 'A field survey of factors affecting the adoption and perceived success of diversity training', *Personnel Psychology*, 48 (1995): 247–70.

63 The statistics cited in support of each trend and the organisational implications are derived from a variety of sources, including: Thomas Jr, 'From affirmative action to affirming diversity', op. cit.; C. Trost, 'New approach forced by shifts in population', *Wall Street Journal* (22 November 1989): B1, B4; M. Greller, 'The changing workforce and organisation effectiveness: an agenda for change', *Journal of Organisation Change Management*, 3 (1990): 4–15; M. Graddick, E. Bassman and J. Giordano, 'The changing demographics: Are corporations prepared to meet the challenge?', *Journal of Organisation Change Management*, 3 (1990): 72–9; Jamieson and O'Mara, *Managing Workforce 2000*, op. cit.; 'Human capital: the decline of America's work force', *Business Week* (19 September 1988): 100, 141; 'Managing now for the 1990s', *Fortune* (26 September 1989): 46; F. Chessman and associates, *Leadership for Literacy: The Agenda for the 1990s* (San Francisco: Jossey-Bass, 1990); in addition, this section benefited greatly from the advice and assistance of Pat Pope, president of Pope and Associates, Cincinnati, Ohio.

64 J. Blair and M. Fotter, *Challenges in Health Care Management* (San Francisco: Jossey-Bass, 1990).

65 K. Warner, T. Wickizer, R. Wolfe, J. Schildroth and M. Samuelson, 'Economic implications of the workplace health promotion programs: review of the literature', *Journal of Occupational Medicine*, 30 (1988): 106–12.

66 H. Hawkes, 'Nice perk if you can get it', *Sunday Life, Sunday Age Magazine* (23 May 1999): 12–14.

67 S. Savitz, 'Mental health plans help employees, reduce costs', *Best's Review*, 96:3 (1995): 60–2.

68 C. Hodges, 'Growing problem of stress at work alarms business', *People Management*, 1:9 (1995): 14–15.

69 Hall and Goodale, *Human Resource Management*, op. cit., 554.

70 J. Spicer, ed., *The EAP Solution* (Center City, MN: Hazeldon, 1987).

71 T. O'Boyle, 'Fear and stress in the office take toll', *Wall Street Journal* (6 November 1990): B1, B3; A. Riecher, 'Job stress: what it can do to you', *Bryan–College Station Eagle* (15 August 1993): D1.

72 D. Allen, 'Less stress, less litigation', *Personnel* (January 1990): 32–5; D. Hollis and J. Goodson, 'Stress: the legal and organisational implications', *Employee Responsibilities and Rights Journal*, 2 (1989): 255–62.

73 D. Ganster and J. Schaubroeck, 'Work stress and employee health', *Journal of Management*, 17 (1991): 235–71; T. Stewart, 'Do you push your employees too hard?', *Fortune* (22 October 1990): 121–8.

74 T. Cummings and C. Cooper, 'A cybernetic framework for studying occupational stress', *Human Relations*, 32 (1979): 395–418.

75 J. French and R. Caplan, 'Organisation stress and individual strain', in *The Failure of Success*, ed. A. Morrow (New York: AMACOM, a division of American Management Associations, 1972).

76 ibid.

77 R. Kahn, D. Wolfe, R. Quinn, J. Snoek and R. Rosenthal, *Organisational Stress* (New York: John Wiley and Sons, 1964).

78 C. Cooper and J. Marshall, 'Occupational sources of stress: a review of the literature relating to coronary heart disease and mental ill health', *Journal of Occupational Psychology*, 49 (1976): 11–28; C. Cooper and R. Payne, *Stress at Work* (New York: John Wiley and Sons, 1978).

79 Cooper and Marshall, 'Occupational sources', op. cit.

80 R. Rosenman and M. Friedman, 'The central nervous system and coronary heart disease', *Hospital Practice*, 6 (1971): 87–97.

81 D. Glass, *Behaviour Patterns, Stress and Coronary Disease* (Hillsdale, NJ: Lawrence Erlbaum, 1977); V. Price, *Type A Behaviour Pattern* (New York: Academic Press, 1982).

82 See, for example, the Addison-Wesley series on occupational stress: L. Warshaw, *Managing Stress* (Reading, MA: Addison-Wesley, 1982); A. McClean, *Work Stress* (Reading, MA: Addison-Wesley, 1982); A. Shostak, *Blue-Collar Stress* (Reading, MA: Addison-Wesley, 1982); L. Moss, *Management Stress* (Reading, MA: Addison-Wesley, 1982); L. Levi, *Preventing Work Stress* (Reading, MA: Addison-Wesley, 1982); J. House, *Work Stress and Social Support* (Reading, MA: Addison-Wesley, 1982).

83 J. Ivancevich and M. Matteson, 'Optimizing human resources: a case for preventive health and stress management', *Organisational Dynamics*, 9 (Autumn 1980): 7–8.

84 E. Huse and C. Barebo, 'Beyond the T–Group: increasing organisational effectiveness', *California Management Review*, 23 (1980): 104–17.

85 I. Dayal and J. Thomas, 'Operation KPE: developing a new organisation', *Journal of Applied Behavioural Science*, 4 (1968): 473–506.

86 Huse and Barebo, 'Beyond the T–Group', op. cit., 104–17.

87 Dayal and Thomas, 'Operation KPE', op. cit., 473–506.

88 House, *Work Stress and Social Support*, op. cit.

89 Ivancevich and Matteson, 'Optimizing human resources', op. cit., 19.

90 J. Zuckerman, 'Keeping managers in good health', *International Management*, 34 (January 1979): 40.

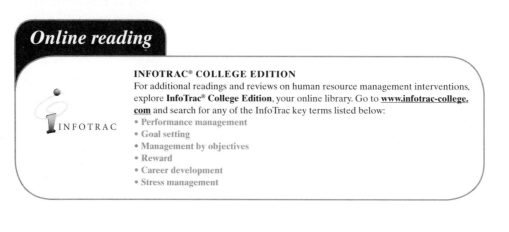

Online reading

INFOTRAC

INFOTRAC® COLLEGE EDITION

For additional readings and reviews on human resource management interventions, explore **InfoTrac® College Edition**, your online library. Go to **www.infotrac-college.com** and search for any of the InfoTrac key terms listed below:

• Performance management
• Goal setting
• Management by objectives
• Reward
• Career development
• Stress management

STRATEGiC iNTERVENTiONS

This chapter is concerned with interventions that are aimed at organisation and environment relationships. These change programs are relatively recent additions to the OD field that focus on helping organisations to relate better to their environments, and to achieve a better fit with those external forces that affect goal achievement and performance. Practitioners are discovering that additional knowledge and skills, such as competitive strategy, finance, marketing and political science, are necessary to conduct such large-scale change.

Because organisations are open systems, they must relate to their environments if they are to gain the resources and information needed to function and prosper. These relationships define an organisation's strategy and are affected by particular aspects and features of the environment. Organisations have devised a number of responses for managing environmental interfaces. The responses vary from creating special units to scan the environment to forming strategic alliances with other organisations.

The interventions described in this chapter help organisations to gain a comprehensive understanding of their environments and to devise appropriate responses to external demands. Open systems planning is aimed at helping organisation members to assess the larger environment and to develop strategies for relating to it more effectively. The intervention results in a clear strategic mission for the organisation, as well as action plans for influencing the environment in favoured directions.

Integrated strategic change is a comprehensive OD intervention. It suggests that business strategies and organisational systems must be changed together in response to external and internal disruptions. A strategic change plan can help members to manage the transition state between the current strategic orientation and the desired future strategic orientation.

Transorganisational development is concerned with helping organisations to enter into partnerships with other organisations in order to perform tasks or to solve problems that are too complex and multifaceted for them to resolve on their own. These multi-organisation systems abound in today's environment and include joint ventures, strategic alliances, research and development consortia, and public–private partnerships. They tend to be loosely coupled and non-hierarchical and, consequently, require different methods from those of most traditional OD interventions that are geared to single organisations. These methods involve helping organisations to recognise the need for partnerships and developing co-ordinating structures for carrying out multi-organisation activities.

ORGANISATION AND ENVIRONMENT FRAMEWORK

This section provides a framework for understanding how environments affect organisations and, in turn, how organisations can impact on environments. The framework is based on the concept described in Chapter 4 that organisations and their sub-units are open systems existing in environmental contexts. Environments provide organisations with the necessary resources, information and legitimacy, and organisations must maintain effective relationships with suitable environments if they are to survive and grow. A manufacturing firm, for example, must obtain raw materials so that it can produce its products, and then use appropriate technologies to efficiently produce them, induce customers to buy them, and satisfy the laws and regulations that govern its operations. Because organisations are dependent on environments, they need to manage all the external constraints and contingencies, while at the same time taking advantage of external opportunities. They also need to influence the environment in favourable directions through such methods as political lobbying, advertising and public relations.

In this section, we first describe the different environments that can affect organisations, and then identify those environmental dimensions that tend to influence the organisational responses to those external forces. Finally, we review the different ways in which an organisation can respond to the environment. This material provides an introductory context for describing the various interventions that concern organisation and environment relationships: open systems planning, integrated strategic change and transorganisational development.

Environments

Organisational environments consist of everything outside organisations that can affect, either directly or indirectly, their performance and outcomes. This could include external agents (such as suppliers, customers, regulators and competitors) and the cultural, political and economic forces in the wider societal and global context. These two classes of environments are called the 'task environment' and the 'general environment', respectively.[1] We will also describe the enacted environment, which reflects members' perceptions of the general and task environments.

The *general environment* consists of all external forces that can influence an organisation or department, and includes technological, legal and regulatory, political, economic, social and ecological components. Each of these forces can affect the organisation in both direct and indirect ways. For example, economic recessions can directly impact on the demand for a company's product. The general environment can also impact indirectly on organisations by virtue of the linkages between external agents. For example, an organisation may have trouble obtaining raw materials from a supplier because a consumer group has embroiled the supplier in a labour dispute with a national union, a lawsuit with a government regulator or a boycott. These members of the organisation's general environment can affect the organisation, even though they have no direct connection to it.

The *task environment* consists of those specific individuals and organisations that interact directly with the organisation and can affect goal achievement. The task environment consists of customers, suppliers, competitors, producers of substitute products or services, labour unions, financial institutions and so on. These direct relationships are the medium through which organisations and environments mutually influence one another. Customers, for example, can demand changes in the organisation's products, but the organisation can attempt to influence customers' tastes and desires through advertising.

The *enacted environment* consists of the organisation's perception and representation of its environment. Weick suggested that environments must be perceived before they can influence decisions as to how to respond.[2] Organisation members must actively observe, register and make sense of the environment before their decisions as to how to act can be made. Thus, only the enacted environment can affect which organisational responses are chosen. The general and task environments, however, can influence whether those responses are successful or ineffective. For example, members may perceive customers as relatively satisfied with their products and may decide to make only token efforts at new-product development. If those perceptions are wrong and customers are dissatisfied with the products, the meagre efforts at product development can have disastrous consequences for the organisation. Consequently, an organisation's enacted environment should accurately reflect its general and task environments if members' decisions and actions are to be based on external realities.

Environmental dimensions

Organisational environments can be characterised along a number of dimensions that can influence organisation and environment relationships. One perspective views environments as information flows and suggests that organisations need to process information in order to discover how to relate to their environments.[3] The key feature of the environment to affect information processing is information uncertainty or the degree to which environmental information is ambiguous. Organisations seek to remove uncertainty from their environment so that they know how best to transact with it. For example, they try to discern customer needs through focus groups and surveys, and they attempt to understand competitor strategies by studying their press releases and sales force behaviours, and by learning about their key personnel. The greater the uncertainty, the more information processing is required to learn about the environment. This is particularly the case when environments are dynamic and complex. Dynamic environments change abruptly and unpredictably, while complex environments have many parts or elements that can affect organisations. These kinds of environments pose difficult information-processing problems for organisations. Global competition, technological change and financial markets, for example, have made the environments of many multinational firms highly uncertain and have severely strained their information-processing capacity.

Another perspective sees environments as consisting of resources for which organisations compete.[4] The key feature of the environment is resource dependence, or the degree to which an organisation relies on other organisations for resources. Organisations seek to manage critical sources of resource dependence, while remaining as autonomous as possible. For example, firms may contract with several suppliers of the same raw material so that they are not overly dependent on one vendor. Resource dependence is extremely high for an organisation when other organisations control critical resources that cannot easily be obtained elsewhere. Resource criticality and availability determine the extent to which an organisation is dependent on other organisations and must respond to their demands, as the 1970s oil embargo by the Organisation of Petroleum Exporting Countries (OPEC) clearly showed many Australian firms.

These two environmental dimensions – information uncertainty and resource dependence – can be combined to show the degree to which organisations are constrained by their environments and consequently must be responsive to their demands.[5] As shown in Figure 10.1, organisations have the most freedom from external forces when information uncertainty and resource dependence are both low. In this situation, organisations do not need to be responsive to their environments and can behave relatively independently of them. United States automotive manufacturers faced these conditions in the 1950s and operated with relatively little external constraint or threat. As information uncertainty and resource dependence become higher, however, organisations are more constrained and must be more responsive to external demands. They must accurately perceive the environment and respond to it appropriately. As described in Chapter 1, modern organisations – such as financial institutions, high-technology firms and health care facilities – are facing unprecedented amounts of environmental uncertainty and resource dependence. Their very existence depends on their recognition of external challenges and their quick and appropriate responses to them.

Organisational responses

Organisations employ a number of ways of responding to environmental demands. These help to buffer the organisation's technology from external disruptions and to link the organisation to sources of information and resources. Referred to as 'external structures', these responses are generally carried out by administrators and staff specialists who are responsible for setting corporate strategy and managing the environment. Three major external structures are described next.

SCANNING UNITS

Organisations must have the capacity to monitor and make sense of their environment if they are to respond to it appropriately. They must identify and attend to those environmental parts and features that are highly related to the organisation's own survival and growth. When environments have high information uncertainty, organisations may need to gather a diversity

Figure 10.1 Environmental dimensions and organisational transactions

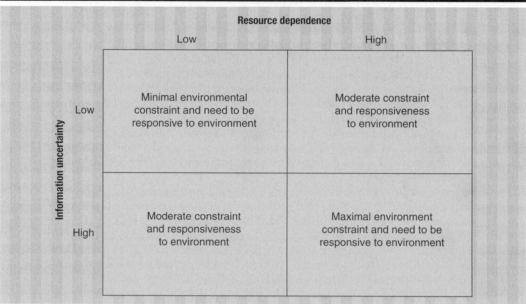

Source: Howard E. Aldrich, *Organizations and Environments*, Prentice-Hall, 1979. Reprinted edition forthcoming in 2008, Stanford University Press, "Business Classics" series, new forward written by the author.

of information in order to comprehend external demands and opportunities. For example, they may need to attend to segmented labour markets, changing laws and regulations, rapid scientific developments, shifting economic conditions, and abrupt changes in customer and supplier behaviours. Organisations can respond to these conditions by establishing special units for scanning particular parts or aspects of the environment, such as departments of market research, public relations, government relations and strategic planning.[6] These units generally include specialists with expertise in a particular segment of the environment, who gather and interpret relevant information about the environment, communicating it to decision makers who develop appropriate responses. For example, market researchers provide information to marketing executives about customer tastes and preferences. Such information guides choices about product development, pricing and advertising.

PROACTIVE RESPONSES

These involve attempts by organisations to change or modify their environments. Organisations are increasingly trying to influence external forces in favourable directions.[7] For example, they engage in political activity to influence government laws and regulations; seek government regulation to control entry to industries; gain legitimacy in the wider society by behaving in accordance with valued cultural norms; acquire control over raw materials or markets by vertical and horizontal integration; and introduce new products and services, using advertising to shape customer tastes and preferences. Although the range of proactive responses is almost limitless, organisations tend to be highly selective when choosing them. The responses can be costly to implement and can appear aggressive, thus evoking countervailing actions by powerful others, such as competitors and the government. For example, Microsoft's dominance in the software industry has drawn heavy scrutiny from the US Justice Department and from competitors. Moreover, organisations are paying increased attention to whether their responses are socially responsible and contribute to a healthy society. The Body Shop, for example, views its business as an important arm of society and devotes a considerable amount of time and corporate resources to charity and pressing social issues. Today, there is much global attention to the ethical and moral implications of organisational behaviours.

COLLECTIVE STRUCTURES

Organisations can cope with problems of environmental dependence and uncertainty by increasing their co-ordination with other organisations. These collective structures help to control interdependencies among organisations and include such methods as bargaining, contracting, co-opting and creating joint ventures, federations, strategic alliances and consortia.[8] Contemporary organisations are increasingly turning to joint ventures and partnerships with other organisations in order to manage environmental uncertainty and perform tasks that are too costly and complicated for single organisations to perform. These multi-organisation arrangements are being used as a means of sharing resources for large-scale research and development, for reducing risks of innovation, for applying diverse expertise to complex problems and tasks, and for overcoming barriers to entry into foreign markets. For example, defence contractors are forming strategic alliances to bid on large government projects; firms from different countries are forming joint ventures to overcome restrictive trade barriers; and high-technology firms are forming research consortia to undertake significant and costly research and development for their industries. Major barriers to forming collective structures in Australia are the organisations' own drive to act autonomously and government policies that discourage co-ordination among organisations, especially in the same industry. Japanese industrial and economic policies, on the other hand, promote co-operation among organisations, thus giving them a competitive advantage in their responses to complex and dynamic global environments.[9] For example, starting in the late 1950s, the Japanese government provided financial assistance and support to a series of co-operative research efforts among Japanese computer manufacturers. The resulting technological developments enabled the computer firms to reduce IBM's share of the mainframe market in Japan from 70% to about 40% in less than 15 years.

An example of how a changed market environment can lead to the need for urgent organisational response is described in Application 10.1.

APPLiCATiON 10.1

SWIPE-CARD SQUEEZE

The fight over banking market share has moved from the front counter to the back office. The big Australian banks have grown accustomed to greater competition in home loans, credit cards, deposits and small-business finance over the past decade, but they have maintained their hold on the transactional side of their business: the authorisation, clearing and settlement of credit, debit and other non-cash payments. But their pre-eminence in payments is now under challenge, thanks to a move by the Reserve Bank of Australia (RBA) to open access to the country's electronic funds transfer system (Eftpos). A new Eftpos access regime came into force on 31 May, and there are several companies ready to challenge the banks in the payment market.

Foreign and regional banks, international technology companies and a handful of hopeful specialist start-ups are lining up to get into the Eftpos system and offer payment services to merchants and other financial institutions. They say the present system is old, expensive and basic. Their promise is lower costs, more flexible systems and more innovative payment options. Companies such as First Data, MoneySwitch, Customers and Pulse International have developed strategies that are based on the idea that merchants will abandon the banks in search of something better.

There is plenty at stake. RBA figures show that non-cash payments are growing quickly. The number of direct debits per capita increased from six to 19 a year between 1997 and 2004, the number of debit-card transactions per capita increased from 24 to 53 a year over the same period, and the number of credit-card transactions increased from 17 to 54. The financial institutions that handle those payments collect a fee with each transaction. Eftpos was developed in the 1980s as a series of bilateral arrangements between banks and merchants. Each institution built its own processing system and linked it to all the other systems in a complex network. Once the system was developed it was not easy for newcomers to get in. They had to pay the banks connection fees, which could be prohibitively high. With the exception of First Data, a big United States payments processing company, few outsiders have made any real impression on the electronic payments market.

▷▷

The RBA reviewed Eftpos as part of an investigation into the credit card, ATM and Eftpos markets that has been going on since the late 1990s. It found that the market for non-cash payments was being distorted by a wholesale pricing structure (what it calls interchange fees) that was not subject to market forces. Restrictive access rules created further distortions. Since 2003, when it made changes to credit-card rules, the RBA has moved to bring down wholesale prices, open up access to payment systems and remove rules governing the activities of merchants.

More change is planned. In November, the RBA will introduce Eftpos interchange pricing, forcing a substantial reduction in costs. And in 2007 it will bring in changes to the ATM market aimed at making user charges more transparent.

For the chief executive of MoneySwitch, Jost Stollmann, the new Eftpos access regime is something he has been working towards for the past two years. The company has been granted a licence by the Australian Prudential Regulation Authority to process debit- and credit-card transactions, and it plans to become an acquirer, competing directly with the big banks in the payments market. In the non-cash payments market, financial institutions play one of two roles: issuing or acquiring. Issuing is on the consumer side of the business: a bank issues a credit or debit card and offers a line of credit or a transaction account for making payments. Acquiring is on the merchant side: an acquiring bank handles the switching, authorisation, clearing and settlement that goes on between a merchant and the consumer's bank when a purchase is made. The big banks are issuers and acquirers.

If and when it picks up its first client, MoneySwitch will be the first specialist payment acquirer in the Australian market. But before it can do this it must get connected to the Eftpos network. Stollmann says he is negotiating with the big banks over access. Part of the new RBA access regime limits the connection fee that established Eftpos companies can charge newcomers such as MoneySwitch to $78 000. No one is saying publicly what it used to cost to get a connection, but sources say it was several hundred thousand dollars.

CHALLENGE AND OPPORTUNITY

Commonwealth Bank (CBA) has the biggest installed base of Eftpos terminals in Australia and stands to lose most from the arrival of specialist acquirers. CBA's head of working capital services, Leslie Martin, says the new access regime is both a challenge and an opportunity for the big banks. It could lose acquiring business to companies such as MoneySwitch, but it could develop a new business as a payment system gateway. MoneySwitch plans to be a full participant in the Eftpos network, but other specialists might baulk at the cost of such an exercise, or they might not see the need. Big banks such as CBA can act as the entry point, or gateway, into the Eftpos system for specialists.

Martin says competition between established Eftpos network participants and the specialists will come down to a choice between 'big, safe and predictable' and 'cheap, flexible and innovative'. Martin concedes that the banks are operating with old systems that are hard to change; the specialist will have the edge in new applications. But she says CBA is making innovations to its system. Last year it introduced BPoint, a service that allows consumers to pay bills through Eftpos terminals.

A couple of the new entrants into the market have already shown their credentials by managing the processing of ATM networks. Pulse operates a network of 2200 ATMs in airports and casinos. The founder of Pulse, Chris van Brugge, says the company runs 20% of the off-premises ATMs in Australia. At the moment Pulse's role is limited to switching transactions. It does not act as an acquirer. Van Brugge says Pulse plans to be an acquirer of debit transactions and it may be a gateway for small financial institutions.

Customers, a company that was established late in 2004, operates a 'fleet' of 1700 ATMs, including all of St George Bank's off-premises machines. It has a contract with Bendigo Bank to handle all the bank's payment processing. Customers' managing director, Greg Baker, says the deals with St George and Bendigo give the company a platform for further expansion into the payment system. Customers has launched a joint venture with Bendigo, Strategic Payment Services, that will operate as a gateway into the payment system, offering switching and processing services for third parties.

'Access reform is a big opportunity for smaller financial institutions and for retailers,' Baker says. 'We will see a lot of change in the market over the next few years.'

THE NEXT STEP

Australia's Eftpos system was developed in the 1980s and has not changed much since then. New participants in the market are promising a revolution:
- New payment processing systems are web-based. This will save merchants money by doing away with the need to have a phone line connecting each Eftpos terminal.
- Processing companies will use wireless technology to make mobile Eftpos possible. A waiter could complete the payment at the table. A hotel guest could complete his registration before arriving at the hotel.
- Web-based systems can bring the Windows computing system into ATMs and Eftpos terminals, turning each device into a computer. This enables the use of loyalty programs at the point of sale.
- Web-based payment systems will allow merchants greater integration between point-of-sale systems and business administration systems.

Source: John Kavanagh, 'Swipe-card squeeze', *Business Review Weekly*, 8–14 June 2006.

Critical Thinking Question: Which of the three organisational response structures described above might be most appropriate for Australia's major banks in this situation?

OPEN SYSTEMS PLANNING

Open systems planning (OSP) helps an organisation to systematically assess its task environment and to develop strategic responses to it. Like the other interventions in this book, OSP treats organisations or departments as open systems that must interact with a suitable environment in order to survive and develop. It helps organisation members develop a strategic mission for relating to the environment and influencing it in favourable directions. The process of applying OSP begins with a diagnosis of the existing environment and how the organisation relates to it. It then develops possible future environments, and action plans to bring about the desired future environment. A number of practical guidelines exist to apply this intervention effectively.

Assumptions about organisation–environment relations

Open systems planning is based on four assumptions about how organisations relate, or should relate, to their environment.[10] These include the following:

1   *Organisation members' perceptions play a major role in environmental relations.* Members' perceptions determine which parts of the environment are attended to or ignored, as well as what value is placed on those parts. Such perceptions provide the basis for planning and implementing specific actions in relation to the environment. For example, a production manager might focus on those parts of the environment that are directly related to making a product, such as raw-material suppliers and available labour, while ignoring other, more indirect parts, such as government agencies. These perceptions would probably direct the manager towards talking with the suppliers and potential employees, while possibly neglecting the agencies. The key point is that organisation and environment relations are largely determined by how members perceive the environment and choose to act towards it.

2   *Organisation members must share a common view of the environment to permit co-ordinated action towards it.* Without a shared view of the environment, organisation members would have trouble relating to it. Conflicts would arise about what parts of the environment are important and what value should be placed on different parts. Such perceptual disagreements make planning and implementing a coherent strategy difficult. For example, members of a top-management team might have different views on the organisation's environment. Unless those differences are shared and resolved, the team will have problems developing a business strategy for relating to the environment.[11]

3   *Organisation members' perceptions must accurately reflect the condition of the
     environment if organisational responses are to be effective.* Members can misinterpret
     environmental information, ignore important forces or attend to negligible events. Such
     misperceptions can render organisational responses to the environment inappropriate, as
     happened to American car makers during the energy crisis of the mid 1970s. They believed
     that consumers wanted large automobiles and petroleum producers had plentiful supplies
     of relatively inexpensive petrol. The traditional strategy of manufacturing a high number
     of large-sized cars was quickly shown to be inappropriate to the actual environment; that
     is, the consumer's growing preference for small, fuel-efficient cars and the decision of
     OPEC member nations to raise the price of crude oil. Such misperceptions typically occur
     when the environment exhibits high levels of complexity and unpredictable change. Such
     turbulence makes understanding the environment or predicting its future difficult.

4   *Organisations can not only adapt to their environment but also create it proactively.*
     Organisation and environment relations are typically discussed in terms of organisations
     adapting to environmental forces. Attention is directed to understanding and predicting
     environmental conditions so that organisations can better react to them. A more
     proactive alternative is for organisations to plan for a desired environment and then to
     take action against the existing environment so as to move it in the desired direction.
     This active stance goes beyond adaptation, because the organisation is trying to create
     a favourable environment rather than simply reacting to external forces. For example,
     when Alcoa first started to manufacture aluminium building materials, there was little
     demand for them. Rather than wait to see whether the market developed, Alcoa entered
     the construction business and pioneered the use of aluminium building materials. By
     being proactive, the company created a favourable environment.

Implementation process

Based on these premises about organisation and environment relations, open systems planning
can help organisation members to assess their environment and plan a strategy for relating to it.
After OSP, they may value differently the complexity of their environment and may generate a
more varied range of response strategies.[12] OSP is typically carried out by the top management
of an entire organisation, or by the management and key employees of a department. This group
initially meets off-site for a two- to three-day period and may have several follow-up meetings
of shorter duration. The OD practitioner helps to guide the process. Members are encouraged to
share their perceptions of the environment and to collect and examine a diversity of related data.
Considerable attention is directed to the communication process itself. Participants are helped to
establish sufficient trust and openness to share different views and to work through differences.

OSP starts from the perspective of a particular organisation or department. This point of
reference identifies the relevant environment. It serves as the focus of the planning process,
which consists of the following steps:[13]

1   *Assess the external environment in terms of domains and the expectations that those
     domains have for the organisation's behaviour.* This step maps the current environment
     facing the organisation. First, the different parts or domains of the environment are
     identified. Listing all the external groups that directly interact with the organisation –
     such as customers, suppliers or government agencies – usually does this. Then each
     domain's expectations of the organisation's behaviour are assessed.

2   *Assess how the organisation responds to the environmental expectations.* This step assesses
     the organisation's responses to the environmental expectations identified in step one.

3   *Identify the core mission of the organisation.* This step helps to identify the underlying
     purpose or core mission of the organisation, as shown by how it responds to external
     demands. Attention is directed at discovering the mission as it is evidenced in the
     organisation's behaviour, rather than by simply accepting an official statement of the
     organisation's purpose. This is accomplished by examining the organisation and those
     environment transactions identified in steps one and two, and then assessing the values
     that seem to underlie those interactions. These values provide clues about the actual
     identity or mission of the organisation.

4   *Create a realistic future scenario of environmental expectations and organisation responses.* This step asks members to project the organisation and its environment into the near future, assuming that there are no real changes in the organisation. It asks what will happen in steps one, two and three if the organisation continues to operate as it does at present.

5   *Create an ideal future scenario of environmental expectations and organisation responses.* Here, members are asked to create alternative, desirable futures. This involves going back over steps one, two and three and asking what members would ideally like to see happen in both the environment and the organisation in the near future. People are encouraged to fantasise about desired futures without worrying about possible constraints.

6   *Compare the present with the ideal future and prepare an action plan for reducing the discrepancy.* This last step identifies specific actions that will move both the environment and the organisation towards the desired future. Planning for appropriate interventions typically occurs in three time frames: tomorrow, six months from now and two years from now. Members also decide on a follow-up schedule for sharing the flow of actions and updating the planning process.

Application 10.2 is an example of an organisation bringing in external expertise to assist with the OSP process.

APPLiCATiON 10.2

THE CHALLENGE OF EXPANSION

Send a Cow is a charity that gives farmers in Africa livestock, training and advice, enabling them to become self-reliant. It also works with some of the most vulnerable groups in Africa. The organisation began to expand after the publicity generated by *The Daily Telegraph*'s 1999 Christmas appeal. As resources poured in, Send a Cow needed a structured approach to manage its growth and ensure its board and management had the necessary competencies to cope. It called in John Vincent, an organisational development consultant who takes part in Cranfield's free management consulting program for small and medium-sized charities. He spent 10 days working with staff and trustees.

Vincent began with a skills audit to identify what the charity was good at and what it needed to be good at in order to expand. He also helped to establish whether different aspects of the organisation were the responsibility of the board or the senior management. 'Send a Cow was clear that it did not want to lose the enthusiasm of trustees, but also wanted the skills and strategy it needed to allow it to develop,' says Vincent.

Staff and board members were asked to fill out self-assessment questionnaires to assess their levels of competence. 'We compared their actual competence with the required competence for what they wanted to achieve as an organisation, and we identified where the gaps were,' Vincent explains.

Martin Geake, chief executive of the charity, knew the evaluation could be intimidating. 'Our team was initially defensive, as I think it's quite natural to be, but John got everyone involved in a way that proved very useful,' he says. A final meeting was held to work out what Send a Cow needed to do about the skills gaps it had, how urgently they needed to be filled and whether personal development of staff and trustees or recruitment was required.

The charity has recruited two trustees to fill the gaps it identified, one with general senior management experience, the second with experience of running a large international NGO.

Source: Graham Willgoss, 'People: People Management: Case Study – The challenge of expansion', *Third Sector*, 22/3/06. This article first appeared in Third Sector, the leading UK weekly magazine for and about charities and the voluntary sector www.thirdsector.co.uk.

Critical Thinking Question: Under what circumstances might it be necessary for an organisation to bring in an outside consultant to assist with OSP?

Guidelines for implementing open systems planning

Practitioners who have applied open systems planning offer a number of suggestions for its effective use.[14] These rules of thumb include the following:

1   *Devote sufficient time and resources.* Open systems planning is time-consuming and requires considerable effort and resources. There is much preparatory work in collecting

environmental information, analysing it and drafting reports for group discussion. Also, participants must be given sufficient time to develop healthy interpersonal relationships so that they can discuss the information openly, resolve conflicting viewpoints and arrive at a sufficient consensus to proceed effectively.

2   *Document all steps.* OSP generates considerable information and people can easily lose track of the data. Written reports of the various steps help to organise the diverse information. They can also keep other organisation members informed of the process and can provide them with a concrete focus for reacting to it.

3   *Deal only with key parts of the environment.* The tendency is to collect and examine too much information, losing track of what is important for organisational effectiveness. Mapping out the existing environment should start with an initial scanning that defines broad environmental domains. Only those domains considered important to organisational or departmental functioning are used for the remaining steps of the process.

4   *Follow the steps in order.* In using OSP, people tend to confuse the existing environment with the future environment. They also tend to mix the realistic future with the ideal future. If the steps are systematically followed, the process will logically lead from the present to the realistic future environment and then to the desired future environment.

5   *View planning as process, not outcome.* Probably the key value of OSP is helping organisation members develop an ongoing process for assessing and relating to the environment. While specific plans and action steps are important, they should be viewed as periodic outcomes of a larger process of environmental management.

INTEGRATED STRATEGIC CHANGE

Integrated strategic change (ISC) is a recent intervention that brings an OD perspective to traditional strategic planning. It was developed in response to managers' complaints that good business strategies often never get implemented. The research suggested that too little attention was being given to the change process and to those human resource issues that were necessary to execute the strategy.[15] For example, the predominant paradigm in strategic planning, formulation and implementation artificially separates strategic thinking from operational and tactical actions; it ignores the contributions that planned change processes can make to implementation. In the traditional process, senior managers and strategic planning staff prepare economic forecasts, competitor analyses and market studies. These studies are then discussed and the firm's strengths and weakness are rationally aligned with the environmental opportunities and threats to form the organisation's strategy.[16] Implementation occurs as middle managers, supervisors and employees hear about the new strategy through memos, restructuring announcements, changes in job responsibilities or new departmental objectives. As a result, there is little understanding of the need for change and little ownership of the new behaviours, initiatives and tactics required to achieve the objectives.

ISC, in contrast, was designed to be a highly participative process. It has three key features:[17]

1   The relevant unit of analysis is the organisation's strategic orientation or the constellation of strategy, structure and process. A business strategy and the organisation design that supports it must be considered as an integrated unit.

2   Creating the strategic plan, gaining commitment and support for it, planning its implementation and executing it is treated as one integrated process. The ability to conduct such a process over and over again when conditions warrant it represents a sustainable competitive advantage.[18]

3   Individuals and groups throughout the organisation are integrated into the analysis, planning and implementation process to create a more achievable plan, to maintain the firm's strategic focus, to concentrate attention and resources on the organisation's key competencies, to improve co-ordination and integration within the organisation and to create higher levels of shared ownership and commitment.

Application stages

The ISC process is applied in four steps:
1   performing a strategic analysis
2   exercising strategic choice
3   designing a strategic change plan
4   implementing the plan.

   The four steps are discussed sequentially here but actually unfold in overlapping and integrated ways. Figure 10.2 displays the steps in the ISC process and its change components. An organisation's existing strategic orientation, identified as its current strategy (S1) and organisation design (O1), is linked to its future strategic orientation (S2/O2) by the strategic change plan.

PERFORMING A STRATEGIC ANALYSIS

The ISC process begins with a diagnosis of the organisation's readiness for change and its current strategy and organisation (S1/O1). The most important indicator of readiness is senior management's willingness and ability to carry out strategic change. Greiner and Schein suggest that the two key dimensions in this analysis are the leader's willingness and commitment to change and the team members' willingness and ability to follow the leader's initiative.[19] Organisations whose leaders are not willing to lead and whose senior managers are not willing and able to support the new strategic direction when necessary should consider team-building processes to ensure their commitment.

   The second stage in strategic analysis is understanding the current strategy and organisation design. The process begins with an examination of the organisation's industry as well as its current financial performance and effectiveness. This information provides the necessary context to assess the current strategic orientation's viability. Porter's models of industry attractiveness,[20] as well as the environmental framework introduced at the beginning of this chapter, are the two most relevant models for analysing the environment. Next, the current strategic orientation is described to explain current levels of performance and human outcomes. Several models for guiding this diagnosis exist.[21] For example, the current strategic orientation can be assessed according to the model and methods introduced in Chapter 4. The organisation's mission, goals and objectives, intent and business policies represent the strategy. The structure, work,

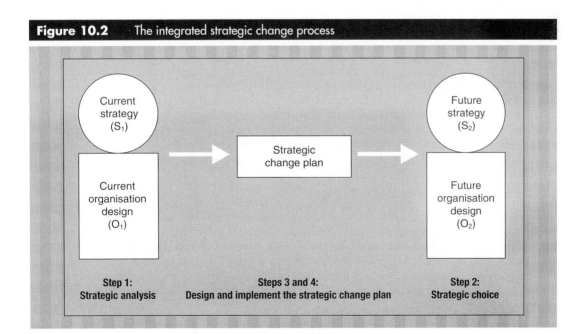

Figure 10.2   The integrated strategic change process

information and human resource systems describe the organisation design. Other models for understanding the organisation's strategic orientation include the competitive positioning model[22] and other typologies.[23] These frameworks assist in assessing customer satisfaction, product and service offerings; financial health; technological capabilities; and organisational culture, structure and systems.

Strategic analysis actively involves organisation members in the process. Search conferences; employee focus groups; interviews with salespeople, customers and purchasing agents; and other methods allow a variety of employees and managers to participate in the diagnosis and increase the amount and relevance of the data collected. This builds commitment to, and ownership of, the change effort; should a strategic change effort be initiated, members are more likely to understand why and be supportive of it.

EXERCISING STRATEGIC CHOICE

The strategic analysis often points out misfits among the organisation's environment, strategic orientation and performance. As the process unfolds, alternative strategies, organisation designs and member preferences will emerge. Based on this analysis, senior management envisions the future and broadly defines two or three alternative sets of objectives and strategies for achieving them. Market forecasts, employees' readiness and willingness to change, competitor analyses and other projections can be used to develop these alternative future scenarios.[24] The different sets of objectives and strategies also include projections about the organisational design changes that will be necessary to support each alternative. Although participation from other organisational stakeholders is important in the alternative generation phase, choosing the appropriate strategic orientation ultimately rests with top management and cannot be easily delegated. Senior managers are in the unique position of being able to view strategy from a general management position. When major strategic decisions are given to lower level managers, the risk of focusing too narrowly on a product, market or technology increases.

This step determines the content, or 'what', of strategic change. The desired strategy (S2) defines the products or services to offer, the markets to be served and the way these outputs will be produced and positioned. The desired organisation design (O2) specifies the organisational structures and processes necessary to support this new strategy. The alignment of an organisation's design with a particular strategy can be a major source of superior performance and competitive advantage.[25]

DESIGNING A STRATEGIC CHANGE PLAN

The strategic change plan is a comprehensive agenda for moving the organisation from its current strategy and organisation design to the desired future strategic orientation. It represents the process, or 'how', of strategic change. The change plan describes the types, magnitude and schedule of change activities, as well as the costs associated with them. It also specifies how the changes will be implemented (given power and political issues), the nature of the organisational culture and the current ability of the organisation to implement change.[26]

IMPLEMENTING A STRATEGIC CHANGE PLAN

The final step in the ISC process is the actual implementation of the strategic change plan. The implementation of the change plan draws heavily on knowledge of motivation, group dynamics and change processes. It deals continuously with such issues as alignment, adaptability, teamwork, and organisational and personal learning. Implementation requires senior managers to champion the different elements of the change plan, which they do by initiating action and allocating resources to particular activities, setting high but achievable goals and providing feedback on accomplishments. In addition, leaders must hold people accountable to the change objectives, institutionalise each change that occurs and be prepared to solve problems as they arise. This final point recognises that no strategic change plan can account for all of the contingencies that emerge. There must be a willingness to adjust the plan as implementation unfolds in order to address unforeseen and unpredictable events and to take advantage of new opportunities.

The retail sector in Australia is highly competitive, particularly between the major department stores Myer and David Jones. Application 10.3 outlines a strategic change at Myer's Melbourne city centre store.

APPLiCATiON 10.3

RETAIL RESURRECTION

A DJ booth in a $900 caravan, jeans in a display fridge, grandma's kitsch, Chesterfield lounges in the cafe, DIY T-shirts and street art are all a part of Myer's youth concept floor in its flagship Melbourne department store. Known as The Basement (with no Myer branding), the store takes up the length of two city blocks and is the innovative solution to how to use a part of the store that struggled to shake off its image as an empty, depressing bargain basement.

Opened on December 1, in time for bidders for Myer to see its potential, the youth concept was devised and realised throughout the stressful sale time. 'The space was a disaster,' says Myer's creative director, Paul Bonnici. 'It was the best retail real estate and it was doing nothing.' After a trip to the legendary department store Galeries Lafayette in Paris, which has a similar youth space, Myer's managing director, Dawn Robertson, suggested moving the store's Miss Shop to the basement. Bonnici and Myer's visual brand manager, Wayne Latham, began researching edgy youth retailers, coming up with voluminous reports on the visuals of this specific retail market. A report was presented to Robertson in May 2005. The following month, a small creative team flew to Paris with Robertson to research the youth retailing trend in department stores.

Bonnici's team had a modest budget and six months to get the store open. There was not enough money to outsource many aspects of the project, so internal staff were involved in adapting fixtures, managing heritage planning issues, creating the design concept, finding new fixtures in junkyards and op shops, and finding new mannequins and recycling old ones. 'We lived and breathed the project,' says Bonnici.

Source: Emily Ross, 'Retail resurrection', *Business Review Weekly*, 8/6/06.

Critical Thinking Question: Why do you think a major department store like Myer would think it important to create a successful youth space in one of its flagship stores?

TRANSORGANISATIONAL DEVELOPMENT

Transorganisational development (TD) is an emerging form of planned change aimed at helping organisations develop collective and collaborative strategies with other organisations. Many of the tasks, problems and issues facing organisations today are too complex and multifaceted to be addressed by a single organisation. Multi-organisation strategies and arrangements are increasing rapidly in today's global, highly competitive environment. In the private sector, research and development consortia allow companies to share resources and risks associated with large-scale research efforts. For example, Sematech involves many large organisations – such as Intel, AT&T, IBM, Xerox and Motorola – that have joined together to improve the competitiveness of the US semiconductor industry. Joint ventures between domestic and foreign firms help to overcome trade barriers and to facilitate technology transfer across nations. For example, the New United Motor Manufacturing, Inc. in Fremont, California, is a joint venture between General Motors and Toyota to produce automobiles, using Japanese teamwork methods. In the public sector, partnerships between government and business provide the resources and initiative to undertake complex urban renewal projects, such as the Docklands project in Melbourne. Alliances among public service agencies in a region – such as the Goulburn rural health services in alliance with the local councils in Albury and Wodonga – can improve the co-ordination of services, promote economies and avoid costly overlap and redundancy.

Transorganisational systems and their problems

Cummings has referred to these multi-organisation structures as transorganisational systems (TSs): groups of organisations that have joined together for a common purpose.[27] TSs are functional social systems midway between single organisations and societal systems. They are able to make decisions and perform tasks on behalf of their member organisations, although members maintain their separate organisational identities and goals. In contrast to most organisations, TSs tend to be underorganised: relationships among member organisations are loosely coupled; leadership and power are dispersed among autonomous organisations, rather than hierarchically centralised; and commitment and membership are tenuous as member organisations attempt to maintain their autonomy while jointly performing.

These characteristics make creating and managing TSs difficult.[28] Potential member organisations may not see the need to join with other organisations. They may be concerned with maintaining their autonomy or have trouble identifying potential partners. Australian firms, for example, are traditionally 'rugged individualists', preferring to work alone rather than to join with other organisations. Even if organisations do decide to join together, they may have problems managing their relationships and controlling joint performances. Because members are typically accustomed to hierarchical forms of control, they may have difficulty managing lateral relations among independent organisations. They may also have difficulty managing different levels of commitment and motivation among members, and sustaining membership over time.

Application stages

Given these problems, transorganisational development has evolved as a unique form of planned change aimed at creating TSs and improving their effectiveness. In laying out the conceptual boundaries of TD, Cummings described the practice of TD as following the stages of planned change appropriate for underorganised systems (see Chapter 2).[29] These stages parallel other process models that have been proposed for creating and managing joint ventures, strategic alliances and interorganisational collaboration.[30] The four stages are shown in Figure 10.3, along with key issues that need to be addressed at each stage. The stages and issues are described next.

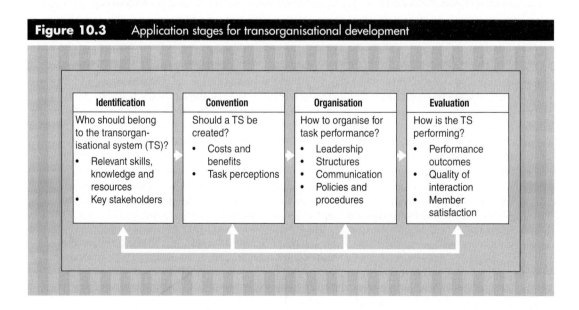

Figure 10.3   Application stages for transorganisational development

IDENTIFICATION STAGE

This initial stage of TD involves the identification of potential member organisations of the TS. It serves to specify the relevant participants for the remaining stages of TD. Identifying potential members can be difficult, because organisations may not perceive the need to join together or may not know enough about each other to make membership choices. These problems are typical when trying to create a new TS. Relationships among potential members may be loosely coupled or nonexistent, and so, even if organisations see the need to form a TS, they may be unsure about who should be included.

The identification stage is generally carried out by one or a few organisations who are interested in exploring the possibility of creating a TS. Change agents work with these organisations to specify criteria for membership in the TS and identify organisations meeting those standards. Because TSs are intended to perform specific tasks, a practical criterion for membership is how much organisations can contribute to task performance. Potential members can be identified and judged in terms of the skills, knowledge and resources that they can bring to bear on the TS task. TD practitioners warn, however, that identifying potential members should also take into account the political realities of the situation.[31] Consequently, key stakeholders who can affect the creation and subsequent performance of the TS are identified as possible members.

During the early stages of creating a TS, there may be insufficient leadership and cohesion among participants to choose potential members. In these situations, participants may contract with an outside change agent who can help them to achieve sufficient agreement on TS membership. In several cases of TD, change agents helped members to create a special leadership group that could make decisions on behalf of the participants.[32] This leadership group comprised a small cadre of committed members and was able to develop enough cohesion among themselves to carry out the identification stage.

CONVENTION STAGE

Once potential members of the TS have been identified, the convention stage is concerned with bringing them together to assess whether creating a TS is desirable and feasible. This face-to-face meeting enables potential members to mutually explore their motivations for joining, and their perceptions of the joint task. They seek to establish sufficient levels of motivation and of task consensus to form the TS.

Like the identification stage, this phase of TD generally requires considerable direction and facilitation by change agents. Existing stakeholders may not have the legitimacy or skills to perform the convening function, and change agents can serve as conveners if they are perceived as legitimate and credible by the different organisations. In many TD cases, conveners came from research centres or universities with reputations for neutrality and expertise in TD.[33] Because participating organisations tend to have diverse motives and views and limited means for resolving differences, change agents may need to structure and manage interactions to facilitate the airing of differences and arriving at consensus about forming the TS. They may need to help organisations work through differences and reconcile self-interests with those of the larger TS.

ORGANISATION STAGE

When the convention stage results in the decision to create a TS, members begin to organise themselves for task performance. This involves establishing structures and mechanisms to facilitate communication and interaction among members and to direct joint efforts to the task at hand.[34] For example, members may create a co-ordinating council to manage the TS and they might assign a powerful leader to head that group. They might choose to formalise exchanges among members by developing rules, policies and formal operating procedures. In cases in which members are required to invest large amounts of resources in the TS, such as might occur in an industry-based research consortium, the organising stage typically includes voluminous contracting and negotiating about members' contributions and returns. Here, corporate lawyers and financial analysts play key roles in structuring the TS. They determine how costs and benefits will be allocated among member organisations, as well as the legal obligations and contractual rights of members.

EVALUATION STAGE

This final stage of TD involves assessing how the TS is performing. Members need feedback so that they can identify problems and begin to resolve them. Feedback data generally include performance outcomes and member satisfaction, as well as indicators of how well members are jointly interacting. Change agents, for example, can periodically interview or survey member organisations about various outcomes and features of the TS and feed that data back to TS leaders. Such information can enable leaders to make necessary modifications and adjustments in how the TS is operating. It may signal the need to return to previous stages of TD to make necessary corrections, as shown by the feedback arrows in Figure 10.3.

Roles and skills of the change agent

Transorganisational development is a relatively new application of planned change and practitioners are still exploring appropriate roles and skills. They are discovering the complexities of working with underorganised systems made up of multiple organisations. This contrasts sharply with OD, which has traditionally been applied in single organisations that are heavily organised. Consequently, the roles and skills relevant to OD need to be modified and supplemented when applied to TD.

The major role demands of TD derive from the two prominent features of TSs: their underorganisation and their multi-organisation composition. Because TSs are underorganised, change agents need to play activist roles in creating and developing them.[35] They need to bring structure to a group of autonomous organisations that may not see the need to join together or may not know how to form an alliance. The activist role requires a good deal of leadership and direction, particularly during the initial stages of TD. For example, change agents may need to educate potential TS members about the benefits of joining together. They may need to structure face-to-face encounters aimed at sharing information and exploring interaction possibilities.

Because TSs are made up of multiple organisations, change agents need to maintain a neutral role, treating all members alike.[36] They need to be seen by members as working on behalf of the total system, rather than as being aligned with particular members or views. When change agents are perceived as neutral, TS members are more likely to share information with them and to listen to their inputs. Such neutrality can enhance the change agents' ability to mediate conflicts among members. It can help them uncover diverse views and interests of, and forge agreements between, different stakeholders. Change agents, for example, can act as mediators, ensuring that members' views receive a fair hearing and that disputes are equitably resolved. They can help to bridge the different views and interests, and achieve integrative solutions.

Given these role demands, the skills needed to practise TD include political and networking abilities.[37] Political competence is needed to understand and resolve the conflicts of interest and value dilemmas inherent in systems that are made up of multiple organisations, each seeking to maintain autonomy while jointly interacting. Political savvy can help change agents to manage their own roles and values in respect to those power dynamics. It can help them to avoid being co-opted by certain TS members, thus losing their neutrality.

Networking skills are also indispensable to TD practitioners. These include the ability to manage lateral relations among autonomous organisations in the relative absence of hierarchical control. Change agents must be able to span the boundaries of diverse organisations, link them together and facilitate exchanges among them. They must be able to form linkages where none existed and to transform networks into operational systems capable of joint task performance.

Defining the roles and skills of TD practitioners is still in a formative stage. Our knowledge in this area will continue to develop as more experience is gained with TSs. Change agents are discovering, for example, that the complexity of TSs requires a team consulting approach, involving practitioners with different skills and approaches working together to facilitate TS effectiveness. Initial reports of TD practice suggest that such change projects are both large scale and long term.[38] They typically involve multiple, simultaneous interventions that are aimed at both the total TS and its constituent members. The stages of TD application are protracted, requiring considerable time and effort to identify relevant organisations, to convene them and to organise them for task performance.

Summary

In this chapter we presented interventions aimed at improving organisation and environment relationships. Because organisations are open systems that exist in environmental contexts, they must establish and maintain effective linkages with the environment in order to survive and prosper. Three environments impact on organisational functioning: the general environment, the task environment and the enacted environment. Only the last of these can affect organisational choices about behaviour, but the first two impact on the consequences of those actions. Two key environmental dimensions affect the degree to which organisations are constrained by their environments and need to be responsive to them: information uncertainty and resource dependence. When both dimensions are high, organisations are maximally constrained and need to be responsive to their environment.

Open systems planning helps an organisation to systematically assess its environment and develop strategic responses to it. OSP is based on assumptions about the role of people's perceptions in environmental relations and the need for a shared view of the environment that permits co-ordinated action towards it. It begins with an assessment of the existing environment and how the firm relates to it and progresses to possible future environments and action plans to bring them about. A number of guidelines exist for effectively applying this intervention.

Integrated strategic change is a comprehensive intervention for addressing organisation and environment issues. It gives equal weight to the business and organisational factors that affect organisation performance and effectiveness. In addition, these factors are highly integrated during the process of assessing the current strategy and organisation design, selecting the desired strategic orientation, developing a strategic change plan and implementing it.

Transorganisational development is an emerging form of planned change that is aimed at helping organisations create partnerships with other organisations to perform tasks or to solve problems that are too complex and multifaceted for single organisations to carry out. Because these multi-organisation systems tend to be underorganised, TD follows the stages of planned change relevant to underorganised systems: identification, convention, organisation and evaluation. TD is a relatively new application of planned change, and appropriate change-agent roles and skills are still being formulated.

ACTIVITIES

Review questions

① What constitutes the organisation's general environment? How would this impact on decisions made by a change agent?

② What is the key dimension of task environment? Give current examples.

③ Through what strategies do organisations gain 'control' over their environments? What implications does this have for how we manage change?

④ What is associated with a transorganisational system? Describe its stages and compare and contrast this with the OD process.

⑤ Explain open systems planning and discuss the advantages and disadvantages of recognising and utilising such a system.

▷▷

⑥ What is the assumption that underlies the integrated strategic change process and what are the steps for implementation? Discuss some of the problems which are likely to be encountered.

⑦ Identify and give examples of the major strategic intervention techniques.

Discussion and essay questions

① How does integrated strategic change differ from traditional strategic planning and traditional planned organisation change? Give examples which will highlight these differences.

② What is open systems planning and what assumptions is it based on? Create a convincing argument for its being accepted as a valid change strategy.

③ How do environmental factors affect the types of interventions that might be carried out in an organisation? What role does the change agent play in determining the most appropriate intervention?

④ What is the role of the change agent in transorganisational development? Identify possible difficulties that may occur in the change agent–client relationship.

NOTES

1 R. Miles, *Macro Organization Behavior* (Santa Monica, CA: Goodyear, 1980); D. Robey and C. Sales, *Designing Organizations*, 4th edn (Homewood, IL: Irwin, 1994).

2 K. Weick, *The Social Psychology of Organizing*, 2nd edn (Reading, MA: Addison-Wesley, 1979).

3 J. Galbraith, *Competing with Flexible Lateral Organizations*, 2nd edn (Reading, MA: Addison-Wesley, 1994).

4 J. Pfeffer and G. Salancik, *The External Control of Organizations: A Resource Dependence Perspective* (New York: Harper and Row, 1978).

5 H. Aldrich, *Organizations and Environments* (New York: Prentice-Hall, 1979); L. Hrebiniak and W. Joyce, 'Organizational adaptation: strategic choice and environmental determinism', *Administrative Science Quarterly*, 30 (1985): 336–49.

6 Pfeffer and Salancik, *The External Control of Organizations*, op. cit.

7 Aldrich, *Organizations and Environments*, op. cit.

8 ibid.

9 W. Ouchi, *The M-Form Society: How American Teamwork Can Recapture the Competitive Edge* (Reading, MA: Addison-Wesley, 1984); L. Thurow, *Head to Head: The Coming Economic Battle Among Japan, Europe and America* (New York: William Morrow, 1992).

10 T. Cummings and S. Srivastva, *Management of Work: A Socio-Technical Systems Approach* (San Diego: University Associates, 1977): 112–16.

11 L. Bourgeois, 'Strategic goals, perceived uncertainty and economic performance in volatile environments', *Academy of Management Journal*, 28 (1985): 548–73; C. West Jr and C. Schwenk, 'Top management team strategic consensus, demographic homogeneity and firm performance: a report of resounding nonfindings', *Academy of Management Journal*, 17 (1996): 571–6.

12 J. Clark and C. Krone, 'Towards an overall view of organisation development in the seventies', in *Management of Change and Conflict*, eds J. Thomas and W. Bennis (Middlesex, England: Penguin Books, 1972): 284–304.

13 C. Krone, 'Open systems redesign', in *Theory and Method in Organization Development: An Evolutionary Process*, ed. J. Adams (Arlington, VA: NTL Institute for Applied Behavioral Science, 1974): 364–91; G. Jayaram, 'Open systems planning', in *The Planning of Change*, 3rd edn, eds W. Bennis, K. Benne, R. Chin and K. Corey, (New York: Holt, Rinehart and Winston, 1976): 275–83; R. Beckhard and R. Harris, *Organizational Transitions: Managing Complex Change*, 2nd edn (Reading, MA: Addison-Wesley, 1987); Cummings and Srivastva, *Management of Work*, op. cit.

14 Jayaram, 'Open systems planning', op. cit., 275–83; Cummings and Srivastva, *Management of Work*, op. cit.; R. Fry, 'Improving trustee, administrator and physician collaboration through open systems planning', in *Organization Development in Health Care Organizations*, eds N. Margulies and J. Adams (Reading, MA: Addison-Wesley, 1982): 282–92.

15 M. Jelinek and J. Litterer, 'Why OD must become strategic', in *Organizational Change and Development*, 2, eds W. Pasmore and R. Woodman (Greenwich, CT: JAI Press, 1988): 135–62; A. Bhambri and L. Pate, 'Introduction – the strategic change agenda: stimuli, processes and outcomes', *Journal of Organization Change*

Management, 4 (1991): 4–6; D. Nadler, M. Gerstein, R. Shaw and associates, *Organizational Architecture* (San Francisco: Jossey-Bass, 1992); C. Worley, D. Hitchin and W. Ross, *Integrated Strategic Change: How Organization Development Builds Competitive Advantage* (Reading, MA: Addison-Wesley, 1996).

16 H. Mintzberg, *The Rise and Fall of Strategic Planning* (New York: The Free Press, 1994).

17 Worley, Hitchin and Ross, *Integrated Strategic Change*, op. cit.

18 P. Senge, *The Fifth Discipline* (New York: Doubleday, 1990); E. Lawler III, *The Ultimate Advantage* (San Francisco: Jossey-Bass, 1992); Worley, Hitchin and Ross, *Integrated Strategic Change*, op. cit.

19 L. Greiner and V. Schein, *Power and Organization Development* (Reading, MA: Addison-Wesley, 1988).

20 M. Porter, *Competitive Strategy* (New York: The Free Press, 1980).

21 R. Grant, *Contemporary Strategy Analysis*, 2nd edn (Cambridge, MA: Basil Blackwell, 1995).

22 M. Porter, *Competitive Advantage* (New York: Free Press, 1985).

23 R. Miles and C. Snow, *Organization Strategy, Structure and Process* (New York: McGraw-Hill, 1978); M. Tushman and E. Romanelli, 'Organizational evolution: a metamorphosis model of convergence and reorientation', in *Research in Organization Behavior*, 7, eds L. Cummings and B. Staw (Greenwich, CT: JAI Press, 1985).

24 J. Naisbitt and P. Aburdene, *Reinventing the Corporation* (New York: Warner Books, 1985); A. Toffler, *The Third Wave* (New York: McGraw-Hill, 1980); A. Toffler, *The Adaptive Corporation* (New York: McGraw-Hill, 1984); M. Weisbord, *Productive Workplaces* (San Francisco: Jossey-Bass, 1987).

25 E. Lawler III, *The Ultimate Advantage* (San Francisco: Jossey-Bass, 1992); M. Tushman, W. Newman and E. Romanelli, 'Convergence and upheaval: managing the unsteady pace of organizational evolution', *California Management Review*, 29 (1987): 1–16; Nadler, Gerstein, Shaw and associates, *Organizational Architecture*, op. cit.; R. Buzzell and B. Gale, *The PIMS Principles* (New York: Free Press, 1987).

26 L. Hrebiniak and W. Joyce, *Implementing Strategy* (New York: Macmillan, 1984); J. Galbraith and R. Kazanjian, *Strategy Implementation: Structure, Systems and Process*, 2nd edn (St. Paul: West Publishing Company, 1986).

27 T. Cummings, 'Transorganizational development', in *Research in Organizational Behavior*, 6, eds B. Staw and L. Cummings (Greenwich, CT: JAI Press, 1984): 367–422.

28 B. Gray, 'Conditions facilitating interorganizational collaboration', *Human Relations*, 38 (1985): 911–36; K. Harrigan and W. Newman, 'Bases of interorganization co-operation: propensity, power, persistence', *Journal of Management Studies*, 27 (1990): 417–34; Cummings, 'Transorganizational development', op. cit.

29 Cummings, 'Transorganizational development', op. cit.

30 C. Raben, 'Building strategic partnerships: creating and managing effective joint ventures', in *Organizational Architecture*, eds D. Nadler, M. Gerstein, R. Shaw and associates (San Francisco: Jossey-Bass, 1992): 81–109; B. Gray, *Collaborating: Finding Common Ground for Multiparty Problems* (San Francisco: Jossey-Bass, 1989); Harrigan and Newman, 'Bases of interorganization co-operation', op. cit.; P. Lorange and J. Roos, 'Analytical steps in the formation of strategic alliances', *Journal of Organizational Change Management*, 4 (1991): 60–72.

31 D. Boje, 'Towards a theory and praxis of transorganizational development: stakeholder networks and their habitats', (working paper 79–6, Behavioral and Organizational Science Study Center, Graduate School of Management, University of California at Los Angeles, February 1982); B. Gricar, 'The legitimacy of consultants and stakeholders in interorganizational problems' (paper presented at annual meeting of the Academy of Management, San Diego, August 1981); T. Williams, 'The search conference in active adaptive planning', *Journal of Applied Behavioral Science*, 16 (1980): 470–83; B. Gray and T. Hay, 'Political limits to interorganizational consensus and change', *Journal of Applied Behavioral Science*, 22 (1986): 95–112.

32 E. Trist, 'Referent organizations and the development of interorganizational domains' (paper delivered at annual meeting of the Academy of Management, Atlanta, August 1979).

33 Cummings, 'Transorganizational development', op. cit.

34 Raben, 'Building strategic partnerships', op. cit.

35 Cummings, 'Transorganizational development', op. cit.

36 ibid.

37 B. Gricar and D. Brown, 'Conflict, power and organization in a changing community', *Human Relations*, 34 (1981): 877–93.

38 Cummings, 'Transorganizational development', op. cit.

Online reading

INFOTRAC® COLLEGE EDITION

For additional readings and reviews on strategic interventions, explore **InfoTrac® College Edition**, your online library. Go to **www.infotrac-college.com** and search for any of the InfoTrac key terms listed below:

- **Framework**
- **Environment scanning**
- **Open systems planning**
- **Integrated strategic change**
- **Transorganisational development**

INFOTRAC

ORGANiSATiON TRANSFORMATiON

CHANGE iN CHAOTiC AND UNPREDiCTABLE ENViRONMENTS

This chapter presents interventions that are aimed at organisation transformation (OT) and describes activities designed to change the basic character or culture of the organisation. These interventions bring about important alignments among the organisation strategies, design elements and culture, and between the organisation and its competitive environment.[1] These frame-breaking and sometimes revolutionary interventions are mostly directed at the culture or dominant paradigm within the organisation and typically go beyond improving the organisation incrementally, instead focusing on changing the way it views itself and its environment.

Organisation transformations can occur in response to, or in anticipation of, major changes in the organisation's environment or technology. In addition, these changes are often associated with significant alterations in the firm's business strategy, which, in turn, may require modifying corporate culture as well as the internal structures and processes in order to support the new direction. Such fundamental change entails a new paradigm for organising and managing organisations. It involves qualitatively different ways of perceiving, thinking and behaving in organisations. Movement towards this new way of operating requires top managers to take an active leadership role. The change process is characterised by considerable innovation and learning, and continues almost indefinitely as organisation members discover new ways of improving the organisation and adapting it to changing conditions.

Organisation transformation is a recent advance in organisation development and there is some confusion about its meaning and definition. This chapter starts with a description of several major features of transformational change. Against this background, three kinds of interventions are discussed: culture change, self-design and organisation learning.

Organisation culture is the pattern of assumptions, values and norms shared by organisation members. A growing body of research has shown that culture can affect strategy formulation and implementation, as well as a firm's ability to achieve high levels of performance. Culture change involves helping senior executives and administrators to diagnose existing culture and make necessary alterations in the basic assumptions and values that underlie organisational behaviours.

Self-designing organisations are those that have gained the capacity to fundamentally alter themselves. Creating them is a highly participative process involving multiple stakeholders in setting strategic directions, designing appropriate structures and processes, and implementing them. This intervention includes considerable innovation and learning as organisations design and implement significant changes. Organisation learning refers to the capacity of an organisation to change and improve.[2] As distinct from individual learning, this intervention helps the organisation move beyond solving existing problems to gain the capability to improve continuously. It results in the development of a learning organisation, where empowered members take responsibility for strategic direction.

CHARACTERISTICS OF TRANSFORMATIONAL CHANGE

During the 1990s a large number of organisations radically altered the way they operated and related to their environment. Increased foreign competition forced many industries to downsize and to become leaner, more efficient and flexible. Deregulation pushed organisations in the financial services, telecommunications and airline industries to rethink business strategies and to reshape how they operate. Public demands for less government and lowered deficits forced public-sector agencies to streamline operations and to deliver more for less. Rapid changes in technologies rendered many organisational practices obsolete, pushing firms to be continually innovative and nimble.

Organisation transformation implies radical changes in the way members perceive, think and behave at work. These changes go far beyond making the existing organisation better, or finetuning the status quo. They are concerned with fundamentally altering the assumptions that underlie how the organisation relates to its environment and functions. Changing these assumptions entails significant shifts in corporate philosophy and values, and in the numerous structures and organisational arrangements that shape members' behaviours. Not only is the magnitude of change greater, but the change fundamentally also alters the qualitative nature of the organisation.

Organisation transformation interventions are recent additions to OD and are still in a formative stage of development. For example, organisation learning was originally discussed in the late 1950s, but did not reach prominence until the early 1990s. Examination of the rapidly growing literature on the topic suggests, however, several distinguishing features of these revolutionary change efforts. They are triggered by environmental and internal disruptions; create systemic and revolutionary change; result in a new organising paradigm; are driven by senior executives and line management; and requires continuous learning and change.

Environmental and internal triggers

Organisations are unlikely to undertake transformational change unless significant reasons to do so emerge. Power, sentience and expertise are vested in existing organisational arrangements and, when faced with problems, members are more likely to finetune those structures than to drastically alter them. Thus, in most cases organisations must experience or anticipate a severe threat to survival before they will be motivated to undertake transformational change. Such threats generally arise when environmental and internal changes that threaten the very existence of the organisation (as it is presently constituted) render existing organisational strategies and designs obsolete. Application 11.1 highlights significant contemporary changes that will have a dramatic impact on organisations.

APPLICATION 11.1

LEADING INDICATORS

Leadership is in; management is out. The changing currency of words routinely reveals alterations in social or economic directions, and the downgrading of 'management' suggests that seminal changes are afoot in business. Just as human resources has replaced personnel, so have managers been replaced by real or incipient leaders.

It is not hard to identify what is causing the rethink. The results-oriented methods of 30 years ago and the process-oriented techniques of 15 years ago have been replaced by far more complex challenges, involving solving basic questions about what the enterprise is, what the market is, and how staff should be treated. In conditions of uncertainty, the need for the decisiveness of true leaders seems self-evident.´

The six trends analysed ... are fundamentally changing the dynamics of firms. Globalisation, especially the entrance into the world economy of China and India, is changing the dynamics of capital and labour everywhere. Complexity is increasing, not least because the old methods of management must be maintained while new challenges, such as more market complexity and uncertain corporate structures, are met. Companies have difficult questions to answer about when to outsource, how to create incentives within flatter organisational structures in which promotion is less available, ands what kinds of internal influence to exert to get the best out of staff.

▷▷

Maintaining staff when the conventional incentives have been removed is a leadership challenge, especially considering the emerging shortages of skilled workers, which is a function of demographic changes that will affect labour markets for at least 20 years.

The conclusion is that greater vision, the supposed principal attribute of leaders, is what is required. Just how much this is really meaningful is questionable. The principal of the consultancy Heads Together, Bruce Watson, suggests that managers may simply have to develop new skills; a wholesale change is not necessary. 'Leadership may just boil down to an ability to influence in an appropriate way, taking into account the context and situational elements of the circumstances,' he says. 'Surely "influence" is something that is distributed throughout the people in organisations, just as learning and knowledge are. The great leader, the individual manager or chief executive managing from the top down as the total unit of analysis in organisational functioning, is well past its use-by date.'

It is not even certain if it is possible to develop the necessary skills and attributes to be dubbed a leader. Leadership consultants are prone to reduce the subject to the features of great leaders, an approach that is necessarily biased. No one wants leaders with the humility of Napoleon, the memory of Ronald Reagan or the imbibing habits of Winston Churchill.

The subject may be ill-defined, but the obsession with leadership does at least pose questions about conventional management. In an environment of heightened uncertainty, the questions are worth asking, even if the answers are likely to remain elusive.

Source: David James, 'Leading indicators', *Business Review Weekly*, 25/8/05.

Critical Thinking Question: What are the six trends mentioned in Application 11.1? With each trend identify how organisations will need to implement OT interventions to remain competitive.

In studying a large number of organisation transformations, Tushman, Newman and Romanelli showed that transformational change occurs in response to at least three kinds of disruption:[3]

- *Industry discontinuities*. These are sharp changes in legal, political, economic and technological conditions that shift the basis for competition within industries.
- *Product life-cycle shifts*. These are changes in product life cycle that require different business strategies.
- *Internal company dynamics*. These are changes in size, corporate portfolio strategy, executive turnover and the like.

These disruptions severely jolt organisations and push them to alter business strategy and, in turn, their mission, values, structure, systems and procedures.

Systemic and revolutionary change

Transformational change involves reshaping the organisation's culture and design elements. These changes can be characterised as systemic and revolutionary as the entire nature of the organisation is fundamentally altered. Typically driven by senior executives, change may occur rapidly so that it does not get mired in politics, individual resistance and other forms of organisational inertia.[4] This is particularly true of changes to such features of the organisation as structure, information systems, human resource practices and work design, which tend to reinforce one another, thus making it difficult to change them in a piecemeal manner.[5] They need to be changed together and in a co-ordinated fashion so that they can mutually support each other, as well as the new cultural values and assumptions.[6] Transformational change, however, is distinguished from other types of strategic change by its attention to the people side of the organisation. For a change to be labelled 'transformational', a majority of individuals in an organisation must change their behaviour.[7]

Long-term studies of organisational evolution underscore the revolutionary nature of transformational change.[8] They suggest that organisations tend to move through relatively long periods of smooth growth and operation. These periods of convergence or evolution are characterised by incremental changes. At times, however, most organisations experience severe external or internal disruptions that render existing organisational arrangements ineffective. Successful firms are able to respond to these threats to survival by transforming themselves to fit the new conditions. These periods of total system and quantum changes represent abrupt shifts in the organisation's structure, culture and processes. If successful, they enable the organisation to experience another long period of smooth functioning until the next disruption signals the need for another drastic change.[9]

These studies of organisation evolution and revolution point to the benefits of implementing transformational change as rapidly as possible. The faster the organisation can respond to disruptions, the quicker it can attain the benefits of operating in a new way. Rapid change enables the organisation to reach a period of smooth growth and functioning sooner, thus providing it with a competitive advantage over those firms that change more slowly.

A new organising paradigm

Organisations undertaking transformational change are, by definition, involved in second-order or gamma types of change.[10] Gamma change involves discontinuous shifts in mental or organisational frameworks.[11] Creative metaphors, such as 'organisation learning' or 'continuous improvement', are often used to help members visualise the new paradigm.[12] During the 1980s, increases in technological change, concern for quality and worker participation led to at least one shift in the organising paradigm. Characterised as the transition from 'control-based' to 'commitment-based' organisations, the features of the new paradigm included leaner, more flexible structures; information and decision making pushed down to the lowest levels; decentralised teams and business units accountable for specific products, services or customers; and participative management and teamwork. This new organising paradigm is well suited to changing conditions.

The role of senior executives and line management

A key feature of organisation transformation is the active role of senior executives and line managers in all phases of the change process.[13] They are responsible for the strategic direction and operation of the organisation and actively lead the transformation. They decide when to initiate transformational change, what the change should be, how it should be implemented and who should be responsible for directing it. Because existing executives may lack the talent, energy and commitment to undertake these tasks, they may be replaced by outsiders who are recruited to lead the change. Research on transformational change suggests that externally recruited executives are three times more likely to initiate such change than existing executive teams.[14]

The critical role of executive leadership in transformational change is clearly emerging. Lucid accounts of transformational leaders describe how executives, such as Sol Trujillo at Telstra, actively manage both the organisational and personal dynamics of transformational change. Nadler, Tushman and others point to three key roles for executive leadership of such change:[15]

1 *Envisioning.* Executives must articulate a clear and credible vision of the new strategic orientation. They must set new and difficult standards for performance and generate pride in past accomplishments and enthusiasm for the new strategy.
2 *Energising.* Executives must personally show their excitement about the changes, and model the behaviours that they expect of others. They must communicate examples of early success in order to mobilise energy for change.
3 *Enabling.* Executives must provide the resources necessary for undertaking significant change and use rewards to reinforce new behaviours. Leaders must also build an effective top-management team to manage the new organisation and develop management practices to support the change process.

Continuous learning and change

Transformational change requires considerable innovation and learning.[16] Organisation members must learn how to enact the new behaviours that are required in order to implement new strategic directions. This typically involves a continuous learning process of trying new behaviours, assessing their consequences and modifying them if necessary. Because members must usually learn qualitatively different ways of perceiving, thinking and behaving, the learning process is likely to be substantial and to involve much unlearning. It is directed by a vision of the future organisation and by the values and norms necessary for supporting it. Learning occurs at all levels of the organisation, from senior executives to lower level employees.

Because the environment itself is likely to be changing during the change process, transformational change rarely has a delimited time frame, but is likely to persist as long as the firm needs to adapt to change. Learning how to manage change in a continuous manner can help the organisation keep pace with a dynamic environment. It can provide the organisation with the built-in capacity to continually fit into its environment.

CULTURE CHANGE

The topic of organisation culture became extremely important to Australian companies during the 1990s, and culture change is now the most common form of organisation transformation. The number of culture change interventions has grown accordingly. Organisation culture is also the focus of growing research and OD application, and has spawned a number of best-selling management books including *Theory Z*, *The Art of Japanese Management*, *In Search of Excellence* and, more recently, *Built to Last*, *Corporate Culture and Performance* and *Beyond the Boundaries*.[17] Organisation culture is seen as a major strength of such companies as AMP, Lend Lease and Arnotts. A growing number of managers have come to appreciate the power of corporate culture in shaping employee beliefs and actions. A well-conceived and well-managed organisation culture, closely linked to an effective business strategy, can mean the difference between success and failure in today's demanding environment.

Concept of organisation culture

Despite the increased attention and research devoted to corporate culture, there is still some confusion about what the term 'culture' really means when applied to organisations.[18] Examination of the different definitions suggests that organisation culture is the pattern of basic assumptions, values, norms and artefacts shared by organisation members. These shared meanings help members make sense of the organisation. The meanings signal how work is to be done and evaluated, and how employees are to relate to each other and to significant others, such as customers, suppliers and government agencies.

Organisation culture includes four major elements existing at different levels of awareness, as shown in Figure 11.1.[19]

1   *Artefacts*. Artefacts are the highest levels of cultural awareness. They are the visible manifestations of the deeper levels of culture, such as norms, values and basic assumptions. They include observable behaviours of members, as well as the structures, systems, procedures, rules and physical aspects of the organisation. At Mono Pumps, a pump manufacturing firm in Melbourne, all members of the organisation are encouraged to believe that they have a valuable contribution to make to the organisation. There is an implied sense of 'Have a go', which results in employees being encouraged to discuss directly with the customer the development of particular products to suit their needs, or to arrange maintenance or service for their pumps. Although this may not be specifically stated, it is, nevertheless, a generally accepted procedure.

2   *Norms*. Just below the surface of cultural awareness are norms guiding how members should behave in particular situations. These represent unwritten rules of behaviour. At Mono Pumps, norms dictate that employees are allowed to go beyond their normal job description in order to satisfy customer requirements.

3   *Values*. The next deeper level of awareness includes values about what ought to be in organisations. Values tell members what is important in the organisation and what they need to pay attention to. Obviously, the norms and artefacts support these values.

Figure 11.1   Levels of corporate culture

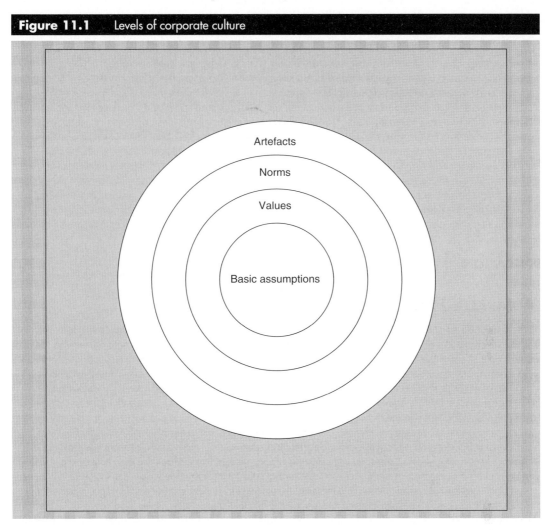

4   *Basic assumptions.* At the deepest level of cultural awareness are the taken-for-granted assumptions about how organisational problems should be solved. These basic assumptions tell members how to perceive, think and feel about things. They are the non-confrontable and non-debatable assumptions about how to relate to the environment, and about human nature, human activity and human relationships. For example, the basic assumption at Mono Pumps is that all the employees are skilled and competent in their tasks. The consequence is that customers are happy about the service they receive and remain loyal to the organisation.

Corporate culture is the product of long-term social learning and reflects what has worked in the past.[20] It represents those basic assumptions, values, norms and artefacts that have worked well enough to be passed on to succeeding generations of employees. For example, the cultures of many companies (including BHP Billiton, CSR and Pacific Dunlop) are deeply rooted in the firm's history. They were laid down by a strong founder and have been reinforced by successive top executives and corporate success into customary ways of perceiving and acting. These customs provide organisation members with clear and widely shared answers to such practical issues as the following:[21]

* 'Who's who and who matters around here?'
* 'Who's "us"?' 'Who's "them"?' 'How do we treat them and us?'
* 'How do we do things around here and why?'
* 'What constitutes a problem and what do we do when one arises?'
* 'What really matters here and why?'

Organisation culture and organisation effectiveness

The interest in organisation culture derives largely from its presumed impact on organisation effectiveness. There is considerable speculation and increasing research to suggest that organisation culture can improve an organisation's ability to implement new business strategies, as well as to achieve high levels of performance.

Organisations in many industries, such as energy, banking and electronics, have faced increasingly complex and changing environments brought about by deregulation, technological revolutions, foreign competition and unpredictable markets. Many firms (for example, Telstra, the Australian Broadcasting Corporation and CSR) have attempted to adapt to those conditions by changing business strategy and moving into new, unfamiliar areas. Unfortunately, efforts to implement a new strategy can fail simply because a company's culture is unsuited to the new business.[22] An organisation culture that was once a source of strength for a company can become a major liability in successfully implementing a new strategy. For example, as depicted in Application 11.2, Australia Post has survived the technology onslaught and has ventured out into other areas of business.

APPLiCATiON 11.2

AUSTRALIA POST HEADS THE CHARGE

After a decade of change, Australia Post continues to cement its position as a successful and reputable company delivering results. The change was brought about by focusing not only on the culture and skills of the workforce but also on the organisation's physical network, product offering and accompanying technology. All this was aimed at providing quality service – and it worked.

Today Australia Post has a reputation of being a successful and reliable business with the proof seen clearly in the bottom line. Net profit jumped 12.2% to $371.1 million in the 30 June year: the sixth consecutive profit rise for the corporation. It reflected a high level of productivity gains and an ability to generate profitable revenue with its customers. General Manager of Australia Post's Commercial Division, Bill Mitchell, acknowledges that his people's motivation is the key to unlocking a lasting relationship with customers, although he recognises that other factors also play a role. 'To create a culture of motivated employees, it is essential that Post gave its workforce new products, new merchandising formats, state-of-the-art counter technology and a new commercial image,' says Mitchell.

'Creating a positive culture among employees is not just about skills, roles and rewards – these are critical – but it is also about giving them the means to achieve high performance. If staff work in high-quality environments, with bright new products supported by positive advertising, they will, in our experience, become the organisation's strongest supporters and go the extra mile with customers. And, importantly, they will probably get a buzz out of work and have some fun along the way.'

Part of the change program has been the refocus around key customers segments and the repositioning within local communities so that Post can get closer to its customers and better understand their differing needs. This has been achieved by harnessing the efforts of the 35 000-strong workforce to focus on the customer and be involved in the selling effort, no matter whether they deliver or sort the mail, serve at a retail counter or handle telephone enquiries. Engaging staff has involved such initiatives as introducing dedicated account management teams to serve the big end of town, establishing specialised retail outlets tailored to the unique needs of business customers and encouraging staff to become more involved in their business community through formalised programs.

As with other companies working on improving customer service, Australia Post runs research and service programs to measure customer satisfaction. The retail arm also introduced a reward-and-recognition program for high levels of performance against such criteria as product and service knowledge, merchandising, how quickly and efficiently they attend to the customer's needs and how effective they are in creating a positive experience for the customer.

Source: 'Australia Post heads the charge', *Management Today*, Jan–Feb 2005.

Critical Thinking Question: Australia Post has changed significantly in the past 10 years. What are some of the changes that you have observed and where do you suggest they go from here? Search the internet and find similar businesses (for example, FedEx) and compare their change strategies.

The growing appreciation that culture can play a significant role in implementing new strategy has fuelled interest in the topic, especially in those firms that need to adapt to turbulent environments. A number of independent consultants and consulting firms have increasingly focused on helping firms to implement new strategies by bringing culture more in line with the new direction.[23] Indeed, much of the emphasis in the 1970s on formulating business strategy shifted to organisation culture in the 1980s as firms discovered cultural roadblocks to implementing strategies. Along with this emerging focus on organisation culture, however, came the sobering reality that cultural change is an extremely difficult and long-term process. Some experts doubt whether large firms can even bring about fundamental changes in their cultures, while those who have accomplished such feats estimate that the process took between six and 15 years.[24] For example, Telstra has struggled for years to change from a service-oriented telephone company to a market-oriented communications business. Its industrial conflict is thought to be partly the result of a dramatic shift in culture from a 'public sector' mindset to one that is more conducive to a market-competitive environment.

Evidence suggests that, in addition to affecting the implementation of business strategy, corporate culture can affect organisation performance. Comparative studies of Eastern and Western management methods suggest that the relative success of Japanese companies in the 1980s could be partly explained by their strong corporate cultures that emphasised employee participation, open communication, security and equality.[25] One study of American firms showed a similar pattern of results.[26] Using survey measures of culture and Standard & Poor's financial ratios as indicators of organisational effectiveness, the research examined the relationship between culture and effectiveness for 34 large American companies over a five-year period. The firms represented 25 different industries, and more than 43 000 people responded to the survey instrument. The results show that firms whose cultures support employee participation in decision making, adaptable work methods, sensible work designs, and reasonable and clear goals perform significantly better (financial ratios about twice as high) than companies scoring low on these factors. Moreover, the employee participation element of corporate culture only showed differences in effectiveness among the firms after three years; the other measures of culture showed differences in all five years. This suggests that changing some parts of corporate culture, such as participation, needs to be considered as a long-term investment.

A study of 207 firms in 22 different industries between 1987 and 1991 examined the relationship between culture and performance.[27] The researchers examined relationships between financial performance and the strength of a culture, the strategic appropriateness of a culture and the adaptiveness of a culture. First, there were no significant performance differences between organisations with widely shared values and those with little agreement around cultural assumptions. Second, there was a significant relationship between culture and performance when the organisation emphasised the 'right' values – values that were critical to success in a particular industry. Finally, performance results over time supported cultures that emphasised anticipation of, and adaptation to, environmental change.

These findings suggest that the strength of an organisation's culture can be both an advantage and a disadvantage. Under stable conditions, widely shared and strategically appropriate values can significantly contribute to organisation performance. However, if the environment is changing, strong cultures can be a liability. Unless they also emphasise adaptiveness, the organisation may experience wide swings in performance during transformational change.

Diagnosing organisation culture

Culture change interventions generally start by diagnosing the organisation's existing culture so as to assess its fit with current or proposed business strategies. This requires uncovering and understanding the shared assumptions, values, norms and artefacts that characterise its culture. OD practitioners have developed a number of useful approaches for diagnosing organisation culture that fall into three different, yet complementary, perspectives: the behavioural approach, the competing values approach and the deep assumption approach. Each diagnostic perspective focuses on particular aspects of organisation culture and together the approaches can provide a comprehensive assessment of these complex phenomena.

THE BEHAVIOURAL APPROACH

This method of diagnosis emphasises the surface level of organisation culture: the pattern of behaviours that produce business results.[28] It is among the more practical approaches to culture diagnosis because it assesses key work behaviours that can be observed.[29] The behavioural approach provides specific descriptions about how tasks are performed and how relationships are managed in an organisation. For example, Table 11.1 summarises the organisation culture of an international banking division as perceived by managers. The data were obtained from a series of individual and group interviews asking managers to describe 'the way the game is played', as though they were coaching a new organisation member. Managers were asked to give their impressions in regard to four key relationships (company-wide, boss–subordinate, peer and interdepartmental) and in terms of six managerial tasks (innovating, decision making, communicating, organising, monitoring and appraising/rewarding). These perceptions revealed a number of implicit norms for how tasks were performed and relationships managed at the division.

Cultural diagnosis derived from a behavioural approach can also be used to assess the cultural risk of trying to implement the organisational changes that are necessary for supporting

Table 11.1	Summary of corporate culture at an international banking division
Relationships	**Culture summary**
Company-wide	Preserve your autonomy Allow area managers to run the business as long as they meet the profit budget
Boss–subordinate	Avoid confrontations Smooth over disagreements Support the boss
Peer	Guard information; it is power Be a gentleman or lady
Interdepartment	Protect your department's bottom line Form alliances around specific issues Guard your turf
Tasks	**Culture summary**
Innovating	Consider it risky Be a quick second
Decision making	Handle each deal on its own merits Gain consensus Require many sign-offs Involve the right people Seize the opportunity
Communicating	Withhold information to control adversaries Avoid confrontations Be a gentleman or lady
Organising	Centralise power Be autocratic
Monitoring	Meet short-term profit goals
Appraising and rewarding	Reward the faithful Choose the best bankers as managers Seek safe jobs

Source: Reprinted from *Organizational Dynamics*, 10, Summer 1981, H. Schwartz and S. Davis, 'Matching corporate culture and business strategy', p. 38, Copyright 1981, with permission from Elsevier.

a new strategy. Significant cultural risks result when changes that are highly important to the implementation of a new strategy are incompatible with the existing patterns of behaviour. Knowledge of such risks can help managers determine whether implementation plans should be changed to manage around the existing culture, whether the culture should be changed, or whether the strategy itself should be modified or abandoned.

THE COMPETING VALUES APPROACH

This perspective assesses an organisation's culture in terms of how it resolves a set of value dilemmas.[30] The approach suggests that an organisation's culture can be understood in terms of four important 'value pairs'; each pair consisting of contradictory values placed at opposite ends of a continuum, as shown in Figure 11.2. The four value pairs are internal focus versus external focus, organic processes versus mechanistic processes, innovation versus stability and people orientation versus task orientation. Organisations continually struggle to satisfy the conflicting demands placed on them by these competing values. For example, when faced with the competing values of internal versus external focus, organisations must choose between attending to internal operations or their external environment. Too much emphasis on the environment can result in the neglect of internal efficiencies. Conversely, too much attention to the internal aspects of organisations can result in their missing important changes in the competitive environment.

The competing values approach commonly collects diagnostic data about the four sets of competing values, using a survey that has been specifically designed for the purpose.[31] It provides measures of where an organisation's existing values fall along each of the four competing values

Figure 11.2   The competing values approach to culture

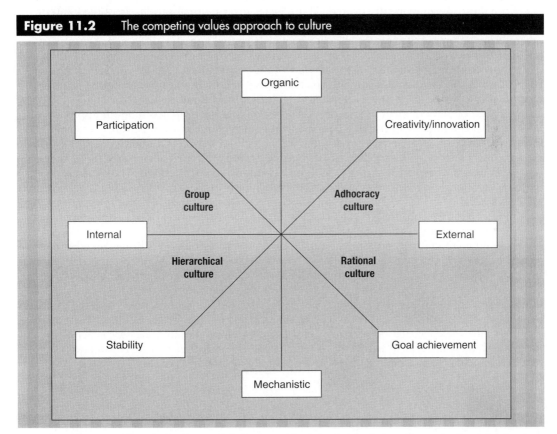

Source: Reprinted from D. Denison and G. Spreitzer, 'Organizational culture and organizational development: A competing values approach', in *Research in Organizational Change and Development*, 5e, eds R. Woodman and W. Posmore, p. 4, Copyright 1991, with permission from Elsevier.

continua. When taken together, these data identify an organisation's culture as falling into one of the four quadrants shown in Figure 11.2: group culture, adhocracy culture, hierarchical culture and rational culture. For example, if an organisation's values are internally focused and emphasise people and organic processes, it manifests a group culture. On the other hand, a rational culture characterises values that are externally focused and emphasises task achievement and mechanistic processes.

THE DEEP ASSUMPTIONS APPROACH

This final diagnostic approach emphasises the deepest levels of organisation culture: the generally unexamined assumptions, values and norms that guide member behaviour and which often have a powerful impact upon organisation effectiveness. A diagnosis of culture from this perspective typically begins with the most tangible level of awareness, and then works down to the deep assumptions.

Diagnosing organisation culture at the deep assumptions level poses at least three difficult problems for collecting pertinent information.[32] First, culture reflects shared assumptions about what is important, how things are done and how people should behave in organisations. People generally take cultural assumptions for granted and rarely speak of them directly. Rather, the company's culture is implied in concrete behavioural examples, such as daily routines, stories, rituals and language. This means that considerable time and effort must be spent observing, sifting through and asking people about these cultural outcroppings in order to understand their deeper significance for organisation members. Second, some values and beliefs that people espouse have little to do with the ones they really hold and follow. People are reluctant to admit this discrepancy, yet the real assumptions underlying idealised portrayals of culture must somehow be discovered. Third, large, diverse organisations are quite likely to have several subcultures, including countercultures that go against the grain of the wider organisation culture. Assumptions may not be widely shared and may differ across groups in the organisation, which means that focusing on limited parts of the organisation or on a few select individuals may provide a distorted view of the organisation's culture and subcultures. All relevant groups in the organisation must be discovered and their cultural assumptions sampled. Only then can practitioners judge the extent to which assumptions are widely shared.

Organisation development practitioners who emphasise the deep assumptions approach have developed a number of useful techniques for assessing organisation culture.[33] One method involves an iterative interviewing process that involves both outsiders and insiders.[34] Outsiders help members uncover cultural elements through joint exploration. The outsider enters the organisation and experiences surprises and puzzles that were not expected. The outsider shares these observations with insiders and the two parties jointly explore their meaning. This process involves several iterations of experiencing surprises, checking for meaning and formulating hypotheses about the culture. It results in a formal written description of the assumptions that underlie the organisation's culture.

A second method for identifying the organisation's basic assumptions brings together a cross-section of senior management, old and new members, labour leaders, staff and line managers for a two-day workshop. The group first brainstorms a large number of artefacts, such as behaviours, symbols, language and physical space arrangements. From this list, the values and norms that would produce such artefacts are deduced. In addition, the values espoused in formal planning documents are listed. Finally, the group attempts to identify the assumptions that would explain the constellation of values, norms and artefacts. Because they are generally taken for granted, these are typically difficult to articulate. A great deal of process consultation skill is required to help organisation members see the underlying assumptions.

Changing organisation culture

There is considerable debate over whether changing something as deep-seated as organisation culture is possible.[35] Those advocating culture change generally focus on those elements of culture that are nearer to the surface, such as norms and artefacts. These elements are more changeable than are the deeper elements of values and basic assumptions. They offer OD practitioners a more manageable set of action levers for changing organisational behaviours. Some would argue, however, that unless the deeper values and assumptions are changed, organisations have not really changed the culture.

Those arguing that implementing culture change is extremely difficult, if not impossible, typically focus on the deeper elements of culture (values and basic assumptions). Because these deeper elements represent assumptions about organisational life, members do not question them and have a difficult time envisioning anything else. Moreover, members may not want to change their cultural assumptions. The culture provides a strong defence against external uncertainties and threats.[36] It represents past solutions to difficult problems. Members may also have vested interests in maintaining the culture: they may have developed personal stakes, pride and power in the culture and may strongly resist attempts to change it. Finally, cultures that provide firms with a competitive advantage may be difficult to imitate, thus making it hard for less successful firms to change their cultures to approximate the more successful ones.[37]

Given the problems with cultural change, most practitioners in this area suggest that changes in corporate culture should be considered only after other less-difficult and less-costly solutions have either been applied or ruled out.[38] Attempts to overcome cultural risks when strategic changes are incompatible with culture might include ways of managing around the existing culture. Consider, for example, a single-product organisation with a functional focus and a history of centralised control that is considering an ambitious product-diversification strategy. The firm might manage around its existing culture by using business teams to co-ordinate functional specialists around each new product. Another alternative to changing culture is to modify strategy to bring it more in line with culture. The single-product organisation just mentioned might decide to undertake a less ambitious strategy of product diversification.

Despite problems in changing corporate culture, large-scale cultural change may be necessary in certain situations: for example, if the firm's culture does not fit a changing environment; if the industry is extremely competitive and changing rapidly and frequently; if the company is mediocre or worse; if the firm is about to become a very large company; or if the company is smaller and growing rapidly.[39] Organisations facing these conditions need to change their cultures in order to adapt to the situation or to operate at higher levels of effectiveness. They may have to supplement attempts at cultural change with other approaches, such as managing around the existing culture and modifying strategy.

Although knowledge about changing corporate culture is in a formative stage, the following practical advice offers guidelines for cultural change:[40]

1   *Clear strategic vision.* Effective cultural change should start from a clear vision of the firm's new strategy and of the shared values and behaviours needed to make it work.[41] This vision provides the purpose and direction for cultural change. It serves as a yardstick for comparing the firm's existing culture and for deciding whether proposed changes are consistent with new values. A useful approach to providing clear strategic vision is the development of a statement of corporate purpose, listing in straightforward terms the basic values that the organisation believes in.

2   *Top-management commitment.* Cultural change must be managed from the top of the organisation. Senior managers and administrators need to be strongly committed to the new values and need to create constant pressures for change. They must have the staying power to see the changes through.[42] For example, Bob Ansett, the former CEO of Budget Rent-a-Car who was famed for his practice of 'management by walking around', now has a successful career on the management lecture circuit.

3   *Symbolic leadership.* Senior executives must communicate the new culture through their own actions. Their behaviours need to symbolise the kinds of values and behaviours being sought. In the few publicised cases of successful culture change, corporate leaders have shown an almost missionary zeal for the new values, and their actions have forcefully symbolised the values.[43] For example, Toyota Australia's implementation of '360-degree performance appraisal' began at the top, giving even the most junior workers a chance to assess the performance of their bosses.[44]

4   *Supporting organisational changes.* Cultural change generally requires supporting modifications in organisational structure, human resource systems, information and

control systems, and management styles. These organisational features can help to orient people's behaviours to the new culture.[45] They can make people aware of the behaviours required to get things done in the new culture and can encourage the performance of those behaviours. For example, when Peter Kirby became managing director of building materials and commodity conglomerate CSR in 1998, he had a clear brief: fix up the company and its share price. He realised that focusing on numbers and balance sheets was not enough. What the company needed was a cultural change: more women, more local nationals in overseas businesses and more accountability in divisions – all changes that reinforce the importance of challenges and being proactive.[46]

5   *Selection and socialisation of newcomers and termination of those with different views.* One of the most effective methods of changing corporate culture involves changing organisational membership. People can be selected and terminated in terms of their fit with the new culture. This is especially important in key leadership positions, where people's actions can significantly promote or hinder new values and behaviours. For example, the arrival of new CSR managing director Peter Kirby in 1998 led to the departure of two senior managers and changes among the executive group.[47] Another approach involves socialising new hires into the new culture. People are most open to organisational influences during the entry stage, when they can be effectively indoctrinated into the culture. For example, companies with strong cultures such as Amcor, CSR and Westpac attach great importance to socialising new members into the company's values.

6   *Ethical and legal sensitivity.* Cultural change can raise significant tensions between organisation and individual interests, resulting in ethical and legal problems for practitioners. This is particularly pertinent when organisations are trying to implement cultural values that promote employee integrity, control, equitable treatment and job security – values often included in cultural change efforts. Statements about such values provide employees with certain expectations about their rights and how they will be treated in the organisation. If the organisation does not follow through with behaviours and procedures that support and protect these implied rights, it may breach ethical principles and, in some cases, legal employment contracts. Recommendations for reducing the chances of such ethical and legal problems include: setting realistic values for culture change and not promising what the organisation cannot deliver; encouraging input from throughout the organisation in setting cultural values; providing mechanisms for member dissent and diversity, such as internal review procedures; and educating managers about the legal and ethical pitfalls inherent in cultural change and helping them to develop guidelines for resolving such issues.

SELF-DESIGNING ORGANISATIONS

A growing number of researchers and practitioners have called for self-designing organisations that have the built-in capacity to transform themselves to achieve high performance in today's competitive and changing environment.[48] Mohrman and Cummings have developed a self-design change strategy that involves an ongoing series of designing and implementing activities carried out by managers and employees at all levels of the firm.[49] The approach helps members to translate corporate values and general prescriptions for change into specific structures, processes and behaviours that are suited to their situations. It enables them to tailor changes to fit the organisation and helps them to continually adjust the organisation to changing conditions.

The demands of transformational change

Mohrman and Cummings developed the self-design strategy in response to a number of demands that were facing organisations engaged in transformational change. These strongly suggested the need for self-design, in contrast to more traditional approaches to organisation change that emphasise ready-made programs and quick fixes. Although organisations prefer the control and certainty inherent in programmed change, the five requirements for organisational transformation reviewed below argue against this strategy:

1   Transformational change generally involves altering most features of the organisation and achieving a fit among them and with the firm's strategy. This suggests the need for a *systemic change process* that accounts for these multiple features and relationships.

2   Transformational change generally occurs in situations where heavy change and uncertainty are being experienced. This means that changing is never totally finished, as new structures and processes will continually have to be modified to fit changing conditions. Thus, the change process needs to be *dynamic* and *iterative*, with organisations continually changing themselves.[50]

3   Current knowledge about transforming organisations provides only general prescriptions for change. Organisations need to learn how to translate that information into specific structures, processes and behaviours appropriate to their situations. This generally requires considerable on-site innovation and learning as members learn by doing: trying out new structures and behaviours, assessing their effectiveness and modifying them if necessary. Transformational change needs to facilitate this *organisational learning*.[51]

4   Transformational change invariably affects many organisation stakeholders (owners, managers, employees and customers). These different stakeholders are likely to have different goals and interests related to the change process. Unless these differences are surfaced and reconciled, enthusiastic support for change may be difficult to achieve. Consequently, the change process must attend to the interests of *multiple stakeholders*.[52]

5   Transformational change needs to occur at *multiple levels of the organisation* if new strategies are to result in changed behaviours throughout the firm. Top executives must formulate a corporate strategy and clarify a vision of what the organisation needs to look like if they are to support it. Middle and lower levels of the organisation need to put those broad parameters into operation by creating structures, procedures and behaviours to implement the strategy.[53]

Self-design change strategy

The self-design strategy accounts for these demands of organisation transformation. It focuses on all features of the organisation (for example, structure, human resource practices and technology) and seeks to design them to mutually support the business strategy. It is a dynamic and an iterative process aimed at providing organisations with the built-in capacity to continually change and redesign features as the circumstances demand. The approach promotes organisational learning among multiple stakeholders at all levels of the firm, providing them with the knowledge and skills necessary for transforming the organisation and continually improving it.

Figure 11.3 outlines the self-design approach. Although the process is described in three stages, in practice the stages merge and interact iteratively over time. Each stage is described below:

1   *Laying the foundation.* This initial stage provides organisation members with the basic knowledge and information needed to get started with organisation transformation. It involves three kinds of activities. The first is to acquire knowledge about how organisations function, about organising principles for achieving high performance and about the self-design process. This information is generally gained through reading relevant material, attending in-house workshops and visiting other organisations that have successfully transformed themselves. This learning typically starts with senior executives or with those managing the transformation process, and cascades to lower organisational levels if a decision to proceed with self-design is made. The second activity in laying the foundation involves valuing: determining the corporate values that will guide the transformation process. These values represent those performance outcomes and organisational conditions that will be needed to implement the corporate strategy. They are typically written in a values statement that is discussed and negotiated by various stakeholders at all levels of the organisation. The third activity is to diagnose

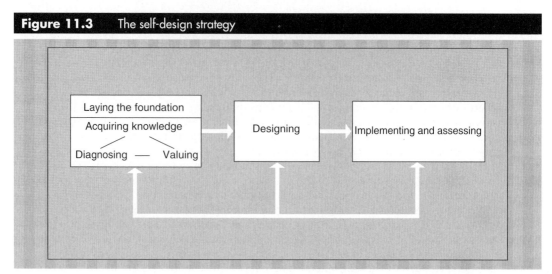

Figure 11.3   The self-design strategy

Source: S. Mohrman and T. Cummings, *Self-Designing Organization: Learning How to Create High Performance*, copyright © 1989 by Addison-Wesley Publishing Company Inc.

the current organisation to determine what needs to be changed in order to enact the corporate strategy and values. Organisation members generally assess the different features of the organisation, including its performance. They look for incongruities between the organisation's functioning and its valued performances and conditions. In the case of an entirely new organisation, members diagnose constraints and contingencies in the situation that need to be taken into account when designing the organisation.

2   *Designing.* In this second stage of self-design, organisation designs and innovations are generated to support corporate strategy and values. Only the broad parameters of a new organisation are specified; the specifics are left to be tailored to the different levels and groupings within the organisation. Referred to as minimum specification design, this process recognises that designs need to be refined and modified as they are implemented throughout the firm.

3   *Implementing and assessing.* This last stage involves implementing the designed organisation changes. It includes an ongoing cycle of action research: changing structures and behaviours, assessing progress and making the necessary modifications. Information about how well implementation is progressing and how well the new organisational design is working is collected and used to clarify design and implementation issues and to make necessary adjustments. This learning process continues indefinitely as members periodically assess and improve the design and alter it to fit changing conditions. The feedback loops shown in Figure 11.3 suggest that the implementing and assessing activities may lead back to affect subsequent designing, diagnosing, valuing and acquiring knowledge activities. This iterative sequence of activities provides organisations with the capacity to transform and improve themselves continually.

Application 11.3 reports on an interview with Andrea Grant who has been given the challenge to align everything concerning the HR department to the business strategy of Telstra.

APPLiCATiON 11.3

CATCHING THE SOL TRAIN

In 2006 the big leadership issue will be managing workforces in a climate of substantial industrial relations change, labour market pressures and the need to downsize. All eyes will be on Telstra in 2006, which faces the greatest challenges in these areas. Its task is to convert the ambitious vision of the *Telstra Strategic Review* into reality. In 2006, reconciling strategy with implementation will be the key.

A big part in transforming the company will be played by Telstra's latest recruit, its new head of human resources (HR), Andrea Grant. Among her important challenges is overseeing up to 12 000 redundancies.

…

She has been contracted to an overtly bureaucratic business that is known for its silos and hierarchies. 'Sometimes people get so frustrated because they can't get things done, even with all the goodwill in the world,' she says. Staff are also prone to cynicism about change. A November 2005 IDC report states that Telstra employees have been subject to reorganisation almost every six months for the past decade. Despite these negatives, Grant's first impressions are of a company with a strong sense of spirit and 'pockets of excellence'.

Trujillo wants to transform Telstra through a combination of organisational simplification, cost-cutting, staff reduction, employee-training programs and technology upgrades. To become a 'one factory', customer-centric, next-generation telecommunications company, there needs to be substantial change to the culture of the business.

While the company prefers to emphasise other aspects of Grant's new role, such as creating a new culture at Telstra, she will have to accept her informal title as Telstra's Grim Reaper. She will oversee the reduction of Telstra's full-time equivalent positions by up to 12 000 over the next five years, one of the most substantial staff reductions in Australia's corporate history. There are 52 000 full-time-equivalent employees, including 6000 individual contractors at Telstra.

Credit Suisse First Boston estimates that the restructuring of Telstra's labour force could save the business $1 billion. Telstra has undergone staff cuts of this magnitude before. Grant holds up a spreadsheet, pointing out that the Telstra workforce has halved since 1996. Seven thousand staff lost their jobs in the 1997–98 financial year alone.

These jobs losses are rationalised by Telstra and telco analysts alike as something that is necessary for the organisation to remain competitive. A telecommunications company analyst and the managing director of Paul Budde Communications, Paul Budde, says that Telstra is lagging behind the rest of the world. Grant also sees the change as inevitable. 'It is not going to go away; it is going to happen and we have to work within that context,' she says. 'It is not evil.'

…

Grant is a person who likes to talk about hard-wiring. This is how she describes the process of incrementally changing the way things are done, identifying exactly the HR processes that need to be rewired so that a different result can be achieved. 'I am a great believer in aligning everything you do in HR to the business strategy,' she says. This is why, she believes, her change-management programs have worked where most have failed. For the new business strategy to work, people and the culture have to be part of the plan.

Source: Emily Ross, 'Catching the Sol train', *Business Review Weekly*, 8–14 Dec. 2005.

Critical Thinking Questions: Andrea Grant has now had time to establish herself within the company. What significant changes have resulted from her implementation of the company's strategy? What problems do you expect will occur and how may they be overcome?

The self-design strategy is applicable to existing organisations that need to transform themselves, as well as to new organisations just starting out. It is also applicable to changing the total organisation or sub-units. The way self-design is managed and unfolds can also differ. In some cases, it follows the existing organisation structure, starting with the senior executive team and cascading downwards across organisational levels. In other cases, the process is managed by special design teams that are sanctioned to set broad parameters for valuing and designing for the rest of the organisation. The outputs of these teams are then implemented across departments and work units, with considerable local refinement and modification.

ORGANISATION LEARNING

The third organisational transformation intervention is called 'organisation learning' (OL), change processes aimed at helping organisations develop and use knowledge to change and improve themselves continually. Organisation learning is crucial in today's rapidly changing environments as it can enable organisations to acquire and apply knowledge more quickly and effectively than competitors, and so can provide a competitive advantage. Organisation learning is one of the fastest-growing interventions in OD and has been used by such firms as BHP Billiton, NEC Australia and AMP to facilitate transformational change.

Organisation learning interventions draw heavily on similarities between individual learning and OL. It is possible for individual members to learn while the organisation does not. For example, a member may learn to serve the customer better without ever sharing such learning with other members. Conversely, it is possible for the organisation to learn without individual members learning. Improvements in equipment design or work procedures, for example, reflect OL, even if individual members do not understand these changes. Moreover, because OL serves the organisation's purposes and is embedded in its structures, it stays with the organisation, even if members change.

Processes of organisational learning

Organisation learning consists of four interrelated processes: discovery, invention, production and generalisation.[54] Learning starts with discovery when errors or gaps between desired and actual conditions are detected. For example, sales managers may discover that sales are falling below projected levels and set out to solve this problem. Invention is aimed at devising solutions to close the gap between desired and current conditions. It includes diagnosing the causes of the gap and inventing appropriate solutions to reduce it. The sales managers may learn that poor advertising is contributing to the sales problem and may devise a new sales campaign to improve sales. Production processes involve implementing solutions, while generalisation includes drawing conclusions about the effects of the solutions and applying that knowledge to other relevant situations. For instance, the new advertising program would be implemented and, if found successful, the managers might apply variations of it to other product lines. Thus, these four learning processes enable members to generate the knowledge necessary to change and improve the organisation.

Levels of organisation learning

Organisations can apply the learning processes described above to three levels of learning.[55] The lowest level is called 'single-loop' (or 'adaptive') learning and is focused on learning how to improve the status quo. This is the most prevalent form of learning in organisations, and it enables members to reduce errors or gaps between desired and existing conditions. It can produce incremental change in how organisations function. The sales managers described above engaged in single-loop learning; they sought to reduce the difference between desired and current levels of sales.

'Double-loop' (or 'generative') learning is aimed at changing the status quo. It operates at a more abstract level than single-loop learning because members learn how to change the existing assumptions and conditions within which single-loop learning operates. This level of learning can lead to transformational change, where the status quo itself is radically changed. For example, the sales managers may learn that sales projections are based on faulty assumptions and models about future market conditions. This knowledge may result in an entirely new conception of future markets with corresponding changes in sales projections and product-development plans. It may lead the managers to drop some products that had previously appeared promising, develop new ones that had not been considered before, and alter advertising and promotional campaigns to fit the new conditions.

The highest level of OL is called 'deuterolearning', which involves learning how to learn. Here learning is directed at the learning process itself and seeks to improve how organisations perform single- and double-loop learning. For example, the sales managers might periodically examine how well they perform the processes of discovery, invention, production and generalisation. This could lead to improvements and efficiencies in how learning is conducted in the organisation.

The learning organisation

Organisation learning interventions are aimed primarily at designing and implementing what is commonly referred to as 'the learning organisation', a term used to describe organisations that are capable of effective OL.[56] Much of the literature on the learning organisation is prescriptive and proposes how organisations should be designed and managed to promote effective learning. Although there is relatively little systematic research to support these premises, there is growing consensus among researchers and practitioners about specific organisational features that characterise the learning organisation.[57] These qualities are mutually reinforcing and fall into five interrelated categories:

1   *Structure.* Learning organisations are structured to facilitate OL. Their structures emphasise teamwork, strong lateral relations and networking across organisational boundaries, both internal and external to the firm. These features promote the information sharing, systems thinking and openness to information that are necessary for OL. They help members scan wider parts of the organisation and its environment and reduce barriers to shared learning. Learning organisations also have relatively flat managerial hierarchies that enhance opportunities for employee involvement in the organisation. Members are empowered to make relevant decisions and to significantly influence the organisation, thus nurturing the personal mastery and efficacy that are essential to OL.

2   *Information systems.* Organisation learning involves gathering and processing information and, consequently, the information systems of learning organisations provide an infrastructure for OL. Organisations traditionally rely on information systems for control purposes. They focus on single-loop learning, where information is used to detect and correct errors in organisational functioning. In today's environments where learning is increasingly directed at transformational change, organisations require more sophisticated information systems to support these higher levels of OL. They need systems that facilitate the rapid acquisition, processing and sharing of rich, complex information and that enable knowledge to be managed for competitive advantage. Examples of information systems that facilitate OL include Monsanto's 'knowledge management architecture', which uses 'Lotus Notes' (now renamed 'Domino') to link salespeople, account managers and competitor analysts to shared customer and competitor databases that are updated continually. Motorola's process of 'Total Quality Management', which relies heavily on external benchmarks and continuous measurement to improve quality, is another example.[58]

3   *Human resource practices.* Because organisation members are the ultimate creators and users of OL, the human resource practices of learning organisations are designed to promote member learning. These include appraisal and reward systems that account for long-term performance and knowledge development; they reinforce the acquisition and sharing of new skills and knowledge. For example, Toyota Australia uses skill-based pay to motivate employees to use multiple skills and do diverse jobs. Similarly, the training and development programs of learning organisations emphasise continuous learning and improvement. They are directed at enhancing human capital and opportunities for OL. AMP, one of Australia's largest insurance organisations, has developed a special relationship with the University of Technology in Sydney in order to undertake the high-quality training of staff.

4   *Organisation culture.* The shared assumptions, values and norms that comprise an organisation's culture can have a strong influence on how members carry out the learning processes of discovery, invention, production and generalisation. Learning organisations have strong cultures that promote openness, creativity and experimentation among members. These values and norms provide the underlying social support needed for successful learning. They encourage members to acquire, process and share information; they also nurture innovation and provide the freedom to try new things, to risk failure and to learn from mistakes. The Wesley Hospital in Brisbane takes this concept even further through the HealthWise project: a computer-based information centre in which patients can interactively research diseases and treatment.[59] Members are encouraged to think and behave differently. Mistakes and errors are treated as a normal part of the innovation process and members actively learn from their failures how to change and improve both themselves and the organisation.

5   *Leadership*. Like most interventions aimed at organisation transformation, OL depends heavily on effective leadership throughout the organisation. The leaders of learning organisations are actively involved in OL. They model the openness, risk taking and reflection necessary for learning. They communicate a compelling vision of the learning organisation and provide the empathy, support and personal advocacy needed to lead others in that direction.

Organisation learning and organisation performance

A key premise underlying much of the OL literature is that OL interventions will lead to higher performance. Although the positive linkage between OL and performance is widely assumed, the mechanisms through which OL translates into organisation performance are rarely identified or explained, but an understanding of this is essential when applying this intervention in organisations.

Based on the integration of existing theory and exploratory field research, Figure 11.4 explains how OL affects organisation performance.[60] This framework suggests that specific

Figure 11.4   How organisation learning affects organisation performance

Organisation characteristics

Structure
Information systems
Human resource practices
Culture
Leadership

Organisation learning processes

Discovery
Invention
Production
Generalisation

Organisation knowledge

Skills
Cognition
Structures

Organisation task

Organisation performance

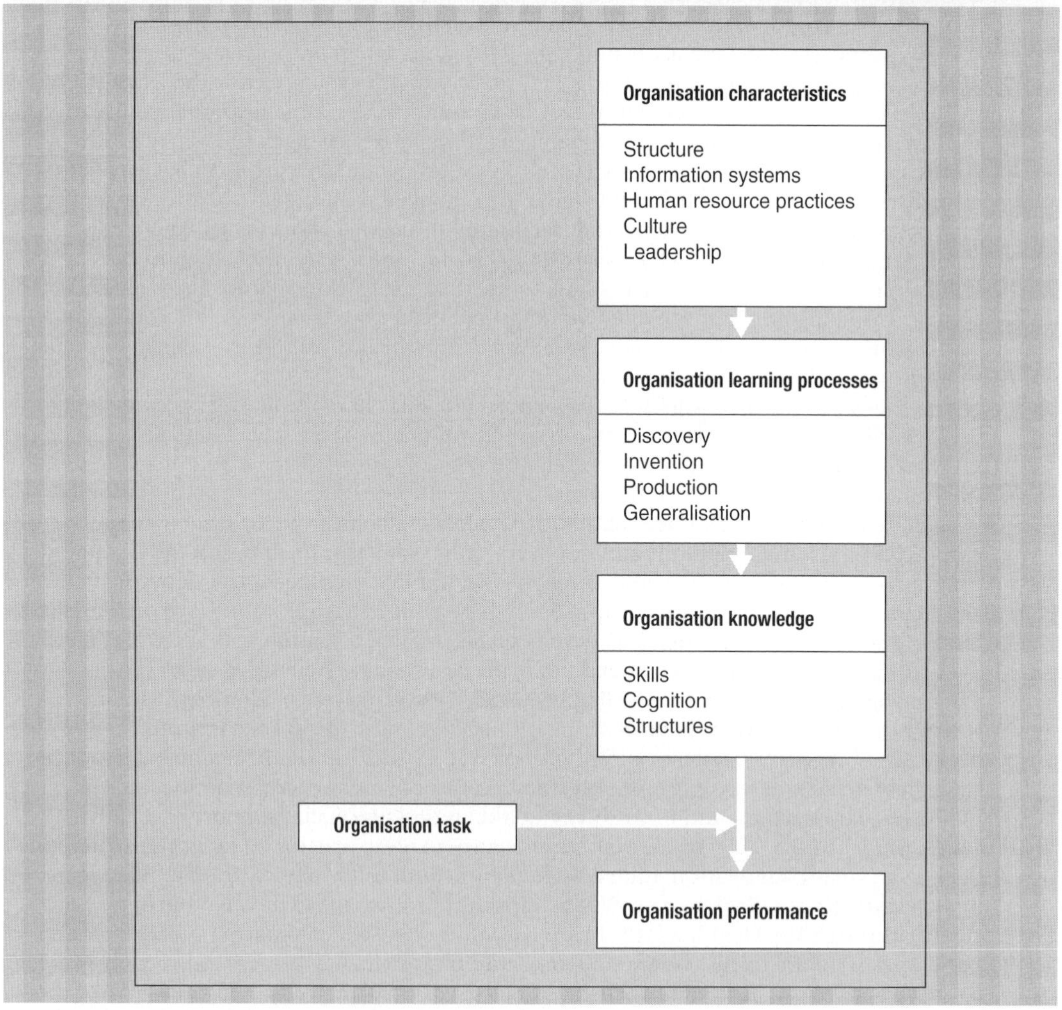

Source: Reproduced with permission from W. Snyder and T. Cummings, 'Organisation learning disorders: Conceptual model and intervention guidelines', Copyright © The Tavistock Institute, London, UK, 1998, by permission of Sage Publications Ltd.

organisational characteristics, such as those described above for the learning organisation, influence how well the OL processes of discovery, invention, production and generalisation are carried out. These OL processes affect organisation performance through their impact on organisation knowledge: the skills, cognitions and systems that comprise the organisation's core competencies. Specifically, the OL processes influence the amount and kind of knowledge that an organisation possesses, and that knowledge, in turn, directly influences performance outcomes, such as product quality and customer service. As depicted in Figure 11.4, the linkage between organisation knowledge and performance depends on the organisation's task or technology. Organisation knowledge will lead to high performance insofar as it is both relevant and applied effectively to the organisation's task. For example, customer-service tasks generally require good interpersonal and listening skills as well as information about customer needs. Successful task performance relies heavily on members having this knowledge and applying it effectively to customers.

Because organisation knowledge plays a crucial role in linking OL processes to organisation performance, increasing attention is being directed at how organisations can acquire and use it effectively. Two of the more popular books on innovation and global competition include the term 'knowledge' in their titles: Leonard-Barton's *Wellsprings of Knowledge: Building and Sustaining the Sources of Innovation*[61] and Konaka and Takeuchi's *The Knowledge-Creating Company: How Japanese Companies Foster Creativity and Innovation for Competitive Advantage.*[62] They show how many Japanese companies and such firms as Hewlett-Packard and Motorola achieve competitive advantage through building and managing knowledge effectively. These knowledge capabilities have been described as 'core competencies',[63] 'invisible assets'[64] and 'intellectual capital',[65] suggesting their contribution to organisation performance. There is growing emphasis both in the accounting profession and in many industries on developing accounting measures that capture knowledge capital. In knowledge-intensive firms, such as Andersen Consulting and Microsoft, the value of knowledge may far exceed the value of capital assets.[66] Moreover, the key components of cost in many of today's organisations are research and development, intellectual assets and services rather than materials and labour, which are the focus of traditional cost accounting. For example, Application 11.4 describes how Kerry Sanderson is leading Fremantle Ports through change while plotting a course for the future.

APPLiCATiON 11.4

LEADING THROUGH CHANGE

'The most important thing in leading an organisation like this is to establish a culture of continuous improvement and ongoing learning,' says Kerry Sanderson, CEO of Fremantle Ports, a Western Australian (WA) government trading enterprise, which has, under her leadership, notched up a series of impressive achievements.

Riding the resources boom, Fremantle Ports is responsible for $18 billion of cargo each year. Managing that sort of complexity is a daunting task, especially since the enterprise itself is fairly small – only about 250 people. In the 1980s, Fremantle Ports had a reputation as a bottleneck, but now it is widely seen as a trade facilitator.

'When I took up the CEO position in 1991, things were pretty bad, especially on the financial side,' says Sanderson. 'In some ways, that was an advantage for a new leader with a reform agenda, because everyone realised that something had to be done. But even there, a lot of the thinking was: Okay, do what you have to do to fix things up, then we can go back to business as usual. The message our management team had to get out was that there was no more 'business as usual'. In a dynamic industry, change has to be an ongoing process, and that point had to be accepted by everyone.'

Sanderson says that the reform agenda is a team effort and has had the support of successive WA governments.

'The strategy has been to set targets, agree on them with government, and work systematically towards them,' she says. 'The relevant ministers have been willing to provide general support and to step back and let us get on with the task of getting there.'

▷▷

The objectives and the means of achieving them were reached after an inclusive approach involving lengthy discussions with employees, senior managers and other stakeholders. The cultural change of the organisation was underpinned by a set of values, also developed through a consultative process.

'Our operational focus has been on efficiency and quality,' Sanderson notes. 'It's been a necessary emphasis, given that since 1991 container trade for the port has grown fourfold. We developed a set of metrics, looking at issues such as ship delays and cargo-handling productivity. This has been crucial; you need good measures if you are to manage effectively. We used the Australian Business Excellence Framework as a guide, and that helped us at every step along the way. Fremantle Ports has achieved Award level within this framework – one of only five organisations in WA to do so.'

…

'At the moment, we are working with our larger customers on 'value chain analysis', to help us understand the costs and benefits of particular actions by the port. At the same time, we are looking at ways to improve the infrastructure that supports our facilities. For example, we are acting as the project manager for the construction of a new rail loop for the port, which will lead to significant efficiency gains. It's another aspect, I think, of seeing reform as a continuing process.'

Source: Derek Parker, 'Leading through change', *Management Today,* April 2006.

Critical Thinking Question: Investigate the Australian Business Excellence Framework. What other companies have won this award and what change processes did they implement?

Organisation knowledge is particularly valuable when it is unique and cannot easily be obtained by competitors.[67] Thus, organisations seek to develop or acquire knowledge that distinctly adds value for customers, and that can be leveraged across products, functions, business units or geographical regions. For example, Target excels at managing its unique distribution systems across a diversity of regional stores. Honda is particularly successful at leveraging its competence in motors across a number of product lines, including automobiles, motorcycles and lawn mowers.

Change strategies

Organisation learning is a broad phenomenon that can be influenced by a variety of structures, processes and performances occurring in organisations. Consequently, many of the interventions described in this book can help organisations develop more effective learning capabilities. Human resource management interventions, such as performance appraisal, reward systems, and career planning and development, can reinforce members' motivation to gain new skills and knowledge. Technostructural interventions, such as process-based and network structures, self-managing work teams and re-engineering, can provide the kinds of lateral linkages and teamwork needed to process, develop and share a diversity of information and knowledge. Human process changes, such as team building, search conferences and intergroup relations interventions, can help members develop the kinds of healthy interpersonal relationships that underlie effective OL. Strategic interventions, such as integrated strategic change and open systems planning, can help organisations gain knowledge about their environment and also help them develop values and norms that promote OL.

In addition to these broader interventions, change strategies designed specifically for OL have been developed. Although these interventions are relatively new in OD and do not follow a common change process, they tend to focus on cognitive aspects of learning and how members can become more effective learners. In describing these change strategies, we draw heavily on the work of Argyris and Schon, Senge and his colleagues, and many Australian researchers such as Hearn and Candy, because they are the most developed and articulated in OL practice.[68]

From this perspective, OL is not concerned with the organisation as a static entity but as an active process of sense making and organising. Members socially construct the organisation as they continually act and interact with each other and learn from those actions how to organise themselves for productive achievement. This active learning process enables members to develop, test and modify mental models or maps of organisational reality. Called 'theories in use', these cognitive maps inform member behaviour and organising.[69] They guide how members make decisions, perform work and organise themselves. Unfortunately, members' theories in use can be faulty, resulting in ineffective behaviours and organising efforts. They can be too narrow and fail to account for important aspects of the environment; and they can include erroneous assumptions that lead to unexpected negative consequences. Effective OL can resolve these problems. It can enable members to learn from their actions how to detect and correct errors in their mental maps and so promote more effective organising efforts.

The predominant mode of learning in most organisations is ineffective, however, and may even intensify errors. Referred to as Model I learning, it includes values and norms that emphasise unilateral control of environments and tasks, and the protection of oneself and others from information that may be hurtful.[70] These norms result in a variety of defensive routines that inhibit learning, such as withholding information and feelings, competition and rivalry, and little public testing of theories in use and the assumptions that underlie them. Model I is limited to single-loop learning where existing theories in use are reinforced.

A more effective approach to learning, called Model II, is based on values that promote valid information, free and informed choice, internal commitment to the choice and continuous assessment of its implementation.[71] This results in minimal defensiveness with greater openness to information and feedback, personal mastery and collaboration with others and public testing of theories in use. Model II applies to double-loop learning where theories in use are changed, and to deuterolearning where the learning process itself is examined and improved.

Organisation learning interventions are aimed at helping organisation members learn how to change from Model I to Model II learning. Like all learning, this change strategy includes the learning processes of discovery, invention, production and generalisation. Although the phases are described linearly below, in practice they form a recurrent cycle of overlapping learning activities.

DISCOVER THEORIES IN USE AND THEIR CONSEQUENCES

This first step involves uncovering members' mental models, or theories in use, and the consequences that follow from behaving and organising according to them. Depending on the size of the client system, this may directly involve all members, such as a senior executive team, or it may include representatives of the system, such as a cross-section of members from different levels and areas.

Organisation learning practitioners have developed a variety of techniques to help members identify their theories in use. Because these theories are generally taken for granted and are rarely examined, members need to generate and analyse data to infer the theories' underlying assumptions. One approach is called 'dialogue', a variant of the human-process interventions described in Chapter 10.[72] It involves members in genuine exchange about how they currently address problems, make decisions and interact with each other and relevant others, such as suppliers, customers and competitors. Participants are encouraged to be open and frank with each other, to treat each other as colleagues and to suspend individual assumptions as far as possible. Organisation learning practitioners facilitate dialogue sessions, using many of the human-process tools, such as process consultation and third-party intervention. Dialogue can result in a clearer understanding of existing theories in use and their behavioural consequences. It can enable members to uncover faulty assumptions that lead to ineffective behaviours and organising efforts.

A second method of identifying theories in use involves the construction of an action map of members' theories and their behavioural consequences.[73] Organisation learning practitioners typically interview members about recurrent problems in the organisation, explanations of why they are occurring, actions that are taken to resolve them and outcomes of those behaviours. Based on this information, an action map is constructed, showing interrelationships among the values underlying the theories in use, the action strategies that follow from them and the results of those actions. This is fed back to members so that they can test the validity of the map, assess the effectiveness of their theories in use and identify factors that contribute to functional and dysfunctional learning in the organisation.

A third technique for identifying theories and surfacing assumptions is called the 'left-hand, right-hand column'.[74] It starts with each member selecting a specific example of a situation where he or she was interacting with others in a way that produced ineffective results. The example is described in the form of a script and is written on the right side of a page. For instance, it might include statements such as: 'I told Larry that I thought his idea was good' and 'Joyce said to me that she did not want to take the assignment because her workload was too heavy'. On the left-hand side of the page, the member writes what he or she was thinking but not saying at each phase of the exchange. For example: 'When I told Larry that I thought his idea was good, what I was really thinking was that I have serious reservations about the idea, but Larry has a fragile ego and would be hurt by negative feedback' and 'Joyce said she didn't want to take the assignment because her workload is too heavy, but I know it's because she doesn't want to work with Larry'. This simple yet powerful exercise can reveal hidden assumptions that guide behaviour. It can make members aware of how erroneous or untested assumptions can undermine work relationships.

A fourth method that helps members identify how mental models are created and perpetuated is called the 'ladder of inference', as shown in Figure 11.5.[75] It demonstrates how far removed from concrete experience and selected data are the assumptions and beliefs that guide our behaviour. The ladder shows vividly how members' theories in use can be faulty and lead to ineffective actions. People may draw invalid conclusions from limited experience, and their cultural and personal biases may distort meaning attributed to selected data. The ladder of inference can help members understand why their theories in use may be invalid and why their behaviours and organising efforts are ineffective. Members can start with descriptions of actions that are not producing intended results and then back down the ladder to discover the reasons that underlie those ineffective behaviours. For example, a service technician might withhold valuable yet negative customer feedback about product quality from management, resulting in the eventual loss of business. Backing down the ladder, the technician could discover an untested

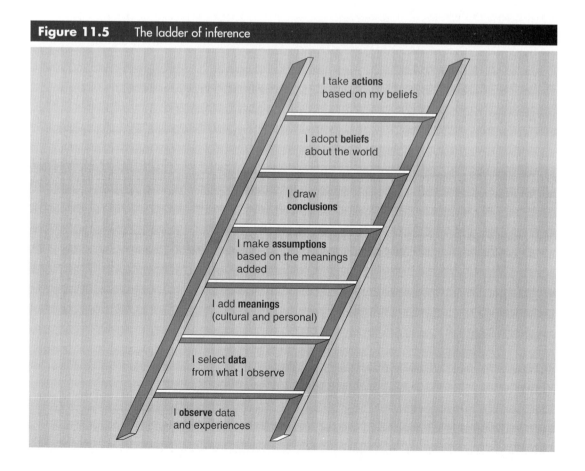

Figure 11.5   The ladder of inference

belief that upper management does not react favourably to negative information and may even 'shoot the messenger'. This belief may have resulted from assumptions and conclusions that the technician drew from observing periodic lay-offs and from hearing widespread rumours that the company is out to get trouble makers and people who speak up too much. The ladder of inference can help members understand the underlying reasons for their behaviour and can help them confront the possibility that erroneous assumptions are contributing to ineffective actions.

INVENT AND PRODUCE MORE EFFECTIVE THEORIES IN USE

Based on what is discovered in step one, members invent and produce theories in use that lead to more effective actions and are more closely aligned to Model II learning. This involves double-loop learning as they try to create and enact new theories. In essence, members learn by doing; they learn from their invention and production actions how to invent and produce more effective theories in use.

As might be expected, learning how to change theories in use can be extremely difficult. There is a strong tendency for members to revert to habitual behaviours and modes of learning. They may have trouble breaking out of existing mindsets and seeing new realities and possibilities. OL practitioners have developed both behavioural and conceptual interventions to help members overcome these problems.

Behaviourally, practitioners help members apply the values that underlie Model II learning – valid information, free choice and internal commitment – to question their experience of trying to behave more consistently with Model II.[76] They encourage members to confront and talk openly about how habitual actions and learning methods prevent them from creating and enacting more effective theories. Once these barriers to change have been discussed openly, members typically discover that they are changeable. This shared insight often leads to the invention of more effective theories for behaving, organising and learning. Subsequent experimentation with trying to enact those theories in the workplace is likely to produce more effective change because the errors that invariably occur when trying new things are now discussible and, hence, correctable.

Conceptually, OL practitioners teach system thinking to members in order to help them invent more effective theories in use.[77] It provides concepts and tools for detecting subtle yet powerful structures that underlie complex situations. Learning to see such structures can help members understand previously unknown forces that operate in the organisation. This information is essential for developing effective theories for organising, particularly in today's complex, changing world.

Systems thinking generally requires a radical shift in how members view the world: from seeing parts to seeing wholes; from seeing linear cause–effect chains to seeing interrelationships; and from seeing static entities to seeing processes of change. Practitioners have developed a variety of exercises and tools to help members make this conceptual change, including: system diagrams for displaying circles of influence among system elements; system archetypes describing recurrent structures that affect organisations; computerised micro-worlds where new strategies can be tried out under conditions that permit experimentation and learning; and games and experiential exercises demonstrating systems principles.[78]

CONTINUALLY MONITOR AND IMPROVE THE LEARNING PROCESS

This final stage involves deuterolearning: learning how to learn. Here, learning is directed at the learning process itself and at how well Model II learning characteristics are reflected in it. This includes assessment of OL strategies and of the organisational structures and processes that contribute to them. Members periodically assess how well these elements facilitate single- and double-loop learning (as described in steps 1 and 2). They generalise positive findings to new or changing situations and make appropriate modifications to improve OL. Because these activities reflect the highest and most difficult level of OL, they depend heavily on the members' capability to do Model II learning. Members must be willing to question openly their theories in use about

OL, and they must be willing to test publicly the effectiveness of their learning strategies and of the wider organisation.

There is little hard evidence of OL's effect on organisations and more evaluative research is needed. For example, Argyris and Schon state that they are unaware of any organisation that has fully implemented a double-loop learning (Model II) system.[79] Even more troubling, they describe and analyse several case studies of change that are not typically labelled as organisation learning examples. As a result, they appear to suggest that organisation learning is equivalent to concepts such as organisation adaptation, innovation and strategic change. This exacerbates confusion about what OL is and is not.

SUMMARY

In this chapter we presented interventions for helping organisations transform themselves. These changes can occur at any level in the organisation, but their ultimate intent is to change the total system. They typically happen in response to, or in anticipation of, significant environmental, technological or internal changes. These changes may require alterations in the firm's strategy, as described in Chapter 15, but are mostly aimed at altering corporate culture, vision and mental models within the organisation.

Corporate culture includes the pattern of basic assumptions, values, norms and artefacts shared by organisation members. It influences how members perceive, think and behave at work. Corporate culture affects whether firms can implement new strategies and whether they can operate at high levels of excellence. Culture change interventions start with diagnosing the organisation's existing culture. This can include assessing the cultural risks of making those organisational changes needed to implement strategy. Changing corporate culture can be extremely difficult and requires clear strategic vision, top-management commitment, symbolic leadership, the support of organisational changes, selection and socialisation of newcomers, termination of people who do not support the changes, and sensitivity to legal and ethical issues.

A self-design change strategy helps a firm to gain the built-in capacity to design and implement its own organisational transformation. Self-design involves multiple levels of the firm and multiple stakeholders, and includes an iterative series of activities: acquiring knowledge, valuing, diagnosing, designing, implementing and assessing.

Organisation learning refers to a process whereby the organisation systematically inquires into the way it operates in order to uncover the patterns in its actions, the assumptions underlying those patterns and the alteration of those patterns. The primary focus of an organisation's learning activities is to increase organisation members' awareness of their theories in use, and then challenge and change their basic assumptions for taking action. An organisation that engages in learning over a sustained period of time creates a learning organisation.

ACTIVITIES

Review questions

① What is transformational change? How does it differ from organisation development?

② What does the behavioural approach to diagnosing culture propose? What are some practical examples of this approach?

③ Describe the three approaches to diagnosing culture. Which is the most difficult to interpret? Why?

④ Define organisational culture. What are the basic assumptions of this definition?

⑤ How does the competing values approach view culture? Do you agree/disagree? Why?

⑥ What are the key roles of leadership in transformational change? How does it differ from leadership in an organisational development context?

⑦ List and explain the criteria for organisation learning.

⑧ What is the focus of a self-designing organisation and how would you lay its foundations? What are the major difficulties that you may encounter?

Discussion and essay questions

① Under what conditions are transformational changes necessary?

② How would a change agent attempt to change an organisation's culture? What would be the most obvious pitfalls that a change agent must consider?

③ How can a change agent help an organisation become self-designing? What expertise is required of such a change agent?

④ Describe how an organisation can use 'double-loop learning' to improve performance. Discuss the difficulties that an organisation may encounter.

⑤ Is it a current management strategy to treat chaos with chaos? Discuss.

NOTES

1 C. Lundberg, 'On organizational learning: implications and opportunities for expanding organizational development', in *Research in Organizational Change and Development*, 3, eds W. Pasmore and R. Woodman (Greenwich, CT: JAI Press, 1989): 61–82.

2 M. Fiol and M. Lyles, 'Organizational learning', *Academy of Management Review*, 10 (1985): 803–13; J. March and H. Simon, *Organizations* (New York: John Wiley, 1958).

3 M. Tushman, W. Newman and E. Romanelli, 'Managing the unsteady pace of organizational evolution', *California Management Review* (Fall 1986): 29–44.

4 ibid.

5 A. Meyer, A. Tsui and C. Hinings, 'Guest coeditors introduction: configurational approaches to organizational analysis', *Academy of Management Journal*, 36:6 (1993): 1175–95.

6 D. Miller and P. Friesen, *Organizations: A Quantum View* (Englewood Cliffs, NJ: Prentice-Hall, 1984).

7 B. Blumenthal and P. Haspeslagh, 'Toward a definition of corporate transformation', *Sloan Management Review*, 35 (3, 1994): 101–7.

8 Tushman, Newman and Romanelli, 'Managing the unsteady pace', op. cit.; L. Greiner, 'Evolution and revolution as organizations grow', *Harvard Business Review* (July–August 1972): 37–46.

9 M. Tushman and E. Romanelli, 'Organizational evolution: a metamorphosis model of convergence and reorientation', in *Research in Organization Behavior*, 7, eds L. Cummings and B. Staw (Greenwich, CT: JAI Press, 1985): 171–222.

10 J. Bartunek and M. Louis, 'Organization development and organizational transformation', in *Research in Organizational Change and Development*, 2, eds W. Pasmore and R. Woodman (Greenwich, CT: JAI Press, 1988): 97–134.

11 R. Golembiewski, K. Billingsley and S. Yeager, 'Measuring change and persistence in human affairs: types of changes generated by OD designs', *Journal of Applied Behavioral Science*, 12 (1975): 133–57.

12 J. Sackmann, 'The role of metaphors in organization transformation', *Human Relations*, 42 (1989): 463–85.

13 A. Pettigrew, *The Awakening Giant: Continuity and Change in Imperial Chemical Industries* (Oxford: Blackwell, 1985); A. Pettigrew, 'Context and action in the transformation of the firm', *Journal of Management Studies*, 24 (1987): 649–70; Tushman and Romanelli, 'Organizational evolution', op. cit.

14 M. Tushman and B. Virany, 'Changing characteristics of executive teams in an emerging industry', *Journal of Business Venturing* (1986): 37–49; L. Greiner and A. Bhambri, 'New CEO intervention and dynamics of deliberate strategic change', *Strategic Management Journal*, 10 (Summer 1989): 67–86.

15 M. Tushman, W. Newman and D. Nadler, 'Executive leadership and organizational evolution: managing incremental and discontinuous change', in *Corporate Transformation: Revitalizing Organizations for a*

Competitive World, eds R. Kilmann and T. Covin (San Francisco: Jossey-Bass, 1988): 102–30; W. Bennis and B. Nanus, *Leaders: The Strategies for Taking Charge* (New York: Harper and Row, 1985); Pettigrew, 'Context and action in the transformation of the firm', op. cit.

16 T. Cummings and S. Mohrman, 'Self-designing organizations: towards implementing quality-of-work-life innovations', in *Research in Organizational Change and Development*, 1, eds R. Woodman and W. Pasmore (Greenwich, CT: JAI Press, 1987): 275–310.

17 W. Ouchi, *Theory Z: How American Business Can Meet the Japanese Challenge* (Reading, MA: Addison-Wesley, 1979); R. Pascale and A. Athos, *The Art of Japanese Management* (New York: Simon and Schuster, 1981); T. Deal and A. Kennedy, *Corporate Cultures* (Reading, MA: Addison-Wesley, 1982); T. Peters and R. Waterman, *In Search of Excellence* (New York: Harper and Row, 1982); T. Peters and N. Austin, *A Passion for Excellence* (New York: Random House, 1985); J. Pfeffer, *Competitive Advantage Through People* (Cambridge: Harvard Business School, 1994); J. Collins and J. Porras, *Built to Last* (New York: Harper Business, 1994); J. Kotter and J. Heskett, *Corporate Culture and Performance* (New York: The Free Press, 1992): D. Dunphy and D. Stace, *Beyond the Boundaries* (Sydney: McGraw-Hill, 1994).

18 D. Meyerson and J. Martin, 'Cultural change: an integration of three different views', *Journal of Management Studies*, 24 (1987): 623–47; D. Denison and G. Spreitzer, 'Organizational culture and organizational development: a competing values approach', in *Research in Organizational Change and Development*, 5, eds R. Woodman and W. Pasmore (Greenwich, CT: JAI Press, 1991): 1–22; E. Schein, *Organizational Culture and Leadership*, 2nd edn (San Francisco: Jossey–Bass, 1992).

19 Schein, *Organizational Culture and Leadership*, op. cit.; R. Kilmann, M. Saxton and R. Serpa, eds, *Gaining Control of the Corporate Culture* (San Francisco: Jossey-Bass, 1985).

20 Schein, *Organizational Culture and Leadership*, op. cit.

21 M. Louis, 'Toward a system of inquiry on organizational culture', paper delivered at the Western Academy of Management Meeting, Colorado Springs, CO, April 1982.

22 E. Abrahamson and C. Fombrun, 'Macrocultures: determinants and consequences', *Academy of Management Journal*, 19 (1994): 728–55.

23 B. Uttal, 'The corporate culture vultures', *Fortune* (17 October 1983): 66–72.

24 ibid., 70.

25 Ouchi, *Theory Z*; Pascale and Athos, *Japanese Management*; both op. cit.

26 D. Denison, 'The climate, culture and effectiveness of work organizations: a study of organizational behavior and financial performance', PhD dissertation, University of Michigan, 1982.

27 Kotter and Heskett, *Corporate Culture and Performance*, op. cit.

28 D. Hanna, *Designing Organizations for High Performance* (Reading, MA: Addison-Wesley, 1988).

29 H. Schwartz and S. Davis, 'Matching corporate culture and business strategy', *Organizational Dynamics* (Summer 1981): 30–48; S. Davis, *Managing Corporate Culture* (Cambridge, MA: Ballinger, 1984).

30 Denison and Spreitzer, 'Organizational culture and organizational development', op. cit.; R. Quinn, *Beyond Rational Management: Mastering the Paradoxes and Competing Demands of High Performance* (San Francisco: Jossey-Bass, 1988).

31 R. Quinn and G. Spreitzer, 'The psychometrics of the competing values culture instrument and an analysis of the impact of organizational culture on quality of life', in *Research in Organization Change and Development*, 5, eds R. Woodman and W. Pasmore (Greenwich, CT: JAI Press, 1991): 115–42.

32 Schein, *Organizational Culture and Leadership*, op. cit.

33 R. Zammuto and J. Krakower, 'Quantitative and qualitative studies of organizational culture', in *Research in Organizational Change and Development*, 5, eds R. Woodman and W. Pasmore (Greenwich, CT: JAI Press, 1991): 83–114; Quinn and Spreitzer, 'The psychometrics of the competing values culture instrument', op. cit.

34 Schein, *Organizational Culture and Leadership*, op. cit.

35 P. Frost, L. Moore, M. Louis, C. Lundberg and J. Martin, eds, *Organizational Culture* (Beverly Hills, CA: Sage, 1985): 95–196.

36 Meyerson and Martin, 'Cultural change', op. cit.

37 J. Barney, 'Organizational culture: can it be a source of sustained competitive advantage?', *Academy of Management Review* (1986): 656–65.

38 Uttal, 'Corporate culture vultures', op. cit.

39 ibid., 70.

40 Schwartz and Davis, 'Matching corporate culture and business strategy'; Uttal, 'Corporate culture vultures'; Davis, *Managing Corporate Culture*; Kilmann, Saxton and Serpa, *Gaining Control*; Frost, Moore, Louis, Lundberg and Martin, *Organizational Culture*; all op. cit.; V. Sathe, 'Implications of corporate culture: a manager's guide to action', *Organizational Dynamics* (Autumn 1983): 5–23; B. Drake and E. Drake, 'Ethical and legal aspects of managing corporate cultures', *California Management Review* (Winter 1988): 107–23.

41 C. Worley, D. Hitchin and W. Ross, *Integrated Strategic Change* (Reading, MA: Addison-Wesley, 1996); R. Beckhard and W. Pritchard, *Changing the Essence* (San Francisco: Jossey-Bass, 1992).

42 B. Dumaine, 'Creating a new corporate culture', *Fortune* (January 1990); C. O'Reilly, 'Corporations, culture and commitment: motivation and social control in organizations', *California Management Review*, 31 (Summer 1989): 9–25; Pettigrew, 'Context and action', op. cit.

43 Dumaine, 'Creating a new corporate culture', op. cit.

44 K. McGhee, *Sydney Morning Herald* (1997).

45 N. Tichy and S. Sherman, *Control Your Destiny or Someone Else Will* (London: HarperBusiness, 2001).

46 *The Age* (26 April 1998): 25.

47 *Australian Financial Review* (10 June 1998): 21.

48 B. Hedberg, P. Nystrom and W. Starbuck, 'Camping on seesaws: prescriptions for a self–designing organization', *Administrative Science Quarterly*, 21 (1976): 41–65; K. Weick, 'Organization design: organizations as self–designing systems', *Organizational Dynamics*, 6 (1977): 30–46.

49 S. Mohrman and T. Cummings, *Self–Designing Organizations: Learning How to Create High Performance* (Reading, MA: Addison-Wesley, 1989); Cummings and Mohrman, 'Self–designing organizations', op. cit.

50 P. Lawrence and D. Dyer, *Renewing American Industry* (New York: Free Press, 1983).

51 C. Argyris, R. Putnam and D. Smith, *Action Science* (San Francisco: Jossey-Bass, 1985); C. Lundberg, 'On organizational learning: implications and opportunities for expanding organizational development', in *Research on Organizational Change and Development*, 3, eds R. Woodman and W. Pasmore (Greenwich, CT: JAI Press, 1989): 61–82; P. Senge, *The Fifth Discipline* (New York: Doubleday, 1990).

52 M. Weisbord, *Productive Workplaces* (San Francisco: Jossey-Bass, 1987); R. Freeman, *Strategic Management* (Boston: Ballinger, 1984).

53 Miller and Friesen, *Organizations*, op. cit.

54 J. Dewey, *How We Think* (Boston: D.C. Heath & Company, 1933).

55 C. Argyris and D. Schon, *Organizational Learning: A Theory of Action Perspective* (Reading, MA: Addison-Wesley, 1978); C. Argyris and D. Schon, *Organizational Learning II: Theory, Method and Practice* (Reading, MA: Addison-Wesley, 1996); Senge, *The Fifth Discipline*, op. cit.

56 Senge, *The Fifth Discipline*, op. cit.; S. Chawla and J. Renesch, eds, *Learning Organizations: Developing Cultures for Tomorrow's Workplace* (Portland, Oreg.: Productivity Press, 1995).

57 M. McGill, J. Slocum and D. Lei, 'Management practices in learning organizations', *Organizational Dynamics*, (Autumn 1993): 5–17; E. Nevis, A. DiBella and J. Gould, 'Understanding organizations as learning systems', *Sloan Management Review* (Winter 1995): 73–85.

58 Nevis, DiBella and Gould, 'Understanding organizations as learning systems', op. cit.

59 *Australian Financial Review* (22 May 1998): 67.

60 W. Snyder and T. Cummings, 'Organization learning disorders: conceptual model and intervention guidelines', working paper, School of Business, University of Southern California, 1996.

61 D. Leonard-Barton, *Wellsprings of Knowledge: Building and Sustaining the Sources of Innovation* (Boston: Harvard Business School Press, 1995).

62 X. Konaka and X. Takeuchi, *The Knowledge-Creating Company: How Japanese Companies Foster Creativity and Innovation for Competitive Advantage* (New York: Oxford University Press, 1995).

63 C. Prahalad and G. Hamel, 'The core competencies of the corporation', *Harvard Business Review*, 68 (1990): 79–91.

64 H. Itami, *Mobilizing for Invisible Assets* (Cambridge: Harvard University Press, 1987).

65 T. Stewart, 'Intellectual capital', *Fortune* (3 October 1994): 68–74.

66 ibid.

67 J. Barney, 'Looking inside for competitive advantage', *Academy of Management Executive*, 9:4 (1995): 49–61; M. Peteraf, 'The cornerstones of competitive advantage', *Strategic Management Journal*, 14:3 (1993): 179–92; Worley, Hitchin and Ross, *Integrated Strategic Change*, op. cit.

68 Argyris and Schon, *Organizational Learning II*; Senge, *The Fifth Discipline*; both op. cit.; P. Senge, C. Roberts, R. Ross, B. Smith and A. Kleiner, *The Fifth Discipline Fieldbook: Strategies for Building a Learning Organization* (New York: Doubleday, 1995); Hearn and Candy in *Management Development in Australia*, ed. B. Smith (New South Wales: Harcourt Brace Jovanovich).

69 Argyris and Schon, *Organizational Learning II*; Senge, *The Fifth Discipline*; both op. cit.; P. Senge, C. Roberts, R. Ross, B. Smith and A. Kleiner, *The Fifth Discipline Fieldbook: Strategies for Building a Learning Organization* (New York: Doubleday, 1995); Hearn and Candy, in *Management Development in Australia*, ed. B. Smith (New South Wales: Harcourt Brace Jovanovich).

70 ibid.

71 Argyris and Schon, *Organizational Learning II*, op. cit.; C. Argyris, *Intervention Theory and Method* (Reading, MA: Addison-Wesley, 1970).

72 Senge, *The Fifth Discipline*, op. cit.

73 Argyris and Schon, *Organizational Learning II*, op. cit.

74 Argyris and Schon, *Organizational Learning II*; Senge, Roberts, Ross, Smith and Kleiner, *The Fifth Discipline Fieldbook*; both op. cit.

75 Senge, Roberts, Ross, Smith and Kleiner, *The Fifth Discipline Fieldbook*, op. cit.

76 Argyris and Schon, *Organizational Learning II*; Argyris, *Intervention Theory and Method*; both op. cit.
77 Senge, *The Fifth Discipline*, op. cit.
78 ibid.
79 Argyris and Schon, *Organizational Learning II*, op. cit., 112.

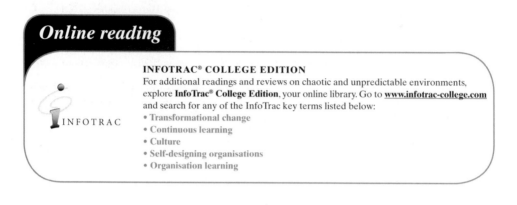

Online reading

INFOTRAC® COLLEGE EDITION

For additional readings and reviews on chaotic and unpredictable environments, explore **InfoTrac® College Edition**, your online library. Go to **www.infotrac-college.com** and search for any of the InfoTrac key terms listed below:

- **Transformational change**
- **Continuous learning**
- **Culture**
- **Self-designing organisations**
- **Organisation learning**

COMPETITIVE AND COLLABORATIVE STRATEGIES

This chapter describes transformation interventions that help organisations implement strategies for both competing and collaborating with other organisations. These change programs are relatively recent additions to the OT field. They focus on helping organisations position themselves strategically in their social and economic environments and achieve a better fit with the external forces affecting goal achievement and performance. Practitioners are discovering that additional knowledge and skills in such areas as marketing, finance, economics, political science and complexity theory are necessary to implement these significant interventions.

Organisations are open systems and must relate to their environments (Chapter 4). They must acquire the resources and information needed to function, and they must deliver products or services that customers value. An organisation's strategy – how it acquires resources and delivers outputs – is shaped by particular aspects and features of the environment. For example, cigarette manufacturers faced with increasing regulation and declining demand in New Zealand and Australia increased distribution to other countries and diversified into other industries, such as foods, beverages and consumer products. Thus, organisations can devise a number of competitive and collaborative responses for managing environmental interfaces. Competitive responses – such as creating or clarifying mission statements and goals, developing new strategies or creating special units to respond to the environment – help the organisation to outperform rivals. Collaborative responses, such as forming strategic alliances with other organisations and developing networks, seek to improve performance by joining with others. These often result in dramatic and chaotic change which is called organisation transformation (OT).

The OT interventions described in this chapter help organisations gain a comprehensive understanding of their environments and devise appropriate responses to external demands. The chapter begins with an elaboration of the organisational environments discussion started in Chapter 4. Then, two categories of interventions are described: competitive strategies and collaborative strategies.

Competitive strategies include integrated strategic change, mergers and acquisitions. Integrated strategic change is a comprehensive OT intervention aimed at a single organisation or business unit. It suggests that business strategy and organisation design must be aligned and changed together to respond to external and internal disruptions. A strategic change plan helps members manage the transition between the current strategic orientation and the desired future strategic orientation. Mergers and acquisitions represent a second strategy of competition. These interventions seek to leverage the strengths (or shore up the weaknesses) of one organisation by combining with another organisation. This complex strategic change involves integrating many of the interventions previously discussed in this text, including human process, technostructural and human resource management interventions. Research and practice in mergers and acquisitions strongly suggest that OT practices can contribute to implementation success.

Collaborative strategies include alliances and networks. Alliance interventions – including joint ventures, franchising and long-term contracts – help to develop the relationship between two organisations that believe the benefits of co-operation outweigh the costs of lowered autonomy and control. These increasingly common arrangements require each organisation to understand its goals and strategy in the relationship, build and leverage trust, and ensure that it is receiving the expected benefits. Finally – and building on the knowledge of alliances – network development interventions are concerned with helping sets of three or more organisations engage in relationships to perform tasks or to solve problems that are too complex and multifaceted for a single organisation to resolve. These multi-organisation systems abound in today's environment and include research and development consortia, public–private partnerships and constellations of profit-seeking organisations. They tend to be loosely coupled and non-hierarchical, and consequently they require methods different from most traditional OD interventions that are geared to single organisations. These methods involve helping organisations recognise the need for partnerships and the development of co-ordinating structures for carrying out multi-organisation activities.

ENVIRONMENTAL FRAMEWORK

This section provides a framework for understanding how environments affect organisations. The framework is based on the concept, described in Chapter 4, that organisations and their sub-units are *open systems* existing in environmental contexts. Environments can be described in two ways. First, there are different types of environments consisting of specific components or forces. To survive and grow, organisations must understand these different environments, select appropriate parts to respond to, and develop effective relationships with them. A manufacturing firm, for example, must understand raw materials markets, labour markets, customer segments and production technology alternatives. It then must select from a range of raw material suppliers, applicants for employment, customer demographics and production technologies to achieve desired outcomes effectively. Organisations are thus dependent on their environments. They need to manage external constraints and contingencies, and take advantage of external opportunities. They also need to influence the environment in favourable directions through such methods as political lobbying, advertising and public relations.

Second, several useful dimensions capture the nature of organisational environments. Some environments are rapidly changing and complex, and so require organisational responses different from those in environments that are stable and simple. For example, breakfast cereal manufacturers face a stable market and use well-understood production technologies. Their strategy and organisation design issues are radically different from those of software developers, which face product life cycles measured in months instead of years, where labour skills are rare and hard to find, and where demand can change drastically overnight.

In this section, we first describe different types of environments that can affect organisations. Then we identify environmental dimensions that influence organisational responses to external forces. This material provides an introductory context for describing two kinds of interventions – competitive strategies and collaborative strategies – that represent ways organisations can change dramatically as a response to their environments.

Environmental types and dimensions

As discussed more fully in Chapter 10, organisational environments are everything beyond the boundaries of organisations that can indirectly or directly affect performance and outcomes. There are two classes of environments: the general environment and the task environment; plus the enacted environment, which reflects members' perceptions of the general and task environments.

The *general environment* consists of all external forces that can influence an organisation, including technological, legal and regulatory, political, economic, social and ecological components. The *task environment* consists of the specific individuals and organisations that interact directly with the organisation and can affect goal achievement: customers, suppliers, competitors, producers of substitute products or services, labour unions, financial institutions and so on. The *enacted environment* consists of the organisation members' perception and representation of its general and task environments. Only the enacted environment can affect which organisational responses are chosen. The general and task environments, however, can influence whether those responses are successful or ineffective.

Environments also can be characterised along dimensions that describe the organisation's context and influence its responses. The key dimension of the environment affecting information processing is *information uncertainty*, or the degree to which environmental information is ambiguous. Another key dimension is *resource dependence*, or the degree to which an organisation relies on other organisations for resources. These two environmental dimensions can be combined to show the degree to which organisations are constrained by their environments and consequently must be responsive to their demands.

Organisations must have the capacity to monitor and make sense of their environments if they are to respond appropriately. Organisations employ a number of methods to influence and respond to their environments, to buffer their technology from external disruptions, and to link themselves to sources of information and resources. OT practitioners can help organisations implement competitive and collaborative responses.

The two types of interventions discussed in this chapter derive from this environmental framework. Competitive interventions, such as integrated strategic change and mergers and acquisitions, focus on sets of administrative and competitive responses to help an individual organisation improve its performance. Collaborative interventions, such as alliances and networks, utilise a variety of collective responses to co-ordinate the actions of multiple organisations.

Application 12.1 is an example of how an organisation integrates all of its knowledge of the environment in order to design strategies for the future.

APPLiCATiON 12.1

MOBILE BATTLEGROUND

Companies in the mobile telecommunications industry are engaged in a fight to the death. It is normal for any company to concentrate on innovation if its products are struggling in the market, but for mobile-phone makers the need to innovate is more primal and urgent. Makers of mobiles, digital cameras, personal computers, iPods, BlackBerrys and small video devices are locked in fierce combat – and the battle draws in companies as diverse as Nokia, Motorola, Kodak, Sony, Philips, Samsung and Apple.

The victors will sell a hand-held device that provides telephony, internet, sound and vision, e-mail and video games. The losers will probably find they have a smaller business or no business at all.

It is small wonder, then, that the Finnish giant Nokia is intense about the way it innovates. It has already shown a stunning ability to re-invent itself. In the mid 1990s Nokia was an industrial conglomerate that earned about half its revenue from telecommunications. The remainder came from pulp and paper, and businesses such as tyre manufacturing.

A decade later, all Nokia's sales revenue is earned from telecommunications. The company is broken into four divisions: networks, enterprise solutions, multimedia and mobile phones.

…

Last year, Nokia's main head-to-head competitor, Motorola, increased its world market share by about 50%, and a less-expected combatant, Samsung, nearly tripled its share. Analysts say Nokia's share is down slightly to about 30%. Motorola and Samsung each have more than 15%.

When it is considered that additional competitive threats will inevitably come from other industry sectors, it is evident that the effort to survive will be intense. The main object of the battle is to win over the mind of the customer, which Nokia attempts in a disciplined fashion.

Nokia's head of insight and innovation, Hannu Nieminen, says the emphasis is on 'co-creation': the boundaries between the company and the customer are dissolving; the consumer does not just consume, but innovates with the company.

'That is new,' he says. 'Because we are taking these steps now [to co-create] we will see where it leads.'

Nokia uses many of the more recognisable demographic analytics in developing its designs, breaking the market into premium, classic and basic, and cross-referencing that with fashion, activity

▷▷

and expression. Other methodologies are product stories, new scenarios, mood boards (a way to identify customer values) and concept formulation.

'We have to look outside the mobile industry,' Nieminen says. 'Then we work with consumers to narrow the choices. One of the key strengths is how wide our portfolio [of products] is. No one else is covering all those areas.'

...

'Anybody can be your competitor or your partner – that is the concept of co-creation. I am not sure that asking who your competitor is, is even the right question any more. The right question is what do you offer customers at this point in time?'

...

Nokia is not just contending with a blistering level of industry convergence, which, although a fierce competitive threat, also represents an opportunity to eat into the markets of other industries. It is also dealing with market saturation, a common problem for global companies.

About two billion people have mobile phones and the figure is expected to be three billion by 2008.

Source: David James, 'Mobile battleground', *Business Review Weekly*, 11–17 May 2006.

Critical Thinking Questions: Nokia is undoubtedly functioning successfully in a saturated market. How may Nokia succeed in the years after 2008? How can the company prepare its employees to 'co-create' with customers? What future do you predict for Nokia?

COMPETITIVE STRATEGIES

These interventions are concerned with choices organisations can make to improve their competitive performance. They include integrated strategic change and mergers and acquisitions. Competitive strategies use a variety of responses to better align the organisation with pressing environmental demands. To establish a competitive advantage, organisations must achieve a favoured position vis-à-vis their competitors or perform internally in ways that are unique, valuable and difficult to imitate.[1] Although typically associated with commercial firms, these competitive criteria can also apply to not-for-profit and governmental organisations. Activities that are unique, valuable and difficult to imitate enhance the organisation's performance by establishing a competitive advantage over its rivals.

UNIQUENESS

A fundamental assumption in competitive strategies is that all organisations possess a unique bundle of resources and processes. Individually or in combination, they represent the source of competitive advantage. An important task in any competitive strategy is to understand these unique organisational features. For example, resources can be financial (such as access to low-cost capital), reputational (such as brand image or a history of product quality), technological (such as patents, know-how or a strong research and development department) and human (such as excellent labour–management relationships or scarce and valuable skill sets). Bill Gates's knowledge of IBM's need for an operating system on the one hand and the availability of the disk operating system (DOS) on the other hand represent a powerful case for how resources alone can represent a unique advantage.

An organisation's processes – regular patterns of organisational activity involving a sequence of tasks performed by individuals[2] – use resources to produce goods and services. For example, a software development process combines computer resources, programming languages, typing skills, knowledge of computer languages and customer requirements to produce a new software application. Other organisational processes include new product development, strategic planning, appraising member performance, making sales calls, fulfilling customer orders and the like. When resources and processes are formed into capabilities that allow the organisation to perform complex activities better than others, a distinctive competence or 'hedgehog concept' is identified.[3] Collins found that a key determinant in an organisation's transition from 'good to great' was a clear understanding and commitment to the one thing an organisation does better than anyone else.

VALUE

Organisations achieve competitive advantage when their unique resources and processes are arranged in such a way that products or services either warrant a higher-than-average price or are exceptionally low in cost. Both advantages are valuable according to a performance–price criterion. Products and services with highly desirable features or capabilities, although expensive, are valuable because of their ability to satisfy customer demands for high quality or some other performance dimension. BMW automobiles are valuable because the perceived benefits of superior handling exceed the price paid. On the other hand, outputs that cost little to produce are valuable because of their ability to satisfy customer demands at a low price. Hyundai automobiles are valuable because they provide basic transportation at a low price. BMW and Hyundai are both profitable, but they achieve that outcome through different value propositions.

DIFFICULT TO IMITATE

Finally, competitive advantage is sustainable when unique and valuable resources and processes are difficult to mimic or duplicate by other organisations.[4] Organisations have devised a number of methods for making imitation difficult. For example, they can protect their competitive advantage by making it difficult for other firms to identify their distinctive competence. Disclosing unimportant information at trade shows or forgoing superior profits can make it difficult for competitors to identify an organisation's strengths. Organisations also can aggressively pursue a range of opportunities, thus raising the cost for competitors who try to replicate their success. Finally, organisations can seek to retain key human resources through attractive compensation and reward practices, thereby making it more difficult and costly for competitors to attract such talent.

The success of a competitive strategy depends on organisation responses that result in unique, valuable and difficult-to-imitate advantages. This section describes two OT interventions that can assist individual organisations in developing these advantages and managing strategic change.

Integrated strategic change

Integrated strategic change (ISC) is a recent intervention that extends traditional OD processes into the content-oriented discipline of strategic management. Discussed more fully in Chapter 10, ISC is a deliberate, co-ordinated process that leads gradually or radically to systemic realignments between the environment and a firm's strategic orientation, and that results in improvement in performance and effectiveness.[5]

The ISC process was developed in response to managers' complaints that good business strategies often are not implemented. Implementation occurs as middle managers, supervisors and employees hear about the new strategy through memos, restructuring announcements, changes in job responsibilities or new departmental objectives. Consequently, because participation has been limited to top management, there is little understanding of the need for change and little ownership of the new behaviours, initiatives and tactics required to achieve the announced objectives.

Mergers and acquisitions

Mergers and acquisitions (M&As) involve the combination of two organisations. The term *merger* refers to the integration of two previously independent organisations into a completely new organisation, while *acquisition* involves the purchase of one organisation by another for integration into the acquiring organisation. M&As are distinct from the strategies of collaboration described later in this chapter because at least one of the organisations ceases to exist. The stressful dynamics associated with M&As led one researcher to call them the 'ultimate change management challenge'.[6]

M&A RATIONALE

Organisations have a number of reasons for wanting to acquire or merge with other firms, including diversification or vertical integration; gaining access to global markets, technology, or other resources; and achieving operational efficiencies, improved innovation or resource sharing.[7] As a result, M&As have become a preferred method for rapid growth and strategic change. In 2002, for example, over 6900 M&A deals worth $458.7 billion were conducted in the United States; globally, over 23 500 deals worth $1.4 trillion were registered according to the Dealogic market research firm.[8] Recent large transactions include Oracle and Peoplesoft, HP and Compaq, AOL and Time/Warner, Chrysler and Daimler-Benz, Ford and Volvo, and Boeing and McDonnell Douglas. Despite M&A popularity, they have a questionable record of success.[9] Among the reasons commonly cited for merger failure are inadequate due diligence processes, the lack of a compelling strategic rationale, unrealistic expectations of synergy, paying too much for the transaction, conflicting corporate cultures and failure to move quickly.[10]

M&A interventions typically are preceded by an examination of corporate and business strategy. *Corporate strategy* describes the range of businesses within which the firm will participate, while *business strategy* specifies how the organisation will compete in any particular business. Organisations must decide whether their corporate and strategic goals should be achieved through strategic change, such as ISC, a merger or acquisition, or a collaborative response, such as alliances or networks. Mergers and acquisitions are preferred when internal development is considered too slow, or when alliances or networks do not offer sufficient control over key resources to meet the firm's objectives.

In addition to the OT issues described here, M&As are complex strategic changes that involve legal and financial knowledge beyond the scope of this text. OT practitioners are encouraged to seek out and work with specialists in these other relevant disciplines. The focus here is on how OT can contribute to M&A success.

APPLICATION STAGES

Mergers and acquisitions involve three major phases as shown in Table 12.1: precombination, legal combination and operational combination.[11] OT practitioners can make substantive contributions to the precombination and operational combination phases.

Precombination phase

This first phase consists of planning activities designed to ensure the success of the combined organisation. The organisation that initiates the OT change must identify a candidate organisation, work with it to gather information about each other, and plan the implementation and integration activities. The evidence is growing that precombination activities are critical to M&A success.[12]

1   *Search for and select candidate.* This involves developing screening criteria to assess and narrow the field of candidate organisations, agreeing on a first-choice candidate, assessing regulatory compliance, establishing initial contacts and formulating a letter of intent. Criteria for choosing an M&A partner can include leadership and management characteristics, market-access resources, technical or financial capabilities, physical facilities and so on. OT practitioners can add value at this stage of the process by encouraging screening criteria that include managerial, organisational and cultural components, as well as technical and financial aspects. In practice, financial issues tend to receive greater attention at this stage, with the goal of maximising shareholder value.

Table 12.1	Major phases and activities in merger and acquisitions	
Major M&A phases	Key steps	OD and change management issues
Precombination	• Search for and select candidate • Create M&A team • Establish business case • Perform due diligence assessment • Develop merger integration plan	• Ensure that candidates are screened for cultural as well as financial, technical, and physical asset criteria • Define a clear leadership structure • Establish a clear strategic vision, competitive strategy, and systems integration potential • Specify the desirable organisation design features • Specify an integration action plan
Legal combination	• Complete financial negotiations • Close the deal • Announce the combination	
Operational combination	• Day 1 activities • Organisational and technical integration activities • Cultural integration activities	• Implement changes quickly • Communicate • Solve problems together and focus on the customer • Conduct an evaluation to learn and identify further areas of integration planning

Failure to attend to cultural and organisational issues, however, can result in diminished shareholder value during the operational combination phase.[13]

Identifying potential candidates, narrowing the field, agreeing on a first choice and checking regulatory compliance are relatively straightforward activities. They generally involve investment brokers and other outside parties who have access to databases of organisational, financial and technical information. The final two activities, making initial contacts and creating a letter of intent, are aimed at determining the candidate's interest in the proposed merger or acquisition.

2   *Create an M&A team.* Once there is initial agreement between the two organisations to pursue a merger or acquisition, senior leaders from the respective organisations appoint an M&A team to establish the business case, oversee the due diligence process and develop a merger integration plan.[14] This team typically comprises senior executives and experts in such areas as business valuation, technology, organisation and marketing. OT practitioners can facilitate formation of this team through human process interventions, such as team building and process consultation, and help the team establish clear goals and action strategies. They also can help members define a leadership structure, apply relevant skills and knowledge, and ensure that both organisations are represented appropriately. The group's leadership structure, or who will be accountable for the team's accomplishments, is especially critical. In an acquisition, an executive from the acquiring firm is typically the team's leader. In a merger of equals, the choice of a single individual to lead the team is more difficult, but essential. The outcome of this decision and the process used to make it form the first outward symbol of how this strategic change will be conducted.

3   *Establish the business case.* The purpose of this activity is to develop a prima facie case that combining the two organisations will result in a competitive advantage that exceeds their separate advantages.[15] It includes specifying the strategic vision, competitive strategy and systems integration potential for the M&A. OT practitioners can facilitate this discussion to ensure that each issue is fully explored. If the business case cannot be justified on strategic, financial or operational grounds, the M&A should be revisited, terminated, or another candidate should be sought.

Strategic vision represents the organisations' combined capabilities. It synthesises the strengths of the two organisations into a viable new organisation. Application 12.2 comments that caution is required, though, as the process of merging and acquiring is not an automatic success.

APPLiCATiON 12.2

HOW TO MAKE A DECISION ABOUT MERGERS AND ACQUISITIONS

The causes of value-destroying acquisitions are frequently traced to a number of factors. These include offering a sizeable premium, overestimation of cost savings and synergies, and poor post-merger integration. One inescapable conclusion, though, is that revenue growth is a key driver of successful merger and acquisition outcomes.

As such, generating accurate and realistic demand, price and revenue forecasts are equally critical factors of success. Improving the chances of success requires the integration of a number of forecasting tools, processes and skill sets that are not commonly hard wired into merger analysis.

…

It should be recognised that the use of forecasting tools and techniques do not always give a definitive answer. In fact, it is not uncommon for these types of analyses to produce divergent views in revenue potential. It is also important to point out that the process of going through revenue analysis in a more systematic way adds significant value to the forecast analysis. By following a moderately more rigorous approach to evaluating candidate assumptions, practical and potentially revealing questions begin to surface. With that, an acquiring company may be able to better distil the differences between a target's plans and forecasts. Consequently, deals may be struck that retain more value for the shareholders of the acquiring company.

Accurate and realistic revenue forecasts are critical to the successful outcome of mergers and acquisitions. Most business combinations fail to achieve their promised payoff in terms of growth and profitability, yet it is revenue that heavily influences the long-term outcome of a merger. By applying a more systematic approach to analysing the demand and pricing assumptions of potential targets during the due diligence process, companies can identify potential 'red flags' and improve acquisition decisions. The causes of value-destroying acquisitions are frequently traced to a number of factors. These include offering a sizeable premium, overestimation of cost savings and synergies, and poor post-merger integration. One inescapable conclusion, though, is that revenue growth is a key driver of successful merger and acquisition outcomes. As such, generating accurate and realistic demand, price and revenue forecasts are equally critical factors of success. Improving the chances of success requires the integration of a number of forecasting tools, processes and skill sets that are not commonly hard wired into merger analysis.

Source: Stephen J. Smith, 'How to make a decision about mergers and acquisitions', *Journal of Business Forecasting*, July 2005, Vol. 24, Iss. 2.

Critical Thinking Question: Much has been written to encourage mergers and acquisitions, but this article suggests that caution should be used when considering this option. Search the internet and find an organisation that has recently undergone a merger or acquisition and has been unsuccessful or encountered several difficulties. What went wrong? Why did things go wrong?

Competitive strategy describes the business model for how the combined organisation will add value in a particular product market or segment of the value chain, how that value proposition is best performed by the combined organisation (compared with competitors) and how it will be difficult to imitate. The purpose of this activity is to force the two organisations to go beyond the rhetoric of 'these two organisations should merge because it's a good fit'.

Systems integration specifies how the two organisations will be combined. It addresses how and if they can work together. It includes the following key questions: Will one firm be acquired and operated as a wholly owned subsidiary? Does the transaction imply a merger of equals? Are layoffs implied and, if so, where? On what basis can promised synergies or cost savings be achieved?

4   *Perform a due diligence assessment.* This involves evaluating whether the two organisations actually have the managerial, technical and financial resources that each assumes the other possesses. It includes a comprehensive review of each organisation's articles of incorporation, stock option plans, organisation charts and so on. Financial, human resources, operational, technical and logistical inventories are evaluated along with other legally binding issues. The discovery of previously unknown or unfavourable information can halt the M&A process.[16]

Although due diligence assessment traditionally emphasises the financial aspects of M&As, this focus is increasingly being challenged by evidence that culture clashes between two organisations can ruin expected financial gains.[17] Thus, attention to the cultural features of M&As is becoming more prevalent in due diligence assessment. The scope and detail of due diligence assessment depends on knowledge of the candidate's business, the complexity of its industry, the relative size and risk of the transaction, and the available resources. Due diligence activities must reflect symbolically the vision and values of the combined organisations. An overly zealous assessment, for example, can contradict promises of openness and trust made earlier in the transaction. Missteps at this stage can lower or destroy opportunities for synergy, cost savings and improved shareholder value.[18]

5   *Develop merger integration plans.* This stage specifies how the two organisations will be combined.[19] It defines integration objectives; the scope and timing of integration activities; organisation design criteria; Day 1 requirements; and who does what, where, and when. The scope of these plans depends on how integrated the organisations will be. If the candidate organisation will operate as an independent subsidiary with an 'arm's-length' relationship to the parent, merger integration planning need only specify those systems that will be common to both organisations. A full integration of the two organisations requires a more extensive plan.

Merger integration planning starts with the business case conducted earlier and involves more detailed analyses of the strategic vision, competitive strategy and systems integration for the M&A. For example, assessment of the organisations' markets and suppliers can reveal opportunities to serve customers better and to capture purchasing economies of scale. Examination of business processes can identify: best operating practices; which physical facilities should be combined, left alone or shut down; and which systems and procedures are redundant. Capital budget analysis can show which investments should be continued or dropped. Typically, the M&A team appoints subgroups composed of members from both organisations to perform these analyses. OT practitioners can conduct team-building and process-consultation interventions to improve how those groups function.

Next, plans for designing the combined organisation are developed. They include the organisation's structure, reporting relationships, human resources policies, information and control systems, operating logistics, work designs and customer-focused activities.

The final task of integration planning involves developing an action plan for implementing the M&A. This specifies tasks to be performed, decision-making authority and responsibility, and timelines for achievement. It also includes a process for addressing conflicts and problems that will invariably arise during the implementation process.

Legal combination phase

This phase of the M&A process involves the legal and financial aspects of the transaction. The two organisations settle on the terms of the deal, register the transaction with and gain approval from appropriate regulatory agencies, communicate with and gain approval from shareholders, and file appropriate legal documents. In some cases, an OT practitioner can provide advice on negotiating a fair agreement, but this phase generally requires knowledge and expertise beyond that typically found in OT practice.

Operational combination phase

This final phase involves implementing the merger integration plan. In practice, it begins during due diligence assessment and may continue for months or years following the legal combination phase.[20] OT implementation includes the three kinds of activities described below.

1   *Day 1 activities.* These include communications and actions that officially start the implementation process. For example, announcements may be made about key executives of the combined organisation, the location of corporate headquarters, the structure of tasks, and areas and functions where layoffs will occur. OT practitioners pay special attention to sending important symbolic messages to organisation members, investors and regulators about the soundness of the merger plans and those changes that are critical to accomplishing strategic and operational objectives.[21]

2   *Operational and technical integration activities.* These involve the physical moves, structural changes, work designs and procedures that will be implemented to accomplish the strategic objectives and expected cost savings of the M&A. The merger integration plan lists these activities, which can be large in number and range in scope from seemingly trivial to quite critical. For example, Westpac's acquisition of the Bank of Melbourne involved changing Bank of Melbourne's employee uniforms, the signage at all banks, marketing and public relations campaigns, repainting buildings and integrating the route structures, among others. When these integration activities are not executed properly, the M&A process can be set back.

3   *Cultural integration activities.* These tasks are aimed at building new values and norms in the combined organisation. Successful implementation melds both the technical and cultural aspects of the combined organisation. For example, Application 12.3 gives a fictional case study where merging two very different companies can be a daunting job, but expert comments suggest that the right investment of time and effort will see it through.

APPLiCATiON 12.3

CULTURE CLASH: A FICTIONAL CASE STUDY

Champagne corks popped and the celebratory drinks flowed in the boardroom of the department store Salingers when the chairman clinched the takeover of his rival company, the trendy retailer Yuppy. But the chief operating officer of Salingers, Rick, was not convinced that this was the merger of the century.

The figures were impressive: paying $600 million for 120 new warehouse-type stores in the up-and-coming suburbs of Australia's boom states of Queensland and Western Australia would balance the 150 established Salingers stores in the southern states. But the transformation to the new Salingers brand depended on combining Salingers' years of retail management experience with the marketing ideas of the Yuppy stores. The combined purchasing power of the group would be important but the true value of knocking out Salingers' only rival was the strength of the new brand rising above the discount general merchandisers that had been eroding the company's profits in the past five years.

Shortly after the merger announcement, Rick was appointed to lead a team to draw up an integration plan. A survey examining organisational culture was a priority.

The first area of difference revealed by the survey was decision making. Salingers made decisions at the executive level and sent out decrees to junior managers. But Yuppy staff workshopped each big product and marketing decision in monthly store meetings. Any employee whose idea was adopted was rewarded, boosting innovation.

A second area of cultural difference was the method of executing the strategy. Salingers' managers drew up lists of project tasks for each team and expected line managers to complete each one. Yuppy appointed a project team to communicate the wider objectives of a project, designate tasks and performance measures for each employee and report on progress during staff meetings.

The last difference was leadership style. Salingers relied on a cadre of older managers to train middle managers over many years in one team. Every Yuppy employee was given a mentor when they started, to guide their development over many years. The Yuppy chief executive boasted that he visited each store twice a year and had an intimate knowledge of the company's operations.

Rick was startled by the differences. How was he to bring two such divergent cultures together? How would he get managers from both companies to work together on the integration? How could he bring employees under a common system without stifling the much-needed injection of creative and innovative thinking? How could Rick judge how long he would need to complete the cultural change?

Rick is justifiably concerned, particularly if he reads the numerous articles that say culture is the reason 60–70% of acquisitions fail. Rick should go back to basics and consider why Salingers thought it was a good idea to buy Yuppy. The number-one priority for Salingers is to ensure that it does not destroy Yuppy's value.

There is no need to rush into cultural integration, particularly as they do not compete in the same geographical markets. Salingers should integrate the back-office functions, such as purchasing, finance, human resources and information technology, that will not put pressure on earnings. This will allow them to streamline the business while maintaining revenue and profit. Yuppy could continue with a separate sales and marketing team.

Over time, they can work out a plan to exploit the best cultural aspects of each business. Rick needs to understand that cultural change is a long-term goal, not a short-term project.

The big differences in leadership styles will be a risk, particularly if egos start to take over, as they often do in these circumstances. Rick could form several functional teams to focus on integration of the back-office activities. He should populate these teams with good people from both sides, but the objective of each team must be to achieve a specific result, and all team members will be held accountable.

This work has to be done fast. Confirming structures and appointing people to roles must be a priority – no more than three months – to minimise anxiety and reduce the risk of losing important talent. But that's not the end of the hard work. The next six to 12 months will require a big effort to achieve true integration, not just on paper.

David Clark, group executive of human resources, National Foods

Would your company ever contemplate a merger or acquisition without undertaking financial due diligence? Of course not. Yet why do most mergers and acquisitions fail? The most common reasons are incompatible cultures, inability to manage the target company and inability to implement the change.

It is a pity that people due diligence was not carried out before this merger, because Rick will require the commitment of budget and dedicated resources that may not have been factored into the true costs and assumed benefits of the acquisition.

Rick needs to start a change-management process to prepare both companies for change, plan and implement the changes and then reinforce the changes.

First Rick needs to be clear about the strategic intent of the merger. What will the successfully integrated organisation look like and deliver? Who are its customers? What is its value proposition? What is the brand after the merger? What are the milestones that need to be achieved and in what time?

With clarity on these issues, Rick and his change team (selected for their solid change-management expertise) can start identifying, planning and implementing the systems, processes and culture that will support this.

It is almost impossible to put a time frame on completing culture change. Clearly defined milestones and constant orientation to the strategic intent are crucial for the journey.

A change in culture only happens when systems and processes support it and the leadership models it. It requires communication, congruency and commitment – with these, the merger of the century will have a chance.

Anne Riches, change consultant

Source: Amita Tandukar, 'Culture clash: a fictional case study', *Business Review Weekly*, 25/5/06.

Critical Thinking Questions: Of the two responses to the case study from David Clark and Anne Riches, which advice do you prefer? Why or why not? Do you have an alternative suggestion?

[22]The OT literature contains several practical suggestions for managing the operational combination phase. First, the merger integration plan should be implemented sooner rather than later, and quickly rather than slowly. Integration of two organisations generally involves aggressive financial targets, short timelines and intense public scrutiny.[23] Moreover, the change process is often plagued by culture clashes and political fighting. Consequently, organisations need to make as many changes as possible in the first hundred days following the legal combination phase.[24] Quick movement in key areas has several advantages: It pre-empts unanticipated organisation changes that might thwart momentum in the desired direction; it reduces organisation members' uncertainty about when things will happen; and it reduces members' anxiety about the M&A's impact on their personal situation. All three of these conditions can prevent desired collaboration and other benefits from occurring.

Second, integration activities must be communicated clearly and in a timely fashion to a variety of stakeholders, including shareholders, regulators, customers and organisation members. M&As can increase uncertainty and anxiety about the future, especially for members of the involved organisations who often inquire: Will I have a job? Will my job change? Will I have a new boss? These kinds of questions can dominate conversations, reduce productive work and spoil opportunities for collaboration. To reduce ambiguity, organisations can provide concrete answers through a variety of channels including company newsletters, email and intranet postings, press releases, video and in-person presentations, one-on-one interaction with managers, and so on.

Third, members from both organisations need to work together to solve implementation problems and to address customer needs. Such co-ordinated tasks can clarify work roles and relationships, and they can contribute to member commitment and motivation. Moreover, when co-ordinated activity is directed at customer service, it can assure customers that their interests will be considered and satisfied during the merger.

Fourth, organisations need to assess the implementation process continually to identify integration problems and needs. The following questions can guide the assessment process:[25]

- Have savings estimated during precombination planning been confirmed or exceeded?[26]

- Has the new entity identified and implemented shared strategies or opportunities?

- Has the new organisation been implemented without loss of key personnel?

- Was the merger and integration process seen as fair and objective?

- Is the combined company operating efficiently?

- Have major problems with stakeholders been avoided?

- Did the process proceed according to schedule?

- Were substantive integration issues resolved?

- Are people highly motivated (more so than before)?

Mergers and acquisitions are among the most complex and challenging interventions facing organisations and OT practitioners.

COLLABORATIVE STRATEGIES

In the prior section, we explored strategies of competition: OT interventions that helped individual organisations cope with environmental dependence and uncertainty by managing their internal resources to achieve competitive advantage and improve performance. Organisations also can cope with environmental pressures by collaborating with other organisations. This section discusses collaborative strategies where two or more organisations agree to work together to achieve their objectives. This represents a fundamental shift in strategic orientation because the strategies, goals, structures and processes of two or more organisations become interdependent and must be co-ordinated and aligned.

The rationale for collaboration is discussed first. Then we describe the process of forming and developing alliances and networks. *Alliance interventions* focus on the relationship between two organisations, while *network interventions* involve three or more organisations. As the number of organisations increases, the scope and complexity of the problems and issues that need to be addressed increase. Alliances can be building blocks for networks, however, and the lessons learned there can be applied to the development of network arrangements.

Collaboration rationale

More and more, organisations are collaborating with other organisations to achieve their objectives. These collaborative strategies can provide additional resources for large-scale research and development; spread the risks of innovation; apply diverse expertise to complex problems and tasks; make information or technology available to learn and develop new capabilities; position the organisation to achieve economies of scale or scope; or gain access to new, especially international, marketplaces.[27] For example, pharmaceutical firms form strategic alliances to distribute non-competing medications and avoid the high costs of establishing sales organisations; firms from different countries form joint ventures to overcome restrictive trade barriers; and high-technology firms form research consortia to undertake significant and costly research and development for their industries.

More generally, however, collaborative strategies allow organisations to perform tasks that are too costly and complicated for single organisations to perform.[28] These tasks include the full range of organisational activities, including purchasing raw materials, hiring and compensating organisation members, manufacturing and service delivery, obtaining investment capital, marketing and distribution, and strategic planning. The key to understanding collaborative strategies is recognising that these individual tasks must be co-ordinated with each other. Whenever a good or service from one of these tasks is exchanged between two units (individuals, departments or organisations), a *transaction* occurs. Transactions can be designed and managed internally within the organisation's structure, or externally between organisations. For example, organisations can acquire a raw materials provider and operate these tasks as part of internal operations or they can collaborate with a raw material supplier through long-term contracts in an alliance.

Economists and organisation theorists have spent considerable effort investigating when collaborative strategies are preferred over competitive strategies. They have developed frameworks, primarily transaction cost theory and agency theory, that are useful for understanding the interventions described in this chapter.[29] As a rule, collaborative strategies work well when transactions occur frequently and are well understood. Many organisations, for example, outsource their payroll tasks because the inputs (such as hours worked, pay rates and employment status), the throughputs (such as tax rates and withholdings) and the outputs occur regularly and are governed by well-known laws and regulations. Moreover, if transactions involve people, equipment or other assets that are unique to the task, then collaboration is preferred over competition. For example, Microsoft works with a variety of value-added resellers, independent software vendors, and small and large consulting businesses to bring their products to customers ranging in size from individual consumers to the largest business enterprises in the world. An internal sales and service department to handle the unique demands of each customer segment would be much more expensive to implement and would not deliver the same level of quality as the partner organisations. In general, relationships between and among organisations become more formalised as the frequency of interaction increases, the type of information and other resources that are exchanged become more proprietary, and the number of different types of exchanges increases.[30]

Cummings has referred to groups of organisations that have joined together for a common purpose, including alliances and networks, as *transorganisational systems* (TSs).[31] TSs are functional social systems existing intermediately between single organisations on the one hand and societal systems on the other. These multi-organisation systems can make decisions and perform tasks on behalf of their member organisations, although members maintain their separate organisational identities and goals. This separation distinguishes TSs from mergers and acquisitions.

In contrast to most organisational systems, TSs tend to be underorganised: Relationships among member organisations are loosely coupled; leadership and power are dispersed among autonomous organisations, rather than hierarchically centralised; and commitment and membership are tenuous as member organisations act to maintain their autonomy while jointly performing. These characteristics make creating and managing TSs difficult.[32] Because members typically are accustomed to hierarchical forms of control, they may have difficulty managing lateral relations among independent organisations. They also may have difficulty managing different levels of commitment and motivation among members and sustaining membership over time.

Alliance interventions

An alliance is formal agreement between two organisations to pursue a set of private and common goals through the sharing of resources, including intellectual property, people, capital, technology, capabilities and physical assets.[33] They are an important strategy for such organisations as Corning Glass, Federal Express, IBM and Starbucks. The term *alliance* generally refers to any collaborative effort between two organisations, including licensing agreements, franchises, long-term contracts and joint ventures. Franchising is a common collaborative strategy. Companies such as McDonald's, Jim's Mowing and Holiday Inn license their name and know-how to independent organisations that deliver the service and leverage the brand name for marketing. A *joint venture* is a special type of alliance where a third organisation, jointly owned and operated by two (or more) organisations, is created. Joint ventures between domestic and foreign firms, such as Fuji-Xerox, can help overcome trade barriers and facilitate technology transfer across nations. Application 12.4 is an example of a joint venture between Aker Kvaerner and Clough Murray & Roberts, which secured a $111 million contract for the expansion of the Boddington gold mine project, southeast of Perth in Western Australia.

APPLiCATiON 12.4

AKER KVAERNER-CLOUGH WINS $111M BODDINGTON GOLD CONTRACT

Aker Kvaerner in joint venture with Clough Murray & Roberts (CMR) has been awarded a contract for the expansion of the Boddington Gold Mine Project, located 130km southeast of Perth, Western Australia.

The contract value is $111 million, of which Aker Kvaerner's scope is about 60%. The award follows the successful completion of the pre-engineering contract of $4 million. The work is expected to be completed in late 2008 and includes engineering design, procurement and construction management (EPCM). The previous, largely oxide operation is being expanded to treat primary ore at a rate of approximately 35 million tonnes of ore per annum producing around 850 000 oz of gold and 200 000 tonnes of copper concentrate per annum. The joint venture is a collaborative effort between CMR and Aker Kvaerner's offices in Melbourne, Australia, and Santiago, Chile. The Chile office will provide established experience and relief from local resource shortages, while performing the bulk of the detailed engineering for the process plant area.

Tom Quinn, Managing Director of Aker Kvaerner Australia, comments: 'This is a great opportunity for CMR and Aker Kvaerner to continue our successful partnership based on leveraging our complementary skills and developing a significant international scale project in Western Australia for major resource clients. The use of high-pressure grinding rolls provides a unique occasion to expand this technology prospect within the Australian gold mining industry.' Dave Lawson, President of Aker Kvaerner Metals, continues: 'This project will be an opportunity to highlight Aker Kvaerner's global engineering and procurement capability on a high-profile gold project.'

Boddington represents one of the world's largest undeveloped gold projects. The project owner, Boddington Gold Mine Management Company, is a joint venture between Newmont Mining Corporation (66.67%) and AngloGold Ashanti Limited (33.33%).This contract was booked as part of the order backlog in 2005.

Source: 'Aker Kvaerner-Clough wins $111m Boddington gold contract', *WA Business News*, 24/4/06
© Business News Pty Ltd.

Critical Thinking Questions: What are the advantages of this joint venture? Do you anticipate any difficulties for either or both companies? Check the current status of the joint venture on the internet.

APPLICATION STAGES

The development of effective alliances generally follows a process of strategy formulation, partner selection, alliance structuring and start-up, and alliance operation and adjustment.

1   *Alliance strategy formulation.* The first step in developing alliances is to clarify the business strategy and understand why an alliance is an appropriate method to implement it. About one-half to two-thirds of alliances fail to meet their financial objectives, and the number-one reason for that failure is the lack of a clear strategy.[34] For example, Collins found that alliance success was heavily influenced by the alignment of the partner to the company's 'hedgehog concept'.[35] If the organisation understood its passion, distinctive capabilities and economic drivers, it was more likely to develop alliances that supported its strategy. Thus, it is important to pursue alliances according to a 'collaboration logic'.[36] The alliance must be seen as a more effective way of organising and operating than: developing new capabilities to perform the work in-house; acquiring or merging with another organisation; or buying the capabilities from another organisation in a transactional relationship.

2   *Partner selection.* Once the reasons for an alliance are clear, the search for an appropriate partner begins. Alliances always involve a cost–benefit trade-off; while the organisation typically gains access to new markets or new capabilities, it does so at the cost of yielding some autonomy and control over its activities.

Similar to identifying merger and acquisition candidates discussed previously, this step involves developing screening criteria, agreeing on candidates, establishing initial contacts and formulating a letter of intent. A good alliance partnership will leverage both similarities and differences to create competitive advantage. Compatible management styles or cultures, goals, information technologies or operations are important similarities that can smooth alliance formation and implementation. However, different perspectives, technologies, capabilities and other resources can complement existing ones and be good sources of learning and value in the partnership. These differences can also be a source of frustration for the alliance. OT practitioners can add value at this stage of the process by ensuring that the similarities and differences among potential alliance partners are explored and understood. In addition, the way the alliance begins and proceeds is an important ingredient in building trust, a characteristic of successful alliances explored more fully in the next step.

3   *Alliance structuring and start-up.* Following agreement to enter into an alliance, the focus shifts to how to structure the partnership and build and leverage trust in the relationship. First, an appropriate governance structure must be chosen and can include

medium-to-long-term contracts, minority equity investments, equal equity partnerships or majority equity investments. As the proportion of equity investment increases, the costs, risk and amount of required management attention also increase.[37] In general, partners need to know how expenses, profits, risk and knowledge will be shared.

Second, research increasingly points to 'relational quality' as a key success factor of long-term alliances.[38] Alliances shift the nature of the relationship from the simple exchange of goods, services or resources with no necessary expectation of a future relationship to one where there is a clear expectation of future exchange. The parties in the relationship must act in good faith to ensure the future. This requires trust – 'a psychological state comprising the intention to accept vulnerability based upon positive expectations of the intentions or behaviour' of another firm or individual representing the organisation. It implies an expectation that the organisation will subordinate its self-interest to the 'joint interest' of the alliance under most conditions.[39]

Trust can increase or decrease over the life of the alliance. Early in the alliance formation process, it can serve as an initial reservoir of comfort and confidence based on perceptions of the organisation's reputation, prior success and other sources. These same factors can also contribute to a lack of initial trust. Trust can be increased or decreased by new assessments of the other's capabilities, competence and ethical behaviour. OT practitioners can assist in this initial start-up phase by making implicit perceptions of trust explicit and getting both parties to set appropriate expectations.[40] During the structuring and start-up phase, trust can increase through direct activities as a function of the number, frequency and importance of interactions; differences between expectations and reality; the nature of mistakes and how they are resolved; and attributions made about partners' behaviour.

4   *Alliance operation and adjustment.* Once the alliance is functioning, the full range of OT interventions described in this text can be applied. Team building, conflict resolution, large-group interventions, work design, employee involvement, strategic planning and culture change efforts have all been reported in alliance work.[41] OT practitioners should pay particular attention to helping each partner in the alliance clarify the capabilities contributed, the lessons learned and the benefits received.

Diagnosing the state of the alliance and making the appropriate adjustments is a function of understanding whether the environment has changed in ways that make collaboration unnecessary, whether partner goals and capabilities have changed the nature of the relationship and interdependence, and whether the alliance is successfully generating outcomes. The long-term success of the Fuji-Xerox joint venture, for example, has been due to the willingness and ability of the two organisations to adjust the relationship in terms of ownership, profit sharing, new product development responsibilities and market access.[42]

Network interventions

Networks involve three or more organisations that have joined together for a common purpose, and their use is increasing rapidly in today's highly competitive global environment. In the private sector, research and development consortia, for example, allow companies to share resources and risks associated with large-scale research efforts. Networks among airlines with regional specialisations can combine to provide worldwide coverage, while Japanese *keiretsu*, Korean *chaeobols* and Mexican *grupos* can enable different organisations to take advantage of complementary capabilities among them. In the public sector, partnerships between government and business provide the resources and initiative to undertake complex urban renewal projects that promote economies, and avoid costly overlap and redundancy.[43]

Managing the development of multi-organisation networks involves two types of change: (a) creating the initial network, and (b) managing change within an established network. Both change processes are complex and not well understood. First, the initial creation of networks recognises their underorganised nature. Forming them into a more coherent, operating whole involves understanding the relationships among the participating organisations and their roles in the system, as well as the implications and consequences of organisations leaving the network, changing roles or increasing their influence. Second, change within existing networks must account for the relationships among member organisations as a whole system.[44] The multiple and complex relationships involved in networks produce emergent phenomena that cannot be fully explained by simply knowing the parts. Each organisation in the network has goals that are partly related to the good of the network and partly focused on self-interest. How the network reacts over time is even more difficult to capture and is part of the emerging science of complexity.[45]

CREATING THE NETWORK

As discussed in Chapter 10, OT practitioners have evolved a unique form of planned change aimed at creating networks and improving their effectiveness. In laying out the conceptual boundaries of network development, also known as *transorganisation development*, Cummings described the practice as following the phases of planned change appropriate for underorganised systems.[46] Due to their significance and the fact that they exemplify the fine line between organisation transformation (OT) and organisation development (OD), the four stages are shown again in Figure 12.1, along with key issues that need to be addressed at each stage and are described below.

1   *Identification stage.* This initial stage of network development involves identifying existing and potential member organisations best suited to achieving their collective objectives. Identifying potential members can be difficult because organisations may not perceive the need to join together or may not know enough about each other to make membership choices. These problems are typical when trying to create a new network. Relationships among potential members may be loosely coupled or nonexistent; thus, even if organisations see the need to form a network, they may be unsure about who should be included.

The identification stage is generally carried out by one or a few organisations interested in exploring the possibility of creating a network. OT practitioners work with these initiating organisations to clarify their own goals, such as product or technology exchange, learning or market access, and to understand the trade-off between the loss of autonomy and the value of collaboration. Change agents also help specify criteria for network membership and identify organisations meeting those standards. Because networks are intended to perform specific tasks, a practical criterion for membership is how much organisations can contribute to task performance. Potential members can be identified and judged in terms of the skills, knowledge and resources that they bring to bear on the network task. Practitioners warn, however, that identifying potential members also should take into account the political realities of the situation.[47] Consequently, key stakeholders who can affect the creation and subsequent performance of the network are identified as possible members.

An important difficulty at this stage can be insufficient leadership and cohesion among participants to choose potential members. In these situations, OT practitioners may need

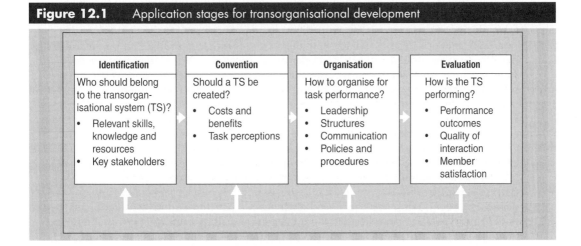

Figure 12.1   Application stages for transorganisational development

Identification	Convention	Organisation	Evaluation
Who should belong to the transorganisational system (TS)?	Should a TS be created?	How to organise for task performance?	How is the TS performing?
• Relevant skills, knowledge and resources • Key stakeholders	• Costs and benefits • Task perceptions	• Leadership • Structures • Communication • Policies and procedures	• Performance outcomes • Quality of interaction • Member satisfaction

to adopt a more activist role in creating the network.[48] They may need to bring structure to a group of autonomous organisations that do not see the need to join together or may not know how to form relationships. In several cases of network development, change agents helped members create a special leadership group that could make decisions on behalf of the participants.[49] This leadership group comprised a small cadre of committed members and was able to develop enough cohesion among members to carry out the identification stage. The activist role requires a good deal of leadership and direction. For example, change agents may need to educate potential network members about the benefits of joining together. They may need to structure face-to-face encounters aimed at sharing information and exploring interaction possibilities.

2   *Convention stage.* Once potential network members are identified, the convention stage is concerned with bringing them together to assess whether formalising the network is desirable and feasible. This face-to-face meeting enables potential members to explore mutually their motivations for joining and their perceptions of the joint task. They work to establish sufficient levels of motivation and task consensus to form the network.

Like the identification stage, this phase of network creation generally requires considerable direction and facilitation by OT practitioners. Existing stakeholders may not have the legitimacy or skills to perform the convening function, and practitioners can serve as conveners if they are perceived as legitimate and credible by the attending organisations. However, change agents need to maintain a neutral role, treating all members alike.[50] They need to be seen by members as working on behalf of the total system, rather than as being aligned with particular members or views. When practitioners are perceived as neutral, network members are more likely to share information with them and to listen to their inputs. Such neutrality can enhance change agents' ability to mediate conflicts among members. It can help them uncover diverse views and interests and forge agreements among stakeholders. OT practitioners, for example, can act as mediators, ensuring that members' views receive a fair hearing and that disputes are equitably resolved. They can help to bridge the different views and interests, and achieve integrative solutions. In many cases, practitioners came from research centres or universities with reputations for neutrality and expertise in networks.[51] Because participating organisations tend to have diverse motives and views and limited means for resolving differences, change agents may need to structure and manage interactions to facilitate airing of differences and arriving at consensus about forming the network. They may need to help organisations work through differences and reconcile self-interests with those of the larger network.

3   *Organisation stage.* When the convention stage results in a decision to create a network, members then begin to organise themselves for task performance. This involves developing the structures and mechanisms that promote communication and interaction among members and that direct joint efforts to the task at hand.[52] It includes the organisations to be involved in the network and the roles each will play; the communication and relationships among them; and the control system that will guide decision making and provide a mechanism for monitoring performance. For example, members may create a co-ordinating council to manage the network and a powerful leader to head it. They might choose to formalise exchanges among members by developing rules, policies and formal operating procedures. When members are required to invest large amounts of resources in the network, such as might occur in an industry-based research consortium, the organising stage typically includes voluminous contracting and negotiating about members' contributions and returns. Here, corporate lawyers and financial analysts play key roles in specifying the network structure. They determine how costs and benefits will be allocated among member organisations as well as the legal obligations, decision-making responsibilities and contractual rights of members. OT practitioners can help members define competitive advantage for the network as well as the structural requirements necessary to support achievement of its goals.

4   *Evaluation stage.* This final stage of creating a network involves assessing how the network is performing. Members need feedback so that they can identify problems and begin to resolve them. Feedback data generally include performance outcomes and member satisfactions, as well as indicators of how well members are interacting jointly.

Change agents can periodically interview or survey member organisations about various outcomes and features of the network, and feed that data back to network leaders. Such information will enable leaders to make necessary operational modifications and adjustments. It may signal the need to return to previous stages in the process to make necessary corrections, as shown by the feedback arrows in Figure 12.1.

MANAGING NETWORK CHANGE

In addition to developing new networks, OT practitioners may need to facilitate change within established networks. Planned change in existing networks derives from an understanding of the 'new sciences,' including complexity, nonlinear systems, catastrophe and chaos theories. From these perspectives, organisation networks are viewed as complex systems displaying the following properties:[53]

1   The behaviour of a network is sensitive to small differences in its initial conditions. How the network was established and formed – the depth and nature of trust among the partners, who was selected (and not selected) to be in the network, and how the network was organised – play a key role in its willingness and ability to change.

2   Networks display 'emergent' properties or characteristics that cannot be explained through an analysis of the parts: 'Given the properties of the parts and the laws of their interaction, it is not a trivial matter to infer the properties of the whole.'[54] The tools of systems thinking and the understanding of emergence in complex systems is still being developed and applied.[55]

3   A variety of network behaviours and patterns, both expected and unexpected, can emerge from members performing tasks and making decisions according to simple rules to which everyone agreed. This is amply demonstrated in Senge's 'beer game' simulation where a retailer, a wholesaler and a brewery each acts according to the simple rule of maximising its own profit. Participants in the simulation routinely end up with enormous inventories of poor-selling beer, delayed deliveries, excess capacity and other problems. Without an understanding of the 'whole' system, the nature of interdependencies within the system, and timely and complete information, each part – acting in its own self-interest – destroys itself.[56] Apparently random changes in networks may simply be chaotic patterns that are not understood. These patterns cannot be known in advance but represent potential paths of change that are the result of the complex interactions among members in the network.

The process of change in complex systems such as networks involves creating instability, managing the tipping point and relying on self-organisation. These phases roughly follow Lewin's model of planned change described in Chapter 2. Change in a network requires an unfreezing process where the system becomes unstable. Movement in the system is described by the metaphor of a 'tipping point' where changes occur rapidly as a result of information processing. Finally, refreezing involves self-organisation. The descriptions below represent rudimentary applications of these concepts to networks; our understanding of them is still in a formative stage.

1   *Create instability in the network.* Before change in a network can occur, relationships among member organisations must become unstable. A network's susceptibility to instability is a function of members' motivations for structure versus agency.[57] *Structure* refers to the organisation's expected role in the network and represents a source of stability. All things being equal, network members tend to behave and perform according to their agreed-upon roles. For example, most routine communications among the network members are geared towards increasing stability and working together. A manufacturing plant in Nike's network is expected to produce a certain number of shoes at a certain cost with certain features. Nike headquarters in Beaverton, Oregon, plans on the plant behaving this way. On the other hand, *agency* involves self-interest which can create instability in the network. Each member of the network is trying to maximise its own performance in the context of the network. Changes in member goals and strategies, the ratio of costs and benefits in network membership, and so on can affect the willingness and ability of members to contribute to network performance. When a plant in Nike's network grows to a sufficient size, it may decide to alter its role in the network. As the ratio of agency to structure increases, the instability of the network rises, thus enabling change to occur.

OT practitioners can facilitate instability in a network by changing the pattern of communication among members. They can, for example, encourage organisations to share information. Technology breakthroughs, new product introductions, changes in network membership or changes in the strategy of a network member all represent fluctuations that can increase the susceptibility of the network to change. Another important aspect of changing the pattern of information is to ask who should get the information. Understanding and creating instability is difficult because the nature of members' connectedness also influences the system's susceptibility. Some organisations are more connected than others; most organisations are closely connected to several others, but relatively unconnected to many. This makes creating a sense of urgency for change difficult. Diagnosis of the relationships among member organisations can provide important information about organisations that are central to network communications.[58]

2   *Manage the tipping point.* Although instability provides the impetus and opportunity for change, the direction, type and process of change are yet to be determined. An unstable network can move to a new state of organisation and performance or it can return to its old condition. At this point, network members, individually and collectively, make choices about what to do. OT practitioners can help them through this change period. Recent studies suggest the following guides for facilitating network change:[59]

a   *The law of the few.* A new idea, practice or other change spreads because of a relatively few but important roles in the network. Connectors, 'mavens' and salespeople help an innovation achieve sufficient awareness and credibility throughout the network to be considered viable. *Connectors* are individuals who occupy central positions in the network and are able to tap into many different network audiences. They have 'Rolodex' power; they are quickly able to alert and connect with a wide variety of people in many organisations. *Mavens* are 'information sinks'. They passionately pursue knowledge about a particular subject and are altruistically willing to tell anyone who is interested everything they know about it. The key to the maven's role is trust. People who speak to mavens know that they are getting unbiased information; that there is no 'hidden agenda' – just good data. Finally, *salespeople* are the champions of change and are able to influence others to try new ideas, do new things or consider new options. Thus, the first key factor in changing a network is the presence of communication channels occupied by connectors, mavens and salespeople.

OT practitioners can fill any of these roles. They can, if appropriate, be mavens on a particular subject and act as a source of unbiased information about a new network practice, aspects of interpersonal relationships that network members agree is slowing network response, or ideas about information systems that can speed communication. Less frequently, OT practitioners can be connectors, ensuring that any given message is seeded throughout the network. This is especially true if the change agent was part of the network's formation. In this case, the practitioner might have the relationships with organisations in the network. Thus, networking skills, such as the ability to manage lateral relations among autonomous organisations in the relative absence of hierarchical control, are indispensable to practitioners of network change. Change agents must be able to span the boundaries of diverse organisations, link them together and facilitate exchanges among them.[60] The OT practitioner can also play the role of salesperson. Although it is in line with the 'activist' role described earlier in the practice of network creation, it is not a traditional aspect of OT practice. The wisdom of having a change agent as the champion of an idea rather than a key player in the organisation network is debatable. The change agent and network members must understand the trade-offs in sacrificing the OT practitioner's neutrality for influence. If that trade-off is made, the change agent will need the political competence to understand and resolve the conflicts of interest and value dilemmas inherent in systems made up of multiple organisations, each seeking to maintain autonomy while jointly interacting. Political savvy can help change agents manage their own roles and values in respect to those power dynamics.

b   *Stickiness.* The second ingredient in network change is stickiness. For a new idea or practice to take hold, the message communicated by the connectors, mavens and salespeople must be memorable. A memorable or sticky message is not a function of typical communication variables, such as frequency of the message, loudness or saliency. Stickiness is often a function of small and seemingly insignificant characteristics of the message, such as its structure, format and syntax, as well as its emotional content, practicality or sequencing with other messages. OT practitioners can also help network members develop sticky messages. Brainstorming alternative phrases, using metaphors to symbolise meaning or enlisting the help of marketing and communications specialists can increase the chance of developing a sticky message. Since the ingredients of stickiness are often not obvious, several iterations of a message's structure with focus groups or different audiences may be necessary to understand what gets people's attention.

c   *The power of context.* Finally, a message must be meaningful. This is different from stickiness and refers to the change's relevance to network members. The source of meaning is in the context of the network. When network members are feeling pressure to innovate or move quickly in response to a customer request, for example, messages about new cost-cutting initiatives or new and exciting information systems that will allow everyone to see key financial data are uninteresting and can get lost. On the other hand, a message about how a new information system will speed up customer communication is more likely to be seen as relevant. When OT practitioners understand the network's current climate or 'conversation', they can help members determine the appropriate timing and relevance of any proposed communication.[61]

When the right people communicate a change, present and package it appropriately, and distribute it in a timely fashion, the network can adopt a new idea or practice quickly. In the absence of these ingredients, there is not enough information, interest or relevance, and the change stalls.

3   *Rely on self-organisation.* Networks tend to exhibit 'self-organising' behaviour. Network members seek to reduce uncertainty in their environment, while the network as a whole drives to establish more order in how it functions. OT practitioners can rely on this self-organising feature to refreeze change. Once change has occurred in the network, a variety of controls can be leveraged to institutionalise it. For example, communication systems can spread stories about how the change is affecting different members, diffusing throughout the network or contributing to network effectiveness. This increases the forces for stability in the network. Individual organisations can communicate their commitment to the change in an effort to lower agency forces that can contribute to instability. Each of these messages signifies constraint and shows that the different parts of the network are not independent of each other.

SUMMARY

In this chapter, we presented interventions aimed at implementing competitive and collaborative strategies. Organisations are open systems that exist in environmental contexts and they must establish and maintain effective linkages with the environment to survive and prosper. Three types of environments affect organisational functioning: the general environment, the task environment and the enacted environment. Only the last environment can affect organisational choices about behaviour, but the first two impact the consequences of those actions. Two environmental dimensions – information uncertainty and resource dependence – affect the degree to which organisations are constrained by their environments and the need to be responsive to them. For example, when information uncertainty and resource dependence are high, organisations are maximally constrained and need to be responsive to their environments.

Integrated strategic change is a comprehensive intervention for responding to complex and uncertain environmental pressures. It gives equal weight to the strategic and organisational factors affecting organisation performance and effectiveness. In addition, these factors are highly integrated during the process of assessing the current strategy and organisation design, selecting the desired strategic orientation, developing a strategic change plan and implementing it.

Mergers and acquisitions involve combining two or more organisations to achieve strategic and financial objectives. The process generally involves three phases: precombination, legal combination and operational combination. The M&A process has been dominated by financial and technical concerns, but experience and research strongly support the contribution that OT practitioners can make to M&A success.

Collaborative strategies are a form of planned change aimed at helping organisations create partnerships with other organisations to perform tasks or to solve problems that are too complex and multifaceted for single organisations to carry out. Alliance interventions describe the technical and organisational issues involved when two organisations choose to work together to achieve common goals.

Network development interventions must address two types of change. First, because multi-organisation systems tend to be underorganised, the initial development of the network follows the stages of planned change relevant to underorganised systems: identification, convention, organisation and evaluation. Second, the management of change within a network also must acknowledge the distributed nature of influence and adopt methods of change that rely on the law of the few, the power of context and the stickiness factor.

ACTIVITIES

Review questions

① What is the difference between 'open' and 'closed' systems?

② There are three types of environments to consider when designing an OT change process. What are they? (Give examples.)

③ The two environmental dimensions – information uncertainty and resource dependence – can be barriers to successful change. How may they be managed?

④ Distinguish between competitive and collaborative strategies. What type of environment would be beneficial for each?

⑤ Explain what is integrative strategic change and give current examples.

⑥ Why would an organisation choose to merge rather than acquire another company?

⑦ What are the advantages and disadvantages of alliances? Give examples where appropriate.

⑧ Are networks the current fad or fashion in management theory? Why or why not?

Discussion and essay questions

① 'Some environments are rapidly changing and complex, and so require organisational responses different from those in environments that are stable and simple.' Do you agree with this statement? Why or why not?

② Explain the importance of the activities (uniqueness, value and difficulty to imitate) in enhancing an organisation's performance. Choose an organisation that you are familiar with and describe how these activities give it a competitive advantage.

③ Investigate further Cummings's 'transorganisational systems (TSs)' theory. How does this theory differ significantly from other change approaches? How would OT interventions assist organisations who intend to enter such an arrangement?

NOTES

1 J. Barney, *Gaining and Sustaining Competitive Advantage* (Reading, MA: Addison-Wesley, 1996).

2 R. Nelson and S. Winter, *An Evolutionary Theory of Economic Change* (Cambridge, MA: Belknap Press, 1982).

3 P. Selznick, *Leadership in Administration* (New York: Harper & Row, 1957); M. Peteraf, 'The Cornerstones of Competitive Advantage: A Resource-Based View', *Strategic Management Journal*, 14 (1993): 179–92; J. Collins, *Good to Great* (New York: HarperCollins, 2001).

4 R. Grant, *Contemporary Strategy Analysis*, 4th edn (Malden, MA: Blackwell, 2001); Barney, *Competitive Advantage*, op. cit.

5 L. Greiner and A. Bhambri, 'New CEO Intervention and the Dynamics of Strategic Change', *Strategic Management Journal*, 10 (1989): 67–87.

6 T. Galpin and D. Robinson, 'Merger Integration: The Ultimate Change Management Challenge', *Mergers and Acquisitions*, 31 (1997): 24–9.

7 M. Marks and P. Mirvis, *Joining Forces: Making One Plus One Equal Three in Mergers, Acquisitions, and Alliances* (San Francisco: Jossey-Bass, 1998).

8 G. Dixon, 'Merger and Acquisition Activity in Canada, World Continues to Decline in 2002', *The Canadian Press* (6 January 2003), http://www.factiva.com (accessed 12 June 2003).

9 A variety of studies have questioned whether merger and acquisition activity actually generates benefits to the organisation or its shareholders, including M. Porter, 'From Competitive Advantage to Corporate Strategy', *Harvard Business Review* (May–June 1978): 43–59; 'Merger Integration Problems', *Leadership and Organisation Development Journal*, 19 (1998): 59–60; 'Why Good Deals Miss the Bull's-Eye: Slow Integration, Poor Communication Torpedo Prospects for Creating Value', *Mergers and Acquisitions*, 33 (1999): 5; T. Brush, 'Predicted Change in Operational Synergy and Post-Acquisition Performance of Acquired Businesses', *Strategic Management Journal*, 17 (1996): 1–24; P. Zweig with J. Perlman, S. Anderson and K. Gudridge, 'The Case Against Mergers', *Business Week* (30 October 1995): 122–30. The research includes: an A.T. Kearney study of 115 multibillion-dollar global mergers between 1993 and 1996 where 58% failed to create 'substantial returns for shareholders', measured by tangible returns in the form of dividends and stock price appreciation; a Mercer Management Consulting study of all mergers from 1990 to 1996 where nearly half 'destroyed' shareholder value; a PriceWaterhouseCoopers study of 97 acquirers that completed deals worth $500 million or more from 1994 to 1997 and where two-thirds of the buyer's stocks dropped on announcement of the transaction and 'a year later' a third of the losers still were lagging the levels of peer-company shares or the stock market in general; and a European study of 300 companies that found that planning for restructuring was poorly thought-out and underfunded. Similarly, despite the large amount of writing on the subject, a large proportion of firms involved in mergers have not gotten the message that post-merger integration is the key to success. For example, in the A.T. Kearny study, only 39% of the cases had set up a management team in the first 100 days and only 28% had a clear vision of corporate goals when the acquisition began.

10 Zweig et al., 'Case Against Mergers', op. cit.

11 Marks and Mirvis, *Joining Forces*, op. cit.; R. Ashkenas, L. DeMonaco and S. Francis, 'Making the Deal Real: How GE Capital Integrates Acquisitions', *Harvard Business Review* (January–February 1998); B. Brunsman, S. Sanderson and M. Van de Voorde, 'How to Achieve Value Behind the Deal During Merger Integration', *Oil and Gas Journal*, 96 (1998): 21–30; A. Fisher, 'How to Make a Merger Work', *Fortune* (24 January 1994): 66–70; K. Kostuch, R. Malchione and I. Marten, 'Post-Merger Integration: Creating or Destroying Value?', *Corporate Board*, 19 (1998): 7–11; A. Kruse, 'Merging Cultures: How OD Adds Value in Mergers and Acquisitions' (presentation to the ODNetwork meeting, San Diego, CA, October 1999); M. Sirower, 'Constructing a Synergistic Base for Premier Deals', *Mergers and Acquisitions*, 32 (1998): 42–50; D. Jemison and S. Sitkin, 'Corporate Acquisitions: A Process Perspective', *Academy of Management Review*, 11 (1986): 145–63.

12 Ashkenas, DeMonaco and Francis, 'Making the Deal Real', op. cit.; G. Ledford, C. Siehl, M. McGrath and J. Miller, 'Managing Mergers and Acquisitions' (working paper, Center for Effective Organisations, University of Southern California, Los Angeles, 1985).

13 Ledford et al., 'Managing Mergers and Acquisitions', op. cit.; B. Blumenthal, 'The Right Talent Mix to Make Mergers Work', *Mergers and Acquisitions* (September–October 1995): 26–31; A. Buono, J. Bowditch and J. Lewis, 'When Cultures Collide: The Anatomy of a Merger', *Human Relations*, 38 (1985): 477–500; D. Tipton, 'Understanding Employee Views Regarding Impending Mergers to Minimize Integration Turmoil' (unpublished master's thesis, Pepperdine University, 1998).

14 Marks and Mirvis, *Joining Forces*, op. cit.; Ashkenas, DeMonaco and Francis, 'Making the Deal Real', op. cit.

15 Sirower, 'Constructing a Synergistic Base', op. cit.; Brunsman, Sanderson and Van de Voorde, 'How to Achieve Value', op. cit.

16 Sirower, 'Constructing a Synergistic Base', op. cit.

17 Ledford et al., 'Managing Mergers and Acquisitions', op. cit.

18 S. Elias, 'Due Diligence', http://www.eliasondeals. com/duedilig.html (1998).

19 Brunsman, Sanderson and Van de Voorde, 'How to Achieve Value', op. cit.

20 Ashkenas, DeMonaco and Francis, 'Making the Deal Real', op. cit.

21 Ashkenas, DeMonaco and Francis, 'Making the Deal Real', op. cit.; Brunsman, Sanderson and Van de Voorde, 'How to Achieve Value', op. cit.

22 Galpin and Robinson, 'Merger Integration', op. cit.

23 ibid.

24 Ashkenas, DeMonaco and Francis, 'Making the Deal Real', op. cit.

25 Kostuch, Malchione and Marten, 'Post-Merger Integration', op. cit.

26 This application was developed by Michael Krup. His contribution is gratefully acknowledged.

27 A. Tsai, 'A Note on Strategic Alliances', 9-298-047 (Boston: Harvard Business School, 1997); B. Gomes-Casseres, 'Managing International Alliances: Conceptual Framework', 9-793-133 (Boston: Harvard Business School, 1993); J. Bamford, B. Gomes-Casseres and M. Robinson, *Mastering Alliance Strategy* (New York: John Wiley and Sons, 2002).

28 Aldrich, *Organisations and Environments*, op. cit.

29 O. Williamson, *Markets and Hierarchies* (New York: Free Press, 1975); O. Williamson, *The Economic Institutions of Capitalism* (New York: Free Press, 1985); J. Barney and W. Ouchi, *Organisational Economics* (San Francisco: Jossey-Bass, 1986); K. Eisenhardt, 'Agency Theory: An Assessment and Review', *Academy of Management Review*, 14 (1989): 57–74.

30 P. Kenis and D. Knoke, 'How Organisational Field Networks Shape Interorganisational Tie-Formation Rates', *Academy of Management Review*, 27 (2002): 275–93.

31 T. Cummings, 'Transorganisational Development', in *Research in Organisational Behaviour*, vol. 6, eds B. Staw and L. Cummings (Greenwich, CT: JAI Press, 1984): 367–422.

32 B. Gray, 'Conditions Facilitating Interorganisational Collaboration', *Human Relations*, 38 (1985): 911–36; K. Harrigan and W. Newman, 'Bases of Interorganisation Co-Operation: Propensity, Power, Persistence', *Journal of Management Studies*, 27 (1990): 417–34; Cummings, 'Transorganisational Development', op. cit.

33 A. Arino, J. de la Torre and P. Ring, 'Relational Quality: Managing Trust in Corporate Alliances', *California Management Review*, 44 (2001): 109–31; M. Hitt, R. Ireland and R. Hoskisson, *Strategic Management* (Cincinnati, OH: South-Western College Publishing, 1999).

34 Bamford, Gomes-Casseres and Robinson, *Mastering Alliance Strategy*, op. cit.

35 Collins, *Good to Great*, op. cit.

36 Gomes-Casseres, 'Managing International Alliances', op. cit.; J. Child and D. Faulkner, *Strategies of Co-operation: Managing Alliances, Networks, and Joint Ventures* (New York: Oxford University Press, 1998).

37 Bamford, Gomes-Casseres and Robinson, *Mastering Alliance Strategy*, op. cit.

38 A. Arino, J. de la Torre and P. Ring, 'Relational Quality', op. cit.

39 C. Rousseau, S. Sitkin, R. Burt and C. Camerer, 'Not So Different After All: A Cross-discipline View of Trust', *Academy of Management Review*, 23 (1998): 395.

40 M. Hutt, E. Stafford, B. Walker and P. Reingen, 'Case Study Defining the Social Network of a Strategic Alliance', *Sloan Management Review*, Winter (2000): 51–62.

41 Marks and Mirvis, *Joining Forces*, op. cit.; Child and Faulkner, *Strategies of Cooperation*, op. cit.

42 K. McQuade and B. Gomes-Casseres, 'Xerox and Fuji-Xerox', 9-391-156 (Boston: Harvard Business School, 1991).

43 R. Chisholm, *Developing Network Organisations* (Reading, MA: Addison-Wesley, 1998).

44 D. Watts, *Six Degrees* (New York: W.W. Norton and Co., 2003).

45 S. Strogatz, 'Exploring Complex Networks', *Nature*, 410 (March 2001): 268–76.

46 Cummings, 'Transorganisational Development', op. cit.; C. Raben, 'Building Strategic Partnerships: Creating and Managing Effective Joint Ventures', in *Organisational Architecture*, eds Nadler et al., (San Francisco: Jossey-Bass, 1992): 81–109; B. Gray, *Collaborating: Finding Common Ground for Multiparty Problems* (San Francisco: Jossey-Bass, 1989); Harrigan and Newman, 'Bases of Interorganisation Co-operation', op. cit.; P. Lorange and J. Roos, 'Analytical Steps in the Formation of Strategic Alliances', *Journal of Organisational Change Management*, 4 (1991): 60–72; B. Gomes-Casseres, 'Managing International Alliances', op. cit.

47 D. Boje, 'Towards a Theory and Praxis of Transorganisational Development: Stakeholder Networks and Their Habitats' (working paper no. 79-6, Behavioural and Organisational Science Study Center, Graduate School of Management, University of California, Los Angeles, February 1982); B. Gricar, 'The Legitimacy of Consultants and Stakeholders in Interorganisational Problems' (paper presented at annual meeting of the Academy of Management, San Diego, CA, August 1981); T. Williams, 'The Search Conference in Active Adaptive Planning', *Journal of Applied Behavioural Science*, 16 (1980): 470–83; B. Gray and T. Hay, 'Political Limits to Interorganisational Consensus and Change', *Journal of Applied Behavioural Science*, 22 (1986): 95–112.

48 Cummings, 'Transorganisational Development', op. cit.

49 E. Trist, 'Referent Organisations and the Development of Interorganisational Domains' (paper presented at annual meeting of the Academy of Management, Atlanta, August 1979).

50 Cummings, 'Transorganisational Development', op. cit.

51 ibid.

52 Raben, 'Building Strategic Partnerships', op. cit.; C. Baldwin and K. Clark, 'Managing in an Age of Modularity', in *Managing in the Modular Age*, eds R. Garud, A. Kumaraswamy and R. Langlois (Malden, MA: Blackwell Publishing Ltd., 2003): 149–60.

53 P. Anderson, 'Complexity Theory and Organisation Science', *Organisation Science*, 10 (1999): 216–32.

54 H. Simon, 'The Architecture of Complexity', in *Managing in the Modular Age*, eds R. Garud, A. Kumara-swamy and R. Langlois (Malden, MA: Blackwell Publishing Ltd., 2003): 15–37.

55 Senge, *The Fifth Discipline*, op. cit.; B. Lichtenstein, 'Emergence as a Process of Self-Organising: New Assumptions and Insights from the Study of Non-Linear Dynamic Systems', *Journal of Organisational Change Management*, 13 (2000): 526–46.

56 Senge, *The Fifth Discipline*, op. cit.

57 Watts, *Six Degrees*, op. cit.

58 P. Monge and N. Contractor, *Theories of Communication Networks* (New York: Oxford University Press, 2003).

59 This section relies on information in M. Gladwell, *The Tipping Point* (Boston: Little, Brown, 2000).

60 B. Gricar and D. Brown, 'Conflict, Power, and Organisation in a Changing Community', *Human Relations*, 34 (1981): 877–93.

61 P. Shaw, *Changing Conversations in Organisations: A Complexity Approach to Change* (London: Routledge, 2002).

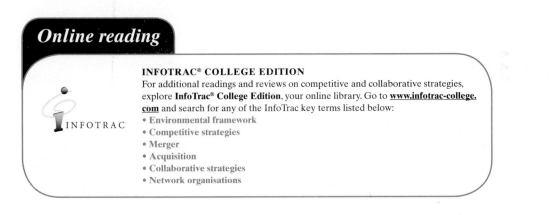

Online reading

INFOTRAC® COLLEGE EDITION

For additional readings and reviews on competitive and collaborative strategies, explore **InfoTrac® College Edition**, your online library. Go to **www.infotrac-college. com** and search for any of the InfoTrac key terms listed below:

- **Environmental framework**
- **Competitive strategies**
- **Merger**
- **Acquisition**
- **Collaborative strategies**
- **Network organisations**

INFOTRAC

iSSUES iMPACTiNG CHANGE MANAGEMENT

13

THE USE OF ACTiON RESEARCH iN ORGANiSATiON CHANGE PROJECTS

By Dr John Molineux, Monash University

Action research as an approach to planned change was first discussed in Chapter 2. As noted there, the action research model underlies most current methods of planned change. Action research has long been identified with the practice of organisational development, and has been in wide use for many decades.

Action research arose from the seminal social research work of Kurt Lewin.[1] Lewin suggested that there was a continual process of a spiral of steps in this form of research that involved planning, acting and fact-finding about the social research situation. Lewin integrated theory with practice by framing social science as the study of problems of real life. The essential relationship of the three elements – the joint existence of research, action and participation – in an ongoing cyclical process make this methodology different from others.[2] In fact, without this relationship, the methodology cannot be called action research. Action research has four major characteristics:

- It is *research*, in that theoretical knowledge from a range of sources is used to discover possible applications to a particular project or problem.
- It is *action*, in that the knowledge must be applied to a problem or situation.
- It involves *participation*, as the researcher must involve others – such as managers, staff or clients – in some way during the project or problem discovery and resolution processes.
- It involves *cycles* of research, planning, action and evaluation.

Action research is a pragmatic approach, where the intended destination or outcome of an intervention is not necessarily the same as the one that develops during the course of the action taken. The pragmatic approach requires an ongoing re-assessment of the impact of the intervention, reflection on this, and subsequent adjustments in direction. This ongoing process is represented as an action research cycle in Figure 13.1.

Various authors label these steps differently. For Example, this author uses *design action*, *take action*, *evaluate* and *reflect* as the action research steps.[3] Coghlan and Brannick use *diagnosing*, *planning action*, *taking action* and *evaluating action* as the steps.[4] At Figure 13.2 is a representation of a model of action research in a series of spirals.

Action research needs to operate with a minimum of two cycles, as the philosophy of action research is built around reflection and adjustment. For example, a manager may plan to implement a change program using action research. Such a design and plan would be the first *design action* step in the cycle. To test the effectiveness of the planned process, a pilot program may be developed, which would be the first *take action* step. The first *evaluate* step of the cycle

Figure 13.1 An action research cycle of steps

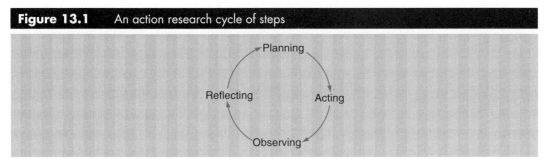

Source: J. McNiff, *Action Research: Principles and Practice* (London: Routledge, 1988): 22.

may occur concurrently with implementation and/or after implementation. This *evaluation* of the pilot program may inform the manager that adjustments may need to be made to the program when implementing it in the rest of the organisation. Also, when the results are analysed, the manager may *reflect* that there is a need for further research before a revised plan can be developed. Subsequently, with the results of the evaluation, a revised plan is developed, which is the second *design action* step. The revised plan is then implemented. Already, there are two cycles in this process. A third may develop in the course of implementation, when further *evaluation* informs the manager of some arising issues that were not previously envisaged. The manager may then *reflect* on it further and adjust the plan, and continue the implementation in a modified path.

It should be noted that these cycles, neatly represented in models at Figures 13.1 and 13.2, are unlikely to follow a smooth or linear path. Cycles can be planned, but they can also arise spontaneously as an emergent property of the system as it is changing. The manager of the process needs to build some flexibility in the system to be able to cope successfully with such spontaneous events.

DIMENSIONS OF ACTION RESEARCH

The use of action research will vary significantly in different organisations. Kates and Robertson[5] note that various approaches of action research vary along three significant dimensions:
* the type of reflective thought required by participants
* the degree of freedom, participation and liberty accorded to them by organisational culture
* the role and capabilities of the action research team.

In some situations, the reflective thought processes may be limited to the management or action research team. In other cases, reflection may be much broader and involve participants in pilot or implementation programs, working together with the action research team.

Figure 13.2 Spiral of action research cycles

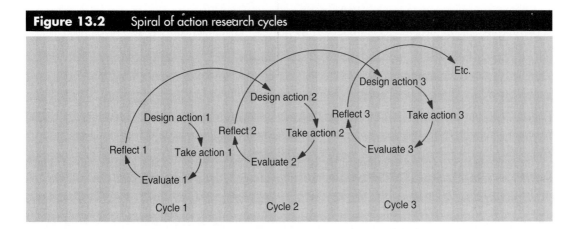

The reflection may be about the issues arising from implementation, it could be about the methodology of implementation or it could even be about the design or aims of the intervention. Issues around reflection are explored later in the chapter.

The extent of participation will significantly vary across organisations. It may involve just the manager and an action researcher, or it could encompass the whole organisation. An appropriate participation level is an important factor that needs to be decided at the commencement of the project, and this issue is also explored later in the chapter.

An action researcher or action research team may have very different roles, depending on the type of intervention and the role given to them by management. The team could consist of external consultants, internal change agents or even a mixed group of externals and internals. They could work alongside management or work in a way that was independent of management. Whatever the role assigned, a limitation is always the capability of the individuals concerned and the extent of freedom allowed by management. The role of the insider is explored later in the chapter.

It is critical that an action research intervention generates improvements for the organisation. Improvements could result in higher levels of efficiency or effectiveness, or sometimes just the generation of a better understanding of the system or problematic situation. Action research may generate small-step incremental improvements, or in some cases is used as a methodology where revolutionary change is driven. Whatever the final outcome, the use of theory in developing understanding, making comparisons with the current situation and generating alternative solutions is necessary. It is here that theory informs action, and action informs theory. In using action research in a particular situation, participants may develop a deeper understanding of the issue or the application of action research to that situation, which may then lead to a broader understanding of how it may apply in similar contexts.

So theory and practice are integrated in an action research program. Action research users need to aim to bring about improvements through making changes in a problematic situation, and also aim to generate new knowledge and new insights as a result of their activities.[6] This new knowledge may be used in other situations in the organisation or it could be published and applied more broadly to other organisations with similar issues.

Benefits of choosing action research

This next section explores the reasons managers may choose action research as a change methodology, and outlines the potential benefits. It also warns that action research is not a quick fix or short-term approach to change, and reinforces the commitment from management that is needed to undertake an action research change project. Action research is a very flexible methodology, which has myriad uses and purposes, and is able to be deployed in a variety of contexts. One aim of action research is expressed by Rapoport,[7] who states that action research:

> … aims to contribute both to the practical concerns of people in an immediate problematic situation and to the goals of social science by joint collaboration within a mutually acceptable ethical framework.

Action research is a practical approach, and its purpose is to produce practical knowledge that is useful to people in the everyday conduct of their lives.[8] This practicality is also recognised as a problem-solving ability in that it aims at solving specific problems within a program, organisation or community.[9] This is because it focuses first on problem solving, and more secondarily on the knowledge generated from the process. The generation of knowledge about a situation leads to improvement, which is usually some form of organisational improvement or the solution of practical problems.[10] Action research is a positive approach to change because of its focus on outcomes and its involvement of people as participants. One of the greatest benefits of using action research is that no other research approach has the power to add to the body of knowledge and deal with the practical concerns of people and organisations in such a positive manner.[11]

Action research is a good methodology to use in gaining an understanding of organisational systems to enable change. This is because it attempts to generate knowledge of a system, while, at the same time, trying to change or develop it and attempts to contribute to general knowledge about systems and the dynamics of changing them.[12] Importantly, action research can become the process of bridging local knowledge and scientific knowledge, and it is therefore a process that will create both new local knowledge and new scientific understandings.[13] The benefits can be both for the organisation and for broader application, in a scientific or research context.

Another key benefit of using action research is in situations with highly uncertain outcomes, as action research allows time to build enough understanding to decide which methods are best suited to the organisational problem context. As action research can be quite adaptive, it allows flexibility in approach and can change direction in these volatile contexts. It has been found that action research offers substantial flexibility and responsiveness to a complex situation, so it is particularly useful for managers and change agents who need responsiveness to complex situations, as it provides an opportunity to achieve some important practical outcomes.[14] A summary of benefits of action research appears in Table 13.1.

Table 13.1   Summary of benefits of action research

Benefits of action research	Reasons
Achieves results	There is a focus on achieving the best outcomes possible in a given context
Bridges local and scientific knowledge	It applies knowledge in specific contexts and builds on local understanding
Useful where there is uncertainty	The cyclical approach can more easily respond to turbulent environments
Integrates thought and action	It brings together thinkers and doers, enabling partnerships
Helps managers' professional development	It enables managers to learn from the reflection built into the cycles
Can be multidisciplinary	It is useful for complex change projects, where a range of disciplines may be needed to develop an appropriate response
Helps implementation of change	Its practical nature makes it ideal for change projects
Allows correction	The reflective cycles enable corrective action to be taken, minimising risk
Helps develop a holistic understanding	This is important for a complete understanding of the context and factors involved in building successful change
Is focused on the problem	It won't get bogged down in unnecessary research or activity
Is future oriented	It focuses on building better systems for the future success of an organisation
Empowers participants	Involvement helps in the engagement and commitment of stakeholders
Deals with practical concerns	Issues raised are able to be dealt with in a logical and practical way
Is flexible in the use of tools	There is no one correct method, so a range of tools can be used within an action research program to suit the context

POTENTIAL PROBLEMS

Although the benefits can be substantial, there are a number of problems that potential users of action research should consider. Action research is not a quick-fix methodology that can bring a speedy resolution to a problem. It is best used as a planned approach to change that involves a number of stakeholders participating at various stages of the project. Because it is anchored around involvement of participants, it requires time. It takes a while to engage appropriate people in a change project, even when there is top management support. Each cycle may take some time to complete, and complex change projects cannot be rushed, otherwise the risk of failure increases. In fact, action research's participatory approach to change can be quite problematic as a methodology. For example, an organisation undergoing change involving a significant reduction in workforce may find that action research is not a very suitable methodology to use. As it is a participatory approach, and aims at improvements in social systems, managers may find it problematic when considering downsizing interventions.

Another issue to consider is the management style of the organisation. Action research is not about applying standard solutions to a known problem. Rather, it unfolds in a participatory process and conversation over time. This emergent aspect of action research may make some managers wary or uncomfortable, as they may prefer the certainty of a step-by-step, controlled, mechanistic approach to change. Action research cannot be controlled in this way, as it is flexible and emergent in nature.[15] A similar issue is the current bias for action and speed in organisations that obviates any interest in reflection and participation.[16] The context of business these days often involves quick decision making and immediate action. The reflective and participative nature of action research does not sit well in these contexts. There are other more direct approaches that managers may prefer to use in these situations.

TOP-MANAGEMENT COMMITMENT

Where action research is suitable for the organisation's change context, it is essential to obtain top-management commitment for an action research change project. However, in situations where the change only relates to a part of an organisation, it may only require the top-management support in that part of the organisation. To achieve this, the impetus for change must be recognised by the top-management group. The management group may set some direction for change, or have engaged a consultant to help implement a change program. The consultant (either external or internal) or change design group must negotiate a realistic time frame with top management. There is no point in launching into a large change program when the organisation's managers are expecting immediate results.

Managers need to be aware that the early stages of the program may require investment in time, money and human resources. Benefits may not be immediately obvious; however, the focus needs to be on the long-term benefits of the program. It is possible that the benefits may not be realised for six months or even up to two years, depending on the nature of the change and the complexity of the organisation and its environment. However, once a major change program has commenced, it is important to keep the long-term outcomes in mind, as problems and issues will occur along the change path that may initially be quite negative. Some of these issues may be expected, such as resistance to change or an initial drop in productivity while learning how to implement a new work system, but others may arise unexpectedly. Ongoing reminders of the long-term benefits may need to be stated and subsequently reinforced by management in the course of the change process.

Roles of the action researcher

This section explores the role of the action researcher in the context of an organisational development consultant, and outlines the role and potential conflicts of an organisational employee (or *insider*) using action research in change management.

ACTION RESEARCH VERSUS CONSULTANCY

An action research practitioner is essentially an internal or external consultant to the organisation. However, a consultant on a change project is not necessarily an action researcher. The difference is that an action researcher uses theory, which is applied to a specific situation in a manner that is participatory with stakeholders in the organisation. On the other hand, a consultant may or may not use theory and may or may not use participation in implementing change. For example, a consultant who uses downsizing as a change program intervention would probably not use participation as a process for change. With this difference in mind, the role of the OD consultant as action researcher and the role of the insider using action research as an approach to change management is explored in the next sections.

THE OD CONSULTANT AS ACTION RESEARCHER

In the context of OD, a consultant using action research has a range of roles. The model of action research for OD outlined by French[17] and reproduced as Figure 13.3 outlines many of these roles, including:

- *Consulting with management.* This is an essential component of any OD practitioner's work, where the consultant will present ideas and findings and work with management. It is a role that is critical at the start of a project, but also at other key times during design, implementation and review.
- *Data gathering.* A major role in action research, as in other forms of OD, this is where the practitioner gathers information about the organisation and its environment, including information on its people and the impact of change. This role is recurring in action research, in accordance with the cyclic pattern of an action research intervention.
- *Diagnosis.* In action research, the diagnostic role is quite similar to other forms of OD, and similar techniques are used.
- *Providing feedback.* Feedback may be provided on an ongoing basis to management and change participants about progress and issues that arise.
- *Joint action planning.* This role is critical, as the action researcher is not just a consultant but also an active participant in developing the change process with others, such as management or staff representatives.

In addition to these, other critical roles are embedded within this model, and need to be drawn out. These are:

- *Undertaking research.* An action researcher embeds their understanding of an organisation's problem in theory and research, bringing rigour and meaning to a particular problem.
- *Providing insight.* Part of the action researcher's role is to reflect holistically on the problem, the data, the theory, the relationships, etc. to bring insight and learning to a particular change program or organisation.
- *Generating solutions.* This role is critical in any OD intervention, and in action research it may often occur in participatory groups of managers and/or project participants.
- *Conducting evaluation.* An action researcher should set up critical evaluation processes, whereby the intervention can be measured at all stages of implementation, allowing for regular feedback and review.
- *Facilitating groups.* This role is critical in action research due to the participatory nature of this type of intervention. An action researcher must be able to facilitate groups in conducting interventions.

While some of these *roles* may instead be considered as *tasks*, it does accentuate the multiple roles that are required of an action researcher. The roles generally fit into an action research process, such as the model described in Figure 13.3.

An insider as change agent

This section reviews the role the insider: an action research change agent working as an employee within the organisation. It reviews some of the problems and possibilities facing

Figure 13.3   An action research model for organisation development

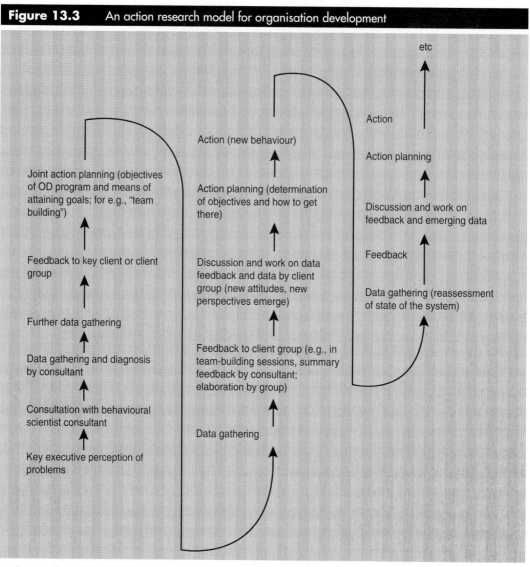

the insider, including the management of working relationships, cultural influences and organisational politics. In relation to the study of organisational culture, Edgar Schein[18] outlines three routes for a researcher:

> (a) infiltration, in which the participant observer becomes a true insider; (b) a formal research role agreed to by the insiders; and (c) a formal clinical role, in which the insiders ask the outsider to come into the organisation as a helper/consultant.

A 'true insider' may not necessarily have infiltrated the organisation, but instead be a staff member of the organisation. This type of role, often called an *internal change agent*, allows for the organisation to control the project more closely and to change course more easily. This is because the organisation doesn't need to renegotiate contracts as it would with an external change agent or consulting company. This type of insider role allows insight and opportunity that could not occur for outsiders. From the inside, a change agent can have the privilege of seeing first-hand the nature of new local, contextual and immediately applied research in action, leading to the generation of new knowledge and organisational improvements.[19] The insider role, however, has the potential to create a dilemma for action researchers. The organisational change role may demand total involvement and active commitment, whereas the research role may require a more detached, theoretic, objective and neutral observer position.[20] In some cases, managers may demand too much action from the action researcher, and not allow enough time for research and reflection, which are essential in this process. This is a dilemma that the insider must resolve. An external change agent would not be faced with the same amount of internal control.

There are also specific issues for managers who undertake insider action research. Managers who undertake action research projects may be located anywhere in their organisation's hierarchy, but their location in the hierarchy has undoubted implications for what may be done and how. For example, higher-level executives may have more access but may be excluded from access to informal and grapevine networks. Middle- or lower-level managers may find upward access difficult and be confined to their function or division.[21] It is possible to lead action research at the highest level of the organisation. For example, in one case the CEO of an organisation undertook and led an action research intervention to improve the organisation's learning and thinking capabilities.[22]

Another issue for the insider researcher is to maintain their status and a desired career path within the organisation.[23] A complicating issue in some projects will be a pre-understanding of knowledge, insights and experiences of the organisation and various participants.[24] This latter issue has the potential to bias the research project, particularly if the insider has some false understandings of the organisation. However, a real advantage of being an insider is that the researcher is already immersed in the organisation, so has built up an extensive understanding of how it works. It can also be a disadvantage, in that the researcher may assume too much and not probe as deeply as if they were outsiders or ignorant of the situation.[25] Other problems that an insider might face include role conflict, and potentially damaging impacts on organisational relationships.

One of the most difficult problems is the possibility of the research being considered political, and it might even be considered subversive by some managers.[26] Political forces in the organisation can undermine research efforts and block planned change. Gaining access, using organisational data and disseminating and publishing information and reports may be seen as intensely political acts.[27] It is therefore critical that the researcher carefully negotiate their access and use of organisational information. There is a need for researchers to be prepared to work the political system and to maintain their credibility as an effective driver of change and as an astute political player.[28] This will add an extra burden on the researcher, so the choice of an insider must be made carefully.

Many of these aspects outlined above were issues for me in undertaking the role of an internal change agent using action research. For example, I was able to access information that would not generally be available to an outsider. I also understood the context and history of the organisation in undertaking change, and had built relationships with key stakeholders. As I wished to maintain a career in the organisation, playing the political system was an important consideration. However, I faced significant issues in relation to the management of implementation projects, including some that were abolished without full completion. This resulted in some staff displacement and consequent disappointment. For an insider, the intensity of the level of involvement of a large project over several years can have emotional and relational impacts. An outsider might be more dispassionate about the work. However, it is important for the insider to become resilient and to work through any setbacks and pitfalls to discover new understanding.

THE SYSTEMIC NATURE OF ACTION RESEARCH

This section explores the systemic nature of action research. Action research is not a linear methodology and its understanding is linked to a holistic view of change, where the business environment and context are matched with the strategy and culture of the organisation. Many change techniques are quite simplistic as they do not consider the impact of the intervention on the whole organisational system in its context. This is particularly true of an intervention that goes through a detailed planning process but does not take into account the feedback resulting from the area of implementation. Such feedback could include information about the impact on people, outputs, clients or competitors. Often a change process will produce unintended consequences. These consequences may be a direct result of the intervention, or they may develop over time as a new set of interactions develop within the organisation's system and its environment.

Any system may develop emergent properties that are the result of interactions within the system. For example, a new low-cost entrant in a market may result in a whole set of reactions where the system becomes destabilised, and some players may leave the market and others join. An outcome of this interaction may be that the system itself may emerge in a quite different form. An example of this is the Australian domestic airline industry. Some years ago, a new entrant, Virgin Blue, destabilised the system. Its entry was a major factor in the demise of an existing player, Ansett, which went out of business. It also later resulted in another existing player, Qantas, to set up a new airline, Jetstar, to compete against the significant loss of market share to the new entrant. The Australian domestic airline system in 2006 is quite different from what it was only a few years before. Of course, it should also be noted that there were other economic, social, political, global and regulatory factors involved in this process. However, the change in the whole system has been quite dramatic.

Action research often takes a more cautious approach to change, where it considers the impact of change on the whole system. Where the impact is uncertain, the action research process carefully monitors the outcomes of the intervention on the system so adjustments can be made and implemented. This is where systemic thinking and the action research cycle play complementary roles. In a systems approach to action research, tentative explanations are being formed as the story unfolds. These explanations provide frameworks to understand the system, its elements and the relationships between them, and to consider possible alternative interventions to enhance the change process.[29]

The use of quick fixes and linear change models might seem a little dated in this world of complexity and change. However, the continuing use of linear change models might be due to the Western culture of managers, based around analytical and mechanistic thinking, which is referred to by Ackoff:[30]

> In our culture, managers are educated to believe that a social system's performance can be improved by improving the performance of each of its parts taken separately – that is, if each part is managed well, the whole will be. This is seldom if ever the case, because parts that appear to be well managed when viewed separately seldom fit together well.

Such thinking is familiar and easy for managers and creates short-term solutions that may bring about quick wins, but in the long-term may cause the system to be dysfunctional, or create the need for more short-term solutions. Peter Senge,[31] a management guru from MIT, warns of this approach:

> Beware the symptomatic solution. Solutions that address only the symptoms of a problem, not fundamental causes, tend to have short-term benefits at best. In the long term, the problem resurfaces and there is increased pressure for symptomatic response. Meanwhile, the capability for fundamental solutions can atrophy.

The systemic thinking required to bring about long-term solutions is difficult, because systems are complex and have many interrelated parts that are hard to understand. Such thinking, though, may deliver significant benefits in the long term. Senge[32] outlines the implications of short-term thinking in the systems archetypes 'Fixes that fail' and 'Shifting the burden'. In Figure 13.4, the 'Fixes that fail' archetype is shown.

The 'Fixes that fail' archetype shows that short-term fixes may resolve immediate problems, but over time develop unintended consequences that were not envisioned by the decision maker due to a lack of systemic thinking involved. A similar issue is raised in the 'Shifting the burden'

Figure 13.4 'Fixes that fail' archetype

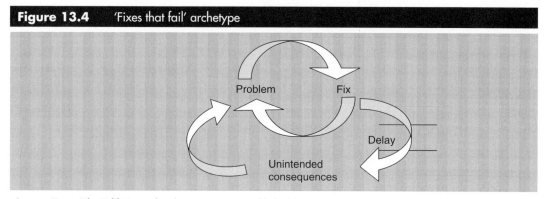

Source: From *The Fifth Discipline* by Peter Senge, published by Century. Reprinted by permission of The Random House Group Ltd.

archetype, shown in Figure 13.5. In this archetype, a problem symptom is dealt with using a symptomatic solution, which causes side effects, while the fundamental solution that may resolve the problem is not considered. The fundamental solution, of course, may take more time to implement to obtain the intended result. Senge[33] notes that:

> The systems viewpoint is generally oriented toward the long-term view. That's why delays and feedback loops are so important. In the short term, you can often ignore them; they're inconsequential. They only come back to haunt you in the long term.

Managers should note the difference between the symptomatic and fundamental approaches. There are places for both. However, a focus on the results of short-term goals for business performance, rather than on high-leverage areas for system-wide redesign and significant improvement in the long term, could be disastrous for an organisation.[34]

Action research provides a methodology that helps understand the systemic links between the change mechanisms and the outcomes for an organisation's system. If used in a systemic and flexible manner, it will help an organisation move away from quick fixes and symptomatic solutions towards longer-term and fundamental solutions.

Figure 13.5 'Shifting the burden' archetype

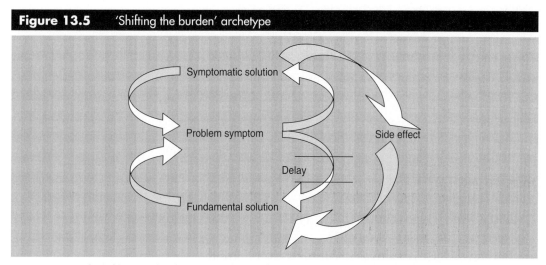

Source: From *The Fifth Discipline* by Peter Senge, published by Century. Reprinted by permission of The Random House Group Ltd.

Soft Systems Methodology

Soft Systems Methodology (SSM) is one of a number of systemic methodologies that can be used within an action research program to enhance its usefulness. SSM was created in an action research process by Checkland[35] and colleagues as an answer to the lack of specific applicability of other systems approaches to the complex area of human activity systems. SSM may be defined as 'an organised way of tackling messy situations in the real world'.[36]

The use of the term 'soft' in systems theory relates to methodologies that concentrate on human activity systems, and soft systems are seen to have sociological, cultural and political properties that are difficult to quantify and measure (for example viewpoints, conflicts, vested interests and other qualitative characteristics).[37] So, SSM is designed specifically to deal with problem situations in human systems where there are pluralist views. SSM is a practical methodology, with a focus on achieving systemically desirable and culturally feasible change.[38] SSM can be used in ill-structured or messy problem contexts where there is no clear view on what constitutes the problem, or what action should be taken to overcome the difficulties. Action in SSM should prevent managers and change agents from rushing into poorly thought-out solutions based on preconceived ideas about an assumed problem.[39]

Allied to action research, SSM is an organised use of systems ideas in a methodology for learning one's way to purposeful action to improve a problem situation.[40] This idea of learning for a purpose of action to improve a problem is critical in relation to the usefulness of both action research and SSM. Also, SSM can be used to guide learning and the understanding of information and its management, leading to more informed decisions about the action that needs to be taken in the problem situation.[41]

THE SSM MODEL MODE 1

A model of a process of SSM, known as SSM Mode 1, is shown in Figure 13.6. The process is naturally organic and flexible in nature and it allows for situational differences among problem contexts, the diversity of views of stakeholders and styles of facilitators. Again, allied to action research, the most stimulating and fruitful way to use SSM is participatively, with the people in the problem situation themselves building models and conducting the debate.[42] SSM Mode 1 follows seven steps in a loosely structured way.[43] These are described in more detail in the next segments.

Checkland separates the methodology into 'real world' activities, which involve people in the problem situation, and 'systems thinking' activities, which may or may not involve those people.

Stages 1 and 2: current state using rich pictures

Stages one and two of the SSM Mode 1 process involve attempts to build up the richest possible picture of the situation in which there is perceived to be a problem.[44] The first stage of the SSM process involves using 'rich pictures', which are drawings contributed to by participants in an SSM process, for the purpose of understanding the current problem context. The use of rich pictures initiates a different and particularly creative process that sets SSM apart from other methodologies. This is because pictures are a better medium than linear prose for expressing relationships, which is required because of the fact that the complexity of human affairs is always a complexity of multiple interacting relationships.[45] The pictures, then, help to encourage holistic rather than reductionist thinking about a situation and attempt to capture the story of the situation using graphics and words.[46]

The second stage of SSM Mode 1 involves 'expressing' the explored situation in a more structured way. In many SSM workshops, including those experienced by the author, this involves expanding on the themes explored in the rich pictures, and subsequently explaining the Stage 1 rich picture diagrams to other participants. This latter process usually involves some challenges from participants and further discovery.

Figure 13.6   Soft Systems Methodology: Mode 1

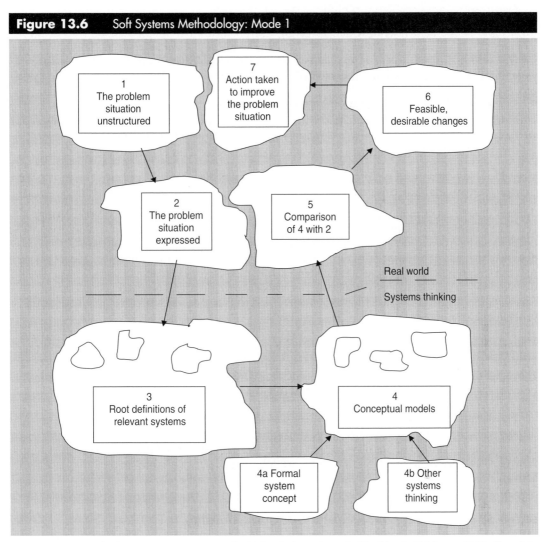

Source: *Systems Thinking, Systems Practice*, John Wiley & Sons, Peter B. Checkland, Chichester 1981. Copyright John Wiley & Sons Ltd. Reproduced with permission.

Stage 3: root definitions of ideal systems

The third stage of SSM Mode 1 moves away from the problem situation to explore the possibilities of ideal systems. This process starts with the 'naming' of various ideal systems, followed by an exploration of one or more of the 'named' systems. In practice, the naming of ideal systems can be quite creative, and can express the values behind the ideal system. Following the naming of systems, and at the heart of stage three of the methodology, is the root definition of ideal systems, which is a statement of what the system is designed to achieve.[47] The basic form of a root definition is:[48]

- a system
- to do X
- by means of Y
- in order to achieve Z.

In an approach developed to assist analysis, the use of the mnemonic CATWOE was introduced to help ensure that root definitions are well formulated.[49] There are six elements contained in the analysis of the root definition. These are: the transformation process (T); ownership of the system (O); actors in the system (A); customers (beneficiaries and victims) of the system (C); environmental constraints on the system (E); and a *Weltanschauung* or worldview of the system (W).[50] In practice, a well-formulated root definition should be 'an O-owned and A-operated system, which, affecting C, transforms T to a new state of T according to some W, within the given constraints E'.[51] At this stage, any system chosen as 'relevant' is selected by the problem solver in accordance with a particular image of the world – a world view (or *Weltanschauung*) – and it is normal to work with a number of models in the one process.[52]

Another version of this, the TWOACES mnemonic, was used by me in several SSM workshops. This mnemonic is simply a reordering of the elements of the CATWOE mnemonic so that the most important element 'T' is considered first. An additional element 'S' is added, to explore the impact of other systems on the ideal system being explored.

Stage 4: conceptual models

The building of conceptual models is a key stage of SSM. Conceptual models are theoretical constructs that embody potential real-world systems.[53] They are designed from a developed understanding of the problem situation and the transformation required. They should be designed around the concept of building an ideal system. It is from the conceptual models that the learning process may be undertaken, as the impetus for change may come as a result of an activity that is identified through any of the conceptual models designed. As models are constructed, the direction of learning is changed and further questions are prompted about the problematical situation.[54]

There is no certainty in the outcome of the conceptual modelling process, as different people will understand the system according to their own worldviews and develop alternative models from any given root definition. This is because individuals will have different abstract concepts about the real world, based on their own education and social environment. This is important, because the models in SSM have an impact and effect in the real world, and may change perceptions of the problem situation.[55]

The design of a conceptual model is that of an activity system, and therefore its elements usually consist of action words – verbs. A conceptual model may consist of a list of verbs covering the activities that are necessary in the ideal system structured in a sequence according to logic.[56] The use of arrow diagrams and workflow maps are often useful in the linking of these activities.

Stage 5: comparing conceptual models with reality

The next stage is the comparison of the conceptual to the real world, which is possibly the most important process in SSM.[57] Checkland[58] notes that SSM models 'are only *relevant to debate about* the real world and are used in a cyclic learning process'. The creation of a model is designed to establish a firm basis for the comparison process, which will also generate a deeper understanding of, and knowledge about, aspects of the problem situation.[59] The comparison process looks at the difference between elements of the ideal system and elements of the existing system to understand the extent of change required. The process usually involves a detailed evaluation of the elements already in place, including those in need of change and those that do not require change. It also extracts further understanding of the new elements of the ideal system.

Stages 6 and 7: implementation

The final stages of SSM Mode 1 involve an evaluation of feasible and desirable changes, and action planning to improve the problem situation. In Stage 6, the changes need to be debated to ensure that they are systemically desirable, culturally feasible and politically acceptable within the organisation.[60] In Stage 7, plans are drawn up to ensure responsibility for change and the process for implementation of the change. This will detail the specifics of the people who are responsible for each of the new elements and processes, and time frame and method as to how the proposed changes should be implemented.

In summary, systems theory offers some alternative approaches for participation in action research projects. SSM was used by me in the course of a large organisational change program.[61] I found that projects that used a co-design approach using SSM had much greater acceptance and success than projects that did not use SSM. This finding was confirmed through a number of interviews with project managers and the implementation team. One of these processes is outlined in Application 13.1.

APPLiCATiON 13.1

THE USE OF SOFT SYSTEMS METHODOLOGY FOR SYSTEM DESIGN

This case gives an example of the use of a systemic methodology – Soft Systems Methodology – in the planning cycle of action research for the purpose of designing improvements to an organisational performance system. It presents a description of the process used and results of its success.

The context was a performance system of a large government agency in Australia. The agency's performance team had been set the task by senior management of redesigning the agency's performance system. A project team had been set up to research and consult with stakeholders. However, the team members were looking for a methodology, and a suitable practitioner who could facilitate design workshops for them.

I was able to convince management of the use of the SSM process, which was previously used successfully in the organisation in a large action research change project. I explained the process to the members of the team, and distributed outlines of the process and SSM approach. The performance team sent out an open invitation to members of a cross-organisational forum that supported the performance system, as well as to other key stakeholders, to nominate to attend one of the workshops or invite other interested staff members to attend. Over 60 people volunteered to attend a workshop, and participants included members of the forum, the performance team, and managers and staff members from various business areas in the organisation.

The design consisted of a two-day workshop, which was run in four different locations, based around a slightly modified SSM Mode 1 design. The introduction of the workshops included a brief explanation of systemic thinking, an outline of the SSM process to be used and an outline of the purpose of the project. Participants were asked to complete an evaluation form at the end of the SSM workshops. The evaluation form contained both open-ended questions and Likert-type scale questions. Completion of the forms was entirely voluntary. A total of 80% of participants completed the evaluation forms. Nearly all (97.1%) participants thought the use of SSM in the workshop was either good or excellent. There was a similar high rating (97.1% either excellent or good) for the delivery of the workshops. Participants also thought they were fully involved (56.3%) or mostly involved (35.4%) in the process, and the workshop also largely met their expectations.

THE ADAPTED SSM PROCESS USED IN THE WORKSHOPS

At each of the workshops, the participants were split into groups of three to five. The process used was as follows:
1   The introduction provided the context of the workshop, the strategic drivers and related broad organisational issues.
2   The facilitator explained some of the basic concepts in systems thinking and outlined the structure of SSM.
3   Participants were asked what they thought were the major elements included in the organisation's performance system.
4   Participants then were led through a seven-stage process, as outlined below.

Stage 1: Problem unstructured

Draw a rich picture of your understanding of the issues and problems in the performance system.

Stage 2: Problem expressed

Explain the picture to the other participants, and respond to questions, clarifications, comments and suggestions by other participants.

▷▷

Stage 3: Ideal systems

Name the sorts of ideal systems contained in the performance system. Make logical links between them and choose one that is important to you, to work on for the next day and a half. Analyse the system in terms of its 'TWOACES'.

Stage 4: Conceptual models

List the verbs or action words required as ideal elements of your subsystem. Link them in an ideal process or flow map.

Stage 5: Compare and contrast

List the action words from the flow map and compare with current reality. Analyse to what extent the organisation does these things now, and explain your reasoning.

Stage 6: Feasible and desirable change

Comment whether your ideal subsystem will work, and respond to the three questions of:
- Is it systemically viable?
- Is it culturally feasible?
- Is it politically acceptable?

Stage 7: Action required

Outline the actions required for the system to be implemented, including:
- What? (the specific actions required)
- Who? (the players involved)
- How? (the process required)
- When? (the time frame recommended).

OUTCOMES OF THE WORKSHOPS

The results of the workshops were very powerful. The client team were amazed at the enormous creativity of the workshops, with 11 subsystems created or redesigned and 73 significant changes suggested. The ideas and designs from the workshops were presented to a further three-day workshop of the cross-organisational forum. The ideas were then evaluated for implementation, and categorised as to their probable time scales. Volunteers from different business areas were called for to trial many of the proposed changes. Following evaluation and testing, many of the suggested changes were implemented or implemented in a modified form. Subsequent to implementation, staff surveys have indicated a significant improvement in the maturity of the performance system, its acceptability in the workplace and the commitment of staff towards the organisation's goals.

Critical Thinking Questions: What are the critical factors in choosing an approach such as SSM? How does the relationship between the action researcher and the client management group make a difference?

PARTICIPATION AND REFLECTION
Participation in action research

Participation, which is an essential component of action research, is explored in this section. It considers the sometimes problematic nature of participation, and discusses the time investment needed for participation while trying to focus on getting results. It then suggests a spectrum of possibilities in relation to participation.

Participation is a fundamental principle of action research. For example, West and Stansfield[62] state: 'Attention to the notion of collaboration is vital in action research.' Also, Reason and Bradbury[63] note that action research:

> ... is only possible *with*, *for* and *by* persons and communities, ideally involving all stakeholders both in the questioning and sense-making that informs the research, *and* in the action which is its focus.

However, there needs to be a balance in action research of three elements – research, participation and action – and this will vary depending on the organisation and its problem context.[64] In action research, the process of generating knowledge through participation is essential, as knowledge that aspires to be of practical use often needs to be developed jointly with the users of the knowledge, and researchers have to form knowledge in interactive relationships with practitioners.[65] While it is noted that participation is an essential part of action research, its use in large organisational change projects is somewhat problematic. This is due to the sheer numbers of people involved or impacted by major change in organisations. In an effort to become more participative, organisations have used techniques such as industrial democracy and representative boards to enhance participation in management. Change management, however, can be much more of a problem as it can be very emotive, and participative management techniques can invoke resistance rather than collaboration. It should be noted, though, that there is a range of possibilities in relation to participation in action research. In fact, there is even a spectrum of participation from which one can choose, which may be done with the style and level of participation that suits the action researcher, the participants and the context situation.[66] In a large organisation, it is not possible to involve everyone as a collaborator in the co-design of change programs. It is more likely that action researchers may involve people in different ways and at different times of the project.

A possible spectrum of action research participation appears in Table 13.2. The spectrum ranges from one type of participation where the researcher conducts a research project with one client or manager, to a very different type involving a fully collaborative action research project with all relevant members of the organisation. It should also be noted that one action research intervention may cut across several different forms of participation in different parts of its cycles. For example, the action researcher may be engaged by the CEO in the first instance, and in the first phase or cycle may be working only with a small team. Later, during subsequent cycles, the researcher may be designing interventions with representative groups, and later be implementing the change in a collaborative way with many organisational members.

Table 13.2	Spectrum of action research participation in a large organisation
Type of action research participation	Examples of participants involved
Client-oriented action research intervention	Researcher and one client or manager
Manager-sponsored action research	Researcher and management team
Project-based action research	Researcher, managers and/or project team
Representative action research	Researcher, managers and representatives from parts of the organisation
Participative action research	Researcher, managers and relevant organisational members participating
Collaborative action research	Researcher, managers and relevant organisation members collaborating
Collaborative action research with co-researchers	Researchers and clients working jointly as co-researchers

I conducted a major change project using action research where the level of participation varied depending on the cycle and the situation context. At times it involved a small group, and at other times it involved larger groups of participants, clients and others. The smaller group of participants consisted of a core group and several project leaders. These participants had a much higher level of participation and involvement than workshop participants and other stakeholders. In relation to the categories suggested in Table 13.2, the design stage of the change project would be categorised as project-based action research, as I worked with managers and a project team. The implementation stage of the project would be categorised as representative action research, where the implementation team worked with representatives from other parts of the organisation. The third phase of the project involved co-design with the collaboration of relevant organisation members, so this part of the research would be categorised as collaborative action research.

Reflection in action research

The importance of reflection in action research is emphasised in this section. It examines the approach to reviewing the results of previous cycles, the integration with research, the success of the use of various techniques, and any feedback for the original strategy that may need some adjustment. This is where action research is at its 'best', and much learning and insight is generated.

Reflection is the process of stepping back from experience to process what the experience means, with a view to planning further action.[67] It is the activity that integrates action and research. Reflection is a critical component of action research and is an integral part of the action research cycles. In fact, doing action research means engaging in a process of mutual action and reflection. Action research practitioners need to continually reflect on experiences from the field, seeking what is necessary to keep a change process moving and tracking what is being learned.[68] Reflection is critically important as it is the dynamic of the reflection phase that incorporates the learning process of the action phase and enables action research to be more than everyday problem solving.[69]

The process involved in reflection may vary depending on the context; however, critical reflection is the way in which a naive understanding of practice is transformed. It is also where the practitioner reflects upon instead of merely experiences practice, and where the process is shared so that others gain an understanding of the practice.[70] The process of reflection is a dialectical process, looking inwards at our thoughts and thought processes, and outwards at the situation in which we find ourselves.[71] Mature reflection has become crucial to progress in action research, for change is unlikely to be simple to achieve, and the way forward is unlikely to be obvious to everyone concerned.[72] Reflection may lead to the uncovering of new interpretations and perspectives, which may challenge prior beliefs and understandings and reframe what participants know.[73] Regular, systematic and critical reflection enables an action researcher to develop the understanding that may contribute to knowledge, and directly or indirectly to action. It is an essential, iterative part of action research.[74] In an action research process, there are always more possible futures than appear at first to be open and therefore effort needs to be made to re-analyse the past, and to consider what other, possibly more desirable, futures may be available.[75]

Two processes of reflection are noted by Donald Schön.[76] One of these is reflection-in-action, which is the ability to reflect on the process while engaging in the action itself. The other is reflection-on-action, which means working through experiences gained from actions after the fact. Both of these types of reflection are essential in action research and a variety of tools exist to examine them.

Techniques for reflection in an action research program include documenting reflections in a journal, facilitated reflection, Mezirow's 3 types of reflection, collaborative off-line reflection, reflection and inquiry, ladder of inference, Checkland's FMA and revisiting mental models. A journal could be considered reflection-on-action, whereas a facilitated process of reflection during an event could be reflection-in-action. Some of these tools will be explored later in the chapter. However, the use of a journal is worthy of special attention here. Journal keeping is a significant mechanism for developing reflective skills as it helps to reflect on experiences, see how you think about them and anticipate future experiences before you undertake them.[77] It is certainly a discipline that action researchers should consistently use.

REFLECTION AND 'MENTAL MODELS'

The term 'mental model' was popularised in management theory by Senge.[78] It could be said that a purpose of reflection is to establish a new mental model of the situation. But what is a mental model? All managers and researchers view data via a particular mental framework, or worldview, and attribute *meaning* to the observed activity by relating it to a larger image we supply from our minds. Such an observed activity is only meaningful to us, in fact, in terms of a particular image of the world, which in general we take for granted.[79] This view, or mental model, of the situation helps an individual to make sense of the world around them and will direct them towards certain types of action that are in line with this view. In reflection, it is important to look beyond this view and especially to perceive alternatives. This is not easy to achieve, as Senge and Sterman[80] state:

> Efforts to improve strategic management often founder because new strategies and structures threaten traditional habits, norms, and assumptions. The problem lies, in part, with failing to recognise the importance of prevailing mental models. New strategies are the outgrowth of new worldviews. The more profound the change in strategy, the deeper must be the change in thinking.

It is often the mental models of the management team that shape strategic change through issue recognition and debate that leads to action plans. These models are networks of facts and concepts that mimic reality and from which executives derive their opinions of strategic issues, options, courses of action and likely outcomes. So, the quality of action plans depends on both the adequacy of mental models (how well they mimic reality) and the use made of participants' knowledge.[81] However, this is problematic for a researcher working with a group of managers who are not open to reflection and challenging long-held assumptions. People conditioned by the mental model of reductionism and causal thinking will find it difficult simply to flip over to a consciousness of systemic awareness.[82] Thus, one major problem with many organisations is that reflection about practices, procedures, effectiveness and processes is seen as a threat.[83] To overcome this lack of double-loop critical thought, action researchers may be advised to anticipate the threats and barriers that might arise if contradictions between espoused theory and theory-in-action are exposed.[84] So, action researchers may need to educate managers over time in the use of reflective techniques and their potential benefits to unlocking new images and mental models about the future.

A possible list of reflective questions appears in Table 13.3. These could be used as a trigger for a reflective discourse following an implementation phase.

LADDER OF INFERENCE

The ladder of inference is a reflection tool developed by Argyris.[85] It is used to make sense of the conversations we have with each other, and the beliefs and meanings we attribute to others, which may or may not be true. In reflection, it is important that these assumptions are uncovered, so that true dialogue can occur to the point where all parties have a shared meaning of the conversation.

The tool may be used directly in examining a particular conversation, or the thinking behind it may be used to respond to others in a different way. The process is detailed in Figure 13.7.[86] At the bottom of the ladder, an individual observes data and experiences going on around them. The individual then selects certain data from this that has meaning

Table 13.3	List of reflective questions

What action has taken place?

How was this action received by organisational members?

What issues arose in the course of its implementation?

What feedback has been provided on the implementation process?

What other ideas have been suggested by participants and recipients?

What do you think was good about the process?

What do others think was good about the process?

What do you think was not so good about the process?

What do others think was not so good about the process?

What would you change?

Have you thought about other research ideas relating to the process?

What are three things you would do differently next time?

for them, and they add their own meaning to it, which is based on their own history of personal experiences. Following this, the individual makes assumptions based on those added meanings and draws conclusions about it, which may or may not be true. Once conclusions are drawn, the individual may adopt a belief about it and then take personal actions based on that belief. This is often how people miscommunicate and attribute meaning to situations without checking their belief with others. Some simple suggestions to overcome this, using an understanding of the ladder of inference, are:

• Become more aware of your own thinking and reasoning (reflection)
• Make your thinking and reasoning more visible to others (advocacy)
• Inquire into others' thinking and reasoning (inquiry)
• What is the observable data behind that statement?
• Does everyone agree on what the data is?
• Can you run me through your reasoning?
• When you said '[your inference]', did you mean '[my interpretation of it]'?[87]

Figure 13.7	Ladder of inference

I take actions based on my beliefs

I adopt beliefs about the world

I draw conclusions

I make assumptions based on the meanings I add

I add meanings (cultural and personal)

I select "data" from what I observe

Observable data and experiences

Source: P. Senge, A. Kleiner, C. Roberts, R. Ross and B. Smith, *The Fifth Discipline Fieldbook* (London: Nicholas Brealey Publishing, 1994): 243.

A CULTURAL CHANGE PROJECT IN A LARGE GOVERNMENT AGENCY

This case outlines the cyclical approach to action research used in implementing a cultural change project through strategic human resource management in a large government agency. It briefly describes the regular cycles used, and presents some of the key outcomes following implementation.

The context of change was the introduction of a major government reform agenda. As a consequence of this, a strategic issue arose around the people of the organisation. It became apparent at the top level of the agency that the internal capability of the agency's people may not be able to implement the reform agenda without substantial change or improvement. This strategic issue became an imperative for the top-management group, who discussed the issues and philosophy regarding the future for the internal capability of their people.

A comprehensive cultural change strategy design was developed iteratively between a design team and the top-management group. Implementation projects were set up and operated for 18 months. The change project was conceived, designed and implemented over a three-year period, with the implementation process consisting of six action research cycles. One of the key aims of the project was to shift the culture of the organisation towards a 'performance culture'.

Initial project leaders were located in six different cities, so regular communication was considered vital, and the interlinking of projects and interdependency of projects was seen as crucial to successful change implementation. An initial workshop of project leaders and their advisers was held, and weekly phone hook-ups were established with project leaders, advisers and a core management team. The phone hook-ups were usually facilitated by a member of the core team. The project leaders were later joined at various stages by a varying number of team members. The number of team members in projects varied from one person to up to eight. At one stage there were around 40 people involved in implementing the projects.

Workshops were held every three months, and these defined the six action research cycles of the project. The action research cycles followed the same model as in Figure 13.2 of this chapter. The workshops brought together the disparate project leaders to review progress, address key linkages and help solve problems. The workshops were the major reflective and planning events for the whole strategy, and each had a major impact on the progress of implementation. In relation to the action research cyclic process, these workshops delineated the specific reflection periods for each cycle. The extent of the projects and logistics required to run them was an indication of the organisation's commitment to implement change. There was significant learning generated during the course of these cycles, particularly during the workshops. These were major catalysts for sharing information and intelligence, developing new approaches to implementation, modifying approaches, evaluating trials and pilots, and building systemic understanding about leverage and relationships in the whole system. Most of these workshops included facilitated reflection sessions, using different techniques in each one. In one session, a project leader was asked to personally reflect on her experiences in leading one of the implementation projects, and the issues raised during the process. Following this, other project leaders were encouraged to undertake a similar reflection process. In another session, the project leaders were taken through a systemic process of reflection on the project objectives, the implementation methodology and the design strategy. Workshop participants found these sessions very effective, and found that the process of implementation was significantly enhanced by these encounters.

There were significant outcomes for the organisation following the implementation process. The agency found that it had actually shifted its culture towards its desired 'performance culture'. Along the way, it had created a more harmonious and co-operative industrial climate, improved productivity, introduced more effective human resource systems and improved a range of indicators relating to governance and integrity.

Critical Thinking Question: Why is the reflective process so important in action research?

ACTION RESEARCH IN PRACTICE
Action research in cultural change

This section reviews the approach I used in an action research cultural change program using strategic human resource management at a large Australian government agency. It presents and describes a model for the use of strategic human resource management in bringing about cultural change. It is my contention that the poor success rate in organisational cultural change is partly due to a lack of systemic thinking by organisational change agents. To help to develop this understanding, I proposed a systemic model of organisational cultural change using strategic human resource management (SHRM). The model is presented as Figure 13.8.[88] Although many of the elements may be found in other models of organisational change, there are three key elements included that are substantially different from other models: (a) business cycles, (b) systemic thinking, and (c) systems practice. All of the elements of the model were used in the implementation of a systemic strategic human resource management cultural change process, with the exception of *business cycles*. This element arose from learning as a consequence of the implementation process. The cultural change process was quite successful, and a shift in the agency's culture from an 'entitlement culture' towards its desired 'performance culture' is noted by Molineux.[89]

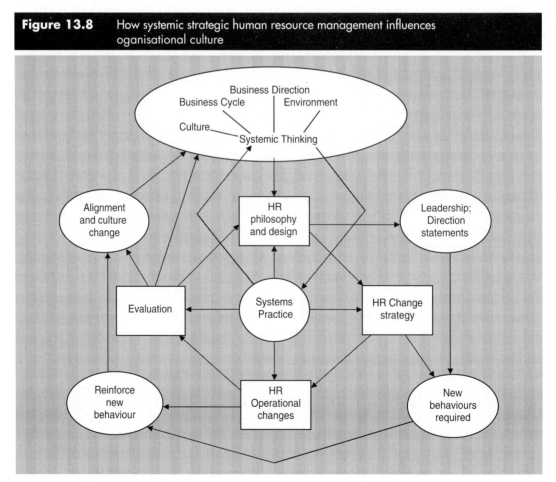

| **Figure 13.8** | How systemic strategic human resource management influences oganisational culture |

Source: J. Molineux, *Systemic strategic human resource management enables organizational cultural change: An action research study* (unpublished PhD thesis, Monash University, 2005).

It should be noted that the model was developed in the context of a major cultural change project in a large and complex organisation. It could be readily applied to other large and complex organisations wishing to undertake cultural change. It may also be adaptable for medium-sized organisations, or organisations that are less complex. Also, some of the thinking and messages that are explained here and are behind the creation of the model could be applied to organisations undertaking any significant change project.

ELEMENTS OF THE MODEL

The elements of the model depicted in Figure 13.8 are defined as follows:
1   *Business direction.* This is the strategic direction and vision proposed by the leaders of the organisation.
2   *Environment (and context).* This refers to the organisation's environment, including its business context, and its technological, legislative, financial and competitive environments.
3   *Culture.* This refers to a shared management understanding of the current state of the organisation's culture.
4   *Business cycle.* This refers to the organisation's pattern of punctuated change, including an analysis of the change initiators.
5   *Systemic thinking.* This allows for the complexity of the whole change program to be understood in the context of the business direction and environment, and for the various stages to be evaluated and modified in an ongoing cycle.
6   *HR philosophy and design.* This refers to the organisation's philosophical intent for the future organisational culture, and the high-level design of a human resources change program.
7   *Leadership and direction statements.* These refer to the ongoing leadership required to initiate and sustain a major change program.
8   *HR change strategy.* This incorporates the methodologies required for change, and the planning, resourcing and co-ordination of strategic change projects.
9   *Behavioural requirements.* These refer to the specific new behaviours that are required of employees by the HR philosophy and leadership directional statements.
10 *Systems practice.* This refers to the specific systems techniques used to help build the changes, using strategic human resource management in a systemic way.
11 *HR operational changes.* This incorporates the actual activities used in bringing about change, and the new infrastructure and systems built and delivered as a result of the change process.
12 *Reinforce new behaviour.* This refers to the process occurring with the impact of operational changes in HR, reinforcing the required new behaviours.
13 *Evaluation.* This incorporates assurance measures, both qualitative and quantitative, as well as ongoing organisational cultural assessment.
14 *Alignment and culture change.* This refers to the impact of the cultural change process on the culture, and its alignment to business outcomes.

EXPLANATION OF HOW THE MODEL WORKS IN PRACTICE

This section describes how the model at Figure 13.8 works in practice. Large-scale cultural change needs to be carried out in the context of a revolutionary period of organisational change, as described by Tushman and Romanelli.[90] Without this impetus, change will only be incremental and slow, as the inertia within the organisation resists attempts at fundamental change. It should be noted that culture is a key to the successful execution of revolutionary change.[91] There is a difference between incremental and revolutionary cultural change in terms of the dynamic contextual environment of the organisation. Where the conditions exist for revolutionary change, then incremental change will not work.[92] The dynamic nature of the context for change requires systemic understanding of all of the factors, in order to understand the relationship between the elements of the model. A failure to understand the dynamic consequences of cultural phenomena results in an under-analysis or misunderstanding of its importance.[93] This realisation underlies the value of systemic thinking in dealing with organisational culture.

In the model shown at Figure 13.8, within the oval at the top of the diagram, the element noted as *systemic thinking* is a critical starting point. Such thinking helps understanding of the impact of the *business direction* of the organisation, the factors in the *environment* surrounding and influencing the business, its organisational and *business cycles*, and the impact of the existing *culture* on the business. Such environmental factors may include: the impact of new technology; legislative and government changes; changes in the market, competitors and predicted consumer behaviour; changes in international relations and trade agreements; labour market and demographic projections; and economic trends. The dynamics of these relationships are driven by business and organisational cycles. An understanding of this comes from an assessment of the factors involved in revolutionary change, and the current state and history of the organisation's business cycles. In the agency's case, these were driven by political cycles. In private-sector organisations, economic and industry cycles may be more relevant.

The *systemic thinking* component is critical to avoiding pitfalls, such as generating a quick-fix solution. Systemic thinking should avoid the 'shifting the burden' archetype, as the understanding of underlying structure, context and culture will enable the leaders of the organisation to develop a philosophy and design that aims to provide a fundamental solution, rather than using a symptomatic solution. To build cultural change takes time, and leaders that understand this will be able to avoid the 'fixes that fail' archetype. For example, an organisation that uses frequent retrenchment and hiring sets up a cycle that appears to use quick fixes. This may cause fundamental problems with an organisation's long-term capability, and the motivation of its staff. The culture of the organisation could also be severely affected, although this would not generally be an intention of management. Such unintended consequences of quick-fix solutions will be avoided if systemic thinking is used. To assist leaders in this type of thinking, systemic techniques such as scenario planning and system dynamics modelling would provide meaningful information.

In Figure 13.8, four 'boxes' represent a cycle of different levels of HR. From the systemic thinking represented in the oval, a new *HR philosophy and design* can be drawn that will include the high-level design of the HR system to be implemented, and images of the future intended culture. Once the design has been created, a *change strategy* and methodology needs to be chosen and implemented. This will include the planning, resourcing and management of new initiatives and projects. Implementation of the change strategy then results in *HR operational changes*, which would be specifically designed to elicit and *reinforce new behaviours* required. Resulting behaviours and organisational performance would then be assessed through *evaluation* processes.

At the core of the model, and underpinning this cycle, is *systems practice*, which enables this to occur in a systemic way. The process for systems practice that I recommended is Flood and Jackson's Total Systems Intervention (TSI).[94] When TSI is chosen, a number of systems techniques can be applied to the various parts of the model. In my research, Soft Systems Methodology[95] and System Dynamics[96] techniques were used. Systems practice can be used at any stage of the change process. The various systems techniques will enable the user to design implementation processes, to engage stakeholders, to analyse contexts, to evaluate complex dynamic information and to evaluate outcomes. The TSI method can guide practitioners in the choice of appropriate system techniques for the relevant situation.

At the outside of the model, the process of behavioural change is indicated. The new philosophy and design requires *leadership and directional statements* to model the new behaviour required. The change strategy and methodology outline the *new behaviours required* for the desired culture to set benchmarks that changes may be measured against. The new HR infrastructure and operations *reinforce new behaviour*. The extent of *alignment and culture change* in accordance with the overall philosophy and business direction can then be measured. This information then feeds back to the systemic thinking about the business and its direction.

The whole operation should not be viewed as static or sequential, however. Feedback from each of the elements should be noted and issues addressed. The implementation of such models rarely run smoothly, so adjustments along the way are to be expected and planned for. The model has been created to enable researchers and organisational change agents to improve the success of organisational cultural change programs. The model, if used in the manner described, should enable better insight into the dynamics of cultural change processes. This, in turn, will enable an appropriate strategy to be developed for the organisation's particular context. Following this, the implementation of the strategy, using the elements as described, should enable cultural change to occur.

The use of FMA as a reflective approach in action research

An interesting approach to reflection in action research is presented in this section. An application and development of this approach by an action research group at Monash University is discussed in Application 13.3.

The FMA approach is presented in Figure 13.9.[97] It is a combination of Checkland's[98] general model of the organised use of rational thought (or FMA) and Mezirow's[99] reflection types. It can be used as a tool for deep reflection and rethinking about the implications of unexpected action that arise during the conduct of action research. In fact, Checkland claims that any research in any mode may be thought of as entailing the elements shown in the FMA model.[100] Checkland and Holwell[101] describe it as:

> Particular linked ideas (F) are used in a methodology (M) to investigate an area of interest (A). Using the methodology may then teach us not only about A but also about the adequacy of F and M.

The importance of this in action research is that a change to or modification of F, M and even A has to be expected in action research.[102] Changing situations, then, are likely to test the adequacy of F and M and the appropriateness of A.[103]

In action research, there is a need to declare the framework of ideas up front. The declared framework is in the sense of research themes within which lessons can be sought, and the researcher enters a real-world situation in which the themes are relevant and becomes involved as both participant and researcher.[104] Reflection of experience on the declared F and M may require some rethinking of earlier phases – and again, it is the declared intellectual framework of F and M that allows this to be done coherently.[105] The reflection can yield findings of various kinds, such as learning about F, M and A, or about the research themes; or new themes may be defined as a result of the experience.[106]

The Monash action research group, as noted in Application 13.3, found that FMA could be used as a reflective tool and that a further enhancement would be the inclusion of Mezirow's three types of reflection.[107] Mezirow[108] notes that transformative learning occurs when fundamental mental frameworks are questioned and revised, and in action research such reflection leads to the uncovering of new interpretations and perspectives. He notes three types of reflection:

- *Content reflection.* This examines the issues and events in the area of action (the *what*).
- *Process reflection.* This examines the methods and processes used (the *how*).
- *Assumption reflection.* This examines the underlying ideas and mental models (the *why*).

These types of reflection are included in the template at Figure 13.9.[109] Content and process reflection may become an integral part of thoughtful action in these processes, but assumption reflection is less common.[110] However, this self-reflection is important and may lead the researcher to eventually reconsider both their theoretical framework and their understanding of the 'problem-solving' activity, from the self-reflection process.[111] Assumption reflection is the dynamic where our belief systems and perspectives on the world can become transformed.[112]

Figure 13.9 Checkland–Mezirow template

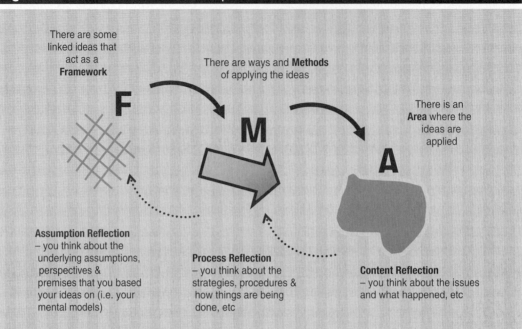

Source: R. Sarah, T. Haslett, J. Molineux, J. Olsen, J. Stephens, S. Tepe and B. Walker, 'Business action research in practice: A strategic conversation about conducting action research in business organizations', *Systemic Practice and Action Research*, 15:6, 2002. Reproduced with permission from Springer Science & Business Media.

APPLiCATiON 13.3

THE USE OF REFLECTION BY A RESEARCH COHORT GROUP AT MONASH UNIVERSITY

This case looks at the action research community at Monash University and, in particular, its use of action research and the reflective use of Checkland's FMA process. The group relied on the use of the Checkland–Mezirow FMA and Reflection Template described in Figure 13.9.

The Monash action research group from the Department of Management consisted of six PhD students and two mentors. The students were engaged in action research in various settings over a seven-year period. The group met monthly as a group of critical friends who provided support, advice and critique of the individual and collective work of the group. Significantly, the group engaged in extensive reflection processes and was able to generate extensive insight and learning in the field of action research.

The FMA template was used as a tool for deep reflection and rethinking about the implications of unexpected action that arose during the conduct action research by members of the Monash action research group. For example, the reflection cycles in the process of one of the group member's research led to new thinking about strategic human resource management and about the relevance of the theory of punctuated equilibrium to the research problem. In this research, reflection was essential and resulted in new understandings of the application of theory in the field, and on the methodologies used.

Within the Monash cohort, the framework of ideas was stated in research propositions relating to each researcher's work. However, circumstances within the area of action meant that the application of the framework of ideas to real projects did not result in the expected outcomes. This was mainly due to environmental factors and circumstances that were beyond the control of the researcher. In one case, this led to the abolition of the original research project. In other cases, the research projects were terminated prior to full implementation. In another, the researcher was retrenched from the organisation. Reflection on evidence from the applied action areas indicated that the original frameworks of ideas may actually require some adjustments. It was during this time that the Monash cohort of researchers discussed and used the FMA template, and discovered that the projects were the subject of larger systems, some of which were being driven by political and economic macro-cycles. In one case, this was found to be in accordance with the theory of punctuated equilibrium. Subsequently, the researchers rethought the framework and the methodology of their research projects and new insights were generated. In a couple of cases, new projects were created and completed.

The Monash group found that FMA could be used as a reflective tool and that a further enhancement would be the inclusion of Mezirow's three types of reflection, as noted in Figure 13.9. All three of these types of reflection were used by the Monash researchers in reflecting on the action research they were undertaking. When the group reflected on content, they were reflecting on what happened in the action area (A). Their reflection on process mapped to the choice and application of their methodologies (M). Their assumption or premise reflection suggested that they explore why they chose to do what they did in the way they did it as a reflection of their various frameworks of ideas (F).[113]

The group members found the FMA template simple to use, yet highly useful in being able to think through some complex change management and research problems. Since the Monash group first used the FMA template in 2001, its use has continued in subsequent action research groups and in other forums.

Critical Thinking Question: How can FMA be used to improve an ineffective change program?

SUMMARY

After reading this chapter, you may think that an action research program is too different from mainstream thinking and too difficult a methodology to work with. Well, action research has been successfully used for many years by organisational development practitioners. In fact, it became integral to the growth of the theory and practice of organisational development.[114] The recent experiences of the Monash University action research cohort would confirm that it is a worthwhile and successful methodology. However, it should not be entered into lightly, as it can challenge the existing mental models and thinking frameworks that may be firmly established in a particular organisation. Yet there are many managers who would want to challenge the thinking assumptions and frameworks embedded in their organisations. These managers may find that action research will aid their quest to bring about significant change and organisational improvement. Managers who are open to new experiences and thinking should consider it as an excellent methodology to bring about widespread change. If done well, the change will be accepted into the organisation and sustained into the future, becoming a new part of the culture and history of the organisation. A number of recommendations are suggested as a result of the understanding on the use of action research outlined in this chapter:

1 *Reflexivity and flexibility.* It is important for an action researcher to critically review their own action and impact on the organisation. The action researcher needs to consider that intent and outcome may be quite different, and needs to be able to be responsive and flexible to deal with changing requirements on the run. This not only involves interaction with others, but also critical reflection on, and re-evaluation of, the researcher's own approach and goals. FMA is recommended as an approach for reflection in this context.

2 *Understand the system.* The action researcher should always remember to view the system on which they are working on a number of levels. The researcher should not just consider the project they are working on, but also its ongoing context in the macro-system of the organisation and its interaction with its environment. Understanding the impact and relationships at this level will help the researcher to implement a more effective approach to change management. It is recommended that the researcher actively advocate the systemic approach, particularly in meetings with organisational management, such as during the design and implementation of a project.

3 *Choose from a spectrum of participation*: There is a range of possibilities in involving people in change programs. The action researcher needs to consider the stage of the project, the relationships with key stakeholders and the appropriateness of involvement of organisational members at these project stages. The researcher can then work out which form of participation would be the most effective for each of the project stages. It is recommended that researchers consider the types of participation noted in the spectrum at Table 13.2.

4 *Positioning oneself in the organisation*: The action researcher needs to place themselves in a position within the organisation where they can most benefit themselves and bring about the desired change. The researcher must first understand their role and the political and social position they have within the organisation. To achieve a place of influence that would benefit the project, the researcher needs to build close relationships with key clients and gain sufficient political and positional support to enable effective contribution to the outcomes of the project. It is recommended that the researcher obtain organisational written agreement about their role and reporting relationships.

ACTiViTiES

Review questions

① What are the essential components of action research?

② Name a version of the four components of the action research cycle.

③ What are the benefits in conducting an action research intervention? What are some of the problems with using action research?

④ What are some of the issues with using an organisational insider as an action research change agent?

⑤ What is the meaning of a systemic view of action research?

⑥ What are the steps used in Soft Systems Methodology?

⑦ Discuss two types of participation noted in the spectrum of participation possibilities in action research and give an example of where they might be used.

⑧ Discuss the importance of reflection in action research.

Discussion and essay questions

① Describe action research. Discuss the benefits and potential problems associated with using this methodology in a change program.

② Participation is an essential part of action research. How can a change agent use participation effectively in an action research change intervention?

③ Discuss the features of Soft Systems Methodology. How may it be used in a change intervention?

④ One of the major debates in organisation change is the use of internal and external change agents. Discuss some of the benefits and potential pitfalls in using insiders as change agents in action research. Discuss whether these pitfalls can be overcome by the use of external change agents.

NOTES

1 K. Lewin, 'Action research and minority problems', *Journal of Social Issues*, 2:4 (1946): 34–46; K. Lewin, *Resolving social conflicts* (New York: Harper, 1948).

2 D. Greenwood and M. Levin, *Introduction to Action Research* (Thousand Oaks, CA: Sage, 1998).

3 J. Molineux, *Systemic strategic human resource management enables organizational cultural change: An action research study* (unpublished PhD thesis, Monash University, 2005).

4 D. Coghlan and T. Brannick, *Doing Action Research in Your Own Organization* (London: Sage, 2001).

5 S. Kates and J. Robertson, 'Adapting action research to marketing: A dialogic argument between theory and practice', *European Journal of Marketing*, 38:3/4 (2004): 418–32.

6 J. McKay and P. Marshall, 'The dual imperatives of action research', *Information Technology & People*, 14:1 (2001): 46–59.

7 R. Rapoport, 'Three Dilemmas of Action Research', *Human Relations*, 23:6 (1970): 499–513.

8 P. Reason and H. Bradbury, *Handbook of Action Research: Participative Inquiry and Practice* (London: Sage, 2001).

9 M. Patton, *Qualitative Evaluation and Research Methods*, 2nd edn (Newbury Park, CA, Sage, 1990).

10 J. Gaventa and A. Cornwall, 'Power and Knowledge', in P. Reason and H. Bradbury (eds), *Handbook of Action Research: Participative Inquiry and Practice* (London: Sage, 2001): 70–80.

11 D. Avison, R. Baskerville and M. Myers, 'Controlling action research projects', *Information Technology & People*, 14:1 (2001): 28–45.

12 R. Chisholm, 'Action Research to Develop an Interorganisational Network', in P. Reason and H. Bradbury (eds), *Handbook of Action Research: Participative Inquiry and Practice* (London: Sage, 2001): 324–32.

13 Greenwood and Levin, *Introduction to Action Research*, op. cit.

14 B. Dick, 'Postgraduate programs using action research', *The Learning Organization*, 9:4 (2002): 159–70.

15 D. De Guerre, 'Doing action research in one's own organization: an ongoing conversation over time', *Systemic Practice and Action Research*, 15:4 (2002): 331–49.

16 ibid.

17 W. French, 'Organization Development Objectives, Assumptions, and Strategies', *California Management Review*, 12 (Winter, 1969): 23–4.

18 E. Schein, 'Sense and Nonsense about Culture and Climate', in N.M. Ashkanasy, C.P.M. Wilderom and M.F. Peterson (eds), *Handbook of Organizational Culture and Climate* (Thousand Oaks, CA: Sage): xxiii–xxx.

19 De Guerre, 'Doing action research in one's own organization: an ongoing conversation over time', op. cit.

20 Coghlan and Brannick, *Doing Action Research in Your Own Organization*, op. cit.

21 D. Coghlan, 'Insider Action Research Projects', *Management Learning*, 32:1 (2001): 49–60.

22 J. Stephens and T. Haslett, 'Action learning as a mindset', *Systemic Practice and Action Research*, 15:6 (2002).

23 Coghlan, 'Insider Action Research Projects', op. cit.

24 ibid.

25 ibid.

26 ibid.

27 Coghlan and Brannick, *Doing Action Research in Your Own Organization*, op. cit.

28 Coghlan, 'Insider Action Research Projects', op. cit.

29 Coghlan and Brannick, *Doing Action Research in Your Own Organization*, op. cit.

30 R.L. Ackoff, 'Systems thinking and thinking systems', *System Dynamics Review*, 10:2–3 (1994): 175–88.

31 P. Senge, *The Fifth Discipline: The Art and Practice of the Learning Organisation* (London: Century, 1990).

32 ibid.

33 ibid.

34 D.H. Kim and P.M. Senge, 'Putting systems thinking into practice', *System Dynamics Review*, 10:2–3 (1994): 277–90.

35 P.B. Checkland, *Systems Thinking, Systems Practice* (Chichester: John Wiley & Sons, 1981).

36 P.B. Checkland and J. Scholes, *Soft Systems Methodology in Action* (Chichester: John Wiley & Sons, 1990).

37 A. Waring, *Practical Systems Thinking* (London: International Thompson Business Press, 1996).

38 P.J. Dobson, 'The SoSM Revisited – the importance of Social Structures', *Proceedings of the 7th Annual ANZSYS Conference* (Perth: 2001): 51–9.

39 R.L. Flood and M.C. Jackson, *Creative Problem Solving: Total Systems Intervention* (Chichester: John Wiley & Sons, 1991).

40 Checkland and Scholes, *Soft Systems Methodology in Action*, op. cit.

41 L.J. Davies and P.W.J. Ledington, *Information in Action: Soft Systems Methodology* (London: Macmillan, 1991).

42 P.B. Checkland and M.G. Haynes, 'Varieties of systems thinking: the case of soft system methodology,' *System Dynamics Review*, 10:2–3 (1994): 189–97.

43 Checkland, *Systems Thinking, Systems Practice*, op. cit.

44 Checkland, *Systems Thinking, Systems Practice*, op. cit.

45 P.B. Checkland, 'Soft Systems Methodology: A Thirty Year Retrospective', *Systems Research and Behavioral Science*, 17:S1 (2000): S11–58.

46 J. Gold, 'Storying Systems: Managing Everyday Flux Using Mode 2 Soft Systems Methodology', *Systemic Practice and Action Research*, 14:5 (2001): 557–73.

47 D. Patching, 'Soft systems methodology and information technology', *Management Services*, 31:8 (1987): 16–19.

48 Davies and Ledington, *Information in Action: Soft Systems Methodology*, op. cit.

49 D. Smyth and P. Checkland, 'Using a systems approach: The structure of root definitions', *Journal of Applied Systems Analysis*, 5:1 (1976): 75–83.

50 Checkland, *Systems Thinking, Systems Practice*, op. cit.

51 B. Bergvall-Kåreborn, A. Mirijamdotter and A. Basden, 'Basic Principles of SSM Modeling: An Examination of CATWOE from a Soft Perspective', *Systemic Practice and Action Research*, 17:2 (2004): 55–73.

52 P.B. Checkland and C. Tsouvalis, 'Reflecting on SSM: The Link Between Root Definitions and Conceptual Models', *Systems Research and Behavioural Science*, 14:3 (1997): 153–68.

53 J. Rose and M. Haynes, 'A soft systems approach to the evaluation of complex interventions in the public sector', *Journal of Applied Management Studies*, 8:2 (1999): 199–216.

54 M.J. Taylor and J.L. DaCosta, 'Soft Issues in IS Projects: Lessons from an SME Case Study', *Systems Research and Behavioural Science*, 16:3 (1999): 263–72.

55 C. Tsouvalis and P. Checkland, 'Reflecting on SSM: The dividing line between "real world" and systems thinking world', *Systems Research*, 13:1 (1996): 35–45.

56 D. Fielden and J.K. Jacques, 'Systemic Approach to Energy Rationalisation in Island Communities', *International Journal of Energy Research*, 22:2 (1998): 107–29.

57 Davies and Ledington, *Information in Action: Soft Systems Methodology*, op. cit.

58 P.B. Checkland, 'Model Validation in Soft Systems Practice', *Systems Research*, 12:1 (1995): 47–54.

59 Davies and Ledington, *Information in Action: Soft Systems Methodology*, op. cit.

60 Checkland, *Systems Thinking, Systems Practice*, op. cit.

61 Molineux, *Systemic strategic human resource management enables organizational cultural change: An action research study*, op. cit.

62 D. West and M.H. Stansfield, 'Structuring Action and Reflection in Information: Systems Action Research Studies Using Checkland's FMA Model', *Systemic Practice and Action Research*, 14:1 (2001): 251–81.

63 Reason and Bradbury, *Handbook of Action Research: Participative Inquiry and Practice*, op. cit.

64 Greenwood and Levin, *Introduction to Action Research*, op. cit.

65 G. Brulin, 'The Third Task of Universities or How to Get Universities to Serve their Communities!', in P. Reason and H. Bradbury (eds), *Handbook of Action Research: Participative Inquiry and Practice* (London: Sage, 2001): 440–6.

66 Dick, 'Postgraduate programs using action research', op. cit.

67 Coghlan and Brannick, *Doing Action Research in Your Own Organization*, op. cit.

68 Greenwood and Levin, *Introduction to Action Research*, op. cit.

69 Coghlan and Brannick, *Doing Action Research in Your Own Organization*, op. cit.

70 P. Lomax, 'Action researchers' action research: a symposium', *British Journal of In-service Education*, 13:1 (1986): 42–50.

71 S. Kemmis, 'Action research and the politics of reflection', in D. Bould, R. Keogh and D. Walker (eds), *Reflection: Turning Experience into Learning* (London: KoganPage, 1985): 139–64.

72 Rose and Haynes, 'A soft systems approach to the evaluation of complex interventions in the public sector', op. cit.

73 A.W. Martin, 'Large-group Processes as Action Research', in P. Reason and H. Bradbury (eds), *Handbook of Action Research: Participative Inquiry and Practice* (London: Sage, 2001): 200–8.

74 Dick, 'Postgraduate programs using action research', op. cit.

75 Greenwood and Levin, *Introduction to Action Research*, op. cit.

76 D.A. Schön, *The Reflective Practitioner: How Professionals Think in Action* (New York: Basic Books, 1983); D.A. Schön, *Educating the Reflective Practitioner: Toward a New Design for Teaching and Learning in the Professions* (San Francisco, Jossey-Bass, 1987).

77 Coghlan and Brannick, *Doing Action Research in Your Own Organization*, op. cit.

78 Senge, *The Fifth Discipline: The Art and Practice of the Learning Organisation*, op. cit.

79 Checkland, *Systems Thinking, Systems Practice*, op. cit.

80 P.M. Senge and J.D. Sterman, 'Systems Thinking and Organisational Learning: Acting Locally and Thinking Globally in the Organisation of the Future', in J.D.W. Morecroft and J.D. Sterman, *Modeling for Learning Organizations* (Portland: Productivity Press, 1994): 196–211.

81 J.D.W. Morecroft, 'Executive Knowledge, Models, and Learning', in J.D.W. Morecroft and J.D. Sterman (eds), *Modeling for Learning Organizations* (Portland: Productivity Press, 1994): 3–28.

82 R.L. Flood, *Rethinking the Fifth Discipline* (London: Routledge, 1999).

83 Kates and Robertson, 'Adapting action research to marketing: A dialogic argument between theory and practice', op. cit.

84 ibid.

85 C. Argyris, *Reasoning, learning, and action* (San Francisco: Jossey-Bass, 1982).

86 P. Senge, A. Kleiner, C. Roberts, R. Ross and B. Smith, *The Fifth Discipline Fieldbook* (London: Nicholas Brealey Publishing, 1994).

87 ibid.

88 Molineux, *Systemic strategic human resource management enables organizational cultural change: An action research study*, op. cit.

89 ibid.

90 M.L. Tushman and E. Romanelli, 'Organisational Evolution: A Metamorphosis Model of Convergence and Reorientation', in L.L. Cummings and B.M. Staw (eds), *Research in Organizational Behavior*, 7 (Greenwich, CT: JAI Press, 1985): 171–222.

91 C.A. O'Reilly and M.L. Tushman, 'Using Culture for Strategic Advantage: Promoting Innovation Through Social Control', in M.L. Tushman and P. Anderson (eds), *Managing Strategic Innovation and Change: A Collection of Readings* (New York: Oxford University Press, 1997).

92 J.B. Sørensen, 'The strength of corporate culture and the reliability of firm performance', *Administrative Science Quarterly*, 47:1 (2002): 70–91.

93 E.H. Schein, *Organisational Culture and Leadership* (San Francisco, CA: Jossey-Bass, 1985).

94 Flood and Jackson, *Creative Problem Solving: Total Systems Intervention*, op. cit.

95 Checkland, *Systems Thinking, Systems Practice*, op. cit.

96 J.W. Forrester, *Industrial Dynamics* (Cambridge, MA: MIT Press, 1961).

97 R. Sarah, T. Haslett, J. Molineux, J. Olsen, J. Stephens, S. Tepe and B. Walker, 'Business Action Research in Practice – A Strategic Conversation About Conducting Action Research in Business Organizations', *Systemic Practice and Action Research*, 15:6 (2002): 535-46.

98 P.B. Checkland, 'From optimizing to learning: A development of systems thinking for the 1990s', *Journal of the Operational Research Society*, 36:9 (1985): 757–67.

99 J. Mezirow, *Transformative Dimensions of Adult Learning* (San Francisco, CA: Jossey-Bass, 1991).

100 Checkland, 'From optimizing to learning: A development of systems thinking for the 1990s', op. cit.

101 P.B. Checkland, and S. Holwell, 'Action Research: Its Nature and Validity', *Systemic Practice and Action Research*, 11:1 (1998): 9–21.

102 ibid.

103 ibid.

104 ibid.

105 ibid.

106 P.B. Checkland and S. Holwell, *Information, Systems and Information Systems* (Chichester: John Wiley & Sons, 1998).

107 Mezirow, *Transformative Dimensions of Adult Learning*, op. cit.

108 ibid.

109 Sarah et al., 'Business Action Research in Practice – A Strategic Conversation About Conducting Action Research in Business Organizations', op. cit.

110 Mezirow, *Transformative Dimensions of Adult Learning*, op. cit.

111 J.E. Yu, 'Reconsidering participatory action research for organizational transformation and social change', *Journal of Organisational Transformation and Social Change*, 1:2/3 (2004): 111–41.

112 Mezirow, *Transformative Dimensions of Adult Learning*, op. cit.

113 Sarah et al. 'Business Action Research in Practice – A Strategic Conversation About Conducting Action Research in Business Organizations', op. cit.

114 D. Coghlan and T. Brannick, *Doing Action Research in Your Own Organization*, op. cit.

Online reading

INFOTRAC® COLLEGE EDITION

For additional readings and reviews on action research, explore **InfoTrac® College Edition**, your online library. Go to **www.infotrac-college.com** and search for any of the InfoTrac key terms listed below:

INFOTRAC

• Systemic nature of action research
• Soft systems methodology
• Participation and reflection

14

ORGANiSATiON DEVELOPMENT AND DiSCOURSE ANALYSIS

By Dr James Latham, Swinburne University

Organisation development is about planned change over time and time is one of the enemies of OD practitioners. How often do change initiatives become unsustainable and fail, even after substantial investment of resources? One reason is that we fail to change the discourse we are operating in. In short, we don't change the way we speak and relate to others as required by the new changes. This chapter will look at discourse analysis as a strategy for understanding how we need to adjust our relations and speech within any OD initiative.

DISCOURSE ANALYSIS AND ORGANISATION DEVELOPMENT

OD is about movement. It is about moving the organisation (or part of it) from its existing position to a previously identified desired position. On the face of it this process seems unproblematic, yet many managers have floundered on the many 'hidden reefs' of OD. Why can it be so troublesome for managers to move their organisation forward to desired ends? One problem (and it is major) is that managers look to existing theory and current 'trendy' techniques to provide them with the ultimate solution to any problem that may arise. Quite often organisations dole out a great deal of money with the intention of buying solutions in the form of consultants, training packages or the latest software in the hope that these will bring the ultimate solutions to organisational problems. Alas, many of these purchases are a recipe for disaster. In this chapter we will argue that to increase your chance of success in any OD initiative, managers must look closer to home and to develop an implicit understanding of the processes operating in their organisation and to realise that there are no pre-packed solutions available outside the organisation. Of particular interest here is an area of study not usually explored in mainstream OD theory. This is the area of discourse analysis and its subsequent contribution to successful OD initiatives.

Discourse analysis is about understanding your organisation in terms of its unique use of language and conversation in the here and now. For example, if your organisation is highly bureaucratic with an emphasis on policy and procedure and you are considering developing a team culture, you will need to compare the current methods of relating and communicating with those required for a team culture to succeed. With this understanding, future directions can be explored based on the limitations and advantages of your organisation's discourses. As noted above, this is a relatively new approach to organisational analysis. However, it is not intended to displace other theories and fields of organisational studies; the intention here is to place this approach alongside other approaches and techniques in order to provide a broader platform from which to launch your OD project. With this in mind, this chapter will first explore discourse as a means of analysing organisation structure and processes by asking: What is discourse analysis? Second, we will explain not only how discourse constructs our identity but also how it regulates our behaviour and relationships with others. Third, we introduce the notion of boundary as a framework of analysis. Fourth, we bring together the concepts discussed above to develop a model of discourse communities. In summary we discuss the implications for OD practice.

What is discourse?

Many of you will be familiar with the question: 'You can talk the talk but can you walk the walk?' Simply put, this means not just talking about doing something, but doing it! However, what is missing here is that you can only 'walk the talk' if the 'talk' and the 'walk' are compatible. And that is where the problem lies for many organisations who wish to develop and change. These organisations say the right things in line with contemporary thinking, then they develop new mission statements through visioning techniques, and discuss, plan and resource their change projects. Everyone is 'fired up', so to speak, and ready to implement the changes, but when it comes to 'walking the talk' something goes wrong: the changes are not sustainable. The new ways are accepted in the beginning, but over time people tend to revert to the 'same old way' (SOW). Why should this be so? One reason is that the organisation failed to work on and change the discourses in use in the organisation.

So what is discourse? It is said that there is some 'terminological confusion' surrounding the term discourse and its analysis.[1] This, they say, stems from the fact that a number of disciplines have developed their own ideas about discourse from a range of theoretical perspectives.[2] One definition suited to the area of change and OD is given by Henriques as: 'a regulated system of statements and practices that defines social interaction'.[3] Legge extends this definition by saying that discourse: 'refers to the way in which things are discussed and the argumentation and rhetoric used to support what is said'.[4] Legge also refers to *reading between the lines* [my emphasis]: what remains unspoken or taken for granted, such as assumptions or evasions. Both definitions of discourse above suggest that discourse is a process and not a structure, although in the Henriques[5] definition the assumption is one of a rule-bound, formalised process. However, Legge's[6] definition is broader in that it identifies clearly the processual nature of discourse when she refers to the 'reading between the lines' feature of discourse. For the purposes of this chapter, Legge's[7] definition of discourse will be adopted, viewing discourse in terms of processes.

An example of discourse analysis is shown by adapting the following dialogue from a film entitled *Brassed Off*,[8] set in a Yorkshire mining town in the United Kingdom. The conversation that takes place nicely illustrates the process of Legge's[9] notion of reading between the lines. The scene is set in a bar where a group of miners have just found out that one of their group (Andy) is courting a girl who works in the mine's survey department, a department that is viewed by the group as being part of 'management'. This situation causes conflict within the group because miners from this community have traditionally viewed 'management' with deep suspicion and hatred, which, over time, has become embedded in their culture both within and outside their work organisation. Jim criticises Andy by accusing him of being a traitor to the 'cause' when he says: 'O aye, old enough to be a *scab* [my emphasis] then.' There is now a deathly silence, not only within the group but throughout the whole bar. The term 'scab' is the ultimate insult to any member of this close-knit community. Andy responds by holding his pool cue in a fashion that represents a swordsman ready to strike a blow on the back of Jim's head. Ernie, another group member steps in to reduce the rising anger:

> Ernie: It's all right Andy, he doesn't mean it.
>
> Andy, still angry over the insult, responds by saying: 'You don't mess around with words like that.'
>
> Jim, sensing the tension created by his statement, but not wishing to back down totally, replies by saying: 'Aye, I'm sorry Andy I tek it back – you're a stupid f**ker!'

Although Jim has substituted his initial insult with a term understood by many as being equally insulting, for Andy it was a lot more acceptable than being labelled a 'scab'. The tension is released within the group when Andy replies: 'That's more like it.' There was not much said in this exchange, but the use of the term 'scab' has been known to strike fear into the hearts of many 'hard-nosed' Yorkshire miners and their families. For the uninitiated, this four-letter word seems harmless enough but for those who legitimately participated in the discourse and through 'reading between the lines',[10] this word or label meant the difference between acceptance into the community or becoming a complete outcast. Within the Yorkshire mining community in this film, the word acted as a very powerful regulator of behaviour, because it implicitly contained the rhetoric of fear. What this one word did for those members of the discourse was implicitly construct an identity (in that it symbolised something undesirable, unsightly and unclean) of anyone who wore that label. Further, the constructed identity was a product of the past, the present and the future,[11] so the term possesses temporal features. It also had the effect of making the discourse members knowable through construction processes, which allowed them to identify any deviants who were subsequently denied a voice and marginalised. Finally, it suggests that language is not a mere carrier of meaning but, in fact, is a constructor of meaning. As Alvesson argues, the traditional view of language is faulty in that it privileges the idea that 'language represents reality'[12]. Language for most social constructionists does not represent reality but, in fact, constructs reality. In short, language is a process.

So what makes up discourse?

In their handbook on organisational discourse, Grant et al.[13] say that 'organisational discourse' is made up of 'structured collections of texts embodied in the practices of talking and writing'. Other texts can be 'visual representations and cultural artefacts'. These texts are not just singular documents but often are also multiple. Organisations by their very nature are informed by multiple texts (for example, financial, human resource and marketing) and many organisational discourses contain what are called metalanguages. In short, a metalanguage is a fabricated version of someone's reality.[14] For example, sociology is a metalanguage created to explain the everyday dynamics and behaviour of groups and communities. Within a metalanguage the subject is 'objectified' through the use of object language. For example, the term 'scab' was a local descriptor of a particular set of values and behaviours, but it was also part of the metalanguage of industrial relations in a Yorkshire mining context.

Mueller, Sillince, Harvey and Howorth[15] introduce rhetoric into discourse analysis and say that rhetorical strategies and devices are used to make general viewpoints more convincing. They go on to say that often you find rhetoric at work when you have competing discourses; for example, commercial versus patient care discourses in the health-care industry. These types of discourse grow to 'dominate' other discourses as they attract support and sponsorship from other powerful agencies. For example, in Australia we have seen a significant shift in workplace relations away from pluralism (an acceptance of difference in motives and aims of the parties within organisations) to a more unitary form (a perspective that claims we should all 'sign up' for the stated objectives and values of the organisation). In doing this we have significantly reduced the effect of trade union discourses and substituted these with discourses based on the individual. In the main this shift has come about through the strong endorsement of successive governments who have actively sponsored these changes. Therefore, in analysing the numbers and types of texts affecting our organisation, we must also look outside the organisational boundaries and identify those external discourse texts that influence the organisation.

If we return to the analysis of the miners' episode and take it a stage further, a number of features of discourse can be identified. These include: the constructionist nature of discourse; the regulation of discourse; the contextual nature of discourse; and communities of discourse.

THE CONSTRUCTIONIST NATURE OF DISCOURSE

Social constructionism has been around for some time now and can be traced through sociological literatures. Mead[16] introduced the notion of symbolic interactionism, which is based on the notion that people construct their own and each other's identities through our everyday encounters with each other in social interaction. Schutz[17] also contributed to this view, but it was Berger and Luckmann's seminal work[18] that brought social construction to the fore. Berger and Luckmann's *The Social Construction of Reality* was an 'anti-essentialist' account of social life that argues that it is human beings together, in relationships, that create and sustain all social phenomena through social practices.

Burr[19] explains that Berger and Luckmann[20] identified three fundamental processes as responsible for this sustainability:

1   *Externalisation*. People 'externalise' when they act on their world, creating some artefact or practice. For example, they may have an idea (such as how to produce defined outputs from defined inputs) and 'externalise' it by telling a story or writing a plan. But this then enters into the social realm; other people re-tell the story or read the plan, and once in this social realm the story or plan begins to take on a life of its own. This then leads to the process of objectivation.

2   *Objectivation*. This is the idea that the story or plan has become an 'object' of consciousness for people in that society ('objectivation') and has developed a kind of factual existence or truth. It seems to be 'out there': an 'objective' feature of the world, which appears as 'natural', issuing from the nature of the world itself rather than dependent upon the constructive work and interactions of human beings.

3   *Internalisation*. Because future generations are born into a world where this idea already exists, they 'internalise' it as part of their consciousness – as part of their understanding of the nature of the world.[21]

A more postmodern explanation of the construction of discourse comes from the work of scholars like Robert Chia, Daniel Hjorth, Robert Cooper, Campbell Jones and Andre Spicer.[22] Chia[23] argues that 'reality' as we know it is socially constructed and has become an accepted truth. We abstract reality from the 'undifferentiated flux of fleeting sense impressions' of our life world. Chia[24] goes on to say that our 'attention carves out and [our] conception names … through [the] process of differentiating, fixing, naming, labelling, classifying and relating – all intrinsic processes of discursive organisation – that social reality is systematically constructed'. This also goes for our identity. So there is an identity construction process at work when we engage in discourse. As Phillips and Hardy[25] claim: 'The things that make up the world – including our very identities – appear out of discourse. To put it another way, our talk, and what we are, are one and the same.' And given the regulative effects of discourse, we do not necessarily have the 'luxury' of choice in regard to our identity, our truth claims and our reality: 'Our view of discourse can be summarised in a sentence: Without discourse there is no social reality, and without understanding discourse, we cannot understand our reality, our experiences, or ourselves.'[26]

Burr[27] states: 'There is no one feature which could be said to identify a social constructionist position.' Rather, social constructionist approaches can be loosely grouped together based on one or more of the following assumptions, which are drawn from Gergen[28] and adapted by Burr.[29] She also suggests that: 'You might think of these as something like "things you would absolutely have to believe in to be a social constructionist".'[30]

APPLiCATiON 14.1

CHALLENGING ESSENTIAL ASSUMPTIONS

A CRITICAL STANCE TOWARDS TAKEN-FOR-GRANTED KNOWLEDGE

Social constructionism insists that we take a critical stance towards our taken-for-granted ways of understanding the world (including ourselves). It invites us to be critical of the idea that our observations of the world unproblematically yield its nature to us; to challenge the view that conventional knowledge is based upon objective, unbiased observation of the world.

Social constructionism cautions us to be ever suspicious of our assumptions about how the world appears to be. This means that the categories with which we as human beings apprehend the world do not necessarily refer to real divisions. Just because we think of some music as 'classical' and some as 'pop' does not mean we should assume that there is anything in the nature of the music itself that means it has to be divided up in that particular way. A more radical example is that of gender. Our observations of the world suggest to us that there are two categories of human being: men and women. Social constructionism would bid us to question seriously whether even this category is simply a reflection of naturally occurring distinct types of human being. This may seem a bizarre idea

▷▷

at first, and of course differences in reproductive organs are present in many species, but we should ask why this distinction has been given so much importance by human beings that whole categories of personhood (that is, man/woman) have been built upon it. Social constructionism would suggest that we might equally well (and just as absurdly) have divided people up into tall and short, or those with ear lobes and those without.

Source: adapted from V. Burr, *An Introduction to Social Constructionism* (London: Routledge, 1995): 3.

Critical Thinking Question: What challenges can you make to the assumptions being made in your own job position? Use your position description as a guide.

HISTORICAL AND CULTURAL SPECIFICITY

The ways in which we commonly understand the world – the categories and concepts we use – are historically and culturally specific. Whether one understands the world in terms of men and women, pop music and classical music, urban life and rural life, past and future, etc. depends upon where and when in the world one lives. For example, the notion of childhood has undergone tremendous change over the centuries. What it has been thought 'natural' for children to do has changed, as well as what parents were expected to do for their children (see, for example, Aries).[31] It is only in relatively recent historical times that children have ceased to be simply small adults (in all but their legal rights). And we only have to look as far back as the writings of Dickens to remind ourselves that the idea of children as innocents in need of adult protection is a very recent one indeed. We can see changes even within the time span of the last 50 years or so, with radical consequences for how parents are advised to bring up their children.

This means that all ways of understanding are historically and culturally relative. Not only are they specific to particular cultures and periods of history, but they are seen as products of that culture and history, and are dependent upon the particular social and economic arrangements prevailing in that culture at that time. The particular forms of knowledge that abound in any culture are therefore artefacts of it, and we should not assume that our ways of understanding are necessarily any better (in terms of being any nearer the truth) than other ways.

Critical Thinking Question: Think about how the nature of workplace relations have changed over the last 20 years. What discursive (new language, new words, new ways of saying things) changes have occurred and which aspects of them are positive and which are negative?

KNOWLEDGE IS SUSTAINED BY SOCIAL PROCESSES

If our knowledge of the world (and our common ways of understanding it) is not derived from the nature of the world as it really is, where does it come from? The social constructionist answer is that people construct it between them. It is through the daily interactions between people in the course of social life that our versions of knowledge become fabricated. Therefore, social interaction of all kinds (and particularly language) are of great interest to social constructionists. The goings-on between people in the course of their everyday lives are seen as the practices during which our shared versions of knowledge are constructed. Therefore, what we regard as 'truth' – that is, our current accepted ways of understanding the world, which of course vary historically and cross-culturally – is a product not of objective observation of the world, but of the social processes and interactions in which people are constantly engaged with each other.

Critical Thinking Question: What interactions with members of your workgroup can you identify where shared versions of knowledge are constructed? These can be either formal or informal interactions.

KNOWLEDGE AND SOCIAL ACTION GO TOGETHER

These 'negotiated' understandings could take a wide variety of different forms, and we can therefore talk of numerous possible social constructions of the world. But each different construction also brings with it, or invites, a different kind of action from human beings. For example, before the temperance movement, drunks were seen as entirely responsible for their behaviour, and therefore blameworthy.

A typical response was therefore imprisonment. However, there has been a move away from seeing drunkenness as a crime and towards thinking of it as a sickness; a kind of addiction. 'Alcoholics' are not seen as totally responsible for their behaviour, since they are the victims of a kind of drug addiction. The social action appropriate to understanding drunkenness in this way is to offer medical and psychological treatment, not imprisonment. Descriptions or constructions of the world therefore sustain some patterns of social action and exclude others.

Critical Thinking Question: Identify instances of social constructions in your workplace that sustain some patterns of social action and exclude others. Why this is so?

DISCOURSE AND LANGUAGE

Language is viewed as the foundation of discourse and identity in social relations. According to Cooper,[32] language serves as a model for 'all systems of communication, including social systems' and can be understood as a 'structure' or a 'system'. Saussure[33] developed a theory based on language as a system of signs. Potter and Wetherell[34] say that Saussure's basic thinking is a distinction between a concept and its associated speech sound; an example of this being the concept of 'tree' (a living object with a trunk, branches and leaves) called the *signified* and the speech sound 'tree', which Saussure calls the *signifier*. Saussure calls the combination of the two linguistic terms the *sign*. His initial thoughts were that signification (the process) was made up of the signifier (the sound image) and the signified (the concept) and that these two terms together made up what is known as the sign. Saussure[35] developed this early systems perspective of language based on the notion that the signifier was merely the carrier of meaning (the signified); that is, language was located in the object. However, as Potter and Wetherell[36] point out, Saussure later changed his view and argued that the sign is not fixed but is arbitrary in nature because the sign 'rests on a demonstration that neither the nature of the signifier, signified or their relationship[s] is fixed or determined'. This argument suggests that there is no essential relationship between the signifier and the signified; between the word 'tree' and an object with a trunk, leaves and branches. To take another example, the popular signifier for sweet confectionary (the signified) is 'candy' in the USA, 'sweets' in the UK and 'lollies' in Australia. In short, the sound used is essentially arbitrary, and humans have the capacity to produce a vast range of sounds, where different languages use certain sounds for conveying meaning and ignore others. There is no necessity that certain sounds should carry some meanings and others not.

Cooper[37] went on to say language is thus described as a process that had no source and was never-ending: 'Language as a system reveals a structure that far from the positivity and fixity of sign as meaning, is essentially incomplete and without solid foundation, with neither beginning nor end.' Saussure[38] also argued that the continuous process of language was based on the concept of difference; that is, what it is not rather than what it is. Cooper[39] then argued that 'we do not experience things in themselves in their full, unitary presence but as transforms or differences of them'. Based on this view we can say that the 'world of form and communication deals only in differences. In the mind there were no objects or events; the mind contains only differences [and that] … Difference, or information, cannot be localised or placed because it is dimensionless [because] … A difference … is a transform of the world, and the mind records the difference.'[40] Cooper[41] used Bateson's[42] notion of map and mapmaker as the recording of differences; for example, altitude to explain the concept of 'difference' and 'mind'. He said: 'What gets on the map, in fact, is difference, be it … a difference in vegetation, a difference in population structure, difference in surface or whatever.'[43]

Both Bateson[44] and Saussure[45] saw information in terms of having no fixed location; where Saussure said that language was a structure of traces, Bateson saw language as 'dimensionless' and thus could not be located. The 'dimensionless', non-locatable nature of language made it 'unameanable' to natural or 'essential' regulation and control.[46] This meant that some action had to be taken to make the 'unameanable' become amenable, or the undecidable become decidable, or extract order from disorder, and this is brought about through the manipulation of information. As Bateson[47] states: 'Information in the technical sense is that which excludes certain alternatives. The machine with a governor does not elect the steady state; it prevents itself from staying in any alternative state; and in all such ... systems, corrective action is brought about by *difference* ... The difference between some present state and some 'preferred' state activates the corrective response.'[48] This notion of 'governor' is an important concept for organisational members in that alternative states are prevented by some predetermined instruction (explicit and implicit in the 'preferred state'). So in everyday organisational life there is not necessarily a 'steady state', but instead 'corrective action' processes brought about by the existence of difference (variance). These alternative states can be described in terms of anti-organisation theories[49] or retro-organisation theories.[50] Cooper[51] concludes that mind should be viewed as a 'circuit of differences' and, like difference, mind is 'not locatable' but is a process that is 'immanent throughout the system of differences'. In short, this means that the 'relationship' between information (or difference) and action is 'affected through exclusion'.

THE REGULATORY NATURE OF DISCOURSE

While we strive to influence the discourses we are part of, our ability to act strategically is limited by the discourses that accompany our intervention and the complex processes of social construction that precede it.[52] This is mainly because within any discourse there are rules of regulation and control, many of which are more likely to be implicit rather than explicit. If you were not part of the miners' discourse you would not necessarily understand the serious nature of the term 'scab', but the term labels a set of behaviours that were deemed 'taboo' by the working community. Drawing on the work of Foucault, Davies and Mitchell[53] analysed these regulation processes in some detail when they argued that discourse regulated behaviour through language and social interaction, and described these processes of discourse regulation in terms of the principles of exclusion, limitation and communication.

Principles of exclusion: external regulation

This principle explains the external regulation of discourse that is from outside a particular discourse. There are three basic principles of exclusion that define and legitimise meaning and rationality within discourse. They are:

* *Prohibition.* This is what can and cannot be said, the manner in which it can be said and which actors can legitimately speak within a discourse.
* *Division.* This distinguishes between those who 'rationally' should have a legitimate right of participation in a discourse and those who should not. Divisional practices seek to manipulate the discourse by the creation of classifications that redistributed the participation in the discourse.
* *Truth and power.* This is the creation of opposition between the true and the false. If truth, in any discourse, was determined then a set of implicit rules can be developed and maintained. These would seek to deny new arguments and contributions through the application of rules, which defined things as false, in opposition to the defined truth.

By use of these principles, individuals who simply wished to voice a contribution could be excluded, as they were rendered ignorant against the knowledge voice of the legitimate.

Principles of limitation: internal regulation

Discourse may be regulated internally through the application of principles that limit participation. These principles operate to classify, order and distribute the discourse to allow for and deal with irruption or unpredictability. The principles are commentary, rarefaction and disciplines.

COMMENTARY

Commentary makes new discourse possible on the understanding that the meaning rules that governed the primary discourse are maintained and that the new is based upon a repetition of the old. This is to prevent the unexpected from entering into a discourse by:

- regulating the speaker who can say something other than what was currently being discoursed but must do so within the genre, style, and language of that discourse
- constant reference to the recent past of the discourse in order to prevent irruptive change, thus constraining the discourse to what was expected and normal practice.

RAREFACTION

Rarefaction regulates the discourse through the speaker conventions, which prescribes the role of a speaker, rather than an individual; that is, it is concerned with the repetition of identity. Rarefaction thus observes and controls the unifying principles of the group(s) within the discourse, the source from which their meanings have been derived and the nature of consistency in the collections of discourse within that group.

DISCIPLINES

Disciplines regulate discourse through the application of rules, definition, techniques and media. A discipline contains a fundamental set of beliefs on which all new work was founded and the truth of a discipline is valid only within a specific context. Disciplines are also constrained in functioning, by the application of other principles, and this needs to be understood in analysis.

Principles of communication: ritual context

These principles are concerned with the conditions in which communication is conducted, including the ritual framework surrounding all discourse.

- *Societies or communities of discourse.* These operate to restrict the discourse to a particular group, social classification or organisational section and is affected by disciplines as the very act of communicating in certain disciplines implies membership of a restrictive group or structure.
- *Social appropriation.* Closely related to societies of discourse, it was the means of appropriating discourse that were in themselves principles of communication that regulated and controlled membership of a discourse. Membership of the discourse could become a political means of maintaining or modifying the appropriation of other discourses.
- *Regulation and control.* This is concerned with systems of regulation and control of discourses. An inherently political process, it leads to the control of production and the manipulation of knowledge objects; that is, those elements of a socially constructed reality that were taken to be relevant in the knowledge domains of those within organisational discourses.

To summarise, it has been argued that discourse is a regulated system of statements, texts and relationships,[54] but one that is not just explicit in nature, as discourse is very much implicit in nature: it is symbolic and its true meaning is often hidden to the outsider. There is a need to 'read between the lines'[55] to interpret and make sense of what is going on. To do this one needs to become an 'insider'; one who is privy to the metalanguage of the discourse (which is often regarded as the undisputed truth itself). Exclusion limits participation and determines status, which often means that outsiders are regarded as being 'less ordered' and 'less unitary'.[56] This suggests the existence of a boundary within discourse and that this boundary is manipulated both covertly and overtly. Organisational discourse is not easy to change because vested interests, and regulation and control, are two of the foundations upon which modern organisations are built.

Discourse and context

It is also suggested above that not only is discourse-regulated, but it is also context-specific in that the context of the discourse is created from the 'discursive interactions' that become the environment in which 'further interactions' occur.[57] For example, in normal times, turning up for work is an acceptable behaviour; in fact, if you do not turn up for work in normal times the same people may call you a 'bludger' (a construction of self by others). In abnormal times (for example, during a strike), turning up for work has a different connotation. Nothing has changed except the context in which the behaviour occurred, but a new construction of self is constructed by others. We can argue, then, that an individual will have multiple identities that are dependent on context. If we return to the movie *Brassed Off* and explore the character of Phil, he exhibits a number of contextual identities: parent, miner, musician, union member, son, circus clown and, when he is admitted to hospital, a patient. Each one of these identities is managed in some way through the tacit and invisible processes of 'reading between the lines' of appropriate discourses.

Because identity is context-specific we can also ask about the number of discourses. How many discourses are we members of and what is our position and role within these? The answer is probably as many as there are identifiable social groups or interactions within an individual's field of experience. A more important question would be: Which discourses are dominant in one's field? In the movie quoted above, there were two clearly dominant macro or meta discourses:

- *Management discourse.* The management discourse was a representation of most classic management discourse with its attendant metalanguage and principles. It was also very much a political discourse, in that management's ultimate aim was to close the mine down according to the government's wishes.
- *Miners' discourse.* The miners' discourse was an alternative discourse to the management discourse[58] and a little more interesting in that:
  1 It existed in opposition to the management discourse; that is, management and miners did not seem to share a common discourse (it was pluralistic and not unitary), which suggests some form of resistance.
  2 It extended beyond the confines of the pit and influenced the mining community; that is, their families and their recreation. For example, the discourse quoted above took place in a public house.
  3 It was as robust as the management discourse in its principles and practices; that is, it was entrenched and not easy to change.
  4 It did not seem to be governed by a sophisticated metalanguage (technical); that is, miners tended to use everyday object language.

The following framework can assist us to structure enquiries about any OD project in terms of how discourse impacts on OD and change.

Communities of discourse

We can say, then, that if organisations are made up of multiple discourses, it stands to reason that it is possible for an individual to have multiple identities based on their location within or external to those discourses. If this is so, then we can begin to understand our organisational discourses in terms of communities of discourse. Within this frame of thinking, Northedge[59] adopts a sociocultural perspective to describe discourse in terms of a community. He says: 'Any grouping that regularly communicates about particular issues for particular purposes develops shared ways of talking about and understanding those issues … become participants in a discourse community.' In terms of Northedge's[60] description of a discourse community, knowledge becomes a tangible product to be transferred to other discourse members. While Northedge[61] describes discourse in terms of a community of sharing (but not necessarily an equal one), he went on to say that specialist discourse communities had hierarchies, which were described in terms of:

- core versus peripheral
- generative versus vicarious
- convergent versus variant understanding.

CORE VERSUS PERIPHERAL

Northedge[62] describes discourse as having membership located from the core to the periphery. At the core are the high-status members of the community, with the 'ordinary members' located away from the centre towards the edge. Forums at the periphery are generally where new members participate. An example here is the Australian Parliament, which comprises the Cabinet (core), the front bench (general membership) and the backbenches (periphery). In organisational terms, the core can be interpreted as senior management, the ordinary members become middle and first-line management, and non-management personnel populate the periphery. In short, membership of the discourse community is described in terms of stakeholder participation based on location and knowledge ownership status.

GENERATIVE VERSUS VICARIOUS

On this dimension, Northedge[63] argues that some stakeholders contribute directly to the discourse (normally senior management), while others participate vicariously (indirectly). For example, much communication within the organisational discourse is carried out through the processes of writing and announcements. For many organisational members the only means of contributing is through vicarious participation. This suggests a differential in stakeholder contribution and power.

CONVERGENT VERSUS VARIANT UNDERSTANDING

Here Northedge[64] talks about shared meaning in situations where there are different levels of understanding. Simply put, what you understand about what is being spoken can be different between discourse members. Northedge[65] goes on to argue that the sharing of knowledge between stakeholders who understand differently is a key function of discourse. From a discourse perspective, this does not mean that the different understandings have equal status. Those stakeholders who are close to the centre or core of the discourse set standards for the community. The more prominent stakeholders of the discourse will tend to converge with the mainstream thinking, while those on the periphery will be more 'variant' in discourse usage.[66] A conceptual model showing discourse and stakeholder membership is shown in Figure 14.1.

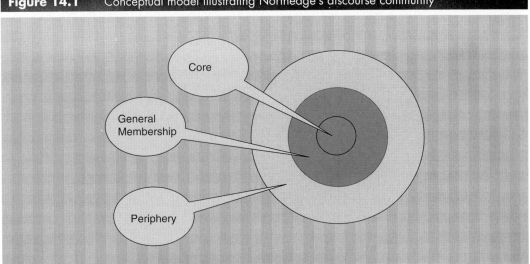

Figure 14.1   Conceptual model illustrating Northedge's discourse community

In this model the three categories of stakeholders are shown: core, general membership and periphery. When applied to an organisation, the core becomes the most senior members of the discourse community who tend to define knowledge and practice within the community. The general membership becomes the appointed managers within the organisation that adopt and distribute the knowledge and practices of the core group, while the periphery stakeholders are the non-management members of the organisation who tend only to contribute in a marginal or vicarious way.

The following application gives an example of an industrial dispute not unlike that in *Brassed Off*. This application provides an opportunity to analyse social interactions using the discourse model described above.

APPLiCATiON 14.2

DISCOURSE ANALYSIS RESEARCH

An example of communities of discourse in action can be found in a research paper based on an industrial relations dispute in a major seaport in Australia. In this research, Selsky, Spicer and Teicher[67] examined the changing employment relationships between employers and employees in the stevedoring industry. Selsky et al.[68] argued that when major disputes occur they unsettle the 'pre-existing ordering of relationships among actors' who were participants in a 'shared field of action', which they called a domain.[69] This unsettling results in forcing the participants to 'engage in complex sense-making processes to understand the new situation'. In short, a new discourse was being implemented (but not without a struggle). In this dispute external parties – members of the media – were identified as playing a pivotal role in the direction the dispute took. Through the media the discourse texts constructed by the parties to the dispute were publicised, which had the effect of shaping the actors' and external parties' interpretation of the situation.

Critical Thinking Questions: Identify instances of social interactions where new replace old discourses. What role did external agencies play in this transition phase? Based on the discourse model above what role did you play in the transition?

Discourse boundaries

Latham and Whiteley[70] argue that a discourse boundary is a conceptual frame within which a certain type of discourse is carried out. Latham and Whiteley[71] go on to say that, for the manager, this is important because when discourse is happening that implicitly defines the structure and process of the discourse, it also has both an inclusive and exclusive effect on the participants in the discourse. This idea is based on the Foucauldian notion that those who are included are subjected to order and behaviour as defined by rules, principles and metalanguage.[72] Those who are excluded create alternative discourses that may or may not influence others. However, those included in the discourse are seen as being privileged, while those excluded are less privileged.[73] In other words, it is reasonable to assume that bosses want to converse with employees in an inclusive way, but if they inadvertently erect discourse barriers, or fail to change existing ones by adopting discourse that is derived from defined rules and regulations, then it would be difficult to attract arguments or even alternative views.

The bond

For every relationship there has to be a bond; that is, something that binds the parties of the relationship together. In a classic bureaucratic organisation the bond is made up of rules, regulations, policies and procedures, and any diversion from the stated norms will initiate sanctions from the authorities above. A bond can be defined as a substance or substances used to bind surfaces together, so we can see that in a formal bureaucratic organisation the relationship boundaries (where the bond occurs) tend to be rigid and well defined. Cooper and Law[74] also say that normally in a human relationship, the surface in the relationship is 'intrinsically unordered and directionless' in nature. Therefore, the rigid nature of a formal boundary requires some kind of force to retain its influence, which is usually achieved through the power implied in formal authority positions. Terms like 'tension' and 'strength' are related to the concept of power. In terms of a discourse boundary the weaker the unity, the more power (adhesive) is needed to maintain the bond. In other words, managers would need to evoke their organisational power and control to preserve the structure of the discourse, but not necessarily the process. The stronger the unity, the less power (adhesive) is required. The power differential can be described as the strength of the unity with and without the adhesive.

From a management perspective it is to their advantage to develop strong discourse relationships, as this will reduce the need to waste scarce resources on maintaining a weak relationship (procedures and control mechanisms). Unity in discourse means that both the boss and the employee are conversing and relating in an informal as well as a formal mode.[75] Therefore, the manager does not need to use power as there are numerous points of unity holding the relationships together. Figure 14.2 is an example of a conceptual model of a complex discourse boundary; one that includes formal and informal elements. This figure shows the boundary's elements and their relationship to the participants in a particularly strong discourse relationship. Each half of the figure represents an individual in the relationship. The thicker vertical and horizontal lines represent the complexity of the boundary in terms of number of points of unity.

Operating within a simple discourse boundary, the manager would expect to need to use more bonding adhesive (formal procedures and control) because there would be fewer points of unity and more gaps that needed something to hold them together. This is because there is a superimposed direction and structure to the discourse. In short, the discourse is a fabrication and not one that would be acceptable in a more natural setting. For example, a position description form (PDF) would define a work role in terms of tasks, duties and responsibilities of a subordinate. Simply put, the relationship is partial through choice by the 'core' discourse stakeholders. However, to maintain an effective discourse relationship with this subordinate, rules, regulations, policies and procedures need to be in place to control the direction of the discourse. Figure 14.3 shows the same elements of a

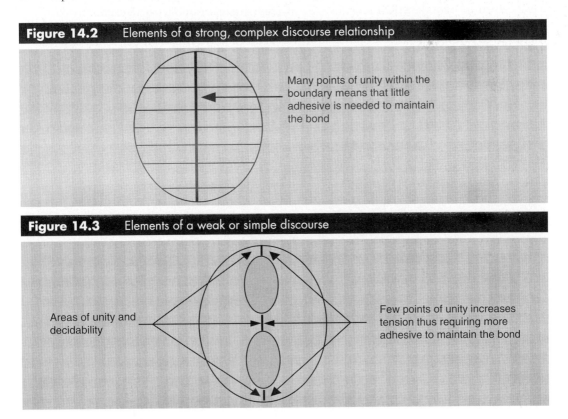

Figure 14.2 Elements of a strong, complex discourse relationship

Many points of unity within the boundary means that little adhesive is needed to maintain the bond

Figure 14.3 Elements of a weak or simple discourse

Areas of unity and decidability

Few points of unity increases tension thus requiring more adhesive to maintain the bond boundary as the previous figure, but in terms of a particularly weak or fragile discourse relationship. There are fewer points of unity, therefore requiring more adhesive to maintain the bond.

In summary, relationship boundaries are complex and in the past, through the application of scientific management principles, managers have attempted to reduce the complexity of these relationships to the minimum interactions necessary to complete the tasks. Latham[76] found that these types of relationships were weak in structure and liable to fracture at any time. In weak relationships managers tended to resort to bureaucratic means to maintain the relationship. In the case where complex relationships were allowed to exist in the organisation, Latham[77] found that organisational members were more friendly and happier in their roles, which in some cases led to more innovation and creativity.

A combined model

The combination of Davies and Mitchell's[78] principles of discourse regulation, Northedge's[79] concept of communities of discourse, and Latham and Whiteley's[80] concept of boundary provides an active process model that reveals important insights into organisational behaviour. Figure 14.4 illustrates the dynamics of the model.

In this model both membership and boundary can be seen. What is also shown is the regulation process of the boundary. Further analysis of these processes should reveal the nature of any constraints affecting the management of these processes. For example, the boundary can be interrogated using the principles of discourse regulation (as described above) as a guiding framework. This analysis can be carried out by identifying the Who? What? Why? How? Where? and When? of a particular discourse process.

A further development to the conceptual discourse model maps functional relationships onto the discourse community to show the distribution of access to the organisational core each function may have. Figure 14.5 shows this development.

From this model the proportions or disproportions of discourse membership can be identified and explored. For example, in this model the finance function is disproportionally represented when compared with the HRM function. Mainstream organisation theory tends not to show these sorts of dynamics. For example, as discussed above, the classic mainstream organisation chart fails to identify the more dynamic processes at work in the organisation. Wider application of the discourse model developed above can provide insight into how the organisation fits into the wider community and thus identifies other stakeholders. Using the existing models shown above, discourse analysis can be carried out to show membership, regulatory processes and proportional contribution of stakeholder membership. This analysis can also provide intra- and

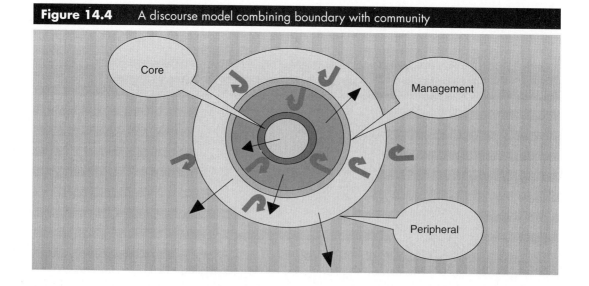

Figure 14.4   A discourse model combining boundary with community

Figure 14.5 Discourse boundary model showing functional membership

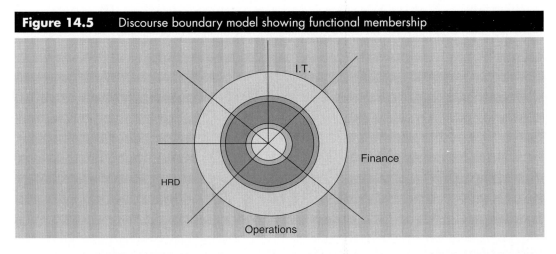

Figure 14.6 Community discourse model illustrating a discourse mapping process

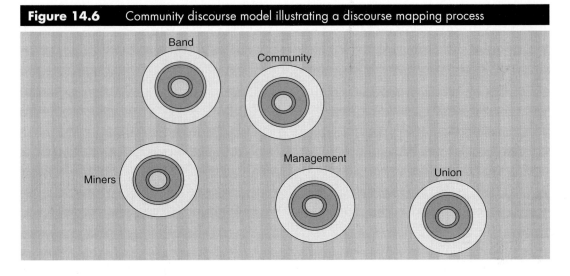

inter-discourse membership links and the effects of change on these links. Figure 14.6 illustrates how a community stakeholder discourse map can be developed, based on the film *Brassed Off*.

The approach to organisational analysis based on community discourse analysis provides an alternative perspective to mainstream approaches. The nature of analysis provides management and other organisation stakeholders with a model to guide them in exploring the lesser visible aspects of relationships that can have a significant effect on organisational behaviour. Such exercises can be built into organisation development and change programs. An example of such a program is briefly described in Application 14.3.

APPLiCATiON 14.3

MANAGEMENT DEVELOPMENT WORKSHOP

A management development workshop was developed and run for a group of senior managers in a major Australian logistics organisation. The theme of the workshop was the management of major organisational development and cultural change. The program was held over a four-day period, with a four-hour session devoted to a discourse workshop. As a way of demonstrating and utilising the community discourse model described above, the film *Brassed Off* (as described above) was used as the source of data for analysis. The film attempts to show the dynamics and effects the threat of

▷▷

closure of the local coal mine has on stakeholders and members of the wider community. One of the outcomes of the workshop was an active commitment to the analysis of community discourses as part of the overall strategic planning process.

Critical Thinking Questions: Watch the movie *Brassed Off* and answer the following:

- What are the core, general and peripheral members of each community discourse?
- What effect does language, both spoken and unspoken, have on community behaviour? Give examples.
- What are the possible effects that the dissolution of one discourse (the mine closure) might have on other societal discourses?
- In what circumstances does the use of principles, values, community membership and culture regulate communities of discourse?

NEW ORGANISATION DEVELOPMENT AND DISCOURSE

In their paper 'Organisational Discourse and the New OD', Marshak and Grant[81] show how discourse analysis can and does contribute to OD theory. To begin with, they state that from the 1980s onwards, constructionist and postmodern approaches increasingly influenced the social sciences and their subsequent contribution to OD and change management. Underpinning this contribution is the notion of multiple realities and challenging the existence of a singular truth: '[I]f there are multiple realities then there can be no transcendent, objective truth to be discovered. [Rather], the issue becomes how agreements about the reality of a situation are actually, or could be most effectively, negotiated among the contending points of view.'[82] It is further argued that realities are subjective, which lend themselves to political influences and the subsequent related power dynamics.[83] A number of what are seen as new OD theories and techniques were identified as being amenable to discourse analysis and included:

- *Appreciative inquiry.* This approach aims for transformational change by focusing on organisation members' positive experiences and appealing to their hopes and aspirations.[84]
- *Large-group interventions.* This aims to seek common ground and gain agreement among a plurality of viewpoints (all considered legitimate versions of reality). In these approaches: 'Data is gathered and used … for the purpose of presenting multiple possibilities and perspectives'.[85] This type of intervention is used in place of bringing objective facts to the discussion (which invokes a particular dominant discourse).[86]
- *Changing mindsets and consciousness.* Some practitioners and academics argue that transformational change 'requires a change in consciousness'[87] and that this orientation 'understands transformation as being primarily driven by shifts in human consciousness'.[88]
- *Multiple cultures, multiple realities and diversity.* This is based on the question: How do various groups establish or reinforce inclusionary and exclusionary standards, practices and paradigms that may favour their own interests? This approach also recognises how power may be involved in the establishment of a version of reality and requirements that may favour some groups and interests over others.[89]

Links to organisational discourse

Many employees of organisations easily and early on recognise the multiple nature of subcultures operating within their own workplaces. Each specialised function, for example, will have its own subculture and methods of discoursing. For example, the finance department may depend heavily on accounting reports, rates, various financial calculation models, and so on, whereas the human resource department may focus on the human elements of welfare, safety, development, and recruitment and selection. From these two examples alone it is not difficult to appreciate the differences likely to occur in discourse use. Several overlaps between new OD and organisational discourse were identified. Some of the elements they seem to have in common include:[90]

- a shift from the more classic, mainstream, objectivist orientation of analysis towards newer and more critical theories and orientations
- a core interest in how discourses, dialogues, conversations and other forms of communication directly and indirectly influence and shape organisational processes, behaviour and change
- a focus of attention on the influence of mindsets in shaping behaviour, and the ways in which language in turn creates and reinforces mindsets
- the existence of multiple socially constructed realities
- the challenging and changing of 'storylines' through the analysis of political and power dynamics at work within discourses.

Within organisations we have competing discourses, each one trying to become the accepted truth based on different knowledges. Some base their truth on economic arguments like the neoliberal economic rationalists, some on values (for example, the unitary perspective of the enterprise culture), while others are based on philosophy (for example, the philosophy of positive science). Application 14.4 discusses three of these competing discourses affecting today's organisations and change.

APPLiCATiON 14.4

THE CLASSICAL MANAGEMENT DISCOURSE

This discourse is over a hundred years old and yet it is still alive and well in many organisations around the globe.[91] For the purpose of this chapter we will focus on two of its pioneers: Henri Fayol and Fredrick Taylor.[92]

HENRI FAYOL AND THE GENERAL PRINCIPLES OF MANAGEMENT

To begin with Fayol was an engineer (as were many of his contemporaries) and with his background firmly rooted in the middle classes, he developed a particular perspective on managing organisations. For Fayol the management function only operated on human resources, and good management depended on conditions, indiscriminately labelled as principles, laws, rules and so on.[93] Fayol identified 14 principles of good management:

1 division of work (more commonly known as job specialisation)
2 authority and responsibility
3 discipline
4 unity of command
5 unity of direction
6 subordination of individual interests to common interest
7 remuneration of personnel
8 centralisation
9 scalar chain (a recognisable line of authority)
10 order
11 equity
12 stability of tenure of personnel
13 initiative
14 esprit de corps (unity).

Fayol advocated intensive management training programs to lift the level of management skill to meet with his principles.

FREDRICK TAYLOR AND SCIENTIFIC MANAGEMENT

Taylor was also an engineer, but unlike Fayol he based his discourse on what he had observed while working, most notably the Bethlehem steel works. One of his key observations was the restriction

▷▷

of output by the workers, an activity Taylor called 'soldiering'. He did not blame the workers for this practice but the management for not encouraging the workforce to increase production through payment incentives. Taylor came up with four principles of management:

1 Develop a science for each element of an individual's work, which replaces the old rule-of-thumb method.
2 Scientifically select and then train, teach and develop the worker.
3 Heartily co-operate with the workers so as to ensure that all work is done in accordance with the principles of the science that has been developed.
4 Divide work and responsibility almost equally between management and workers, where managers take over all work and the greater part of responsibility.

Critical Thinking Question: In what ways would workplace discourse be affected if scientific management principles were introduced?

These principles raised in Application 14.4 are in fact the basis for particular organisational discourses that were very powerful within management circles. Throughout the 20th century, the majority of management practices in organisations were carried out based on the principles stated above.[94] The 1980s, however, saw the emergence of an alternative management discourse that was to challenge the dominant discourse for the management crown. This was based on the philosophy of the 'enterprise culture', an anti-bureaucracy culture led by Peters and Waterman[95] with one of its main aspects being total quality management (TQM).

The discourse of total quality management

It was Edwards Deming who pioneered this approach to organisational management. He based his philosophy around the elimination of what he saw as being retroactive management practices that he argued were the cause of poor performance because of defective management systems. Some of those defects in the old style of management included:

- lack of constancy of purpose (the organisation is just drifting along)
- emphasis on short-term returns
- evaluation by performance, merit rating or annual performance review processes
- management mobility (short-term tenure of managers leading to 'job hopping')
- decision making based on visible figures alone (no evaluation of hidden effects of good organisation; for example, satisfied customers normally return)
- over-reliance on surveillance and control systems and techniques.

In his foreword to the book, *The Deming Management Method*,[96] Deming did not hold back in condemning those contemporary management practices of the day, which were based on classical management theories and principles: 'The follies of the systems of management that thrived in the expanding market … are now all too obvious. They must now be blasted out, new construction commenced. Patchwork will not suffice.' In its place, Deming recommended the implementation of an all-inclusive system of management based on 14 principles:

1 The creation of a constancy of purpose.
2 Adopt the new philosophy.[97]
3 Cease dependence on mass inspection.
4 End the practice of awarding business on price tag alone.
5 Implement continuous improvement practices.
6 Institute training and retraining.
7 Institute leadership.
8 Drive out fear.
9 Break down barriers between functions and departments.
10 Eliminate slogans and poster campaigns aimed at the workers.
11 Eliminate numerical quotas.
12 Remove barriers to doing a good job.
13 Institute robust education and retraining programs.
14 Work together to implement the above points.

All three of the contributors shown above can be viewed as discourses – each one a product of a social construction process. If you read a little of the history of these contributors you begin to get a 'feel' about what social factors were influencing their rationale; for example, middle class, engineering and mathematically oriented, with objective worldviews. Table 14.1 shows the three discourses together and highlights the differences and hence the struggle between the three for supremacy. Notice how very similar these discourses are. They are saying similar things using different terms; for example, esprit de corps – heartily cooperate – work together.

Enter stage right yet more management discourses including reflexive studies and a reassessment as to where the business world is heading. Handy[98] was a contributor to this perspective and painted a pessimistic picture of the future if we go on producing and consuming the same way as we currently are. Handy questioned the viability of organisations that stand alone and advocated for a more federally based structure to the new global economy. So here we are seeing another discourse being created (one based on political principles) in an attempt to construct an alternative way of discussing and managing modern workplaces. As Handy[99] states: '[F]ederalism is particularly appropriate since it offers a well recognised way to deal with paradoxes of power and control: the need to make things big by keeping them small; to encourage autonomy but within bounds; to combine variety and shared purpose, individuality

Table 14.1 Comparison of management discourses in the 20th century

Fayol	Taylor	Deming
1 division of work (more commonly known as job specialisation) 2 authority and responsibility 3 discipline 4 unity of command 5 unity of direction 6 subordination of individual interests to common interest 7 remuneration of personnel 8 centralisation 9 scalar chain (a recognisable line of authority) 10 order 11 equity 12 stability of tenure of personnel 13 initiative 14 esprit de corps (unity)	1 Develop a science for each element of an individual's work, which replaces the old rule-of-thumb method. 2 Scientifically select and then train, teach and develop the worker. 3 Heartily co-operate with the workers so as to ensure that all work is done in accordance with the principles of the science that has been developed. 4 Divide work and responsibility almost equally between management and workers, where managers take over all work and the greater part of responsibility.	1 The creation of a constancy of purpose. 2 Adopt the new philosophy. 3 Cease dependence on mass inspection. 4 End the practice of awarding business on price tag alone. 5 Implement continuous improvement practices. 6 Institute training and retraining. 7 Institute leadership. 8 Drive out fear. 9 Break down barriers between functions and departments. 10 Eliminate slogans, poster campaigns aimed at the workers. 11 Eliminate numerical quotas. 12 Remove barriers to doing a good job. 13 Institute robust education and retraining programs. 14 Work together to implement the above points.

and partnership, local and global, tribal region and nation state, or nation state and regional bloc.' Here we see a challenge to the old order on management discourse. In this case there is a call to reshape organisations and their relationships with each other. So the focus of this discourse is external whereas those described above are internally focused. This has some serious implications for OD and change management, because many of the techniques are internally focused.

SUMMARY

In this chapter we have attempted to bring together theory and processes from different discourses to show how they can be linked in such a way as to provide alternative perceptions about organisation structure and behaviour. We do not suggest that these approaches be adopted and all other OD and change initiatives abandoned, but instead that the approaches described above be used alongside prevailing initiatives as a way of emerging wider and richer understandings of the wide variable nature of behaviour in organisations. In doing this you are likely to begin to see new and different issues and behaviours that are often left unseen and missed.

ACTIVITIES

Review questions

① What is the difference between realist and constructionist worldviews?

② How is discourse regulated? Give examples.

③ How does language influence organisational behaviour through discourse?

④ How does discourse construct identity?

⑤ How are knowledge and social actions related?

⑥ Why is it important to understand discourse in context?

⑦ Describe discourse communites in terms of: core versus peripheral; generative versus vicarious; and convergent versus variant understanding.

Discussion and essay questions

① Scene: The delivery room in a maternity hospital.
Pregnant woman: What do I do?
Doctor: Nothing dear, you're not qualified!
(From Monty Python's *The Meaning of Life*)
Discuss this dialogue in terms of competing discourses and accepted social mores.

② Give examples of communities of discourse in an organisation of your choice. Identify members and their location within the communities.

③ Analyse a discourse of your choice and discuss the effects the regulatory process has on discourse membership and behaviour.

④ Using examples, discuss ways and means that discourse analysis can assist in the management of OD and change projects.

NOTES

1 J.W. Potter and M. Wetherell, *Discourse and Social Psychology: Beyond Attitudes and Behaviour* (London: Sage Publications, 1987).
2 D. Grant, C. Hardy. C. Oswick and L. Putnam (eds), *The Sage Handbook of Organizational Discourse* (London: Sage, 2004); N. Phillips and C. Hardy, *Discourse Analysis: Investigating Processes of Social Construction* (Thousand Oaks, London and New Delhi: Sage, 2002); T.A. Van Dijk, 'The study of discourse', in T.A. Van Dijk, ed., *Discourse as structure and process: Discourse studies*, vol. 1: 'A multidisciplinary introduction' (London: Sage, 1997): 1-34; T.A. Van Dijk, 'Discourse as interaction society', in T.A. Van Dijk, ed., *Discourse as a structure and process: Discourse studies*, vol. 2: 'A multidisciplinary introduction' (Newbury Park, CA: Sage, 1997): 1-38.
3 J. Henriques, W. Hooloway, C. Urwin, C. Venn. and V. Walkerdine, *Changing the Subject* (London: Methuen, 1984).
4 K. Legge, *Human Resource Management – Rhetorics and Realities* (London: MacMillan Press Ltd, 1995).
5 Henriques et al., *Changing the Subject*, op. cit.
6 Legge, *Human Resource Management – Rhetorics and Realities*, op. cit.
7 ibid.
8 M. Herman, *Brassed Off* (London: Channel Four, 1997).
9 Legge, *Human Resource Management – Rhetorics and Realities*, op. cit.
10 Legge, *Human Resource Management – Rhetorics and Realities*, op. cit.
11 T. Keenoy and C. Oswick, '"To Explain is to Destroy": Some Reflections on the Discursive Reconstitution of HRM', 3rd International Critical management Studies Conference (Lancaster University School of Management, 2003).
12 M. Alvesson, *Postmodernism and Social Research* (Buckingham, PA: Open University Press, 2002): 67.
13 Grant et al., *The Sage Handbook of Organizational Discourse*, op. cit: 3.
14 R. Cooper, 'Organization/disorganization', in J.P. Hassard and D. Pym (eds), *The Theory and Philosophy of Organizations: Critical Issues and New Perspectives* (London: Routledge, 1990): 167–97.
15 F. Mueller, J. Sillince, C. Harvey and C. Howorth, 'A Rounded Picture Is What We Need', *Organization Studies*, 25:1 (2004): 75–93.
16 G.H. Mead, *Mind, Self and Society* (Chicago: University of Chicago Press, 1963/1934).
17 A. Schütz, *Collected Papers 1: The problem of social reality* (The Hague: Martinus Nijhoff, 1973): 207-59.
18 P. Berger and T. Luckmann, *The Social Construction of Reality* (London: Penguin, 1967).
19 V. Burr, *An Introduction to Social Constructionism* (London: Routledge, 1995).
20 Berger and Luckmann, *The Social Construction of Reality*, op. cit.
21 Adapted from Burr, *An Introduction to Social Constructionism*, op. cit.
22 See, for example: R. Chia, 'Discourse Analysis as Organizational Analysis', *Organization*, 7:3 (2000): 513–18; R. Cooper, 'Information, Communication and Organization: A Post-structural Revision', *Journal of Mind and Behaviour*, 8:3 (1987): 395–416; C. Jones and A. Spicer, 'The Sublime Object of Entrepreneurship', *Organization*, 12:2 (2005): 223–46; D. Hyorth and C. Steyaert, eds, *Narrative and Discursive Approaches in Entrepreneurship* (Cheltenham: Edward Elgar, 2004).
23 Chia, 'Discourse Analysis as Organizational Analysis', op. cit.
24 ibid.
25 Phillips and Hardy, *Discourse Analysis: Investigating Processes of Social Construction*, op. cit.
26 ibid.
27 V. Burr, *An Introduction to Social Constructionism*, op. cit.
28 K. Gergen, 'The social constructionist movement on modern psychology', *American Psychologist*, 40 (1985): 266–75.
29 Burr, *An Introduction to Social Constructionism*, op. cit.
30 ibid.
31 P. Aries, *Centuries of Childhood: A social history of family life* (New York: Vintage, 1962).
32 Cooper, 'Organization/disorganization', op. cit.
33 F. Saussure, *Course in General Linguistics* (London: Fontana/Collins, 1974).
34 Potter and Wetherell, *Discourse and Social Psychology: Beyond Attitudes and Behaviour*, op. cit.
35 Saussure, *Course in General Linguistics*, op. cit.
36 Potter and Wetherell, *Discourse and Social Psychology: Beyond Attitudes and Behaviour*, op. cit.
37 Cooper, 'Organization/disorganization', op. cit.
38 Saussure, *Course in General Linguistics*, op. cit.
39 Cooper, 'Organization/disorganization', op. cit.
40 ibid.
41 ibid.
42 G. Bateson, *Steps to an Ecology of Mind* (New York: Chandler Publishing Company, 1972).
43 G. Bateson in Cooper, 'Organization/disorganization', op. cit.: 176.

44 Bateson, *Steps to an Ecology of Mind*, op. cit.

45 Saussure, *Course in General Linguistics*, op. cit.

46 Cooper, 'Organization/disorganization', op. cit.

47 Bateson, *Steps to an Ecology of Mind*, op. cit.: 176.

48 G. Bateson cited in Cooper, 'Organization/disorganization', op. cit.: 176.

49 G.M. Burrell and G. Morgan, *Sociological Paradigms and Organisational Analysis: Elements of the Sociology of Corporate Life* (London: Heinemann, 1979).

50 G. Burrell, *Pandemonium* (London: Sage Publications, 1997).

51 Cooper, 'Organization/disorganization', op. cit.: 176.

52 Phillips and Hardy, *Discourse Analysis: Investigating Processes of Social Construction*, op. cit.

53 L. Davies and G. Mitchell, 'The Dual Nature of the Impact of IT on Organizational Transformations', in R. Baskerville, S. Smithson, O. Ngwenyama and J.I. DeGross, *Transforming Organizations and Information Technology* (Amsterdam: Elsevier Science B.V., 1994).

54 Henriques et al., *Changing the Subject*, op. cit.

55 Legge, *Human Resource Management – Rhetorics and Realities*, op. cit.

56 Cooper, 'Organization/disorganization', op. cit.

57 Burr, *An Introduction to Social Constructionism*, op. cit.; Potter and Wetherell, *Discourse and Social Psychology: Beyond Attitudes and Behaviour*, op. cit.

58 A. Whiteley, *Managing Change – A Core Values Approach* (Melbourne: MacMillan Education Australia Pty Ltd, 1995).

59 A. Northedge, 'Rethinking Teaching in the Context of Diversity', *Teaching in Higher Education*, 8:1 (2003): 17–32.

60 ibid.

61 ibid.

62 ibid.

63 ibid.

64 ibid.

65 ibid.

66 ibid.

67 J. Selsky, A. Spicer and J. Teicher, '"Totally Un-Australian!": Discursive and Institutional Interplay in the Melbourne Port Dispute of 1997–98', *Journal of Management Studies*, 40:7 (2003): 1730–60.

68 ibid.

69 A domain is a field of relations among a set of organisations that interact around some shared issues or set of concerns (Hardy, 1994; Selsky and Barton, 2000; Trist, 1983), not unlike the 'communities of discourse' discussed above.

70 J. Latham and A. Whiteley, *Managerial Discourse: learning the boundary*, 17th ANZAM Conference (Fremantle, Western Australia, 2003).

71 ibid.

72 Cooper, 'Organization/disorganization', op. cit.; Davies and Mitchell, 'The Dual Nature of the Impact of IT on Organizational Transformations', op. cit.

73 Cooper, 'Organization/disorganization', op. cit.

74 R. Cooper and J. Law, 'Organization: Distal and Proximal Views', in S. Bacharach (ed.), *Research in the Sociology of Organizations* (Greenwich, CN: JAI Press, 1995).

75 Cooper, 'Organization/disorganization', op. cit.

76 J. Latham, 'Boundary Management in Organisations – The Use of Discourse as a Framework of Analysis' (unpublished PhD thesis, Graduate School of Management, Perth: Curtin University of Technology, 2002): 321.

77 ibid.

78 Davies and Mitchell, 'The Dual Nature of the Impact of IT on Organizational Transformations', op. cit.

79 Northedge, 'Rethinking Teaching in the Context of Diversity', op. cit.

80 Latham and Whiteley, *Managerial Discourse: learning the boundary*, op. cit.

81 R. Marshak and D. Grant, 'Organizational Discourse and the New OD', unpublished paper given at the Discourse 06 Conference (The Free University, Amsterdam, Holland, 2006).

82 ibid.

83 See, for example: Berger and Luckmann, 1967; Berquist, 1993; Hancock and Tyler, 2001; Hassard and Parker, 1993; Linstead, 2004; Searle, 1995.

84 F. Barrett and D. Cooperrider, 'Generative Metaphor Intervention: A New Approach for Working with Systems Divided by Conflict and Caught in Defensive Perception', *Journal of Applied Behavioural Science*, 26:2 (1990): 219–39; G. Bushe and A. Kassman, 'When is Appreciative Inquiry Transformational? A Meta-case Analysis', *Journal of Applied Behavioural Science*, 41:2 (2005): 161–81; D. Cooperrider and S. Srivastra, 'Appreciative Inquiry in Organizational Life', in R. Woodman and W. Pasmore (eds), *Research in Organizational Change and Development* (Stamford CT: JAI, 1987).

85 Marshak and Grant, 'Organizational Discourse and the New OD', op. cit.

86 See also: Ackerman et al. (2001); Adams (2005); Beck and Cowan (1996); Senge et al. (1994); in Marshak and Grant, 'Organizational Discourse and the New OD', op. cit.

87 Marshak and Grant, 'Organizational Discourse and the New OD', op. cit.

88 L. Ackerman-Anderson and D. Anderson, 'Awake at the Wheel: Moving Beyond Change Management to Conscious Change Leadership', *OD Practitioner*, 33:3 (2001): 4–10, cited in Marshak and Grant, 'Organizational Discourse and the New OD', op. cit.

89 Marshak and Grant, 'Organizational Discourse and the New OD', op. cit.

90 Adapted from Marshak and Grant, 'Organizational Discourse and the New OD', op. cit.

91 For example; the McDonald's philosophy of management is very much based on the principles of scientific management and Fayol's principles of management. See G. Ritzer, *The McDonaldization of society: an investigation into the changing character of contemporary social life* (Thousand Oaks, CA: Pine Forge Press, 1996).

92 For a fuller background of theorists in this category see J. Shafritz and J. Ott (eds), *Classics of Organization Theory* (Orlando: Harcourt Brace & Company, 1996).

93 H. Fayol (1916) in Shafritz and Ott, *Classics of Organization Theory*, op. cit.

94 Other discourses were introduced during the 20th century; for example, the discourse of the social or human factors in organisations, based on the work of Elton Mayo and the Hawthorne studies. However, they did not replace the classical principle-based practices, but only supplemented the dominant discourse.

95 T. Peters and J. Waterman, *In Search of Excellence* (New York: Harper & Row, 1982).

96 M. Walton, *The Deming Management Method* (London: Allen Mercury, 1989): x.

97 ibid.

98 C. Handy, *Beyond Certainty: The Changing Worlds of Organizations* (London: Hutchinson, 1995).

99 ibid.

Online reading

INFOTRAC® COLLEGE EDITION

For additional readings and reviews on discourse analysis, explore **InfoTrac® College Edition**, your online library. Go to **www.infotrac-college.com** and search for any of the InfoTrac key terms listed below:

- **Discourse**
- **Constructionist nature**
- **Language**

INFOTRAC

15

RESiSTANCE TO CHANGE

By Dr Margaret Heffernan and Anne Smythe, RMIT University

There is a proliferation of resources on 'resistance' in the context of change management. This chapter is not definitive, but draws on academic research, theory and the insights of practitioners and our own practice as management educators, researchers and practitioners. It offers different perspectives from the traditional views of resistance and places it as an integral component in the formative and implementation planning stages of change management. It attempts to diffuse the notion that the employee is at fault if seen to resist, and instead places resistance with the change planning framework as an identifier of ineffective or incomplete change planning.

Before you begin reading this chapter, reflect on what you think resistance is in a change management context. Consider the two opinions below, and then compare them with your opinions. What drives your resistance paradigm, and how is that similar to or different from that of Burnes, and Jick and Peiperl?

> Resistance is a signal that something is wrong with the change process.[1]
>
> Resistance is part of the natural adaptation to change. When resistance is seen as natural it can be seen as a preliminary step to adaptation.[2]

RESISTANCE TO CHANGE: REALITY OR MYTH?

While there is no doubt that resistance is a central concept in organisational change from the perspective of all involved – practitioners, researchers, managers and leaders, and organisational members dealing directly with the impact of change – this chapter will present a view that while resistance may be a legitimate expectation in change management thinking, rethinking human responses to change identifies many outcomes of which resistance is one, albeit one that is very important and often misunderstood. Hence, the focus of this chapter is an attempt to help understand resistance better and, in doing so, how to respond to it more effectively.

Clarke and Clegg[3] propose that because continuous incremental change has been displaced by discontinuous change, organisation environments are less predictable and more complex to manage. Old ways of operating are no longer effective in dealing with the new levels of complexity and require new ways of thinking and practice, especially in the way that organisations manage change. This calls for new paradigms, deconstruction of the old order and development of new assets. Change managers should be mindful that implementing change is complex, and that multiple stakeholders have diverse needs and that no one change implementation strategy is going to satisfy them simultaneously.

Waddell and Sohal[4] note that the research literature recognises resistance as a critical variable in influencing the success or failure of change efforts and some authors attribute the failure of some large-scale corporate change programs directly to employee resistance[5]. Practitioner accounts also feature it as a highly influential and usually very problematic factor[6]. Some accounts refer to it as negative and antithetical to effective change management,[7] others grudgingly acknowledge its presence in the range of responses to change[8] while others regard it as a natural, normal and useful part of the human response to change.[9] Underpinning this is the premise that if change managers continue to use 'resistance' as a generic phrase in a traditional paradigm, and with an expectation that it will have a negative outcome, then this in effect intensifies real resistance. This raises some interesting questions. Does an expectation that resistance to change is natural or negative, that it will occur and that it will require skilled management to overcome actually hinder change implementation processes? Or does the recognition that resistance is a *positive* element of change enhance the change process? And is resistance the most useful framework, or mental model, to categorise human responses to change?

Dent and Goldberg[10] tracked the evolution of the term 'resistance to change' and showed how it found its way into mainstream thinking. Lewin introduced the term as a *systems* concept; as a force affecting managers and employees equally. Misinterpretation of this research saw the term evolve into a psychological concept, creating subjectivity between employees and managers. Dent and Goldberg[11] further suggested that people do not resist change, per se. Rather, people resist the *impact* of the change on their personal status quo, such as feared loss of status, loss of pay or loss of comfort. However, this is not the same as resisting change in its totality. The pervading belief that people do resist change creates psychological and systemic barriers within organisations that can stall the process and progress of change. Just because employees are uncertain about aspects of the impact of change and require more detailed information to allay the uncertainty, this does not mean they are resisting the change. Carnall[12] supports this, suggesting that resistance is a complex element requiring positive and optimistic attitudes from change managers, but in essence resistance is more a response to the change management process. Organisational members may not be resisting the change itself, but are resistant to the *uncertainty* that the change engenders, especially in the formative stages of implementation. Change processes that depend on changing employee attitudes and beliefs are less important than helping employees manage perceptions of the relevance of the change, as well as the likely success of the change outcome and the credibility of the change proposal in terms of organisation strategy and capability to implement it. Managing employee perceptions, especially in the formative stage of implementation when they can arise through the change process, will then assist ongoing performance, self-esteem and success for the change project. Bridges'[13] notion of transition suggests it is not the change that does us in, but rather the transition and the psychological adjustments that people go through to come to terms with the new situation along with other responses. Resistance is a product of this adjustment during transition and Bridges argues that this is a normal, healthy psychological response.

So what do we mean by 'resistance'?

The following section will attempt to address why resistance has been applied as a negative construct in change management thinking and ask that if resistance is an outmoded and limited concept, what do we need to do to shift our thinking to view it more usefully and what are the most effective ways for those leading and managing change processes to respond to it? Causes and manifestations of resistance as one of a range of responses to changes are explored, as well as the impact it has on the implementation of change. In addition, we show that an understanding of these issues enables us all to deal personally with change in a more confident and wise manner.

APPLICATION 15.1

RESPONSES TO RESISTANCE

What does the term 'resistance' mean to you when thinking about organisational change? Write examples drawing on what the organisation situation was, the particular change that was being implemented and your responses to it. Why did you respond that way? Were your responses to the change typical of other colleagues, or did they respond in different ways?

Critical Thinking Questions: Conduct a quick survey with your colleagues. When they are part of organisational change do they resist it, or respond to it in other ways? What patterns emerge in your findings?

Pietersen[14], a change practitioner who has operated at the highest levels of organisations and is currently a Professor of the Practice of Management at Colombia University Business School, is one of the relatively few leadership practitioners who directly and strongly acknowledges that 'we dislike change'. He argues that 'change hurts' and that paradoxically this is the case even if we know the organisations we work for must change, innovate and adapt to survive and that the change is often beneficial. The human response to this, especially when confronted with significant change, is to resist the dislocation that any change inevitably causes because it always triggers feelings of anxiety, threat and loss.[15] We all call upon our defences; consciously and unconsciously, and directly or indirectly, to protect ourselves and help us deal with these feelings.[16] While protective, these defences can also stop an individual or group from adapting to change and when widespread or poorly managed can undermine the very success of the change itself.[17]

Why does 'resistance' remain in the forefront of change management as a negative construct? In the *organisational* context resistance 'is an expression of reservation which normally arises as a response or reaction to change'.[18] It usually refers to employee actions that delay, stop or in some fashion get in the way of a change effort and it is usually associated with negative attitudes or counterproductive behaviours. Waddell and Sohal[19] briefly and usefully track the historical development of our understanding of resistance. They explain that the concept benefitted from a growing diversity of discipline perspectives, becoming more sophisticated as we moved from the notion of obliterating resistance to make way for the change, to avoiding it as an expression of dysfunction, and then perceiving it as a complex response driven by a range of factors. These included rational assessments of the merit of the change, non-rational judgements based on preferences, political factors such as favouritism, management issues such as management style, and organisational factors such systems processes and structures. So resistance is now seen as complex, multidimensional and triggered by a variety of factors. There is also a view that it can play a useful role in organisational change rather than the entirely negative role suggested by classical management theory.

Managerial responses to resistance

This raises the whole issue of the organisational, and especially managerial, responses to individual and group resistance. How as managers we think about resistance, and the assumptions we bring to it, has a significant impact on our capacity to deal with it productively. Most authors regard resistance as an inevitable part of the change process and to be expected. Some welcome it as a natural and necessary human response,[20] bringing positive benefits as well as difficulties, and others reluctantly accept it, sometimes with a hint of irritation, thereby sending a somewhat mixed message.[21] Still others take a rather pejorative approach and declare it to be futile and that people really need to accept change and move on![22] The latter view sees resistance as 'the enemy of change … a foe which must be overcome'.[23] This reflects some of the diverse views that abound in organisations that often confuse the organisational response to resistance as they are not sufficiently surfaced, discussed or resolved. One of the most consistent findings in the literature is that it is not possible to deal effectively with change or resistance if the strategy and key messages are not coherent, focused and very clear.[24]

Waddell and Sohal[25] point out that despite considerable acknowledgement of the significance of resistance and the need to manage it effectively, as well as the lack of theoretical support for the adversarial approach to dealing with resistance, there is still little recognition of the notion of utility in resistance or recognition of its positive qualities and what it takes to work with it. The accounts of Pietersen[26] and Iskat and Liebowitz[27] are recent exceptions to this. Our work with many practitioners, who have undertaken study through action learning and research-based leadership and management Masters programs, strongly indicate that it is the adversarial and mixed message approach to resistance that still dominates the implementation of change programs in organisations. Part of this is because most organisational change is managed from a technical perspective (strategies, action plans, resource allocation and so on) with a persistent tendency to either neglect or ignore the human element or account for it in a token or instrumental manner. As Bovey and Hede[28] note that in this situation, 'resistance becomes something to be resisted'. As Maurer[29] says, this is in effect meeting force with force and often that is achieved through the force of reason via information 'sharing'. This is typically experienced by recipients as being 'battered' with vast amounts of information rather than genuine engagement. They cite many authors who recount change programs in which significant resources are invested in planning and execution, but demonstrate a failure to invest adequately in the people aspects: training, communication and follow-up. Such approaches are characterised by an unwillingness to seriously consider and treat employee views with respect. The result is mistrust, resentment and the strengthening of resistance. As the message of this book states, leading change requires human and organisational needs to be constructively balanced. This is not as easy as it sounds and requires commitment and skill.[30] It also requires leaders and managers who are able to take up their personal authority and their organisational authority so that they are able to act confidently in their roles.[31]

Concrete responses to change

Atkinson[32] usefully looks at some concrete responses to change. He explains that people's first response is often to ask 'How is this going to affect me?' and that they are often susceptible to unsubstantiated rumours at this stage. They understand it will mean more work, different and sometimes unknown work practices, new things to learn, loss of an imagined future and possibly no future with the organisation. A view can develop that this is yet another 'flavour of the month', especially if there has been a history of short-term and poorly supported change efforts, and that it might go away if ignored. Middle managers can feel very much like the meat in the sandwich[33] and often have trouble owning and supporting the change with their staff on behalf of senior management, especially if they do not feel supported themselves. There is also sometimes a tendency to wait for someone else to commit and lead: to go first, in effect. The resistance that these responses represent can be displayed overtly and covertly, the latter is often the case and difficult to identify or deal with. Rarely articulated is the real concern that they will discover that what staff have been doing for years is 'wrong'. Sometimes this is because there were no clear accountabilities, that what is now required has indeed changed or that the wrong things were in fact rewarded. Either way, it is all particularly unsettling and potentially very threatening. Personal uncertainty thrives in this situation: expectations are unclear, which undermines the sense of competence staff feel and their ability to adapt to new requirements. As Bridges[34] notes, this can extend to a questioning of their very identity as organisational members and as people if they are particularly identified with their roles.

It is interesting to note the language Atkinson[35] uses in discussing reactions to change: he refers to them as *symptoms* of resistance. This medical analogy indicates a situation of disease, which is often implicit in the mixed message view of resistance. The further implication is that these symptoms need to be cured with a metaphorical 'pill', which in turn can encourage more instrumental, problem-solving approaches to quickly resolve the contradictions and paradoxes inherent in change and resistance to it.[36] These include how to combine top-down and bottom-up approaches, learning and working, individual and organisational ambitions, structure and empowerment, and motivational approaches with those directed at resistance reduction. As Smith and Berg[37] argue, it is not always the best strategy to try to resolve paradoxes, as more authentic and lasting outcomes arise from working through the genuine complexity of organisational life that they represent. However, this takes awareness and skill.

THE NATURE OF RESISTANCE

This chapter takes the view that what we know from research and practice makes it clear that managers in organisations must take a more sophisticated and informed approach to resistance if they are to make change successful and sustainable. This includes understanding it as part of the spectrum of responses to change. Strategies and interventions can then be built on these understandings and are more likely to appropriately address the issue and encourage successful outcomes. An analysis of the nature of resistance provides useful clues as to how it might be most productively worked with.

Just as responses to resistance differ, resistance can also be directed from different sources. There are four main types of resistance:

1   *Psychological*. Resistance is often perceived as a negative human reaction as discussed elsewhere in this chapter. However, Russell-Jones[38] suggests that resistance can display healthy characteristics that result in early acceptance of the change plan. Figure 15.1 depicts phases that 'positive' resisters move through; however, keep in mind that not all people react or respond in the same way, in the same sequence or in a linear fashion as this model implies. Phase 1, 'Uninformed optimism', is where the organisation member embraces the opportunity that the change presents. At Stage 2, 'Informed pessimism', the person is now thinking through the consequences and impacts of the change, but this should not be read as a negative reaction. This level of analysis demonstrates a rational approach to the change and allows for a range of scenarios to be dealt with. After analysing the evidence the member then moves through to Stage 3, 'Hopeful realism', where they are quite realistic about the opportunities and consequences the change will have on the organisation. By Stage 4, 'Informed optimism', the member has moved further to accepting the change and will now be seen by change managers as a useful advocate. At Stage 5, 'Completion', the member is satisfied that the change is most beneficial for the organisation and internalises its value.

2   *Systemic*. This rejects the view that people are not, in fact, resisting the change as they can perceive the benefits to the organisation's internal operations, and therefore these systems are not creating the anxiety. Change can be successfully implemented providing information about the new system is given.

3   *Institutional*. When resistance becomes institutionalised it is often because of an entrenched counterproductive culture. Values and norms become so embedded in the way the organisation operates and therefore resistance is often covert.

4   *Individual perception*. Coming from substantial experience in key leadership roles in large-scale corporate change programs, Pietersen[39] refers to the 'FUD Factor' or the *f*ear, *u*ncertainty and *d*oubt that change produces. He notes that change involves many losses: certainty, the comfort of the known, our sense of feeling competent, financial security, status and, most powerfully, our sense of control when change is imposed as in organisations (it most often is). People need to be persuaded that ultimately the gains will outweigh the losses so that the driving forces outweigh the restraining forces. He notes that this needs 'people skills of the highest order'[40] so that the organisational and human dynamics are shifted from resistance to support. Later we will discuss some of the strategies that enable this to occur.

The psychodynamic perspective

The psychodynamic perspective is another approach to organisational studies that argues instrumental approaches to dealing with resistance are often ineffective and fail to recognise the deeper human response to the anxiety generated by all change. The issue of organisational and human dynamics identified by Pietersen[41] is almost always overlooked in the literature on change and resistance, except in the specific psychodynamic literature on organisations.[42] Only occasionally does mainstream change literature make the link with psychodynamics, and it is rarely explored in any depth. In this context, Bovey and Hede's[43] discussion of the role of defence mechanisms is unusual. Their study usefully explores the role of both adaptive and maladaptive defence mechanisms in driving resistance to change, and offers intervention

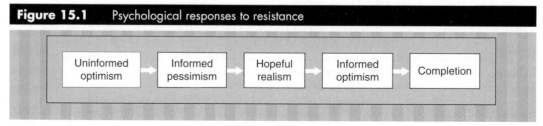

Figure 15.1   Psychological responses to resistance

Uninformed optimism → Informed pessimism → Hopeful realism → Informed optimism → Completion

Source: N. Russell-Jones, *The Managing Change Pocketbook*, Management Pocketbooks, London, 1999.

strategies to address them. Most of the time, however, these ways of thinking remain in splendid isolation from one another, despite together having much to offer practitioners and researchers.

The psychodynamic perspective draws on psychoanalytic theory, which provides a well-established and credible framework for understanding how unconscious processes operate. It is important to acknowledge that much of the human response to change is based on our unconscious response to anxiety, and becomes behaviourally apparent through the way we defend and protect ourselves. What we often see then is resistance at both the individual and at the group level.[44] It can have more impact on people's behaviour than conscious processes, particularly in times of stress such as change, and it directs energy away from the task of change towards self-protection. One of the most common manifestations of this is the use of projection or the tendency to falsely put blame and place responsibility on others rather than owning our own impulses.[45] This behaviour is very evident in many change programs. Until the individual or group and their managers are aware it is occurring and why, they will not be able to work through it to move on, as all management efforts will continue to be seen as an external threat. Much resistance management and the change itself become stuck at this point or people regress to this point after outward but surface compliance collapses.

What resistance has to offer us

Waddell and Sohal[46] remind us that resistance can play an important role in influencing the organisation towards greater stability. It does this by forcing the organisation to balance the external demand for constant change with the need for some maintenance and stability so that the work can be established, consolidated and evaluated with some degree of predictability and control. The delicate challenge is to achieve the right balance. They also remind us that resistance draws attention to those aspects of change that are poorly thought out, ill-conceived, missing critical data or just plain wrong or dangerous. Resistance in this sense is data – data the organisation often does not want to see or hear but ignores at some risk. This is supported by Jackson and Harris's[47] case studies of organisational change programs in e-business settings that investigate how one can reconcile traditional values while transforming the business to survive. Essentially they advise that such changes should not be framed as a simple technical matter, but rather as a significant social and cultural re-design. This then requires a robust change management process paying thorough attention to the micro-political, behavioural and cultural dimensions, and the need to take account of the multiplicity of stakeholders involved. They emphasise that people should be the centre of attention, advocating a 'hearts and minds approach' led by visible, credible change leadership. Interestingly, the lesson they take away from the experience of e-businesses – that faced enormous internal and external pressures to change radically and very quickly – was that the most durable today are the ones that took a more considered, incremental approach. They took time to deal with the complexity, particularly the people issues that presented, which were often expressed through resistance. This goes against the more driven, reactive approach that advocates immediate change, the squashing of resistance.[48]

Another benefit of resistance is that it can contribute to an injection of energy, creativity and innovation. The management and leadership practitioners we have worked with often refer to how difficult it is to implement and sustain change with a passive or low-energy workforce: they find this much harder to manage than direct resistance. Resistance can also encourage the generation of a wider range of alternative approaches and outcomes, but only if conflicting opinions are worked through rather than quashed.[49]

Resistance is not restricted to a particular sector of the organisation and can manifest at all levels and at various stages in the change process depending on the perceptions of the individual or the department. Balogun and Hailey[50] concur that because change is an *emotional* process, resistance should be seen as natural and anticipated as it is an indicator of the quality of the planning of the change process. The challenge for change managers is to recognise overt resistance, expect covert resistance and develop actions that will help people move through their resistance to acceptance of the change. Resistance is sometimes caused by lack of 'people preparation' and as Balogun and Hailey[51] state: 'Lack of readiness for change should not be confused with resistance.' Furthermore, Smith[52] maintains that blockages and resistance to the change are rarely overt and are more often disguised or subsumed, but over time their existence becomes apparent as the change implementation progresses. Later we shall examine further ways in which change

Table 15.1	Drivers of responses to change
Factors	Indicators
Economic	• Job loss or job security and impact on self-image • Economic future for family • Reduction of value of existing skills for future promotion • Transfer of organisation or components of the organisation to less costly locations • Vested interests in position, or salary benefits
Uncertainty	• Doubt about the stated benefits of the change • Doubt about ability to undertake new role or tasks • Rumours that destabilise the benefits of the change • Impact on relationships and values
Inconvenience	• Additional load to current role • Relocation of office or home • Loss of security of the familiar • Challenge to familiar routine
Threats to interpersonal relationships	• Status among employees • Threat to work team • Impact on morale of work team • Impact on organisation culture • Impact on social relationships
Impact on internal processes and systems	• Technology • Structure and dependencies • Inadequate communication to explain the change • Impact on resources
Impact on social psychological	• Cognitive dissonance or incompatibility with new values • Fear of the unknown

Source: adapted from F. Graetz, M. Rimmer, A. Lawrence and A. Smith, *Managing Organisational Change* (Milton: Wiley, 2006): 289.

managers can appropriately prepare people for change and lead them to a level of understanding that will enable them to work with resistance. It is imperative that resources are applied in the pre-implementation phase to enable the development of change planning strategies that will prepare organisational members for the capacity and readiness to change.

APPLiCATiON 15.2

SOURCES OF RESISTANCE

People resist change for many reasons. This list includes typical reasons for resistance:

Ignorance	Disagreement
Personal cost	Anxiety
Loss of authority	Mistrust
Alienation	Reward (or lack thereof)

Source: Adapted from MP de Val & CM Fuentes, 2003, 'Resistance to change: A literature review and empirical study', *Management Decision*, 41(2), pp. 148–55. Republished with permission, Emerald Group Publishing Limited, www.emeraldinsight.com.

Critical Thinking Question: Is 'change really a vision of a new future and should be exciting'[53] or is it more of a response to a crisis? Discuss.

Table 15.2	Maslow's hierarchy of needs
Maslow's hierarchy	Possible response to change
5 Actualisation	• Change approach • Cultural bias • Historical organisation factor
4 Status (esteem)	• Psychological reasons • Change approach • Cultural bias • Historical organisation factor
3 Love / belonging	• Employee self-interest and power/politics • Recipient perceptions • Historical organisation factor
2 Safety	• Psychological reasons • Recipient perceptions
1 Physiological (biological needs)	• Emotional reasons • Recipient perceptions

Resistance to change caused by many factors and often depends on the paradigm or framework that each individual or department is operating within. Particular life stages may have direct impacts on how members respond. For instance, if we apply Maslow's hierarchy of needs (see Table 15.2) as a basic framework, a member at level 2 may have different responses to change than a member at level 5.

SO WHAT DO MANAGERS OF CHANGE DO?

> 'Resistance' is often not that at all – it is a potential source of energy as well as information about the change effort and direction.[54]

> It is important to recognise that there will be a time lag between the announcement of a change and an emotional reaction to it … it is easy to mistake the apparent calm of the 'immobilisation' and 'minimisation' phases for acceptance of the change.[55]

How to make sure resistance will happen every time:
• begin with an 'us' versus 'them' mindset
• believe that it is always 'them' at fault
• adopt an attitude of resistance as 'baditude' rather than it being 'gratitude'.

There are, of course, no generic formulas that will work in a particular way as a change management template in all settings. This book and this chapter has shown the change process and its management as multifaceted, complex and influenced by many contextual variables; these include the nature and scale of the change, its drivers and the characteristics of the organisation and the groups and individuals involved. It is very clear, however, that the role of leadership and what managers and leaders pay attention to is absolutely crucial[56]. The response to and management of resistance is no different. Accounts of change programs, studies of what helps or hinders them[57] and practitioner accounts,[58] without exception, reinforce this. Pietersen[59], in particular, is very direct about what is required and draws on his experience of leading significant and difficult, large-scale organisational change, providing examples from this to illustrate his learnings. He offers a framework that is supported by other practitioners and researchers[60]. While

Table 15.3	Creating successful change	
Approaches to avoid		**Approaches to action**
1 No sense of urgency		1 Create a simple, compelling statement
2 Lack of powerful coalition		2 Communicate constantly and honestly
3 Lacking a vision		3 Maximise participation
4 Under-communicating		4 Reflect on the change process thus far
5 Not removing obstacles to new vision		5 Modify the implementation processes if needed
6 Not systematically planning for and creating short-term wins		6 If all else fails, remove those who resist
7 Declaring victory too soon		7 Generate short-term wins
8 Not anchoring changes in the corporate culture		8 Set a shining example

Source: adapted from B. Senior, *Organisational Change* (London: Prentice Hall, 2002); W. Pietersen, 'The Mark Twain dilemma: The theory and practice of change leadership', *The Journal of Business Strategy*, 23:5 (2002).

he argues that leaders need to transform resistance into support by attending to certain principles, we also propose that if adequate resources are committed at the planning or pre-formation stage that organisational and employee support for the change will quickly follow.

The attitude of senior management towards the change project is important in managing resistance. Strategic concepts which are at first strongly resisted by organisational members can gain acceptance and support over time if senior executives act as advocates for the change and do not display hostility either towards the change or organisational members who are displaying resistance. It is important in planning change processes that consideration is given to the type of 'anchors' that can be implemented for people to hold on to during the change process. One such 'anchor' could be to communicate how stability can be maintained during the change process, acknowledging simultaneously that the change will cause some disruption, especially to organisation control.[61]

The Pietersen framework

Pietersen's framework is based on six principal elements that can minimise resistance and assist the successful implementation of change.

1   *Create a simple, compelling statement.* It is essential that the starting point is a corporate strategy that is 'based on clear logic, rooted in the realities of the marketplace and represents a compelling cause for change'.[62] If this is lacking then the problem is not change leadership or resistance and needs separate attention. This is a threshold requirement and the leader's job is to explain what the change will be, why it is required and invite people to join the future. Pietersen notes that 'simplicity and clarity of vision is crucial here and is strongly correlated with superior performance'. This statement should not be complex or convoluted but a single, key idea that people can grasp and rally around. He advises to avoid laundry lists of priorities, focus on the top five and be strategic in thinking and action.

2   *Communicate constantly and honestly.* The logic for change should be repeated over and over in a variety of ways and contexts. Pietersen insists the honesty is absolutely critical. To be otherwise, or to obfuscate, heightens the fear, anxiety and uncertainty – people will always invent their own versions of the truth if it is hidden or disguised. He notes that this is particularly important when communicating the bad news. He also notes that managers must be prepared with supporting strategies such as provisions for outplacement, retraining, personal counselling and incentives such as bonus systems to maintain productivity.

3   *Maximise participation.* Pietersen[63] notes that it is important to recognise that leading change is not a one-person role, as 'people will support something they help to build'. He

advises paying close attention to people's responses, expected and unexpected; listening to and actively engaging with their concerns; and responding honestly. It is not an option to hand it over to HR or a change team to implement and to leave it to them alone.

4   *If all else fails, remove those who resist.* It is just as important to acknowledge that despite all efforts some will not be able to align themselves with the change and see themselves as fitting in. It is hardest when this is underground or passive. This cannot be ignored despite the difficulties involved. Leadership actions in relation to this aspect of resistance are highly symbolic[64] and impact on the entire change effort. He advises leaders to be sure the person is in fact in this category, confront the issue directly and fairly, and set a timetable for either change or departure. A range of HR strategies to support these options is needed as dramatic, sudden removal causes much wider damage.

5   *Generate short-term wins.* As change can take some time it is helpful to punctuate this with some short-term gains. These can create self-confidence and a belief that bigger successes are possible. He notes that this 'builds a psychological momentum' to sustain the overall effort. Bridges's[65] work on transition also supports this.

6   *Set a shining example.* Pietersen[66] regards this as 'the essence of leadership': the willingness to lead by example. For both managers and leaders at all levels of the organisation, a strong engagement with all aspects of the change, a positive orientation and enthusiasm helps spread a similar response to others. Bridges's[67] seminal work on transitions clearly echoes Pietersen's advice. He did not mince words when he advised managers that it was not an option to fail to deal with 'that personal stuff', and that while transition management is not easy, it is essential. Specifically, he refers to four crucial rules: (1) show up, (2) be present, (3) tell the truth, and (4) let go of outcomes (that is, don't try and control everything).

Essentially Pietersen[68] and Bridges[69] argue an approach to leadership that is strong, decisive and confident but not arrogant or dismissive. Those writing about leadership and change from a psychodynamic perspective[70] refer to this as a willingness to step into a role and a preparedness to exercise the personal and organisational authority located in that role.[71] In considering Pietersen's[72] advice, it is important to be cognisant of the issues raised in this chapter; of how we think about resistance and how this affects our ability to respond to it effectively and constructively, with consideration and judgement. Many of the authors discussed here advise thorough consideration of the many issues involved and the need to take a critical and more sophisticated perspective on what is a complex and often poorly understood concept.[73] Bovey and Hede[74] recommend, for example, that two types of interventions are needed to deal with the impact of the defence mechanisms typically associated with responses to change: information-based interventions and counselling interventions. The former are designed to create awareness of unconscious processes and how these impact on the individual's response to change, and the latter to support these factors. Counselling interventions are designed to assist individuals and groups to understand their defence mechanisms in relation to change, and how these affect their behaviour, which of course is often manifested in various types of resistance. Managers are as caught up in this as anyone else and have the added task of managing others through it.[75]

Table 15.4   Organisational responses to resistance

	Psychological resistance	Systemic resistance	Cultural resistance
Strategic choice	Manage people	Manage systems	Manage values and attitudes
New institutionalisation	Change forced on organisation members by the environment	Change forced on organisation systems by the environment	Change forced on organisation values and attitudes by environment

Source: F. Graetz, M. Rimmer, A. Lawrence and A. Smith, *Managing Organisational Change* (Milton: Wiley, 2006): 289.

So what is needed to do this? There's one easy way to effective change management, every time: communication. If we accept that resistance is expected, and that it can be overt or covert, that it has both positive and negative impacts on organisation outcomes, the negative impact of resistance can be minimised but relies on particular strategies and plans being in place. Walsh, Lok and Jones[76] suggest that different circumstances among groups and departments within an organisation require different approaches to managing resistance and these often depend on the time frame or urgency of the need for change, the power base or status of the change agent and the source of resistance.

For instance, if we examine Graetz, Rimmer, Lawrence and Smith's[77] (2006) analysis of the sources of resistance in Table 15.5, we find different reactions and responses at different stages of the change process.

However, if the change is large scale and will transform the organisation considerably, we must be mindful that restructuring 'psychological contracts'[78] – depending on the level of disruption to the status quo – involves extensive commitment and trust and takes time. The

Table 15.5   Examples of resistance

Stage of change	Source of resistance	Examples/manifestations
Formulation stage	Distorted perceptions of change need, barriers to interpretation and vague strategic priorities	• Myopia • Denial • Refusal • Implicit assumptions • Communication barriers • Organisational silence
	Low motivation for change	• Direct costs of change • Benefits equal disadvantages • Past failures • Different interests between employees and employers
	Lack of creative response	• Fast, complex change • Resignation to change • Inadequate strategic vision or commitment of top management
Implementation stage	Political and cultural deadlocks	• Department politics • Disagreement about the nature of the problem and proposed solutions • Deep-rooted values and loyalty • Lack of awareness of the social dimension of change
	Other	• Leadership inaction • Embedded routines • Problems with collective action • Lack of necessary capabilities • Cynicism

Source: *Managing Organisational Change*, F. Graetz & M. Rimmer, John Wiley & Sons Australia, Ltd; © 2006. Reprinted with permission of John Wiley & Sons Australia.

amount of time given to building commitment and trust will often determine both short- and long-term effectiveness of the change, and levels of resistance.[79]

PATTERNS OF ORGANISATIONAL RESISTANCE

Jones[80] suggests that among the most powerful impediments to change implementation are power and conflict agendas between individuals and groups, which are often driven by group norms and characteristics. Adding to this are the differences in departmental characteristics, such as whether their structural orientation is functional, mechanistic or organic. This, in turn, influences departmental or organisational subcultures, which have the potential to produce resistance to change. Therefore, the strength of resistance can demonstrate the degree to which the change has the potential to alter perceptions on the level of disruption to something valuable to individuals and departments within the organisation. As any change will have different implications for individuals and groups in the organisation, and at different times, not all groups and departments will progress through the change cycle simultaneously. Because of this managers can expect that the management of the resistance at various stages of the change cycle will be an ongoing process. The challenge, therefore, is to determine what level of impact the change will have on each department, anticipate the likelihood of resistance and resource accordingly.

Organisation change is often implemented in unrealistic time frames, and, being time-poor, managers run the risk of assuming that organisation members have the same levels of awareness, understanding and acceptance as themselves in an effort to implement the change. One way of determining awareness, understanding and acceptance is to factor in reflection and checking strategies in the change process. Ongoing communication at all levels – individual, group and department – will enhance acceptance and therefore lower levels of resistance.

APPLICATION 15.3

CHARACTER TYPES WITHIN ORGANISATIONS

Russell-Jones has developed a range of categories of character types that accept change at different rates of change within organisations. The five categories are:
- innovators/visionaries
- early adopters
- early majority
- late majority
- laggards.

Source: N. Russell-Jones, *The Managing Change Pocketbook* (London: Management Pocketbooks, 1999): 90.

Critical Thinking Question: How true is this for members in your organisation?

If we briefly pursue the notion of organisation culture being a driver of resistance to change, departmental subcultures need to be understood in the change planning process. Brown and Harvey[81] argue that resistance can emerge out of shared behaviours or habits, and that an inappropriate department culture, for instance, is often the biggest stumbling block to adaptation. The resistance that is driven by this subculture can prevent a company from remaining competitive due to its inability to embrace change. Therefore, the subculture of the stakeholder group or department undergoing the change process needs to be taken into account when communicating the goals, values and underlying assumptions of the benefits of the change to the affected people. There may need to be differentiated styles of communication determined by the subculture characteristics. For instance, if a subculture has formal and directive characteristics, the group may need facts, figures and comparisons. Conversely, if the subculture is more organic and empowering in its characteristics, that group may need to be encouraged to participate as partners in the change process to excite them about the organisation's future potential.

Managers also need to understand that as organisations undergo life cycles in their strategic activities, resistance also has a 'life cycle' pattern.[82] At the initial phase of the change life cycle, few see the need for change, and levels of resistance towards the change can be high. After a time those resisting and supporting the change merge. However, there may be direct conflict between the opposing groups depending on how successfully the resistance has been managed. Resisters may be seen as stubborn and a nuisance, and therefore marginalised and alienated. However, depending on the power and control held by the resisters, they may be sufficiently influential to mobilise enough support to shift the balance of power and therefore sabotage the change process. Of concern to change managers in anticipating resistance are the 'hedgers'[83] or 'fence sitters'.[84] These are those individuals who, often through fear of job security or loss of status, refuse to openly voice their objections and allow others to, but at the same time refuse to support the change: having a bet both ways! Robbins and Finley[85] suggest that resistance does not even have to be a conscious act. Because nearly every organisational problem has a solution, they argue that mass resistance can be more easily addressed than small groups of resisters. As discussed elsewhere, mass resistance often indicates that the change plan is flawed or not communicated well.

Management approaches

Kotter and Schlesinger recommend a range of what they term 'competencies' that change managers can apply. We recommend that these be considered at the pre-implementation phase of the change management process. This requires organisation resources being available to enable their appropriate application. The competencies are:

1   *Education and communication.* This may need to be stratified through the organisation depending on department need, group norms within those departments and the capabilities of internal people to facilitate this.
2   *Participation and involvement of individuals and groups.* Even if change agents think they have all the answers, organisation member involvement will minimise resistance.
3   *Facilitation of support.* Participation and involvement of individuals and groups will assist in identifying which groups need priority support.
4   *Negotiation and agreement.* This may be needed if feedback from organisation members indicates the change plan is not feasible or is flawed.
5   *Manipulation and co-option.* This can be used if there are still people resisting the change and the change is systems-driven. Try to avoid this approach.
6   *Explicit and implicit coercion.* Avoid this approach at all costs unless there is the potential of physical risk for employees who do not adapt to the change. There is always a solution!

It is important *not* to underestimate what is involved: the management of resistance needs commitment and effort but also an understanding that it can and must be engaged with, and be positively and actively managed. Realistic expectations are important – it is simply naive to expect change and the responses to it to be all plain sailing and straightforward if managers follow a recommended model and adhere systematically to the steps. This clockwork or machine view of an organisation does not prepare us well for the complex and messy realities of change management. Similarly, a common misapprehension is that resistance will only occur in the early stages of the change process.[86] While there isn't scope within this chapter to comprehensively discuss what it takes to implement recommended strategies, there are some capabilities that can be usefully considered. These include:

•   the willingness and capacity of those managing and leading change to assess and constantly reassess the situation (for example, keeping their antennae tuned, ongoing monitoring of responses to change, and anticipating and responding with continued sensitivity to events)

- an awareness of our own strengths and vulnerabilities as people affected by the change as well as responsibility for its success (that is, the management of dual and sometimes conflicting ideas)
- the capacity to make clear, self-aware judgements (that is, a commitment to reflective practice through action learning cycles of observation, reflection, thought and action-taking, so considered, adaptive and reality-based decisions are more likely)
- an ability to tolerate anxiety and ambiguity, and to engage with one's own and others' responses, rather than to block or deny them
- an understanding of the opportunities, constraints and responsibilities afforded by our role as managers and an ability to act strongly within these.

THE REFLECTIVE PRACTITIONER

It is important to acknowledge that managers in organisations are time-poor and subject to a multiplicity of pressures and demands. This is magnified when change programs are underway. The capacity to deal with these in a self-aware and practical manner is crucial, no more so than when dealing with resistance. The reflective practitioner is able to make such judgments, call on resources such as supervisors to support them, and keep going along the program's path. The fostering of such capabilities calls for a reflective practice approach to management and leadership.[87] In essence, this refers to the process of critically examining one's practice by taking the perspective of an external observer, to identify assumptions and feelings underlying that practice, how these impact practice, and to determine if the practitioner needs to change to be more effective.[88] Given our discussion so far, this approach is particularly important in the management of organisational change and the resistance it triggers, which is, by its very nature, characterised by strong emotional responses both positive and negative and, commonly, considerable anxiety.[89] It also unleashes complex individual, group and organisational dynamics that are unconsciously driven and difficult to deal with unless one is aware of such possibilities and how they manifest and play out.[90] Personal resilience – emotionally and physically – is crucial[91] when adapting to change. This needs to be strengthened by the support offered through human resource development strategies such as supervision, coaching and mentoring.[92] Managers in planning and implementing change often underestimate the demands of the process and do not put such support mechanisms in place for themselves and their staff: Bridges[93] highlighted this many years ago. And the managers, the staff and the change process suffer as a consequence.[94]

SUMMARY

Understanding that resistance to change is a complex issue that is caused by many factors can substantially assist managers in the change process. The recognition and understanding that resistance is often driven by a paradigm or framework that each individual or department is operating within, and may not have common associations, adds to the complexity of managing resistance.

Knowing that resistance is to be expected when implementing organisational change, and that it can manifest itself in various forms with both positive and negative impacts on organisation outcomes, can reduce the impact of resistance on the change management process.

Resistance cannot just be placed on the individual or group affected by the change; it also relies on managers understanding the nature of resistance. By being more aware that resistance is one of a range of human responses to the change management process, it can then be managed and worked with effectively but this requires committed leadership.

It is also helpful to understand that resistance is an ongoing process and may manifest itself at various stages of the change cycle. Organisations need to be aware that the effective management of resistance requires management and leadership skills, plus appropriate human resource development strategies and support mechanisms to be put in place. With appropriate support managing resistance, the change process need not be as complex or difficult.

ACTIVITIES

Review questions

① Describe some of the factors that lead to 'resistance'.

② Summarise the variety of ways in which resistance can be managed.

③ Explain the differences between 'overt' and 'covert' resistance.

④ Discuss the ways in which resistance can have positive or negative impacts on the change management process.

Discussion and essay questions

① Describe ways in which managers can positively and actively manage resistance, and what managers need to understand when undertaking this.

② Discuss the overall role of the change manager in managing resistance during the change process, and the critical knowledge they and the human resource department need to apply.

③ Do types of resistance differ between types of organisations? Reflect on the type of resistance that might occur in those organisations that are: board-directed, family-owned, governmental and not-for-profit.

④ Which of Kotter and Schlesinger's six competencies can be classified as either 'soft' or 'hard'? Discuss which would be effective in the short term but not for long-term organisational acceptance of the change. List what other competencies are required to create ownership and commitment to make the change last.

NOTES

1 B. Burnes, *Managing Change* (London: Pitman, 2004).

2 T.D. Jick and M.A. Peiperl, *Managing Change: Cases and Concepts* (New York: McGraw Hill, 2003).

3 T. Clarke and S. Clegg, *Changing Paradigms: The transformation of management knowledge for the 21st century* (London: Harper Collins, 1998).

4 D. Waddell and A. Sohal, 'Resistance: a constructive tool for change management', *Management Decision*, 36:8 (1998): 543.

5 W.H. Bovey and A. Hede, 'Resistance to organizational change: The role of defence mechanisms', *Journal of Managerial Psychology*, 16:7/8 (2001): 534.

6 W. Pietersen, 'The Mark Twain dilemma: The theory and practice of change leadership', *The Journal of Business Strategy*, 23:5 (2002): 32; P. Jackson and L. Harris, 'E-business and organizational change: Reconciling traditional values with business transformation', *Journal of Organizational Change Management*, 16:5 (2003): 497; P. Castka, C.J. Bamber and J.M. Sharp, 'Measuring teamwork culture: the use of a modified EFQM model', *The Journal of Management*, 22:1/2 (2003): 149; S. Palo and S. Panigrahi, 'Managing change during a transition period', *Development and Learning in Organisations*, 18:6 (2004): 7.

7 J. McLean, 'Responding to change ensures survival', *The British Journal of Administrative Management*, Dec 2004–Jan 2005: 16.

8 P. Atkinson, 'Managing resistance to change', *Management Services*, 49:1 (2005): 14; P.R. Simons, J. Germans and M. Ruijters, 'Forum for organizational learning: Combining learning at work, organizational learning and training in new ways', *Journal of European Industrial Training*, 27:1 (2003): 41; Castka, Bamber and Sharp, 'Measuring teamwork culture: the use of a modified EFQM model', op. cit.

9 Waddell and Sohal, 'Resistance: a constructive tool for change management', op. cit.; Jackson and Harris, 'E-business and organizational change: Reconciling traditional values with business transformation', op. cit.; Jick and Peiperl, *Managing Change: Cases and Concepts*, op. cit.

10 E.B. Dent and S.G. Goldberg, 'Challenging Resistance to Change', http://polaris.umuc.edu/~edent/resist4.html (accessed 1 November 2006).

11 ibid.

12 C.A. Carnall, *Managing Change in Organizations* (Harlow: Prentice Hall, 2003).

13 W. Bridges, *Managing Transitions: Making the Most of Change* (Massachusetts: Addison-Wesley, 1997).

14 Pietersen, 'The Mark Twain dilemma: The theory and practice of change leadership', op. cit.

15 W. Bridges, *Managing Transitions: Making the Most of Change*, op. cit.; Bovey and Hede, 'Resistance to organizational change: The role of defence mechanisms', op. cit.

16 L. Hirschhorn, *The workplace within* (Cambridge: MIT, 1988); R. de Board, *The psychoanalysis of organizations*, op. cit.; Y. Gabriel, *Organisations in depth* (London: Sage, 1999).

17 Bovey and Hede, 'Resistance to organizational change: The role of defence mechanisms', op. cit.

18 P. Block, 'The Empowered Manager: Positive Political Skills at Work', (Singapore: Jossey-Bass, 1987); cited in Waddell and Sohal, 'Resistance: a constructive tool for change management', op. cit.

19 Waddell and Sohal, 'Resistance: a constructive tool for change management', op. cit.

20 W. Bridges, *Managing Transitions: Making the Most of Change*, op. cit.; Bovey and Hede, 'Resistance to organizational change: The role of defence mechanisms', op. cit.

21 Atkinson, 'Managing resistance to change', op. cit.

22 McLean, 'Responding to change ensures survival', op. cit.

23 Waddell and Sohal, 'Resistance: a constructive tool for change management', op. cit.

24 Pietersen, 'The Mark Twain dilemma: The theory and practice of change leadership', op. cit.; Atkinson, 'Managing resistance to change', op. cit.; Palo and Panigrahi, 'Managing change during a transition period', op. cit.; G.J. Iskat and J. Liebowitz, 'What to do when employees resist change', *SuperVision*, 64:8 (2003): 12; Jackson and Harris, 'E-business and organizational change: Reconciling traditional values with business transformation', op. cit.

25 Waddell and Sohal, 'Resistance: a constructive tool for change management', op. cit.: 543.

26 Pietersen, 'The Mark Twain dilemma: The theory and practice of change leadership', op. cit.

27 Iskat and Liebowitz, 'What to do when employees resist change', op. cit.

28 Bovey and Hede, 'Resistance to organizational change: The role of defence mechanisms', op. cit.: 2

29 cited in Waddell and Sohal, 'Resistance: a constructive tool for change management', op. cit.

30 Jackson and Harris, 'E-business and organizational change: Reconciling traditional values with business transformation', op. cit.; Pietersen, 'The Mark Twain dilemma: The theory and practice of change leadership', op. cit.

31 L.J. Gould, 'Contemporary perspectives on personal and organisational authority', in L. Hirschhorn and C.K. Barnett, *The psychodynamics of organisations* (Philadelphia: Temple University Press, 1993).

32 Atkinson, 'Managing resistance to change', op. cit.

33 S. Smith, *Create That Change* (London: Kogan Page, 1997).

34 Bridges, *Managing Transitions: Making the Most of Change*, op. cit.

35 Atkinson, 'Managing resistance to change', op. cit.

36 P.R. Simons, J. Germans and M. Ruijters, 'Forum for organizational learning: Combining learning at work, organizational learning and training in new ways', *Journal of European Industrial Training*, 27:1 (2003): 41; Bovey and Hede, 'Resistance to organizational change: The role of defence mechanisms', op. cit.

37 K.K. Smith and D.N. Berg, *Paradoxes of Group Life: understanding conflict, paralysis and movement in group dynamics* (San Francisco: Jossey-Bass, 1987).

38 N. Russell-Jones, *The Managing Change Pocketbook* (London: Management Pocketbooks, 1999).

39 Pietersen, 'The Mark Twain dilemma: The theory and practice of change leadership', op. cit.

40 ibid., 3.

41 ibid.

42 De Board, *The psychoanalysis of organizations*, op. cit.; Gabriel, *Organisations in depth*, op. cit.; Hirschhorn, *The workplace within*, op. cit.

43 Bovey and Hede, 'Resistance to organizational change: The role of defence mechanisms', op. cit.

44 Smith and Berg, *Paradoxes of Group Life: understanding conflict, paralysis and movement in group dynamics*, op. cit.; W. Bion, *Experiences in groups and other papers* (London: Tavistock/Routledge, 1989); L. Wells Jr., 'The Group-as-a-whole: a systematic socio-analytical perspective on interpersonal and group relations', in C.P. Alderfer and C.l. Cooper, *Advances in Experiential Social Processes, Vol 2* (John Wiley & Sons, 1980).

45 Hirschhorn, *The workplace within*, op. cit.; Bovey and Hede, 'Resistance to organizational change: The role of defence mechanisms', op. cit.

46 Waddell and Sohal, 'Resistance: a constructive tool for change management', op. cit.

47 Jackson and Harris, 'E-business and organizational change: Reconciling traditional values with business transformation', op. cit.

48 McLean, 'Responding to change ensures survival', op. cit.

49 Waddell and Sohal, 'Resistance: a constructive tool for change management', op. cit.

50 J. Balogun and V. Hope Hailey, *Exploring Strategic Change* (Essex: Prentice Hall, 2004).

51 ibid.

52 Smith, *Create That Change*, op. cit.

53 L. Clarke, *The Essence of Change* (New York: Prentice Hall, 1994).

54 Jick and Peiperl, *Managing Change: Cases and Concepts*, op. cit.

55 J. Hayes, *The Theory and Practice of Change Management* (New York: Palgrave, 2002).

56 Balogun and Hope Hailey, *Exploring Strategic Change*, op. cit.; Burnes, *Managing Change*, op. cit.; Carnall, *Managing Change in Organizations*, op. cit.; Jick and Peiperl, *Managing Change: Cases and Concepts*, op. cit.; L. Hirschhorn, *Reworking authority: Leading and following in the post-modern organization* (Cambridge: MIT Press, 1997).

57 Jackson and Harris, 'E-business and organizational change: Reconciling traditional values with business transformation', op. cit.; Bovey and Hede, 'Resistance to organizational change: The role of defence mechanisms', op. cit.

58 Pietersen, 'The Mark Twain dilemma: The theory and practice of change leadership', op. cit.

59 Pietersen, 'The Mark Twain dilemma: The theory and practice of change leadership', op. cit.

60 Jackson and Harris, 'E-business and organizational change: Reconciling traditional values with business transformation', op. cit.; Iskat and Liebowitz, 'What to do when employees resist change', op. cit.; Atkinson, 'Managing resistance to change', op. cit.; Bridges, *Managing Transitions: Making the Most of Change*, op. cit.

61 C. Mabey and B. Mayon-White, *Managing Change* (London: Paul Chapman, 1993).

62 ibid., 3.

63 ibid.

64 L.G. Bolman and T.E. Deal, *Reframing organizations: artistry, choice and leadership* (San Francisco: Jossey-Bass, 2003).

65 Bridges, *Managing Transitions: Making the Most of Change*, op. cit.

66 Pietersen, 'The Mark Twain dilemma: The theory and practice of change leadership', op. cit.

67 see notes 67 and 68.

68 Pietersen, 'The Mark Twain dilemma: The theory and practice of change leadership', op. cit.

69 Bridges, *Managing Transitions: Making the Most of Change*, op. cit.

70 Hirschhorn, *The workplace within*, op. cit.; de Board, *The psychoanalysis of organizations*, op. cit.

71 L.J. Gould, 'Contemporary perspectives on personal and organisational authority', in L. Hirschhorn and C.K. Barnett, *The psychodynamics of organisations* (Philadelphia: Temple University Press, 1993).

72 Pietersen, 'The Mark Twain dilemma: The theory and practice of change leadership', op. cit.

73 Waddell and Sohal, 'Resistance: a constructive tool for change management', op. cit.; Bovey and Hede, 'Resistance to organizational change: The role of defence mechanisms', op. cit.

74 Bovey and Hede, 'Resistance to organizational change: The role of defence mechanisms', op. cit.

75 Bridges, *Managing Transitions: Making the Most of Change*, op. cit.

76 P. Walsh, P. Lok and M. Jones, *The Measurement and Management of Strategic Change* (Frenchs Forest: Pearson, 2006).

77 Graetz et al., *Managing Organisational Change*, op. cit.

78 Jick and Peiperl, *Managing Change: Cases and Concepts*, op. cit.

79 Jackson and Harris, 'E-business and organizational change: Reconciling traditional values with business transformation', op. cit.

80 G.R. Jones, *Organizational Theory, Design, and Change* (New Jersey: Pearson, 2004).

81 D.R. Brown and D.F. Harvey, *An Experiential Approach to Organization Development* (New Jersey: Prentice-Hall, 2006).

82 ibid.

83 C. Mabey and B. Mayon-White, 'Managing Change', op. cit.

84 Block, 'The Empowered Manager: Positive Political Skills at Work', op. cit.

85 H. Robbins and M. Finley, *Why Change Doesn't Work* (London: Orion, 1998).

86 H.S. Schwartz, *Narcissistic Processes and Corporate Decay* (New York: University Press, 1990); G. Morgan, *Images of organization* (California: Sage Publications, 2006); Hirschhorn, *The workplace within*, op. cit.; Gabriel, *Organisations in depth*, op. cit.

87 C. Agryris and D.A. Schon, *Organizational Learning 11 – Theory, Method and Practice*, Addison-Wesley OD Series (Reading, MA: Addison-Wesley, 1996); D. Kolb, *Experiential learning: experience as the source of learning and development* (Englewood Cliffs, New Jersey: Prentice Hall, 1984); W. Doyle and J. Young, 'Management development: Making the most of experience and reflection', *Canadian Manager* (Fall, 2000): 18–20; I. Gardner and C. Boucher, 'Reflective practice: A meta-competency for Australian allied health managers' (paper presented to Seventh Annual International Conference on Advances in Management, Colorado Springs, 12–15 July 2000).

88 W. Doyle and J. Young, 'Management development: Making the most of experience and reflection', op. cit.

89 Bovey and Hede, 'Resistance to organizational change: The role of defence mechanisms', op. cit.

90 Bovey and Hede, 'Resistance to organizational change: The role of defence mechanisms', op. cit.; Gabriel, *Organisations in depth*, op. cit.; de Board, *The psychoanalysis of organizations*, op. cit.

91 R.S. Rubin, 'Leading from within: the effects of emotion, recognition and personality on transformational leadership behaviour', *Academy of Management Journal*, 48:5 (2005): 845–58.

92 A. Smyth, D. Legge and P. Stanton, 'Learning Management', in M.G. Harris & Associates, *Managing Health Services: Concepts and Practices*, 2nd edn (Elsevier, NSW: 2005); C. Boucher and A. Smyth, 'Up close and personal: Our experience of supervising research candidates who are using personal reflective techniques', *Reflective Practice*, 5:3 (2003): 345–56; B.L. Delahaye, *Human resource development: adult learning and knowledge management*, 2nd edn (Milton, Qld: John Wiley & Sons, 2005).

93 Bridges, *Managing Transitions: Making the Most of Change*, op. cit.

94 Bovey and Hede, 'Resistance to organizational change: The role of defence mechanisms', op. cit.; Atkinson, 'Managing resistance to change', op. cit.

Online reading

INFOTRAC® COLLEGE EDITION

For additional readings and reviews on resistance, explore **InfoTrac® College Edition**, your online library. Go to **www.infotrac-college.com** and search for any of the InfoTrac key terms listed below:

- **Responses to resistance**
- **Nature of resistance**
- **Pietersen Framework**
- **Reflective practitioner**

iNTEGRATiVE CASE STUDiES

Case study A

NORTHERN STOCK FEED SUPPLiES

By Dr Cheryl England, James Cook University

BACKGROUND

Northern Stock Feed Supplies (NSFS) was established as a family-owned and -operated business in regional north Queensland 30 years ago. The company sells stock feed (horse, cattle, dog and poultry) and maintains a limited range of equine products and fencing supplies for cattle and horses, as well as gravel and mulch products. It is owned and operated by Meg and Tom Overton as a family business with an annual turnover of approximately $3.5 million. NSFS operates from a large storage shed with accompanying office, set on 100 acres on the outskirts of a major regional town in north Queensland.

The immediate business – which includes the shed, office, two small trucks, a forklift truck and a Toyota Landcruiser – is located on the southern part of the property and is surrounded by a six-foot barbed-wire fence. The Overton's house and kennels are located to the back of the business side of the property. The remaining 80 acres hold several stock horses that Tom uses for mustering as the Overton's hold a lease on an additional 200 acres, 10km to the north of the business. On their leased property they keep a small herd of Brahmans, which Tom sells to the local abattoirs when prices are high. Prices for beef fluctuate depending on supply and demand.

Brahmans were selected as they are valued as drought- and tick-resistant stock. However, they still require maintenance and mustering for the meat market. At such times the Overtons hire stock hands (ringers) from the local employment agency or employ experienced riders from the local horse clubs. The property is also used for agistment purposes. While income from agistment is not high, it has been useful to supplement earnings from other sources. When first established the company was surrounded by a thriving farming and rural/residential community.

Northern Stock Feed Supplies does not advertise extensively as it is situated on the main road in and out of town. Anyone living in this rural community has to travel past the store when going into town from the southern side. Tom works at loading feed and materials onto customer's vehicles while Meg manages the books in the office, which is located in a demountable shed beside the large aluminium shed used to store feed and equipment. They also employ a farmhand, Boris, who assists Tom with loading equipment. He also accompanies Meg when she does the weekly run to outlying areas delivering feed and equipment to customers unable to collect the produce themselves. This service operates free to regular customers and is seen by many locals as one of the unique aspects of the company as other competitors charge for this service. However, with the increased cost of fuel, the Overton's are considering charging customers a small fee for this service, although it goes against their company philosophy and culture, which is to provide a friendly, relaxed, country way of conducting business. Many of their older customers see this service as a chance to sit down with a cup of tea and catch up on local gossip.

In addition to the stock feed business, Meg's hobbies include maintaining a small kennel where she has been breeding and training working kelpies for over 20 years. Kelpies have long been bred and trained for herding sheep and cattle. In the early years of settlement in

Australia kelpies and horses were used extensively on large properties but were then replaced by motorised vehicles such as agricultural bikes. With the increased cost of fuel, some property owners have returned to using horses and dogs for mustering stock. In the last few years Meg has found a niche market selling her kelpie pups to property owners out west. Recently one of her adult working dogs sold to a property owner in Hughendon for just under $6000. Also, many of the property owners out west are experiencing difficulties employing suitably experienced stock hands and ringers for mustering cattle and have found that a good working dog can muster both sheep and cattle at a fraction of the cost. Compared with wages for employing a farmhand or ringer, a good working dog is very cheap as it requires only a handful of feed. Meg has always been keen on developing her hobby into a business but Tom is sceptical that it can sustain a profit and wants Meg to remain keeping the books for NSFS. While he 'tolerates' employing Boris to assist loading and other duties around the business, he is not keen to employ other staff. Tom does not have formal management skills, although his relaxed, sardonic humour is appreciated by his customers who frequently tap into his vast knowledge. What Tom doesn't know about fencing and stock feed is not worth knowing, as one customer put it recently. However, over the years the company has had to accommodate changes both within the industry and from external influences.

COMPETITION AND MARKETING STRATEGY

Northern Stock Feed Supplies does not have any systematic marketing strategy although there are other competitors in the market. Two similar companies operate in the same area from their offices in the centre of town, while there are another two companies who are in the same business and who have premises on the northern outskirts of town, in the opposite direction to NSFS. The competitors in the town centre were established prior to the entry into the market of Northern Stock Feed Supplies, but the two companies on the outlying regions of town are new entries into the market. The Overtons consider that marketing is just a waste of time and money, and that if people want a product, they will just come and buy it. The only 'marketing' conducted by Northern Stock Feed Supplies is a donation to the local horse clubs when events such as the annual fun day and barrel racing carnivals are held. These events attract many pony and horse club enthusiasts from around the district and banners supporting the company are displayed on the arena fence with an announcer broadcasting the sponsors for the day and suggesting that it is in the interests of all participants to support the local company. An additional form of advertising occurs when special events such as 'bareback riding' competitions occur, which attract a number of competitors from throughout the state because of the large 'purse' attached to winning first place. During this competition, riders wear competition jackets with the sponsoring company's logo. However, there has been no systematic follow-up to see if this marketing technique brings new custom.

Northern Stock Feed Supplies operates within a climate of friendly, open communication, and when visiting the company to collect supplies, customers are frequently provided with a cup of tea while supplies are loaded onto the vehicle. Conversation revolves around the weather, price of grass and politics – the atmosphere is a friendly, relaxed, country style of doing business. Tom is in his element and loves talking with customers. He has a wealth of knowledge on anything relating to the land and he is keen to share his knowledge and experience with customers.

CLIMATIC AND ENVIRONMENTAL IMPACTS

The weather is one of those elements that impact significantly on the stock feed industry. It has been reported both by the government and in the press (*Country Life* and *North Queensland Register*) that Australia, and particularly northern Australia, is in the grips of one of the most severe droughts in its history (see Figure A.1 and Table A.1).

Figure A.2 indicates rainfall (millimetres) in Australia for September 2006. The lack of adequate rainfall affects both the growing and harvesting of feed in the form of grass, hay,

Figure A.1   Queensland drought-declared areas

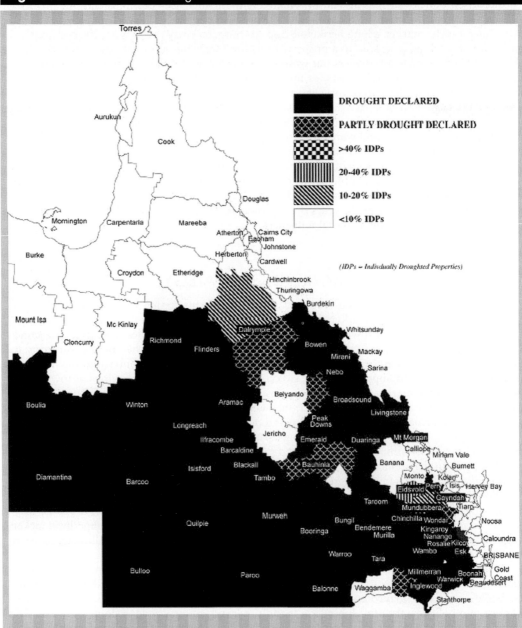

Source: The State of Queensland, Department of Primary Industries and Fisheries, 1995–2005.

lucerne, oats and chaff, all of which form the main products sold by Northern Stock Feed Supplies. Also, price is determined by the rainfall, which affects not only the quality of the harvest but also the supply. It has long been a concern for the Overtons to be able to have adequate supplies to sell to customers.

    NSFS often experiences difficulty maintaining adequate supplies of stock feed when the regular sources are unable to meet demand because of seasonal fluctuations in rainfall and the lack of producing quality round bales. Not only is drought affecting supply of grass but ironically in one small section of the state (Atherton Tableland), which is another major supplier for Northern Stock Feed Supplies, during the wet season they were unable to supply feed as they were experiencing too much rainfall. This meant they were unable to harvest the grass

| **Table A.1** | Queensland drought situation as at 30 September 2006 |

QUEENSLAND DROUGHT SITUATION
as at 30th September 2006

SHIRE	DATE DECLARED	SHIRE	DATE DECLARED
Aramac	01.01.2003	Kingaroy	15.06.2005
Balonne	01.08.2002	Laidley	18.10.2002
Barcaldine	01.02.2003	Livingstone	22.05.2002
Barcoo	19.08.2002	Longreach	01.01.2003
Bauhinia	❑ 01.01.2003	Mackay	17.12.2002
Belyando	♠ 01.01.2003	Millmerran	25.05.2005
Bendemere	01.05.2005	Mirani	17.12.2002
Blackall	01.02.2003	Mount Morgan	22.05.2002
Boonah	19.08.2002	Murgon	28.10.2000
Booringa	01.11.2002	Murilla	26.07.2001
Boulia	⚥ 24.05.2005	Murweh	01.02.2003
	⊠ 12.04.2006	Nanango	15.06.2005
Bowen	01.01.2003	Nebo	24.05.2002
Broadsound	24.05.2002	Paroo	28.06.2002
Bulloo	23.09.2002	Peak Downs	24.05.2002
Bungil	01.05.2005	Perry	20.06.2005
Burdekin	15.10.2003	Pittsworth	18.04.2005
Cambooya	31.10.2000	Quilpie	✗ 01.09.2002
Chinchilla	✦01.05.2005		• 11.11.2002
	✖01.06.2006	Richmond	⚫31.01.2003
Clifton	28.10.2000		◔ 06.08.2003
Crows Nest	02.12.2002	Rockhampton	22.05.2002
Dalby Town	01.06.2005	Roma Town	01.05.2005
Dalrymple	⊕ 01.02.2003	Rosalie	◼ 28.10.2000
Diamantina	11.11.2002		◆ 15.06.2005
Duaringa	22.05.2002	Sarina	17.12.2002
Emerald	01.01.2003	Tambo	01.02.2003
Esk	01.08.2006	Tara	01.06.2005
Fitzroy	22.05.2002	Taroom	☉ 26.07.2001
Flinders	⊕ 31.01.2003		☽ 06.05.2005
	✚18.03.2005	Waggamba	⚘ 01.08.2002
Gatton	18.10.2002	Wambo	✼ 28.10.2000
Ilfracombe	01.02.2003		⚫ 01.06.2005
Inglewood	08.08.2002	Warroo	01.05.2005
Ipswich	01.05.2005	Warwick	23.04.2005
Isisford	01.02.2003	Whitsunday	01.01.2003
Jondaryan	28.10.2000	Winton	01.01.2003
Kilcoy	01.08.2006	Wondai	28.10.2000
Kilkivan	⊠ 28.10.2000		

⊠ That part of the Shire of Kilkivan west of the Wide Bay Creek.

☉ South of the area revoked as the 'northern part of Taroom Shire', described as that part of the shire being from the eastern side heading west, the northern side of the Red Range Road, eastern side of the Nathan Road, north of the Bungaban Seven Mile Road, down the Leichhardt Highway, north of Murrays Road continuing west along the stock route to the Yeovil Road taking in all properties north of the Yeovil Road and the Taroom Roma Road.

☽ The remainder of the shire of Taroom not covered by the 26.07.2001 declaration.

✗ That portion of Quilpie Shire located south of the Charleville to Quilpie Road and then to the south and west of the Quilpie to Windorah Road.

• The remainder of the shire of Quilpie not covered by the 01.09.2002 declaration.

♠ The remainder of the shire of Belyando not revoked on 02.03.2005. The revoked area being the area south and west of a line beginning at the point where the Peak Downs Highway intersects the boundary of Belyando and Peak Downs Shire and following the Peak Downs Highway from this point north west to the Clermont roundabout and continuing along the highway to the junction of the Peak Downs Highway where it meets the Gregory Development Road (Charters Towers Road) and north west to the junction of the Gregory Development Road and the Kilcummin Diamond Downs Road and north along the Kilcummin Diamond Downs Road to the point where it meets the shire boundary.

⊕ That part of the shires of Flinders, Dalrymple and Richmond south of the Flinders Highway.

✚ The remainder of the shire of Flinders not covered by the 31.01.2003 declaration

◔ The remainder of the shire of Richmond not covered by the 31.01.2003 declaration.

⚘ That part of Waggamba Shire east of the Leichhardt Highway (Goondiwindi to Moonie)

❑ The remainder of Bauhinia Shire apart from the area that extends south from the township of Rolleston, west of the Comet/Brown River and Clematis Creek, east of the Carnarvon Development Road, Rewan Road and O'Briens Road, which was revoked effective 20th May 2004.

◼ The remainder of Rosalie Shire west of the Great Dividing Range not covered in the 08.06.2004 revocation.

◆ The remainder of Rosalie Shire east of the Great Dividing Range.

✦ The southern portion of the Chinchilla Shire (south of the Dingo Barrier Fence).

✖ The remainder of the shire of Chinchilla not covered by the 01.05.2005 declaration.

✼ That portion of Wambo Shire NOT revoked on 04.06.2004. The revocation was described as being the area located north and west of the Dalby/Jandowae/Wondai Road and to the south and west of the Dalby to Toowoomba Road (the Warrego Highway).

⚫ The remainder of the shire of Wambo not covered by the 28.10.2000 declaration.

⚥ That part of Boulia Shire south and west of the following roads: Urandangie North Development Road, Kennedy Development Road, Diamantina Development Road and Springvale Road.

⊠ The remainder of the shire of Boulia not covered by the 24.05.2005 declaration.

Source: The State of Queensland, Department of Primary Industries and Fisheries, 1995–2005.

and process it into round and square bales for delivery. Also, as competitors are becoming increasingly aggressive at obtaining supplies of grass, lucerne and chaff products, a 'war' has developed in the pricing of these products. While this price war means good news for consumers, it is having a detrimental effect on profits for Northern Stock Feed Supplies.

One way that the Overtons have overcome the shortfall in feed supply is to irrigate several acres of their property. This improved pasture is then cut, dried and harvested into bales for local

Figure A.2   Australian rainfall as at 30 September 2006

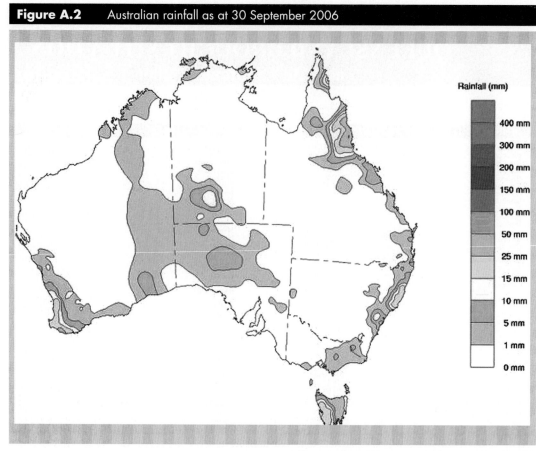

Source: Bureau of Meteorology, http://www.bom.gov.au/weather/qld.

supply. At this stage they have not considered selling grass fodder to other suppliers as they have only planted sufficient feed for their immediate customers' needs. They have only five acres under cultivation and the irrigation equipment, which is quite expensive, will only service an area of approximately 10 acres. While the quality of their grass is not of a high standard, it has been useful for consumers wanting feed to be used as bulk feed for their cattle. Another problem is that the shed that houses the stock feed is not large enough to accommodate more than 50 bales at one time. This presents a problem when it does rain as any bales not under shelter are spoiled and can not be sold as stock feed. However, they can be sold at a reduced price for use as garden mulch.

IMPACT OF EXTERNAL INFLUENCES ON SUPPLIES

NSFS operated with a handsome profit in the early years when competition for stock feed was not as aggressive as it is today, but profit margins are being reduced with the onset of the prolonged drought. Round bales of grass, used as stock feed, are increasing in price to the point that many customers often travel long distances to the agricultural college where they are able to purchase grass in bulk at reduced prices. In some cases they order large quantities and on-sell to the local horse club members. This competition is detrimental to NSFS. Prices have also fluctuated over the years. For example, a round bale of Rhodes grass in 2002 sold for $25 a bale, whereas in 2006 it was selling for approximately $40 a bale depending on availability. By comparison, lucerne/chaff sold for $15 a sack in 2002 and $40 a sack in 2006, depending on quality. The quality depends on how succulent the lucerne/chaff remains after harvesting as it can dry out very quickly in the summer months. An additional concern is the increased price of fuel, which has added to freight charges.

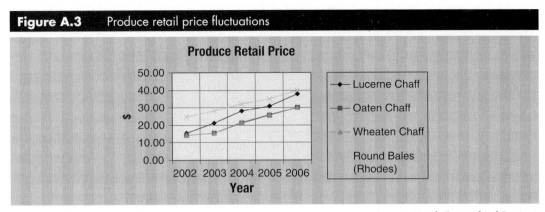

| Figure A.3 | Produce retail price fluctuations |

Source: North Queensland Register.

CHANGING DEMOGRAPHICS

As mentioned previously, when the company was originally established, it serviced a large, regional, rural community where there were many large cattle and horse properties and a large rural/residential community. There are four horse and pony clubs within a 30-kilometre radius of NSFS and all clubs are well supported and attended by the local communities and surrounding areas. However, while still patronised, the horse clubs are losing membership as teenagers grow older and leave the district to seek work.

According to the Australian Bureau of Statistics, 10 years ago the median age of the local population was 45–55 years of age with families who were between 10–18 years of age. These demographics have changed as there has been an influx of young adults into the area. The average age of residents is now between 25–29 years of age with either no children or with children under the age of five years. This has occurred as many of the surrounding large properties have been sold and subdivided into small residential blocks, thus attracting a different sector of the population. The needs of these residents are different from previous landholders. The landholders on large holdings and acreage properties running cattle and horses wanted stock feed, fencing, cattle and horse panels. However, the sector of the population attracted to the smaller residential size blocks of land are looking to purchase landscaping products such as soil, sand, turf, mulch and trees.

CHANGING PRODUCT LINES: DIVERSIFICATION

Therefore, Northern Stock Feed Supplies has now diversified its range of products to meet current demand. As consumers of livestock feed diminish, the company is altering its range of products. While the company always retained a small amount of gravel, soil, sand, turf and other landscaping products, it has now greatly expanded this side of its business. Not only do

Table A.2	Produce retail prices				
	2002	2003	2004	2005	2006
Lucerne Chaff	15.60	21.00	28.00	31.00	38.00
Oaten Chaff	14.30	15.40	21.00	25.50	30.00
Wheaten Chaff	14.30	15.50	21.50	26.00	30.00
Round Bales (Rhodes)	25.00	28.00	32.00	35.00	40.00

Source: North Queensland Register.

they sell all types of turf and soil, but also they sell a variety of pavers, pebbles and palm trees for use in landscaping. Initially this part of their business was small and accounted for a minor part of the overall business – only 10% of sales – but now it is expanding rapidly to cope with the increased local demand. Present estimates indicate that in the next few years over 70% of the business will be devoted to landscaping.

With this shift in product lines has come a change in the service needs of consumers. Consumers purchasing landscaping supplies are a different type of client. These people do not want to sit and chat over a cup of tea. Many of them are younger people working in town and they require a service that is quick and convenient.

Both Tom and Meg Overton have had to re-think the way they operate their business and this has meant changes not only to the product line of the business but also to the management styles and practices. Tom is most affected as he is now reaching retirement age. He is finding it difficult to work the longer hours required as well as lifting heavy materials. Customers patronising the landscape side of the business want the company to remain open longer, particularly on the weekend. If the company is to remain profitable, management will have to comply with these longer hours. One thing that both Tom and Meg appreciate is that the landscaping supply business is much more competitive than the livestock feed business and profit margins are generally a lot lower.

SUCCESSION PLANNING

As Northern Stock Feed Supplies has been a small family-operated business, both Meg and Tom are reluctant to sell at this stage, despite Tom's impending retirement. They have two sons: David, who is 29 years old and working in town; and Toby, who is 34 years of age. Toby has been travelling Australia working as a pastoral assistant before becoming a station manager for a large cattle property at Katherine in the Northern Territory, while David has shown no interest in the company and couldn't wait to leave home and the family business to work for a construction company in town. David holds a driver's license for fork lift trucks and heavy-rigid (HR) vehicles. Toby was originally interested in the family business but due to a disagreement with his father decided to go his own way. In fact, both Tom and Toby disagreed about how the business should be managed.

Toby has a Bachelor of Business degree, majoring in marketing, from a university in southern Queensland, and he disagreed with his father's outdated practices when it came to marketing the family business. Toby felt that both Meg and Tom were no longer keeping pace with new technology and methods of marketing and managing, and that NSFS has much unexplored potential to diversify and expand. NSFS is now at the crossroads and if it is to remain financially viable, it needs to re-position itself within the recently expanding landscaping industry. The newly established residential subdivision is virtually on their back doorstep, and the Overtons want to ensure that they are the first place that customers visit for their landscaping supplies.

Meg, particularly, has a very astute knowledge of the business and while she has no formal education, she has been managing the business successfully: balancing the books, doing the accounting and ordering supplies. She has established quite a network and while the target market and needs of the consumers have changed, she has worked hard to retain old networks and foster new ones. Because of her close networks and astute business sense she can often obtain supplies when her competitors are having difficulty. She has mastered using a computer to operate the business but lacks the technological skills when it comes to inventory control and accounting packages – all skills that could save considerable time. However, Tom is ready to acknowledge that the company culture needs to change and keep pace with the changing products and consumers.

FUTURE DIRECTIONS

Both Meg and Tom have decided that it is time to re-think the direction that NSFS should take in the years prior to their retirement, and also to include both David and Toby in the planning process as it is their hope that one or both will manage the company when they retire. This has been prompted by Toby's recent return to north Queensland as he has some new ideas on management and marketing that he thinks will be of benefit to the family company. Also, both Meg and Tom agree that they need to capitalise on the opportunity presented by the landscaping boom. They are also aware that they must fully utilise their property, which could include selling a 50-acre section for real estate development. At this stage, they are unsure whether this would be a wise decision or whether they should retain the land but use it more effectively.

REVIEW QUESTIONS

1 What do you think the future holds for Northern Stock Feed Supplies?
2 Discuss, using the theoretical concepts, processes and models covered in the text, the problems experienced by the company.
3 Discuss the forces for and against change for the company and its owners.
4 Recommend how NSFS can maintain its viability and profitability in this changing market.

Online reading

INFOTRAC® COLLEGE EDITION
For additional readings and reviews on Northern Stock Feed Supplies, explore **InfoTrac® College Edition**, your online library. Go to **www.infotrac-college.com** and search for any of the InfoTrac key terms listed below:
• Environmental impacts
• Changing demographics
• Diversification
• Succession planning

Case study B

QANTAS AiRLiNES

By Dr Quamrul Alam,[1] Monash University

BACKGROUND

The airline industry in Australia has encountered major changes in its operating environment over the past 16 years. These changes include the collapse of the Ansett group, the absorption of Impulse Airlines into Qantas, then the entry and rapid growth of competitor Virgin Blue and the demise of Australian Airlines, Freedom Air and Jetconnect. The deregulation of Australasian air services in the 1990s has continued in stages since the establishment of the 'Open Skies' agreement between Australia and New Zealand. To compound an already turbulent industry where volatility is ever-present through government deregulation and the difficulty of driving profits year-in year-out, terrorist attacks in the United States in 2001, and the Iraq war and the SARS crisis in 2003, led to significant downturns in the Australian airline industry, resulting in further change.

The industry's turbulence has been ubiquitous in the 16 years that have elapsed since the termination of the two-airline policy in 1990. Unsustainable growth has occurred in the domestic airline industry marked by a cycle of the entry of new players (Compass, Impulse, Freedom), the collapse of some players (Ansett, Compass, Impulse), and the unsuspecting emergence of others (Virgin Blue, Jetstar). Extreme capital costs have additionally contributed to the high-entry costs into the domestic airline industry, ultimately increasing the market power of the big players such as Qantas and Virgin Blue. In this highly competitive environment Qantas has to pursue policies and practices for organisational change and development to reposition itself. In this case study an attempt has been made to discuss some key organisational change and development strategies that Qantas pursued to stay competitive.

Changes in the airline industry

The airline industry has gone through turbulent times since 2001. The government tightened security laws in both international and domestic sectors to prevent terrorist attacks, but this has brought about a dramatic drop in passenger volume leading to increased competition in the Australian airline industry as airlines compete aggressively to try to attract customers to gain a small share of the pie. Although the airline industry is recovering, oil prices have surged to an all-time high, threatening the aviation sector's profitability. Like many airlines, Qantas had to respond to these market conditions by raising its fuel surcharge on both domestic and international flights, which raised concern as to what may happen to its passenger volume.

Airlines are pursuing changes with an emphasis on aggressive containment of cost to sustain highly competitive fare levels.

QANTAS: AN OVERVIEW

Qantas was founded in Queensland on 16 November 1920 as Queensland and Northern Territorial Aerial Services Limited. It specialised in airmail services subsidised by the Australian government, linking railheads in western Queensland. In 1934, Qantas Limited and Britain's Imperial Airways (the forerunner of British Airways) formed a new company, Qantas Empire Airways Limited. Each partner held 49%, with 2% in the hands of an independent arbitrator. Qantas Empire Airways, the sole Australian international carrier, commenced services between Brisbane and Singapore using de Havilland DH-86 (now a strand of now Boeing) Commonwealth Airliners. Imperial Airways operated the rest of the service through to London.

By the 1960s, Qantas was operating round-the-world from Australia to London via Asia and the Middle East, and to South America via the USA and Mexico. Many of these routes were dropped in the 1970s following the airline slump after wide-body aircraft were introduced. Qantas purchased Australian Airlines in 1992 and integrated its domestic operations into the company. In its current form the Qantas Group employs approximately 38 000 staff across a network that spans 142 destinations.[2] Qantas was privatised in 1995.

The Qantas Airways Group has extensive commercial and ownership links with various regional carriers, and Qantas has code-sharing[3] and alliance agreements with international carriers through the 'oneworld' alliance, which is the second-largest airline alliance and underpins true globalisation in the airline industry. Hamel[4] (1989) noted the need to collaborate with one's competitors to win. Qantas used alliances to gain market share as the international airline industry moved to reach a globalising industry. It is these alliances that have enabled Qantas to maintain a significant share in the international airline market through connecting customers internationally with renowned airline carriers.

Although the company's main business continues to be the transport of passengers, the Qantas Group refers to a diverse portfolio of airline-related businesses, including engineering, catering, freight and travel wholesaler subsidiaries. In conjunction with this, Qantas Airways Limited owns 44.5% of Orange Star, which owns and operates the value-based intra-Asia airlines Jetstar Asia and Valuair, based in Singapore. Qantas also holds a 46.3% shareholding in Air Pacific, the international airline of Fiji.[5]

As part of their strategy since 2004, the flying businesses of the Qantas Group have been branded under two major labels – Qantas and Jetstar – which domestically operate over 500 flights a week serving 62 city and regional destinations in all states. Internationally it operates nearly 700 flights a week, offering services to 80 international destinations (including code-share services) in nearly 40 countries. Despite recent turmoil in the aviation industry, Qantas has remained surprisingly profitable, and was recognised as 'Airline of the Year 2004' by *Air Transport World* magazine.[6] Recently celebrating its 85-year anniversary, Qantas has maintained its reputation for providing a premium aviation service, which has grown to cater to all aspects of the market. Prior to Ansett's liquidation, Qantas encompassed approximately 55% market share; however, it now has approximately 70% of the travel market on the domestic trunk route network.[7]

With the entry of Virgin Blue into the Australian domestic market, Qantas has had to respond to the growing popularity of discount air travel to competitively challenge Virgin Blue's 'low-far' end of the market. To meet such competition in such a turbulent industry, Qantas had to build on the low-cost operating model it inherited in May 2001's acquisition of Impulse Airlines. By retaining Impulse Airlines (which has evolved into Jetstar) as a stand-alone unit, Qantas has been able to derive cost savings from utilising Impulse's low operating cost, all-economy class and streamlined staffing/labour practices. The change in policy has enabled Qantas to implement some of its strategic learnings from this low-cost model to develop Jetstar.

DEVELOPMENT AND CHANGE IN QANTAS

The Australian government deregulated the domestic airline industry in 1990 with a staged termination of the two-airline agreement. The primary driving force for the deregulation initiative was to promote increased competition and pricing flexibility, aiming for greater efficiency in the industry and benefits to the customer.[8] Since deregulation, Qantas has faced additional competition from regional carriers, especially Air New Zealand. Through the government reducing the entry barrier from a legislative point of view, it enabled smaller airline carriers to gain market share from major players like Qantas.

The deregulation shifted the airline industry from guaranteeing exactly two airlines, with parallel schedules and identical planes and prices on major domestic routes, to almost complete freedom of entry to the market, subject only to safety restrictions.[9] The Prices Surveillance Authority (PSA) estimates that the real cost of air travel declined by 24%.[10] However, further strategic analysis is required when investigating how the deregulation impacted the competitive dynamics of the Australian airline industry.

A major problem identified with the airline deregulation is that the structure of the industry has not been modified like the government anticipated. Under the deregulation, two airlines still serve the same domestic routes without any divergence in the pricing, market share and greater efficiency in scheduling. Despite government deregulation attempting to lower the entry point for competitors into the industry, the entry barrier remains high as the market is mature and dominated by an oligopoly such as Qantas and Ansett in pre-2001 and Qantas and Virgin Blue in post-2001 period.

With the revoking of the two-airline agreement under the *Airline Agreement Termination Act*,[11] Compass Airlines entered the domestic market with a low-cost operating model, offering a single class of service at industry-low prices. The established airline carriers had to respond with deep price cuts and special discount offers. The new entrants were poorly capitalised and the expensive barriers to entry forged by the incumbents, such as their control of terminals, and external environmental factors resulted in Compass's demise.

Since deregulation encouraged new entrants into the market, the incumbents were forced to build up other alternative barriers to entry by offering services that new entrants could not match due to operating on a low-cost provider model. Other factors determined change in the airline industry:

1 Existing competitors struggle to make profits.
2 The industry is highly volatile, risky and uncertain.
3 The market is mature.
4 Buyer demand is slowing due to external factors (terrorism, war, interest rates etc.).

Another factor that helped Qantas to develop and grow was that the attempt by regional airline Impulse to enter the capital city market failed in 2000. Shortly after Impulse commenced service, a fourth player, Virgin Blue, also entered the market. Unlike previous entrants, Virgin Blue had the backing of an international carrier. The success of Virgin was largely due to Ansett's collapse. The entry of Virgin has resulted in the replacement of the symmetrical oligopoly imposed under the two-airline policy.

Qantas's main defence mechanism to remain competitive is to continually upgrade its core competencies across the multitude of customer service platforms and to continue to pioneer innovations such as the CityFlyer services on key trunk routes. It is reportedly considering investing about $1.5 billion to expand its fleet of Boeing 737-800s to around 30 aircraft. This development strategy allows Qantas to remain competitive with Virgin Blue's all-economy configuration.[12] Qantas's introduction of new products/service such as frequent flyer programs, club lounges, holiday packages and upgrades of IT systems were dynamic development initiatives introduced at intervals (spacing) according to a set schedule. Greene, Walls and Schrest[13] believe such a development strategy should be based on the similarities between new and existing products/services in order to ease the absorption process and to ensure that ongoing successes lend credibility to the overall internal promotion strategy.

There are some unique factors that Qantas introduced as developmental initiatives to achieve unique market attractiveness. OzJet was launched in November 2005 to target business travellers on the Sydney–Melbourne route, the third busiest in the world,[14] with prices equivalent to Qantas economy fares. Unsurprisingly, OzJet failed to win enough of the market to affect pricing and was unable to make sustainable returns; barely three months after beginning operations, the airline was transformed into a charter fleet. This led Paul Stoddart, OzJet founder and main financier, to proclaim: 'Would I recommend anybody else try it? Not particularly … It has certainly proven to me that Australia is a duopoly and it always has been.'[15] Three of the four low-cost carriers failed in a year, while the one that did survive had the advantage of circumstance, the demise of Ansett and much deeper pockets. With so little competition, the duopolists invariably remain profitable in Australia.

The value of the duopoly profitability is only compounded by the geography of the continent. In fact that was one of the driving factors for Qantas.[16] Considering the size, borders, isolation and urban dispersion, air travel is a necessity in Australia unlike any other country on earth. Therefore, the threat of substitutes in the form of other modes of transport (bus, train, boat etc.) is effectively negligent, especially with the advent of low-cost air travel. Despite a population of just 20 million people, Australia is ranked fourth in the world concerning domestic passenger-kilometres performed, which is indicative of the viability of the domestic aviation market (see Table B.1).

While Europe, Asia and the US markets are drowning in red ink, with both discount carriers and incumbents struggling to survive, Qantas has the undeniable benefit of a stranglehold on the albeit small Australian market. Given such a stranglehold Qantas has not been averse to deploying predatory behaviour in restricting entrants.[17] In May 2002, the Australian Competition and Consumer Commission (ACCC) investigated Qantas for alleged predation on its Brisbane–Adelaide route.[18] Responding to Virgin Blue's arrival, Qantas changed its fare policy and increased capacity from two to three flights per day. The additional capacity meant an operating loss for Qantas at the expense of more significant losses for Virgin Blue. The ACCC could not find any misconduct but it is indicative that due to a limited number of popular routes it is difficult for new entrants to squeeze any significant market share from Qantas. Qantas's policy changes helped the company to withstand market pressure.

In Australia, Qantas and Virgin Blue are the two main players. A major reason for the continual profitability of Qantas is its policy to initiate and implement changes. Qantas offers the full-service carrier and Virgin Blue offers a low-cost carrier without any major competition from any other airline carriers. The collapse of Ansett left a large gap in services in the Australian airline industry. Lacking capacity and operating on a very limited number of routes, Virgin Blue was unable to 'fill Ansett's shoes'. Nor was Virgin Blue willing to modify its low-cost provider model and provide an in-flight service. In the absence of competitors, Qantas restructured its management team, outsourced non-core services, implemented contract management and managed to increase its domestic market share to 70% in 2005.[19]

Responding to the ever-changing Australian airline industry, Qantas implemented developmental policies in a proactive manner. The sudden upsurges in demand required rescheduling more flights and using smaller aircraft to cater for the increased demand at lower costs.[20] When international terrorism impacted on the global airline industry, Qantas diverted its international fleet to domestic routes to further capitalise on the domestic upsurge in demand. A key factor that further has galvanised the oligopoly in Australia is the small number of routes. While the United States is characterised by a population and geographic diversity that allows an entrant to capitalise on literally thousands of routes, Australia has only eight capital cities with a handful of other smaller centres.

Table B.1	Top 10 countries by air traffic: passenger-kilometres performed (millions)			
Country	Rank	Total	International	Domestic
USA	1	1244694	337354	907340
China	2	201961	44603	157358
United Kingdom	3	200333	190543	9790
Germany	4	182508	172799	9709
Japan	5	153289	82227	71062
France	6	135017	107526	27491
Australia	7	99614	56275	43339
Canada	8	94680	55650	39030
Singapore	9	82904	82904	0
Netherlands	10	82269	82258	11

Source: adapted from 'Annual Review of Civil Aviation 2005', *ICAO Journal*, 61:5 (September/October 2006).

DEVELOPMENT STRATEGIES AT QANTAS

In 1999, Brett Godfrey, an Australian executive of Virgin Express, proposed to Richard Branson (Virgin guru) the establishment of a 'Virgin-branded, low-cost, low-fare carrier operating in the Australian domestic market'.[21] This low-cost carrier was similar to Southwest Airlines (SWA), which was renowned for being a 'no-frills' airline. Godfrey said: '[T]he airlines that are clearly succeeding are those that have stuck to the consumer-friendly Southwest low-fare model'.[22] Qantas continued to introduce changes to execute its broad differentiation strategy. This strategy was based on it 'seeking to provide products or services unique or different from those competitors in terms of dimensions widely valued by buyers'.[23] The unique offerings by Qantas were different classes, frequent flyer programs, club lounges, catering services and corporate freight-carrying services, truly bracketing itself as a broad differentiation strategic organisation.

Since Virgin Blue's aggressive expansion was based on lower costs, which were 30–40% lower than Qantas's,[24] Qantas CEO, Geoff Dixon, drew a 'line in the sand' by creating Jetstar to restrict Virgin Blue and other carriers from taking more than 35% of the domestic market.[25] Qantas adopted a broad differentiation strategy that included 'pincer-movement' tactics. Qantas's strategic platform had three principles:

1   establishment of a low-cost carrier, Jetstar, to compete with Virgin Blue
2   growth in the leisure markets, through expanding Qantas Travel agencies and inclusive holiday packaging with airfares
3   maintenance of its quality as a full-service carrier.

Qantas used a market segmentation strategy, adopting two brands to target different markets to bridge the gap at the low-end of the domestic market, a concept that occurred in the UK with British Airways and its low-cost carrier, GO.[26] Qantas's broad differentiation strategy in the low-cost carrier market seemingly strengthened the competitiveness of the oligopoly market, as prices became increasingly competitive to retain and regain market share. When investigating types of competitive low-cost strategies, Virgin Blue adopted the Southwest Airlines low-cost carrier model, whereas the Qantas Jetstar model was a selection of the best features from the leading low-cost carriers around the world, tailored to meet the demand of the Australian market. Qantas aimed to adopt the efficiency (cost) of Ryanair, the branding of easyJet, the innovation of JetBlue and the customer service of Southwest Airlines.[27]

Implementation of change

Qantas Airlines has been effective in using its core competencies to provide premium customer service across a variety of platforms to numerous customer types. Due to specialisation Qantas has a reputation for providing quality service to its customers. Additionally, its efforts with internal marketing were aimed at providing optimum levels of satisfaction to customers. The combined efforts acted as a key enabler to providing all streams of customers with a greater travel experience.

A survey conducted on Qantas[28] shows that the organisation has a repeat customer level of 42% of their airline sales. This relatively wide base of regular customer activity and a revenue-generating market base highlights that customer service is an integral component of Qantas's policy goal.

Qantas has been good at establishing and maintaining a network of agents. Qantas sells itself through highly developed networks of established agents around the world. This major strength allows the business to maintain desirable relations with its agents.

Qantas's breadth of sales and marketing channels has also allowed it to provide exquisite customer service across a number of platforms. Qantas enters corporate contracts for major business travel to be sold via e-commerce. Qantas has an online ticketing system for regular customers for convenience, combined with Qantas stores providing collaborated travel and holiday packages, and various customer service centres in-house and outsourced. This reiterates that Qantas has developed an organisational system and an operational network to support its broad differentiation strategy.

The change in competitive dynamics in the post-deregulation period forced Qantas to introduce aggressive structural changes. Since deregulation, Qantas senior management has transformed the organisation from a government-run reactive organisation into a high-performing strategic corporate organisation. In 1993, Qantas CEO James Strong took the challenge to build a new partnership between staff and management. The challenge was to instil a need for 'staff understanding that it is necessary to make a profit'[29] by contributing to a profitable company. Strong immediately implemented business strategies to drive profits by reducing costs and building up a customer-service focus. Key initiatives such as an extensive training program, development of work teams, new classification structures, a share ownership scheme, changes in the management structure, 'road shows' communicating company performance, outsourcing, competitive tendering and downsizing were introduced to improve company performance.

There was a strong emphasis on implementing an integrated approach by appointing various group and general managers to manage the turbulent organisational and industrial changes that Qantas had to pursue. This strategic restructuring at the top allowed Qantas to implement policies for change, downsize its labour force and reduce costs. The reduction of labour cost has been a central plank of employee management in Qantas since deregulation. Senior executives in the industry regarded reduced labour costs as one of the necessary features of survival. It is not the sole means of ensuring profitability[30] and a competitive edge, but is part of an overall corporate strategy, and has been on the agenda in Australian airlines since the pilots' dispute of 1989–90.[31] Qantas has been very effective in implementing change without major disruptions in the post-deregulation period.

On the international front, Qantas took some targeted measures to withstand market pressures. Due to the lull in the industry in the post 9/11 era and because of spiralling fuel costs, Qantas withdrew from a number of infeasible routes (for example, Buenos Aires, Rome and Paris) in favour of growing markets such as Mumbai and Shanghai.[32] In 2001–02 Qantas deferred a number of infeasible Asian and trans-Tasman routes to newly established low-cost alternatives: Australian Airlines and Jetconnect. The redirection towards international low-cost carriers was further emphasised by Qantas in 2004 when it agreed to a partnership (49.9%) based in Singapore, and the launch of Jetstar International in December 2005. Qantas has built a bigger footprint with the maximum range of price options to help cope with the recent turmoil in the industry.[33]

On the domestic front, the leisure market has grown from 35% to 60%.[34] Qantas launched the low-cost carrier, Jetstar, in May 2004 to restrict Virgin Blue's inexorable growth and to alter industry attractiveness, warding off new entrants from the domestic duopoly that delivers 57% of its earnings.[35] Through a new reservation system that emphasised direct distribution channels, new low-cost ground handling and catering alternatives, more favourable labour agreements and higher aircraft utilisation through a production-driven schedule, Jetstar aimed to achieve the lowest cost base in the market.[36] With the addition of Jetstar and low-cost international affiliates, Qantas exploited their competence for market reach to broaden its differentiation strategy. It now covers all aspects of the market (regional, domestic and international), offering both low-cost and premium services. Peter Gregg, the CFO of Qantas, proclaimed: 'The success of our domestic operations is due principally to our differentiated business and leisure product.'[37] Due to its competitive position, Qantas was able to replicate Virgin Blue's low-cost leadership strategy, while maintaining an inimitable broad differentiation strategy. Thus, through aviation expansion, Qantas's uniqueness was protected and a strategic competitive advantage was achieved.

Management of related businesses

Aside from their main purpose of carrying passengers, Qantas has also invested in related business opportunities as part of its development and growth strategy. For instance, through a joint venture with Australia Post, Qantas operates Australian Air Express and road freight operator Startrack Express. In October 2006, Express Freighters Australia, a newly formed subsidiary, was set up to support their growth in domestic freight operations.[38] Since Qantas relies heavily on logistics throughout the business, the benefit from co-ordinating and centralising these businesses is significant for greater efficiency and cost-effectiveness. As Dixon proposed, 'We are trying to build an integrated transport company' with a number of specialities.[39] Most recently this has involved discussions with the country's second-biggest freight operator, Lindsay Fox, to buy his trucking business, Linfox. With the Department of Transport forecasting freight transport in Australia to increase 73% by 2020, Qantas is looking to make sure it has the biggest piece of the pie.[40]

Meanwhile, other related businesses (Qantas Engineering, Holidays, Flight Catering, Express Ground Handling, and Qantas Defence Services) have consistently outperformed the core business in terms of scale,[41] providing returns above their collective cost of capital for relatively little incremental capital expenditure.[42] By building the company around businesses whose value chains possess competitively valuable strategic fits, Qantas has a competitive advantage of cross-business resource transfer and lower costs, all while building brand recognition. As Porter argues: 'Interrelationships among business units are the principal means by which a diversified firm creates value.'[43] This also spreads investor risk across a broader business base, protecting the organisation from the full extent of variations in operating conditions. Given the maturity of its main business, the strategic investment in vertically integrating profitable segments of the value chain was vital in sustaining profitability. Investing aggressively in creating such sustainable competitive advantages was Qantas's single most dependable contribution to above-average profitability. The change management capability of Qantas has provided it the ability to implement pioneering technology and maintain flexibility in organisational structures and employee management.

Management of employees

Due to entrenched union positions, Qantas was operating with higher than market pay for less productive work. For instance, B737 captains were getting paid 36% more than at Virgin Blue.[44] Consequently Dixon stressed to Qantas's 14 unions that they were 'going to have to realise that some employment practices contributed to Ansett's demise',[45] and pointed to wage reductions of 16% at Singapore Airlines since 9/11 as indicative of where the airline had to go.[46] In order to align its labour costs more closely with those of its rivals, Qantas enforced increased redundancies, increased use of accumulated leave to reduce staffing numbers, began an expanded leave-without-pay program and increased use of part-time workers. Qantas signed agreements with unions to set up Jetstar, like Virgin Blue. The three union agreements and its slim-line union status provided the template for Qantas to further challenge established labour agreements. In this regard, the strategic implementation of Jetstar was not only a means to differentiate the brand and restrict competitors but also to influence labour reform.

Qantas introduced a bold policy initiative in February 2003 to use overseas labour markets as part of its cost-cutting strategy. When the union staged a 14-hour strike, a well-prepared Qantas drew strike-breaking labour from four different sources, including Thailand and New Zealand. Qantas management argued that the reality of the aviation industry today requires relocating work offshore. Since 2004, Qantas has shifted a fifth of its long-haul flight attendants offshore in an effort to cut $18 million annually.[47]

Management of a sustainable cost-reduction program

Following unsustainable growth in net operating expenses (from $7.8 billion in 1999 to $10.7 billion in 2002–03),[48] there was increasing pressure to eradicate costs from the supply chain. In addition, given the substantial competitive advantage Virgin Blue had in its cost structure – about 30% less than Qantas – management argued that this 'differential is not a situation that can continue'[49] and devised the 'Sustainable Future Program' in August 2003 to reduce operating costs by $1.5 billion through productivity initiatives and re-engineering processes. In the six months up until December 2003, alterations towards labour productivity resulted in a 13% improvement in domestic cabin crew utilisation, while net operating cost per available-seat kilometres (ASK) fell by 7.2%.[50] By introducing new efficient aircraft, savings were made on fuel and maintenance while also improving punctuality; on-time arrivals domestically during January 2004 were 90%.[51] Internet sales increased significantly, accounting for 30% of domestic and 9% of international sales in 2004.[52] Technology costs were drastically reshaped under a $1.4 billion outsourcing push to IBM and Telstra, aimed at reducing computer and communications fixed costs from 70% to 30%.[53] Commissions paid to travel agents were reduced to as little as 1% in September 2004, expected to result in cost savings of $100 million annually.[54] Pursuing an aggressive fuel hedging program, Qantas recently boosted its fuel hedging level to 90% of its needs for 2006–07.[55] A fleet renewal program has been instituted to provide Qantas with not only the most up-to-date and efficient service, but also an increasingly flexible fleet that allows them to manage yields more effectively and at little cost.[56] The updated fleet also addresses corporate social responsibility concerns through a reduction in carbon emissions.[57]

The Sustainable Future Program resulted in an 89% lift in the airline's bottom-line profit in its first year, despite a decline of 0.2% in consolidated revenues. The best practices of Virgin Blue made the operating inefficiencies of expense-bloated Qantas identifiable, and thus provided the impetus for this cost-structure strategy. But more importantly the cost-cutting strategies didn't undermine Qantas's competence for providing a full-service product; rather, they enhanced efficiency.

Management of restructuring program

Given a new corporate strategy, modifications to corporate structure are required. So commencing in 2003, Qantas undertook a restructuring process that involved the establishment of eight different businesses in three categories: flying businesses, flying services and associated businesses. While maintaining a corporate centre to provide information technology, human resource and financial services, all businesses were to stand alone and compete for investment. Aimed at optimising accountability, collaboration and agility, Qantas management was convinced that adapting to evolving market conditions would be difficult with a traditional organisational structure. As Porter[58] suggests, success in strategy lies in the realisation that nothing lasts forever: only change and regeneration are constants. This is a contention Dixon endorsed: 'I believe the reorganisation will better enable us to manage the constant change and drive initiatives now in place – and others that will be required – so we maintain our reputation for excellence in everything we do.'[59]

Management of partnerships and alliances

The restructuring emphasis on collaboration was also reflected in Qantas and Singapore Airlines uniting to share costs on new training and maintenance facilities for the super-sized Airbus-380. Doz and Hamel[60] argue that a strategic partnership is an effective way to pursue opportunities that are uneconomical to pursue alone. The alliance of Qantas and Singapore Airlines was also emblematic of the global shift from the days of national flag carriers towards consolidation. This was first made evident through strategic alliances: the only viable means to gain access to foreign markets since getting airline mergers past competition authorities and complex bilateral air rights remains virtually impossible. Qantas was a founder of the oneworld alliance in 1998, which aimed to unify code-sharing so capacity utilisation and domestic hub traffic could be optimised, while realising savings in combined marketing and customer loyalty programs. The oneworld alliance represented another means for Qantas to expand its network while reducing its costs.

LESSONS FROM THE QANTAS CHANGE MANAGEMENT STRATEGY

In a period where global aviation has suffered $43 billion in losses[61] Qantas has become the most profitable airline in the world,[62] largely because it has been strategically well managed. On a global stage, Qantas has led the way in effective utilisation and management of its asset base, effectively reducing costs by addressing inefficient practices and expanding networks through bold diversification.

Despite sustained profitability, Qantas has lost some ground since privatisation in 1995. Back then it had 45% of Australia's international airline business, compared with 31% now.[63] The plan for Jetstar Asia (of which Qantas owns 44%) drafted in 2004 is far from the reality of its $27.4m losses in the final half of 2005.[64] Subsequently, complicated questions arose in the alliance about 'how to divide efforts among partners and about who has effective control'.[65] Unfortunately because of its less than majority stake, Qantas is incapable of assisting through scheduling, capacity or fare decisions, and has called on the ACCC to revise international regulation.

The Australian airlines have responded to entry in much the same way as airlines in North America and Europe. They have been selective, and this has limited the cost to them. When entrants offer low fares, Qantas has matched the fares. Qantas has not had to reduce the fares for all traffic, however. The low-cost entrants typically offer inflexible fares, which appeal to leisure travellers; they may offer higher-priced flexible fares to appeal to business travellers (Virgin Blue), but they do not offer higher-quality service (business class, executive lounges). In the recent entry period (2000), the spread of fares increased; Qantas lowered their discount fares but increased their higher fares, on which they were not experiencing much competition.[66]

Qantas has restructured itself to focus on the important business priorities. The company is happy with the cost structure, and is now planning transition from cost centres to profit centres. Adopting best practices and striving for continuous improvement, Qantas instituted a cost-cutting program to create a leaner company. Qantas has been able to restructure its business with minimal unrest. One of the reasons for this was good communication informing people at work of what was happening and why it was taking place. Waddell et al.[67] rightly argue that effective communication about changes and their likely consequences can reduce speculation and unfounded fears.

Leadership plays a key role in Qantas. Margaret Jackson, the Chair of the Qantas board, and Geoff Dixon, the CEO, have formed a formidable partnership. They have been able to lead the company through some difficult times in the market and still deliver on its strategy. The success over this period shows that the company's senior executives support their leaders and helped drive the message through to the rest of the company.

CHALLENGES AHEAD

The consensus in the airline industry seems to be that both competition and collaboration will soon be inevitable in all parts of the world. Qantas already has partners in oneworld, and it has American Airlines as its strategic US partner and British Airways as its strategic UK partner. A new change environment is emerging in which strong regional giants are not only becoming stronger, but are also teaming up globally to form larger and more formidable global partnerships/alliances. By 2010, the process may converge into a state of a small number of strong and strategically networked global partnerships/alliances.

The formation of such strong and strategic global airline partnerships/alliances will result in competition being elevated up to the highest levels. This means that size will be of strategic significance, and will be used as a strategic weapon. With global consolidation occurring on a grand scale, only a small number of consortia/alliances, each comprising lead airlines from all key regions of the world, would ultimately supply most of the world's air transport demand. It is critical that Qantas throws its hat into these global consortia/alliances and wields considerable power, highly differentiating it and expanding its clientele base and market share. Faced with the competitive challenges, Qantas may transform itself into a lean and sleek marketing- and strategy-led powerhouse. The 2006 takeover bid, and the management decision to accept the offer, demonstrates that Qantas has developed organisational and strategic capabilities to accept challenge and manage changes.

One of the key challenges for these global players will be to offer and compete on the basis of consistency/compatibility of products, service standards and operational integrity throughout their global/strategic network. With its alliance with oneworld, Qantas appears placed to meet this challenge because the major airlines in the alliance have similar strategies implemented in their domestic market; therefore, transference of clientele can be easily made.

With the omnipresent driving force of cost efficiency, Qantas management considers that it is at a disadvantage to its mostly 'subsidised' competitors in the global market. The market has changed since 2003. The combined share of Qantas and Air New Zealand has fallen from 90.5% to 77.2%, largely because of the growing shares of Emirates (9.8%) and Pacific Blue (7.7%).[68] As such Qantas has been lobbying the government in recent years demanding more comparable taxation (currently Qantas aircraft depreciate over 10 years; in Singapore it's three years), continuing restrictions on rival foreign carriers (Qantas and Air New Zealand's proposed 'Tasman networks agreement' is a grossly anti-competitive price-and-capacity-fixing contrivance), and revising the *Qantas Sale Act*, which restricts foreign ownership to 49.9% (this depresses the company's share price and therefore increases its cost of capital by about 3%).[69]

Moreover, Qantas will face corporate social responsibility pressures to reduce noise pollution and other emissions even further; global warming and climate change is now very much a social and corporate issue. Preservation of the environment is paramount and the government may further introduce regulation that may require Qantas to refine its noise pollution and current emissions from fuel consumption. There will be cost involved in any change in policy to comply with corporate social responsibility obligation.

REVIEW QUESTIONS

1 Critically discuss the changes that Qantas implemented to become one of the most profitable airlines in the world.

2 Identify the developmental features and evaluate their impact on Qantas's success.

3 What challenges will Qantas face in the 21st century? What change initiatives would you recommend for Qantas?

NOTES

1 The author wishes to thank Mathew Marchingo and Nicholas Doble for their support in collecting information and co-operation in the preparation of this case.
2 Qantas Fact File, www.qantas.com (2006).
3 www.aviationaustralia.net.au (accessed 15 October 2006).
4 G. Hamel, 'Collaborate with your competitors and win', *Harvard Business Review* (January–February, 1989).
5 Qantas Fact File, op. cit.
6 www.atwonline.com.
7 IBISWorld, 'Qantas Report: 2006', www.ibisworld.com (2006) (accessed 12 October 2006).
8 Australia, House of Representatives (1990): 650.
9 J. Quiggin, 'Evaluating Airline Deregulation in Australia', *The Australian Economic Review*, 30:1 (March, 1995).
10 Prices Surveillance Authority (1994).
11 P. Forsyth, 'Low-cost carriers in Australia: experiences and impacts', *Journal of Air Transport Management*, 9 (2003): 277–84.
12 J. Kain and R. Webb, 'Turbulent Times: Australian Airline Industry Issues' (2003).
13 W. Greene, G. Walls and L. Schrest, 'Internal marketing: the key to external marketing success', *Journal of Services Marketing*, 8:4 (1994): 5–13.
14 S. Creedy, 'Another crash landing', *The Australian* (14 March 2006).
15 ibid.
16 Qantas Fact File, www.qantas.com (2006).
17 B. Sandilands, 'Airlines take aim as low-cost war heats up', *Australian Financial Review* (24 February 2001).
18 Forsyth, 'Low-cost carriers in Australia: experiences and impacts', op. cit.
19 G. Bamber, *Marketing Strategies and Labour-Market Behaviour of Full-Service and Low-Cost Airlines: An Australian Study* (Brisbane: Griffith University, 2006).
20 Kain and Webb, 'Turbulent Times: Australian Airline Industry Issues', op. cit.
21 Virgin Blue, 'Prospectus', www.virginblue.com.au/pdfs/investors/shareoffer/Virgin_Blue_Prospectus_17nov03.pdf (accessed 13 October 2006).
22 ibid.
23 G. Johnson and K. Scholes, *Exploring Corporate Strategy: Text and Readings*, 5th edn (Hemel Hempstead: Prentice-Hall, 1999).
24 www.afr.com.au (accessed 21 October 2006).
25 T. Harcourt, 'Qantas in Radical Plan for Jetstar', *Australian Financial Review* (25 February, 2004): 1.
26 www.ba.co.uk (accessed 17 October 2006).
27 A. Joyce, 'Address to National Aviation Press Club', media release (22 July 2004).
28 www.qantas.com.au (accessed 15 October 2005).
29 Interview with James Strong (1995), in J. McDonald and B Millett, 'A Case Study of the Role of Collective Bargaining in Corporate Change – Qantas Airways Limited', University of Southern Queensland (1998): 1–21.
30 D. Jenkins, 'Evolution in the Airline Industry: The Impact of Structural Change on Productivity and Reorganization', George Washington University International Institute of Tourism Studies and Travel Technics (1995).
31 J. McDonald, 'Some features of industrial relations in the deregulated airline' (1992).

32 www.qantas.com.
33 R. Myer and C. Dorman, 'Air Wars', *The Age*, Business (17 December 2005).
34 P. Gregg, 'Qantas Presentation', UBS Australian Transport Conference (31 March 2004).
35 J. Durie, 'Dixon can now run his own race', *Australian Financial Review* (9 September 2004).
36 www.qantas.com.
37 Gregg, 'Qantas Presentation', op. cit.
38 www.qantas.com.
39 J. Flottau, 'New Horizons', *Aviation Week & Space Technology*, 161:2 (December, 2004): 42.
40 A. Ferguson, 'Dixon delays departure', *Business Review Weekly* (25 May 2006).
41 www.ba.co.uk.
42 G. Dixon, '2002/03 Full Year Results: Presentation to Investors' (21 August 2003).
43 M.E. Porter, *Competitive Advantage* (New York: Free Press, 1985): 97.
44 S. Washington, 'The Secret Qantas', *Business Review Weekly* (10 July 2003).
45 A. Ferguson, 'Blue sky for Qantas', *Business Review Weekly* (27 September 2001).
46 T. Harcourt, 'Qantas seeks help to fight rivals', *Australian Financial Review* (20 August 2004).
47 Washington, 'The Secret Qantas', op. cit.
48 Harcourt, 'Qantas seeks help to fight rivals', op. cit.
49 Washington, 'The Secret Qantas', op. cit.
50 Gregg, 'Qantas Presentation', op. cit.
51 ibid.
52 ibid.
53 D. Crowe, 'Qantas contracts worth $1.4bn', *Australian Financial Review* (18 May 2004).
54 Harcourt, 'Qantas in Radical Plan for Jetstar', op. cit.
55 R. Myer, 'Qantas raises fuel hedging, new delay for super jumbo', *Sydney Morning Herald* (28 September 2006).
56 G. Dixon, '2003/04 Full Year Results: Presentation to Investors' (19 August 2004).
57 J. Macken, 'Fresh Take: Airlines rise to climate challenge', *Australian Financial Review* (11 August 2006).
58 Porter, *Competitive Advantage*, op. cit.
59 Dixon, '2002/03 Full Year Results: Presentation to Investors', op. cit.
60 Y.L. Doz and G. Hamel, *Alliance Advantage: The Art of Creating Value through Partnering* (Boston: Harvard Business School Press, 1998).
61 Durie, 'Dixon can now run his own race', op. cit.
62 Harcourt, 'Qantas seeks help to fight rivals', op. cit.
63 Myer and Dorman, 'Air Wars', op. cit.
64 A. Ferguson, 'Troubled Flight', *Business Review Weekly* (30 June 2005).
65 C.K. Prahalad and Y. Doz, *The Multinational Mission: Balancing Local Demands and Global Vision* (New York: The Free Press, 1987).
66 IBISWorld, 'Qantas Report: 2006', op. cit.
67 D. Waddell et al. (2004).
68 P. Kerin, 'Good for Qantas, not good for us', *Business Review Weekly* (8 June 2006).
69 T. Harcourt, 'Turbulent times unite Qantas, Singapore', *Australian Financial Review* (4 August 2004); Kerin, 'Good for Qantas, not good for us', op. cit.

Online reading

INFOTRAC® COLLEGE EDITION

For additional readings and reviews on ???, explore **InfoTrac® College Edition**, your online library. Go to **www.infotrac-college.com** and search for any of the InfoTrac key terms listed below:

• Development strategies

CLOTHiNG COMPANY PTY LTD: MAiNTAiNiNG AN ORGANiSATiON'S CULTURE DURiNG A PERiOD OF RAPiD GROWTH

By Lindy Henderson, University of Newcastle; Glenda Strachan, Griffith University; and John Burgess, University of Newcastle

THE COMPANY

Clothing Company Pty Ltd designs, produces and distributes clothing, accessories and related products for young-minded people and develops brands that represent a casual lifestyle. It prides itself on its innovative products, events and retail environments across the globe. Its beach and leisure wear brands are dominant in their market sector.

Today the company has interests around the world. Clothing Company (CC) is fully owned by its USA parent. CC Asia Pacific operates in Australia, New Zealand, the Philippines, Thailand, Malaysia, Singapore and Hong Kong. It also owns or licenses retail stores under the three brands. It derives about 12.5% of its total revenue from its Asia/Pacific segment.

History

In the 1970s, intent on earning a living while residing at the beach, two Australians formed CC in a coastal town. A few years before, they had begun to design and manufacture beach wear to suit their own requirements for function, durability and comfort. Their product had attracted favourable attention from Australia and overseas consumers with similar needs, allowing the business to grow from a home-based operation to a viable enterprise.

In 1976 two Americans gained the USA license for CC and opened an office, warehouse and distribution centre in California. While continuing their business in Australia, the founders sold licenses for the CC brand around the world, and ownership was diluted. The USA arm of the business eventually became dominant and obtained control of the CC license in the USA in the late 1980s. CC Inc was listed on the New York stock exchange in 1986. In 1991 the Smart brand of clothing for active young women was launched in the USA. The company purchased the European licensee to CC in 1991, the international licensee in 2000 and the Australian one in 2002. The Australian founders each retained a 6% holding in CC Inc, making them the corporation's largest individual shareholders. They remain connected to the Australian business via their shareholding and longstanding association.

Current operations

Today the corporation has total annual revenue in excess of $US2 billion and is the top-selling beachwear brand. The company expanded its product lines through the purchase of a French winter sports manufacturer and distributor in 2005, and has also added footwear and golf equipment companies to its portfolio. CC operates in three regional segments: Americas, Europe and Asia Pacific. The board of directors of CC Inc includes representatives from Europe and USA.

Over the three decades of its operations, CC has expanded its business. During the late 1980s and the early 1990s the product range was developed with sportswear for teenage girls, clothing for toddlers, boys, girls and men, and accessories. Later acquisitions added footwear, clothing and equipment for winter sports and golf. The company branched into retailing and expanded the number of company-owned retail outlets (including some in Australia) as well as licensing stores to carry their merchandise. The organisation has thus grown by a mixture of expansion of its original products and markets with the acquisition of other organisations in other related areas: the design, manufacture, distribution and sale of sportswear and sporting equipment. This growth has been rapid and the company operates in the highly competitive fashion industry which is dependent on the changing whims of the consumer.

THE COMPANY IN AUSTRALIA

The primary focus of the Australian segment of the organisation is design, wholesale and distribution operations. Most of the business is conducted at the wholesale level, that is, as business-to-business, even allowing for recent expansion in retail operations.

Its Australian origins notwithstanding, CC Manufacturing is only part of a global operation. Asia Pacific, of which Australia is the biggest and most significant part, represents about 10% of the corporation's total profits. At the same time it is a growing market segment for the company. In 2004-2005, the Asia Pacific revenues rose by 49% and showed rapid growth of 17% in revenue in the nine months ending 21 July 2006. In 2005 CC acquired Beachlife, which operated eleven retail stores in New South Wales. The profit margin in the Australian operation is somewhat lower than is the case in Europe or America, reflecting lower margins.

The last few years have thus been a period of rapid growth together with a change in ownership and direction for CC Manufacturing. In the early 1990s the company ceased manufacturing in Australia, but it still undertakes the detailed design process in Australia, supervises manufacturing which is done off-shore, and manages merchandising, marketing, distribution and much of the retailing, together with all the administration, financial and human resource management aspects of these processes. This takes place in a local market, but in a global context.

Operations for Australia are concentrated in the small coastal town where the company started, with other operations in the nearby large regional centre. The coastal town is a small, supportive community dependent on just a few local industries to provide year-round employment, while an influx of tourists in the summer months represents the other major source of economic activity. At various times the company has secured government assistance for investment in rural and regional areas.

Design of fashion garments and accessories, from concept to detailed pattern and checking the finished product takes place at the coastal town. There are three main product ranges produced each year, one in winter and two in summer. In addition, some new lines are added during each season to satisfy demand and offer variety to retail customers. The design phase takes one to 15 weeks before detailed design specifications are prepared using complex, computerised methods. These designs are then sent to Hong Kong, where samples are made and returned to Australia for checking of accuracy, quality, fit and so on before large scale manufacturing takes place.

The process from design to manufacture takes approximately seven months. The shelf-life of a fashion garment is only six months. As a range is prepared for release, the samples, which have been made overseas, are made into kits for the sales representatives to use. Forty such kits must be prepared to a tight deadline, and may involve last minute changes or corrections. This may involve considerable overtime in the warehouse. Sales representatives then have the task of presenting the latest range to major retail chains and independent retailers. Orders then have to be filled, the goods received from the overseas factory and distributed to retailers.

At the coastal town there is a commitment to staff flexibility and the company is proud of its achievements in having equal numbers of men and women on the payroll, a change from the company beginnings when the workforce was almost exclusively male. Although the workforce might be seen as young and 'hip', with the opportunity to be flexible in terms of time spent in the workplace and in the surf, the company has a diverse workforce that includes workers of all ages with varying family and community obligations. The needs of an employee with an elderly parent or a young child, or one with a desire to go surfing, are equally respected.

CC Manufacturing has a policy of promotion from among existing employees where possible, and has a good record for locating and promoting talented and dedicated people from within its ranks. It has also made a point of providing training, which might be in-house in the retailing division, or sourced from one of the Universities or Colleges in the regional town. The end of manufacturing in Australia in the early 1990s meant a change in direction for the company's workers, some of whom secured positions in the warehouse while others undertook education programmes supported by the company. Two women were found to be highly educated although they were working as sewing machinists. They became sample machinists who had to make up a specific garment from a piece of fabric to completion. With the move to samples being made off-shore based on specifications like architectural drawings (a computerised process), staff became involved in this process

Structure of CC Manufacturing in Australia

The workforce has grown rapidly, and the addition of a retailing operation has added hundreds of employees across Australia. Indeed the total workforce has increased substantially (see Table 1).

The organisation in Australia has three divisions. Within each division, the management structure is typically a flat one with three levels of responsibility. Sales offices in Queensland, New South Wales and New Zealand are supplemented by the use of wholesale agencies in other states. A profile of the full-time workforce is contained in Table 2.

Head office operations

This division controls the development of the company as well as day-to-day functions such as marketing, financial management, IT and human resource management. The executive team consists of a small group of men, with a small number of women having joined the senior management ranks recently.

The company's financial operations are led by the Chief Financial Officer with a department of approximately twelve people. The takeover of the company by its USA parent brought some changes in the statutory reporting requirements and resulted in growth in this department. This has increased the complexity of the work as well as the pressure of work which includes

Table C.1 Total Workforce Numbers, CC Manufacturing	
Year	Number
2001	184
2002	223
2003	223
2004	327
2005	730

Table C.2 Workplace profile, full-time employees, by category

Work category	Number of employees	% female
Retail division		
Sales assistant	54	46
Assistant manager	25	64
Store manager	26	50
Area manager	4	50
Admin/support	5	60
Management	8	50
Distribution		
Warehouse floor employees	58	18
Warehouse floor supervisors	17	43
Admin/support	5	75
Management	4	0
Head office operations		
Admin/support	26	65
Sales professionals	29	52
Finance/human resources/information technology	20	40
Marketing	16	25
Management	7	43
Senior management	11	0
Executive team	6	0
Design		
Designer/merchandiser	53	74
Senior designer/merchandiser	11	55
Management	6	33

Source: Equal Opportunity for Women in the Workplace Agency report (2005).

compliance with USA standards. However, this has also meant greater recognition of the importance of the finance team because of the requirements of being a publicly owned company. As a result of these changes the Division has been provided with significantly increased resources.

The small human resource department is responsible for all the HR for Australasia and also provides support to the wider Asia Pacific region. The majority of the employees are based in the central locations of the coastal town, regional centre, Sydney and the Gold Coast, with other staff scattered in retail stores throughout the country. Many HR functions are therefore handled by local store managers who are able to consult the central HR department by telephone. Recruitment and retention strategies emphasise staff involvement in a company that is 'fun' and where they are learning and progressing. The HR philosophy aims to have informed employees who have ownership of what they are doing.

Design and merchandising division

Design is the core of the business and the task of this department is to make the designs, provide detailed specifications for off-shore manufacturers (this involves preparing coloured, computer-assisted designs) and to ensure that the fit, quality and 'look' of the finished products meet the company's standards. The design team consists of a mixture of youth, enthusiasm and experience. It is a competitive labour market and the most talented designers are highly sought after. This department comprises about 70 people, most of them full-time and three quarters of them women. At the most senior management level within the department there are four men and two women, but at the intermediate management level the numbers of male and female employees are approximately equal.

The design process takes approximately seven months from concept to creation of the final product, and there is constant pressure to meet a series of deadlines. While there is a degree of flexibility in terms of hours and days worked, these deadlines have to be met, and this places the responsibility for work arrangements in the hands of the employees in this department. The designers work closely with the merchandisers to prepare the range of clothing for each new season. A number of junior merchandisers assist their more senior colleagues and the sectional merchandisers. The sections cover men's clothing, women's clothing, men's accessories, women's accessories and children's clothing. The structure of this division is fluid with changes occurring to meet demand. Senior designers and senior merchandisers together are responsible for 35 to 40 designers, plus design support staff such as pattern makers, technical drawing and fitting people.

Retail division

This division is led by a retail specialist with extensive experience. Located in Sydney, this manager is directly responsible for 27 stores owned by the company, a permanent staff of 70 in the shops, and a total of almost 500 employees in the division. The stores are located all over the country, but predominantly on the eastern seaboard.

This division is also responsible for opening new stores, buying, visual merchandising, staff training and other tasks associated with the operational side of retailing. The seasonal nature of the fashion industry, with increased demand during the summer and at holiday times, necessitates the flexibility afforded by casual labour in this division. Approximately 60% of the sales assistants (some 300 individuals) are employed on a casual basis. The division involves them in training and casual work in the retail stores is a primary recruitment tool for employment with CC Manufacturing.

Distribution

One division manager is responsible for all movements of physical product throughout the Asia/ Pacific region. This includes product which is manufactured overseas, chiefly in Hong Kong, and their distribution to retail stores. There are approximately 60 employees in the division, divided into various units. Supply and distribution has been handled in-house for the last few years, although prior to this it was contracted to another company.

The seasonality of the work presents particular challenges in managing this division. Peaks and troughs of demand occur throughout the year, but as demand is growing the 'down time' is decreasing and the demand peaks are growing. CC Manufacturing utilises a combination of paid overtime and casual employment to manage the peak demand periods.

COMPANY CULTURE AND LEISURE CULTURE

From the beginning, CC promoted itself to its employees and customers as being integral with a particular way of life associated with surfing, the beach, leisure, youth and a carefree attitude. The ethos within the organisation is derived from the founders' concept of a flexible blend of working with beach activities and was consequently oriented to leisure and youth, specifically young men and the surf. This has reflected the employee profile of the company and its customer base. In addition, the company has been active in supporting surfing by sponsoring and promoting surf competitions for men, women and juniors. This remains an important part of the company's commercial profile.

Traditionally, workers at CC Manufacturing have been encouraged to continue surfing and have been able to take time off to go surfing, resulting in the adoption of an (apparently) casual approach to work with an emphasis on fun and the outdoors. Reinforcing this idea, the company's web site boasts that board meetings may be scheduled at a variety of attractive sporting and recreation resorts on the basis that this keeps employees involved in using and hence developing its products. Locally, promoting work-life balance is central to the company's culture, and arrangements for staff have included flexible start and finish times, extended leave and gradual return from maternity leave. At the same time, tight deadlines must be met and seasonal demands satisfied.

Historically, the beach apparel and accessory industry has been male dominated and this is reflected in the composition of the senior management and executive positions within the company: there are currently no women in these roles. In the last two or three years, the proportion of CC's Australian income derived from the female-oriented Smart brand has risen from 25 % to 40 % of total revenue. Greater participation of women in senior management is regarded as a safeguard for the continued growth of this brand. Apart from the retail division, most of the workforce is full-time, although there are a few part-time and casual designers or merchandisers. Women far outnumber men among part-time and casual workers (189 females and 100 male casuals) and, as would be expected, this is especially so at the shop assistant level. In contrast, half the store managers and other managers within the retail division are women.

The culture might be laid-back and leisure-oriented, but the industry is highly competitive with an ever-increasing number of labels supplying the same market. New designs are seasonal, have a short shelf-life as fashionable and desirable items, and are subject to the whims of the consumer; production is seasonal with marked peaks and troughs in demand; quality control is vitally important in the design and manufacturing process to protect the labels' reputation and costs must be contained. With CC Inc's revenue for the region at $US222 million and operating income at $US30 million this is a large and complex organisation, ultimately answerable to the USA-owned parent company and its shareholders.

THE CHALLENGES

Many senior staff started when the company was very small with relatively few employees, a flat management structure and a 'can-do' attitude. As roles have become larger and more specialised, the development of existing staff to fill expanding roles has been a feature. There has also been considerable recruitment from outside the organisation, and this has included individuals at most levels of seniority. For example, the company was not involved originally in retailing. Undertaking this function meant recruiting staff and managers externally, as well as gradual understanding of the needs and demands of this function within the company.

Current challenges for the organisation are:
1   maintaining the organisation's culture during a period of rapid growth
2   increasing the number of women in the highest ranks of the organisation to reflect its customer and overall employee numbers.

Rapid growth

All divisions of the organisation have seen rapid growth in number of employees and the scale and scope of the work undertaken. For instance, in the financial/accounting division, not only have there been increases in the number of workers, but a change in the procedures and timescale of financial reporting. The design and merchandising team has similarly had to deal with rapid growth both in numbers and responsibilities. The addition of a retailing operation has added hundreds of employees across Australia. Indeed the total workforce has increased substantially (see Table 1).

Increasing the number of women

Beach sports and culture are traditionally male-dominated. The founders of the company were young men, and young men were also the end users of the product. Endorsement by leading male sports people was the key to marketing, and many keen beach sportsmen became employees. In 1991, the company launched the Smart brand which was innovative in creating functional and fashionable clothing for teenage girls. CC Manufacturing began to sponsor female sportspeople and beach sport competitions for women as part of the marketing strategy for the brand.

In response to this changed product mix, and to comply with Australian equal opportunity legislation, efforts have been made to increase the number of women at senior levels within the organisation. Approximately half the employees are women, and this has been the case for some years. In 2005, women made up 55% of the workforce, 27% of managers, but were not represented at the most senior executive level roles.

REVIEW QUESTIONS

1 How can the company manage the transition from being a small organisation with many informal practices to a larger one with formal policies and practices, while maintaining the characteristics of the culture that are valued and promoted by the organisation?

2 How can the company increase the representation of women across the organisation and in senior management? What policies and practices could the company use to recruit, retain and promote women within the company? You could link these practices to compliance with anti-discrimination legislation and equal opportunity legislation, specifically the Equal *Opportunity for Women in the Workplace Act 1999*.

Online reading

INFOTRAC® COLLEGE EDITION
For additional readings and reviews, explore **InfoTrac® College Edition**, your online library. Go to **www.infotrac-college.com** and search for any of the InfoTrac key terms listed below:

INFOTRAC
• **Equal opportunity**
• **Company culture**
• **Managing diversity**

Case study D

TEACHiNG AND TECHNOLOGY: UNiVERSiTY OF THE SUNSHiNE COAST

By Selina Tomasich and Paul Corcoran, University of the Sunshine Coast

BACKGROUND

The University of the Sunshine Coast was the first 'greenfield' university established in Australia for more than 20 years and has enjoyed the fastest growth of any Australian university during the 10-year period of its operations. It grew from a simple organisation with a handful of staff and no students to a complex organisation of more than 400 staff and nearly 5000 students in a little over a decade. This growth is all the more remarkable given that the main funding agency, the Federal Government, did not wish it to be established as an independent campus.

A major concern of the new university was how it could differentiate itself from other universities, three of which were around one hour's travel from the new campus. During the construction stage the university identified the potential of differentiating itself through its use of information technology in its teaching. The university's governing body decided to include state-of-the-art technology in the lecture halls to enable the delivery of real-time intensified learning for students. It was also proposed that the university develop teaching materials that maximised the use of the new technologies.

TEACHING AND TECHNOLOGY: MARK I

A project officer was engaged to examine the technologies that were available in Australia and to identify those that would be most effective in the emerging environment. The selection of technologies was not made in conjunction with the academic staff that would be using the teaching spaces. These staff were yet to be appointed at the time of the campus construction. Instead, the project officer examined the technologies then available in other universities and talked to suppliers about the latest equipment coming onto the Australian market.

It was recommended that the university adopt both old and new technologies. The old technologies would include standard video outlets, 35mm film players, slide projectors and overhead transparencies projectors, as well as live reception of free-to-air television and FM and AM radio frequencies. The new technologies would include high-end computer graphic systems as well as the latest digital equipment. When the campus opened for business there was confidence that the combination of old and new technologies would meet the demands of the incoming staff.

The first University Council was cautious in its arrangements for staffing. It determined that all full-time staff would be appointed on one-, three- or five-year fixed-term contracts. This provided a measure of flexibility should the organisational structure need to be varied as a result of some teaching areas being discontinued or some administrative functions being outsourced. However, there was a risk, in an environment where ongoing employment was standard, that many experienced staff in the higher education sector would be turned off by the fixed-term contracts offered by the university. However, fixed-term contracts would not be a turn-off to all potential applicants. It was possible that this approach of providing less-secure employment would attract individuals who were prepared to take risks, back their own abilities and who were prepared to think creatively and innovatively about their teaching.

The university was successful in attracting a core of experienced staff, but the majority were new academics albeit drawn from well-established institutions. As the new courses were rolled out over a three-year period, there was never a critical mass of new staff; they tended to be appointed a few at a time with staggered starting dates. As a result, a comprehensive training program on either the new or old technologies was never developed for lecturing staff. Rather, one-on-one demonstrations could be given to newcomers by the sole technical officer in the university or by other academic staff by request.

With, in some cases, only a basic knowledge of how to use the new technology, much of the technical capability of the equipment was not used. Complex operating systems greeted teaching staff at lecterns that controlled all of the audiovisual devices installed in the lecture theatres as well as lighting. A lack of training or familiarity with the controls meant that students were often required to sit through one-quarter of their lecture time while academic staff tried to readjust the instrument panel to their requirements. Frequently the technical officer was telephoned to attend physically to complete the readjustment. The lack of understanding of the equipment led many teaching staff to reduce the scope of the lectures and to become 'talking heads' rather than risk the technology.

Even older technology, such as the free-to-air television facilities in the lecture theatres, was not effective. Live broadcasting into lecture theatres is only useful where the course content and the television program content are compatible. Otherwise, videotaping from any television for later use during lectures would have been sufficient. As a result, this capability of the lecture theatres was not used. The provision of 35mm film facilities was also not effective as most academic resources in this format were out of date or difficult to obtain. In any case, the majority of staff did not have the experience to operate the equipment. Those that did have the knowledge found that time restraints restricted the use of this type of technology. As a result it, too, was not used.

This first attempt to combine teaching and technology was directed largely at the provision of equipment in the hope that academic staff would maximise its use and develop innovative teaching approaches. This did occur in some cases but a lack of support services, clear direction from senior staff and adequate training resulted in the initial failure to achieve objectives. Instead, this approach emphasised the divide between those who were technologically savvy and those who relied on traditional 'chalk and talk' teaching methods.

TEACHING AND TECHNOLOGY: MARK II

Over the first five years of teaching the use of on-campus learning technologies had limited success. In time, staffing stabilised and academic staff became more proficient in the use of the equipment and its use became standard in all courses. The use of audiovisual materials in lectures to supplement PowerPoint slides became more usual and accepted by the students. There was still no formal training provided to new academic staff by the university. The technical officer or other academic staff continued to provide one-on-one demonstrations as the principal means for training new staff. The technologies were used but it is doubtful that they were used to their optimal effect. However, as the staff numbers grew there were increasing numbers of more experienced academics, many of whom were able to maximise the use of the equipment available in the university. This group of staff became more concerned that the technologies initially installed did not keep pace with emerging educational technologies. In their view, as advancements in educational technology were identified, plans needed to be adjusted to accommodate them.

Courses that used online learning technologies as the sole mode for delivery had been in place for nearly seven years, but these had been limited to postgraduate business courses. In developing a Master of Business Administration, the Faculty of Business had chosen to pursue a totally online delivery approach: the first in Australia to do so. However, the organisational focus was on the delivery of on-campus courses using the physical infrastructure that had been developed. Therefore, in developing this approach the Faculty of Business needed to establish its own expertise and support services. It chose a learning management system (TopClass), hired an instructional designer to ensure that teaching materials were of an appropriate quality and developed internal processes for delivery.

In some first-year courses there had been use of the technologies as a support for face-to-face teaching. The university had determined that, as part of its mission, it would pursue international standards in teaching. In order to do so it would need to address the emerging problems of its existing approach and develop a more focused approach to the use of online learning technologies.

In 2001 the university secured a major project. The project involved a range of partner universities all around the world and IBM. Using IBM speech-recognition software, the project involved the translation of a lecture in real time by converting the speech into digitised text and then displaying the text on a screen in the lecture theatre. The project was clearly a benefit for students with certain types of disabilities, such as hearing impairment, and for students from non-English-speaking backgrounds. The project provided a renewed opportunity for the university to pursue cutting-edge technology and innovative educational practice. However, the securing of the project was largely the result of a single individual's tenacity. The university decided to house the project within the Faculty of Business as it appeared to have the most interest in new educational technologies.

The initial trial of audio processing and speech recognition for lecture content was conducted during real-time lecture delivery. The majority of the group, however, was not hearing-impaired nor from a non-English-speaking background. The trial resulted in distractions for these students as they tended to watch the display of the conversion from voice to text rather than concentrate on the lecture content. A further problem was the lag between speech and displayed text and incorrect translations being displayed. These problems restricted the information exchange during lectures and resulted in negative feedback from students. Difficulties proved too great and the process was abandoned as a live exercise. However, the technology fitted well with the Faculty of Business's delivery of postgraduate course work, which involved large numbers of students from non-English-speaking backgrounds. These students gave positive feedback when lectures, using the software, were provided on DVDs.

The project continued for a number of years as an organisational unit within the Faculty of Business and made some positive contributions to its postgraduate teaching. However, the project did not impact on the organisation as a whole and nor did other organisational areas benefit noticeably from the project's output.

TEACHING AND TECHNOLOGY: MARK III

The third attempt at maximising the use of technology in teaching coincided with the university's establishment of a central organisational unit: the Office of Teaching, Learning and Research. Part of the office's role was to co-ordinate the development of teaching and to develop and monitor operational plans and action plans to support improvements to teaching practice. The university also established teaching and learning co-ordinators in each faculty as a conduit for communication and also as a means for ensuring that unit-level activity was focused on strategic outcomes. Each of the teaching and learning co-ordinators, as well as other academic staff with an interest in teaching and learning, was appointed to a new university committee: the Learning and Teaching Management Committee. The committee was responsible for the development of relevant policy as well as the development and monitoring of an operational plan for teaching and learning.

The Office of Teaching, Learning and Research brought a new focus to the use of technology in teaching. In particular, the office saw the potential of promoting e-learning as a point of differentiation from other universities and included it as an issue in the operational plan. One of the barriers to implementation was identified as the 'tension between a desire to move ahead and support innovators and the realities of limited staff and technological resources and support'.[1]

Initially the key issues in introducing an e-learning approach were identified as:

- the need to develop a common understanding of the meaning of e-learning and approaches to it
- the need to determine a pace of change that would not alienate either the staff or the students
- the need to consider a range of educational models
- identification of the things that excite or turn off (push and pull factors) staff involvement in e-learning
- the need to manage and promote involvement in e-learning processes
- the need to identify and receive appropriate levels of resources for the implementation of e-learning approaches/strategy.

It was recognised that the university needed to keep pace with technology, but it was also noted that implementation needed to be a whole-of-university initiative. It could not be done by 'expecting novices to dramatically increase their e-learning skills at an unrealistically fast pace'.[2] Expanding the technology to incorporate a new portal for e-learning needed to be undertaken in a methodological manner so that it did not aggravate staff or students, many of whom had previously experienced the negative impacts of technology on campus.

Through the new Learning and Teaching Management Committee a three-year functional plan was developed. The Office of Teaching, Learning and Research would have responsibility for ensuring that the goals contained in the functional plan were met. One of the major goals of the plan was to enable all courses to be delivered with online access for students. As a first step, a uniform learning management system for the university needed to be identified and implemented. A review of available systems resulted in the choice of the BlackBoard Learning Management System (BLMS). The Faculty of Business, which had participated in the review, was required to replace the system that it had been using and provide the test environment for the new choice. The trial by the Faculty of Business did not use the full capabilities of the learning management system. Most staff tended to migrate what they had been doing on the old system to the new. However, the potential for the new system was proven and formally adopted as the basis for further university-wide development. With the purchase of some additional components, the BLMS could be expanded to support flexible delivery of all courses at the university within a three-year time frame.

To test-drive the full capabilities of the BLMS, a newly created foundation course (a mandatory course for all undergraduate students) called Innovation, Creativity and Entrepreneurship was selected. The choice of this course had a number of benefits. The course was located within the Faculty of Business, which had some relevant expertise. The course itself was about innovation and creativity and was, therefore, philosophically aligned to the use of new technologies. The concern with this was that some 500 new students would be required to access the system within four months and the whole system needed to be functional within that time frame. An additional concern was that all students coming in would be first-year, first-semester students and it was important that the delivery of the course 'reflects educationally innovative and creative curriculum design and instruction' via the BLMS.[3]

A working party, the Application Support Group, was established to oversee the project and it highlighted a number of operational issues. First, the information technology support team had limited skills in instructional design and multimedia.[4] Second, the support team did not have experience in production development at the level required to facilitate the project.[5] Third, the University network bandwidth could not support student access from off-campus (although there were plans to increase the bandwidth significantly in the near future). Fourth, wireless access was not available on campus and this limited the flexibility of use of the new system. Fifth, academic support for the project was minimal; probably due to the fact that the initial use of technology in teaching had been problematic. Sixth, not all computers on campus had the ability to accommodate the new system, nor did the majority of classrooms. Last, training options for the new system were costly and user-specific, meaning staff and students would have minimal motivation to access the technology once installed. Funding needed to be obtained to secure additional components of the Learning Management System, and the existing environment needed to be stabilised. Resources needed to be identified to ensure that the new technology would be supported, not only in the existing online learning courses but also for all future courses. The chair wanted to see the working party integrated into the established committee structures of the university and not be seen as a stand-alone group. He sought a name change to reflect the core purpose and standing of the working party. He also sought the establishment of a second group to deal with policy and planning activities. Neither the name nor the status changed but the second group, with a similar membership, was established.

The working party also concentrated its initial discussions on administration issues. The major issues here were who would be able to access the BLMS (potential privacy issues), the development of its own terms of reference and a determination of the exact role for the working party as the BLMS was rolled out for all courses. However, having made this progress the working committee did not then meet for a further nine months. By this time the Innovation, Creativity and Entrepreneurship course had been running for a full semester. Numerous problems had been encountered with the BLMS. Staff and students were providing negative feedback to the working party. To minimise the negativity being experienced by the majority of users and to stop the feedback getting to potential users of the system, the working party decided to focus on the day-to-day practical aspects of using the BLMS and to identify solutions to the immediate issues.

The working party undertook a compilation of common concerns and found that:

- Students and staff did not know where to direct BLMS queries. Requests for help were being received at four different organisational locations.
- Most students could not log on to the BLMS. Those that could log on had no idea how to use it.
- Some staff and students had software clashes that prevented them from using the system.
- Not all computers on campus could support BLMS and these machines needed to be upgraded.

The working party's solutions to these concerns were to:

- prepare a troubleshooting flowchart to identify the first port of call for assistance
- train staff in the use of the system
- provide a link to e-learning on the corporate website
- identify a staff member in each faculty to be the point of contact for BLMS queries
- upgrade student computers.

The University of the Sunshine Coast has three faculties but the only experienced staff were located in the Faculty of Business. This meant that the Faculty of Arts & Social Sciences and the Faculty of Science needed to identify staff to participate in the BLMS implementation process. These staff would then be given a higher level of instruction so that they could also act as the local point of contact for queries. However, this was not seen as a priority and it was many months before the staff were identified. To ensure that there was adequate time for the identification to occur, a staged rollout of the system was determined as the best option. In the intervening period the experienced staff in the Faculty of Business were the only support available.

Four levels of access were planned for the rollout of the BLMS.

LEVEL 1: ONE-WAY TRAFFIC

- All courses, course co-ordinators and students are put into BLMS, but the course co-ordinator has to elect to 'switch it on'.
- BLMS replaces the student intranet, and is used to make announcements to students and to house the course outline.
- There are limited resources, so knowledge of BLMS or additional teaching strategies are required.
- Course co-ordinators build in time to experiment with the system.

LEVEL 2: AUGMENT FACE-TO-FACE TEACHING

- Academics utilise course cartridges (BLMS-designed courses) supplied by publishers of course textbooks.
- Limited BLMS functionalities are used; for example, submission of assessment as word documents and communication forums set by the course co-ordinator.
- Limited additional curriculum design or teaching strategies are employed.
- Students are encouraged to become familiar with BLMS.
- BLMS supplements face-to-face teaching.

LEVEL 3: INTEGRATED ONLINE PEDAGOGY

- Online curriculum design is integrated into courses.
- Time requirements are increased for course co-ordinators in designing curricula.
- Consideration is given to learning and teaching practices in an online environment.
- Interactivity between the course co-ordinator and students is achieved primarily, or entirely, online.
- Student responsibility is increased.
- More sophisticated technologies are integrated into courses.
- BLMS may extend from individual courses to the whole-program level.
- Increased budget levels for BLMS courses.
- The impact on academics' workload is assessed.

LEVEL 4: 'ROLLS ROYCE'

- BLMS is totally interactive.
- BLMS can be applied to any learning and teaching concepts.
- The principles and practices of good pedagogy are embodied in the system.

The working party identified that any new courses added to the BLMS needed to be restricted owing to the need to test the capabilities of the current technology and due to the limited understanding of what the new system could handle. No procedures were in place to support new courses being added, and only a limited number of staff knew how to accomplish this. A staged rollout was determined as the best option, which required staff to determine the timeliness of this coupled with staff abilities. Other areas needed immediate attention to allow for the implementation process to progress smoothly. Resource requirements needed to be identified to allow for a case to be presented to the Vice-Chancellor.

As the new system would be the main access point for staff and students, a request for a dedicated and clearly identifiable link on the university's corporate website was made. The link would provide the main pathway into the BLMS for all staff and students. Initially this was refused by the organisational unit responsible for the website. The reasons cited included that they would prefer not to change the existing general link because staff and students were familiar with this wording. The concern with not having a specific link on the corporate website was raised by the working party with the Vice-Chancellor and it was agreed that specific link would be put in place.

As the implementation team delved further, the capabilities of the new system were found to be lacking in some areas. As the system was developed in America, some aspects were not required for Australian students. It was found that these could not be disabled within the system and unless all required fields of information were entered into the system it would not operate. In addition, other resources were required, such as specifically formulated templates that staff could use to develop course materials. These templates would make loading new information onto the system easier. It was decided that the committee members needed to participate in a demonstration of an academic adding a new course to the BLMS to see the problems that were occurring at the next meeting as they had limited knowledge of how the system operated.

Time restrictions were making an impact now as the new system was due to go live within three weeks. However, the committee determined not to 'advertise this widely' as not all the support personnel were in place. Even though not broadly advertised, those students who did use the BLMS noted that it was slow to load on campus and even slower to load off campus. Over time, each of these issues was addressed and the Level 1 access objective was achieved.

Within two years of the initial working party meeting, the initial rollout plan had been completed, the system had been upgraded and an additional 14 courses were being run via e-learning strategies. Trained staff were in place in the three faculties (but the strongest group was in the Faculty of Business). Problems of access had been resolved and, after considerable effort, a dedicated link to the BLMS was placed on the university website. Although a successful implementation, the current use of the BLMS reflects the four stages of access identified earlier in the project. Some courses, like the Innovation, Creativity and Entrepreneurship course, have based their curriculum delivery around the capabilities of the system. Others, however, have little to do with the system, preferring to deliver their curriculum in a traditional manner.

CONCLUSION

The initial attempt to instil a teaching approach based around emerging technologies did not succeed. The 'if we build it, they will come' view lacked a clearly defined objective and was not well supported at a strategic level. The second attempt was localised to a single organisational unit. Notwithstanding some of the problems, it achieved a measure of success in that courses were developed and delivered using cutting-edge technology. This attempt was successful for several reasons. It had the support of senior staff within the organisational unit, and it was also central to the unit's strategic plan. Most importantly, and resulting from these two reasons, it was appropriately resourced. The third attempt benefited from a clear objective but suffered from the desire to balance the needs of multiple stakeholders. It is considered a success – it has achieved Level 1 access – but more work will need to be done to optimise the results. It is likely that a fourth attempt will emerge in the next few years. This attempt should benefit from, and build upon, the successes in the third attempt, using those successes as models for the future.

NOTES

1 University of the Sunshine Coast, 'Interim e-Learning Plan for 2005–2006' (2005).
2 University of the Sunshine Coast, 'Interim e-Learning Plan for 2005–2006', op. cit.
3 University of the Sunshine Coast, 'Interim e-Learning Plan for 2005–2006', op. cit.
4 University of the Sunshine Coast, 'Interim e-Learning Plan for 2005–2006', op. cit.
5 University of the Sunshine Coast, 'Interim e-Learning Plan for 2005–2006', op. cit.

Online reading

INFOTRAC® COLLEGE EDITION

For additional readings and reviews on teaching and technology, explore **InfoTrac® College Edition**, your online library. Go to **www.infotrac-college.com** and search for any of the InfoTrac key terms listed below:

INFOTRAC
• Teaching
• Technology

Index